Rules for the Endgame

PARALLAX RE-VISIONS OF CULTURE AND SOCIETY

Stephen G. Nichols, Gerald Prince, and Wendy Steiner,
SERIES EDITORS

Rules for the Endgame

The World of the *Nibelungenlied*

Jan-Dirk Müller
Translated by William T. Whobrey

The Johns Hopkins University Press
Baltimore

Originally published as *Spielregeln für den Untergang: Die Welt des Nibelungenliedes*, © 1998 Max Niemeyer Verlag, Tübingen

Printed in the United States of America on acid-free paper
9 8 7 6 5 4 3 2 1

The Johns Hopkins University Press
2715 North Charles Street
Baltimore, Maryland 21218-4363
www.press.jhu.edu

Library of Congress Cataloging-in-Publication Data

Müller, Jan-Dirk.
[Spielregeln für den Untergang. English]
Rules for the endgame : the world of the Nibelungenlied / Jan-Dirk Müller ; translated by William T. Whobrey.
p. cm. — (Parallax, re-visions of culture and society
Includes bibliographical references and index.
ISBN-13: 978-0-8018-8702-4 (hardcover : alk. paper)
ISBN-10: 0-8018-8702-X (hardcover : alk. paper)
1. Nibelungenlied—Criticism and interpretation.
2. Nibelungen. I. Whobrey, William T., 1956– . II. Title.
PT1589.M8513 2007
831'.21—dc22 2007011945

A catalog record for this book is available from the British Library.

Contents

Preface to the English Translation

Unlike in the natural sciences, national borders still play an important role in the humanities. It continues to be disappointing for German scholars to discover in bibliographies of English-language books that scholarly studies written in German rarely find their way to the international community. The same is true of other European languages; perhaps a bit less so of French—but even there it is true that scholarship has a hard time getting noticed outside its linguistic borders, with the possible exception of intellectual fashions like poststructuralism. The exception to this is anglophone literature in the spheres of other languages, even though English does not have the status of a lingua franca in the humanities as it does in the natural sciences. International conferences and anthologies of papers have begun to offer some relief in this regard. It is always surprising to participants, then, how productive a look over the fence can be, and how many scholarly developments outside one's own language can lead to similar questions and solutions. If the increasing marginalization of the humanities is to be stopped, then it is incumbent on us to intensify exchanges beyond conferences and to create other modes of continual knowledge transfer.

I am therefore all the more pleased that an American colleague of mine suggested that my work on the *Nibelungenlied* ought to be translated into English and so made available to anglophone scholars who would otherwise be little inclined to read a dense work in another language. I am also pleased that the beginnings of such considerations go back to several months I spent at Washington University in St. Louis and the chance to engage with young American students over the text in a way that was not colored by decades of German interpretative attempts and traditions. The attempt over the following years to continue such an unprejudiced reading of the text may have led to certain convolutions and overstatements in my original book that I would now avoid. Nevertheless, I decided against making deletions and changes in this American edition so as not to erase the original intent of the project, which is to gather information in a "thick description" of a literary text about a historic culture's imaginary world (*l'imaginaire*). The literature is not used as a "source" for historic conditions (for example, political or social conflicts around the year 1200), but as an independent medium that reworks historical experience, which is to be understood as more or less close to historical fact and can even function as a counterversion of it. I am concerned with the uniqueness of the literary text, that is, the special way in which it gives structure and perspective to experiences and imagination, and with this path to one (and I emphasize only one) aspect of medieval laity's fictions. Other contemporary texts from related genres must therefore be employed alongside the *Nibelungenlied.*

This general interest is also the reason why my 1998 book was chosen to be translated and not my shorter guide, *Das Nibelungenlied* (Klassiker-Lektüren 5, 2002; rev. ed., Berlin, 2005), which goes beyond some of the positions presented here. It did not seem advisable to add these newer considerations to my older concept of the text. The bibliography has been updated, however, with some of the more important recent literature.

Translating an investigation in the humanities into another language is a difficult and tricky undertaking. Over the past 150 years, German has developed into a scholarly language in the field of culture studies. As such, it has at its disposal certain advantages in differentiation and precision. These are not easily transferred to another language, however, and they may thus not always make up for the unavoidable losses in translation. I am thankful to the translator for having done his best. There are also additional, pedestrian kinds of problems. German and English vary greatly, on matters ranging from the word order in an ordinary sentence to the options for complex clauses. Compromises are certainly possible, but they remain compromises. What is a flexible and lively style in German may end up sounding rather Teutonic and pedantic in English. We have tried to avoid this as much as possible, but a German study in English translation will always bear the marks of the scholarly culture from which it originated, or it would simply not be the same book.

In contrast to the German, the English version has been enhanced with translations of the Middle High German texts. These translations are not from existing dual-language editions but have instead been tailored to each particular argument. This has sometimes resulted in more tedious and ungainly translations than those that would be more considerate of the narrative context. This has been necessary in order to impart the foreignness of the medieval text to the reader, whereas a dual-language edition also has the legitimate task of bringing the text closer.

This has been a challenging collective effort involving many compromises. I hope that the result is true to the original intent, and that it will stimulate new efforts at interpreting this fascinating text. I would like to thank Hans Ulrich Gumbrecht and Stephen Nichols for their efforts in having the book published by the Johns Hopkins University Press, Michael Lonegro for his engagement at the publishing house, Brigitte Badelt for her support from Germany, and, last but not least, William Whobrey for his hard work in translating a cumbersome book.

Preface

Long before I knew more than a few bits of the *Nibelungenlied,* a question caught my attention. It hooked me as early as grammar school—to be precise, in composition. As is well known, the outline plays a major role in any expository essay: the introduction, three points for and three against, followed by one's "own opinion," and finally the conclusion, with the theme repeated in the form of a question between the introduction and the main body. In my case, the paradigm for such a restatement was: "How did Kriemhilt become a villain?"

Well, how did she? I must admit that I have been haunted by this question ever since. I suppose I was first fascinated by this sentence because of its solemn incomprehensibility; then perhaps because of the way it marked an important standard for correct outlining; then possibly because the inertia of human memory drags all sorts of useless clutter along with it; and, finally (and by this time I must already have been a medievalist), because of the realization that it raises some of the problems that continue to haunt Nibelungen philology. The question not only reflects a middle-class unease about how a nice girl from a good family could fall so low but also implicitly contains a hypothesis about how stories should be told. If Kriemhilt *became* a villain, then she was apparently not one at first. Something had to happen that made the transition from one to the other plausible. I began to search for individual events that, with the help of "covering laws" and plausible assumptions about human character and the ways of the world, could explain how Kriemhilt the non-villain became Kriemhilt the villain.

Analytical historical theory concerns itself with the structure of such stories and examines their ability to explain events. The *Nibelungenlied* was read as a historical report, as the theory presumed it should be. Any expectation of plausible explanations was continuously frustrated, however. This must be some other kind of story, namely, a story of the kind that does not concern itself with seamless causal linkages like the psychological novels of the past 250 years. It is a kind of story that is completely uninterested in psychological development and does not share in the assumptions that support such developments. And so this book starts with a foolish question but refuses to provide an answer. Instead, it will show that the question itself is wrong.

The warning against employing empathetic commonsense psychology in dealing with old epics is not in itself groundbreaking (which does not prevent common sense from sometimes incorporating what is foreign to it). And so this book has a positive as well as a negative goal. It hopes to describe the rules of the world in which the *Nibelungenlied* unfolds and to determine the credit that must be given to its narrator, as to all narrators. It is therefore important to examine the supposed contradictions in this story closely. There are many such contradictions in the plot, and many of these will be the subject of commentary. They will not be viewed as "mistakes" with which we can establish the aesthetic failure of the epic, but rather as clues that lead us to another view of the world, as well as to another aesthetic.

This requires turning away not only from the worldly norms of naïve realism but also from the more demanding "realistic" poetics of the novel as they became the literary norm between 1750 (the era of the rise of the novel) and 1880 (the era of the consolidation of German philology, or *Germanistik*). The scholarship of modern literature has long since assumed that the novel's program is invalid for the literature that precedes and follows it, and it has demonstrated that even the literature of nineteenth-century realism was a subtle poetic episode suffused with its own mimetic demands. The study of heroic epic can no longer, as it did in its beginnings, appeal to a seemingly timeless program of poetic mimesis that is beholden to a nineteenth-century aesthetic.

One point of inquiry is the special contract between the narrator and the audience, the prerequisite of every narrative. Hitherto, total distrust ("Where has he gone wrong this time?") has often enough replaced the "suspension of disbelief" required by every serious text from Homer to James Joyce (and beyond). Great literature has certainly never cared much about the petty reactions of some of its readers. Statements along the lines of "This is where Goethe was mistaken" derive from—and owe their modicum of humor to—this fact. For the past 150 years, Nibelungen scholarship has devoted itself with uncommon zeal to showing where things remain open, dark, ambiguous, or even contradictory. It is much more difficult to explain why these kinds of problems exist in this or that section of text, and what aesthetic principles suggest solutions that "we today" might not expect and that cannot readily be reconciled with what we know now. These are the principles that matter here, and—this has to be said up front—there is no single solution that reveals the text's timeless meaning.

This book has long been planned. I discussed the idea of describing "rules" for medieval behavior in the early 1980s with Gerd Althoff, who at the time was finishing his book on political and social bonds in medieval Europe.[1] Althoff has since then completed a whole series of studies of such "rules." The idea that the *Nibelungenlied* might be the focal point for such a study began to take more definite shape during preparations for the Passau Nibelungen Symposium organized by Fritz Peter Knapp in 1985, and my earlier thoughts were redirected by discussions with the experts gathered there. The results of the conference were published in 1987. A visiting faculty position in St. Louis then gave me the opportunity to study the text of the vulgate version for two months and to teach it to a small group of curious American students. Along with many other things, the book slowly took shape, and an additional sabbatical from the Deutsche Forschungsgemeinschaft in the winter semester of 1996/1997 gave me the time to complete the manuscript. A final revision took place during the semester break in 1997.

I have tried to make my investigation accessible to those who are not familiar with all the details of the pertinent scholarship. I have often referred to such scholarship in general terms and only gone into more detail when I found myself in conflict with it. The secondary literature, of which there is by now an overwhelming amount, is therefore cited only selectively. Working with a subject for years often has the effect of making certain thoughts seem original, notwithstanding that they have been thought before. I have attempted to draw the line here, but I don't believe that I have been entirely successful. Moreover, it seemed superfluous to attempt—as so often done in dissertations—to find the first citation for every detail, even when it had a very different meaning in another context. Likewise, it seemed unnecessary to list the name of everyone who ever had anything to say about a particular matter, since this tends to distract attention from the overall context, which is then more blurred than clarified. The fact that philological work has to maintain a precisely documented discussion with its predecessors remains uncompromised by this.

I hope that this book will be read not only by specialists in older German literature but also by experts in related philological and historical disciplines, and perhaps even by a larger audience interested in foreign cultures. Such readers should skip the arguments with current scholarship and go directly to the examination of the text. Such arguments, which do not as usual try to explain epic narrative in a sequential retelling, might prove impenetrable for such a wider circle of readers. The argumentation instead views the text from a different perspective, from the side, as it were. A short overview of the text would have been helpful so as not to discourage such readers, though it would have been superfluous for the expert. I decided against such an approach, because one of the basic tenets of this book is that narration creates meaning, which leads to the conclusion that any retelling, no matter how much it may reject evaluation, gives the story a new meaning, the meaning of the critic. This creates a coherence that still needs to be demonstrated. In addition, there are several good summaries of the *Nibelungenlied* (e.g., Schulze 1997a, pp. 86-89), which, each in its own way, contain important aspects of the text, and the basic outline of the epic is still known outside a smaller circle of experts. Reading the text in the excellent translation by Siegfried Grosse (1997), for example, cannot be replaced by a summary of its contents.

This book has been preceded by a series of individual studies. Readers of these will encounter some familiar terrain. Nevertheless, it seemed important to me to show that there is a concept behind these individual questions, and that they are connected. It has become common in Germany to favor the specific monograph to the overarching representation of a book. Publications from the Anglo-Saxon world have often been criticized for a handling of differentiations and details that is sometimes all too lax (including the collection of individual studies into a book in all too loose a way). The opposite might likewise be criticized: focusing only on details is often justified in terms of lack of time and space, or by limited goals, but the author is then unable to deal with the consequences of his or her observations. I believe that this criticism is more valid than the former. This is why I have always returned to previous investigations and interpretations, sometimes to modify them so as to test their relevance for a new interpretation of the text as a whole.

"Interpreting the text as a whole" is not an interpretation of form and content that claims that all details agree with one another, nor is it part of an overarching concept that attempts to fix the meaning of the epic once and for all. The price of such an absolute interpretation has been revealed by critical Nibelungen philology. The postulated meaning derives from the whim of the critic, who manipulates the text and its many transmissions. I would like to show that this justified criticism does not proscribe the "interpretability" of the text.

The following effort is based on a number of theoretical considerations, which are applied on a case-by-case basis. Those who think they can do without such considerations are only fooling themselves with regard to the (unconsidered) theoretical assumptions that guide their own work. Theory does not mean, as some scholars seem to think, the invention of a model that is then superimposed on the text, but rather a reflection on the circumstances under which these objects can be experienced and interpreted to begin with. The construed conflict between "theory" and "textual work" or philology is imagined. There is no philology or work with a text that is not implicitly or explicitly guided by theory and whose results are not dependent on the validity of a theory. Likewise, there is no theory of literary criticism that is independent of its object of study and that does not have to defend its value by confronting texts.

There are many whom I would like to thank. This includes all those who helped me in writing this book, most especially Ute von Bloh and Udo Friedrich, whose tireless discussion always prompted me to ask new questions; the students of various courses who were tolerant of these unfamiliar inquiries; and Céline Hofer and Cornelia Herberichs, who read the final corrections with me. Last, but not least, thanks to all those philologists and enthusiasts who encouraged my contradictions, and whom I (unsuccessfully) tried to talk out of believing that it makes sense to ask: How did Kriemhilt become a villain?[2]

Rules for the Endgame

1 Introduction

"Do you know the legend?" I asked her.
"Of course," she said. "The tragic story the Germans spoiled with their latter-day Nibelungen."

Jorge Luis Borges, "Ulrica"

The National Epic and Its Critics

Books on the *Nibelungenlied* are legion, and there certainly seems to be no need for more. The legend is more popular than practically any other from the German Middle Ages. Its adaptation by Richard Wagner still guides current reflections on power and property, love and hate, anarchy and rule. The Nibelungen epic from the late twelfth century, however, is less evident today. It has disappeared, albeit more slowly, from the curricula of most secondary schools in Germany, which have banished most older literature as a whole. The little known *Nibelungenlied* is today a questionable educational relic in the national aberrations of recent German history.[1] The proverbial Nibelungean loyalty (*Nibelungen Treue*) was linked to World War I, the first catastrophe of German history in the twentieth century, which pitted the "fraternal" Hohenzollern and Habsburg monarchies against the rest of the world.[2] The rulers of the Third Reich also tried to give the second, even worse catastrophe something of a mythological dimension with allusions to the destruction of the Nibelungen. When the horror had passed, the epic, too, seemed compromised. It was relegated to the ivory towers of Germanic studies, where it remains the object of the relentless efforts of a few.

The *Nibelungenlied* owes its place in Germany's cultural memory and its association with German history above all to the "national" origin and tradition of its material, making it distinct from the Latin-Mediterranean–West European tradition. The epic's form seems to reinforce this peculiarity even more. Both facts explain the interest in the text since the Napoleonic Wars.[3] They also explain why the *Nibelungenlied* is still the most widely known work of the German Middle Ages and why its material is still to be found today in pop culture, novels, and movies.

After World War II, the *Nibelungenlied* lost its central role among academic specialists in German philology. The more "European"-oriented, somewhat less martial view of humanity developed by courtly poetry came to overshadow the bloody story of the destruction of the Nibelungen. There were certainly plenty of attempts to rehabilitate the epic and to free it from its nationalistic deformities.[4] After overblown glorification came a sobriety that also raised questions about the literary quality of the text. Symptomatic of this is the skepticism that asks if the epic wasn't just a failed attempt to paste a contradictory heroic tradition together in a manner that was halfway plausible.[5] This reaction is understandable in light of the excessive national and aesthetic significance attached to the *Nibelungenlied* by its national eulogists, politicians, and even philologists.

From the time of its rediscovery by Johann Jakob Bodmer in the eighteenth century, and at least since the German national uprising of the Napoleonic era, the *Nibelungenlied* in theory exemplified the national epic, heroic self-confirmation, and a genuine national character and the values and goals ascribed to it.[6] This political actualization only accounts for a small part of the history of its reception as a whole. Friedrich Heinrich von der Hagen was able to describe the national virtues of Germans and their conflict with foreign archenemies based on the *Nibelungenlied.* In the context of the international tensions preceding World War I, German Chancellor Prince Bernhard von Bülow was able to appeal to a mutual "Nibelungen loyalty" between the cheerful Danubian monarchy (= Volker) and the fierce German empire (= Hagen). Subsequently, Hermann Göring tried to encourage German soldiers by reminding them in the final stages of World War II of the willingness of the Nibelungen to fight to the last man, all of this accompanied by a moral investment in a supposed Nibelungian character, instigated by nationalistic educators and professors.[7]

Independent of such distortions, Germans were interested in the "autochthonous" legend as material from their own ethnic past in which the traits of national character might be found. Not just a particular story but the entire world of the Nibelungen offered itself for identification. The epic was translated and reworked as a book for the whole people (*Volksbuch*), which was invariably splendidly illustrated. How successful this was and what consequences it had is another question. Scholarship in any case reaped some benefits from this popular interest. Up until the middle of the nineteenth century, Germanic philology dealt with the *Nibelungenlied* more than with any other work of the German Middle Ages. The quarrel over the best manuscript led to bitter academic enmities, worthy of the Nibelungen themselves. The scholarly geography of the German Reich could be measured according to the point of view taken by scholars on the "Nibelungen question," that is, which of the epic's competing versions was closest to the "original" text. Some universities were dominated by the "Berliners," others by the "southern Germans," and between these stood the "Leipzigers," with each group favoring one of the great Nibelungen manuscripts of the thirteenth century.[8]

Up until World War II, *Nibelungenlied* philology was the most important measure of competence in Early Germanic studies, whether in editions or in commentaries, in mythological or linguistic scholarship. The *Nibelungenlied* supported the importance of the discipline itself, responsible as it was for preserving the national heritage of the Middle Ages. It would therefore be too easy to explain the history of *Nibelungenlied* philology only in terms of the national frenzy and public uproar that accompanied it from its beginnings. Lasting results were gained apart from this, sometimes in the form of an explicit stand against political utilization. The privileged position of the text in the literary history of the German Middle Ages cannot be understood without these accompanying phenomena. After World War II, when scholars began to distance themselves from the political positions that had mistakenly been thought to be part of the epic, the consequences affected the *Nibelungenlied.* A book like Gottfried Weber's *Das Nibelungenlied: Problem und Idee* (1963), which, in a kind of vulgar existentialism, advocated a Nibelungian-type heroism in the face of a godless present day, was a curious exception. The stories of the strong Siegfried and the horrible Kriemhilt ended up being trivialized in books, films, and television programs.

Nonetheless, important monographs and articles continued to be written on the medieval epic, even more so than before. Free of the political ballast of Germanic prehistory, the main issue became the interpretation of the text as a literary work. The characters were meant to inspire an emotional involvement independent of their heroism. Their conflicts, motivated by all-too-human impulses such as love, jealousy, hatred, envy, hunger for power, and trust, were to be analyzed with the help of the sparse words of the epic poet, which were without commentary and often seemingly contradictory. Aside from a few studies,[9] scholars were less interested in the epic of the late twelfth century than in the timeless work of art whose emotional conflicts could be directly understood by a modern public.

Many complex and subtle insights have been gained from these efforts, especially in terms of structure, representation, characterization, and motivation. Common to most of them, however, is that they have not sought an approach that takes the more circuitous route of historical terms of cognition. Instead, they chose to empathize with the constellation of actions that seem directly accessible to modern understanding. The goal has been up until recently to make the actions and feelings of the characters, especially those of Kriemhilt, comprehensible to a modern reader, and to create a psychologically transparent reconstruction of the epic's plot.[10] The theoretical foundation of such a reconstruction is seldom made explicit. In reality, it is generally based on the critic's intuition, his or her experiences as a spouse or a friend, on current concepts of how young people should behave, on assumptions about courtliness or female nature, and so on.

In the most comprehensive interpretations, the Middle Ages and the present are not naïvely confused.[11] Historical factors are considered, such as the obligation of revenge, the greater intensity of affect and acts of will, a worldview that has room for giants, dragons, and water fairies. But despite consideration of all these special circumstances, the eternal themes of love and hate, loyalty to friends and fealty to a lord, power, and rivalry remain paramount. The claim to interpret the *Nibelungenlied* as a text from around 1200 (and not as the result of the long history of an archaic legend) paradoxically resulted in a dehistorization of the epic and a false, anthropological view of its conflicts.[12] The most political grand epic of the German Middle Ages became the object of the decontextualization of close readings and appeared to its modern critics as very close to, and at its core deeply interrelated with, their own world. At its extreme, everything that seemed strange and alien in the story was transformed into familiar everyday psychology. A good example is Walter Falk's assertion that the mythic-archaic remains of the story line that resist a clear interpretation are the expression of an "interior world."[13] When Sivrit hands over the legendary treasure of the Nibelungen to Kriemhilt as a dowry, this is declared to be "impossible" in reality but nevertheless true, because "Sivrit's internal wealth becomes external through his marriage."[14] Thanks to such interpretive acrobatics, the medieval epic becomes indistinguishable from a nineteenth-century adaptation of mythological material.

Even when the political focus was on the core of the epic, the historical content was pushed aside in favor of the timeless circumstances of political action, based on the main characters and their personal interests.[15] The political problem was reduced to the question of whether Kriemhilt acts out of ambition or love, and whether the epic is mainly about a struggle for power or the revenge of a woman in love.[16] No matter what the answer is, Kriemhilt appears as a representative of common human entanglement. What was normally lacking in these political reinterpretations was a concrete historical basis. Epic characters were stylized as representatives of political power, weakness of character as a political trait, and positive or negative appraisal was "translated" from one sphere into the other.[17]

A psychologization, unconsidered in its foundation but successfully practiced, to some extent supported the epic's claim to a place in the current literary canon and seemed to compensate for its loss of importance following World War II. It was suggested that the attempt at historical distancing and reconstruction suffocates everything with the dust of academic studies. Actually, just the opposite is true. Read as quasi-contemporary but timeless history, the epic seems a barbaric collection of contradictions, a psychological net full of holes, the incomprehensible remains of an opaque legend centered around problems that are either somewhat trivial (the marital drama) or not particularly pertinent (its embeddedness in sociopolitical relationships). Such things can from time to time be gazed at in amazement, with a respect for age, but that's about all.

As apolitical as it might seem, this actualization of a timeless and universal human nature, which had turned its back on unholy nationalistic attempts, remained bound to the same ahistorical reception. Surely long gone are the naïve and appropriating projections of nationalism that block the way to the text. But the misunderstanding remains the same. The epic could only be misappropriated by ill-considered propaganda because it seemed to recount a way of life thought to be relevant even "today," even if exaggerated as grand and heroic. This is also presupposed by a psychological reading.[18] The philologist, critical of the heroicized falsifications that result from the nationalist appropriation of the epic, rightly points to the text-immanent description of heroic destruction and seeks to work out its critical potential, but he is still using his own understanding of the world and of humans as a standard. In this way, Kriemhilt may represent the tragedy of a woman in love who has lost what is dearest to her, Hagen may shock us with the inhumanity of his icy scheming for power, the Burgundian family of kings represents the entanglements of political action and the weaknesses of political decision makers, and Sivrit lays bare the delusion of those who believe only in themselves.

This is hardly less distant from the world of epic than the storms of steel [*Stahlgewitter]* in the clash of nations.[19] In fact, the acting characters and the conflicts in which they are entwined can only reveal themselves to our understanding in their historical concreteness. Only historical alienation makes a world that is no longer ours transparent, a world that, for precisely this reason, narrates alternatives to what is true today. It is this alienation that opens the door to a story that is neither flat nor antiquated, but rather well motivated, even in its immanent aporia. A new book on the *Nibelungenlied* is justified by an appeal against a false actualization that colonializes the Middle Ages and transforms them to meet one's own preconceived notions, as happened with the alien world beyond Europe.

Aporias of Interpretation

Our point of departure is the historical uniqueness of the Nibelungian world, whose supposed timeless constellation depends on presumptions that no longer hold true for us. What seems close to us often only seems that way through a trick of perspective. To resist this requires a different way of thinking that can only partially succeed, because we can never completely give up our own historical position, but only try to suspend some common notions. The prerequisites for this are fairly propitious today, because the tempo of modernization, on the one hand, and the continual relativization of Eurocentric thinking, on the other, constantly force us to question the general applicability of our everyday understanding, and whatever had previously been taken for granted as fact. From the perspective of a world that is continually being overtaken by the future and problematized at its margins, there is scant comfort to be found in the past, either in the reliability of valued traditions, whether national, cultural, ethical, or whatever, or in the promise of constant progress along teleologically determined lines, on which history rides toward the critic's point of view as if on railway tracks. Trying to take the viewpoint of the other, the stranger, the unexpected and new becomes a question of survival, and historical thinking must also search for an answer to the question, "What if . . . ?"

I have attempted to approach the *Nibelungenlied* with the question, "What if this or that, although seeming valid to me, were not true?" I want to set aside assumptions about "how I would act in place of the epic characters" or "what I would say about their behavior," assumptions about their habits, their means of perception, the presumed relationship in the epic between "interior" and "exterior," about the normal ways of the world, and about sufficient causal links. Medieval studies lacks the preparatory work for such an attempt. The critic finds himself instead directed to works on archaic Greece or modern ethnology.[20] In any case, I continue to pursue some of my own efforts related to the individual oddities of the epic.[21] These attempts were sometimes incorrectly understood as arguments for replacing a "psychological" reading with a "sociological" one.[22] Instead, my intentions are much more ambitious, aiming at a historical reading of the *Nibelungenlied* that would also consider the historical construct of what modern scholarship distinguishes as "psychological" or "sociological" as being historically inadequate.

The first thing that must be done is to suspend the current concept of literature that refers to and yet is dependent on the actual culture of writing. Whenever the *Nibelungenlied* is measured by this yardstick, supposed "shortcomings" are immediately exposed. The epic, most likely created shortly before or around 1200, presupposes a centuries-long tradition that was either never written down or, if it was, failed to survive. It has to be assumed that the narrator knew at least parts of this tradition and attempted to integrate it into his epic. But the grand epic design was his work alone.[23] This version became the object of further revision. This permanent reworking must be seen as the basis for the work's literary status (and not just as an explanation of the supposed shortcomings that distinguish the epic from a more recent literary text). There is no "original" single text that is complete, and the "poet" of an epic is not fully in control of the text in any case.

Presuming expectations of coherence, agreement, and integrity derived from modern literature to be normative for medieval epics is therefore problematic. Disruptions occur more frequently in the reworking of a multivocal tradition, and expectations of agreement, or at least the absence of contradiction, are likely to be more easily disappointed. A narration that brings divergent traditions together is less exacting in connecting these elements.[24] In vain, scholarly readers of the *Nibelungenlied* expect seamless connections and "probable" motivation, as required by everyday experience and defined by modern narrative theory, instead of asking about other types of motivation and narrative coherence. What is "probable" or "contradictory" is usually only postulated intuitively. Almost never discussed are the historical and aesthetic criteria themselves, which sometimes call to mind a legal transcript or a run-of-the-mill crime novel. They are inadequate even for most of the great texts of modernity, from Cervantes to Goethe, Kleist, and Kafka. Here, too, they would lead to verdicts of "improbable" and "contradictory."

However, in recent years, the expectation of wholeness and integrity has often been completely abandoned, and attempts to make the epic's "total concept" plausible have been rightly criticized.[25] Correspondingly, commentaries on individual scenes have come to the fore. They seem more appropriate to the text, but they are limited in scope. In the end, they are simply an expression of embarrassment. Implicitly scholars admit that the linkage of "realistic" scenes was apparently not yet mastered in the *Nibelungenlied,* which is why some latitude should be allowed when attributing a literary quality to the epic. Instead, a historically adequate reading must recognize this theory's inherent expectations of coherence as historically limited and therefore inappropriate to the Middle Ages.

The ground for approaching the older narrative form was prepared in 1932 by Clemens Lugowski's analyses of late medieval prose narration.[26] His approach remains to be transferred to medieval literature. This is all the more astonishing in that the unquestioned assumption of the novel's timeless aesthetic, whose relevance for the premodern is questioned by Lugowski, has been abandoned in newer narrative theory. This "realistic" type of narration, the standard by which the *Nibenlungenlied* and its relationship to legend is still latently measured, is a phenomenon of the eighteenth and nineteenth centuries. The psychological-anthropological basis of this type of narration in everyday experience has long since been destroyed by twentieth-century science, by psychoanalysis, sociology, and linguistics. It continues to exist only in trivial genres.

The suspension of familiar cultural patterns must therefore include those aesthetic norms that are only seemingly obvious. A more adequate descriptive model for the narration in the *Nibelungenlied* must be developed.

Only in this way can conclusions that basically question the epic's interpretability be repudiated. Their argument is this: when a redactor was bound to a contradictory and, insofar as it was oral, possibly shifting and unreliable tradition, he could not produce a closed text. Every interpretation of the whole, as well as of individual scenes, runs the risk of constructing connections where divergent material was simply painstakingly stuck together.[27] These kinds of constructions only succeed, so the thinking goes, with the help of massive additions and the critic's smoothing of the text by playing down breaks, filling gaps, and silently correcting "mistakes" in the adaptation of the legend history. These kinds of modifications can be found in abundance in some interpretations of the *Nibelungenlied.* I have called them "interpolations."[28] Joachim Heinzle calls them "insinuations of meaning" (*Sinnunterstellungen*).[29]

Such interpolations should not only be criticized as a methodologically questionable consequence of a lack of narrative material, that is, as a hapless attempt at repair, but as a wrong aesthetic concept of premodern narratives. They are undertaken in the name of logical coherence of plot and psychological correctness, that is, the standard of modern narrative texts. Most critics are beholden to this principle. "Insinuations of meaning" are stimulated by elements of the text that seem to be unintelligible and contradictory in and of themselves, and they therefore seem to suggest an interruption or an inappropriate contamination in the legend, or prompt the critic to write a new and improved version of the text.

Heinzle's suggestion of doing away with interpretations altogether comes to terms with this dilemma, since in his opinion any interpretation harmonizes what is dissonant. The critic is, after all, dealing with a work that only superficially integrates a long, deficient, diverse tradition. Heinzle suggests instead a reflection on the history of the legend. He does not return to the speculations of older scholarship about lost versions and the original form of the work,[30] but rather emphasizes the accidental nature of the legend's transmitted form. The history of transmission does not permit going back, through textual criticism in its "original" form, to a single, closed, and at most only marginally corrupted and therefore nearly "original" text. Rather, it documents a series of basically solid, but, in their actual form, heterogeneous, structures that have been patched together more or less successfully out of a legend that can no longer be reconstructed. Every interpretation must fail at the fissures unless it attempts to paste these structures into some kind of harmonious whole.

In my opinion, Heinzle's alternative, a "unique and original work of art," as opposed to a divergent tradition that prevents unequivocal assertions, is too simple.[31] To be sure, it does consider literary types as represented by the *Nibelungenlied*, but the implicit standard of comparison remains the same aesthetic norm at the heart of the criticized attempts to "insinuate meaning." Instead, one should look for norms and aesthetic concepts that appropriately reflect a medieval type of literacy. Heinzle's warning against interpretation has its corollary in the structurally closed artwork that assigns a meaning both complete and exclusive, in which every element is subsumed by an organized and conceptual whole. The justified criticism of "insinuated meaning" does not exclude all hermeneutic-interpretive efforts.

Newer literary theory has asserted that the structural integrity of a work of art is an illusion, or at best a dramatic effect that eliminates the diversity and fractured nature of linguistic structures, at least on the surface. This is most certainly true of premodern texts that are in no way beholden to the ideal of structural integrity and organic harmony—which does not, of course, mean that they are impervious to any analysis of their semantic latency. Corresponding to the "open" text are "open"—but not arbitrary—interpretations, and the fact that a modern aesthetic concept fails to explain a medieval text does not mean that there is no other, more adequate concept. It seems to me too early to give up hope.

"Insinuations of meaning" grow out of the inconsistencies and contradictions of the text. But should we not first question whether these are in fact inconsistencies and contradictions; whether the critics' "interpolations"—regardless of what kind—are justified, even necessary; whether or not there are possible explanations other than harmonizations or assumptions of error on the part of the epic's material? Such a different reading remains inaccessible so long as the norm remains a narration that is linearly progressive, causally linked, based on everyday experiences, and syntagmatically coherent.

In the end, it does not matter whether the intermediate links of Kriemhilt's story, the tale of the young Sivrit, or the theft of the treasure hoard—all elements that the epic narrator withholds—are supplemented by "insinuated meaning" as a necessary part of normal narrative, or if their absence is explained by a heterogeneous heroic tradition that ultimately defeats all attempts at interpretation. In both cases, the distinctiveness of premodern literacy is ignored. One may agree with Heinzle's critique but not with its conclusions and aesthetic assumptions.

That's not all. Investigations of the "realistic" novel have shown that literary texts necessarily always work with "empty spaces," to be filled in by the reader's own imagination, and that the "act of reading" consists of the interaction between the given of the text and the interpretive activity of the reader.[32] A text that explicates the many presuppositions that are necessary to understand what is being narrated, leaving no room whatsoever for its recipient's imagination, is only imaginable as an exception, and in the end would be an unconsumable literary monstrosity. Lawrence Sterne parodies such a text in *Tristram Shandy*. Every text stimulates the reader's fantasy through "empty spaces" and at the same time restricts it through what it says. A reading that does not allow itself to be restricted by what is specified by the text is in danger of becoming arbitrary and only serving the reader's associations.[33] On the other hand, a reading without any involvement on the part of the reader is impossible. The difficulty lies in controlling the (necessary) activity of the recipient in some historically adequate way, which means proceeding from the text's own instructions.

Behind the many attempts to show the epic narrator's gaps and contradictions, there is almost always the idea of a "correct" linkage that has simply become corrupted. The rules of such a linkage are believed to be valid for all time. A historical argument—the possible development of a legend—is thus ahistorically justified. This circumvents the need to read these supposed breaks and gaps as traces of a foreign concept of the world, of commonplaces that are now strange, of another way of forming coherence. This task requires that one's own expectations of how a story can be plausibly told be suspended as long as possible, and that what is actually told is, as much as possible, taken to be conclusive.

In view of the *Nibelungenlied*'s successful dissemination, it is hard to believe that it is nothing more than a patchwork of legends for philologists to unravel, and that recipients and scribes have missed the point for centuries. Or are we back to attributing all its inconsistencies to the medievals' "childlike credulity" and "aesthetic indifference"? The fact that medieval recipients themselves had difficulties with some of the breaks, gaps, and contradictions[34] will be a subject for further comment when talking about the variants of the manuscripts. In trying to make sense of the narration by improving the text, medieval scribes demonstrate that the story, on the whole, was accepted. Simplifying a complex structure in order to make it fit one's own understanding is so common in the history of literature that it hardly qualifies as an argument against such complexity and the acceptance of the simpler version as the original and correct one.

The basic question of this book is whether the aporia described by Heinzle is based on a problematic concept of interpretation, a historically inappropriate model of narration, and a modern view of the world and society. Instead, I propose a reading that elucidates meaningful linkages, close variants, and structural recurrences on the epic's different levels and thematic subjects. This should be done without claiming that these attempts lead to an interpretation that is closed and conclusive, that integrates everything that is disparate, and glues together all breaks. These very breaks and contradictions (as seen from a contemporary perspective) are what make the *Nibelungenlied* fascinating to begin with.

The Dilemma of the Legend's History

The history of the *Nibelungenlied* profoundly challenges a reading such as that outlined above. "Without a . . . sense [of the legend's prehistory], anyone who wants to understand the work is lost," Heinzle writes, because the poet must "submit himself to the material at hand, with its tradition and its claim to tell an accurate history, and has to accept it as an objective fact."[35] Indeed, in the Middle Ages, the poet was tied to a tradition that limited room for creativity. Even Gottfried von Straßburg, the author of the medieval romance most deeply rooted in Latin literary culture, worked against a background of tradition and reacted to both literary versions and orally circulating stories. He claims to "read" (*lesen*) the story better than his predecessors, who read it "incorrectly."[36] A fortiori, this must also be true of a tradition-bound genre such as heroic epic.

Nevertheless, narration, even oral narration, and most certainly narration according to an epic concept, is not simply a registration of everything and everyone, but rather a selective, amplifying, and interpretive undertaking. Its scope is larger or smaller, depending on the genre. For Chrétien's Arthurian romance, the consensus is that it was large enough to incorporate the circulating tales of Celtic origin into a *bele conjointure*.[37] Even texts with claims to historiography, which have to tell as completely as possible what is transmitted, give a unique structure to their material through critical selection and organization. In the heroic epic, both tendencies exist: the attempt to reshape the material in a meaningful and new way and the attempt to keep what is transmitted. Even when heroic epic was seen as ancient history, it was always newly adapted to changing interests.[38]

Another question is how convincingly the integration of what is transmitted succeeds, and this is the decisive point in determining what sort of relationship the author of the *Nibelungenlied* might have had to the narrative tradition. If he really just got tangled up in the threads of a tradition that could no longer be unraveled, then the *Nibelungenlied* would simply be a bad text—as with so many of the Dietrich epics.[39] Before him undoubtedly stood a broad, diffuse heroic tradition. As to the story it told and the poet's knowledge of it, at best, only a few suppositions can be made.

The "model" that Andreas Heusler invented to explain the creation of the *Nibelungenlied*, postulating just a few intermediate stages, was an attempt to come to terms with a complicated problem through reduction. Heusler was guided by completely modern concepts in that he first limited the transmission of heroic material exclusively to a few texts of differing lengths, fixed by poets (heroic lay, short epic, book epic).[40] Second, he attributed the integration of these texts to a single text, the so-called *Ältere Not*, a shorter epic he thought had been created some decades before the *Nibelungenlied* and to which he denied all the mistakes and modernisms that were bothersome in the *Nibelungenlied.* Heusler hoped to gain some sort of idea of the content of the *Ältere Not* from Norse poetry, especially the *Elder Edda* and the *Thidreks saga*, a prose work of the thirteenth century.[41]

This hypothetical construction of the *Ältere Not*, in which earlier adaptations of the legend, perhaps in the form of heroic lays, are supposed to have come together, has for a long time blocked work on an adequate understanding of the text. Everything in agreement was attributed to it, and everything wanting to the *Nibelungenlied.* The plausibility of such a "missing link" and assumptions about how it might have looked in detail are dependent on how much credit is given to latent Darwinistic evolutionary theories in the area of culture studies. In any case, the *Ältere Not* quickly became treated in epic scholarship as a matter of fact, as though it actually were a transmitted text.[42]

How certain is this construction? The transmission in the centuries between the Migration Era and the assumed time of the creation of the *Nibelungenlied* is lost in darkness. That the legend was handed down and told orally is made probable by traces in genealogical-dynastic tradition.[43] But all tangible beginnings are based on unverifiable hypotheses.[44] Also unverifiable is the assumption that Nordic Nibelungen compositions are closer to the original form of the legend, so that with their aid one can decide what is "old Nibelungian" and what is an "addition." That would take for granted that the cultural circumstances of Scandinavia only marginally influenced the legends, whereas the culture of continental Europe forced massive interventions. Even if the Nordic versions retain an older form of the legend, this entails neither the conclusion that this is the "authentic" version nor that it is the standard for all later adaptations. Do we evaluate Goethe's "mistakes" based on Euripides?

Talk of the "primitive bedrock" (*Urgestein*) of the old Nibelungen tradition assumes a model of original form that is basically romantic: there is one true origin from which everything takes shape, and all the rubble must first be cleared away to get there. The "primitive bedrock" therefore represents not only the oldest but also the most valuable layer, the untainted source, the "crown jewel."[45] This implies the opposite conclusion that whatever seemed to the scholar to be the most valuable was by definition also the oldest. But why do the "qualitatively best" songs have to be at the beginning? Why, Heinrich Beck asks, does the path necessarily lead from a "short, erratic representation to the more complete, smoother prose"?[46] What justification is there for seeing the adaptations on the continent as worn out and defective?[47] If what was transmitted could not simply be shoved aside by the author, then we have to ask how it was received, crafted, and reinterpreted. Crafting and interpretation are not the superfluous plastering of "primitive bedrock," just as the so-called primitive bedrock itself is not an annoying atavism.[48]

Finally, abandoning the model of mythical origin does not fail to recognize the immemorial efforts that fashioned the *Nibelungenlied*. Dynastic political and sociohistorical constellations undoubtedly had an effect on the legend.[49] It is known that political constellations of the early Middle Ages left their trace.[50] The idea that we might reach the core by stripping away layer after layer is nonetheless an illusion. Different versions were presumably known to the author. This does not lead to the conclusion, however, that one or other more or less accidentally surviving version can indicate with "considerable evidence" what was told in the other versions but was then painstakingly suppressed by the author at the cost of "many inconsistencies."[51] This is why the elder and younger *Atlilied*, *Völsunga saga*, and *Thidreks saga* have nothing to contribute to a story in which Sivrit is not disloyal, Gunther is not a cuckold, and Etzel is not greedy for gold. If the prohibition on defloration is missing in the *Thidreks saga*, this argues neither that the prohibition in the *Nibelungenlied* is an addition nor that the *Thidreks saga* "forgot" about it. Both texts only give different interpretations of the plot. Contemporary poems are therefore "sources,"[52] but represent different possibilities of selecting from the tradition. There is no matter in and of itself, and therefore no version of a text that does not subscribe to a particular interpretive perspective,[53] and so the matter controls the narrator only within certain boundaries.[54] The individual text should be seen as a distinct answer to a tradition that collected various answers. Parallel texts show the spectrum of possible appropriation, not "how the story should in fact go." The legend should in no way be used as a wild card that can always be played whenever the critic fails to create a logical, psychological concord.

If the history of the legend cannot be used as a source for details of the plot, it can, nevertheless, point to certain general conditions for the process of putting the Nibelungen matter into writing. Instead of starting with single hypothetical texts that might have preceded the *Nibelungenlied*, one has to imagine the literary type at the transition point from orality to writing.[55]

The tradition of the legend includes individual and collective appropriations, poetically formed and unformed narrations. Whereas "within a few decades from the beginning of the thirteenth century," five written versions of the story of the downfall of the Burgundians were circulating in Nordic lands, where "new compositions" were possible alongside simple "transmission,"[56] on the continent, the *Nibelungenlied* alone was successful (without losing the traces of other epic versions completely), supplemented in almost all manuscripts by the *(Nibelungen-)Klage.*

The framework of tradition is present here, too. The narrators are always playing on the general knowledge of what else is narrated about the Nibelungen.[57] They depend on tradition, proving their trustworthiness by recourse to what one knows. By incorporating plundered single verses or verse segments into his own text and utilizing material that is or seems to be ingrained, the epic composer shows that he has traditional poetic stock at his disposal. But he cannot be controlled by tradition, simply because tradition does not speak with a single voice.[58]

In some passages of the *Nibelungenlied,* it is possible to hear a dialogue with tradition. The narrator detaches himself from it and attempts either to eliminate it, to wipe it away, or to interpret it anew or fashion it better. Every oral performance presumes such an implicit dialogue with tradition. With writing, the text leaves behind the turmoil of voices that sound over each other and inscribes itself in the consciousness of the reader as the "authentic" version, at least until the next text claims this status. The text wants to be understood as the "correct" version, without recourse to what is being discarded. Nevertheless, its acceptance also depends on its compatibility with what is generally known, with a tradition that guarantees trustworthiness and authority. Without tradition, the text lacks integrity, without a distinct shape, it lacks clarity and currency for the recipient and the present time.

Attempts to dispel so-called contradictions within a mythical-genetic perspective can, as demonstrated by Joachim Bumke, bear interpretive fruit, if they bring attention to what is odd in contemporary thinking and what points to the scars of various appropriations.[59] But they can only offer hypotheses about what came before. It is hardly possible to determine what parts of the legend the composers knew in some detail, what elements they perhaps assumed to be general knowledge, or perhaps even what they found in an already formed text.[60] It is uncertain what the narrator's heroic preknowledge amounted to, but it was certainly less than that of philologists and scholars of mythology. We should not even assume an exact acquaintance with the story line. If one takes a look at what kind of knowledge of the legend is present aside from the *Nibelungenlied* in the late Middle Ages, for example, about Kriemhilt, then one will not overestimate the exactness and level of detail of such knowledge.[61] To what extent this knowledge limited the narrator in his possibilities and to what extent it acted as a stimulus for going beyond such limits is very difficult to decide. The completely negative picture of Kriemhilt outside of the *Nibelungenlied* supports the latter possibility. The narrator of the epic, and most certainly of the *Klage*, told a tale contrary to the common knowledge of the evil Kriemhilt (*übele Kriemhilt*), and they did this in terms of Kriemhilt's reputation without much success, despite the widespread circulation of their works.[62]

Normally one assumes two different types of legend transmission. One type is formed in specific texts, and the other is told without being reworked in a text. The second kind is mostly only hypothetically postulated as a necessary intermediate link between two actually transmitted versions. This assumes two contradictory models of development. The premise of the first lies in a "comprehensible psychological progression." "The logic of the legend follows a psychological reasoning, a development from the simple to the more complex," it relies on "elaboration," "intensification," and "continuation," Beck writes critically.[63] The second type conversely relies on misunderstanding, banalization, harmonization, or abridgment of what was once a meaningful plot. The first premise is most often used whenever representations of a myth are to be brought into a chronological order, as "steps in a development." The second premise is employed when something that is incomprehensible actually appears in a transmitted text. Both types of reconstruction are, each for itself, and most certainly in combination, highly problematic in text-genetic argumentation. Why should transforming a myth run in only one direction? A constellation might plausibly be a secondary formation,[64] a psychologically more consistent late addition, or, on the other hand, less plausibly, it may not be corrupted but original.

Every adaptation takes place in a concrete historical context, and this can be quite distant from the time when the story was first told. Stories of the Migration Era, the early Middle Ages, and the more recent past have been reworked. This makes shifts likely. Stories have their own time index. What the impact of the historical context is in a new adaptation can only be evaluated in each individual case. The heterogeneity of the living conditions, values, and human characterizations thematized in the *Nibelungenlied* has been examined by scholarship under different aspects since early on. No interpretation of the epic "in its own time" can argue away this heterogeneity; any new approach must work with this assumption. It does seem possible to find a different perspective, using this heterogeneity neither as an argument for the construction of a supposed original nor as the worthless result of a failing contemporary integration. Rather, it should be understood as a basic premise for the wide span of the epic's structure that attempts to overcome contradictions in precarious ways.

Every narration presumes and refers to other narrations. In telling a story that is known, the narrator is prevented from being completely arbitrary. Since he is competing with others who have given the story poetic form, he can follow them, or he can show how his version is superior to theirs. Both can be accomplished when he incorporates their advantages (the accomplished verse, the keen metaphor) and adds them to his own. This is done within a horizon of tradition that is only partially transmitted in writing.

"Vocality" and Cultural Knowledge

The *Nibelungenlied* is an epic that was fed from oral sources.[65] The relationship of the written literary work to orality is complicated. The problem was barely recognized by older orality scholarship. Perhaps because at first the theory of oral formulaic epic, developed with preliterary societies in mind, was all too directly translated to the semi-oral Middle Ages, the impulses of oral literature scholarship have found little response in the philology of the *Nibelungenlied*.[66] The vernacular heroic epic of the Middle Ages is not genuinely oral and only secondarily fixed in writing; it represents a conceptually guided writing down of a former oral tradition.

It was consequential that medieval scholarship interpreted the relationship between orality and writing mostly in terms of alternatives. The notion that a text like the *Nibelungenlied* was unthinkable without the use of writing implied that its embeddedness in a mostly oral, illiterate lay society was set aside and its dependence on oral transmission was reduced to the problem of the origins of certain motifs or a "formulaic" style of narration. The status of the *Nibelungenlied* cannot be adequately described within the dichotomy orality/literality. To describe it more precisely, I therefore employ the term "vocality," introduced by Paul Zumthor and Ursula Schaefer.[67]

This concept is appropriate to a society that is not completely illiterate ("primary orality"), but in which writing is limited to certain groups, institutions, and language uses ("secondary orality"). Some of those who are illiterate have access to writing (mostly the nobility), while those who are literate (e.g., the clergy) participate in the oral communication of the lay society, where writing is again turned into voice through the oral delivery of texts.[68] The illiterate noble lay society around 1200 lived in a culture that transmitted significant amounts of knowledge without writing, but it was able in specific instances to use the skills of the clerics.[69] Literary communication in the vernacular was accomplished predominantly orally. Conversely, there was a Latin culture of *clerici* whose production of writing was at the disposal of a predominantly illiterate society, of which they were part and on which they depended.[70] Medieval Europe was therefore a "semi-oral or secondary oral culture."[71] It was not completely illiterate. Those who could not write could nonetheless take advantage of writing. Thus orality and literality are inseparably connected in medieval lay culture.[72] At first, forms of communication, patterns of perception and interaction, and the handling of transmission change only in certain sectors of society when writing is introduced to vernacular culture, whereas those cultural patterns that are genuinely a part of orality continue to exist in other areas.[73] In addition, the slowness of historical processes in traditional societies explains how the consequences of literalization appear only gradually. The oral preservation of tradition is the norm in certain areas until at least the late Middle Ages and early modern period.[74]

The *Nibelungenlied* explicitly thematizes vocality, that is, dependence on what is written and translatable into voice. It is beyond dispute that the epic uses "formulas" that are typical of oral poetry: preformed sets of words, syntactical elements, metrical units, situational patterns, narrative schemes, and so on, whose basic structure is identical, but whose concrete word fill is variable. The formula is to be understood functionally, as a resource for poetic production and an aid to memorization and reception.[75] This means that the formulas for crafting, for performance and its preparations, and finally for the reception and understanding of the epic can have different meanings and functions. Formulaicness implies "improvisation" only under the conditions of primary orality, when the ad hoc invention of text is based on preexisting patterns, and not necessarily even in that case. Formulas can just as easily work against free improvisation and warrant unambiguous fixing and memorization.[76]

Formulas change their function in a semi-oral society. The author of a written work can employ formulas as a traditional inventory of elements of oral composition in order to make his story appear to be a traditional oral one, thereby evoking in his listeners the impression of something familiar.[77] One must distinguish between a "production problem," a "transmission problem," a "reception problem," and a "stylistic problem," the consequences of which do not necessarily coincide.[78]

In written texts, the emphasis shifts to the latter two aspects.[79] Where oral production can be excluded,[80] oral and literate practices can still continue to interfere in the transmission. The repertoire of "formulas" of completely different kinds makes it easier for the poet (or the arranger) to pursue his craft by using predetermined patterns. More important, however, is the reception side. During the presentation, formulas that become literate are once again realized through voice; they are led back to orality, and can thereby have an effect similar to genuine oral poetry. The formula enables the listener to recognize in the new what he already knows; it reduces uncertainty and limits the possibilities of interpretation.[81] It presumes a common cultural knowledge that is shared by the narrator and actualized in the narration.

Such an implicitly assumed knowledge plays a greater role in oral communication than in writing. If knowledge is not fixed in writing, then special tools are required to transmit it and to save it from being forgotten. Narrations are part of cultural memory.[82] The most important aid to remembering is, next to the ritual, the stereotypical, formal creation of relevant linguistic units. The transience of the spoken word is counteracted by the recurrence of the same or related elements. The formula guarantees the reliability of information and its applicability to what was previously known. It recalls knowledge of the ways of the world and the normal method of interpreting them and thereby assures the transmission and preservation of this knowledge.

With the introduction of writing, this form of preservation loses some of its importance. But even in the developed, modern literate culture, it is not completely pushed to the margins. In the Middle Ages, writing was limited to certain sectors of society, but the older form of knowledge remained dominant and was only supported by writing. Written formulas also reassure the literate listener of the coherence of his experience.[83] The conformity of what is known and what has forever been true is therefore just as important, even for a written text such as the *Nibelungenlied*, as the concord of narrative progression and the motivated linear arrangement of the plot.

An illiterate listener to a written text does not need to be concerned with the complicated rules of literate communication. Narration can facilitate comprehension by employing familiar patterns. The context in which a written text is supposed to be valid must be made verbally explicit if it is to be understood beyond its primary communication situation. Oral speech can bypass this requirement by referring, as in everyday communication, to the shared experience of speaker and listener, about which one can communicate not only in words but also through action and direction.[84] Oral speech can also appeal to a cultural knowledge beyond the commonly experienced situation, and this knowledge can be assumed between communications partners who know each other. Provided that it is unambiguous and stable, subject at most to long-term and thus barely noticeable changes, this knowledge does not have to be explicit and can be kept present through allusions. In contrast, since the homeostasis of archaic cultures began to dissolve with writing, the elements of this knowledge were less significant in written communication and, in the case of changes in the context of reception, had to be continually augmented. The reoralization of written texts in oral performance that occurred between the two types of communication succeeded all the better the more the text referred back to the unproblematized knowledge presumed in oral communication.

The stability and comprehensiveness of knowledge in oral societies continues to apply under conditions of vocality.[85] Texts that originate from orality, or that are tailored to oral communication, therefore seem more stereotypical than written texts on the one hand, and more fragmentary on the other. They are more stereotypical because they build on the reliability of common knowledge, and more fragmentary because they need be less explicit.[86] But this is distinguished only where texts are seen in their written form, which is precisely the case in the *Nibelungenlied.* Only with the gradual success of writing does the implicitly presumed horizon of understanding fade away; competing contexts of understanding become imaginable, and understanding has to be ensured explicitly.[87]

Cultural knowledge is concerned with norms of action, rules of behavior, and assumptions about the ways of the world. These make up the background to any story and are called upon for explanation and interpretation. With this knowledge, one can fill in what remains open horizontally in the motivational connections of the plot. The fact that it can remain open does not just mean that anyone may simply supplement whatever he or she assumes, based on his or her own cultural competency. Instead, a competency must be activated that the narrator can presume for his listeners. In this way, the frame of reference about what is to be imagined remains relatively stable.

Listening requires less of a clear, complete connection of plot elements (syntagmatic coherence) than reading (where one is able to turn back to earlier pages and compare text).[88] During the act of listening, any violation of common cultural knowledge is immediately apparent, for what is said must be plausible in the light of what has always been true (paradigmatic consistency). A contravention would be serious in this case and is therefore less common. Where it nevertheless occurs, it is often explicitly marked by the narrator, because it disturbs the concord between speaker and listener and endangers the success of the communication. The orally performed epic must also speak in terms of what is self-evident as perpetuated in proverbs and maxims, stock phrases of praise or reproach, and stereotypical situations and plots. This is the basis of the "stereotype" of heroic poetry.

The *Nibelungenlied* is marked by vocality and partakes of both literality and orality.[89] If its creation without the help of writing is hard to imagine, it nevertheless seems to have been destined for performance, that is, oral actualization, in which it could rely on unspoken common knowledge without making that knowledge explicit. An appropriate understanding is impossible without the presumptions that the narrator requires of his listeners.

The modern critic for his part is in a difficult position, because he neither shares the situation for which the epic was conceived nor—and this is more important—possesses the cultural knowledge of the original addressees.[90] He must attempt to reconstruct this knowledge if he wants to understand the text. The *Nibelungenlied* in this respect contains more and different "empty spaces" than a literary text,[91] not the kind that give the recipient room for individual appropriation, but the kind that must be filled up with collective cultural knowledge. To disregard this knowledge would mean viewing the text as a work of contemporary literate culture, which would be ahistorical.[92]

From this, we must draw conclusions about the text of the *Nibelungenlied* as it is extant in written form. True, its exact position in the written transmission can no longer be determined. It is probable that the epic of the twelfth century was preceded by earlier written stages, but none of these remain, and it is therefore difficult to base any argument on them. We only know that the *Nibelungenlied*, as it is transmitted in manuscript B, is situated fairly close to the transition from an oral stage into writing and was probably performed orally. An orally received epic would neither depend on purely literary techniques nor manifest the typical characteristics of oral poetry alone.

A written text by no means puts an end once and for all to a living oral tradition. The *Nibelungenlied*, as a grand epic disposed to broad themes, is certainly not thinkable without writing, but writing does not mean a final fixing, authorization, and cohesiveness of the text. The attempt to integrate new material continues, as will be shown in Chapter 1. The (written) text continues to remain open to addenda and corrections, to new motivations and interpretations.[93] It occupies a zone between orality and literality that is hard to define.[94]

In the period of "transition" from orality to literality, each text has only one possible position, but its components do not necessarily belong completely to only one of these two cultures. Various combinations are conceivable: the text is either written or it is not; it is only meant for reception in one or the other context; it falls under one or the other type of composition; it has grown out of orality, but it uses gestures of oral language and aims at a situation of oral performance.

Book Epic Integration as Characterized by Vocality

A book epic in the zone between orality and literacy should not be assessed with the criteria of literate genres such as the modern novel.[95] When the narrator sought to integrate a multivocal heroic tradition into his concept, he merely concentrated, among other things, on a linear connection of the plot, and this in both the macro ("biographical" aspect, as J. J. Bodmer remarks disparagingly) and the micro (apparent in the web of cross-references, as in the foreshadowing that overlays the text). Coherence in such widely scattered branches does not mark the beginning of heroic tradition, but is an end product that can only be attempted when the legend is written down. Earlier Nibelungen scholarship tried to reconstruct the original, presumably coherent, legend. This attempt was inherited from romanticism, but paradoxically it remained aesthetically dependent on the literary classical canon based on the internally and externally closed and harmonious text. Changes were only conceivable as text corruption, a result of repeated copying. The transmission of the text seemed to have been a process of degeneration, similar to the children's game of "telephone," when a sentence passed in a whisper from one player to another turns into ever-increasing nonsense.[96]

The performance situation, on the other hand, allows for a certain independence from the written text, and the interaction with the cacophony of tradition can always begin anew. Both possibilities also existed for the courtly romance around 1200. This is evident from its early transmission, where "two or more manuscript groups, formed relatively early, . . . remained set for centuries."[97] But here the variance seems to be more limited, since the stricter construction and sharper focus on a problem connects every element to the whole. From the very beginning, the courtly romance distances itself from the many voices of the older narrative traditions, as cited in the first verse of the *Nibelungenlied* in the plural. Here, as opposed to the courtly romance, the free alterations of the tradition are excluded, as is their reshaping according to a single concept.

Was the downfall of the Nibelungen ever the complete story that the author of a historical novel would have made of it? Stories have gaps and dark, blind spots that always invite new explanation, breaks that can only be overcome with effort. They challenge everyone who tries to tell them anew. One must complete what is incomplete, illuminate what should remain dark, explain what not only the passage of centuries has made seem inexplicable. This is the situation in which those seeking to tell an old oral narrative find themselves. They have to make connections in an unwieldy field of partially known, partially half-known stories that are out of sync with each other. As shown just by the coexistence of several versions of the *Nibelungenlied* and *Nibelungenklage*, this could succeed only in the course of several attempts.

Rather than trying to cover up what is problematic, I'll make it the starting point of reflection, to interpret overdetermination as well as undermotivation as a sign that a problem had to be solved, not to criticize the *Nibelungenlied*'s fissured construction as an aesthetic shortcoming, but to explain it by the overlapping and competing orders and contradictory strategies, in short, to capture the epic's potential for uneasiness and provocation. The places where the smooth flow of the plot seems to falter, where what came before does not seem to be in concert with what comes after, or where spontaneous understanding halts, deserve special attention. They should neither be prematurely subsumed into a supposed grand concept nor trivialized as mere negligence.[98] They most certainly should not be eliminated as "mistakes" just because they disrupt the horizontal linkage.

All forms of everyday communication, consisting of many more or less fragmentary speech utterances, are based on what is generally known and taken for granted, as is formed speech in the context of vocality. Conformity is guaranteed to a high degree, more than the textual coherence required in literacy. This is also true of epic books that have sprung from orality and are still realized orally. Early writing only occasionally and only incompletely fulfilled the requirements of literary integration and agreement.[99] This raises the question of the textual unity of the *Nibelungenlied*.

Ursula Schaefer rejects the term "text" for cultures of vocality and would like to replace it with "utterance," which is common to oral speech.[100] This is awkward so long as "utterance" is also used for everyday communication.

What is lost is exactly how the term "vocality" describes a situation between orality and literality.[101] More recent linguistic scholarship distinguishes between the unstable everyday utterances of language embedded in action (an "effective" use of language) and "oral texting,"[102] that is, a unit of speech that is detached from everyday communication and committed to memory for suprasituational cultural purposes, but is still entirely realized in orality. These texts can be secondarily embedded "effectively" (for example, in ritual); they are often stored by specialists of tradition (such as a clerical caste). They are in any case every bit as fixed and separated from the ephemeral nature of everyday speech acts as is the text fixed in writing.[103] This type of text includes "sacred" texts, legal texts, and genealogies. They receive their permanence mostly through poetic fabrication. Poetry is the most important medium of cultural transmission in oral societies. It can only accomplish this task reliably, however, if it fixes the important parts of the information, which does not rule out that certain parameters of the text will remain variable and can be adjusted to changing social and cultural conditions.[104]

The linkage of "text" and "writing" is understandable from the perspective of literary culture but historically false. Unlike "utterances" in everyday speech, the oral epic is also "textually whole."[105] Orality that is supported by writing has been all the more detached from the *hic et nunc* of the situation to which everyday utterances refer. (Re-)vocalized writing is more fixed and, of course, not deictic in the same sense as oral speech in everyday situations.[106] An epic like the *Nibelungenlied* is less textually complete than a purely literary work but of greater durability than a purely orally fixed text. It is therefore even less comparable to everyday utterances than the former.[107]

The "fictitious orality"[108] of the *Nibelungenlied* presumes a different concept of text, even though it still represents a text. The epic is a long way from the instability and arbitrariness of everyday utterances. Single formulations are not yet protected, however, in the script that again becomes voice. More important than the wording is the meaning to which the words refer, which allows, as in oral speech, for more than one actualization and yet remains the same as long as the content does not change.

The vocality of vernacular poetry in the Middle Ages should therefore not refer to "literature" when the term is etymologically correctly bound to letters and writing. Such a restriction is hardly practical, however, because it excludes poetic texts that have been formed orally. In what follows, the term "literature" will therefore be expanded to include the ensemble of vernacular texts characterized by vocality.

To the extent to which the textual narrator replaces the physically present narrator (or in the case of a performance, the performer's voice), and the listeners are replaced by an implicit audience,[109] then, formulas—as known from oral formulaic poetry—appear as consciously chosen means of poetic form alongside other genuinely literary forms.[110] The recipient is referred by the "pseudo-oral-formulaic style" to a frame of reference for understanding and to a world that poetic production has already left behind, since its resources are freely available.

What impact does the literary tradition have in comparison? Everyone who wrote anything in western Europe around 1200 certainly took part in the schooling of the Latin culture of writing. Is it even possible to imagine a written conception of a previously oral legend without the model of Latin literacy? As far as specific written skills are involved, certainly not, but the segment of literary dependencies is much smaller than in later, fully formed European literacy, and the linguistic and educational barriers of Latin remained high even after Latin letters were adapted for vernacular texts.

A privileged practice of literary scholarship—reconstructing the relationship between (written) texts, even if their mutual influence still has to be worked out—bumps up against its limitations when confronted with the vernacular literature of the twelfth century There have been many attempts.[111] All these attempts can be criticized in that they do not give enough weight to the diverse difficulties involved in cultural transfers. If, still in the field of heroic epic, the epic of antiquity is a natural model for the Latin *Waltharius*, because phrases, images, and rhythmic figures can be transferred directly,[112] then the adaptation of these elements by a vernacular epic would be much more difficult and their success much less probable, given that the two languages are so different. This is true even in cases of related subject matter: the medieval romance of antiquity, for example, is oriented on sources, but has little to do with their content, structure, and rhetorics. Why look for a Latin model that is difficult to adapt when autochthonous types existed as well? The influence of Virgil is always argued whenever vernacular epic is put into writing, although the motifs can be found as easily in the most distant literatures.[113]

Supposed dependencies on Latin literature usually remain nonspecific. Joachim Heinzle, for instance, thought he had discovered the "programmatic formula for the Troy legend" in the first strophe of the *Nibelungenlied*. "Many heroes must lose their life on account of a woman." He then admits that the formula has limited applicability, since the story soon takes a very different course. Is this really "symptomatic" of "an attempt to literacize the matter" that "could only partially succeed?"[114] Is the idea that many men die on account of a woman so unusual that it must be transmitted from the fall of Troy—especially when it turns out that the model doesn't fit? If an author schooled in Latin literary culture and cognizant of school texts in which Troy appeared often as an exemplum saw a connection, did this obligate him to use the material, even if in the end he failed? A reminiscence of Troy seems to me less important in terms of textual genetics than as a clue to the missed opportunities inherent in the material.

In reference to other vernacular literatures, for example the French chansons de geste,[115] similar traditions made a "translation" from one vernacular to another unnecessary. The cultural memory of an illiterate lay society does quite well without the crutch of writing. With regard to the theme of vassality, for example, which separates continental from Nordic heroic epic, it seems unnecessary to consider the influence of French literature, if—regardless of regional special developments—similar social structures existed in western and central Europe. The "vassal problem" in heroic epics is a political commonplace.[116] Of course, recourse to texts of a neighboring literature is conceivable, but proof requires a more precise correspondence than just the similarity of a gesture[117] or the sequence of a military campaign.[118] Gestures are much more codified in primary and secondary oral societies than in modern ones, so their correspondence in two texts only attests to the identity or similarity of the practice in which they were embedded. For sequences of action, such as battles, societies develop stereotypical schemes of perception and representation that allow the complexity of contingent events to be reduced to the point where they can be recognized, understood, and memorized. Trivialities thematized in a literary text, such as the shift from day to night, or certain kinds of fighting, do not require a written model.[119] The literary parallels can be enlightening in textual analysis, but they say nothing about dependencies.

Much the same is true of motif connections between heroic epic and chronicles.[120] Historiographic representations use similar schemes of perception, structure, and meaning, which spring from the collective experiences of a historic society. Instead of looking for filiations between texts, it would be better to ask about the *outillage mental* of schemes of perception, experience, order, and interpretation.[121] Historic events and fantasy worlds could be drafted with their assistance.

Most hypotheses of literary influence lack a believable explanation for how the author of one text happened to know another text in a foreign language.[122] The "island-like" nature of vernacular writing makes such connections extremely unlikely unless there are positive indications to the contrary. Where such connections can be demonstrated, they are usually explicitly transmitted through a manuscript that has been translated or edited.

Literary scholars tend to favor and even overrate the connections between (written) texts and other (written) texts, as opposed to other possible connections.[123] This amounts to professional self-deception. The marginality of writing in medieval lay societies makes it likely that the narrator would take advantage of other forms of knowledge than just literary texts, especially since the orally performed vernacular text would not meet the expectations of a public formed by Latin literacy. The attempt to replace a diffuse heroic history, which is susceptible to all kinds of projections, with the assumption of a transmitted heroic tradition as a referential frame of epic production may free Nibelungen scholarship from its ideological fetters of earlier Germanic speculation, but it is hardly methodologically less problematic. The instruments of intertextual analysis developed for the courtly romance are mute when confronted with vocality.

Alterity: The Challenge of Ethnology

The conclusion to be drawn from this is that implicit preconditions are more meaningful for this type of literature than preconditions that are explicit and literary. The implicit cultural knowledge that the epic presumes must be reconstructed in its outline so that the view of the foreign text is not blocked by our own cultural commonplaces. Hans Robert Jauß first called attention to the "alterity" of medieval literature by seeing in this alterity its "modernity," in the sense that "alterity" prompts and even forces a revision of what are presumably unquestioned contemporary notions of art, humanity, and the world.[124] What Jauß related to literature has been generalized to all of medieval culture. Jauß never had a strict dichotomy or radical opposition of alterity and modernity in mind. Alterity is always relative.[125] Some things continue over time, other things change radically. Culture is formed by asynchronous tendencies and elements. Medieval culture is not an intransigent entity but a constellation that is constantly in flux, or, more precisely, is an uncoordinated interaction of different components within different constellations.

The alterity of medieval literature and culture should not be exaggerated so as to seem unreachably alien and exotic,[126] that is, so to speak, to find the natives just around the corner. But no longer are the Middle Ages suited to offer a place of refuge or dreams for an alienated modernity. What matters is neither the thrill of the exotic[127] nor the lure of lost origins, neither dramatic changes nor spectacular actualization, but rather the patient description of the foreign within the customary and familiar. Hasty identifications are as inappropriate as is radical distancing. The difficulty lies in the fact that many things in the medieval world, for example, in the culture of the clergy, still seem to us to be directly accessible, precisely because they belong to our own history.

Historical and cultural scholarship has much to learn from ethnology with regard to these kinds of problems. Ethnology long ago left behind its phase of exoticism and search for curiosities. With the exception of a few, ever more rare and isolated areas, its objects of study are part of complex environments of asynchronous cultural formations. Even if the naïveté that was the rule in nineteenth-century Europe, and that carried over to the outside world, still forms the basis for certain historical culture studies, ethnology has outgrown it.

The historical cultural sciences should be encouraged to practice "thick description" as theoretically described and demonstrated by Clifford Geertz in a series of splendid studies. Geertz also pointed out analogies between his methodology and object of study and those of literature and literary criticism. Transferability is therefore already embedded in ethnology.[128] Geertz's famous description of cockfighting in Bali uses the paradigm of literature.[129] Historical investigation should orient itself on certain principles of his methodology.

I am concerned first with the reconstruction of a cultural framework, the circumstances in which what the *Nibelungenlied* narrates seems possible and plausible, the reconstruction of an "ordinary" world from which the extraordinary activities in the epic spring. One guideline is formulated in Geertz's comment: "Understanding a people's culture exposes their normalness without reducing their particularity. . . . It renders them accessible: setting them in the frame of their own banalities, it dissolves their opacity."[130] In order to understand the normalcy of the foreign, I should not interpret away my spontaneous nonunderstanding; instead, I should make it the starting point for a more exact examination.

Second, causal deductions should initially be deemphasized.[131] If I am again to take up a project I began in 1974 with a first attempt at the *Nibelungenlied*, then I would like to change its assumptions. I thought previously that I could demonstrate direct dependencies and similarities between certain constellations in the *Nibelungenlied* and contemporary political conflicts.[132] This attempt was too direct in its approach and did not sufficiently take into consideration the fact that the world of the epic is a conglomerate of different cultural, to some extent literary, traditions and asynchronous social experiences. Between these, there are interrelated, diffuse dependencies and influences, rather than single, clear ones. So the makeup of the epic world should first be described in its complexities before interrelationships between it and other discourses can be made plausible.

Third, this investigation does not presume a closed, internally consistent, coherent social and cultural system and worldview of a particular group, from which all particulars are derived.[133] As Geertz observes:

> Whatever, or wherever, symbol systems "in their own terms" may be, we gain empirical access to them by inspecting events, not by arranging abstracted entities into unified patterns. A further implication of this is that coherence cannot be the major test of validity for a cultural description. Cultural systems must have a minimal degree of coherence, else we would not call them systems; and, by observation, they normally have a great deal more. But there is nothing so coherent as a paranoid's delusion or a swindler's story.[134]

Fourth, I do not claim that what follows is a description of ordinary rules of thought, speech, or behavior in the High Middle Ages. The object of my interest is not "medieval culture around 1200," but rather a world of symbols, that is, the conception of such a culture in a text. The text simulates a cultural configuration and can therefore be read as such semiotically. A literary conception does not originate in a vacuum. It competes with and refers to other contemporary conceptions that are also available in texts. It must therefore be examined in comparison with other "texts," both literary and extraliterary.

If this investigation often stops before going beyond the level of discourse, then it does so in the interest of methodological consistency and with the awareness that it can only illuminate a small segment of high medieval culture. I understand that literature relates to and is dependent on social praxis, and that it can formulate solutions and aporias that answer deep, general deficits and problems in the medieval culture of nobility. Therefore, I shall certainly refer to this culture, if necessary, and so this book is intended to be a contribution on high medieval culture despite these limitations.

Literature is a part of this culture, a special part, but in constant exchange with other parts. The concept of culture in recent ethnology is an important step in solving the ancient Marxist "mediation problem" [*Vermittlungsproblem*], that is, the problem of how social structures influence discourse. In this concept it is no longer literary scholarship that again imports only (as so often in its history) problems and solutions that have been worked out in other disciplines. On the contrary, methods and theories from literary studies can be applied as a model for the analysis of culture.[135] If culture is understood as text,[136] then literary texts are only part of a larger body of signs. Hence, what must be determined is the relationship between related configurations (i.e., "texts"), and not between heterogeneous constellations (i.e., "literature" and "society"). Such an expansion of the concept of text is all the more crucial for the culture of medieval laity, for there the written text is marginal in comparison to other systems of signs and kinds of sign usage. The written text is more closely interwoven with and dependent on other cultural sign systems in the western European Middle Ages than in other times.[137]

The discussion of "cultural poetics" has to retain its metaphorical character. Culture is composed of different "regional" systems of symbols and is the overarching structure that relates them to one another, embedded as they are in social practices and institutions. In its different sectors there are texts of many different kinds, consisting of different sign elements. Whoever reads a culture like a text must consider the differences in various types of text, to include the type that is summarized as "literature." Common to all of these "texts" is their "being made." Culture as the summary of the sign systems of a particular time, along with their attitudes, rituals, practices, and social orders, is a construct whose "rules of production" can be explicated like those of a poetic text.

If, as the discussion of "cultural poetics" suggests, cultures should be read as texts, then texts can also be read as segments of cultures, namely, as models of possible worlds that stand in a describable relationship to other models of the world—the practical model of everyday belief models, normative models, and so on. The difference between cultural phenomena and the special status of literary texts does not have to be suspended, but the conventional distinction between "objective reality" and "plain fiction" is blurred. In a certain regard, even "reality" is constructed and can be comprehended as an ensemble of signs. The rules of the use of signs and the participants in the exchange of signs are not the same on all levels of cultural discourse, but different sign systems do have a mutual relationship. A semiotic analysis of literature will—because of the special nature of literature—capture only parts of medieval culture, but its results will be compatible with other semiotic analyses.

This distinguishes my methodology from the earlier history of mentalities, which examined all sources of an epoch as material for the dominant dispositions, attitudes, and habits—*l'imaginaire*—of an era.[138] Insofar as literary texts were included, they represented one kind of source among many. Their special status with respect to other texts was smoothed over, only their testimony was accorded a somewhat lower degree of reliability in the reconstruction of an era-specific "imaginary."[139] This risks a circular logic, namely, that what is found in literary texts is interpreted as historical mentality, and this mentality is used as the interpretive instrument for these same texts. Instead of understanding "historical mentality" as an average, gained from as many and as different "sources" as possible, it should be understood as a plural *tantum*, as intertwined and contrary complexes, integrated in different ways, consisting of habits, schemes of behavior, values and norms, world and societal views, all differentiated in varied groups and types of texts and sign systems.

Literature is to be understood as a separate and distinctive part of "cultural poetics."[140] This is also true of "literature" in a culture characterized by vocality, which is concerned with pointed constellations and risky solutions that should not be confused with what is normal,[141] that is, constellations and solutions that react to what everyone believes to be real and true. At issue is a special system of symbolic action that may more clearly bring the preconditions and contradictions of the normal system into focus.[142]

My attempt builds on earlier investigations of heroic epic. It has been said that heroic poetry thematizes the "exorbitant."[143] Literature has thus already left behind the normal structures of a culture, but it remains bound to them as a condition for the possibility of excess. The "exorbitant" is only seemingly an atemporal category, because it changes under concrete conditions and always challenges the measure of the ordinary world.[144] By pointing to the "exorbitant," literary concepts say something about extraliterary cultural commonplaces. This reconstructing is why a new narrative interpretation of an old legend, as represented by the *Nibelungenlied*, is always a bit of "ethnography."[145]

The investigation should begin with segments and proceed "topically," that is, it should thematize certain problem areas from different perspectives, without always telling how these areas come together. This means starting with particular elements of the text and beginning with different levels of representation. The rules to be examined have only limited validity, and they are intersected by competing rules. My aim is not a so-called immanent interpretation of the *Nibelungenlied*, but the reconstruction of (fictional) conditions according to which the plot proceeds, conditions that go beyond the text. So that the argumentation does not become circular (what is used to explain the text is what is extrapolated from the text), it will be necessary to consult other contemporary texts as a kind of control. In order to gauge the historical potency of such a virtual world, other contexts would have to be considered. Such contexts cannot simply be found just anywhere, as an earlier social history of literature thought. These contexts are themselves products of reconstructions; they are for the most part also transmitted by texts. In order to make the preconditions similar, I shall refer to contemporary texts, both literary and nonliterary. Investigations in other areas will have to follow in order to examine to what extent the demonstrated results are really elements of a medieval anthropology.

I hope to be able to show that such an attempt is not a game of intellectual whimsy, as opposed to the hard science of philology (certain things could be said about traditional philology's reliance on assumptions that are not problematized). One can indeed say what one likes about any text, but not in the technical language [*Sprachspiel*] of philological science, where the foundations of the argument must be laid bare and specific proofs must be supplied.[146] The difficulties with this are not to be overlooked. In view of the need to develop a conceptual instrument first, this investigation must admit to its incompleteness as well as to its need for enhancement and correction.

Rules for the Endgame

My investigation will take up the challenge of ethnology's interpretive method in three ways. First, it will attempt to reconstruct the rules that make plausible what is narrated: a past world thematized by the text (implicitly assumed, explicitly accepted, criticized, employed, and used as interactive material). The aim is to show that the text does not follow a single, consistent set of rules, but functions as a locus where conflicting rules meet, rules that are "asynchronous" in origin and validity. Such a set of rules does not emanate directly from a "historical" substrate, nor can it be dissected into historical "strata." The *Nibelungenlied* is not a "source" for something else (for a sociocultural constellation around 1200, for instance), but must itself be understood as a "cultural text"[147] that configures an imaginary world in a certain way, while coexisting with other similar models.

Second, I will examine the connection between these "rules" and the rules according to which this world is thematized and narratively developed. In this, there is a similarity to the investigations of Clemens Lugowski and their continued development in recent narrative theory. Lugowski demonstrates that the "improbability" of early modern narrative was not a "mistake," and that it was in fact constituted according to rules and is analogous to what has been called "formal myth."[148] His argument was latently grounded in the philosophy of history and its aim, the developed form of "individuality" in modernity, but he also indirectly proved the historically limited range of the concepts that are linked to this individuality, namely, those of exceptionality, comprehensiveness, and sufficient motivation, along with their related narrative forms. Implicitly, it was also demonstrated that the form of the modern novel, Lugowski's tacit measuring stick, was itself only a particular historical phenomenon,[149] discarded by the avant-garde of the twentieth century. The rules of narrative analyzed by Lugowski are not identical with the rules that govern the Nibelungian world, but they are related, and in attempting to indicate what these relationships are, Lugowski's project should be further developed: what he calls "artificiality," as an "extraordinary," alien configuration of the world,[150] and what he describes in his "formal analysis" seem to be the (historical) condition of every narrative.

Third, I would like to present the epic—or its various redactions—as the result of a series of interpretive processes, starting with contemporary considerations around 1200. Herein lie the points of reference to extraliterary cultural and social constellations. In order to limit the argumentation, this aspect will normally be only briefly covered. Reception does not end with the first written version. It continues up to present-day attempts at interpretation. There are no solutions that are valid for all time. Instead, there are problem areas that constantly call for renewed examination from different perspectives.[151]

The frame for such an examination is a cultural anthropology that does not subscribe to a view that human nature remains constant over time, as was the case with anthropology formerly,[152] but presumes different historical cultural patterns and corresponding discourses. My examination relies more on differences and breaks than identities (these are not excluded, but at least initially more in the background). To be suspended as much as possible are the usually unspoken, often even unconscious assumptions that determine the common awareness of a European scholar at the end of the twentieth century. On the contrary, we have to attempt the more difficult deciphering of clues whose symbolic character has become opaque.

By "rules" I do not mean a system fixed for all time, but a framework for what is possible that allows some things and rules other things out, that leaves open a broad but still limited repertoire of options. As a whole, they combine to create a (fictitious) anthropological context. These "rules" originated and were predominant at different times, at the time of the matter concerned, at the time of the (supposed) written version of the text, and from eras that lie between. These kinds of dissimultaneities appear on the surface of the text as breaks, overdeterminations, doubled motivations, and undermotivations that are not to be eliminated as "mistakes," but should be made transparent as consequences of a synchronous reworking of diachronous shifts.

The fact that the *Nibelungenlied* thematizes what is asynchronous has been one of the commonplaces since the time of its rediscovery. Friedrich Neumann worked out its "strata of ethics."[153] Otfrid Ehrismann pointed to "archaic" elements in certain clearly defined areas of the epic world.[154] My earlier attempt (1974) tried to show that, at Sivrit's first appearance in Worms, two "asynchronous" concepts of rule and kingship come into a conflict that determines the progression of the plot up until the feud of the queens.[155] Stephen Jaeger, finally, saw an opposition between strongly traditional groups (the clergy?) and "modern" courtly culture,[156] and Walter Haug used the conflict between a "modern," "courtly" narrator and an "archaic" heroic as the key to interpretation.[157]

These questions will have to be discussed in detail, but one has to understand that the sketched oppositions are scientific constructs for the purposes of analysis. This was not always clear. Neumann's layer metaphor basically mirrors the view of earlier scholarship that layer upon layer had to be peeled away, from the time around 1200 to the Migration Era, in order to reach the "core" of the epic. It is true that the younger "layers" are undoubtedly evidence of a contemporary reception, and are not simply to be regarded as counterfeits, but they are further removed from the "original" conflict and might cover or distort the original "core." Ehrismann's term "archaic"[158] implies, on the other hand, a perspective of progress and makes claims about the relationship between real historical periods.[159] "Archaic" is the term for a prehistoric time that cannot be determined, whose only characteristic is that everything differed from what it later became.[160]

It would make more sense to use the term "heroic age." A "heroic age" is not dateable.[161] It can only be identified from a later period that is different (which is not to say that they are not genealogically related). In this sense, certain constellations in the *Nibelungenlied* can be distinguished as "heroic," that is, typical of an imaginary past and different from the world "nowadays" thematized in the same text. On the other hand, any attempt to substantially characterize "the heroic" is doomed to failure.

Jaeger's observations on the critique of "courtliness" in the *Nibelungenlied* can be interpreted relationally, too, as a critique of a world that collapses under the pressure of heroic action.[162] Jaeger contends that the *Nibelungenlied* articulates a clerical protest against the soft worldly, courtly code of conduct. But why should clerics have clung to a heroic-feudal paradigm against which the Church had fought since the early Middle Ages?[163]

The conflict I examined in 1974 between different ideals of rule and models of action also must be understood in relational terms. Contrary to what I thought then, there is no direct, point-for-point link to a sociohistorical conflict (e.g., old nobility vs. ministerials). But there is the polarization of alternatives of action and conduct, which were still simultaneously available in the late Middle Ages.

Haug suggests, not a historical, but rather a literary-historical dating when he describes the replacement of the "heroic," "antiquated" narrative paradigm by a "courtly," typologically "younger" one, which was then finally overhauled by the "older" model. Haug takes up the polar tension that is in fact the key attribute of the epic from the beginning, in which the emphasis switches from one pole to the other.[164] His description also has a primarily heuristic value, with whose help differences and movements in the epic can be described.

Instead of speculating about a "not yet" and "not anymore," the main emphasis should be on pointing out the alternatives presented within the text itself. If, in what follows, the discussion focuses on "asynchronous" rules of worldviews and "asynchronous" ways of narration, then this is not meant as a chronological before and after, but as the simultaneous appearance of antagonistic concepts up to apparent contradiction. The current investigation differs from my previous one in that the breaks get more attention. Several years ago, when I first attempted to explain the "logic" of the *alten mæren* by trying to protect it from the sound common sense of its interpreters, I was primarily concerned with demonstrating that what seemed to be the product of divergent legends could make sense under the conditions of medieval society. It might seem that the title of this book, *Rules for the Endgame*, points in this direction, that of a feudal warrior society's one "alternative" logic. But any attempt to reconstruct a homogeneous logic is bound to fail in the face of the immanent tension of the narrative world. If one seeks to grapple with the problem in a less global way, from the margins instead of from a "whole concept," from the many small and strange assumptions and suggestions of the text, then any "logic" is lost in a myriad of competing logics, whose coexistence is to be understood as a result of a reworking and rewriting.

The tension in an interpretation that does not hide or ignore breaks and does not try to correct contradictions is appropriate for an epic whose author(s) felt bound to an immemorial multivocal tradition. It is more difficult to reconcile a unifying interpretation of the heroic epic with its many voices than in the courtly novel, where the author dominates the material. This allows us, however, to employ some insights of recent literary theory. It has been shown for modern authors, too, that what is seemingly independently and sovereignly worked up from existing material remains dependent on what already exists—on the subjects, motifs, methods, and genres, as well as on the contemporary discourse in which the author is socialized, so that not just the single voice that bears the name of the author is speaking. In heroic epic, these other voices are even more prominent and audible. As much as the author may be the "lord of signs" in his work (and this is true to a lesser extent than in the courtly novel, but to a greater extent than oral formulaic theory would want us to believe), he hides himself behind an anonymous narrator. This makes it easier to describe "rules" of narration than in the case of a very individual style.

On Methodology

If divergent, possibly conflicting aspects of the Nibelungian world are to be discussed, if it is not assumed from the outset that constellations of action, representations of characters, concepts of society, norms, and values are all integrated in a single, closed construct, if we are concerned with the opening of spaces instead of with making unequivocal statements, with the tension between alternatives rather than with their dissolution, then the investigation cannot follow the story line. This distinguishes this attempt from previous ones. There is the disadvantage for the reader that he or she must already know the story in its entirety in order to understand particular arguments, but a recapitulation of the story will not be undertaken here.

Instead, I shall examine individual paradigms of situation and interaction, concepts of personal identification, concurrent norms systems, and ideas of time and space without regard to the sequence of the story. The epic's progress will be viewed from different perspectives that do not necessarily have a point of convergence. Some scenes will therefore need to be examined from several perspectives. I shall try successively to broaden the text's horizon of meaning, whereas past attempts have been intent on inscribing one and only one meaning on the epic. An index of cited verses will allow the reader to find commentaries on certain lines more easily.

There remains the question of the basic text version. The certainty that

Helmut de Boor's text provided the "original" version, relying mostly on manuscript B, which was inspired before Helmut Brackert's (1963) investigation, is now a thing of the past. Even if it were possible,—contrary to Brackert[165]—regarding the relative stability of the text, to see a consistent version behind the many manuscripts,[166] such a version is unattainable, and the many different variants transmitted by the manuscripts, some of which may represent "special material" [*Sondergut*] from an "old" tradition, must be taken into account as well.[167]

Accomplishing this in a comprehensive manner is impossible, given the vast amount of material. Even "regionally" operating text analyses must despair. My attempt to open a new view on the *Nibelungenlied* will therefore deal mainly with what is more or less secure. Certainly, there are critical editions of the main manuscripts, but it does not suffice to use these alone. The remaining tradition shows diverse intersections between the main manuscripts. Ever since Joachim Bumke debunked the philological wild card of contamination,[168] these kinds of intersections have had to be reinterpreted. One must also consider the possibility of lost manuscripts that might reflect different combinations of characteristics from existing ones. Whoever relies on the three main manuscripts alone rejects *a limine* other combinations as exhibited in later traditions. On the other hand, a more or less fixed core text is clearly recognizable, from which certain more important variants (mainly in the group around *C) are clearly identifiable as secondary.[169] I shall therefore proceed on a dual track.

I do not believe that the philological considerations that inform the Karl Bartsch–Helmut de Boor edition are obsolete. Certain cases can be disputed, but this edition presents a text, based on manuscript B, that is more than a snapshot of transmission in a (carefully revised)[170] single manuscript and represents the redaction of an entire manuscript group. It has to be made clear that this text is not to be found in any manuscript, and it is therefore necessary to note the relevant deviations from B as the lead manuscript [*Leithandschrift]*. But it must also be acknowledged that a great many of the preserved manuscripts are related to the text documented in manuscript B[171] and confirm it within a certain tolerance of variants.[172]

The edition of de Boor's vulgate version, in the format that was still edited by him, forms the basis for what follows, and not just because it is readily available. Where it varies significantly, I use the text of ms. B according to Michael S. Batts's transcription, which is also cited for ms. A, ms. C, and other manuscripts, with the exception of mss. w, n, and m, with sigla, strophe, and line numbers. These have all been consulted where the argumentation requires it.[173] The version *C is—with a few well-founded exceptions—cited according to ms. C.[174]

This is certainly an unsatisfactory but necessary compromise. The current state of edition theory makes it necessary, however, to check the edition not only against the *Leithandschrift* B, but, insofar as available and important for the argument, also against other concurrent manuscripts. The *Klage* is cited according to the edition by Bartsch, with reference to the critical apparatus and above all the version by Bumke (1996c). In contrast to Bumke, I am not of the opinion that any discussion of the texts must wait for revolutionary revelations by editorial philology to show the way,[175] because it is Nibelungian philology in particular that offers many examples where editors made mistakes or at least thought the transmitted text to be in need of correction because they did not understand it. Edition and hermeneutic discussion are mutually dependent.

1 Variations of the Legend

Collective Memory?

The stories that the *Nibelungenlied* tells reach far back into the Migration Era. Other stories from other times seem to have joined them. Given the popularity of the material, it seems odd that among the many Nordic and continental variants, there remains no clear "core meaning" that provides the stories of the Nibelungen with a "fundamental ideology."[1] The legend of the Nibelungen cannot be linked, either genealogically or fundamentally, to the Holy Roman Empire of the High Middle Ages or to contemporary forms of sociopolitical activity.[2] This distinguishes the legend generally and the *Nibelungenlied* specifically from other heroic legends and their epic composition, from the *Iliad* and its concept of pan-Greek action,[3] for example, or the French heroic epic of the chansons de geste, with its references to the Carolingian dynasty, the political tensions between king and nobility, and the struggle of Christianity against the Saracens.[4]

This also distinguishes the *Nibelungenlied* from the Dietrich epics (including *Ortnit* and *Wolfdietrich*), whose material refers to a Roman-Germanic kingdom before the Carolingian empire, in other words, to the empire's own genealogy. The Dietrich epic can be exploited for dynastic history, but this is not true of the legend of the Nibelungen.[5] In the *Book of Bern* or in *Biterolf*, there are elements of a foundation legend that make the story part of cultural memory. It is not until the late Middle Ages that one finds a Siegfried cult in Worms, probably already influenced by literature.[6] Only in the early Middle

Ages does the legend seem to have left traces in the genealogical consciousness of noble families in eastern Bavaria, evidenced by "Nibelung" names.[7] If ever it had a memorial function, then this was it.

At the time when the *Nibelungenlied* was created, there was, however, no comparable dynastic interest. The Passau Pilgrim cult, established by the bishop of Passau in the late twelfth century, may well have encouraged the memorialization of Pilgrim, the uncle of the Burgundian kings of Worms and, according to the *Klage*, the sponsor of their *memoria*, but the role of this Pilgrim in the *Nibelungenlied* is much too marginal to think that his commemoration could have been the decisive impulse for the creation, much less the circulation, of the epic. It is certainly an insufficient explanation for the literary stylization of the story. This does not exclude the possibility that the name Pilgrim provided a link [*Ansippung*]— perhaps even politically desirable—between legend and history, for which reliable authority was found in *meister Kuonrât*.[8]

It is certainly possible that the *Nibelungenlied*'s narrator, like other composers of vernacular stories, sought to make a direct connection to a world known to his contemporaries. Group conflicts and social constellations around 1200 may certainly be represented in the configuration of certain episodes,[9] but they probably only influenced the adaptation of the legend in some specific instances. They hardly provide sufficient cause for the choice of this material and its treatment in this form.[10] It is also difficult to understand the epic as a panegyrical *memoria* of great heroic deeds. What is narrated in no way celebrates the *mos maiorum*; rather, it tells of a world's final dissolution. At the end, the narrator has nothing left to tell. We find not undying renown—*klea andron*—but lamentation, and nothing else.

The ending is so apodictic that it required some compensation, and so, in spite of the rough transition[11] in virtually the entire transmission tradition,[12] the Nibelungen *Klage* was appended to the epic.[13] The *Klage* tells a version that not only differs in some details but also includes things the *Nibelungenlied* leaves out. The first part of the *Klage* contains an awkwardly told *memoria*, and the second part provides a continuation that goes beyond the catastrophe's laconic breaking off.

The *Klage* also cannot be understood as a medium for heroic *memoria*, typical of literary interests in the Middle Ages [*literarische Interessenbildung*].[14] In recounting elaborate rituals of mourning and laudatory memorials of the fallen, the *Klage* makes memorialization an object of the story itself by shifting it from the epic's audience to the event's surviving protagonists. It tells how praise memory works, and how it is secured for all time.

The proverbial *Kriemhilden hôchgezît* [Kriemhilt's festivities] sums up in a phrase what matters in the epic.[15] Described is a particular kind of celebration, a celebration that does not sow harmony but instead ends terribly, even though the participants are *vriunde* [friends, relatives], and for which a woman, the *übele* [evil] Kriemhilt, is responsible. There is obviously an impulse to tell this incredible story: how such a catastrophe could happen and why it occurred despite all efforts to avoid it. *Kriemhilden hôchgezît* is "exorbitant."[16] The *Klage* calls the downfall of the Nibelungen the greatest event that ever occurred in the world [*grœzeste geschiht / diu zer werlde ie geschach*] (Kl 3480–81), even though its narrator does everything he can to bring the story down to earth. In this, he continues the revision of the epic that was itself already a revision of revisions.[17] I would therefore like to proceed from the different attempts to tell the story as available in the manuscripts (not from a hypothetical preliterary epic). In principle, they are equally valuable versions, even if more or less comprehensive, whose special "createdness"—*poiesis* in the literal sense—is a reaction to other versions.

The *Nibelungenlied* and *Klage* testify to a continual dialogue with a difficult legend. They "attempt, although at first more or less independently of each other, to make the old indigenous material literate, that is, to rework it in a literary way," Michael Curschmann writes. "[T]he *Klage* is a reflective poem written from the perspective of a clerical-didactic, originally Latin, literacy. In this respect the *Klage* probably represents a final and decisive achievement for the 'lay': only with the *Klage* does the 'lay' finally become a book."[18] Epic and *Klage* represent two very different "layers of literary language," Burghart Wachinger observes.[19] The *Klage* corresponds to the normal type of narrative around 1200 with its poetic form of rhyming couplets, while the stanzaic form of the epic is more closely allied with the older orality.[20] Both have taken up elements of a broad heroic tradition that we can no longer apprehend, others have been discarded, and they all are ordered into a more or less meaningful story. The *Nibelungenlied*'s lack of everything programmatic as spelled out in courtly epics should not deceive us. With respect to Sivrit's death and the downfall of the Burgundians, both held together by allusions and portents and by the incessant varying of related constellations, the narrator is intent on telling and interpreting the well-known story.

The *Nibelungenlied* recalls an "old" world, different from that of the new courtly novel, but it does so by forming this world out of the "new" one. It begins with an ideal courtly world, from which entanglements arise that end in the catastrophe at the court of Etzel (Atilla). This presumes a decisive revision of the legend, traces of which may not be always wiped away and whose basis we cannot precisely gauge. Adaptations of the material, however they may have appeared, will have tried to make the narrated circumstances more plausible. These different attempts are not necessarily related to each other, nor should they be organized under a "leitmotif." In any case, the work of the narrator of epic and *Klage* would have to go a good deal further.

In traditional epic, the position of the author is weaker than in more modern literature, weaker, too, than that of the courtly poet. On the other hand, he has greater authority, because he can refer to something that has been said since time immemorial.[21] It is against this background that the story is told. But scholars generally ignored the fact that the Germanic heroic tale even in its earliest recognizable form is a revision. In the oldest traditions, the aggressor Theoderich is an exile, and Attila, the scourge of God, is the patron of exiled heroes and sits at the center of an ideal courtly world. It is inappropriate to interrupt this process of revision at some point to declare a certain stage of the adaptation to be the "original." The legend has always been interpreted and reconfigured in a discourse with such interpretations.

Narration Between Orality and Literality

In what form did the Nibelungen legend exist? Around 1200, the reception and revision of oral material in a book obviously needed justification. How this could have happened is answered by the *Klage*. Although this answer may have very little to do with the actual creation of the *Nibelungenlied*, it is nonetheless important for an understanding of contemporary ideas about the transition from orality to literality. It is less important whether and to what extent the narrator incorporated material from outside the *Nibelungenlied*. What matters is how he envisioned the tradition.[22] The source references of the *Klage* display a confusing spectrum of statements, which are difficult to reconcile, but taken together suggest an interference of orality and literality.[23] The narrator of the *Klage* refers to what is known and what his listeners have already been told (*Iu ist wol geseit daz*, KL 71),[24] then to *der rede meister*, who revises the *mære* (Kl 44–45), and finally to a book (Kl 19).[25] Book and legend mutually support each other: *als uns ist gesaget sît/und ist uns von den buochen kunt* [as has been told us since/and as we know it from books] (Kl C 66–67).

The role of the different authorities, especially of the *meister* who "controls" the tradition, is anything but clear: an anonymous tradition, one "I" present in the text, the first-person speaker who presents the narration, the authority of a *tihtære* or *meister*, and his written work, all of these stand side by side but are unconnected.

Without further transition, the text starts after the last strophe of the epic:

> *Hie hevet sich ein mære*
> *daz wær vil redebære*
> *und wære ouch guot ze sagene,*
> *niwan daz ez ze klagene*
> *den liuten allen gezimt.* (Kl 1–5)
>
> [Here begins a tale
> that would be interesting to speak about
> and would also be worth recounting,
> only that it is more appropriate
> that people lament because of it.]

It is unclear to what these verses refer. Something new begins (*Hie hevet sich* . . .). Since the verses are foreshadowing, it seems that what is meant is the *mære* told by the *Klage*. Does this fit the characterization of the *mære*? It is not primarily the content of the *Klage* that provokes lament, but the just-completed epic. Do the verses point back? The other signals of the opening (*ditze alte mære*, etc.) can also, at this point—in the interior of a Nibelungen manuscript, after the epic, and as an introduction of the literary rhyme poem *Klage*—be taken in two ways, first, in reference to the tearful story that follows, and, second, in reference to the events described previously in the epic, which are to be lamented. The question is easier to decide if one assumes that there existed an independent version of the *Klage* that referred in general to the events told by the epic.[26] The formulae of the introduction point to the performance of the *Klage*. The introduction of this independent composition would then have been included in a part of the Nibelungen transmission.[27]

Who speaks the introductory verses? The passive form corresponds to the epic's narrative style. The *mære* "narrates itself": *ez ist von alten stunden/her vil wærlich gesaget* [since long ago it/has truly been told] (Kl 12–13). It is oral tradition.[28] Whoever takes up this subjectless speech takes the risk, as is stated, that although it may be *guot ze sagene* [well worth speaking about], it will be the cause of lament. Obviously a speaker is present, one who controls this "narrating by itself" and is related to an anonymous tradition. This first-person narrator has already introduced himself with a *captatio benevolentiae*: *hette ich nu die sinne . . .* [had I but the wit . . .] (Kl 9). Behind him stands another authority, an individual poet:

> *Ditze alte mære*
> *bat ein tihtære*
> *an ein buoch schrîben.*
> *des enkundez niht belîben,*
> *ez ensî ouch noch dâ von bekant.* (Kl 17–21)
>
> [This old story
> was written in a book
> at the behest of a poet.
> It could hardly avoid being
> known in this way.]

The story was put into writing in a book by a single *dictator*.[29] This is the condition for further distribution, because as a book, the story will not remain hidden. *Kunde* (*bekant*) is derived from it. This does not necessarily mean a dissemination of the text fixed in the book. The process of being *bekant*—or in a comparable location in *Herzog Ernst*, the *erkennen* (HE 4319)—could also denote an informal dissemination of the content, which Curschmann, for example, suspects to be one of the sources of the *Thidreks saga*.[30] This would match exactly what is later stated about *meister Kuonrât* as a person who scrutinizes circulating stories.

The *tihtære* and the book (their texts must again be kept separate, since "book" does not necessarily mean the word-for-word representation of a dictation) are not in any way authorities for one authentic version, which the speaker might reproduce as precisely as possible. They represent only two—decisive, of course—voices.

In the *C version, the situation is more clearly transferred to written language. In place of the *tihtære* (in the *B version), we find in *C: *het ein schrîbære/wîlen an ein buoch geschriben/latîn, desn ist ez niht beliben* [a writer/wrote (the story) in a book/in Latin, in which it did not stay] (Kl C 18–20). There is no distinction made between *tihtære* and writer, because the ability to write and the competency to conceive a text in Latin (*tihten*) go together. To put into writing means to write in Latin. The Latin language (or does it mean only Latin writing?) provides the text with a learned authority. The Latin version is also not the final version, rather just another station (*desn ist ez niht beliben*) on the path of dissemination (*bekant*), possibly in the vernacular. These vernacular versions would then have authority based on their written (Latin) source. What is told "now" has passed through several stages of oral and written versions, to include in *C the vernacular and Latin.

So from the beginning, writing plays a role in the *Klage* that is clearly marked by literality. This is hardly the case with the epic, which refers exclusively to "what is said."[31]

How Was the Legend Written Down?

The early dominance of orality and the later arrival of writing are explicitly thematized in the *Klage*. Its epilogue tells how a learned man, a *schrîber, meister Kuonrât* (Kl 4315) wrote the story at the behest of the bishop of Passau.[32] The bishop *hiez scrîben ditze mære/wie ez ergangen wære,/in latînischen buochstaben* [ordered that this story be written down,/how it all happened,/in Latin letters] (Kl 4297–99).[33] In the Latin form, as the bishop's intentions are paraphrased, the report becomes trustworthy: *daz manz für wâr solde haben,/swerz dar nâh erfunde* [that it should be deemed true,/by whoever finds it later] (Kl 4300–301); the scholar gives it authority.[34] His source is an oral informant, albeit an eyewitness, somebody who was there, in this case, Etzel's minstrel:

> *wand im seit der videlære*
> *diu kuntlîchen mære,*
> *wie ez ergie und gescach,*
> *wand erz hôrte unde sach,*[35]
> *er unde manec ander man.* (Kl 4309–13)
>
> [For the minstrel told him
> this tale, well worth knowing,
> how everything happened,
> since he had heard and seen it himself,
> along with others.]

Why exactly the *videlære* and not someone else? The *videlære* is obviously trusted to give an orderly account of the events. This is why Etzel and Dietrich choose the *videlære* to be their messenger as someone who is supposed to provide a faithful account of what has happened. A *videlære* is not just a musician but also a poet. Swemmel is not just an eyewitness but also a representative of the lay oral culture.[36] Before he becomes the informant of the learned *schrîbære*, he is constantly under way as a messenger to Vienna, Bechelaren, Passau, and Worms to report what happened. When his mission as messenger ends, he returns to the bishop of Passau, who is not satisfied with a report that might soon be forgotten.

Swemmel reports what he has seen for himself. He is not the only eyewitness, but he is predestined to become the story's guarantor. The bishop has other news from other eyewitnesses who have come from the land of the Huns: *swer iht dervon gesagen kan* [anyone who can say anything of it] (Kl 3474; cf. 3471–77). Since there are several witnesses, it is necessary to question them to obtain an accurate version. Even before Swemmel was able to report on his mission, the rumor of what had happened began to spread uncontrollably. Swemmel, Etzel's messenger, can set things right. The oral report is from the beginning in competition with other reports. Thanks to the bishop's initiative, Swemmel is "authorized" by becoming the informant of the written version and revision (*prieven*, Kl 4314).[37] The authentic work is a result of the combined efforts of an eyewitness, who is a representative of lay oral culture, and clerical writers. Their cooperation is made possible by a spiritual patron who, being related to the high lay nobility, is responsible for their *memoria*. The bishop assigns the task *durh liebe der neven sîn* [compelled by his love for his nephews, i.e., the Burgundian kings] (Kl 4296). The recording serves their dynastic memory and is therefore part of an illiterate lay society's cult of the dead. The written version, authentic thanks to the cooperation of eyewitness and writer, then becomes the secondary point of departure for the vernacular composition:

> *getihtet man ez sît hât*
> *dicke in tiuscher zungen* (Kl 4316–17).[38]
>
> [it has since been set in poetry
> in the German language.]

The report of the *Klage* on how the story of the downfall of the Nibelungen became a vernacular epic develops an ideal-type relationship of (authentic) legend and (authentic) written text. Reliability is guaranteed by a scholar, the chaplain of the bishop of Passau, although he stands at neither the beginning nor the end of the transmission. Dependent on eyewitnesses, his learned work again becomes the object of further revision in the vernacular. This process documents the repeated interference of orality and literality, of clerical and lay culture, and a multiphased revision process that fails to come to any final conclusion. The existing versions depend on the valid, written, Latin version of Magister Kuonrat, but they are not identical with it. Both oral lay culture and scholarly literary culture have played a part in the genealogy of the *mære*, and this cooperation is to be understood as a concurrent process, not a sequential one. Even the *Klage*, strongly characterized as it is by literality, standing at the end of this process as it does, and claiming a Latin literary basis, is called a *liet* by the narrator (Kl 4322), and so it remains within the horizon of orality.

Such mutual interference of oral transmission and scholarly literary culture seems to be typical of early vernacular epic and the conception of its origin. This is confirmed by *Herzog Ernst*, which has long been compared with the *Klage*.[39] In *Herzog Ernst B*, a similarly complicated fiction of authenticity is invented. It does not refer to the whole of the story, for it is taken as "legend,"[40] based on the oral report of Ernst to the emperor and written down at the emperor's command (HE 6003–7). This report furthermore is based on physical evidence—the wondrous creatures Ernst has caught in the Orient and brought with him to the emperor's court (HE 5970–81). More closely related to the *Klage* is the authentification of the precious gem Ernst acquires, the *weysen* that is set in the crown of the empire (HE 4462–65). The *liet* claims a written source for this information: concerning the gem, *luget vns das buch nycht* [the book does not lie to us] (HE 4466).[41] Should someone hold *diese rede . . . /Vor leugenliche wercke* [this text to be a false work] (HE 4468–69),

> *Der kome hin zu Bamberg;*
> *Da vindet er syn eyn ende*
> *An alle myssewende*
> *Von dem meister der esz getichtet hat.*[42]
> *Latin esz nach geschrieben stat:*
> *Da von*[43] *esz an falschen list*
> *Eyn vil wares liet ist.* (HE 4470–76)[44]
>
> [If someone would take this to be a lie,
> he should come to Bamberg.
> There he will find an answer
> without doubt
> from the master who has written it down.
> It is written in Latin.
> Therefore, it is without falsehoods
> and a very true lay.]

The *liet,* that is, the vernacular *Herzog Ernst,* stems from a learned tradition, which in turn is based on an authentic *historia,* the story of Ernst's travels. Latin literate culture inserts itself at some point between orality and orality—

the witness's oral report and oral poetry (*liet*). The parity of vernacular poetry, however, is expressed in the fact that writing is only an intermediary stage that endows the *liet* with a higher authority.

There seems to have been a need to tie literary traditions outside of the clerical culture to their own institutions. In the case of the *Klage* and *Herzog Ernst*, this is the episcopal seat; in that of *Wolfdietrich D*, it is the monastery. Here, too, we find the interference of orality and literality. In this case, the book is at the beginning of the tradition, even though the text that is recounted is explicitly defined as oral:[45]

Hie mügent ir gerne hœren singen unde sagen [!]
von kluoger âventiure, sô müezent ir gedagen.
ez wart ein buoch funden,[46] *daz sage ich iu für wâr,*
ze Tagemunt in dem klôster. dâ lac ez manic jâr. (Wo C I)

[Here you may gladly hear sung and spoken
of difficult adventures, you have to be silent now.
There was found a book, this I tell you truly,
in Tagemunt in the monastery, where it lay for many years.]

It is told how the book was sent to the bishop of Eichstätt, who was entertained by it for seventeen years (Wo C 2,2–3). It was then found again ten years after his death by his *cappellân*, who read it over (*überlas*, Wo D 4,1) and then carried it to the Eichstätt Walburg monastery, from where the story was spread:

merkt von dem guoten buoche wie ez sich zerspreitet hât

Diu eptissîn was schœne, alsô uns ist gesaget.
sie sach daz buoch gerne, wan ez ir wol behaget.
sie sazt für sich zwên meister, die lertenz durch hübscheit:
daz sie dran funden geschriben, daz brâhtens in die kristenheit.

Nâhen unde verre fuoren sie in diu lant.
sie sungen unde seiten, dâ von wart ez bekant.
die seltsæne âventiure wolten sie niht verdagen.
êrst mügent ir gerne hoeren von einem rîchen künege sagen. (Wo D 4,4–6,4)

[See how the great book was spread.

The abbess was noble, as we are told.
She enjoyed looking at the book, because it gave her pleasure.
She called two masters to her, they taught the story in a courtly manner:
What they found written there they carried to all of Christendom.

Near and far they traveled through the land.
They sang and spoke, and this made it known.
The strange adventure they did not want to hide.
First you shall hear told of a rich king.]

Here the authentication by eyewitnesses is missing, but otherwise the process is imagined in a similar way. The written text (the book) does not stand at the end of the transmission. Instead, it is the guarantee for truth and the starting point for oral dissemination and therefore at the beginning. The book is "ancient," and so is the story which it tells; it was hidden for a long time (*manic jâr*) until it was found, then it spent seventeen years in the bishop's possession, and another ten years among his effects, and was thereafter widely disseminated (*zerspreitet*). Its authority is supported by clerical institutions, by the monasteries of Tagemunt and St. Walburg, and by the episcopal seat in Eichstätt. Its attraction is shown through clerics: by the seventeen-year, that is, lifelong, interest of the bishop, who kept the book for himself, by the examination of the chaplain, and by the care of the (*schœnen*, noble) abbess, whom it pleased (*wol behaget*, Wo C 4,2), and who looked to disseminate it.

Religious institutions first made it known throughout Christendom. In the beginning, it served as noble entertainment. The step outside the clerical world of writing into an obviously illiterate Christian society, where the story was "sung and told," was accomplished with the help of learned people. The abbess called upon two *meister*—scholars or simply skilled men? The story is then artistically revised by experts, who participate at least passively in the culture of writing. And why two? Since there were two, it is said, the story was quickly and effectively spread, but also that the transmission was from the beginning not unanimous.

The prologue of *Wolfdietrich D* reacts, as does the *Klage*, to a multivocal oral tradition by projecting it back to the (supposed) point of departure of a dissemination based on writing. With the step into orality, the previously linear filiation of textual transmission is at an end, a transmission that the prologue describes as the path of one single book from one hand to another. In writing, there exists only the one story, which is bound to the book, but when it is performed before a broad public audience, the transmission begins to split. Authenticated by its learned origin, the story lives on in orality, in *singen* and *sagen*. The two *meister* travel far and wide (*nâhen unde verre*) and proclaim what they have learned from the book. The story then becomes general knowledge, a part of collective memory: *dâ von wart ez bekant* (this is how it became known) (Wo C 6,2). The actual narrative is connected to an anonymous *singen unde sagen*, to an undefined and multivocal tradition, which at some time in the past came from a book.

The *Klage*, *Herzog Ernst*, and *Wolfdietrich* secure orally performed poetry in a written text (that stands at its beginnings but does not replace it) and at the same time "explain" the multivocality of what has been "sung and said." The suspicion of lying, with which vernacular poetry is confronted in the early Middle Ages, is thereby put to rest. The reference to writing guarantees reliability, even if not a word-for-word fidelity to one (and only one) version.

The difference between this authentic tradition and plain fable is the eyewitness. Eyewitness accounts and the reference to multiple sources qualify the *mære* as *historia*, something that must follow the *ordo naturalis*, as every *historia* must: *wie ez sih huob und ouh began,/und wie ez ende gewan* [how it all started and began,/and how it all came to an end] (Kl 4304–5).[47] The trustworthiness of the *historia* is also related. The eyewitness is supposed to correct what is general rumor. The reports concerning the downfall of the Burgundians begin immediately following the catastrophe. Dietrich of Bern tries to fashion the many voices into one authentic voice. At first, he forbids Etzel's messenger to say anything at all in Bechelaren. The reason for this is plausible—the messengers are in danger should anything become known about the collapse of the Huns and their power. This is only half the truth, however: Dietrich wants to control the story himself. In fact, his prohibition fails, in that the messengers, who are overwhelmed by the painful memory, are incapable of maintaining the diplomatic lies. The truth escapes them in the form of an inarticulate cry of pain. The first attempt to control dissemination fails.

How oral knowledge is channeled is shown at the arrival of the messengers in Worms. There, Swemmel does not tell just anyone what he knows. He waits for the right moment to give his report:

jane sol ich iu der mære
sunderlingen niht sagen:
ich solse pillîche verdagen,
niwan da ich si sagen sol. (Kl 3568–71)

[I shall not tell each one of you
separately what happened:
I should rather leave it be,
until the time is right.]

Prünhilt and her court are a suitable audience and can guarantee the official nature of Swemmel's report. Yet even in this forum, he at first only submits an abridged version of his story, that is, the outcome, along with the news of the kings' death. Only when the whole land of the Burgundians is called together at a court diet (Kl 3723) does he tell his story in its authoritative form:

> *alrêrst hiez man dô für gân*
> *die boten zantwurte stân,*
> *daz sie sageten diu mære,*
> *wie ez ergangen wære.* (Kl 3771–74)
>
> [only then did they let the messengers come forward
> to answer questions,
> that they might tell the story
> of what took place.]

And now Swemmel gives a lengthy presentation of everything that happened, beginning with Sivrit's death.

This demonstrates how, under the conditions of orality, an authentic story is created out of rumor. The truth is bound to specific authoritative figures, first, the king, then the minstrel, who is responsible for the collective memory in an oral society, and, finally, in the written text, the bishop and his scribe. At first, we have an informal narration of what happened. The news spread from Etzel's court around the land. It is a loss of control when the story bursts out of the messengers, although they were told to keep silent. Their narration is not haphazard, but it is also not completely controllable. Swemmel, on the other hand, is a professional messenger and can therefore report in an orderly manner. He does not do so at just any time. First, the proper audience must be assembled, then a suitable framework must be provided. His report acquires its authority by being embedded in the rituals of feudal rule. Only what is offered to "the entire land" can be the legitimate version of the downfall of the Burgundians.

The triple attempt to lead a cacophony back to a single, true voice mirrors the efforts of the narrator to secure an authorized truth in the text. The attempt fails once (Dietrich's attempt to channel the news), then it succeeds, also under the conditions of orality, but just for this one occasion (Swemmel's report at the court), and, finally, it succeeds a second time, this time under the premises of literacy (the writing of the eyewitness report). Multivocal transmission is anything but diffuse and arbitrary. It is the result of a complicated transmission process. The *Klage* tells as little as *Herzog Ernst* or *Wolfdietrich D* of how the epic came to be, but it does tell us how the true essence of what happened was secured.

Traces of Work on the Legend

A lyric stanzaic model, "formulaic" narrative style, and the designation of all communication as speech bind the *Nibelungenlied* to orality more clearly than the *Klage*. There is no attempt in the epic to base the *mære* on written text, and any commentary, typical of the written medium of revising an older tradition, is lacking.

The realization that we cannot count on a binding and definitive work as the starting point of the textual tradition has led to the hypothesis that there was a "Nibelungen workshop." According to Curschmann, this might be imagined to have been in the vicinity of Passau, where various redactors tackled the material under a "Nibelungen master."[48] Bumke has followed this theory in his investigation of the *Klage*,[49] linking the various versions of it to such a "workshop."[50] This takes into consideration both texts' "openness" to change, the impossibility of approximating an archetype, and the process of working with tradition. The idea of a workshop raises new questions, however, about the relationship of the transmitted texts to one another. It seems to me more reasonable not to assume a simultaneous and institutionally homogeneous revision, but rather a process that was successive and more widespread in time and space. This would have been an uncoordinated, discontinuous process, in which work was ongoing, resulting in different but closely related outcomes.[51] Perhaps the architectonic model of the *Bauhütte* ("builder's workshop or guild") would be appropriate, as is explicitly stated in the *Jüngere Titurel* with respect to the multigenerational construction of a literary work.[52] It would be wrong to think of one single spatial locality where such a *Bauhütte* (or a workshop) was situated. The revision *C does not complete an earlier "workshop" version, but puts itself in place of such a version. A comprehensive and demanding project could only take shape, or better yet, take shapes, in drafts and revisions with the collaboration of many people over a long time.

The changes the legend underwent prior to being written down are no longer discernible. We must limit ourselves to the point from which the oldest manuscripts have come down to us. They already combine, even if in different forms, at least two heterogeneous results, epic and *Klage*. Three relatively clearly distinguishable versions of the epic from the thirteenth century are transmitted in the manuscripts A (München SB, Cgm 34), B (St. Gallen, Stiftsbibliothek, Ms. 857), and C (Karlsruhe Landesbibliothek, formerly Donaueschingen, cod. 63). Several other texts from the two great manuscript families *AB and *C provide evidence of the continued efforts for a "better" version of the material.[53]

Mss. A and B are closely related, but the older and shorter of the two (A) contains an independent version of the first part of the epic.[54] More clearly distinguishable vis-à-vis *AB is the redaction *C. The oldest and almost complete ms. C has added text in many passages, but shortened or corrected it in others.[55] Along with these manuscripts, there are eight other virtually complete manuscripts along with a number of fragments. Some undertake conceptually new initiatives, above all the so-called *Darmstädter Aventiuren-Verzeichniss* (n) and the complete version in the *Heldenbuch Lienhard Scheubls* (k). Other less spectacular expansions or abridgments in manuscripts, considered less valuable for textual criticism, exhibit a continual process of adaptation as well. In this way, even stories foreign to the epic, such as those of *hürnen Seifrid* that link the fight with the dragon with the conquest of Kriemhilt, can be taken up in the story line of the *Nibelungenlied.*

Redactional changes in the Nibelungen tradition have up to now been examined primarily in conjunction with the *C version. Here the redactor intervened in certain passages where the vulgate version (according to B) is difficult to understand. In this way, he provided a version closer to the expectations of a modern audience, but he proceeded mostly on a case-by-case basis and therefore offered only superficial improvements. Seen from a broader perspective, these improvements resulted in new and more serious "mistakes." This seems to confirm indirectly the assumption of a valid, relatively good text that was subsequently corrected.[56] Despite shortcomings in details, manuscript B seems to be closer to the first written text, since it was not yet tainted by these corrections. Manuscript B was recognized in Braune's investigation as the basis for the "vulgate version."[57] Brackert's criticism of Braune's manuscript stemma, in which Braune wanted to prove that ms. B was relatively close to the archetype, has changed nothing with regard to this manuscript's importance. It has only corrected the assumption that ms. B represents the original work and its related history of production. In fact, ms. B is only one (especially important) stage of the story's appropriation, concurrent with others, including oral versions.

The transformation to book form is not, and this point is unanimously agreed upon, simply a written "archiving" ([*Verschriftung]* "transliteration") of what was previously oral. It is instead a new concept ([Verschriftlichung] "literization").[58] This is evident already in ms. B. Ms. A, with great similarity to ms. B, is more concise in the first part, above all in the Prünhilt fable, and was probably shortened. The impulses for revision are clearer in the *C group. Empty space is filled, contradictions are smoothed over, scenes are coordinated, and a less ambiguous image of the characters has been developed. This was continued in the commenting retrospective of the *Klage*,[59] which, given variations in the details, thoroughly builds on the more even *C version.[60] There are various stages of a book revision of older material in the *AB group, in the *C group, and in the *Klage*. The revision continues in some later manuscripts, not consistently, but in single variants, abbreviations, and augmentations. Manuscripts (n and m), including other traditional materials (around the fight with the dragon), and the complete retelling in Lienhard Scheubl's *Heldenbuch* (k) already go well beyond the adaptation process being discussed here.

This process was able to integrate heterogeneous elements of oral tradition beyond the first written form of the epic. Where expectations of coherence are especially frustrated, it has been considered whether different performance variations were simply implemented sequentially.[61] It is also possible that the manuscripts selected and combined different oral texts and text segments. Even if such considerations must admittedly remain hypotheses,[62] they can describe oral and written narrative strategies (and the mutual interference of both). They teach us not to assume a uniform and definitive text under conditions of vocality, and to suspend demands for narrative finality, which a developed literate culture takes for granted.

Given that a fundamental equality of concurrent versions is possible, the question of what is dependent on what becomes less important.[63] The revision process begins to take shape only if one queries the different concepts of the individual versions and what details make sense in which variant. There are many textual elements "that can change without defining these changes as disruptions,"[64] and a series of text parameters seems to be arbitrary.

It was a fault of early editorial philology to base its work primarily on the comparison of single parts (detailed differences in variant readings, so-called conjunctive errors [*errores coniunctivi*], etc.) and to ask whether deviations were more likely to have run in one direction or the other, in order to reconstruct the original text. Even if a conclusion were possible, this does not resolve the question of the concept of the younger (i.e., "worse") manuscript.

Instead of preparing a "better" story line and excising supposedly later material,[65] we must examine how certain motifs, situations, and scenes, known from other sources of the story's transmission, are reworked and given new meaning. The knowledge of what was once told about the Nibelungen legend in different languages and cultures, and the supposition of what could have been told additionally, do not help. How is it possible to decide which version and which type of motivation the narrator followed from one case to the next, what competition they had, or how controversial they were, or whether the storyteller knew of a particular detail? The question of what was originally true can no longer be answered,[66] and the direction of change is only seldom determinable.

Elements transmitted from other sources should therefore always be questioned with regard to their place in the new concept. There is no "original" legend or metatext in which everything that the written version renders incompletely and contradictorily makes sense.[67] The written legend is not a cluster of senseless fragments of older stories, taken out of their previous context, which the redactor has painstakingly tried to glue together. Instead, the book concept is realized in exchanges with a legend whose branches and variants we can no longer firmly grasp. Gaps in the story line, blind motifs, and so-called contradictions are all to be interpreted as "symptoms" of the difficult adaptation of the tradition and are not to be set aside by recourse to a metatext or by cleaning up a text's "foreign matter."

These kinds of symptoms should be the starting point of analysis. They are signs that the narrator does not want to tell a certain fact or wants to tell it differently. The critic should not interpolate what the narrator could have told. There are, of course, examples in the Middle Ages of simple mechanical additions of fragments. Yet, until the contrary can be proven, it must be assumed that the narrator of the story tried to create a plausible, sometimes novel, connection of plot and meaning that relates to what others have said before and what he can assume his audience expects. He seems to have inserted "spoils" from his text's tradition, including single formulations, but in doing so he has given them a new poetic function.[68] He is engaged in an intertextual dialogue that is so difficult for us to reconstruct because it has left only partial traces in the written record.[69] These traces, however, must be deciphered as traces of deliberate revision. The knowledge of legend is simply the "horizon of reference" for the narrator's special interpretation of the story.[70] It does not determine the epic adaptation, but it does limit its room to maneuver.

Storytelling Against the Tradition

It is possible that the narrator was bound by a certain constellation of conflict even after its rationale had long since disappeared. The narrator was obligated to deal with the latent tension between Sivrit, Gunther, and Prünhilt even though this constellation was no longer based on an erotic triangle in his version.[71] But we cannot rely on motifs the narrator avoids, we can only work with transmitted texts. Those passages deserve special interest where discarded alternatives can still be recognized.

It is generally acknowledged that one such passage is strophe 1912 of the so-called vulgate version:

> *Dô der strît niht anders kunde sîn erhaben*
> *(Kriemhilde leit daz alte in ir herzen was begraben),*
> *dô hiez si tragen ze tische den Etzelen sun.*
> *wie kunde ein wîp durch râche immer vreislîcher tuon?*[72]
>
> [Since the fighting could not be provoked in any other way
> (Kriemhilt's ancient pain was still buried in her heart),
> she ordered Etzel's son to be brought to the table.
> How could a woman act more cruelly for the sake of vengeance?]

De Boor's Commentary states: "In the *Ältere Not*,[73] Kriemhild causes the youth to slap Hagen in the face, whereupon Hagen draws his sword and beheads the boy. Here Kriemhild has actually sacrificed her child for the sake of revenge. The courtly poet of the *Nibelungenlied* no longer dared to attribute such a deed to a woman; the death of her son is for him the consequence of Dankwart's appearance after the murder of the court (1981ff.). Still, the poet did not want to do away with the powerful old strophe. The reviser of C smoothed the passage out."[74] Less to the point is the certainty with which a text can be cited that may have never existed, as well as stating the intentions of a compiler of whom we can know nothing. Undoubtedly, the story de Boor tells is more even than what is told in the epic. Above all, it can be supported by parts of the *Thidreks saga* and late medieval heroic prose [*Heldenbuchprosa*], even if in the latter the planned provocation of Hagen does not necessarily mean that Kriemhilt "instigated" the murder.[75] De Boor's version more clearly explains why Hagen kills the Hunnish prince in the following scene and then slays his tutor (1961–62). Ortliep has insulted Hagen, and the direct responsibility for this disrespect would fall on the tutor, as we know from Konrad of Würzburg's *Heinrich von Kempten*.[76]

The only problem is that the narrator did not tell this story. It is therefore a mistake in method to transfer a motive from one story to another in order to substitute the connection in the story with the one the critic prefers.[77] Strophe 1912 of the *Nibelungenlied* (B 1909) only hints that there is a connection between the appearance of the Hunnish prince and the inexorable revenge. Perhaps there was a story like the one de Boor suspects, but if we look at the chain of murders that set off the violence in B, we have another, much more convincing motivational connection. Kriemhilt instigated the underhanded attack of the Hun Blœdelin on the Burgundian servants, and this attack provokes the revenge of the Burgundian nobles at the dinner (1952–57). The Hunnish prince is the focus of the conflict when Dancwart brings the news of the attack, and he thereby becomes the object of revenge. He must be present, because once he has become the first victim of revenge, the conflict can no longer be stopped.

The causal relationships are connected differently than in de Boor's retelling. There are two motivational types that cross, "frontal" motivation [*Motivation von vorne*] (the attack will provoke a counterattack) and "from behind" motivation [*Motivation von hinten*] (the counterattack requires a very prominent victim, who must be within easy reach).[78] This would only be a mistake if the preparatory motivation, as is predominant in modern stories, is the only possible and most normal type. This is apparently not possible in medieval narratives.

If the closing verse of strophe 1912 is tied to the three preceding verses, then Kriemhilt is given the responsibility not only for the intentionally instigated killing of the Burgundian servants by Blœdelin, but also for the fate of Ortliep. Even though it was not a foreseeable and therefore intentional event, Kriemhilt provides the impetus by bringing the child into the dangerous center of possible confrontation.[79] A direct provocation of Hagen by Ortliep is not necessary in this complex motivation. The strophe is therefore not only a "fossil," a badly healed scar that points to an amputated motivation, but also a tribute to a knowledge of the legend the narrator simply cannot ignore. It takes up a new position in the preparation of the conflict, in the mesh of aggressive plotting, unabashed provocation, and half-hearted conciliation. It cannot be denied that another, faded connection may be recognizable, one behind the nexus presented here, whose traces—still evident in the *Thidreks saga*—have been lost, but it is then discarded and replaced by another nexus.

The *Thidreks saga* has another motivation for the outbreak of the fighting. The massacre of the servants does not yet have the desired effect for the queen, so she has to resort to a more severe provocation through her son. In the *Nibelungenlied*, on the other hand, the attack on the servants provokes the counterattack against the Hunnish prince. The two motives are intertwined without being directly connected. Since Kriemhilt has, for the first time, found in Blœdelin a helper for her revenge, the conflict (*strît*) has already begun in her own mind, as strophe 1911 makes clear. At the festive meal, she simply has to await the results:

> *Dô diu küneginne Blœdelînen lie*
> *in des strîtes willen, ze tische si dô gie*
> *mit Etzel dem künege und ouch mit sînen man.*
> *si hete swinde ræte an die geste getân.* (1911)
>
> [After the queen had left Blœdelin
> ready for combat, she went to the table
> with Etzel the king and all of his warriors.
> She had devised a deadly plot against her guests.]

The following temporal clause *Dô der strît niht anders kunde sîn erhaben* (1912,1) could even summarize strophe 1911. "Since the conflict could not be [as was told before] provoked in any other way," and the accusation of *vreis-lîcher* [terrible] revenge, which concludes the following strophe (1912,4) does not necessarily have to refer only to bringing in Ortliep, but can just as well, as in 1911,4, refer to Kriemhilt's unscrupulousness in the instigation of her revenge.

The dinner festivities and the attack go together, because the attack will expose the peace to be a deception, regardless of how it ends. There is no way to predict that Dancwart will be the only one left alive and will burst into the dinner festivities to tell the news. In any case, the outbreak of violence is to be expected. Kriemhilt makes sure that Ortliep is present.

The scene at the dinner makes it possible to show off the contradictory relationship between Huns and Burgundians. Although the conflict is already under way, they still eat together, and Etzel announces that he wants to send his son to be mentored by his wife's brothers. He demonstrates a functioning clan society, while Kriemhilt and Hagen are already working on the confrontation. Kriemhilt uses the king's brother, and Hagen the king's son, so that Etzel himself is sucked into the conflict. This instrumentalization of close relatives is told by strophes 1911 and 1912.

The first provocation that uses Ortliep as a pawn in this game does not even originate with Kriemhilt, but rather with Hagen, when he brutally rejects Etzel's wish to have Ortliep raised by the Burgundians, predicting that he won't live long.[80] This openly questions Etzel's rule and its dynastic future. By having the prince brought in to attend the meal, Kriemhilt offers her opponent a second opportunity to strike at Etzel.

From a genetic textual perspective, the starting point might have been: Ortliep is present when the fight begins and is its first victim. This provokes questions, assumptions about intentions and correlations, and accusations. The narrator cannot get around the "facts." In place of one possible motive for the outbreak of the fighting (Ortliep's insult to Hagen), he injects another motive that also has precedent (the attack on the servants). The one motivation does not unobtrusively replace or wipe out the other. Instead, it is superimposed and connected. The metaphor of the palimpsest, introduced by the intertextuality debate, denotes this process quite precisely.[81] In a palimpsest, the one (usually older) text does not disappear completely, but is weakly visible in a washed-out form. As such, it can still be present as something that has been erased.[82]

This metaphor, developed as an instrument to describe postmodern art, helps us understand the work of putting oral tradition into writing. The written voice of the narrator does not marginalize the voices of other narrators before him; rather, it enters into competition with them. The narrator presents his own—better—version. The knowledge of Kriemhilt's treachery, of the confrontation between Hagen and Ortliep, and of another motive that provokes Hagen, is taken up and reinterpreted. The goal is obvious: responsibility is divided between Kriemhilt and Hagen. Kriemhilt brings her son within reach of the covertly prepared conflict, and Hagen commits the first act of aggression, making Ortliep the first victim. The result, Ortliep's death, is the same, but a straightforward intrigue has turned into a complex intertwining of action and reaction.

The redactor of version *C seems to have found the direct indictment of Kriemhilt to be awkward. So he replaces strophe 1912, which condemns Kriemhilt's terrible (*vreislîche*) revenge, with four new strophes (C 1960–63). The result—Ortliep takes part in the festive dinner—remains the same, because the prince will be needed later for revenge, but the motivation is different. There is no indication that Ortliep might be included in Kriemhilt's calculations. The additional stanzas at first portray the ceremonial preparation of the dinner, the regal pomp (C 1960,2), the table order in the hall (C 1961,2), the different dishes for Christians and non-Christians (C 1961,3), and the care of the servants (1962,1). When it is finally told that the king's son is carried into the hall, it is simply the culmination of the festive display:

Do die fvrsten gesezzen warn vber al
vnd nv begvnden ezzen, do wart in den sal

> *getragen zů den fvrsten das Ezeln kint;*
> *da von der kunec riche gewan vil starchen iamer sint.* (C 1963)
>
> [Now that the nobles were seated all around
> and had begun to eat, Etzel's child
> was carried into the hall to be with the nobles;
> from this the mighty king would gain much grief.]

The narrator is satisfied with expressing the opposite direction of the actions. What will crown the meal—the presence of the prince—is to prove itself to be especially devastating. The fact that Ortliep is present is simply a fact; it is no one's intent. He is in the proper place.

While we can only speculate about the "original" motives for the outbreak of the fighting, the redactions *AB and *C show the continued attempt to deal with this "fact." A mother risks the life of her child. Is it intentional or unfortunate coincidence? Whereas manuscripts D and b follow the *B version, and manuscript a follows the *C version, other manuscripts (Jdh) have an interesting mix.[83] Contrary to *C and its undetermined prefiguration of future sorrow (*iamer*, C 1963,4), they highlight—along with the *AB version—Kriemhilt's ruthless will to revenge (cf. 1912,4). They replace the first verse that could point to treacherous intent (*Dô der strît niht anders kunde sîn erhaben* [because the fight could not be initiated otherwise], 1912,1; after ms. B 1909,1) with one closer to the ms. C version (*Do die fvrsten gesezzen warn vber al* [when the princes were seated all around], C 1963,1).[84] The criticism of Kriemhilt remains, but the rug is pulled out from under the suspicion that the arrival of the Hunnish prince might have been cunningly made to serve the outbreak of open hostilities.

This passage is not only problematic, and therefore controversial, for modern philologists. It provoked alterations already in the manuscripts. Modern attempts to obtain a "correct" version have wiped away traces of any dialogue with tradition. The text constitutes itself by means of delineation from other texts that contain the same material. Early vernacular narration often disputes concurrent versions. The *Straßburger Alexander*, for example, reminds us of the—false—claim that Nectanebus is the hero's father (*Noch sprechent manige lugenêre* . . . [Some liars still claim . . .], Al 83–91). Even Gottfried von Straßburg cannot simply leave out the story of Mark's love for the owner of a golden hair, which a bird has brought his way. Instead, he has to state that the story of the golden hair is not true (Tr 8601–23). The narrator of the *Nibelungenlied* must also confront expectations and occurrences that he cannot, for the sake of his own credibility, simply ignore. He can shape them to his own intent, however. As opposed to Gottfried, he does not explicitly comment on tensions and deviations. Such a commentary would require the self-aware narrator of a courtly romance, who views what is told from a distance and picks and chooses as he pleases.[85] By writing the text, the results can be improved, focused, and made more precise, but also trivialized, watered down, broken up, shortened, and made literally questionable.

Marked Substitutions

Sivrit's bridal quest for Prünhilt is ultimately responsible for his death and creates a special and highly problematic relationship between the two protagonists in the various versions of the legend. The Nordic versions, however, operate on completely different presumptions than the *Nibelungenlied*, many elements of whose story line require explanation. For example, how does Sivrit know about Prünhilt? How can he know her castle, and her as well, when he—as explicitly stated—has never been there before? Why do people know him at Prünhilt's court? Why does Prünhilt honor him before his travel companions? What is the purpose of the notorious fiction that he is Gunther's *man* (386,3)? Answers will be suggested for each of these questions, but the first thing to note is this: all of them lack a preparatory motivation, and different versions provide different solutions.[86] Only the legend tradition, in which at least two sources are corrupted, seems to offer a way to resolve the confusion and restore a comprehensible story line.[87] If one is of this opinion, then the epic narrator failed to reconcile his sources, perhaps because their elements were already deformed or were at least in part unknown to him, or because the transmitted details formed an insurmountable obstacle to what he was trying to accomplish.

I shall limit myself to a single problem manifest in the Prünhilt story. Sivrit "is in the know" about the way to Isenstein and about how things are there. From a modern perspective, the easiest explanation is that he has been there before, as is told in certain stories,[88] but nowhere in the *Nibelungenlied*.[89] The meeting between Sivrit and Prünhilt in the concurrent stories occurs in contexts that the *Nibelungenlied* has completely excluded. This begins with the fact that Isenstein is "far away from the known world," and ends with the fact that a former engagement to be married just does not fit into the biography of the hero.[90] It is not possible to simply take an isolated element from one version of the legend and situate it in a new context where it loses its meaning.

In the *Nibelungenlied*'s version, Sivrit is not a vagabond hero who comes from "outside" and is more than a match for everyone in the known world, but never completely accepted because of his origins. He saves the existing order only to threaten it himself, thereby causing his own death. This legend belongs to a cultural myth in which a developed civilization is confronted with what lies beyond its borders, something it both needs and fears. The *Nibelungenlied* does not relate this myth. While it is true that Sivrit is an intruder in Worms, which is why he introduces himself so provocatively, the "intruder" does not come from beyond the border, but belongs to the same kind of world as the Burgundians. This is also why he does not leave the Worms court, but remains associated with it. Yet he also has an affinity for the "outside" world, where the Nibelungen and Prünhilt exist, and he knows how to live in that world. This is why he knows Prünhilt's ins and outs. His knowledge of the other world is an expression of this affinity. For him to have known Prünhilt before is therefore completely unnecessary within the narrative logic of the *Nibelungenlied.*

The confrontation between "secure rule within" and the "wild world outside" (the kings against the intruder) has become a confrontation within the known world (the court at Worms). This is complicated and exacerbated by a double bridal quest, Sivrit's within this world and Gunther's outside of it. In the bridal quest scheme, the stability of the political order is normally put to the test in the cooperation of the king and the ruling class. Securing the dynasty through exogamy is related as a dangerous collective task.[91] Along with the questing ruler, the actors involved normally include the likewise courageous and loyal vassals. The fact that Sivrit pretends to be merely an assistant, whereas he actually solves the challenges posed to the suitor, is the first decisive "miscasting" of the system in the *Nibelungenlied.*[92] The second is that he is a voluntary helper of the king and not really his vassal, since he only belongs to the Burgundians for a limited time and will depart again as a king in his own right. The third is that there are two suitors, but one bride (Kriemhilt) can only be won through the quest of the other (Prünhilt). As in the analysis of strophe 1912, the *Nibelungenlied* complicates an initially simple structure. Thanks to this complication, the scheme is subverted and sows conflict.

This disruption is thematized in a narrative scheme that is normally intent on integration, namely, of king and subjects in their joint fight against the outside. In this case, however, a split results, and this is why it must be recast. The act of recasting the suitor with the helper is revised in different ways in the manuscripts, but in a way that makes it apparent to everyone that "something is not right." When Sivrit undertakes the quest on Gunther's behalf to promote his own quest elsewhere, he has to hide behind Gunther. The substitution of the extraordinary hero Sivrit for the king's usual assistant—Hagen—is also at issue. This double substitution proves itself to be twice as problematic, openly so in the replacement of Gunther, latently so in the marginalization of Hagen.

The exchange of roles with Gunther is accomplished through a curious trick with a cloak of invisibility (*Tarnmantel*) that enables Sivrit to take the place of the contestant Gunther without being seen. This exchange of roles is cheating and is later the motif by which the double bridal quest develops into a story of treachery. In Isenstein, the prop guarantees a successful result, just as it does later on the wedding night. The cloak of invisibility, mentioned before only briefly as Sivrit's prize in his fight with Alberich, must now be explicitly brought into play during the departure to seek out Prünhilt: *Sivrit der muose füeren die kappen mit im dan* [Sivrit had to take the cloak with him] (336,1). The vulgate version explains the meaning of this in a few verses: the cloak makes the wearer invisible and gives him the strength of twelve men (337–38). It transforms Sivrit so that he can effectively support Gunther. Ms. C adds two additional stanzas:

> *Von wilden getwergen han ich gehőret sagen,*
> *si sin in holn bergen, vnd daz si ze scherme tragen*
> *einez heizet tarnkappen, von wnderlicher art.* (C 342,1–3)
>
> [I've heard stories about wild dwarves,
> who live in mountain caves, and that they carry for protection
> an object called an invisibility cloak that is of a magical nature.]

It is not the details of the effect of the cloak that are interesting,[93] but the indication that its origin lies in the "legend" of a "wild" world whose character is "strange." The line demarcating what might normally be expected has been crossed. We have an ambivalent warrant of truth for the authenticity of this world: *als uns diu âventiure giht* [as the adventure tells us] (C 343,4). The *âventiure* in the courtly romance stands for the narrator's ability to create truth out of fiction. Here it refers to something that lies outside of the possibilities of our own world. It refers to a (*wunderlîch*) crossing over and points for the first time to the confusion of the normal course of events that comes with Gunther's replacement by Sivrit, and that continues in the Isenstein episode.

Hagen's replacement seems less conspicuous. The most important character between *Âventiure* 6 and *Âventiure* 12 is Sivrit, not Hagen. Sivrit speaks decisively in council, has an answer to every question, and takes on everything. Hagen, in contrast, seems unsure of himself in Isenstein, is fearful and unseemly, is lectured by Sivrit on the customs there (406,4), is afraid of the outcome (430,4; 447–48), and makes pointless demands (446–47).[94] The exchange of roles with Hagen is foreshadowed in the introduction to the Isenstein episode through a variety of repetitions. In the council on the Saxon war, the old configuration of the king in the circle of his followers, with Hagen at their head, still applies. Sivrit is not even present. It is Hagen who brings up his name in the discussion. In the war, however, Sivrit becomes the main figure. At the council of the Burgundians on traveling to Isenstein, he then takes part from the beginning, although he initially advises against the journey (*Daz wil ich widerrâten,* 330,1). This would fit the scheme and exclude him from the undertaking.[95] Hagen, on the other hand, advises in favor of it (*Sô wil ih iu daz râten,* 331,1), while at the same time giving up his place and suggesting Sivrit as an aide, *sît im daz ist sô kündec wi ez um Prünhilde stât* [since he knows so much about Prünhilt's situation] (331,4). This exchange of roles is then marked in different ways. Where the vulgate version reports Sivrit's knowledge of Isenstein before the journey:

> *daz was ir deheinem niwan Sîvride erkant* (382,4),
>
> [this was known to no one except Sivrit]

the *C group emphasizes in addition that someone else, Hagen, is at the end of his rope, because he does not possess this knowledge:

> *daz het von Tronege Hagene ê vil selten bekant.* (C 390,4)
>
> [this was completely unknown to Hagen of Troneck.]

The greater knowledge wins.

Sivrit finally agrees, but he makes sure that Hagen and Dancwart, the other *Tronegære*, share the risk and accompany him. This is structurally—not as a result of the narrator's presentation—a conflict-laden situation. The one who advised against the journey becomes the decisive aide; he who advised in favor is squeezed out into a subordinate position. Changing roles is the result of what is initially a harmless disagreement of counselors. The fact that one nominates the other for a dangerous undertaking would suggest based on the model—the *Rolandslied* comes to mind—that he is seeking to get rid of a rival, but none of this is intimated. The scene creates a rivalry, with the substitution of Sivrit for Hagen in the role of the aide, but it also deflects possible conflicts, because Sivrit voluntarily takes on the task, and Hagen voluntarily vacates his place without giving up the journey.

Viewed from a later perspective, the counselors' dissent and role change are not entirely harmless. They are preludes to the break that will lead to Sivrit's death. Upon returning to Worms, the change of roles is made in the other direction. In ms. B, this is not a smooth process either. According to Burgundian conventions and the normal distribution of roles, Gunther wants to assign Hagen the task of bringing the news to Worms:

> *Uns wære ze der selben verte niemen sô bereit*
> *als ir, friunt her Hagene . . .* (530,2–3)
>
> [No one would be more welcome to us on this journey
> than you, dear friend Hagen . . .

Hagen declines, however, by claiming to be *niht bote guot* [an inadequate messenger] (531,1), because he wants to stay *bî den frouwen* [with the women] in order to *behüeten ir gewant* [protect their property] (531,3). He advises that Sivrit be asked to take the role *durch iuwer swester liebe* [for the sake of your sister's love] (532,4).

In the transition zone between Isenstein and Worms, the assignment of roles proves to be uncertain. The necessary role change in Isenstein is over for Gunther. He assumes the conditions to have returned to what they were in Worms. Hagen, on the other hand, still holds fast to the new constellation. Sivrit cannot rid himself of his new role so easily (something that will turn out to be much more inauspicious). He resists at first by refusing to go. Gunther has to persuade him to accept the mission by appealing to his *minne* for Kriemhilt, in other words, to the second quest, whose prerequisite is the success of the first. The two quests are thereby linked a second time, but this time the linkage is problematic.

The precarious nature of the role change, which puts Sivrit's status in doubt, is evident from the discussion about the messenger mission. The problem is shown in Sivrit's reluctance, as well as in Hagen's supposed responsibility for the *kamere* [household] of the queen.[96] The reversal is then resolved only after the return to Worms. Sivrit and Hagen again become what they were before. This is precisely what rouses Prünhilt's distrust and leads to the discovery of the treachery. The delay in returning to the old roles makes it possible to play out what is not right with these roles and underlines the precarious complication of the bridal quest scheme.

Correspondingly, ms. B and its related manuscripts recount the latent conflict as a delayed replacement. In ms. C and the *C group, on the other hand, it has been rendered unrecognizable. Ms. A, too, tells of the fact that Sivrit takes Hagen's place on the journey, because this is necessary for what follows. The problematic of the exchange, however, evident only when it has been reversed, is downplayed. The narrator limits himself to stating that Gunther has asked Hagen to perform the mission of messenger. Hagen immediately recommends Sivrit, and he in turn performs the mission without complaint. Only the seemingly unnecessary detour (why is Hagen asked first?) points to a not-so-straightforward solution. In that neither Sivrit nor Hagen refuses the mission, there is no longer any reason to suspect that might be in some way disagreeable.[97] The plot is in the end the same and moves ahead even more directly, but the paradigmatic role of the scene for the entire story has been weakened.[98]

The function of the reversed role change is also weakened in ms. C. Hagen is asked first to undertake the mission as messenger, since he normally performs such duties (*wande wir in disen ziten ander niemen han* [since we have no one else at this time], C 538,3). He is therefore supposed to return to his old role, but as in ms. B, he rejects the suggestion (C 539,1) and recommends that the king ask Sivrit, who will not refuse *dvrch iwer swester liebe* [out of love for your sister] (C 539,4). In fact, Sivrit does not resist. He is immediately ready to perform the mission (C 541,4) without Gunther's *vlegen* [pleas] being necessary (B 531,4). The role distribution during the journey to Isenstein is extended by a further episode, an essential link in the chain of events, inserted in such a way as to be minimally invasive. A conflict whose time has not yet come is removed for the sake of a smoother narration. The story line is not even, it is just evened out.

These seem to be marginal touchups, yet they stand for different ways of working with the legend. There is a tendency to link blocks of narrative through various recastings of structural patterns (B), or by filling in motivational gaps to create a smoother sequence of events, sometimes also accomplished by filling out the context (C). But even in the book form, both tendencies may be missing in certain passages, and the sequence of events simply follows "and then . . ." (A).

These kinds of differences can also be observed in small details. Few heroes travel to Isenstein. This is normal with this kind of adventure. Already in Sivrit's journey to Worms, the (proposed) military expedition has been replaced by travel *in recken wîse* [in the manner of heroes] (57–58). This is consistent with Sivrit's role as a hero who wants to meet with the Burgundians on his own, but it seems unusual given the relationship between the kingdoms of Worms and Xanten, and in the end, it is unsuccessful. On the other hand, it is necessary to travel to Isenstein *in recken wîse* (cf. 341,1), for it is an adventure only heroes can dare. But traveling *in recken wîse* is inconsistent with an undertaking led by Gunther. Originally, Gunther wants to take 30,000 men with him. His plan has to be corrected explicitly as well: Sivrit tells him that such an army would be useless in Isenstein (340).[99] In ms. B, the correction remains implicit. Ms. C emphasizes Gunther's miscalculation: to be successful there, four of Gunther's type would not suffice (C 335–36). In contrast, ms. A again lacks any marking of disproportion, in that Gunther's inappropriate suggestion (A 338) is not even expressly rejected. Instead, Sivrit only names the four who will actually travel together (A 339). The difference from what is expected is evident but not especially emphasized.

Even more trivial is the replacement of Uote by Kriemhilt. Why does Gunther, before his bridal quest journey, announce his intent to go *zuo mîner lieben muoter* [to my dear mother] to ask for assistance with preparations (345,2–3), only then to be directed by Hagen *mit hêrlîchen siten* [in a lordly manner] to his sister (346,1)? This strange detour can be explained in that Kriemhilt as *vrouwe* is from now on at the center of affairs at the Worms court. Uote is replaced as *vrouwe* and is reduced to a minor character. Ms. A avoids the detour.[100] Gunther immediately calls for his sister (A 326) without having to be dissuaded by Hagen from taking his mother into his confidence. It makes no difference to the rest of the story.

Syntagmatic and Paradigmatic Integration (On the Isenstein Episode)

The introduction of the Isenstein episode is doubly marked by the formulaic opening *Ez was ein küneginne gesezzen über sê* [There was a queen ruling beyond the sea] (326,1) and the preceding strophe *Iteniuwe mære sich huoben über Rîn* [New reports were heard along the Rhine] (325,1).[101] Curschmann has considered whether an older song might have been worked into the book at this point and that a second introductory strophe was added in order to integrate it better.[102] On this point, all three main manuscripts agree. But in ms. C, the attempt to smooth out the transition goes even further: an extra strophe that establishes the plot linkage is inserted between the two introductory strophes.[103]

As for the more concise ms. A, whose gaps are most apparent from *Âventiure* 6 to *Âventiure* 11, those concerning Prünhilt, Curschmann believes he sees clearer contours of an older oral poetic episode that was not yet bound up in the larger book structure. The version in ms. A would not represent an oral poem,[104] but it might be an abbreviation, because it presumes general knowledge of such a poem.[105] Ms. A might therefore testify to the interference between an implicitly shared knowledge of the legend that might silently fill up obvious gaps and written explication by the epic narrator.[106]

This allows us, in the three main manuscripts, to study stages of coherence in working with the traditional sources. In many points, they conform to one another, even where there are obvious gaps in motivation; in other places, they diverge, even in passages that seem fairly innocuous. Sivrit's false claims about his rank fit into this category.[107] The status fiction is based, according to *communis opinio*, on different versions of the legend and is thought to be poorly motivated, but necessary for the continuation. The conditions are clear: only he who defeats Prünhilt can win her hand. This can only be accomplished by the strongest man. In Isenstein, the strongest rules, even though she is a woman, whereby it follows that the strongest man must also be a ruler, otherwise there would be someone stronger still. If the deception of Prünhilt is to succeed, then the equation of strongest = ruler = suitor must be upheld. If Gunther is supposed to play the role of the suitor successfully, then he must be the strongest, stronger than the *starke Sîvrit*, and this must be expressed in the fact that he is the ruler and that Sivrit is beholden to him, which would mean, according to the same logic, that Gunther must have defeated Sivrit. This makes the status fiction necessary for the desired role change between suitor and helper.[108]

There is a second aspect as well. There is no allowance for an assistant in the contest with Prünhilt. Sivrit's strength would normally disqualify Gunther. The usual distribution of roles in the bridal quest must disappear at least on the surface. The narrator thus has a threefold task: he has to modify a common narrative scheme, the bridal quest; he has to show that the fulfillment of this scheme is based on a lie; and he has to explain how this lie can be plausible. This threefold task determines the treatment of the scene in the main manuscripts.

The fiction that Sivrit is not the challenger, not the strongest, and not the lord, is expressed in ms. B both scenically and verbally in a hyperdramatization. First, Sivrit makes his companions swear to maintain his cover story that he is Gunther's *man*. Second, he leads Gunther's horse to land by the reins in plain sight of the Isenstein court, in other words he fulfills the duty of such a *man*.[109] Finally, he allows Gunther to precede him when received by Prünhilt.

Gunther stands "in front of Sivrit" (420,3) for all to see. This should make everything clear. But all of these dramatizations are useless, because Prünhilt still believes that Sivrit is the suitor.[110] Her greeting of Sivrit simply pushes aside all the signs that are supposed to point to his subordination. She must be deceived a second time, this time in words, and Sivrit expressly rejects her greeting. Pointing to Gunther, *wand' er ist mîn herre* [because he is my lord] (420,4), Sivrit identifies him as the suitor (421,3) and defines his own role as that of companion on the dangerous journey, one who has followed the orders of his lord: *möht' ich es im geweigert han, ich het iz gerne verlân* [if I could have refused to come with him, I would have let it be] (422,4).[111] The hyperproduction of the status fiction is not very convincing for the recipient and shows that the narrator is less concerned with the plausibility of the sequence of events than with the elucidation of the paradigmatic content. Such syntagmatic inconsistencies, like Prünhilt having to be told twice of the arrival of the foreigners, could easily have been avoided.

And so it is: in ms. A, the scene is presented to make logical sense, without the useless service and the strange circumstance that Prünhilt observes the staging exactly.[112] This also avoids the curious "contradiction" that Prünhilt is informed once again, even though she has already seen "everything" for herself.[113] In this goal-oriented description, the separate introduction of the companions is also superfluous.[114] It is unimportant whether ms. A straightened the story line or if the missing elements were subsequently added. In either case, the rejection of the hyperproduction is imaginable, and so it is fair to ask why the other manuscripts did not also choose this simple solution.

In the version represented by ms. B, the fact that "something isn't right" is emphasized on several occasions at the cost of a linear and plausible linkage. What the narrator provides in three consecutive sequences is a drama of falsehood, so that every listener can clearly distinguish between the desired fiction and what is "actually" true. It is not a question of the believability of the lie. What matters is the fact that it is a lie, that the lie is repeated several times, and that it is enforced in the end despite the knowledge of Prünhilt and the listener. Rather than hinting at his former inferior status,[115] Sivrit's acting follows a poetic strategy that enhances the paradigmatic meaning of the scene at the expense of the logical consequences. In ms. B, the dual character of the main figure is called to mind, a character that is, from the second *âventiure* on, in contradictory ways, both hero and courtly knight.[116] The one face of Sivrit—the hero who is dependent on no one—must be elaborately made to disappear so that Prünhilt believes that Sivrit serves Gunther.

This strengthens the link to the following plot. It explains Sivrit's conspicuous behavior within a larger context, that of *minne* service: *Jane lob' ihz niht sô verre durch die liebe dîn/sô durch dîne swester . . . /ich wil daz gerne dienen, daz si werde mîn wîp* [I do this not so much for the sake of your friendship/as for the love of your sister . . . /I shall gladly serve so that she becomes my wife] (388,1–2; 4). The hyperproduction emphatically underlines how the hero keeps his royal status a secret under the duty of *minne*. This explicit reservation is notably missing in ms. A;[117] here, the change in behavior is only noted.

Sivrit will lie explicitly one more time, when he takes off the cloak of invisibility after the succcssful contest. Upon returning from the ship, he acts as if he had no idea that the games were already over. He is therefore not only absent from the contests but rather brashly acts out his absence and ignorance for all to see: *Wes bîtet ir, mîn herre? Wan beginnet ir der spil* [Why are you waiting, my liege? When will you start the contest?] (471,1). He therefore provokes the queen's surprised question and gives Hagen the opportunity to "explain," with yet another lie, why he was not present. Here, too, the passage—the overinstrumentalization of lying—is missing in ms. A.[118]

There are thus remarkable differences between mss. A and B in this narrative sequence. The solutions in ms. B can be traced back to two fundamental principles. The meaning of the scene is more important than the linear connection of one event with the following one (hyperdramatization of lying); and beyond this, the scene is more closely related to the deception story altogether. What seems to produce contradictions on the surface can be understood based on these principles. Sivrit's status fiction is not ad hoc, but belongs to a chain of deceptions,[119] which can be remembered by Prünhilt and can be repeated under different circumstances. The wide-ranging book integration requires that "regionally" necessary deceit and "universal" class realities are both simultaneously kept in mind.

This logic-defying production is missing in ms. A, although it does not otherwise leave out any significant components of the event nexus. It is merely not interested in (partly negligible) interlinking. In preparation for the journey, Kriemhilt's question about the goal of the bridal quest, for example, remains unanswered.[120] The answer is subsequently presumed to be obvious.[121] More detailed circumstances of courtly life are missing,[122] and links of the plot's chain are eliminated.[123] Apart from that, only what is shown on the surface is narrated. The indication that Sivrit is absent from the contest, the curious contact between Gunther and the invisible Sivrit, and his encouraging words to Gunther are missing.[124] The ambivalence in the contest between play and violence is ignored: Sivrit averts the deadly consequences of the fight by turning the spear around in order not to harm Prünhilt.[125] The agreement to lie, Prünhilt's "mistake" at the reception, its "correction," and the desired outcome of the contest all form a linear story line. Plot elements that have an implicit function of commentary, as when the deceived and self-deceiving Prünhilt in the arrival scene prefigures the deceived and self-deceiving Prünhilt in Worms, are absent.

The version found in the *C group goes in another direction. Ms. C, in contrast to ms. B, has a greater tendency to linear coherence and emphasizes single actions and situations through doubling. The variants are not very spectacular in the scenes discussed above. There is doubling in some additional strophes, for example, when Gunther praises Prünhilt's incomparable castle upon arrival (C 392), or when the narrator insists on his *sorge* [worry] before the contest (C 452,1)[126] or when Prünhilt comments in an aside on how little the Burgundians' weapons will help them (C 458). There is only occasionally reason to intervene for greater precision and, for example, to clarify once more that Sivrit is the one who frees everyone from danger (C 480,4), or that Prünhilt's court is conquered out of fear (C 480,3). Once, an unmentioned but still obvious link in the plot is appended: that Gunther—and only he—is armed for the contest (C 452,2). Instead of striving for a "more likely" version, as is usually the case, the episode emphasizes the excessiveness of all actions in Isenstein.[127]

In one case, however, the principle of far-reaching constitutional linkage comes to the fore, even if the outcome is least plausible. In the vulgate version, Sivrit asks his companions to refer to him as Gunther's *man*. The term *man* is unclear and open to different interpretations, from legal dependence to servitude, but the common meaning is vassal or liegeman.[128] Prünhilt, in a conspicuous departure from this broad definition, one that does not necessarily discriminate according to class, will later choose a formulation that is not prepared by the scene told in Isenstein. She will identify Sivrit as *eigen*, or unfree (821,2–3). The misalliance that Prünhilt senses between Sivrit and Kriemhilt is emphasized by an exaggeration of class difference. The redactor of *C obviously noticed that Prünhilt does not repeat what she had heard. He corrected this by having Sivrit recommend to his companions in Isenstein that they tell Prünhilt that *Gunther si min herre; ich si sin eigen man* [Gunther is my lord; I am his unfree vassal] (C 395,3–4). This prepares the way for Prünhilt's later words.

This only seemingly serves syntagmatic coherence, and the price is high. The situation in Isenstein requires subservience of the strong to the strongest, but it does not require servitude. The correction turns Sivrit's assertion into a freakish and redundant notion and Gunther's later defense—originally justified by the indeterminate *man*—into a helpless and unlikely excuse. Above all, Sivrit does not use the word *man* with Prünhilt, but rather with his companions, so that Prünhilt's later words are not really prepared. In reality, they rely on the "unlikely" but typically heroic presumption that whatever is said somewhere to someone is valid for everyone. Because in this case the switch goes wrong, it shows the new, only partially realized narrative principle of *C. This principle strengthens the literary tendencies by developing the single episodes separately, not just arranging them in terms of structural analogies and variants. It is only supposedly a preparatory motivation, since Sivrit's words are actually determined by the outcome. He has to say that he is an *eigen man*, because Prünhilt will later claim him to be *eigen*.[129]

This observation can be transferred to the epic as a whole. A tendency toward isolated scenic expansion, typical of oral or orally stylized epic (as in some passages in ms. A), is reformed by different techniques of wide-ranging integration: ms. C corresponds most closely to modern expectations through a syntagmatic linkage of the plot's single elements, even though it often still fails.[130] The *B group realizes an alternative possibility, a kind of "scenic commentary," through layering situational or plot patterns, aggregation of divergent situational and story elements, and contradiction between scenes, words, and gestures. In this way, complexity is established and distant parts of the story are related to each other. In the history of transmission, this method seems to not always have been understood, so that attempts at normalization began early on.

Deproblematization, Proliferation, Amputation

The smoothing out of the story's logic in the *C group is often part of a deproblematization that cuts off detours and eliminates ambivalences for the sake of linear progress. In Sivrit's ambassadorship to Worms, the disruptions of ms. B are missing. The tendency to deproblematization is especially evident in the partition of the Burgundian inheritance. In ms. B, Kriemhilt insists on an appropriate part of the inheritance, despite Sivrit's refusal, and above all she demands to take Hagen and Ortwin as *Burgonden degene* [Burgundian warriors] (698,1).[131] She is met with stiff resistance, not from the kings, but from Hagen in the name of the *Tronegære*. The scene ends, as so often, without any decision, thereby suspending the conflict: *Daz liezen si belîben* [they let it be] (700,1)—a signal of latent disruption. But even the problem just avoided seems to have been problematic. In ms. C, the partitioning scene is retained but bereft of its potential conflict. The initial gestures of unity in ms. B are retained: the kings are prepared to give; Sivrit demands nothing; Kriemhilt nonetheless wants *Buregonden degene* (C 705,2); Gernot offers a third of them, whomever she chooses. Then the redactor intervenes to smooth things out. Kriemhilt no longer makes the demand to take Hagen along, but instead is quite content with Gernot's offer: *daz was ir liebe getan* [this was done for her pleasure] (C 706,4). Nothing is said about what consequences this will have. There is no scandalous demand, and consequently no appalled rejection and no undecided outcome. The story moves right along: *Si bereite sich zir verte* [she prepared for her journey] (C 707,1). The conflict is pushed aside as long as possible for the sake of a smooth progression, with the result that the division of inheritance becomes an inconsequential detour.

The division of Prünhilt's possessions prior to the journey to Worms leads to a conflict in ms. B, which is also in the end avoided (514–21). Dancwart is assigned to exercise *milte* [generosity, largesse] for Prünhilt, but in her eyes he gives away too much. This is why she removes him from the task and makes sure that she retains a part of her possessions. Hagen and Gunther laugh at the turn of events. Squandering the treasure is a part of the disempowerment of Prünhilt.[132] The scene points to the conflict-laden background of the bridal quest, which raises its head again during the wedding night. The just-avoided squandering of the treasure is an unnecessary detour, but the scene thereby becomes a waypoint in the fight for Prünhilt's power. Again, in *C, the conflict is eliminated in favor of an unimpeded demonstration of generosity:[133] Dancwart's excess, Prünhilt's mistrust, Gunther's and Hagen's amused remarks over her concern all disappear.[134] Prünhilt expresses the desire to manage her own possessions; Hagen points to Gunther's wealth; she nevertheless wants to take treasures along with her, and this is in fact what happens. A supplemental strophe (C 532) even reports on her military retinue, which is equal in number to Gunther's. This is a smooth and orderly transition from Isenstein to Worms without the dangerous signs of future conflict.

Attempts at normalization in the *C group often get stuck after a few strophes, or they lead to new incongruities. There are also traces in mss. A and B of attempts to make sense of the nonsensical, as in hypermotivations where linkages seemed to be missing. The reworking of the story created not only sense but also new oddities, for example, when Blœdelin, misled by Kriemhilt's promises, ambushes Dancwart and the servants and then pays for it with his life. Dancwart leaves him with a few derisive words concerning the missing reward he was to have received from Kriemhilt had the attack succeeded. How can Dancwart know about Kriemhilt's promises to Blœdelin? The narrator therefore adds a few words of explanation:

> *ein vil getreuwer Hiune het im daz geseit,*
> *daz in diu küneginne riet sô grœzlîchiu leit* (1928,3–4)
>
> [a faithful Hun had told him
> that the queen had plotted such great harm]

This has its price. The anonymous, otherwise unknown "faithful Hun" is not only an awkward solution but creates a new problem. How could Dancwart, if he already knew everything, be surprised by Blœdelin when he appears armed at the festival, and then even greet him in a friendly manner, though he must fear an attack (1922,3–4)? As the redactor of *C does even more frequently, the narrator bends to the demand of causal motivation here and does not rely on the implicit contract of heroic narration (that what was once said openly is known by all). This occurs point for point and without consideration of the former or later events, so that the result is even more disruptive than the previous gap.

In the adaptation process of the legend, the narration is converted to a different motivation type. The narrator is intent on ensuring that cause and effect appear in the right order. From case to case, everyday experience plays a part in confronting what was previously unquestioned. These are often inconsequential details that prompt such questioning. Ms. C, for example, in a two-strophe insertion, asks: how are the many heroes that Sivrit maintains in Nibelungenland supported logistically?

> *Nv sprichet liht ein tvmber: ez mach wol lvge wesen.*
> *wie mŏhte so vil ritter bi ein ander sin genesn?*
> *wa namen si die spise, wa namen si gewant?* (C 518,1–3).
>
> [Perhaps a naïve person could say: it seems to be a lie.
> How could so many knights together have been supplied?
> Where would the food and the clothing come from?]

This is a seemingly sensible question that aims at a "probability" dimension, given the medieval problems with logistics. The answer is simply one of legendary proportion, however, not one that is plausible in the real world. Sivrit's treasure is inexhaustible: there is no limit to the resources available.

A similar case is the inserted strophe ms. a 1609,[135] which attempts to find a sensible and probable relation between the number of soldiers and the size of the ship used in the Danube crossing. The crossing cannot be accomplished with a paltry little boat,[136] but requires a 400-man ship. This is plausible, but it does not take into consideration that the ferry operator and Hagen are able to maneuver the ship by themselves.

The attempt to create logical and plausible connections always fails. Instead of eliminating questions, it draws out new ones.[137] The *Klage* goes the furthest in attempting to integrate everything that resists such logic, at the cost of watering down everything that is problematic. The attempt to explain the predominant tradition risks eliminating it altogether.[138] In the different versions, which thanks to Joachim Bumke (1996c) can now be more clearly distinguished, we see that the need for normalization could manifest itself in very different ways, and that the continuation of the downfall of the Nibelungen went to various lengths in the individual manuscripts. Whereas the oldest ones add the proper lament for and burial of the dead, information on the survivors, and news of the writing down of the story, later redactors were satisfied with parts of the normalization program.

In the drastically shortened version *J, there is only "a briefly narrated postscript to the terrible end of the *Nibelungenlied*."[139] The prologue and introduction (Kl 1–70) are missing, along with the "lamentation" of the combatants, so that the first part is completely focused on Kriemhilt, a positive assessment of her, and finally her burial. The effort at normalization is concentrated on the main character and softens the dissonance of her end. This is followed by Swemmel's message (with elimination of unneeded episodes), the reactions of Gotelint and Prünhilt, and the report of the story's composition. This brings to an end what can be said about the continuation, and it is left at that.

The opposite, the elaborative augmentation, is also possible, as manifest in the *D version.[140] Ms. D (fourteenth-century), however, breaks off just as the "lamentation" by those who are innocent of the events is finished, namely, when the news of the catastrophe arrives in Bechelaren: *daz beweinte wîp unde man* [this was mourned by women and men alike] (Kl 3140). This, too, is a possible ending.[141] The laments to follow and explanations in Bechelaren do not add anything new; the continuation of Swemmel's journey (Kl 3287ff.) is apparently not of interest.

In two other manuscripts, the notification of those in Worms and their laments (b) are added to the story line in ms. D,[142] or the text breaks off (d) after Etzel's boundless sorrow is reported.[143] On the other hand, Dietrich's entry into Bechelaren is missing, as is the sorrow of the bishop of Passau in memory of his relatives.[144]

Omissions and additions are traces of an active process of continued reworking. In the manuscripts of the epic, too, there are variations, although not as severe, that are centered around a core theme, namely, the betrayal and the downfall of the Burgundians. These deserve just as intensive an examination as that of the *Klage* by Bumke (1996c). Aside from the text-critical problems in the narrower sense, alternatives of meaning by way of larger additions or—as is more often the case—gaps should be investigated. I shall provide only a few observations on the process of rewriting to demonstrate that it was by no means arbitrary.

There are seams in the epic where the story begins to get out of hand, so to speak, in that redactors are virtually incited to elaborate. Most additions belong to version *C, but in principle, they can appear in other manuscripts as well. The divide between the first and the second part after *Âventiure* 19, between Kriemhilt's low point after the theft of the treasure and her resurgence at Etzel's side, makes it possible for the *C group to insert strophes about Kriemhilt's return to Worms and her concern for Sivrit's *memoria* (cf. C 1158–65). These insertions reinforce the impression of a closed plot all the more. The epic also busts its seams in other places, however, for example with the beginning of the Prünhilt story in *Âventiure* 6, where Gunther's desire to confer with his vassals (C 328) and the conference (C 332) are elaborated, the dispute over the danger of the mission is lengthened (C 335–36), and information on the cloak of invisibility from the realm of the dwarves is appended (C 342, 343).[145] Another example is the transition from courtly harmony to conflict before the queens' dispute erupts (C 821 and C 822). The most detailed outgrowth is a passage in ms. b that expands the reception of the Burgundians at Etzel's court by the Amelungs in twelve supplemental strophes.[146]

Often the expansions are concentrated in a single strophe nestled into the lacunae in the story line, linking to unfinished action or contradictory material and announcing that the telling of the legend is not over once and for all. Sometimes a situation can invite the interpolation of a joke, as when someone is split by a sword so cleanly that he only notices after bending over and falling apart.[147]

The opposite is also possible: the renunciation of the unnecessary. The discussion has been about omissions in ms. A; other manuscripts have even more spectacular gaps. In ms. J, the absence of the beginning of the journey to Etzel (Rumolt's counsel, the crossing of the Danube, the battle with the Bavarians) is subsequently obscured by a change in the text.[148] Some versions leave out entire parts of the complex story line or shorten it radically, mainly in the first part, which obviously was seen by many redactors as simply a prologue to the story really worth telling, namely, that of the downfall of the Burgundians.

Ms. a, for example, only begins with strophe 326 (= B 324),[149] that is, with the Prünhilt story, *Es was gesezzenn . . . .* This is preceded by a prose headline that dates the story historically, namely, to the time of Pipanus, who allegedly was Roman emperor in 714, and Dietrich of Bern, his prefect (*vogt*) in Rome, who threw Boethius in prison: *Pein herdietrichs/zeittenn dez romischenn vogtz vergienng sich die auennteur/dez pueches vonn denn rekchenn vnd vonn kreymhilldenn* [in Lord Dietrich's day,/he was Roman prefect, the adventure/of the heroes and of Kriemhild in the book took place].[150] This spans events from the first fateful betrayal to the downfall. Everything that explains Sivrit's participation in the journey to Prünhilt with its life before at the court of Worms is thus lost. Faithful to the scheme of bridal quest, the news of the ruler *über sê* (326,1) marks the beginning of the heroic epic.

The cuts in ms. n are even more radical.[151] Here the entire preface to the downfall of the Burgundians—the contest of the queens, Sivrit's murder, the theft of the treasure—is reduced to twenty-three strophes, of which only five are concerned with the main events. The manuscript begins with the dispute of the queens, referring vaguely to an initial formula for heroic epic:

> *[F]rauw Brünylt und frauw Kremhylt da zusamen gesaßen.* (n 1,1)
> [Lady Brünhild and Lady Kriemhilt were there together]

Without any lengthy detours, with speech and counterspeech, accusation and proof, mobilization of the courtly public and judgment, the story moves forward to the murder of Sivrit by his *swager* (n 10,2);[152] two strophes (n 14 and n 15) are devoted to Kriemhilt's grief and four others to Etzel's wooing and marriage to Kriemhilt, as well as the invitation of his relatives (which is motivated differently). Without the debate about whether or not the invitation should be accepted, four more stanzas lead to the Burgundians' journey to their doom (*Âventiure* 25). Sivrit, the main character of the first part, only provides the impetus, without playing a role himself. The redactor has little patience with the complex web of contingencies in which the relationship between Sivrit and the court at Worms slowly shifts the center of power and values. What remains is the terrible story of the downfall of the Burgundians, for which, as in the *Klage*, Sivrit's murder is only an ill-defined precondition.

The Opening Âventiure

Alongside such an important selection, the interventions of "complete" manuscripts seem much less meaningful. Upon closer inspection, however, this proves to be deceptive, especially in the epic's opening. The first *âventiure* must set the stage for the perspective on Sivrit's death and the demise of the Nibelungen. It contains three components: the programmatic strophe *Uns ist in alten mæren*, the introduction of the Worms court around Kriemhilt, and Kriemhilt's dream. Each of these components is handled differently in the tradition.

The programmatic strophe that situates the story in the past is found only in mss. ACDd, but not in ms. B.[153] Following this, the epic starts with the introduction of a courtly world (mss. ABCDJd). The first to be named is a woman, then come her royal brothers and the heroes at the court. The story's descent is thus marked by the image of the courtly ideal. The frame is drawn somewhat differently in each of the manuscripts. In one part of the transmission—mss. ADJd—the unusual opening with a heroine as opposed to a hero (2,1) is emphasized in an additional strophe (= *Der minneclîchen meide triuten wol gezam* [the lovely maiden was suited for love], 3,1). After the naming of the Worms kings,[154] information on the genealogy of the royal house and the hierarchy of courtly offices in Worms (7–12) is missing in two manuscripts (Jd). These manuscripts are content with naming the protagonists (Jd) and the place where they live (d) and then move on directly to the third part, that is, Kriemhilt's falcon dream.

The manuscripts that contain the first *âventiure* at all come together again with the dream passage, but mss. J and d leave out two strophes of Kriemhilt's talk with her mother,[155] in which Uote criticizes Kriemhilt's decision to live without *minne*. These are the strophes that remember Veldeke's *Eneit,* but they are irrelevant for the continuation.[156] What has been erased is an allusion to the courtly romance. Finally, strophe 19, where the narrator interprets the dream (mss. ABCDd) is missing in ms. J.[157]

The three components of the prologue that frame the events "historically"—the balance between the female protagonist and her heroic environment, the introduction of the ruling clan at Worms, and the dream and the literary reminiscences that the discussion of it evokes—are always combined and accented differently, and the view of what is to follow is changed a little each time. Only after this does the story of Sivrit begin.[158]

The entryway to the epic seems to lead to considerably different things: to a distant past (1), to an unusual female protagonist (2), to an ideally ordered court (4ff.), and to the fate of a well-known hero (13ff.). Aside from the programmatic strophe, there is a sketch of the social context and the fateful dream in each manuscript, but what is worth telling about each varies, whether without whatever seems to be incidental (the introduction of the Worms court? the continuation of a dialogue that is irrelevant to the story?) or augmented by what seems to be memorable (a supplemental praise strophe for Sivrit?). In this way, the complex structure takes different shapes.

Horizons of Legend

Alongside selection, accenting, and concentration on fundamental story lines, there is also the reverse, namely, the linkage to other stories. Admittedly, the stories surrounding Sivrit and the downfall of the Burgundians prove themselves to be far less open than the chansons de geste, and only in one case—the version in ms. k—have they become an integral part of a book of heroic tales. The tendency toward book form countered appendage to other texts.. There are, however, figures that the *Nibelungenlied* shares with other heroic epics: the Amelungs.

Curschmann sees a connection to the Amelung legend in the *Bůch Chreimhilden* (D) from the fourteenth century.[159] In ms. b, the first confrontation between Dietrich and Kriemhilt invites a vast expansion with supplemental stanzas (shorter, but with a similar tendency in ms. n) that describe the reception of the Burgundians by the Amelungs.[160] And the supplement at the end of ms. b (after 2376) that jokes about Kriemhilt's execution by Hildebrant reinforces the confrontation between the two groups. The same impulse to building cycles is shown in ms. a,[161] without the part preceding the Prünhilt adventure, and it creates a connection with the Dietrich legend by using the dating in the heading (*Pein herdietrichs/zeittenn*). In the *Ambraser Heldenbuch* (d) the context—the "double epic" *Nibelungenlied–Klage* preceding the "double epic" *Book of Bern–Rabenschlacht*—moves the downfall of the Nibelungen into the perspective of a "Life of Dietrich."[162]

A syncretism of the epic tradition was more successful where it separated itself from the *Nibelungenlied*, as in the fusion of the two legend cycles around Dietrich and around Kriemhilt in the *Wormser Rosengarten*. The confrontation and the demise of two empires in the *Nibelungenlied* is transformed into a tournament that makes it possible for various groups of heroes from different legends to fight each other.[163] Here the latent tension in the *Nibelungenlied* actually grows into a clear "rivalry of legends" and a "natural opposition."[164]

Where the *Rosengarten* narrates the linkage of the two legend cycles as a bloody, arbitrary game that has been set up by the evil Kriemhilt, *Biterolf and Dietleib* transforms the military confrontation between Etzel's and Dietrich's heroes, on the one side, and Gunther's and Sivrit's, on the other, step for step into a tournament, in which there are only a few, mostly insignificant casualties and where everything ends in a grand festival. A deadly opposition is transformed into play. *Biterolf* is a completely deproblematized variant of the Nibelungen conflict. Here the proverbial *hôchgezît* of Kriemhilt is finally overcome, but also trivialized into literary irrelevance.

This is neither a necessary nor an obvious development. It is impossible to claim a literary sequence of *Nibelungenlied*, *Wormser Rosengarten*, and *Biterolf and Dietleib*. Rather, the three epics circle around a related constellation that may possibly reach far back into orality. The *Heldenbuchprosa*, too, revises a diffuse and contradictory, but by all accounts very old, material from Nibelungen and Amelungen legends.[165] The transformation into a game is countered there by the stylization of the Nibelungen legend according to a wild and archaic prehistoric time. The *Heldenbuch* also develops the confrontation between Dietrich and Kriemhilt. Above all, it tells of the downfall of the Burgundians as the final end to the heroic age, as a story of a violent world inhabited by larger-than-life heroes, giants, and dwarves. The late medieval adaptations go far beyond these constellations as they appear in the *Nibelungenlied*, and they either trivialize them or stylize them into a completely foreign world. Unlike these watered-down alternatives, the epic with the *Klage* seems to be a concept that is relatively whole.

2 *Heroic Narration and Epic Composition*

Endless Speech: An Epic Begins

In the so-called vulgate version, the *Nibelungenlied* employs a narrative style that can no longer be attributed to orality yet still does not satisfy the demands of a literate culture. This intermediate status seems to have been the subject of some attention at the beginning of the thirteenth century. The impulse to revise certain passages was frequently evident, and the story told by the epic was announced as something unusual:

Uns ist in alten mæren wunders vil geseit. (*1,1*)

[Ancient tales tell us of many marvels.]

It is precisely this programmatic stanza that is missing in ms. B, the manuscript that is the basis for the vulgate version. This stanza is, however, significant in terms of the narrative perspective within the framework of a literate culture. Presumably, the stanza was subsequently added to the beginning.[1] Whereas oral narration can be started by the voice of the narrator, in writing, the place of what is told must be determined explicitly. An ancient story is announced, and the speaker seems to be speaking from a position in which telling the story is no longer normal. When *alte mæren* are identified, there are also others that are less old. The narrator opts for the former. "'Old' (*alt*) is a venerable label in written transmission. Since oral transmission does not recognize the need for such a characterization, age itself is a foreign concept."[2] The programmatic strophe thus presumes literality, even if it begins as if it were oral speech, in the presence of a community that includes a speaker and listener (*uns*). This *uns* is split in the fourth verse; the speaker marks his distance from the listeners: *muget ir nu wunder hœren sagen* [may you now hear of wonders told].[3] Whoever put this strophe at the beginning of the epic demonstrates that the *Nibelungenlied* has left behind the collective memory of "we" and no longer presumes a common horizon of narrator and audience.[4] The object of narration and the audience move apart. The distance between them is "stretched out"[5] to become a condition of reporting a strange story, made known by an expert across a hiatus of time. What he announces are *wunder* (1,1; 1,4), something that takes the audience away from the everyday here and now.

The story of the downfall of the Burgundians is put into historical perspective. A characteristic of oral and semi-oral societies is that they do not form a historical awareness and do not know fixed temporal relations that change along with the present.[6] The past appears in the same form as the present; what counts as a past worthy of memory therefore shifts unnoticeably with the march of time. There are degrees, however: the past can seem more or less foreign and more or less removed from one's own point in time.

In the Middle Ages, writing corrects the cultural tradition of an illiterate laity. Vernacular literality, however, remains influenced by the cultural framework of a society that is overwhelmingly oral in its communication. The reception of the foreign in vernacular writing therefore proceeds as it does under the requirements of orality.[7] Written tradition does not necessarily create an idea of the past as a whole. A semi-oral culture is no longer simply "bereft of the past," as Franz Bäuml puts it,[8] but its relationship to the past is usually not articulated as a process. Often there is just the awareness of distance, of alienation, of the *wunder*.

The programmatic stanza hints at this.[9] It states that the song's story has been told since ancient times. Narration here is *sagen*, oral speech, that has for a long time been directed at "us." The narrator does not mark a new beginning, but claims only to continue what was already said long before him. The strophe makes the requirements of heroic epic explicit: it must remember (or pretend to remember) what everyone has known for a long time. In this regard, writing is linked to the unwritten *mémoire collective*. By making this link explicit, the epic already stands outside of the oral tradition it claims to continue. The narrator does not simply continue; he states that he will continue. He cites the type of narration that he wants to perform, refers to oral speech in a gesture of remembering, but does both already in writing. There is a gap that separates the book form from the old heroic tradition. Writing begins by referring to something that it is not.

Legend has always been spoken, and its beginning is therefore absolute. The *mære* can begin at any point in a never-ending speech without having to worry about what preceded it. Everything that is the object of its attention is coexistent in timelessness. The narration of heroic epic is continuation, without having to make what is continued a topic. The *Hildebrantslied* is already representative of this type:

> *Ik gihorta dat seggen, dat sich urhettun ænon muotin*
> *. . . untar heriun tuem.* (Hi 1–3)
>
> [I heard it said that two warriors met to fight
> . . . between two armies.]

Without any apparent preparation, two warriors meet, and it only becomes clear after some time what has preceded this meeting, and what lasting effects it will have. In the *Nibelungenlied*, certain initial formulas are preserved, marking a beginning in the flow of never-ending speech. Those formulas are frequently to be found elsewhere in heroic epics.[10] In the introductory strophe of ms. B, strophe 2, we find the first type:

> *Ez wuohs in Burgonden ein vil edel magedîn.* (2,1)
>
> [In Burgundy a very noble girl grew up.]

Parallel to this, the second *âventiure* begins:

> *Dô wuohs in Niderlanden eins edelen küneges kint.* (20,1)
>
> [In the Netherlands the child of a noble king grew up.]

A place is marked that is known or could be known, as well as a starting point of the events that are to be narrated. The action begins. The *Ez-wuohs* formula reminds us that what is reported is preceded by other events that are not—or at least not here—worth remembering. As opposed to the in medias res technique canonized by the poetics of classical epic, the formula orients itself on a natural chronology. The in medias res technique already presumes literality and the ability of the epic book form to achieve a wide-ranging disposition that separates itself from chronological sequences. The formulaic introduction, on the other hand, dissimulates literality and seeks to mimic oral narration.

The formula is common. At the beginning of the *Ortnit*, we read in the third strophe:

Ez wuohs in Lamparten ein gewalteger künec rîch. (Ot 3,1)[11]

[In Lampart there grew up a mighty and powerful king.]

The *was-gesezzen* formula competes with the *wuohs* formula. It does not use the end of preceding events (which are not narratively expanded themselves) as the narration's starting point, but rather a sort of static situation:

Uf Kunstenobel ze Kriechen ein gewaltiger künic saz. (Wo A 1)

[A mighty king ruled/lived in Constantinople among the Greeks.]

Ez was ze Berne gesezzen
Ein degen sô vermezzen. (La 1f.)

[There ruled/lived in Bern
a hero quite bold.]

This formula can also be found outside of heroic epic, in related texts:

Bi deme westeren mere
Saz ein kuninc, der heiz Rother. (KR 1–2)

[Near the western sea
ruled/lived a king, whose name was Rother.]

Ein konig hie bevorn saz
Zu Kornevaliz der hiz Marke,
der orlôgete starke. (Trt 54–56)[12]

[A king ruled/lived here in former times
at Cornwall, whose name was Mark,
he fought in many battles.]

Both formulas can also be combined with each other, as in *Orendel*; after a prologue—prologues again characterize an epic book form—we find first that the starting point of the action is Trier:

dar inne was gesezzen
ein here wol vermezzen,
konic Ougel was er geheizen. (Or 161–63)

[there a lord ruled/lived
who was quite bold,
his name was King Ougel.]

And after the description of the ideal rule of Ougel, the real hero, Ougel's son Orendel, is introduced by the *wuohs* formula:

In zoch der kunic, daz ist war,
volleclichen uf druzehen jar. (Or 176–77)

[The king raised him, it is true,
until he was thirteen.]

With the use of the *Ez-wuohs* or the *was-gesezzen* formula, new sequences of events can be developed out of the heroic world. The *was-gesezzen* formula takes as its starting point the solid foundation of legitimate rule. The *wuohs* formula describes the entry of the hero or his opponent into heroic action. The story before can remain unknown. Heroic epic can always create new connections in the heroic world and can always choose new starting points for new circumstances.[13]

In literality, such an abrupt beginning can seem inappropriate. This would explain programmatic stanzas or stanzas that detail sources, as well as explicit deviations from the schema. Perhaps the narrator does not want to leave what precedes his story in a nebulous nowhere. The unpreceded beginning has to be supported. In *Biterolf*, the narrator, before he gets to his hero and names him,[14] declares in a rather complicated manner why he does not tell the story of his hero's family:

Von sînen alten mâgen
Darf mich nieman frâgen . . .
Der dise rede tihte,
Der liez uns unberihte . . .
Hæte er iht dâ von geschriben,
daz lieze wir iuch unverdeit:
uns hât des nieman niht geseit. (Bit 19–20; 23–24; 26–28)

[No one should ask
me about his kin . . .
The one who composed this story
left us in the dark . . .
If he had written anything at all about this,
we would not conceal it from you:
But no one told us anything.]

Here a new kind of narrative type has appropriated heroic personalities. Heroic epic is thought of as written history, and history requires of the medieval chronicler an exact establishment of time and the succession of generations. The narrator complains of his inadequate sources (these sources are understood to be written—*geschriben*).[15] By saying that he does not know what is expected of him, he distances himself from a narrative type that can begin absolutely and without a premise.

In the *Nibelungenlied*, too, the formulaic beginning is not interested in any "before." It is enough that someone rules or grows up somewhere. But this is combined with a reflection on such narratives and the attempt to create historical and genealogical links to the premiseless beginning. The narrator immediately delivers in the beginning what the narrator of *Biterolf* painfully lacks: details about the family, familial relationships, and the household of those who are the object of his story (strophes 3–12).[16] He is differentiated in his approach. The most detailed introductions are for the dynastic and ruling groups to which Kriemhilt belongs. The listener is already given less information on Sivrit's heritage. Of Etzel (for whom there is no formula), we at least learn the names of his father and brother. There is no genealogical or historical introduction of the Nibelungen kings at all. We only hear that they are *küneges kint* (87,3), and we hear nothing of Prünhilt's history except for the traditional beginning: *Ez was ein küneginne gesezzen über sê* [there was a queen who ruled/lived across the sea] (326,1). At least the abrupt beginning is softened by an additional bridging strophe (325) in the spirit of written structural coherence. So, the measure of historical-dynastic grounding (as typical for a writing culture that is beginning to control the past) declines if one moves from the "normal" world to the alien locales of legend.

Epic Book Form and Initial Formula: Repressed Movement

The two typical formulas of epic beginnings, one more "dynamic" (*Ez wuohs*) and the other more "static" (*Ez was gesezzen*), introduce the transition from (relative) quiet to (heroic) action.[17] This transition is accomplished in the *Nibelungenlied* several times, twice in the opening *âventiure* alone. The action that seems to begin with the initial formula (*Ez wuohs*) ends with the picture of the Worms court (3–12) describing the *êren* [honors] of the protagonists in considerable detail. Then the narrator begins a second time, now apparently telling a story:

> *In disen hôhen êren troumte Kriemhilde . . .* (13,1)
>
> [Living in such great esteem, Kriemhilt dreamed . . .]

The opening of the narration of Kriemhilt's dream thematizes anew the tension of condition (*êren*) and event (*troumte*). What kind of event is it? The dream still does not bring about the expected action. It only points to an action to be narrated and again presents an image. The image must be interpreted, and it is only with the mother's interpretation that future events are announced.

Dreams that portend disaster, often insolently or frivolously pushed aside, are typical elements of heroic narration. What is peculiar here is the placement in the story, since the dream remains separated from the nexus of the following events. It has no consequences (customarily, for example, attempting to avoid the danger only to fall victim to it all the more certainly).[18] Later on, the dream seems to be completely forgotten by the actors. The beginning of the narration is deceptive. Nothing is set in motion. What is told is only at first glance an event, but in reality the dream contains a metaphor. With its interpretation, the listener can preview what is still to be told. The action is frozen a second time in a tableau. Instead of a tableau of *êren*, as in the first case, this time it is one of misfortune.

The tension between quiet and action is less pronounced in the second *âventiure*. Here, too, the directness of the beginning, marked by the *wuohs* formula, is absorbed in the sketch of the familial and local ("historical") context in Xanten. Here, too, the image of an ideal court is reported in "durative" speech, with repeated reference to events that are not specific as to time: *In sînen besten zîten, bî sînen jungen tagen* [in his best years, in his younger days] (22,1), *vil selten* [often] (25,1), or in circumstances without temporal adverbs. Here, too, an event, introduced three times, only seemingly ends the description of permanent courtly harmony (*Er was nu sô gewahsen daz . . .* [He was old enough that . . .],[19] 24,1; *Nu was er in der sterke daz . . .* [Now he was strong enough that . . .], 26,1; *Dô hiez sîn vater Sigmunt künden . . .* [His father Sigmunt proclaimed . . .], 27,1). This event—the knighting—only brings up a further image of the courtly ideal. The epic is having problems getting started.

This does not change until the third *âventiure*: the young hero leaves the court of the father (*er hôrte sagen mære* [he heard tales told], 44,2; *Dô gedâht ûf hôhe minne* [His thoughts intent on high *minne*], 47,1; *dô sprach* [then he spoke], 48,4). The motif of distant love initiates a shift to the schema of the dangerous bridal quest and promises heroic action. But again, before Sivrit has the opportunity for his first test, the action is interrupted to give Hagen a chance to recount Sivrit's earlier deeds. The listener is told that the just-begun initial *âventiure*, the quest for Kriemhilt, is not an initial *âventiure* at all. Sivrit is already a hero in heroic *memoria* before he can even set foot on center stage.

His long-delayed martial arrival in Worms is over as soon as it begins. Instead of fighting out a violent confrontation, Gunther steers action and provocation back to courtly harmony. Sivrit becomes a member of the Burgundian court and subordinates himself to its rules.

> *Sus wont' er bî den herren, daz ist alwâr,*
> *in Guntheres lande volleclîch ein jâr.* (138,1–2)
>
> [And so he lived with the kings, this is true,
> a whole year in Gunther's realm.]

Strophes 3–12 of the first *âventiure* undercut the absolute beginning of the heroic epic by placing it in a well-known environment. Whereas the programmatic stanza recounts completely indeterminate events, which are repeated again and again and can continue in unpredictable ways—*fröuden, hôchgezîten, weinen, klagen, küener recken strîten*—the narrator begins with descriptions of an almost actionless ideal that is only briefly disturbed three times: by the dream, Sivrit's decision to go on the bridal quest, and his challenge of Gunther. None of these actions leads to a result. A new state of suspension commences. In Worms and Xanten, two equally ideal, ahistorical worlds seem to have been melded together.

The introductory formulas point in the wrong direction. Instead of getting the story going, they help to build up a scenery of peaceful quiet, in which the story only hesitatingly continues.[20] The independent parts of the story are integrated through the parallelization of the introductory formulas, by which isolated actions and action fields are connected to each other. First the heroine is introduced, then the hero, then, in the sixth *âventiure*, their foil, Prünhilt. The formulas refer back to each other, creating an intratextual latticework. Parallelism is complementarity, and the characters are identified as belonging together. Literary cross-reference is thereby created using the means of oral traditional epic.

All events told of prior to Prünhilt's appearance stabilize the equilibrium established at the beginning. The story line starts anew in the fourth *âventiure* with *Nu nâhten vremdiu mære* [Then strange tales were heard] (139,1) and the victorious battle against the external foe, only to come to rest again at the end of the fifth *âventiure* in a grand celebration. The result is again a standstill. The hero continues to remain at court, actionless (324,1). Not until the sixth *âventiure* does the shift begin.

Now the action starts again for a fifth time, and this time the starting point is conspicuously doubly marked: *Iteniuwe mære* . . . [A certain new tale . . .]

(325,1)[21] and—with the alternative initial formula—*Ez was ein küneginne gesezzen über sê* [There was a queen who ruled/lived across the sea] (326,1). The ill-fated journey to Isenstein begins with Gunther's decision (*Dô sprach der vogt von Rîne* [The ruler on the Rhine spoke], 329,1). The alternatives of quiet and action manifest in the *wuohs* and in the *was-gesezzen* formulas are used by the narrator in a paradoxical way. The "dynamic" *wuohs* formula merges with the description of a peaceful state of affairs: the solid rule in Worms and the courtly world in Xanten. The "static" *was-gesezzen* formula introduces the Prünhilt story that will eventually cause the downfall of the stable order of Worms and Xanten.

Looking at the events up to this point, what is striking is their loose connection. They are only weakly integrated in "syntagmatic" terms. The rhythm of quiet and action seems to be precisely calculated. The images of courtly harmony are from the beginning placed against a background of dark premonitions. But wherever a turn for the worse might threaten, the action stops short. The threat from the dream seems to be averted with Kriemhilt's decision to reject *minne*. We only learn of Sivrit's dangerous adventures after they have long since been accomplished. His challenge to Burgundian power morphs into a peaceful invitation, the Saxon war into a brilliant victory celebration. *Weinen unde klagen* are always averted in the foreground but remain constant threats in the background. The adaptation of the old narrative tradition and its avoidance are closely interwoven from the very beginning.

The heroic pattern is announced for a second time with the journey to Prünhilt. The Prünhilt story line extends over the course of almost six *âventiuren* (6–11). This is the first real challenge that takes place center stage. It, too, merges in a celebration—the wedding—that is supposed to demonstrate the newly achieved harmony, but this time it actually carries in it the seeds of division. The disruption does not come from outside but rather from within, and it refers to the festival itself, which threatens to fail.[22] But once more the turbulence is calmed. The calming seems to be successful: *des wart diu vreude guot* [there was great joy] (685,2). It is followed by a ten-year period, described in nine stanzas (715–23) as a peaceful, unheroic reign.

The potential antagonists are far apart in space. The introductory formula for the story (*In disen hôhen êren troumte Kriemhilde* [Living in such great esteem, Kriemhilt dreamed . . .], 13,1) seems to have turned into a closing formula: *In disen grôzen êren lebet'er* [Sivrit lived in high esteem] (715,1) and *Er het den wunsch der êren* [He possessed all the honor one could desire] (723,1). But, in fact, neither court any longer represents what they did at the beginning, namely, mutual courtly ideals; instead, they are bound together by a common story with unexplained ambiguities.

This motivates another attempt to get the story line going (*Nu*), this time through Prünhilt: *Nu gedâht' ouch alle zîte daz Guntheres wîp* [Gunther's wife was thinking all the time] (724,1). What is set in motion is at first described iteratively (*alle zîte*), but Prünhilt's continuing doubt merges in an event, the invitation to the celebration. This initiates the intrigue around Sivrit's death, this time encompassing seven *âventiuren*. The action accelerates for a short time. Now there are only a few stops, the ceremonial reception and the peaceful scenes before the outbreak of the queens' dispute (800–813). After the open confrontation between Kriemhilt and Burgundian power and the failure of any legal clarification, the action seems to come to a halt. The phrase *Dô liezen siz belîben* [they let it be] (871,1) is deceptive, however. It expresses a kind of limbo in which only the guests enjoy the delights of court, while the murderous intrigue moves forward *in allen zîten* (870,2).

There is a short period of hectic activity, then everything comes to a halt. Sivrit's death, more than anything before, creates a break, this time a condition of paralysis, not of equilibrium. Kriemhilt prevents the completion of revenge, Sigemunt disappears from the epic, and Sivrit's son is no longer a topic of interest. After the hero's death, there is nothing left in Xanten worth telling. In Worms, things come to a standstill:

> *Prünhilt diu schœne mit übermüete saz.* (1100,1)
> [The beautiful Prünhilt lived in great pride.]

The initial formula (*was gesezzen*), on which the verse turns, seems to be reversed in its meaning. It no longer marks the starting point of an action but its seemingly irreversible end, from Prünhilt's point of view, a victory (without consequences); from Kriemhilt's, complete stagnation. Actually, a new impulse does go out from this moment of illegitimate triumph, but Prünhilt is no longer affected by it. The formula marks the standstill of the end and the standstill from which new deadly battles will emerge.

Prünhilt in her *übermüete* [pride] and Kriemhilt, heard *z'allen zîten . . . klagen* [lamenting all the time] (1099,2), are both left over from the Sivrit story. The antagonism fossilizes, victor and vanquished are set. The standstill is expressed through "sitting." It is said of Kriemhilt: *dâ si mit ir gesinde sît âne vreude saz* [there she lived/ruled with her household bereft of joy] (1102,3). The situation of the beginning is reversed—Prünhilt is no longer in distant isolation in Isenstein, Kriemhilt is no longer at the center of a powerful royal clan and its retinue. The initial formula is now a closing formula, the complete negation of action:

> *Sus saz si nâch ir leide, daz ist alwâr,*
> *nâch ir mannes tôde wol vierdehalbez jâr.* (1106,1–2)
>
> [So she lived with her pain, this is true,
> three and a half years after her husband's death.]

Several stanzas (1099–1106) are dedicated to this condition of inertia, as those before were to an uneventful happiness.

Then Hagen ends the standstill "at some point": *Dô sprach der helt von Tronege* [Then the hero of Troneck spoke] (1107,1). This is the same phrase that launched the Isenstein adventure (*Dô sprach der vogt von Rîne*, 329,1). It seems that the harmony in the ruling group is to be restored, but in actuality a new conflict arises, now regarding the Nibelungen gold left over from Sivrit's rule. A few stanzas talk about negotiations that go back and forth. Shortly thereafter, *Dar nâch vil unlange* (1116,1), the hoard is brought to Worms. This short period of action leads to a new, violent act: the hoard Kriemhilt wanted to dispose of is stolen. The culprits are not clearly identified. What follows is a judicial proceeding and a renewed standstill: *Nâch Sîfrides tôde . . . si wonte in manigem sêre driuzehen jâr* [After Sivrit's death . . . she lived in great despair for thirteen years] (1142,1–2): a period of paralysis, apparently permanent. In C 1162–63, a second mother-daughter conversation (concerning Kriemhilt's withdrawal to the monastery at Lorsch) evokes the opening scene of the epic, but instead of Kriemhilt's permanent rejection of a husband, this time the subject is the constant nearness to his grave. The circle seems to have been completed.

After the end of *Âventiure* 19, in the middle of the epic, we find the greatest break. Kriemhilt seems permanently robbed of a chance at vengeance. She becomes a petrified icon of pain:

> *dône gestuont ir klage*
> *des lîbes nimmer mêre unz an ir jungesten tage.* (1141,3–4)
>
> [her lament never ceased
> for the rest of her life, until the day she died.]

Whereas *iteniuwe mære* (325,1) had aroused the desire for "unbelievable" adventure, now *iteniuwe leit* (1141,1) is a circumscription of an endlessly repeating, cyclical condition of loss. The impulse to action that was present from the beginning seems to have been finally exhausted.

The opening of *Âventiure* 20 links two originally separate legend cycles. It forms the axis of the epic and divides its two approximately equally long parts (1–19; 20–39). In the first part, four segments can be distinguished: a problem-free, hardly threatened ideal (1–5), the victorious, although deceptive, fight for Prünhilt (6–10), the contradictory attempts at enlightenment and satisfaction (11–14), and finally the murder of Sivrit and humiliation of Kriemhilt (15–19).

The transition to the following plot sequence does not ensue from what precedes it and does not use a variant of one of the initial formulas. The new conflict must come from outside. The narrator chooses the palest formula of epic transition, one that makes no claim to connection or causality, but only expresses simultaneity:

> *Daz was in einen zîten dô vrou Helche erstarp.* (1143,1)
>
> [This was in the days when Lady Helche died.]

By Etzel's wooing of Kriemhilt, her story has a chance of being continued. From this point on the pace quickens with ever fewer pauses to the downfall: (1) Kriemhilt's restitution as queen, (2) a second treacherous invitation, (3) the departure and journey of the army of Burgundians—this time not just individual *recken*—to a dangerous adventure, and (4) the destruction of the entire world that had been constructed up to this point. The overall scheme of events repeats that of the first part, whereas the single sections are structured as mirror-images of each other. The harmony of the beginning is answered by the destruction at the end; the adventure around Prünhilt and its ambivalent development, by the expedition to Etzel with its ambivalent signals; the treacherous invitation of Prünhilt, by that of Kriemhilt; and—in the middle of the epic—Kriemhilt's extreme humiliation, by her shining rise as the queen of the Huns.

The sections are of different lengths and differently arranged. Helche's death and Etzel's wooing (*Âventiuren* 20–22) arrive at their conclusion in six stanzas, 1385–90,[23] which show Kriemhilt at the height of *êren* in exactly the reversal of the situation after the theft of the hoard:

> *Mit vil grôzen êren, daz ist alwâr,*
> *wonten sî*[24] *mit ein ander unz an daz sibende jâr.* (1387,1–2)
>
> [They lived in great esteem, this is true,
> together for seven years.]

The action begins again in *Âventiure* 23, this time as Kriemhilt's intrigue and marked by the temporal adverb *nu* (*Nu het si wol erkunnen* [She now realized fully], 1391,1). This segment (*Âventiuren* 23–24) is characterized by contradictory signals: a friendly invitation and an insidious trap, preparations for a *hôchgezît* and for a clash of arms. This continues on the way to Etzel and in the first scenes at court (*Âventiuren* 25–31): bloody battles and friendly receptions, the equivocal greetings by Kriemhilt, Etzel, and the heroes of Etzel's court, the festival among relatives and the constant threat of violence. The result is at first undecided, but charged with conflict. Then the indecisiveness comes to an end. The last *âventiuren* (32–39) tell how one character after another is sucked into the vortex of death and how almost all must die in the end.

The narrator seems to hesitate in getting the plot under way. The dark clouds at first seem to be insignificant and are quickly dealt with. The disturbances increase from case to case, however. The sections that threaten the equilibrium get longer and longer, the states of peace that they terminate become ever more precarious. All attempts to calm the situation fail to take hold. The conflict is covered up, overcome by silence, kept under wraps by edict, only to break out all the more fatefully. Blocks of uneven lengths that slowly build up and then hesitatingly relax the conflict have short phases of quiet inserted, at first still those with a courtly background, then nothing more than an empty time of simple endurance. If the link between the single episodes sometimes still lacks coherence, causal dependence, a plan, and larger plot segments, then at least the structure as a whole is planned in a thoughtful way.

There is no incisive conclusiveness of the *mæren* about Sivrit's death and the downfall of the Burgundians as preserved in the Eddic lays. What seemed almost necessary there proves itself to be full of alternative possibilities: things could have turned out very differently. In the opaque change of action and quiet, there is in some scenes the impression of contingency, whereas in the macro sense, everything runs as it must, as people have always known it must. The *Nibelungenlied* uses different means to harness all actions toward the well-known ending, but the links do not at first inevitably lead to catastrophe, but seem to avert it instead.[25]

The open time of the heroic legend is measured precisely here. Determinations of shorter and longer spaces of time specify exactly how much of a gap lies between episodes. Sivrit is in Worms for a year before he sees Kriemhilt (138,1–2). Six weeks after the return from the Saxon war, the victory celebration is held (257,2). Gunther's and Kriemhilt's wedding lasts fourteen days (686,1). Sivrit and Kriemhilt live happily in their own land until the tenth year (715,2). Kriemhilt mourns Sivrit's death for thirteen years (1142,2). Kriemhilt has a son with Etzel after seven years (1387,2). These kinds of temporal indicators also have paradigmatic meaning. They do not want to establish an exact chronological framework for the story, but serve as an epic qualification of certain events. Kriemhilt mourns "for a long time," the hoard is "immeasurably great," which is why its transport "takes a long time" (1122,2–4). Especially in the second part, the indications show how narration time and narrated time approach each other, how the empty times of quiet become shorter, and destruction accelerates. After Kriemhilt has ruled happily "for years," things happen ever faster after the departure of the Burgundians. The journey to Etzel (*Âventiuren* 25–28) offers the last retarding moments; the stops are always short ones: *einen tac / und ouch die naht mit vollen* [one day / and also through the whole night] in Passau (1630,1–2), *unz an den vierden morgen* [until the fourth morning] in Bechelaren (1691,2): *Ez enkunde niht wern langer, si muosen dannen varn* [They could not stay any longer, they had to depart] (1692,1). The rest takes place in three days: the day before the *sunewende* [solstice] (1816,1), when the conflict is prepared (*Âventiuren* 28–30), the *sunewende* itself (*Âventiuren* 30–36), which is the start of the conflict, and the following day (*Âventiuren* 37–39) when everything is destroyed. Times of quiet now are only phases of exhaustion until the slaughter resumes.

With this acceleration, more and more plot alternatives, formerly stuck in long phases of inaction, are lost. That the narrator does in the end follow the lines of the legend is less remarkable than that for a long time, other, less fateful, but also less memorable outcomes seem possible.[26] Just before the fateful hunt for Sivrit, we read:

> *noch heten ez gescheiden genuoge 'sküniges man:*
> *dône wolt' et Hagene nie des râtes abe gân.* (882,3–4)
>
> [plenty of the king's men still would have settled the conflict,
> but Hagen did not want to give up the plot.]

Later in the tense atmosphere of Etzel's court, shortly before the outbreak of violence:

> *het iemen gesaget Etzeln diu rehten mære,*
> *er het' wol understanden daz doch sît dâ geschach.*
> *durch ir vil starken übermuot ir deheiner ims verjach.* (1865,2–4)
>
> [If someone had told Etzel the truth,
> he might have still been able to stop what happened afterwards.
> Because of their great pride, not one of them told him.]

How such a solution would have appeared and what about it would have been worth telling is not as important as the fact that it is mentioned at all. The *mære* should not be narrated as absolutely necessity. The written epic allows us to see alternatives, even if they remain unrealized.

The End and Its Denial

At the end of the epic, any continuation would seem impossible:

Diu vil michel êre was dâ gelegen tôt.
die liute heten alle jâmer unde nôt.
mit leide was verendet des küniges hôhgezît,
als ie diu liebe leide z'aller jungeste gît.

[All their great honor was lying there dead.
The people all suffered from great grief and distress.
The king's feast had ended in sorrow,
as love always turns to sorrow in the end.]

Ine kan iu niht[27] *bescheiden, waz sider dâ geschach:*
wan ritter unde vrouwen weinen man dâ sach,
dar zuo die edeln knehte, ir lieben friunde tôt.
hie hât daz mære ein ende: daz ist der Nibelunge nôt. (2378; 2379)

[I am unable to tell you what happened after that,
except that knights and ladies were seen,
along with noble squires, to be crying for the dead among their loved ones.
Here the story has its end, and that is the downfall of the Nibelungen.]

The end of the story, the end of the world of which it tells, and the completion of the epic are all one and the same. With one and the same gesture, the narrator recapitulates that whatever was worth telling about, metonymically taken as *êre*, is dead, with the exception of Dietrich and Etzel. The theme that was announced in the first *âventiure* is thereby fulfilled, *liep* has become *leit*; joy, lament; celebration, destruction. The narrator knows of nothing more to tell except that all of the survivors are crying (2377,3) and that all courtly order, the sign of which is joy, has been destroyed. Finally, the story has a name: *der Nibelunge nôt*. With this title, the world of the epic sinks into the absolute past.[28]

The narrative process always defers the finality of the ending. In the end, however, postponement is pushed aside. There are no perspectives, no "edificatory" and "consolatory" reconciliations, as achieved by the Christian adaptations of heroic patterns in the saints' lives of the early Middle Ages.[29] Any view beyond the end is denied. Almost none of those who copied the epic accepted the four attempts at final conclusion, as evident in the final stanzas. Almost everyone appended the Nibelungen *Klage* to the epic. The beginning of the *Klage* rejects the absolute ending that has just been decreed: *Hie hevet sich ein mære* [Here begins a tale] (Kl 1).[30] The epic leaves uncomfortable questions open, which the *Klage* attempts to answer through its own loquaciousness.

As *Rosengarten*, *Biterolf*, and certain passages of the Dietrich epic (*Book of Bern*) show, the story of the Nibelungen was part of an endless narrative, which could be continued in other stories. Continuations in the heroic world can be added without preconditions. In the *Virginal*, we read:

> *nu hât daz buoch ein ende.*
> *hœrent wie ez dô ergienc:*
> *dô disiu arbeit ende nam,*
> *ein ander schiere ane vienc.* (Vi 1097,10–13)
>
> [Now the book comes to an end.
> Hear what happened afterwards:
> Once this travail came to an end
> another soon began.]

There is always something worth remembering. Narration is based on heroic memory, where many stories are stored alongside one another, and from where they can be recalled at any time.

The epic's continuation by the *Klage* is distinctly different from how the legend is stored memory. With an accountant's precision, the *Klage* registers the laments over and burial of the heroes, the less than spectacular events that followed, and the concern about a final recording of the events. The story tells *waz sider dâ geschach* [what happened afterwards] (2379,1), but in a way completely foreign to the epic. The many lost threads are taken up again, even if nothing of note is actually told. Gunther and his court, on their way to Etzel, left behind the courts of Worms, Passau, and Bechelaren, and these must be notified one after the other, and a kingdom like Etzel's cannot be completely destroyed. All in all, we are left with a heroic vacuum.

The *Klage* is witness to an irritation, a trauma that never ceases to be talked about. The largest part is made up of speeches of survivors about what happened in the epic: lamentation of the dead, comments on the inevitability or avoidability of the catastrophe, stories about the events for those who were not present. Here the "consolatory" function of a renewed heroicism comes to the fore. The "norms of noble and warrior society, seated in heroic poetry," are freed of their ambiguity, and their "norm-setting character" is affirmed,

Wolfgang Haubrichs observes.[31] The figures are sorted into those who went to heaven or hell, the morally good and bad. It is explained who the culprits were, who the victims, and what place each can occupy in heroic remembrance. Once the heroes are all dead, the empty time after the absolute end has to be filled with wordy laments, in which Kriemhilt remains silent, elaborate burial ceremonies, in which the epic leaves the characters frozen in pain, and banal developments of secondary importance, which have no sequel. How far—based on the individual manuscript—this continuation goes has been shown above.[32] But in every case, the downfall as ending seems completely unacceptable.

The *Klage* establishes the historical context by reporting the fate of the survivors. It proceeds to Dietrich's adventures when he returns home and opens up the heroic space to the usual feudal history, telling how Gunther's son became king in Worms.[33] The catastrophe seems to have made little difference to the Burgundian realm, despite the streams of tears. In this way, the events are contextualized, and the downfall of the protagonists is wrapped in a network of dynastic relationships, which are expanded when they are already present in the epic (e.g., Bishop Pilgrim of Passau). Developed even further is above all the possibility of imagining alternatives. If only Etzel had been informed in time, then he would have . . . :

> *man möht ez lîhte erwendet hân.*
> *der Etzeln hete kunt getân*
> *von êrste diu rehten mære.* (Kl 283–85)[34]
>
> [it could easily have been avoided,
> if someone had told Etzel
> the real story from the beginning.]

If only Sivrit and Kriemhilt had never met, then . . . :

> *man sol undanc der wîle sagen*
> *in der diu nôt geschæhe,*
> *unt daz Kriemhilt ie gesæhe*
> *des edelen Sîfrides lîp.* (Kl 546–49)
>
> [the time should be cursed
> when all this grief came to pass,
> and that Kriemhilt ever saw
> the noble Sivrit.]

Even Hagen's fury was avoidable:

het diu künegîn daz eine lân
daz si Blœdelînen
Hagenen den bruoder sînen
ze tôde niht heizen slân:
sone wær es alles niht getân. (Kl 1304–8)

[If only the queen had left one thing undone,
if she had not commanded Blœdelin
to kill Hagen's brother.
Then none of this would have happened.]

Wherever in the epic the nexus of the legend persists, despite all attempts at distraction, in the *Klage* even the most insignificant changes are supposed to avert the catastrophe.

These kinds of considerations, as banal as they may seem, point to a completely revised narrative concept: every event exists in close relationship to other events. Every event influences other events, as it is influenced itself. There is always another possibility. Time is a continuum in which there are no empty phases of standing still. The *Klage*, as a work of literate culture, does not have to handle capacities of memory economically, but instead can record everything that happens. It knows neither absolute beginning nor complete ending. It not only comments on and corrects what the epic narrates;[35] it also alters the type of story that is told.

In detail, too, what seemed awkward is put in order. This starts with the introduction of the characters. Whereas the epic is unconventional in starting with Kriemhilt, then transitioning to her royal brothers, and then to their family, the *Klage* maintains the proper, that is, dynastic, order: first, the family (represented by the old king Dancrat), then, his heroic sons and Queen Uote, who wears the crown along with them, and then, finally, the *swester*, Kriemhilt, who is the main character.[36] This kind of correctness continues.

All this distinguishes the *Klage* from an older narrative type that had already been transformed in the *Nibelungenlied* and is valid only at the very margins of the Nibelungen world. This transformation is nearly completed in the *Klage*. Only on one occasion is the older type preserved: in the narrator's comment on what became of Etzel. First, he confirms that nobody knows anything about it

des enkan ich der wârheit
iu noh niemen gesagen. (Kl 4326–27)

[I can't tell you or anyone else
the truth about that.]

This gesture of rejection is only seemingly identical with the final verses of the epic. With Etzel's disappearance, a character who has no place in the enlightened world of the *Klage* exits. Etzel disappears without a trace from the story, just as the people of Xanten do at the end of the first part of the *Nibelungenlied*, but for a completely different reason. In the epic, characters leave the stage without comment if they are finished as heroes and no longer needed. Writing, on the other hand, must make some accounting of these gaps. Etzel's further fate falls into just such a gap.

The abrupt words of the *Klage* about his future juxtapose the transparency of a (clerically controlled) literate culture against the wild world of the legend preserved in oral heroic literature. What the narrator offers as more or less absurd alternatives for Etzel's end is a confused legend in which no one really knows what is right and everyone claims something else: *sümelîche jehent . . . : sô sprechent sümelîche nein* [some say . . . others say no] (Kl 4328–29). Considered first are versions of Etzel's end appropriate to heroic epic (some say, he was killed, others think not), but then the narrator brings in increasingly ridiculous alternatives: maybe he went up to heaven, maybe down to hell, maybe he went mad, maybe he crawled into the earth. Curschmann has pointed out the learned cleric's distancing from what is told: "These are (almost ironic) rationalizations of a literary man who does not make the effort to literacize in the appropriate genre."[37] This seems to me to be programmatic and points to a literary awareness that distances itself from oral tradition. These suggestions are much below the level of the narrator's interest.

In the turmoil of the legend, it is impossible to distinguish between *lüge* and *wârheit* (Kl 4331–32), because the only authority, the written text authorized by the *tihtære*, is silent, as much as the narrator would like to have told us more about Etzel:

> *Uns seit der tihtære,*
> *der uns tihte ditze mære,*
> *ez enwær von im sus niht beliben,*
> *er het iz gerne gescriben,*
> *daz man wiste diu mære,*
> *wie ez im ergangen wære.* (Kl 4349–54).
>
> [The poet tells us,
> the one who composed this tale,
> that he would not have left it this way,
> he would gladly have written it,
> so that one would know the story
> of what happened to him.]

The narrator prevents Etzel—the only one who does not return to the calming mode of feudal normality—from taking part in literary *memoria* (which is necessarily under the purview of the *clerici*). In this way, the *Klage* provides a literary answer to the "openness" of the epic world. It leads the story, to the extent that it lies outside its horizon of interest, quickly toward its sad ending. The heathen Etzel remains where he belongs, stuck in the absurd cacophony of the legend.

The narrator in the *Nibelungenlied* does not know how to proceed, because after the catastrophe, there is nothing left worth telling. The narrator of the *Klage* falls silent concerning Etzel's end, because he has no source for it. The authorities, those who deserve to be trusted, know nothing. The (written) attempt to provide meaning is significantly broken off where the Christian world ends.

The shifting position of the passage about Etzel's end in the *Klage* manuscripts points to the fact that this part of the legend does not really belong to the story of the Nibelungen: in the *C version, the passage precedes the news of the written fixing of the story. Here, writing has the final word. In the *B version, the comments about Etzel are appended at the very end. In this way, what is resistant to a Christian contextualization remains shut out. By not accepting the absolute end of the epic, but still providing Etzel with an inglorious end, the *Klage* fills an empty space with meaning, a space that has been ripped open for a Christian conscience by the *alten mæren*. The borders of the world coincide with the borders of Christianity.[38]

The Book Epic and Remembering Legend

It becomes possible in writing to relate various registers of narration to each other. In the *Nibelungenlied*, there are spaces and episodes in which forms of narration dominate that seem to point more to the "legend" than the "book." There is, of course, no empirical evidence that any given episode in the written text was taken from oral poetry, and, more important, such evidence would in any case say nothing about the episode's function in the new medium. Narrative strategies and structures can be described, however, that differ significantly from written narrative. Perhaps it gives the narrator too much credit to assume that he consciously distinguished these registers. But even when the difference does not result from aesthetic calculations, we have to consider it. The question is not whether we are really dealing with legend in such cases, but whether the narrator is narrating, or letting someone else narrate, as was done "according to tradition."

There have been up to now no investigations of different narrative registers in the *Nibelungenlied.* The criteria for such an investigation are also difficult to apply. This is never as conspicuous as in the ironically pointed confusion of the comments about Etzel's end in the *Klage.* But even in the epic, there are indications of "another" kind of narration.[39] In any case, such disruptions should not be prematurely dismissed as aesthetically flawed.

That the change in register in the heroic poetry of the thirteenth century can be meaningful will first be demonstrated with another epic that put heroic legend into writing: *Kudrun.* Here we find an odd allusion to heroic legend in the part dedicated to King Hagen. Again, we can observe the tension between a later, literate culture and the heroic world of which it tells.

The passage is at the transition from Hagen's youth in the wild to his rule as king. At this point, Hagen, Kudrun's grandfather and the first hero whose story is told in detail, is dubbed *Vâlant aller künige* [the devil of all kings] (K 168,2; 196,4). This name is not justified by anything that has been or will be told about him. It is obviously the name by which Hagen is known in other stories: *dâ bî was er bekant* [this is how he was known] (K 168,2). Hagen is a famous figure of legend:

> *des hôrte man in dem lande von dem helde sagen oder singen.* (K 166,4)
>
> [this was heard said or sung of the hero throughout the realm.]

An element of heroic legend is transposed into the written text, where it makes no sense at all, but it links the literal and oral traditions. The Hagen of legend is supposed to be the same as the hero in *Kudrun.*

Hagen was kidnapped as a child by a griffin. He rescues three virgins in the wilderness, with whom he eventually returns to his father's court. He marries one of them, and together they have a daughter, who will continue the dynasty. After the daughter is married, against the father's wishes, in a standard bridal quest, Hagen disappears from the story. All of this hardly justifies his legendary fame as the dread of all kings. Moreover, what is said of his powerful rule and judgments—*inner einem jâre enthoubet er ahzig oder mêre* [in the space of a year he beheaded eighty or more] we are told (K 194,4; cf. 194–96)[40]—does not adequately explain the name, but only rationalizes its meaning. It translates the hero's wildness into the more familiar language of feudal jurisprudence through the quantitatively measurable effectiveness of capital punishment. A strong command of the legal system is the mark of a good ruler, but it is not the basis for legendary fame like that of Sivrit (714), who owes his renown as a hero to the acquisition of the hoard and the fight with the dragon.

The name opens a window onto a narrative tradition that is not thematized by the narrator. But in the same context, we have other significant deviations from the usual narrative. These are signals of an overlap of legendary material and the dominant literary concept. The zone of this overlap is approximately stanzas K 163–96, which link the two segments of Hagen's biography, his youth and his investiture as a legitimate ruler. There is a clear seam between the two narrative segments, one life in the wilderness and one in civilization. The links are the knighting ceremony, coronation, and choice of a bride.

This sequence of events is told in a strangely incoherent way, with shifts of some elements and with seemingly redundant repetitions. The prevailing method of creating coherence in the *Kudrun* is abandoned again and again. The narrator proceeds associatively by reaching back and forth, but does not progress in a linear fashion. The temporal sequence becomes convoluted: some stanzas recapitulate what was told long before, such as Hagen's deeds in the wild (*Dar zuo wart er sô küene . . .* [above all he became so bold], K 166,1; *Er wuohs in einer wüeste . . .* [he grew up in a desert], K 167,1), as if they were telling it for the first time.

We have the impression that a new story is beginning. The narrator reminds us in an abbreviated way of what has gone before. This impression corresponds to the varied epic initial formula that starts the episode:

> *Wahsen er begunde bevollen ze einem man* (*K* 163,1).
>
> [He began to grow to be a real man.]

This *wahsen* does not continue the just-finished story of youth—Hagen is already an adult. It points to events that would normally precede heroic action but that are not reported at all. The previously told adventures in the wilderness are not put into any clear relationship to this growing up. They might be part of it, or they may have preceded it. The hero and future king is introduced again as a new character.

The inserted stanzas, which remind us of the legendary hero at the beginning of his courtly career, simulate orality by jumping back and forth, giving up causal motivation or the attempt to establish connections between story lines. By the formula *des hôrte man in dem lande von dem helde sagen und singen* [this people in the land heard said and sung of the hero] (K 166,4), the narrative situates itself in orality, confirmed in other formulations: *daz lobeten schœne frouwen* [this was praised by beautiful women] (K 165,3), *als uns ist geseit* [as we are told] (K 166,1), *sît wart er genant* [later he was named] (K 168,1), *dâ bî was er bekant* [this is how he was known] (K 168,2).[41] The content of what is learned from what "one sings and says" (his growing up in the wild, his handling of animals, his speed) has all been heard in greater detail before. It appears in retrospect of these stanzas as just a vague allusion, spatially and chronologically indeterminate, and the only thing that remains of the heroic king, the *vâlant aller künige*, is the name.

With K 169,1 (*Im rieten sîne mâge, er wurbe umb ein wîp* [His family advised him to look for a wife]) and then more definitely with K 171,1 (*Sîn vater hiez in gâhen* [His father told him to hurry]), the epic composer turns away from legend and goes back to the point his story had reached once before: the story of Hagen's elevation to ruler and his marriage. The counsel of his *mâge* [relatives] to take a wife could evoke the narrative pattern of a (dangerous) bridal quest. This has already taken place, however, and the bride Hagen brought with him from the wilderness has long since been won. After Hagen's return to his parents' court, heroic actions no longer seem appropriate, so that the announcement of the scheme remains unfulfilled. Instead, a completely undramatic wooing begins. The bride *was im dâ vil nâhen* [lived close by to him] (K 169,2), and to win her does not require heroic deeds. The marriage peacefully integrates Hagen into the dynastic order.

From now on the genealogical story, which will peak with Kudrun and her peacemaking, moves forward in an orderly way from one ruler to the next. The chronological order of a written text, also reporting the unspectacular, wins out over what the legend formula seemed to promise. But the retrospective of the world of legend, which is only alluded to, in which Hagen spent his youth—these are the only parts in *Kudrun* with mythical and fairy-tale elements—is presented with a distinctly narrative gesture associated with orality, the world that *Kudrun* dismisses.

In the *Nibelungenlied*, too, there are passages of legend-like narration, as in the double story of Sivrit's youth.[42] The composer of the epic proceeds more subtly than in *Kudrun* to link his book concept with "legend."[43] The legend of the dragon slayer is neither left out nor fully integrated into this concept.[44] It is told as "legend," that is, as something that someone in the know "has to tell." The story of the dragon slayer, as told by Hagen, points back to something that the written book relegated to the background.

The Double Story of Sivrit's Youth

There are two versions of Sivrit's youth, namely his courtly upbringing, which is related by the composer of the epic, and his winning of the hoard and fight with the dragon, which is told by Hagen.[45] Generally, the first is thought to be the younger of the two, whereby the narrator has incompletely realized his intent of giving the hero a new identity. It is still curious that the two versions are linked by two different "voices," the voice of the book's narrator, and the voice of Hagen, who recounts the story orally to an audience.[46] Other rules apply to oral speech, and there are other demands on coherence than those to which the composer of the epic is beholden. Unlike *Kudrun*, the *Nibelungenlied* thematizes legend not only in a special form of narration but also as bound to a certain situation for telling. The composer of the epic changes registers when passing from one world to the other. In so doing, he temporarily hands over his role to one of the protagonists.[47] Much more so than the transitional stanzas in *Kudrun*, Hagen's story of Sivrit the dragon slayer and possessor of the hoard is produced as an oral narration of precisely calculated vagueness. It disregards what is expected of a coherent literary narration.

Hagen's knowledge is "legend knowledge," a collective knowledge of things that are important to everyone. Hagen therefore soon transitions from *ich* to *wir*. Hagen's knowledge does not need to be "explained" in a logical way.[48] The fact that Hagen's narrative is injected as an erratic segment, and not narratively linked with what preceded it, calls for attention. In this way, it has "the effect of something 'outrageous,'"[49] because Hagen's knowledge contrasts sharply with the knowledge of the narrator, who has just recounted something quite different about Sivrit's youth: his courtly upbringing by his parents and others at court, the celebration of his knighthood, and the renunciation of his own claims on rule in favor of his father's.

Sivrit enjoys the same type of courtly upbringing and careful oversight (719,1) as does the younger Sivrit, Gunther's son, who is never stylized as a hero. There is, according to the words of the narrator, little room for the deeds of the future hero. Only strophes 21 and 22 let a different picture of the hero shine through, and one can assume that it was the better-known picture:

er versuochte vil der rîche durch ellenthaften muot.
durch sînes lîbes sterke er reit in menegiu lant.
hey waz er sneller degene sît zen Burgonden vant! (21,2–4)

[He tested many different realms by his brave heart.
He rode to many lands with his great strength.
What courageous warriors he found in Burgundy!]

In sînen besten zîten, bî sînen jungen tagen,
man moht michel wunder von Sîvride sagen,
waz êren an im wüehse und wi scœne was sîn lîp.
sît heten in ze minne diu vil wætlîchen wîp.[50] (22)

[In his greatest times, in the days of his youth,
many marvels were told of Sivrit,
how his honor increased and how handsome he was.
Later, many women of great beauty came to love him.]

Here, too, is a reference to what "is said" (22,2). But it tells what strophe 21 implies, and not of the deeds of a dragon slayer, as the term *wunder* might suggest. Typical of a young courtier, he acquires *êren*, beauty, and success in the service of women (22,3–4). One might even get the impression (21,4) that Worms is the goal and crowning achievement of his career. The wooing of Kriemhilt seems to be an initial adventure within the narrative context, undertaken by a young Sivrit, grown up and promoted to knighthood, with a few companions (44, 47–48, 50–51). His decision (43) to prove himself as a knight before taking the responsibilities of king has nothing to do with winning the hoard and fighting a dragon, but schematically justifies the decision to undertake a dangerous bridal quest.

His youth consists of an education to become the perfect courtier:

Man zôch in mit dem vlîze als im daz wol gezam. (23,1)

[He was educated with the vigor that befitted him best.]

Er was nu sô gewahsen daz er ze hove reit. (24,1)[51]

[He was now mature enough to ride to court.]

Vil selten âne huote man rîten lie daz kint.
in hiez mit kleidern zieren Sigmunt und Siglint.
sîn pflâgen ouch die wîsen, den êre was bekant. (25,1–3)

[The young man was rarely allowed to ride out without an escort.
Sigmunt and Siglint had him finely clothed.
Masters who knew of honor took him under their wing.]

Whereas the young knight must always be in the presence of those at court, the hero in Nibelungenland, according to the rules of the legend world, must act alone:[52] *Dô der helt al eine ân' alle helfe reit* [Once when the hero rode out alone without any escort] (88,1). This, according to 25,1, should be impossible.[53] Up until the knighting ceremony, we hear of no other adventures. The journey from Xanten to Worms ends already on the seventh morning *[An dem sibenden morgen]* (71,1) after its commencement, without any significant incidents. Where would there be room for the hoard and the dragon?

But Hagen, as the spokesman for collective knowledge, is right. What he recounts is on a different level from what the narrator has previously reported. Hagen can rely on the general knowledge of legend, which the narrator seems to spurn when he has the courtly image of *Âventiure* 2 precede the image known to legend. Whereas it is normal to attribute what is said to the current speaker, in a written text there are several speakers from the outset. The bifurcation of the narrator's role enables two related, but completely different narrative techniques, introducing two—at first incompatible—aspects of the hero.[54] Hagen's speech cannot be "perspectively" attributed, and thereby relativized, to Hagen the individual.[55] Narration is not dependent on perspective, chance knowledge, or even the interests of a single individual. Narrators like Hagen do not speak for themselves, but for what "is said." There is basically no difference in terms of claim to truth and validity between what the narrator and what his characters say.[56] The exact correspondence between the two versions, however, remains undiscussed.[57]

If content alone is considered, as is usually the case, then the failed attempt at a courtly transformation of a wild prehistoric hero will be evident. How could the well-behaved young man be the winner of the renowned Nibelungen gold and a dragon slayer?[58] It thus came to be generally held that the narrator failed more often than not in these kinds of transformative attempts, falling into one trap after the other.[59] Yet it would have been easy for the narrator (and dozens of lesser poets have invented expedients in similar situations) to reconcile the two stories and to find a place for the fight with the dragon and the winning of the hoard sometime and somewhere in the youth story or on the way from Xanten to Worms. Why did so conspicuously he reject this? Why is he so often openly uninterested in meeting expectations?[60] It is no explanation to assume that medieval audiences did not care much about plausibility, since there were obviously questions about this point early on. The *C version tries to smooth things out with a supplemental strophe and to open up the possibility of a second career for Sivrit alongside the courtly one:

E daz der degen chvne vol whse ze man,
do het er solhiv wnder mit siner hant getan,
da von man immer mere mac singen vnd sagen,
des wir in disen stunden mvzen vil von im gedagen. (C 21)[61]

[Before the hero had grown to full manhood,
he had accomplished so many wonders with his own hand,
that ever more was sung and said about this,
there is much about him that we cannot include now.]

A second supplemental strophe, which follows the story of the knighting, determines a possible timeframe:

In dorfte niemen schelten; sit do er wafen genam,
ia gerẘete vil selten der reche lobesam
svchte niwan striten. Sin ellenthaftiv hant
tet in zallen ziten in vremeden richen wol bekant. (C 43)[62]

[No one could reproach him. Since he took up arms
the praiseworthy hero hardly rested,
but always sought out new battles. His courageous hand
made him renowned for all times in foreign realms.]

The explanation remains, as is often the case in *C, simple and vague. The redactor of *C points to a diffuse oral tradition, to what people "sing and say" (C 21,3). By trying to cover up the scar, he reminds us of its origin. We are not told what is important about these *wnder*, and the supplement manifestly contradicts what was reported in *Âventiure* 2, also in *C, about Sivrit's sheltered courtly upbringing.[63] The additional strophes therefore provide no evidence of an "actual" presupposed plot structure.[64] They simply show that there was a difficult seam that the narrator could have basically connected fairly easily. How easily is shown by the so-called Darmstadt *âventiuren* register, where the legend is built into the story of Seifrit's youth: *Abinture wie siferit wusch zu stride und wie er hurnyn wart/vnd der nebůlunge hurt gewan E er ritter wart* [The chapter on how Sivrit grew to fight and how he became vulnerable/and how he won the Nibelungen hoard before he became a knight].[65] The problematic, but easily correctable, connection between the two narrative segments is thus evened out.

The late revision ms. k from Lienhard Scheubl's *Heldenbuch* also shows how acceptable this was. Sivrit's upbringing as a courtly knight at the court in Xanten is completely left in the background. The second strophe that tells of Sivrit corresponds to the version of the legend:

> *Er pflag vil grosser sterke der edel ritter gut,*
> *Nach stürm und hartem striten stund im sein sinn und mut;*
> *Durch streit und abenteure durchzog er manig lant,*
> *Bis er kam gen Burgunden der wunderkun weigant.* (k 22)
>
> [The noble knight used to employ his great strength,
> his heart and mind were intent on attack and hard battles;
> in the cause of battles and adventures he traveled through many lands,
> until he came to Burgundy, the marvelous hero.]

Here, the violent appearance in Worms is the goal of establishing the hero, which Seifrit has been from the beginning: Seifrit, who *in seiner jugent vil mange tode schlug* [in his youth killed many] (k 27,2), whose mind is set only on attacks and battles [*Auf sturmen und auf streiten*] (k 27,3), and who, although he is constantly under the oversight [*wol in hute*] of his parents (k 26,1), is more than just a young courtier who is constantly watched. In ms. k, the tension, which the vulgate version had developed by stylizing the dragon slayer as a courtly knight, is relieved in a chronologically plausible way, so that it is always possible to integrate the story of the hero and the courtly knight. Where a marginally talented redactor could succeed in doing this, as in ms. k, the rejection of such an easy answer in the vulgate version should be taken seriously.

The two versions of the story of Sivrit's youth represent different kinds of narration. One is the careful, dimensional, literary kind of the book, and the other is the informal, oral kind that is put into the legendary character's mouth. The legend knowledge of the dragon slayer is suspended until it is retroactively confirmed by Hagen. This does not simply set aside the courtly world established by the narrator; instead, it remains a counterpart to what Sivrit is to the legend.[66]

Narration in Simulated Orality: Hagen's niuwemære

Hagen's report of Sivrit's youth is not told poorly, just differently.[67] Hagen does not arrange what he has to tell either spatially or chronologically in relation to what has already been told. The deed that makes Sivrit a hero (*die küenen Nibelunge sluoc des heldes hant* [the hero's hand defeated the brave Nibelungen], 87,2) has neither time nor place. It falls out of the sequence of events told up to this point. The disruption of linear coherence, which had been the norm up to this point,[68] corresponds to the transition to another world.[69] The spatial dispositions are unclear. Where is the land of the Nibelungen (the epic normally does not spare geographical details, even if they are, from a modern point of view, imprecise)? How does one get there (Sivrit is suddenly "there")? The surroundings are a rudimentary sketch: Sivrit meets warriors *vor einem berge* [by a mountain] (88,2); the hoard is carried *ûz einem holen berge* [out of a cave in the mountain] (89,2)—the same? Is it also the same mountain at which Sivrit later clashes with Alberich, when both run *an den berc* [to the mountain] (97,2) like lions? These are questions that heroic narration does not ask. Spatial uncertainty is anything but uncommon in heroic epic; "the" mountain, "the" tree, "the" fountain suffice as settings, without having to be further defined in their relationship to one another. What counts is the meaning these kinds of spatial segments and objects provide to the action, not their place in a time-space continuum. In some passages, the *Nibelungenlied*, too, knows this kind of representation. What is curious about Hagen's story is the number of such oddities.

Hagen's report is "speech" and as such makes use of communicative license. Its method of narration is adequate to the alien world. When Sivrit later returns there, *ze einem* [!] *lande* [to a realm] (484,2), as it is strangely called again, the space, this time in the narrator's speech, is again similarly indefinite ("an" island, "a" mountain, "a" castle, 485,1–3).

The temporal relationships are equally vague. This distinguishes the passage from other narrative segments of the epic related to each other with exact (even if improbable) indications of time. According to Hagen, what Sivrit brings with him is "new" (*niuwemære*), since in fact the knights in Worms have not heard of it, but this *niuwemære* cannot be dated. *Niuwemære* cannot be associated with a recent past, because what Hagen tells is not related to any particular now. Between the extraordinary event "in the past," the slaying of both kings, and "today" lie other heroic deeds that are even less fixed in space, time, and circumstances: *er frumte starkiu wunder mit sîner grôzen krefte sint* [since then, he accomplished great deeds with his immense strength] (87,4). After telling the story of the winning of the hoard, Hagen transitions to the fight with the dragon:

> *Noch weiz ich an im mêre daz mir ist bekant.*
> *einen lintrachen den sluoc des heldes hant.* (100,1–2)
>
> [I remember something else that I know about him.
> The hero's hand slew a dragon.]

Wagnerites are used to the hoard and the dragon being linked as the treasure and its guardian. Since the winning of the one must cost the other its life,

Hagen need not ask whether the fight with the dragon has already happened or follows later (*sint*), or whether it occurs where the hoard is found or somewhere completely different. What connection exists between the dragon and the Nibelungen kings?[70] At what "frequent" (*dicke*) opportunities has it been proven (100,4) that Sivrit has become invulnerable? The epic does not say. The relationship between individual events remains unclear. The temporal adverb most often used is the unspecific *sît*, which distinguishes a "later" event from an "earlier" one but does not determine a clear sequential order (94,3; 96,2; 97,3).

In the world Hagen speaks about, there are no exact space-time facsimiles and logically linked sequences of events. Sivrit "is," when he appears in Worms, "he who has killed the dragon and conquered the hoard." How he became what he is remains unclear. The royal prince from Xanten has a history. He was properly raised, grew up, became a knight, refused to be king instead of his father, and decided to participate in a bridal quest. The dragon slayer, on the other hand, has no history that can be located in a time-space continuum. Sivrit is, from the beginning, he of whom one knows. In a certain somewhere, he "finds" the foreign warriors King Nibelunc and King Schildunc: *die wâren im ê vremde, unz er ir künde dâ gewan* [they were unknown to him previously, until he learned there more about them] (88,4). The scene becomes even more puzzling. Sivrit arrives in a completely foreign environment, with which he becomes familiar, but this does not preclude that *ir einer*[71] [one of them] already knows him and can say: *hie kumt der starke Sîvrit, der helt von Niderlant* [here comes Sivrit the Strong, the hero of Netherland] (90,3). Sivrit becomes famous bearing this name and epithet—for example, Prünhilt later immediately addresses him as *der starke Sîfrit* [the strong Sifrit] (416,2)—but why is he already called this here, before he has demonstrated his strength and without any mention that his name and his reputation are already known beyond Xanten? It seems that *ir einer* is not just any individual who shares his chance knowledge with his companions. Rather, what *ir einer* says counts for all.[72] "One" knows who Sivrit is, and this is why no one needs to ask to whom the speaker refers with *der starke Sivrit.* Sivrit is identified from the outset as the hero, even if he actually still has to become one by performing some heroic deed. Before and after lose all meaning.

The cause and progression of the coming events are unclear, too. Sivrit "sees" the attempt to divide the Nibelungen treasure. He is received in a friendly manner and is invited to control the division. He agrees, receives the sword *ze miete* [as a reward] (93,1), but fails in the task (*er'n kundez niht verenden* [he was unable to complete it], 93,4). Those who assigned the task become angry (93,4). Their giant *friunde* [allies] are suddenly present (94,1)[73] with 700 other warriors, who are all defeated by Sivrit and his new sword, Balmunc. Then it is said that the two kings are slain. Later—or as a result?—(*sît*: when is this? 96,2), Sivrit is threatened by Alberich.

This is anything but clear, especially with respect to cause and effect. What is Sivrit's role? He is known by the Nibelungen, although he has yet to become known. He is only qualified to be a judge in his role as the *starke Sîvrit*, but he does not become the *starke Sîvrit* until he does battle with a vastly superior number of warriors. After the division fails, he uses the sword that was to be his reward (if it is the same).[74] It is primarily this sword (and the *küene man*, 95,3, is only secondary) that forces the two kings' men to submit. What is the point? Is it a division of inheritance? Why does it fail? We only learn of the result: *er'n kundez niht verenden: si wâren zornec gemuot* [he was unable to complete it: they were angry] (93,4). Attention should be paid to the verb *wâren* (rather than *wurden* [became]), because it does not place Sivrit's action and the kings' reaction in any kind of chronological-causal relationship, so that, if taken exactly, it remains unclear whether the anger is a reaction to the failure of the division or whether the division fails because the opponents are already angry [*zornec*]. The situation "is" a potential conflict and consequently degenerates into violence. The fight has already begun without it having been said when it started.

Many other things remain vague. From where does Alberich suddenly appear (*er kom von Albrîche sît in grôze nôt* [he had great difficulty with Alberich since], 96,2)? When and in what form should one imagine an event described this way: *daz lant zuo den bürgen si im tâten undertân* [the land and the castles were made subject to him] (95,4)? The development of the narrative would suggest that this happened before the death of the kings (96,1) and before the fight with Alberich (96,2ff.) Perhaps before the return of the treasure and the appointment of Alberich as treasurer? If one follows Hagen's account, then the submission of the land is already a fact before it is mentioned, almost as an aside, that Sivrit has also slain the kings. At the end is the résumé: *Die dâ torsten vehten, die lâgen alle erslagen* [those who dared to fight all lay there dead] (98,1). To what does this refer? Alberich, with whom Sivrit has also fought according to the following stanza (97), cannot be meant, because he survives. Does the verse refer to the events leading up to the kings' deaths (96,1)? Why does the verse follow two stanzas later, after the fight with Alberich?

There are, of course, intuitive answers to all of these questions, which a skeptical reading would evoke. The mountain mentioned must always be the same one. When sons fight over a treasure that belonged to their father, and this father is nowhere to be seen, then he is most likely dead, and so the conflict is about inheritance. Alberich was most likely given the task of protecting the treasure by the old rulers, and so on. Questions as sketched above are rightfully rejected by scholarly readers of the *Nibelungenlied*, because there is agreement that the heroic epic does not tell a story in every detail, with the requirement of complete causal linkage. While this is also true moreover for some other passages in the *Nibelungenlied*, nowhere is this heroic style as radical as in Hagen's story, where cause and effect, before and after, far and near lose all distinction. Hagen's story cites oral epic in its purest form. It presumes an understanding of causality that, although described by Ernst Cassirer as "mythical," obviously goes beyond true myth.[75] Rather, it is what Lugowski calls a "mythical analog."[76] In myth or "mythical analog," the time structure "before-after" is eliminated or becomes meaningless. A connection exists, even if it cannot be precisely articulated chronologically, for instance, as a "development." The relationship of Hagen's heroic legend to the story of the courtly Sivrit in Xanten cannot be determined in a chronological-causal way, because it does not concern a relationship in time. It is instead a statement about the contradictory nature of the hero.

That this narrative style was already felt to be deficient in the century of the courtly novel is shown by later modifications that fill some gaps. The reviser of *C saw it necessary to insert a stanza to link the failed division of the treasure with the outbreak of the fighting:

> *ern kundes niht verenden; do wart der helt von in bestan.*
>
> *Den schatz er vngeteilet beliben mvse lan.*
> *do begunden mit im striten der zweier kunige man.*
> *mit ir vater swerte, daz Palmvnc was genant,*
> *ez streit ab in der chune den hort vnd Nibelung lant. (C 93,4; 94)*[77]
>
> [he was unable to complete it; then the hero was attacked by them.
>
> He had to leave the treasure undivided.
> The two kings' men began to fight with him.
> With their father's sword, it was called Balmunc,
> the bold man won all the treasure and the Nibelungen land from them.]

This establishes a clear causality and responsibility, which is missing in the vulgate version.[78] Even the sword is clearly identified. This is pedantics in the service of literary coherence.

Lienhard Scheubl's *Heldenbuch* (k) seeks to shed even more light on some of these events. The conquest of the hoard does not just happen, but is an intentional act of Seifrit's from the beginning. He plans to steal the treasure from its owners: *Den schleich er nach mit listen, bis er den schatz gewan* [he followed them secretly, until he won the treasure] (k 87,4).[79] Seifrit waits until he can go on the offensive:

> *Daz merkt gar wol Seifride und eilet schnelligleich.*
>
> *Er kam in also nahen, daz er den schatz ersach*
> *Under den Nibelunger.* (k 88,4–89,2)
>
> [Seifrit noticed this and hurried along.
>
> He came closer and then saw the treasure
> among the Nibelungen.]

As a referee he immediately sets out to cheat and puts himself above what he has promised to the Nibelungen:[80]

> *Si wurden keiner trewe da von dem held gewert:*
> *Er globet in mit trewen, er wolt si han in hut;*
> *Daz brach an in der degen und traib groß ubermut.* (k 92,2–4)
>
> [They were not dealt with fairly by that hero:
> He promised faithfully that he wanted to protect them.
> The warrior broke that promise and was very selfish and arrogant.]

The battle, which he wins against the giants, the *künen recken* (k 95,1) and Alberich, who seeks to avenge them, breaks out because of Seifrit's treachery.[81]

Given the outline of ms. k, the undermotivation in Hagen's story becomes obvious. This undermotivation is apparently intentionally used as an artistic technique. Hagen's report remains an alien construct mounted onto the story of Sivrit's youth. Elements of orality are intentionally applied.[82] Hagen's story is presented as "speech," which reminds us of what is "said by everyone." Hagen again and again gives his source as the knowledge of "what people hear" (*niuwemære,* 87,1; *daz ist mir wol geseit,* 88,2; *sô wir hœren sagen,* 92,1; but also: *daz mir ist bekant,* 100,1; *daz ist dicke worden scîn,* 100,4). Legend is marked stylistically in the concept of the *Nibelungenlied.* It appears as an erratic insertion in the courtly atmosphere of the first *âventiuren.*

Hagen's story does not necessarily, of course, have to be a relic of lost orality. But it refers to another kind of narrative technique. Hagen (and through him, the narrator) can appeal to a "knowledge" of his listeners that fills up gaps. The story of Sivrit's heroic deeds is therefore accepted as consistent. As in oral speech, anticipations and addenda, spatial and temporal leaps can be relativized through accompanying gestures. "One understands" the speaker. At the same time, however, the narrator draws attention to another kind of world, radically different from the known world. It is a world where dragons are killed and magical treasures are won. The heroic world, which threateningly penetrates Worms in the form of Sivirit, soon to be violently unleashed in the first confrontation with the Burgundian kings, exists under "other" rules, which are also narrative rules. These other rules are addressed as *wunder* (already 1,1; here 89,1; 101,4), initiating *wundern* (89,4), as *seltsæniu mære* [strange stories] (90,4).

Doubling

This kind of clear stylistic designation is otherwise rare. In the *Nibelungenlied,* literary contextualization and overall coherence often compete, however, with the representation of single scenes that are unconnected and without context. It has been shown, in discussing the so-called formulas, how narrative schemes and elements of oral poetry are employed in the service of a book concept and how they are connected to an artistic idiom, a kind of "Nibelungian" style, which the author uses in order to point to an already foreign orality.[83] "Nibelungian" is a literary language that consists of special composition strategies.[84] The *Nibelungenlied* develops grand connections less through the use of logical-linear linkages than through seemingly redundant doubling. At a closer look, these doublings turn out to be variations. Redundancy and repetition of things that are always the same are typical for orality.[85] Construction of a complex structure out of different building blocks, however, is an achievement of literary culture.[86] Doubling allows literary coherence in material that originates out of orality.[87]

In other heroic epics, the transition from oral to literary structure can be clearly observed. Larger structures are at first only created by the addition of the same or similar elements. In the *Book of Bern*, Dietrich's return battle must be fought three times (four times if we include the *Rabenschlacht*). Every time, victory turns to defeat. In this way, the same structure, in which Dietrich appears as the hapless victor, is used time and again. With the exception of the final battle in the *Rabenschlacht,* the variations have no perspective. Simple repetition brings events into an epic book dimension without employing literary strategies to create new meaning: orality transitions to writing.[88]

The *Nibelungenlied*, on the other hand, is more clearly a part of literary culture. Varied doublings have three functions: to represent complex constellations, to express the simultaneity of antagonistic motifs, or to make "changes" clear, through repetition of a partly unchanged, partly modified constellation. Often the three functions work together. What has been criticized about repetitions as being redundant or even contradictory becomes mostly functional and meaningful. This kind of representation has been called "aggregatory." Aggregatory representation denotes a development out of relatively independent blocks. It is a nonsystematic method that uses abrupt "leaps" instead of linear progression from one block to the other. Instead of an integration of elements in an overarching sequence or structure, it creates referential meaning by adding together similar or contradictory but mutually related components.[89] Complexity arises from the configuration of isolated elements, aggregate figures, scenes, and episodes.

First, a simple example: the reaction when Hagen attacks the chaplain of the Burgundians—seemingly for no reason:

> *Gîselher der junge, zürnen erz began.*
> *er'n wold' iz doh niht lâzen er enhet im leide getân.*
>
> *Dô sprach von Burgonden der herre Gêrnôt:*
> *"waz hilfet iuch nu, Hagene, des kappelânes tôt?"* (1576,3–1577,2)
>
> [Young Giselher began to be angry.
> But Hagen wouldn't stop hurting him.
>
> Lord Gernot of Burgundy then said:
> "What good is the chaplain's death to you now, Hagen?"]

The one rages, the other speaks, but both point in the same direction. Why then is there not only one reaction? By dividing the same reaction among two characters, it loses any individuality. Gernot and Giselher are the two who are consistently considered to be positive members in the Worms ruling clan. Their reactions metonymically represent a collective. The right-minded in Gunther's army condemn the act of violence, but they do nothing except talk and get angry. Splitting and doubling express the complexity of these reactions.

The same gesture, divided among different characters, can also express opposition. When the Burgundians arrive at Etzel's court, Etzel and Kriemhilt each seem to be happy:

> *Kriemhilt diu vrouwe in ein venster stuont:*
> *si warte nâch den mâgen, sô friunt nâ friunden tuont.*

von ir vater lande sach si manigen man.
der künic vriesc ouch diu mære; vor liebe er lachen began.

"Nu wol mich mîner vreuden," sprach Kriemhilt.
"hie bringent mîne mâge vil manigen niuwen schilt
und halsperge wîze: swer nemen welle golt,
der gedenke mîner leide, und wil im immer wesen holt." (1716–17)

[Lady Kriemhilt stood looking out a window:
she was watching for her family, as friends will look out for friends.
She saw several men from her father's land.
King Etzel heard of this, too; happy, he began to laugh.

Kriemhilt said, "How great is my joy,
my kin bring new shields
and white hauberks: whoever wants gold
should think of my grief, and I'll be forever grateful."]

The royal couple's joy seems to be appropriate among relatives *sô friunt nâch friunden tuont*; Etzel's laughter emphasizes this. He believes that Kriemhilt's *vreude* is similarly motivated. Kriemhilt ascribes another meaning to the event: the chance for revenge. The doubling expresses ambivalence.

Splitting a sequence into two scenes makes it possible to emphasize different aspects. When, for example, Gotelint finds out about Rüedeger's mission to Worms, she is first informed by a messenger (1160,3). Rüedeger is to perform the bridal quest for Etzel, and this rightly upsets her, because bridal quests are dangerous. When, later, in a moment of spousal intimacy, she asks for more details (1168–69), the bridal quest is brought into the more common context of dynastic history. This time, Gotelint is happy about the news. This kind of splitting is not necessary for the plot, but it allows Gotelint to mirror two aspects of the event.

Doubling can express opposing aspects. This explains a "contradiction" toward the end of the epic. Dietrich's vassals ask the Burgundians for the return of Rüedeger's corpse in order to bury him appropriately, and Gunther replies with praise: *nie dienest wart sô guot/sô den ein vriunt vriunde nâch dem tôde tuot* [never was a service so worthy/than what a friend may do for a friend after he is dead] (2264,1–2). But Volker prevents the service to the dead by denying the corpse to the Amelungen. Later, however, when Dietrich blames Hagen and Gunther for this rejection, it is suddenly Gunther who takes responsibility for the refusal:

den hiez ich in versagen
Etzeln ze leide, und niht den dînen man,
unz daz dô Wolfhart dar umbe schelten began. (2335,2–4)

[I refused them the corpse
to hurt Etzel, and not your men,
until Wolfhart began to be abusive about it.]

This is not a "mistake," but instead shows contradictory claims on the king. Gunther does them both justice in a dual solution: through praise for the concern that an enemy demonstrates for a dead friend and through the rejection of a gesture that might be interpreted as weakness. Since the consequences rule each other out, they are first assigned to two characters, Gunther and Volker. The one praises, the other refuses. Both obligations are valid, so there is fundamentally no disagreement between Gunther and Volker, and the king can later take Volker's refusal as his own order.

Varied doubling can establish wide-ranging links, like between Sivrit's wooing of Kriemhilt, Gunther's wooing of Prünhilt, and Sivrit's journey to Nibelungenland (*Âventiure* 8), which was taken to be a variant of the conquest of the hoard.[90] The three episodes can be understood as transformations of the bridal quest scheme, answering the question of who will win the best woman and who proves by this to be the rightful ruler.[91] According to Sivrit and Prünhilt and the narrator's implicitly presumed norms, it should be the strongest.

In Sivrit's wooing of Kriemhilt, the two motifs—fighting for rule and fighting for a woman—are so naturally linked that they can substitute for each other. The fight for Gunther's land should—this seems to be Sivrit's understanding—also win him the woman on whose account he came to Worms. This is received with incomprehension and denial by the Burgundians. The principle that the strongest gets the most beautiful and that whoever gets the most beautiful has to be the strongest is contested. It cannot be realized in the complex system of rulership in Worms.

In Gunther's wooing in Isenstein, on the other hand, the fight for the woman is the primary purpose from the beginning, but it also gains the winner a realm. The scheme takes hold. This time the roles are miscast, however, in that Sivrit secretly acts for Gunther. The weaker, not the stronger, protagonist wins the most beautiful woman. The fulfillment of the scheme is based on a lie, and Prünhilt's attempts to clear this up cost Sivrit his life.

This is again different in the third variation, in Nibelungenland, where Sivrit proves himself to be the strongest and consequently must be seen as identical with the ruler. When Sivrit overcomes his own guard, although the land already belongs to him, the guard verifies *daz ir von wâren schulden muget landes herre wesen* [that you have every right to be the lord of this land] (500,3). Here the roles are properly cast. Only the woman is missing as a prize. Sivrit's fight serves him indirectly in his bridal quest. By supporting Gunther with his warriors, he again ensures the success of Gunther's quest and promotes his own wooing of Kriemhilt. Only by this detour is the scheme fulfilled: Sivrit succeeds outside the ordinary world, and this success must be dissimulated upon his return. In this respect, too, the scheme is deficient.

A related constellation is thus played out three times, and the components are never quite right. As to the question of who should rule, an answer is intimated but never really fully realized in epic terms. Thus, the conflict, which breaks out with the dispute of the queens, builds up over a long period in three stages. Variation creates connections.

In recognizing this narrative style, supposed contradictions are solved. The motif for Sivrit's bridal quest is doubled. The two impulses, Kriemhilt's love and the battle for rule, are simply put side by side without any connection. The subjugation of Prünhilt is doubled, in Isenstein and Worms. Kriemhilt's revenge is doubly motivated by the murder of Sivrit and the theft of the hoard. This strategy should not simply be explained as a "psychology of oral composition."[92] Instead, the "aggregation" of uncoordinated or even opposing motivations is typical of early vernacular literality as well. The doublings presume wide-ranging dispositions. The listener is not privy to how a character moves from one circumstance to the next, but is shown two images, which, by overlapping, make up a whole.

Disruptions

Another way in which a discursive commentary can be replaced by structural complexity is with strangely inconsequential disruptions. Kriemhilt's fight for her inheritance (693–700) is of interest in this regard. In this scene, the actual protagonists for power, Sivrit and the Burgundian kings, are determined to come to an agreement from the start.[93] Kriemhilt's brothers are prepared to share (693) and allow Kriemhilt—a woman—to keep more than would be left for each of the male heirs (697,3).[94] Sivrit wants nothing at all, because he has enough of his own (694–695). Only Kriemhilt insists on her share, at least in terms of the vassals (696,1). This conflict, too, is over before it has even begun, because Gernot immediately agrees (697). Kriemhilt asks for Hagen and Ortwin (697,4–5). Hagen, however, refuses to follow Kriemhilt and Sivrit. Kriemhilt has to acquiesce: *Daz liezen si belîben* [they let it be] (700,1). The disruption does not disturb the lasting harmony. Even Hagen's supposed resistance is caused by his loyalty to the court and the king.[95] It is a marginal and inconsequential episode, and the solution is peaceful and without any real decision. So why then the detour?

Behind all this lies a strategy: a latent conflict is foreshadowed in a seemingly redundant disruption. This is less a personal conflict between Kriemhilt and Hagen than one of governance, between Sivrit and the Burgundian royal house. In the future power struggle, Sivrit's and Kriemhilt's share in Burgundian power is never remembered. Rather, the issue is whether they themselves will be devoured by this power. The disruption only becomes potent much later, but then all the more fatefully.

In a similar fashion, a later scene, the quarrel over the handover of the rest of Kriemhilt's wealth, brings the future antagonists into position. Kriemhilt wants her property, Hagen refuses it. This conflict is also seemingly only a detour, since it is prematurely defused by Rüedeger. It seems to be solved in Kriemhilt's favor, without having the effect that Hagen fears,[96] and it leaves no traces either with the kings (who support Kriemhilt) or Hagen (who wants to deprive her once again). Nothing is really solved, however. The pragmatic agreement is not a substitute for revenge. The fact that something has been left unresolved is stated by Kriemhilt in a supplemental strophe of the *C redaction:

> *ein mort vnd zwene rovbe, die mir sint genomen,*
> *des mohte ich vil arme noch ze liebem gelte chomen.* (C 1785,3–4)[97]
>
> [a murder and two robberies that have been done to me,
> I, the victim, would still like to have restitution for these.]

The disruption on the surface, which is quickly overcome, is a symptom of a deeper disturbance.

This is also true of less spectacular rough spots that so often stick out from their surroundings. On Kriemhilt's journey to Etzel, one festive reception follows after another. It is therefore all the more surprising when Kriemhilt's men suddenly speak of their displeasure:

> *Wes si dâ mêre pflægen, des enkan ich niht gesagen.*
> *daz in sô übele zogete, daz hôrte man dô klagen*

> *die Kriemhilde recken, wan iz was in leit.*
> *hey waz dô guoter degene mit ir von Bechelâren reit!* (1321)
>
> [What else they did, I cannot say.
> One heard them complain that things were going so slowly,
> Kriemhilt's warriors, because it annoyed them.
> What great heroes rode out of Bechelaren with her!]

If one asks what it was that was *leit* for Kriemhilt's company, one learns from the commentary on *zogete* "that the journey was moving ahead so slowly," which is not a very strong explanation. Or should it be the opposite: "that they were so rushed"?[98] What is important is only that something on the journey is running *übele* and is *leit* to them. Despite the succession of splendid appearances, friendly receptions, and endless displays of honor, the expedition, seemingly so brilliant, has some sort of flaw, which the company's reaction brings to light. In this way, the verse seems to point to future calamity, as does the oft-cited strophe in which Kriemhilt remembers tearfully, despite the magnificence: *wie si ze Rîne sæze* [how she ruled/lived on the Rhine] (1371,1).[99]

Such seemingly inconsequential disruptions accompany the Burgundians' expedition to Etzel. They are not limited to spectacular scenes like the crossing of the Danube, which turns into the first armed conflict, but come to light in seemingly unimportant details: the border of Etzel's realm is guarded by Eckewart, a *Kriemhilde man* (1642,3), but he is asleep. The scene is based on a strange contradiction. The possibility of violence is implied (the border must be guarded against incursions from the west) and taken back at the same time (the guard proves to be ineffective): *die marke Rüedegêres di fundens' übele bewart* [Rüedeger's border land was poorly guarded] (1632,4). Emphasizing the weakness of the defense only makes sense when there is a danger of battle. Why should a guard be posted against the invited guests? Because the guests are already latent enemies? Why does Hagen disarm Eckewart, even though he is a compatriot, even though it might be expected that Etzel's official emissary would provide a suitable reception, as is then actually the case?

Taking away Eckewart's weapons is both a precaution and an insult; consequently, Eckewart falls into *einen trûrigen muot* [a despondent mood] (1632,2), although there is suddenly a completely different reason given for this *muot:*

> *"Owê mir dirre schande," sprach dô Eckewart.*
> *"jâ riuwet mich vil sêre der Burgonden vart.*
> *sît ich verlôs Sîfrîde, sît was mîn freude zergân.*
> *ouwê, herre Rüedegêr, wie hân ich wider dich getân!"* (1633)

["Oh, the shame," said Eckewart.
"I regret the journey of the Burgundians sorely.
Since I lost Sivrit my joy has vanished.
Oh, Lord Rüedeger, what have I done to you!"]

Eckewart laments his *schande* [shame] and the Burgundians' journey to Etzel—because it is dishonorable for him or dangerous for his compatriots?—then the death of his previous master, Sivrit, and finally his failure to fulfill his duty to his lord, Rüedeger. It is a summary of what is not right here. Again the conflict is immediately settled, in that Hagen gives him his weapons back and six gold rings into the bargain: *daz du mîn friunt sîst* [so that you might be my friend] (1634,3). Still the disruption is not completely alleviated. Now Eckewart warns the Burgundians about their hosts:

doch riuwet mich vil sêre zen Hiunen iuwer vart.
ir sluoget Sîfrîden: man ist iu hie gehaz. (1635,2)

[I am still unhappy about your journey to the Huns.
You killed Sivrit. People here hate you.]

When he rushes to announce the Burgundians as guests to Rüedeger, things again go awry, because there is a misunderstanding: Rüedeger suspects that Eckewart is announcing not friends but war: *daz die vîende im heten leide getân* [that the enemies had done him wrong] (1642,4). The reception of Etzel's guests is overshadowed until the very end by the fear that Etzel's kingdom is going to be attacked—and, of course, this is exactly what happens.

Even the "idyll" of Bechelaren presents such a break. At the end of the orgy of gift-giving that demonstrates Margrave Rüedeger's *milte* [generosity, largesse], there is a puzzling scene. Among the gifts is an exceptional case, the gift of the margravine to Hagen. At first, Hagen wants no part of any gift (1697,4)—again a foreshadowing of future enmity?—but then he asks for a shield that is hanging on the wall. This shield interrupts the joy of the courtly gift exchange in a unforeseen way, which is left by the narrator in the shadows of legend memory,[100] because Gotelint starts to cry:

ez mante si ir leides: weinen si gezam.
do gedâht si vil tiure an Nuodunges tôt.
den het erslagen Witege, dâ von sô het si jâmers nôt. (1699,2–4)

[It reminded her of her grief, and she had to cry.
She thought heavily of Nuodung's death.
Witege slew him, and this caused her much sorrow.]

The shield reminds Gotelint of someone who is dead:

> *den muoz ich immer weinen, des gât mir armem wîbe nôt.* (1700,4)
>
> [I always have to cry for him, this is my fate as a poor woman.]

Behind the brilliant lady of the court suddenly appears the other woman, who must "always" lament the dead. This logically unjustified disruption is altogether reminiscent of the disrupted invitation; the perfect hostess Gotelint reminds us of the conniving hostess Kriemhilt and the gift of death. Gotelint and Kriemhilt each weep over the loss of a man. Hagen carries the sword of one of them, and he receives the shield of the other. The gift for Hagen is stigmatized, and only Hagen can receive such a stigmatized gift. The possessions of the dead are intended for those who are bound to die.[101]

Disruptions of this kind can recount an alternative that was rejected by the narrator.[102] Why, for example, does Sigemunt come with Sivrit to Worms, when he disappears without a murmur from the story after Sivrit's death? Sigemunt provides a justification as to why he starts out with Kriemhilt and his son:

> *sît daz iuch mîn sun Sîfrit ze vriunde gewan,*
> *dô rieten mîne sinne, daz ich iuch solde sehen.* (790,2–3)
>
> [since my son Sivrit gained you as a friend,
> my thoughts told me that we should have to meet.]

His presence emphasizes the close familial ties between the two dynasties. It corresponds to the harmonious condition that has been achieved. Right after the arrival in Worms, he can therefore recede into the background, because he only accentuates what the other actors stand for. He is only needed again after Sivrit's death (1014). The previous double proximity has now given way to a double *untriuwe* [disloyalty] (1074,1). He stands by Kriemhilt in her sorrow; but above all he calls for revenge, his bounden duty as the closest male relative. This is exactly the reason that he must be present, even if only to show that he is not needed anyway, because the usual obligation for revenge here is only brought up in order to be diverted. There is more behind this than Kriemhilt's tactical argument (1033–34) that any attempt at revenge would have to fail in light of Burgundian superiority. It is emphasized that the *Nibelungenlied* deviates from what is expected. Sigemunt must be there in order to remove him, so that Kriemhilt can be alone with her desire for revenge. The murder of Sivrit does not set in motion the normal mechanism of strike and counterstrike. Sigemunt's diverted readiness to fight shows that, after the natural solution of revenge by male relatives is discarded, something remains unresolved.

No commentary is necessary to show how previous alternatives were mismanaged. Logically senseless disruptions and opaque scenes are narrative techniques to point out actions and tendencies that underlie the manifest text.

Calculated Uncertainty

A further narrative principle has been especially irritating to modern critics. The narrator favors deliberately imprecise terminology where certainty is called for. There are many examples of this.

Hagen's commentary on Sivrit's rich gifts to the Burgundian messengers when they bring news of his arrival in Worms is seen as an early sign of the growing power struggle:

> *"Er mac," sprach dô Hagene, "von im sampfte geben.*
> *er'n kundez niht verswenden, unt sold' er immer leben.*
> *hort der Nibelunge beslozzen hât sîn hant.*
> *hey sold' er komen immer in der Burgonden lant!"* (774)
>
> [Hagen said, "It's easy for him to give.
> He couldn't spend all of it, and if he lived forever.
> He possesses all of the Nibelungen hoard.
> If only it [he] could come to us in the Burgundian lands!"]

The last verse above all is seen as a sign of Hagen's appetite for power and his strategy for getting his hands on the hoard. Yet the grammatical reference of *er* to *hort* is by no means as certain as some critics would like. Given the loose syntactic structure of the epic, *er* could also refer to Sivrit (774,1 and 2).[103] Hagen would then participate in the general happiness and joy over the high and mighty visit (775,1): "Well, if only Sivrit would come to our land!" Such a visit honors the king, the court, and the land. Only in hindsight does another meaning offer itself. The acceptance of one or the other possibility, however, is not important. The ambiguity of Hagen's words is what matters. Something else may be hiding behind their seeming innocence, and as is so often the case, something actually is hiding there. The world of the courtly festival and peaceful familial manners can be read in two ways, and it is this double readability that spells its doom.

Some of the most controversial passages of the epic can be interpreted as results of narrative strategies that do not aim at clarity, but at ambiguity. The suggestion of an imprecisely known legend allows the narrator to open a space for competing interpretations. He can try to put his version in its place, as with the death of Ortliep. He can also keep other alternatives open and create the impulse for development out of uncertainty.

According to common opinion, Hagen actively pursues the reconciliation with Kriemhilt in order to gain possession of the hoard. He therefore says to Gunther:

> *möht ir daz tragen an,*
> *daz ir iuwer swester ze vriunde möhtet hân,*
> *sô kæme ze disen landen daz Nibelunges golt.*
> *des möht ir vil gewinnen, würd' uns diu küneginne holt.* (1107)
>
> [would that you could arrange it,
> that your sister were again your friend,
> then the Nibelungen gold would come to our land.
> From this you would gain much, if the queen liked us.]

Based on later events, the connection between this advice and the theft of the hoard seems clear, but is it still in Hagen's words in 1107,4? The verse can be interpreted in several ways. The first part is not clear: is it "from this [i.e., from the hoard] you can then gain much"? or, more generally: "this would give you great advantage"? Later events speak for the first possibility (and this is how the words have been understood in ms. C), but the subsequent half line speaks more for the second possibility: "if we[104] gain the queen's *hulde* [grace], again establishing peaceful relations with the queen." Hagen's words could then just mean that the break in the ruling house must be healed in the interest of the king, because then Kriemhilt's endless wealth would become part of Burgundian power.[105]

There is a clue: in order to remove the uncertainty, the redactor of the *C version stepped in: *des wrde vns vil ze teile, wær uns div kuniginne holt* (C 1118,4; similarly only ms. a), that is, "from this—from the hoard—much would we gain; we would gain a great possession." Why does the redactor make this change if everything is so clear? But a new problem arises: if Hagen has from the beginning admitted to planning to steal the hoard from Kriemhilt, then it is incomprehensible why Gunther later incredulously rejects his proposal to take it from her: *ja erwarp ich daz vil kûme, daz si mir wart sô holt* [I had enough trouble getting her to like me] (1129,3). The unscrupulous exploitation is a possible consequence of the reconciliation that Gunther is concerned about, but it is in no way clear from the beginning that this consequence was intended. Not until it is established that Kriemhilt is using the hoard in a way that might threaten the king's power does Hagen begin to sound warnings (1128). Gunther understands what conclusions he should draw (1129) before Hagen explicitly spells out the consequences (1130) and before Gunther can remember his oath, which prevents him from acting directly against Kriemhilt (1131). The "open" situation created by the *suone* [reconciliation] is closed step by step; its uncertainty is removed until the only remaining consequence is a new crime.

The tradition knows the theft of the hoard, and the narrator must therefore include it as a central motif in the story line. He has to reach far and wide to contrive circumstances that put the hoard in reach of Hagen and the kings, which are created by the reconciliation of Kriemhilt and Gunther. The reconciliation, however, is not only a means of intrigue. It simultaneously fits into a series of events that seemingly stop its march to catastrophe. As in similar cases, in the end, this turns out to be an illusion. Nevertheless the *suone* is at first ambiguous as to its consequences.[106] What will become of it remains to be seen. Hagen's uncertain words fit both possibilities. The appropriate reconciliation, which would reestablish the familial peace in the royal house, seemingly averts the danger of Kriemhilt's revenge on her brother. At the same time, it also opens up the possibility of another crime. The ambiguity makes it possible to develop the revenge a bit further and at the same time to insert a pause that may give hope that it can be prevented altogether.

The procedure of only clarifying an open meaning after the fact seems to have caused some changes as early as the thirteenth century. The redactor of *C determined the value of the *suone* explicitly. It is simply lip service for Kriemhilt (*mîn mvnt im giht der sûne; im wirt daz herce nimmer holt* [my mouth talks of reconciliation; my heart will never embrace him], C 1124,4), and Gunther feigns, too, since his and Hagen's true intentions are clear:

> *Durch des hordes liebe was der rat getan;*
> *Dar vmb riet die sv̂ne der vil vngetriuwe man.* (C1127,3–4)
>
> [That counsel was given for the hoard's sake;
> this is why the deceitful man advised a reconciliation.]

The whole thing is mendacious playacting (C 1128,1–2). Later, another stanza is inserted about the kings' *gemeine[n] rat[]* and *giteklichen mv̂t,* who together want to have the hoard at their disposal (C 1151), and another stanza about Hagen's *vntriuwe,* since his greed for the hoard has from the beginning directed him selfishly against his lords: *er wande in niezen eine* [he thought to use it for himself alone] (C 1153).[107] It is only through the redactor of *C that a clear motivational link is created, in that from the beginning, the *suone* is a means of stealing the hoard, so that attempts at a peaceful solution are just a farce. The story's linear connections now tend toward greater precision. The apparent openness of an event, marked by alternatives, is eliminated. In the end, though, the story takes its fateful course. *C is clearer but also uninteresting.

The most ingenious use of this method is in a scene whose controversial interpretations have long led to the conclusion that the narrator did not control the divergent traditions. Kriemhilt's demand for satisfaction in the final confrontation with Hagen plays even more spectacularly with calculated uncertainty.[108] Kriemhilt's proposal to Hagen and Gunther is:

> *welt ir mir geben widere daz ir mir habt genomen,*
> *sô muget ir noch wol lebende heim zen Burgonden komen.* (2367,3–4)
>
> [if you give me back what you took from me,
> then you might still return home to Burgundy alive.]

Based on what has been told up to now, these lines can be interpreted in two ways. Two different legend motifs are combined: revenge for the plundered hoard and for the murder of Sivrit. The critic can therefore find arguments for one or the other motif in the following scene without giving up either one completely. There are "inconsistencies" that seem to result from the fact that the narrator has not decided himself on one of the two versions of the legend.[109]

Is such a choice even necessary? The wording of the verses the narrator has Kriemhilt speak can have two meanings.[110] They do not allow any sure interpretation of the demand—whether it be for the hoard or for the dead Sivrit: "If you will return to me what you have stolen from me, then . . ." Why should the question be decided with the help of the "legend tradition," "with which the poet and audience were familiar"? Does this kind of knowledge dominate in such a way that it forces us "to understand the demand as, at least primarily, a demand for the hoard," as Joachim Heinzle puts it?[111] Kriemhilt's words are ambiguous. The narrator supplies no context that would clarify them. One has to postulate the context as a general "knowledge of the legend." But this is completely speculative. The ambiguity does not arise from an awkward attempt to reconcile an unclearly known legend with the purposeful concept of the composer of the epic.[112] Rather, it expresses the unresolvable mixture of different impulses with a great deal of finesse.

The hoard is not present in Kriemhilt's words. She very ambiguously demands the return of "what was taken from her." This is not possible in the full sense, because if Sivrit is included, then reparation is impossible, as Dietrich perhaps suggests (*wie wol er iuch ergetzet*[113] *daz er iu hât getân!* [how well he will repay what he has done to you!], 2355,3).

If Kriemhilt's demand is to be understood broadly, then the attempt at a legal solution is doomed from the beginning. If her words refer specifically to the hoard, however, such a solution might become reality, even if the quest for revenge remains incomplete.

This demand would also provoke Hagen's insolence, as occurred previously at the reception at Etzel's court. Kriemhilt uses a dual approach that once more presents Hagen as a relentless and violent criminal (or, more improbably, exposes him as a braggart whose resistance has been broken).[114] In either case, she would be the victor. Her promise that Hagen and Gunther could return home if her demands are met is nothing more than a disingenuous offer attached to unrealistic conditions (*muget ir noch wol* [you might still], 2367,4), and the narrator thus characterizes her words as *fientlîch* [hostile] (2367,2). The offer is meant to serve the need for revenge, which lurks in the background as a constant presence (2365,3; 2366,4).

Hagen's answer clarifies Kriemhilt's words by relating them to the hoard alone. With this, he once again defines her role as the gold-hungry queen, which Werner Schröder correctly interprets as the final insidious insult,[115] and he presents himself as a faithful vassal who is steadfast in his word:

jâ hân ich des gesworn,
daz ich den hort iht zeige die wîle daz si leben,
deheiner mîner herren, sô sol ich in niemene geben.

[For this I have sworn,
that I shall not reveal the hoard as long as they live,
any of my lords, therefore I shall give it to no one.] (2368,2–4)

Hagen's answer is again ambiguous and permits two conclusions, the one being: "I can't give you anything back, because I'm bound by my oath," and the other: "Nothing can be done as long as I am bound by my oath; you would have to eliminate its source." It remains open to debate whether Hagen thus deliberately causes the death of his lord or demonstrates the eternal *triuwe* bond one last time. The allegation that Hagen sacrifices the life of his lord with his words cannot be supported and in fact assumes that a favorable outcome is still possible in this power play of calculated ambiguities.

This speech contains a sinister insinuation but does not articulate it openly. Kriemhilt, however, picks up on Hagen's words in exactly this sense and redefines them as a challenge to Hagen, the *man*, to kill his *herre*. Kriemhilt labels Hagen a traitor. Everything else follows from this unambiguous interpretation: the execution of Gunther, Hagen's triumph, and Kriemhilt's final act of violence.

The redactor of the *C version, without understanding the narrative strategies of his text, was once again determined to clarify things. The end is already predetermined when he says about Hagen: *Er wiste wol div mære sine liezen in niht genesen* [He knew well that she would not let him live] (C 2428,1). When he wants to mark Hagen as an evildoer, he has to plainly mark his words as treasonous: *wie mohte ein untriwe iemer stercher wesen* [could there be a greater betrayal?] (C 2428,2), and he adds Hagen's unsubstantiated fear that Kriemhilt might let her brother live once he has been eliminated. This supports the motivation that Hagen is out to end Gunther's life.

The vulgate version resists such clarity. The *ende* that is Kriemhilt's choice is a cynical conclusion based on Hagen's words, which she interprets *malam partem*. She wins the next round of the game. And like a good chess player, Hagen recognizes the decisiveness of her move (*als ich mir hête gedâht*) and that his opponent is one step closer to her goal (*z'einem ende*). But the move allows him to triumph one last time with his countermove:

> *du hâst iz nâch dînem willen z'einem ende brâht,*
> *und ist ouch rehte ergangen als ich mir hête gedâht.*
>
> *nu ist von Burgonden der edel künec tôt,*
> *Giselhêr der junge, und ouch her Gêrnôt.*
> *den schaz den weiz nu niemen wan got unde mîn:*
> *der sol dich, vâlandinne, immer wol verholn sîn.* (2370,3–2371,4)
>
> [you have ended it all according to your will,
> and it has all transpired as I thought it must.
>
> Now the noble king of Burgundy is dead,
> as is young Giselher, and also Sir Gernot.
> Only God and I know where the hoard is:
> it will remain forever hidden from you, you devil.]

This victory permits two conclusions from Hagen's point of view: "You will get nothing out of me, as long as I live"; and from Kriemhilt's perspective: "There is no reason for keeping Hagen alive, since he won't reveal anything anyway." The conclusion for Kriemhilt is clear. Her reply plays one last time with the ambiguity of her own demand. Now, however, vengeance (*ergetzen*) takes the place of reconciliation:

> *Si sprach: "sô habt ir übele geltes [!] mich gewert.*
> *sô wil ich doch behalten daz Sîfrides swert.*
> *daz truoc mîn holder vriedel, do ich in jungest sach,*
> *an dem mir herzeleide von iuwern schulden geschach."* (2372)
>
> [She said: "you have made my revenge bitter indeed.
> But I shall keep Sivrit's sword.
> My dear lover carried it when I saw him for the last time,
> the cause of my bitter grief is all your fault."]

Kriemhilt's right to satisfaction—unattainable for Sivrit, frustrated for the treasure—takes possession of what is closest to her of Sivrit's, namely the sword, which Hagen has appropriated. She takes what she can from what has been denied her. This symbol has many meanings: the sword is a part of Sivrit's Nibelungen property, which is claimed by Kriemhilt; it is what is left of the hero; it metonymically represents Sivrit and his heroic strength; but it is also the metaphorical symbol of revenge. By showing the sword in *Âventiure* 29, Hagen demonstrates his rejection of Kriemhilt's right to vengeance by virtue of his superior strength (1782–84). Now in Kriemhilt's hands, it can defeat Hagen. Kriemhilt's words give the sword another meaning, namely as a memorial to her *herzeleide* (2372,4). When Kriemhilt takes the sword, her gesture is as ambiguous as is her speech: saving the ruins of her possessions, the memory of Sivrit, and revenge. The next act is unambiguous: Kriemhilt decapitates Hagen. The game of deceptive ambiguities and mean-spirited inferences is over.

A legend does not have to understand the final scene as a banal solution in one or the other direction, but as a final demonstration of an unsolvable contradiction that can no longer be kept in balance. The epic stages this contradiction in the final scene as a power play for ambiguity. By taking the special narrative strategies of the epic into account, most of the supposed contradictions resolve themselves.

3 *Nibelungian Society*

Personal Bonds—The Fellowship

The loyalty [*triuwe*] of the Nibelungen has given the epic a sad reputation. Transferred from the heroes Volker and Hagen to the collective subjects of the Austro-Hungarian monarchy and the German empire, it reflected the mythologization of the modern state through the heroic individual. Medieval studies has had to learn the hard lesson that the structure of the state is an achievement of the modern era and its theoretical trailblazers of the late medieval period.[1] In the Middle Ages, political order consisted rather of a fellowship that united the feudal lord and his vassals and bondsmen in a complex network of horizontal and vertical dependencies.[2]

The actual hero of the *Nibelungenlied*, and Kriemhilt's antagonist, is not the individual, but this alliance or bond of individuals.[3] This distinguishes the *Nibelungenlied* from the roughly contemporary courtly romance. In such alliances of persons, contractual relationships (*triuwe*)[4] guarantee social cohesion. A tight network of personal relationships determines the actions of the protagonists. At its center are "bonds of kinship, both agnatic and cognatic in nature," of *mâgen* and *konemâgen*.[5] Its margins are fuzzy, but this network forms the basis of feudal relationships. Without organizing this association "according to the distinctions of feudal law," the *Nibelungenlied* defines it as the "fundamental characterization of dominion and dependence: lord and vassal."[6] There are, in addition, special allegiances, friendships, and communal responsibilities, especially in the form of the brotherhood of arms. All of these relationships can be called *vriuntschaft*. Additionally, at the margins of this network, bonds can be created through gifts among unequals, for example, messengers. The heart of the collective can essentially be described as the overlap of the three abovementioned circles: kinship, rule, and, in the broadest sense, the communal.[7]

Among *vriunden*, special emphasis is given to *mâgen*, relatives, but the delineation of the two types remains somewhat unclear.[8] The more open association of persons of the early Middle Ages, which included blood relatives of differing degrees, as well as bondsmen and allies,[9] seems to gravitate toward a concentration on narrower agnatic relationships starting with the eleventh century (although this is not yet the nuclear family). In the *Nibelungenlied*, the Burgundian royal family is the center around which Kriemhilt's story revolves up until Etzel's courtship. She relies on its guarantees and even trusts Hagen as a relative: *du bist mîn mâc, sô bin ich der dîn* [you are my kin, and so I am yours] (898,1). Even after Sivrit's death, she remains under the protection of her kinsfolk by accepting her younger brothers' offer of safekeeping, and she refuses to follow Sivrit's father to where she has *lützel künnes* (1081,4) and *niemen mâge* (1085,3), that is, no blood relatives, even though this means that she must live with those who killed Sivrit, and even when she is offered rule in Xanten. In Worms, she has the support of her brothers Giselher and Gernot and goes along with the reconciliation with Gunther. Even Etzel's courtship is promoted by the brothers, since it is in the interest of the dynasty as a whole, as Gunther emphasizes:

> *des sol ich ir wol gunnen: si ist diu swester mîn.*
> *wir soltenz selbe werben, ob ez ir êre möhte sîn.* (1204,3–4)
>
> [I should certainly grant it to her: she is my sister.
> We should propose it ourselves if it means honor to her.]

These kinds of bonds are linked by the reciprocity of *hulde* (*familiaritas*).[10] Kriemhilt can legitimize her treacherous invitation with her bond to her *mâgen*, and the Burgundians, should they accept, can trust in it as well. It is on this account that Etzel remains unsuspecting.

The confidence in the kinship bond is problematic, but not a problematized prerequisite of the action. Sivrit's trust in his wife's *mâgen* (923,2) is not simply a foolish delusion but relies on the relationship into which he entered with marriage.

ine weiz hie niht der liute, die mir iht hazzes tragen.
all dîne mâge sint mir gemeine holt,
ouch hân ich an den degenen hie niht anders versolt. (923,2–4)[11]

[I know of no one here who bears me any enmity.
All your kin are well disposed to me,
and I have always acted so that I merited it.]

His murder stains all his relatives, even his own completely uninvolved son, of whom it is charged (*itewîzen*) that *sîne mâge iemen mortlîche hân erslagen* [his kin are murderers] (995,2–3). Etzel is related to the Burgundians through Kriemhilt by *vriuntschaft* (1406,2–3). This is why he speaks of Kriemhilt's relatives (*vriunden dîn*, 1407,2) as his own (*friunde mîne*, 1861,3). In the *Klage*, he regrets the loss not only of wife and son, but also of their relatives, his *konemâgen* (KL 825), even though these were in fact responsible for her death, along with the deaths of his own people. Kinship serves in other medieval texts as a cognitive model for various kinds of connections.[12] To question it would be to undermine one of the foundations of medieval life.

Hagen's actions are explained not so much by the bonds of kinship as by his bonds to his lords. Kriemhilt's trust in kinship (898,1) is exploited by him to commit a murder that would serve the Burgundian king. Kriemhilt's salutation: *vil lieber vriunt* [dearest friend] and her appeal to his mercy [*genâde*] are fatal mistakes. He is more rightly called *vriunt* by the kings.[13] Even in the context of rulership, *vriunt* means a relationship of virtual equals, based on reciprocity, as happens when Kriemhilt lays claim to Hagen as her vassal as part of the royal Burgundian inheritance and Hagen refuses her demand:

jane mac uns Gunther zer werlde niemen gegeben.

Ander iwer gesinde daz lât iu volgen mite,
want ir doch wol bekennet der Tronegære site:
wir müezen bî den künigen hie en hove bestân.
wir suln in langer dienen den wir alher gevolget hân. (698,4–699,4)

[Gunther may not give us to anyone in the world.

Other courtiers may follow you,
but you know very well the custom of Troneck:
We must stay with the kings here at court.
We shall continue to serve them, as we have served them until now.]

The limited authority of the kings does not imply the independence of vassals. Hagen acts against Sivrit in the king's stead in the affront to the queen's honor. He is protecting Burgundian rule from the danger posed by *unkunde[] recken* (1127,2) and properly gauges the threat posed by Etzel's power. He even takes part in an enterprise he condemns in order to protect the kings: whoever invites his lords also invites him, as he has accompanied them on every court journey: *die heizent mîne herren, sô bin ich ir man* [they are called my lords, and so I am their vassal] (1788,3).

Hagen represents a common type of heroic figure in medieval epic on whom the survival of the community depends: the always loyal vassal, such as Wate, Berhter, Hildebrant, and so on. Lord and vassal are each nothing without the other. In Germanic epic, the dependency of the lord on his vassal is dominant, but the vassal must always prove his *triuwe* to be unimpeachable.

Reciprocal obligation is driven to extremes, so that all other social bonds tend to be obscured. Dietrich, in the *Book of Bern*, gives up his entire empire to save the life of his most trusted vassals.[14] In Eilhart's *Tristrant*, which is still closely related to heroic epic, the vassal goes so far as to encourage his lord's adultery to save him from deadly lovesickness.[15] Conversely, Tristrant avoids Isald for a year for the sake of his vassal.[16]

In this context, Hagen's radical bond to his lord is not extraordinary.[17] His disdain for Kriemhilt, his decision to risk his own life by journeying to Etzel, and his rigorous obstinacy lead him to sacrifice the last of the Burgundian survivors for the sake of the sanctity of his oath. On account of this close relationship it is impossible that he be the only guilty party sacrificed for Kriemhilt's revenge (2104–7). The kings have to protect him, too. The mutual obligations of lord and vassal are absolute and valid to the point of self-destruction. There is no such thing as individual responsibility outside of this bond. This remains unquestioned until the *Klage* (KL 259–69). There, by placing the blame on Hagen alone, a more abstract principle of guilt and responsibility wins out in the epic at the cost of the principle of complete reciprocity.[18]

Contractual connections between persons who are neither related nor in a relationship of subordination to a lord are essentially the least fixed. Included here is the brotherhood of arms between Sivrit and Gunther, and above all between Hagen and Volker. The first proves to be unstable, because it is confused with dependencies of rule. At the end of the epic, it is the second relationship, however, based strictly on an informal promise of mutual support (1777–78), that is the idealized counterproposal to the perversion of kinship and to the final catastrophe of rulership. In contrast to these, it proves itself free of conflict until death. The most perfect bond is *vriuntschaft* where it has freed itself from other types of social bonds.

These three types of bonds guarantee social order. The epic relates how they come into conflict with each other, since webs of relationship are constructed through the linkage of individual elements, and there are no abstract or general bonds beyond these linkages.[19] There is no absolute reliability of relatives and vassals, because the one relationship can be contrary to the other. Today's *vriunt* can be tomorrow's enemy. This manifests itself in paradoxical wording, as in Etzel's relationship to Hagen:

> *sînen friunt von Tronege den het er rehte ersehen,*
> *der im in sîner jugende vil starken dienest bôt.*
> *sît frumt' er im in alter vil manigen lieben vriunt tôt.* (1757,2–4)
>
> [He recognized his friend from Troneck,
> who served him well in his youth.
> Later, when he was older, he was to slay many a dear friend of his.]

Is Hagen now a *vriunt*—as a guest and bondsman of the *konemâgen*? Or because he was once in Etzel's service? Or an enemy, because he will later kill other friends of Etzel's—relatives, vassals, and bondsmen?

The chainlike linking of individual elements of society has disastrous consequences. Kriemhilt can be certain that the invitation of her brothers will bring Hagen along, that his *vriuntschaft* with Volker will involve him, too, in the conflict, with which he had nothing to do in the beginning, and that one after another, the Hun vassals will become embroiled in the battle. In the beginning, the intermediate links are still missing, so that the chain is interrupted, but then circumstances develop that create the right links. Etzel is only eventually made suspicious of his Burgundian *vriunden*, for he is bound to Sivrit only by *verriu sippe*, as Hagen scoffs (2023,1), and is therefore not obliged to seek revenge until the murder of his son pulls him in as well (2095). At first, Dietrich declines to fight for Kriemhilt, since her relatives have done him no wrong (1901,3). However, the *leit* (2319,1) that the death of his own men causes him forces him to intervene.

Kriemhilt's efforts are above all directed at supplying the missing links and forcing everyone to comply with her plans for revenge. If two links of the chain pull in opposite directions, then before the one can take effect, the other must be undone: Kriemhilt's bond with Giselher, Etzel's bond with his wife's *vriunde*, and that of Rüedeger's with his guests.

The connections between the links of the chain prove to be of varying strength. The ranking is: brotherhood of arms, vassality, kinship, and obligation by way of reward (*miete*). These connections are of different value. In first place is a voluntary bond of equals that is not based on aristocratic, vassalic, or economic grounds, such as that between Hagen and Volker, which represents the principle of personal bonds with an emphatic purity: *swâ sô friunt bî friunde friuntlîchen stât* [if a friend helps a friend in a friendly way] (1801,2). It is all the more praiseworthy because stability is actually most endangered and not supported by any sort of material interest.[20] Emotional orchestration replaces what is lacking in institutional guarantees. Its caricature is the temporary alliance between Gunther and Sivrit, which falls apart once the common purpose has been achieved.

Obligations that must be bought with gold are worth least. It is true that Hunnish power surpasses all that has gone before,[21] and even Sivrit never possessed so many *recken edele* as Etzel (1368,4), despite his immeasurable wealth.[22] When it comes to battle, however, the entire might of the Huns is only a faceless mass, which may be slaughtered without great regret. The greater political system fails with Etzel's power in the face of the close relationship of heroic *triuwe*.

The crusader epic's cliché of the heathen as a coward is transferred to the Huns (even though the other characteristics of a pagan counterworld are completely repressed). The Burgundian brotherhood of arms is confronted by a heathen army that though numerically superior is nevertheless constantly in danger of dissolution. As in the crusader epic, the heathens must be compelled to engage in battle with threats and force, whereas the Burgundians (Christians) press on with fearless confidence to victory (martyrdom). On the Hunnish (heathen) side, fighting is motivated by lowly greed.

Etzel's Christian warriors in exile are different. Their prowess resembles the Burgundians', and they are bound by a similar fellowship. Irinc and his men's honor is impugned (*schande*, 2027,4) when Volker accuses them of enjoying Etzel's hospitality without helping him in his *nôt*. Irinc almost instinctively throws himself into the hopeless fight:

> *ich hân ûf êre lâzen nu lange mîniu dinc*
> *und hân in volkes stürmen des besten vil getân.*
> *nu brinc mir mîn gewæfen: jâ wil ich Hagenen bestân.* (2028,2–4)
>
> [I have long pursued honor as my cause
> and have performed the best deeds in great battles.
> Now bring me my weapons: I am determined to fight Hagen.]

His decision binds his men so firmly to follow him and to risk their lives with his that he must plead with them on bended knee, *daz si in eine liezen den recken bestân* [that they would let him fight on his own against the hero] (2035,2). As opposed to the Huns, they do not have to be bribed in order to fight, but can hardly be restrained from fighting. The dying Irinc's warning not to fight against the Burgundians has no effect (2068), because they are not concerned with *golt*, but with avenging their *vriunt*. So Irinc's *mâge* and allies throw themselves into battle, and all perish.

Kriemhilt only succeeds in overcoming her guests to the extent that she can oppose them with the fellowships of Danes, Rüedeger's men, and finally Dietrich and his troops.

Conflicts of Loyalty

The portrayal of Nibelungian society is archaic compared with the situation around 1200. It devalues economic and political structures beyond personal bonds, which are idealized and harmonized above all others. Hagen turns into a positive figure by virtue of his unconditional friendship for Volker. The same is true of Rüedeger, who, even in following his obligations of vassality, can once again demonstrate his bond to his Burgundian *vriunde*. Unlike in the rebel epics of the chansons de geste, bonds of rulership are never questioned, but they are pre-harmonized with the "horizontal" bonds to the *vriunt*. This is only superficially connected to the power struggles and the process of class differentiation in the Holy Roman Empire and its territories around 1200. Political interpretations have therefore necessarily failed.

Looking at the consequences of such unrestrainedly positive bonds, what is reflected above all is their endangerment. Their representatives triumph time and again, but the result is their own downfall. In the case of Hagen, there is no conflict between his *triuwe* to Volker and to his lords, but he leads both to ruin. In the case of Rüedeger, similar obligations contradict each other with deadly consequences. The brotherhood of arms between Sivrit and Gunther is misinterpreted in terms of the subordination of the one to the other. The attempt to harmonize "horizontal" bonds (with equals, e.g., with relatives and guests) with "vertical" bonds (with superiors, e.g., the king) results in a an incongruous composite that is at the narrator's mercy and has fatal consequences.

These obligations are not all compatible. The epic plays through alternatives that are partially antagonistic. At best, as in Rüedeger's case, there is a sentimental gesture that expresses aporia. To rupture personal obligations in the name of others is in any case treacherous and disloyal. The criticism of

Sivrit's murder is unanimous. Gunther objects to the plan at the murder conclave: *er was uns ie getriuwe* [he was always loyal to us] (868,4), and the mortally wounded Sivrit repeats this word for word: *ich was iu ie getriuwe* [I was always loyal to you] (989,3). The narrator can hardly do enough to decry the murder of Sivrit as *die starken untriuwe* [the great disloyalty] (876,2), *grôze[n] meinrât* [great treachery] (906,3), and *ungetriuwen tôt* [death by disloyalty] (988,4). He warns: *sus grôzer untriuwe solde nimmer man gepflegen* [such great disloyalty should never again occur] (915,4).[23] Treachery strikes at the very foundation of fellowship, the epitome of social order. This is why its effects reach far beyond those directly involved: *ir habt an iuwern mâgen leider übele getân* [you have done wrong by your kin] (989,4). All those who are connected by personal bonds to the perpetrators are concerned, and even future generations are stigmatized (990).

This is unambiguous, but still the murder of Sivrit is explained by a competing *triuwe* bond, that of Hagen to Prünhilt. And if other *triuwe* obligations are unscrupulously sacrificed to avenge the treachery, even this is based on *triuwe.* Moral verdict is helpless against the social system. It is often demonstrated, in constantly new constellations, how personal bonds cross and can still be mutually exclusive. Every time, the consequence is betrayal.

Hagen follows a social norm of similar constraints to the bond that should bind him to Sivrit—the *friunt* of the kings, the ally, the brother in arms. He decides in favor of the royal house. He does not act as Kriemhilt's *mâc* (898,1), but as Gunther's *man.*[24] His decision remains problematic in the narrator's and the characters' commentary. It is only revalued when another, more problematic decision raises its head: Kriemhilt's intentions toward her next of kin. This moves Kriemhilt into the treacherous role that Hagen occupies in the first part of the epic.

A similar conflict is played out in the controversy surrounding Rüedeger, which has often been discussed and does not need to be gone into here.[25] The conflict is a medium that reflects the aporias of fellowship. The result is that duty to the feudal lord Etzel (hence the oath to Kriemhilt) is stronger than the bond to the Burgundian *friunde.* The decision is clear, but the basis for it not at all. The vote for feudal obligation is not to be equated with "right." Rüedeger must violate the law.[26]

The bond of rulership appears as an inevitable requirement, as the narrator has Rüedeger assert time and again: *ez muoz hiute gelten* [today the cost has to be paid] (2163,2); *ich muoz iu leisten als ich gelobet hân* [I must serve you as I have pledged] (2166,3); *die küenen Burgonden die muoz ich leider bestân* [I must unfortunately stand against the bold Burgundians] (2167,4); *Jane mac ichs niht gelâzen* [I cannot do otherwise] (2178,1); *ich muoz mit iu strîten, wande ichz gelobt hân* [I must fight you, for so I have pledged] (2178,2); *mich enwoldes niht erlâzen des künec Etzelen wîp* [King Etzel's wife did not want to allow me to do otherwise] (2178,4). What prevails is experienced as an overmighty constraint from outside.[27] Nevertheless, prevail it must and will.

The bond to the feudal lord is effectively staged in the pathetic prostration of Etzel and Kriemhilt before Rüedeger, a scene that might play on the emperor Friedrich Barbarossa's prostration before Henry the Lion of Saxony or comparable rituals.[28] This act is only a counterpoint to the earlier prostration of Irinc before his vassals. It reestablishes the balance of mutual obligations by reversing the former scene. If the main concern now is to cause Rüedeger to intervene on behalf of his lord, then the previous goal was to prevent the vassals from supporting their lord, who wanted to fight without their help. The gesture of subordination emphasizes the obligatory nature of the bonds of rulership, visible in a reversal of the legitimate hierarchy, and shows again the mutual dependence of lord and retinue.

Both times the gesture of surrender to the partner succeeds by blocking all alternatives. Rüedeger can still try to dissolve the feudal bond (which fails).[29] He can lament his situation (which he does vociferously). He cannot question the obligatory nature of Etzel's demand, however. On the other hand, the former promise to Kriemhilt, to *büezen* her *leit* [avenge her hurt] (1257,2–3), plays only a subordinate role, and only in the beginning.[30]

Rüedeger openly does what is his duty as a vassal, and he unexpectedly emerges from the conflict unscathed. Since there is no pragmatic solution, he must die. But he is not guilty either, which is why he is granted undying fame.[31] Whereas he had believed *mich schiltet elliu diet* [everyone will blame me] (2154,3), he will, in fact, be praised by all. This is not so much a result of his decision in favor of his vassalic bond, but can be explained by the exemplary way in which he copes with an aporetic situation. Seen objectively, any decision or nondecision will break the law (2154). Rüedeger, however, can show that his actions respect the law on both sides.

When Rüedeger appears armed, Volker immediately understands it as the fulfillment of his feudal obligation: *an uns wil dienen Rüedegêr sîn bürge und sîniu lant* [Rüedeger wants to serve his towns and lands at our cost] (2173,4). The opposing obligations to the Burgundians—Giselher puts his hopes in familial ties (2172), Gunther remembers *der vil grôzen triuwe* [the great loyalty] (2177,3) and recalls the *triuwe unde minne, die ir uns habt getân* [loyalty and love you have granted us] (2179,3), Gernot speaks of the right of the guest and gifts (2182; 2184)—have no effect. The expectation of the actors is, by the way, exactly balanced according to status, in that each one speaks from the class position of the other: the vassal Volker cites the strength of the bond to the lord as the stronger, whereas the kings express the hope that the legal relationships between equals will be the deciding factor.[32] This, too, underscores an equilibrium.

The conversation with the Burgundians repeats, on the opposite side, the conflict with Kriemhilt and Etzel. Analogous to the failed *diffidatio* in that case, Rüedeger asks here, too, for the dissolution of legal obligations, of marriage, guest right, free passage, and gift giving: *ê do wâren wir friunde: der triuwen wil ich ledec sîn* [once we were friends: I now want to be free of this loyalty] (2175,4).[33] This attempt likewise fails, as does the hope that the bond of *vriuntschaft* can withstand the battle.

The prospect of a double break of obligations rears its head. Hagen's intervention,[34] however, allows both sides to be warranted. Hagen's request for Rüedeger's shield reactivates the bonds that Rüedeger is forced to violate.[35] Rüedeger fulfills Hagen's demand just as willingly [*willeclîchen]* (2197,1) as Etzel ordered him to do (2231,1). The weights are "balanced,"[36] at the price of annihilation, of course.

The mutual obligation of the gift is expressed in Hagen's and Volker's retreat from battle. They decide—again a reversal of the starting constellation—against their lords and for the alternative that Rüedeger had rejected. Giselher's reluctance to fight against his relative once more confirms the validity of the legal standpoint that Rüedeger is forced to give up (2208,3). The fact that Rüedeger dies by the sword that he himself gave to his opponent shows the deadly consequence of the opposing obligations. He is praised, not by Etzel and Kriemhilt, for whom he fought—on the contrary, Kriemhilt doubts his trustworthiness (2228–29)—but by the Burgundians, whose *vriunde* he killed, to whom he also voluntarily demonstrated his generosity.

In Rüedeger, we see the triumph of personal bonds, even in their contradictory nature. What opposes his decision is staged as of even greater value, but has to be given up under a stream of tears (2197,2). Rüedeger's downfall celebrates the heroic world at the expense of the victor; his moral triumph is identical with the catastrophe of the social system in whose web he is caught.

The *Klage* maintains Rüedeger's exemplary nature[37]—he is found lying on his shield, the one that replaced the shield given to Hagen—but leaves out his conflict completely. It remains the ideal battle for Etzel. The contradictions and potential conflicts that arise from the structure of the fellowship seem to have not interested the thirteenth-century poet. It is a sad heroic fate, but nothing more.

Making triuwe *Ambiguous*

Triuwe was the principle intended to guarantee the cohesion of the fellowship of persons.[38] *Triuwe* of kinship (*triuwe* within the family or clan), of a feudal nature (*triuwe* between lord and vassal), contractual and emotional (*triuwe* between equals who are bound to each other for a certain purpose), is more than an individual feeling, although it is distinguished by degree and is less than an institutionally secured obligation. In this sense, *triuwe* is the quintessence of all reciprocal bonds between people.[39] "Internal" (that is, relating to individual people) and "social" components are inextricably linked to each other and can only be loosely differentiated.[40] In any particular case, the one or the other can predominate. In the *triuwe* between Hagen and Volker, the element of social obligation is weaker than in a feudal relationship. Between these two types lies the solidarity within the Burgundian ruling elite, which will not deliver any single member to the enemy, even at the cost of self-destruction. Components of rule are always supported by the personal. Missing is any clear hierarchy of different types of bonds, those that are more strongly collective and social and those that are more individualized. In the confrontation of Huns and Burgundians at Kriemhilt's *hôchzît*, however, all emphasis falls on the group in which both types are indistinguishable: the Burgundians.

The horizontal bonds are positively imbued throughout, above all those within the clan, along with others between men, the brotherhood of arms between Hagen and Volker, the hospitality between Rüedeger and the Burgundians, the initial agreement between the Burgundians and the exiled heroes at Etzel's court, and, of course, the—later to be betrayed—*vriuntschaft* between Sivrit and Gunther. Such bonds can span the membership of various, even hostile, political groupings. Even as the Burgundians are still engaged in the battle with Etzel's men, Rüedeger calls them *vriunde* (1996,4), and Giselher confirms this: *sît ir sît triuwen stæte* [since you remain loyal] (1997,3). The agreement between the Amelungen and the Burgundians is only destroyed in the conflict over Rüedeger's corpse. Rüedeger, Hagen, and Volker prove even in the deadly battle that they are still *friunde* (2200,3).

The various relationships that can be characterized as *triuwe* have a common social core. Only gradually does this core shift to a more individually modeled relationship in the literature of the twelfth and thirteenth centuries.[41] There are moves in this direction in the *Nibelungenlied* without explicit reflection, but with clear problematization. Kriemhilt's *triuwe* to Sivrit is uncontested: *si was im getriuwe, des ir diu meiste menige giht* [she remained loyal to him, and that was acknowledged by most] (1142,4). Even this *triuwe* is by no means lacking a social moment, however. Kriemhilt's place in the ruling structure is determined first by Sivrit's place as king, then by her membership in the Burgundian ruling clan. But then the statement: *getriuwer wîbes künne ein helt nie mêre gewan* [never a hero gained a more loyal woman] (1126,4), holds true regardless of Sivrit's power, strength, and wealth (1126,3). Because Kriemhilt's *minne* for Sivrit is no longer motivated by Sivrit's position, but is his regardless of who he is and what he has, it falls outside the framework of normal *triuwe* bonds. The bond to the *holde[n] vriedel* [sweet beloved] (2372,3) can and will destroy all others, including the bonds to family and *vriunde*. The term *vriedel* denotes a relationship beyond legal distinctions (lover, husband).[42] From the narrator's perspective, as well as his characters', this asocial *triuwe* is perverted into a monstrosity.

This kind of *triuwe* comes into play only gradually. If the epic is read from the end, and if one imagines, where the epic is silent, a certain depth of emotion, then it is easy to overlook how conventionally the bond with Sivrit was initially justified and how closely it was linked to the rules of feudal alliance. Sivrit's role as an aspiring knight may be tinged by courtly service of a lady, and Kriemhilt's reaction may be influenced by elements of *amor de lonh*, but Kriemhilt is not the sovereign courtly *vrouwe* who decides on accepting *minne* service based on merit. She stands under her brothers' authority to give away her hand in marriage[43] and is used by her brothers for political purposes. Her *gruoz* [greeting] will reward Sivrit for his services to the king; she is the price for Sivrit's help in Isenstein, and she has to redeem Gunther's sworn obligations when Sivrit demands his reward. When she speaks to Sivrit, she assesses his person primarily according to his services to her relatives and their "favor" (303). She bows to her brothers' wishes unconditionally (613). Her marriage is an act of state, as is shown in the conflict with Prünhilt. Her own role is completely dependent on the social role of her husband.

Surely, the preparation of this normal feudal marriage is colored by *minne* as an individual choice of a specific partner. Kriemhilt's love is expressed in stolen glances, in her interest in the victor of the Saxon war (225, 241), and in blushing (292,2). Erotic closeness is embedded in the courtly greeting ritual

(293–94), and we are told about affection in the official matrimonial ceremony *an dem ringe* (614–15). The *Nibelungenlied* quotes *minne* symptoms, as the courtly romance will continue to develop, but always in conjunction with the usual constellations of feudal betrothal. At first, *minne* seems just to complete the marriage on an emotional level. Only gradually does *minne* become the focus, however, and the social framework vanishes step by step.

The prominence of personal bonds beyond a conventional network of collective responsibilities seems at this time to have been a general stimulant to narration, as well as being a source of bewilderment in early vernacular epic literature. A key role is played by the Tristan legend. In the conventional bond between the king of Cornwall and the king's daughter from Ireland, the marriage, based on convenience, status, and politics, must be enhanced by an individual affection between the partners. This is originally the task of the love potion, which—I am following Eilhart's version—Marke and Isalde are supposed to drink (cf. Trt 2266ff.). It is all the worse that the wrong man drinks the potion, whereby the natural connection between *minne* and expediency, person and status, is no longer provided. The two sides therefore oppose each other in discord. A purely personal love is only imaginable as a negation of convenience. In Eilhart, it is removed from everything that could make Tristrant worthy of love according to collective norms. Only after she is already in love—a love caused by magic—does Isalde discover in Tristrant the usual merits of nobility, beauty, strength, and great deeds. Isalde's passion for this one person has the same destructive effect as Kriemhilt's fixation on avenging Sivrit.

Kriemhilt's *minne* does not develop into the same kind of passion until after Sivrit's death. She remains in proximity to the grave, close to her relatives, but only until she has the opportunity to exact revenge on these same relatives. Her option against family is different from Hagen's. Hagen does not leave the current order but decides for one side, the queen's, at the expense of the opposite side, that of the king's sister and brother-in-law, with whom he cuts his ties. This results in his well-known cynicism: *lât mich den schuldigen sîn* [let me be the guilty one] (1131,4) and *nu rechez swer der welle* [let whoever will avenge this] (1791,3). Nonetheless the consequences of his betrayal are not as devastating as Kriemhilt's, who sacrifices, not just a certain kind, but all other bonds—those to her vassals, Etzel's heroes, her brothers, her son, and her husband—for that to Sivrit. Unlike that of the men to each other, Kriemhilt's *triuwe* to Sivrit is therefore ambivalent; it is only unconditionally positive as long as she is embedded in other *triuwe* networks (as before her marriage to Etzel). This gradually diminishes the more she threatens other *triuwe* bonds, and in the end she destroys them all.

Their elimination is narrated systematically. She cuts the bond to Sivrit's kin first and without complications. She prevents them from exacting revenge and then separates herself from them. In this way, her vengeance becomes her own business and is no longer a matter for the clan. Sivrit's son is forgotten. Still, Kriemhilt seems to be able to rely on another, generally accepted *triuwe* network, her relatives (1078,4). There, disrupted ties are repaired so that the members of the familial group are again *holt*, as they should be (1129,3).[44] Revenge cannot succeed in such a network, however, because it must be aimed at its own destruction. Kriemhilt's *getriuwen* are obligated to familial relationships, against which she must act. So she tries to act on her own by spending the hoard, but is robbed and experiences new *leit* (cf. 1141,1), for which she can find no assistance from her relatives: *wær' er niht mîn mâc, ez gienge im an den lîp* [if he were not family, he would be in mortal danger] (1133,3) is how Giselher rejects the expectation that he should punish Hagen for having taken away the Nibelungen gold. Since Kriemhilt's *triuwe* to Sivrit (cf. 1142,4) includes the plan to avenge him, she is hampered by the *triuwe* to her relatives and those between them and others.

This *triuwe* still exists as Kriemhilt embarks to meet Etzel, apparent in the rituals of leave-taking. The separation from her *guoten friunden* (1291,4) is tear-filled. Giselher assures Kriemhilt again of his services, should she need help, and Kriemhilt gives her relatives, *die ir mâge wâren*, the kiss of peace upon leaving. Here Kriemhilt is still tied to the fellowship of *vriunde*.

Not until she can count on Etzel's men does the *triuwe* to Sivrit become the absolute motif that destroys all other social bonds. How she comes to give up her brother—Gunther, but also Giselher[45]—is told in the grand soliloquy at the beginning of *Âventiure* 23. It is satanic, prompted by the devil [*vâlant*] (1394,1–3), who is used where a normal understanding of the world ends.[46] The criticism of Kriemhilt is increased in that she also violates the right of hospitality.[47] Kriemhilt's *triuwe* is radically individualized, directed at only one person, and ignores social considerations. She must remove herself from the network of *getriuwen* that constitutes feudal society, and this can only happen under clearly negative signs.[48]

Kriemhilt realizes that a norm that is unquestioned in the world of the Nibelungen is being shattered. She is ashamed when Dietrich calls her *vâlandinne* (1748,4) because he knows that she is determined to exact revenge on her closest relatives:

> *Des schamte sich vil sêre daz Etzelen wîp.* (1749,1)
>
> [Etzel's wife was very ashamed of this.]

Shame is knowing that one has violated a rule that one also acknowledges to be valid. Again and again, the narrator hammers home the dishonorable nature of the plan:

> *diu bete dich lützel êret, vil edeles fürsten wîp,*
> *daz du dînen mâgen rætest an den lîp.*
> *si kômen ûf genâde her in diz lant.* (1902,1–3)
>
> [This wish (to slay the Burgundians) does you little honor, dear noble lady,
> that you conspire against the life of your kin.
> They are coming here in good faith.]

Since *der grôze mort* takes place *an ir næhsten mâgen* (2086,1; 3),[49] the trust in the social order (*gedingen*) is fundamentally in doubt. Giselher reproaches her:

> *Ich was dir ie getriuwe, nie getet ich dir leit.*
> *ûf solhen gedingen ich her ze hove reit,*
> *daz du mir holt wærest* . . . . (2102,1–3)
>
> [I was always loyal to you, I never caused you grief.
> In this trust I rode here to court,
> that you would be well-disposed to me . . . .]

The final scene insists on the terms of kinship (*vil liebiu swester*, 2363,1; *bruoder*, 2366,3; 2369,2), and plays them off of the *holde[n] vriedel* (2372,3). Kriemhilt's death mirrors this violation:

> *ze stücken was gehouwen dô daz edele wîp.* (2377,2)
>
> [The noble woman was hacked to pieces.]

Dismemberment is the punishment for traitors, those who destroy order.[50] Hagen, who is branded a traitor in the first part, is only beheaded, the form of execution that privileges the nobility, since it does not taint one's honor. When, later on, the *Klage* praises Kriemhilt as the epitome of *triuwe*, it must cancel the punishment of a traitor and come up with a more honorable means of death. In fact, Kriemhilt is only beheaded here: her head is found separated from her torso (Kl 796–97). She is exonerated of the worst charges.[51]

Triuwe, introduced without discussion as the highest virtue and unconditionally valid, proves itself to be disastrous in Kriemhilt's case when applied to a single individual. Only the *Klage* puts a positive spin on Kriemhilt's exclusive bond to Sivrit under the concept of *triuwe*. Kriemhilt is therefore granted the salvation of her soul (Kl 139–58 and elsewhere). From a religious perspective, *triuwe* here becomes an individual virtue. With the authority of *Des buoches meister*, the narrator declares: *dem getriuwen tuot untriuwe wê* [according to the master of the book, disloyalty is hurtful to those who are loyal] (Kl 569–70). Norbert Voorwinden identifies an allusion to the Bible (Prov. 29:27) in this summing up.[52] Kriemhilt is judged according to a religious (and not feudal or clan-related) definition of *triuwe*.

Even here, the connection to the central medieval principle of social order is not completely rejected. Kriemhilt's justification begins with:

> *Sold er [!] des engelten,*
> *der rehter triuwen kunde phlegen,*
> *der hete schiere sich bewegen*
> *daz er mit rehten dingen*
> *möhte niht volbringen*
> *dehein getriulîchen muot* . . . . (Kl 140–45)
>
> [Should he who practiced a proper loyalty
> be punished for that,
> he would quickly give up
> what he could achieve in a right way
> through a sense of loyalty . . . .]

Kriemhilt's *triuwe* is discussed as a general—and this means masculine (*er [*!*]; mannes lîp* [!]), and at the same time social—virtue. It is only secondarily discussed as a woman's (also social) virtue. It is initially not explicitly expressed in terms of a bond to a beloved:

> *triuwe diu ist dar zuo guot:*
> *diu machet werden mannes lîp* [!],
> *und êrt ouh [!] alsô schœniu wîp*
> *daz ir zuht noch ir muot*
> *nâch schanden nimmer niht getuot.* (Kl 146–50)
>
> [Loyalty is a quality
> that makes a man worthy,
> and it also honors beautiful women,
> so that both their behavior and their intentions
> are never dishonorable.]

The narrator tells his audience what it should be thinking about Kriemhilt:

> *swer ditze mære merken kan,*
> *der sagt unschuldic gar ir lîp,*

wan daz daz vil edel werde wîp
tæte nâch ir triuwe
ir râche in grôzer riuwe. (Kl 154–58)

[Whoever can understand this story,
he will proclaim her innocent,
because the noble and virtuous woman
acted out of loyalty
to avenge, full of grief.]

Kriemhilt's justification through the central virtue of feudal society has surreptitiously changed it from an element of social connectivity to a personal asset. Only under this condition can the opinion that Kriemhilt is damned to hell be refuted (Kl 556–65):

Sît si durch triuwe tôt gelac,
in gotes hulden manegen tac
sol si ze himele noch geleben.
Got hât uns allen daz gegeben,
swes lîp mit triuwen ende nimt,
daz der zem himelrîche zimt. (Kl 571–76)[53]

[Since she was killed because of her loyalty,
she will find God's grace forever
in heaven.
God has given us all assurance
that whoever ends his life in loyalty
will earn the kingdom of heaven.]

Here the external reference to *triuwe* is capped. If Kriemhilt "is" *triuwe* by nature, then there is no question to whom the obligation applies and what other bonds she violates.

The *Klage* reverses the ambiguity of *triuwe*, but its social content is sacrificed as a result. In the epic this personalization of *triuwe* is only evident in a few passages, but always in competition with other *triuwe* relationships that are more juridically defined. This is how the concept is problematized. The *Klage* attempts to clarify what the epic discusses as an open problem. The *Nibelungenlied* and *Klage* react in opposite ways to what is obviously perceived as a critical social relationship with immanent contradictions (Hagen) and manifest limitations (Kriemhilt). The catastrophe of the *Nibelunge nôt* (2379,4) makes questionable the individualization that *triuwe* experiences through Kriemhilt.

Who Shall Rule?

It is certainly not possible to develop a model of political rule that reflects the situation around 1200 from the *Nibelungenlied.* Attempts to extract some sort of political message from the epic have failed, whether one looks for parallels to imperial politics around 1200, seeing in the *Nibelungenlied* the conflict between the head of the empire and the most powerful nobles,[54] or whether one relates the *alten mæren* to the canonistic discussion of the *idoneitas* of the ruler,[55] or whether, as I myself once asserted, a conflict between ministeriality and the old nobility is assumed.[56] It is true that the political organization of an aristocratic warrior society and its latent antagonisms is part of the story, but there are no definitive solutions, and the conflicts cannot be read simply as a commentary on the contemporary situation.

In the actual opening scene of the story in *Âventiure* 3, the question of who the rightful ruler is plays a decisive role.[57] The starting point is the stable rule in Worms and in Xanten. On the one hand, Gunther is the ideal feudal king,[58] on the other hand, his rule is based on tradition. According to the premises of this system, it is inexplicable that Sivrit, a king's son from Xanten, appearing in Worms to woo the king's daughter, proposes combat with the king that will decide who has the right to rule both kingdoms. Whoever wins, says Sivrit

> *dem sol ez allez dienen, diu liute und ouch diu lant.* (114,3)
>
> [all shall serve him, the people and also the land.]

Sivrit wants to show that he owns *von rehte liute unde lant* [the people and the land by right] (109,3), by proving his ability to secure peace through his personal strength (*ellen*). The same, he suggests, should be true of Gunther:

> *Ine wil es niht erwinden . . .*
> *ez enmüge von dînen ellen dîn lant den fride hân.* (113,1–2)
>
> [I do not want to yield . . .
> unless your land can gain peace through your strength.]

The basis of the rule in Worms is, however, the rule of law: *diu dienent uns von rehte* [they serve us by right] (115,4), objects Gernot. Rulership is secured by dynastic tradition (*des mîn vater lange mit êren hât gepflegen* [which my father held for a long time in an honorable way]) and is not to be jeopardized by *iemannes kraft* [anybody's strength] (112,2–2).[59] Legitimate power is based on the lineage of the royal house, and above all on the hierarchically differentiated ruling elite (strophes 9–12). Sivrit's royal rule in Xanten is elaborated in less detail, but it is essentially the same structure: a ruling elite of *vriunden* based on descent and vassalage.[60] Sivrit also refers to the inherited right to the crown (109,1), but he emphasizes that the ruler's rights and his personal qualifications should coincide.

Sivrit cannot prevail with his challenge, but he does later become entangled with Gunther's bridal quest in a world where what he demanded without success in Worms is valid. In Isenstein, the strongest man rules, and rule is decided in single combat, where only the strongest wins.[61] Sivrit must dissimulate his strength if he does not want to be seen—which is what actually happens—as the contestant. He must deceive Prünhilt. Gunther wins a woman and land thanks to strength, but of course, it is someone else's strength. If Sivrit's symbolic service for Gunther is seen as an allusion to the rein and stirrup service [*Zügel- und Bügeldienst*] of Emperor Friedrich I Barbarossa to Pope Hadrian IV and the resulting dispute over the supremacy of sacred or secular power,[62] then it marks an illegitimate act, and Gunther's role is a deceitful pretense. To what extent Gunther arrogates to himself a role that he does not deserve will be clear after the fight, when political normalcy is reestablished.

The rule is not yet won with Gunther's supposed victory. The transference of power must be accomplished before the entire ruling group, and a relative of the queen steps in to take her part. The principle of rule by physical superiority is augmented by a dynastic principle. This seems to be superfluous,[63] since Prünhilt has subjugated herself and her *mâge* and *man* to Gunther after the contest (466,4). Why does she suddenly demand, before she will follow Gunther to Worms: *ez müezen ê bevinden mâge unt mîne man* [first, my kin and my men must all know] (475,2) and *di mîne besten friunde müezen werden ê besant* [first, my best friends must be sent for] (475,4)? Why does Hagen suddenly mistrust this assembly, as if Prünhilt wanted to reverse the result of the contest? Why does Sivrit go to get help that is never needed, for a gathering that never takes place?[64]

The difficulties increase if one sees that the discussion of legitimate rule is continued. Prünhilt is a queen, as Sivrit had imagined, who rules thanks to her personal strength. Nonetheless, this rule is no more dependent on her alone than is any other in the Middle Ages. The vassals must participate. Prünhilt's desire to have her subjugation to Gunther confirmed by her land corresponds to normal political structures. Simultaneously, she comes closer to the conditions in Worms, where the royal power rests on a complex social structure. Even in Isenstein, Gunther needs a large company of knights so that he can act as an equal. In order to obtain them, Sivrit hurries to Nibelungenland. Thanks to Sivrit, the "public" side of the event—taking control of the land with military power—can to some extent be made up. Once more, Sivrit must demonstratively subordinate himself. This is why he advises Gunther, *daz ir mich habt gesendet, daz sult ir Prünhilde sagen* [that you sent me away, that is what you should tell Prünhilt] (481,4).

In this way, two models of rule become corrupted. Gunther wanted to woo Prünhilt with 30,000 men, a considerable increase over the army needed in the Saxon war (161,1). Sivrit knew better. Prünhilt could only be won *in recken wîse* (341,1), by the strength of single heroes. This is in fact what happens, and the quest should thereby be completed. The return to the order of Worms is prepared, however, and there things are different. In the bridal quest scheme, personal affirmation and demonstrations of power by the political elite go together. In Worms, as Sivrit has to learn, strength plays a secondary role. This is reversed in Isenstein, but in the end it is impossible to forgo without involving the "land."

The countertype, in which strength alone decides, is represented by the *Nibelunge lant*. This was once ruled by a dynasty, but since Sivrit eliminated the heirs, there is neither a ruling elite nor a hierarchy. Here, strength alone is the prerequisite for legitimate rule, as Sivrit proposed in Worms,[65] and it is always put to the test. This is why Sivrit must, even though he is already lord of the *Nibelunge lant*, conquer again what belongs to him. The fight with Alberich is not necessary in terms of the story, but it serves to maintain a principle.

In Nibelungenland, Sivrit can prevail in the latent competition with the established power qua tradition, as represented by Gunther, and he does so on Gunther's own playing field, in his rule over a larger apparatus. His warriors (and not Gunther's men) are the counterweight to Prünhilt's company.[66] It is therefore a further deceit when Gunther unabashedly claims the Nibelungen army for himself: *ez sint mîne man* [they are my men] (509,1). Worms and Nibelungenland mark the extremes in a conflict about dynastic tradition and legitimate rule. Isenstein shifts from one extreme to the other.

In the character of Sivrit are combined opposing options of legitimate rule. Whereas in Nibelungenland, he has gained his own *lant zuo den bürgen* [land, including its castles] (95,4), and thanks to his strength rules as a *landes herre* (500,3), he is still not a king in Xanten, even though he is genealogically predestined to be its ruler. While his parents are still alive, Sivrit declines rule (43,1–2),[67] but he already performs the "most important obligation of rule," which is to protect others from harm.[68] He is both *recke und solde krône tragen* [a hero and inheritor of a crown] (109,1). Only after his actions for Gunther and after his marriage do the two come together, and he becomes king in *Niderlant.* Sigemunt proclaims: *er sol vor disen recken die mîne krône tragen* [he will wear my crown in the presence of these warriors] (713,3).

> *sît was er ir aller meister die er ze rehte vant*
> *unt dar er rihten solde, daz wart alsô getân*
> *daz man sêre vorhte der schœnen Kriemhilden man.* (714,2–4)
>
> [since he was the ruler of all those who belonged to his jurisdiction
> and where he should judge, this was done
> so that the husband of the beautiful Kriemhilt was feared by all.]

The right of succession is marginal when Sivrit finally gains the role of ruler, and he fulfills it as he had previously proclaimed (721–23). Since the old king is still living, and since he accompanies Sivrit to Worms and even follows him in his rule, the natural dynastic succession is again shown to be secondary. The line of succession is maintained only with regard to Kriemhilt, for Sigelint dies during the ten-year pause, making room for her: *dô het den gewalt mit alle der edeln Uoten kint* [the noble Uote's child now had absolute rule] (717,2). The fact that—and this is completely unimportant to the story—Sigelint and not Sigemunt dies, points again to the combination of genealogical and heroic principles in the new rulers of Xanten. In this way, with Sivrit, who wants to rely on his own strength as ruler, there remains until the end a difference from Gunther's kingdom and its transmission through hereditary succession.

The type of *hêrschaft* represented by Sivrit is not to be confused with the *idoneitas* of scholarly political theory in the twelfth century. *Idoneitas* represents a rational principle in the transmission of rule in place of natural hereditary succession. *Idoneitas* is seen in ethical-moral terms, as well as—and this is weaker—the intellectual capacity to govern. Both aspects are argued in the investiture conflict in the Church's political interests and raised against imperial hereditary succession as well as against claims of those (militarily) superior. Rules of secular political action are thereby derived from religion-based ethics (for example, for securing the peace), and the spiritual power is responsible for watching over its implementation. This program of verifiable qualifying criteria is part of a rationalization process that was fostered by the Church in the eleventh and twelfth centuries. In this respect, it argues against the feudal legitimacy of rule through superior force as discussed in the *Nibelungenlied.*[69] A show of strength as suggested by Sivrit would be senseless in light of the political conditions in the late twelfth century. It would be disastrous for the land, because the constant testing of military superiority would result in never-ending warfare.[70] Unlike what the heroic epic and its sympathies might imply, Sivrit represents a highly problematic principle in the politics of 1200. This principle can prevail in the confusion of the territorialization process at best de facto but in no way programmatically. It runs counter to institutionalization and rationalization: its potential for legitimacy can be attributed to a heroic age, and therein lies its paradoxical attractiveness.

Heroic epic maintains older ideas of political rule without having to subject them to a discussion of current politics. The conflict that breaks out in *Âventiure* 3 is not a relic of legend tradition. It does not just cause a "break" in Sivrit's "character," but rather belongs in the center of a worldview that tells anew the story of the superior hero in an inferior environment.[71] It can be found in a different form in Greco-Latin heroic legend, as well as in the chansons de geste, and it can also—sometimes as a misunderstood scheme—be traced to late medieval heroic epic.

This scheme seems to be a pièce de résistance of the heroic world that is inherited even in its deproblematized variants. In *Wolfdietrich D,* for example, it is told how the young Wolfdietrich—a wandering hero like Sivrit—comes to the court of Emperor Ortnit, and how, unprepared and completely superfluous to the story, his simple appearance leads to a conflict about rule. Like Sivrit, Wolfdietrich has set out for Ortnit's court without plans of conquest. Unlike Sivrit, he does not explicitly challenge the lord of the court for his rule. The provocation is indirect. Wolfdietrich lies down under a tree to sleep, although no hero had yet dared go beneath this tree (Wo D 541,1). He thereby penetrates a "protected" realm,[72] which is at the same time a *locus amoenus* and the place of royal judgment. Ortnit feels himself challenged, because Wolfdietrich's behavior can only mean that he lays claim to Ortnit's lands.

> *Er bart, sam wer sin aygen di lut und auch di lant.* (*Wo D* 545,3)
> [He behaves just as if the people and lands were his own.]
> *Ir paret, sam daz riche gancz ewer aigen si.* (Wo D 552,2)
> [You behave as if the kingdom is yours alone.]

Again, this is a conflict between an ordinary, established rule and a strong hero who comes from outside. Wolfdietrich's gesture includes, without saying as much, a claim to a woman, Ortnit's wife—which is why Ortnit suspects her as well, although there is no reason to do so. Ortnit, unlike Gunther, immediately reacts to the challenge:

> *Auch traw ich wol beschirmen vor euch di mynen rich.* (Wo D 553,1)
>
> [I am sure I can protect my lands from you.]

Wolfdietrich agrees immediately to fight him, even though he has sought out Ortnit for completely different reasons. He states, appropriately to the situation:

> *Dar umb ich her zu lande mit euch zu fechten rait.* (Wo D 554,2)
>
> [This is why I have come here to fight with you .]

Rulership will depend upon personal strength. However, as in the *Nibelungenlied*, the situational scheme that has been evoked remains without consequence, and the clash is avoided. The heroes even become allies. The hidden rivalry and the opposition of the various forms of rule they represent, however, are only put aside: later, Wolfdietrich will actually replace Ortnit in his rule and with his wife, because Ortnit will prove incapable of effectively protecting his lands.

This unnecessary scene has paradigmatic meaning for a discussion about legitimate rule from the perspective of the warrior class. The Roman emperor will have to give way in the long term to the intruder, so that the "heroic" type of legitimacy can finally prevail. In the late medieval work, the destructive consequences of this model are eliminated, possibly because such a conflict has no serious connection to political options. Therefore the hero will not destroy legitimate rule but save it, and this rule is not threatened by him but rather by other, subhuman aggressors, this time, the dragons. In addition, the substitution of the one type of rule by the other is bound to a generational change, so that the consequences of the conflict are diffused.

The typology of ruler and rule corresponds to those in the *Nibelungenlied*, but the conflict is blurred in its conclusions. Wolfdietrich's rule does not rival Ortnit's but succeeds and supersedes it—a heroic epic atavism. In the older *Nibelungenlied*, the principle is seriously discussed, too, but proves itself to be fairly unsuccessful. It is only reconciled with the existing order in the short phase of Sivrit's rule in Xanten, when he receives *krône, gerihte und ouch daz lant* [crown, courts, and also the land] (714,1). Here personal and dynastic legitimacy come together, and the "best knight" is also the "best ruler." All admit

> *daz er wære ein der beste, der ie ûf ors gesaz.*
> *man vorhte sîne sterke unt tet vil billîche daz.* (723,3–2)
>
> [that he was one of the best who had ever sat upon a horse.
> People feared his strength and were right to do so.]

Even if it is fully realized only in the marginal zones of Isenstein and Nibelungenland, sometimes in the known world, too, the hero and the ruler are one and the same. This is shown when the king must defend the borders of his land. In the Saxon war, Gunther stays at home instead of leading the Burgundian contingent. The opposing kings are personally engaged. Liudegast himself occupies the *warte* (182–83). Sivrit has to take him prisoner. It is characteristic that some of the Saxons falsely attribute this deed to Gernot and not Sivrit. Liudeger, the other opposing king, alone knows who it really was:

> *wol wesser [Liudeger] daz ez tæte daz Siglinde kint.*
> *man zêh es Gêrnôten: vil wol ervant er ez sint.* (209,3)
>
> [Liudeger knew well that it was Siglinde's son who did it.
> Others thought it was Gernot. Later, he found out that he was right.]

The false assumption, seemingly a functionless ornament, underlines how naturally the first role of hero is attributed to the king (Gernot replacing Gunther here), and how strange the change of roles between Sivrit and Gunther is. King Liudeger must also be personally overcome in battle by the Burgundian leader, Sivrit. Liudeger knows who has beaten him: *Sîvriden den starken hân ich hie bekant* [I have learned that it was Sivrit the Strong] (216,3). In war, outside of the courtly world of Worms, superior strength is linked to the office of the king, and this is why Sivrit's deeds are ascribed to the king.

Sivrit's claim remains a challenge that the king at Worms is ultimately not up to, even though it is never aggressively pressed and in pure form can only be realized "outside," in the heroic world. It fails in the murderous intrigue at Worms. The answer to the question, who shall rule, varies depending on perspective, whether of what should be or of what prevails in the end.

Hero, Nobility, Ruler

The problem of rule and strength is linked to the problem of strength and status through the bridal quest intrigue. It is the consequences of taking up Sivrit's claim to rule in a place where it would have actually been appropriate that lead to open conflict, not the claim itself. Prünhilt maintains that only the strongest can be the pretender and future ruler—as Sivrit claims. By virtue of the betrayal, however, Gunther and the traditional order represented by him are victorious even there. After the return to Worms, Prünhilt integrates herself into the traditional order.[73] Her doubt about Sivrit's status is based on his own words in Isenstein and on the principle, which has prevailed since

Âventiure 3, that a traditional order assigns status independent of personal qualities. This makes it possible that the friction between Sivrit's strength and his status continues, even though it is played down in the political sphere. Once more, Sivrit's superiority is played out in fields where an individual's strength must be proven directly, but where political consequences are excluded: in the royal bedchamber and in the tournament. This proves to be problematic in a number of ways. At stake in the first case is not Gunther's royal rule, but his honor as a man. Sivrit's physical involvement in the wedding night must be hidden from Prünhilt. Brought forward by Kriemhilt as an argument in the dispute over rank, it ultimately results in his murder. In the second case—in the tournament—Sivrit's strength may be demonstrated before the entire court, but in a situation meant to exclude claims of rulership, and so it is not really suited to playing a role in the debate over rank. Prünhilt is not supposed to know the one, the other is of no consequence to her, and he certainly does not get his way.

Prünhilt's direct connection between strength and status results from a faulty deduction. According to her words, it seems that the only alternatives are rule or serfdom, which is why she treats the *man* Sivrit (this is what she calls him in 423,1) at the marriage festival in Worms as *eigenholt*.[74] A political model that only knows subordination as serfdom is archaic and simply unacceptable to the complex feudal order, with its varied and different bonds of dependence between lord and man, both the Nibelungian order in Worms and lay society around 1200. If Prünhilt only knows the alternatives of to order and to obey, lord and servant, it demonstrates her misunderstanding of the world of nobility into which she has married, as shown by Gunther's reaction:

> *des ersmielte Gunther, dô si daz gesprach.*
> *er'n jahes im niht ze dienste, swie dicke er Sîfriden sach.* (728,3–4)
>
> [Gunther smiled at what she said.
> He didn't claim it as a service, as often as he saw Sivrit.]

With Prünhilt's interpretation of Sivrit's status based on what she had heard in Isenstein, a typical theme for heroic epic comes into play: the (false) claim of the king versus his powerful vassals. But, unlike in the chansons de geste, it is told, not as a vassality conflict, but as a conflict between two "kings," or, rather, between a king and a queen.

It is possible to see in this a diffusion of a latent political conflict, which is much more starkly recognizable in other heroic epics. For instance, in the

Book of Bern, a commentary attributes an unjust claim to rule to a new generation of princes who threaten the freedoms of the nobility. The story of the *Nibelungenlied*, on the other hand, emphasizes the accord between the king and his most powerful vassals.[75] The exemplary cooperation of king and vassals and its mortal endangerment through treachery is a central theme, not only of heroic epic from the Migration Era, but also generally of early feudal epic before its courtly makeover.[76]

The endangerment of such harmony is thematized in Sivrit, whose status is blurred. It would be worth considering whether the archaic model, which Prünhilt tries to implement, does not in reality encode the consequences of the contemporary territorialization process, in which the many independent rulers fall victim to one superior ruler.[77] Hagen's words concerning Sivrit's rule, his treasure, and possible advantages for Gunther (774,4; 870,3; 1107,3–4) can be read against the background of those processes precisely because they do not have any specific consequences in the epic story: *wol mich deich sîner hêrschaft hân ze râte getân* [I did well when I ended his magnificence] (993,4).[78]

In Prünhilt's image of society, nobility—along with and in competition with the king—does not exist. She does not assume, as in courtly romances, exclusive equality within the nobility, which is not abrogated through dependence on a ruler. Kriemhilt will therefore refute her claim by insisting on being *adelvrî* [free nobility] (828,1). Nobility, in the epic, is a condition for epic valuation and therefore a natural basis for Sivrit's superiority. As an *eigenholt*, he would be excluded from the ranks of heroes. The quality of nobility takes precedence over everything else. In Eilhart's *Tristrant*, for example, Morolt offers single combat to settle rightful claims only to *der von adele sî so vrî / daz er mîn genôze sî* [anyone who is noble and free, that he might be my equal] (Trt 413–14). He at first rejects Tristrant for this reason as *ungenôz* (Trt 627), and provokes him to the extent that he gives up his incognito and proves that he is *von adele wol vrî* (Trt 632).[79] In Biterolf, Sivrit rejects Heime as an opponent:

> *"der von arde ein künic sî,*
> *dem sult ir wan slege drî*
> *bieten und deheinen mêr;*
> *wan ir sît," sprach der fürste hêr,*
> *"eines küneges eigen man,*
> *ir sult von mir wîchen dan . . . ."* (Bit 10883–88)

> ["To him who is a king by birth
> you should offer only three strokes

and no more,
for you are," said the splendid prince,
"a king's unfree vassal,
you should give way to me . . . ."]

Prünhilt's claim is a fundamental attack on the system of co-, super-, and subordination in feudal society and therefore also attacks the foundations of the Nibelungian world.

Sivrit and Gunther do not have to be engaged in a power struggle, and the murder of Sivrit cannot be explained by the fact that Sivrit is "blinded by greed for honor."[80] Sivrit will never attempt to take Gunther's place. On the contrary, those at Worms take the initiative to rid themselves of him, and to do so exactly when Gunther's kingship no longer needs to be supported by the foreign *künec*, but is threatened by the insult of the queen.[81] The institution proves itself to be—as in the question of the legitimacy of rule—stronger.

In the *Nibelungenlied*, there is no "reduction and weakening of the function of sovereignty" at the cost of the "warrior function."[82] Gunther's much-lamented "weakness" does not entail a crisis in the political institution of the kingdom.[83] The system that Sivrit falls victim to must, on the contrary, be all the stronger the weaker its representative is. The fact that this representative proves to be weak to the point of being laughable does not change his success. When the narrator steers sympathies toward the hero and against the intrigue to which he falls victim, then, as is so often the case in the *Nibelungenlied*, the sympathy is for the underdog, and antipathy goes to the victor. Even Hagen, who carries out the victorious deed, appears up to the end of the first part as a cunning and cowardly representative of a power that cannot hold its own in open confrontation. Not only Gunther, but Hagen as well will profit in the second part from the fact that he no longer stands on the winning side.

Gunther's rulership remains unthreatened until the ruling clan starts off for Etzel. Up until then, danger has always been successfully diverted without the ruler exposing himself to the challenger Sivrit, the Saxons, the heroic virgin Prünhilt, Kriemhilt's attack on the queen's honor, and the misuse of the hoard.[84] Even in the punishment of Hagen for the theft of the hoard, the royal (rightful) power prevails.[85]

Heroes in Exile

The political structure seems to change from this point on. In the second part of the epic, the holders of court offices disappear from the story, with the exception of the marshal, Dancwart, who is still needed in his official capacity,[86] but later only as a hero and Hagen's brother. Volker, who plays no role in the first part of the epic comes aboard. Where did the others go? In the case of Rumolt, the absence is explained. The derision he is shown is also meant for the institutionalized form of rule that he represents.[87] The other officeholders are not much better off. The redactor of *C has at least noticed the absence of the steward Ortwin,[88] none other than the eager spokesman of the Burgundians against the aggressor Sivrit (116–17), who refuses to go on the dangerous journey, because he has to take care of *des geschaftes hie haime* [business at home] (a 1502,2).

Apart from this, the entire ruling elite sets out on the journey. Travel is not performed *in recken wîse*; instead, a huge military force is assembled. Once they arrive at Etzel's court, however, it quickly disappears. The baggage train plays a secondary role and is written off at the first opportunity. The personnel are quickly reduced to epic heroes and even most of these remain nameless, numbers to be crossed off. Hagen and, later, Volker take over. In the case of Etzel's courtship, Hagen is still clearly the loser. After receiving the invitation, his advice is at first not accepted, but after being provoked, he himself becomes an advocate of the journey. From then on, starting with the journey to Etzel's realm, he takes the lead. Gunther and his brothers become extras. Hagen conveys the army across the Danube; Volker leads it through Bavaria; Hagen and Dancwart defend the rearguard from enemy attacks.

This does not mean that the feudal powers fatefully prevail against the monarchy, as in the contemporary Holy Roman Empire, and that the *Nibelungenlied* tells of the tragic downfall of the feudal system.[89] Vassal subordination is never called into question. On the contrary, it triumphs in Rüedeger's decision for the king, as it does in Hagen's self-destructive service to Gunther, Gernot, and Giselher. The disintegration of royal power does not depend on the standard conflict of heroic epic as in the French usurper epics; on the contrary, vassals remain constantly true and kings are never the enemies of vassals.[90] Nowhere is there rebellion, yet still Gunther's and Etzel's kingdoms are destroyed.

As the distance from Worms increases, the Burgundians seem to become more and more a company of equals. This is evident in Bechelaren with the conspicuous marriage between the youngest king, Giselher, and the daughter of Margrave Rüedeger, Etzel's vassal. This striking *connubium* becomes the explicit subject of discussion. Volker remarks on Rüedeger's equality with a prince.

> *"Ob ich ein fürste wære," sprach der spilman,*
> *"und solde ich tragen krône, ze wîbe wold' ich hân*
> *die iuwern schœnen tohter . . . ."* (1675,1–3)
>
> ["If I were a prince," said the minstrel,
> "and should I have a crown, even then I would want to have
> your beautiful daughter as a wife . . . "]

Rüedeger contradicts this. He understands *fürste* as *künec* (1676,2) and emphasizes the difference in rank: *waz hülfe grôziu schœne der guoten juncvrouwen lîp?* [what would extraordinary beauty matter for the good young lady?] (1676,4),[91] but his opinion is rejected at once. A king—Gernot—would overlook this (1677,2), since *schœne* is by itself already a quality of nobility. And Hagen recommends the marriage with Giselher (1678,4).[92] This leveling of social differences is more pointed in ms. C, where even the absence of property is regarded as completely unimportant. Rüedeger bolsters his objections there once again by stating: *vnd haben niht ze gebene* [and they have nothing to give] (C 1715,4), but only so that Gernot can strengthen the daughter's royal rank with the statement that he would even take her *ane guot ze wibe* [as a wife without property] (C 1716,3).

At Etzel's court, the king's power vanishes more and more. Gunther attempts in vain to prevent (1887) Volker from killing a Hun courtier. There is no hint of sanction. In the ensuing chaos, the king stands by his man. King Etzel can still smooth out the incident, but then he, too, loses control, like the Burgundian kings, when the battle is finally joined:

> *sine mohtenz mit ir sinnen dô niht understân,*
> *dô Volkêr unde Hagene sô sêre wüeten began.* (1967,3–4)
>
> [They were unable to stop it with reasonable argument,
> when Volker and Hagen began to rage.]

In the regression to direct violence, the political order breaks down.

Now only heroes count: Dietrich of Bern, Hildebrant and the Amelungen, Rüedeger, Irinc, Irnfrit, Hagen, and, on the same level, the kings from Worms. Differences of status are not disregarded in this group, as shown by the Amelungen, but they are less important. Everyone tries to do his best. In *Biterolf*, it is stated once what a king should be in such a situation:

> *sô was er einer drunder*
> *unde iedoch besunder*
> *der beste den man dô vant.* (Bit 1343–45)

[So he was one of them,
yet still above them,
the best to be found then.]

On the Huns' side, aside from the king and his brother, only the exiled heroes, including the *ellende* margrave Rüedeger, count.[93] On the Burgundian side, the alliance between Hagen and Volker forms the core of the company. At Etzel's court, all heroes are *ellende*, that is, uproooted from the social context into which they were born. Under these conditions, feudal *milte* is no longer a means of rulership, but an *acte gratuit*. Therefore it is not the king, but a vassal, the margrave, who most excels in *milte*. He is called the *vröude ellender diete* [the joy of exiled men] (2258,4), because *er ist den ellenden holt* [he is generous to the exiles] (2245,4). He was, in fact, once one of them. Etzel's Burgundian guests are called *ellende*,[94] too, inasmuch as they enjoy Etzel's hospitality (1812,4). They are on the same level as the other heroes in exile. The meaning of *ellende* moves from "alien" to "without protection" and "standing outside the ordinary (Hunnish) order."[95] The decisive final battles only take place between those exiled, the Amelungen (*Wir sîn ouch ellende als Rüedegêr der degen* [we are also exiles, like the hero Rüedeger], 2263,1), Dietrich (2329,3; 2345,4) and the *ellenden* Burgundian survivors (2364,4). They all have fallen out of the normal political world.

Solidarities within this heroic world function beyond the borders of adversaries, but they do not form lasting social relationships. The assembly of exiled heroes is finally anarchic. Vassalic and familial bonds are marginalized. When Rüedeger executes the will of the king, this does not prevent him from giving the enemy Hagen a shield. Hagen also suspends the obligation to his kings in favor of that to his *vriunt*, and Volker also joins in the *fride* [peace] that Rüedeger grants *mîn geselle Hagene* (2203,2).

In the literary topography of the heroic epic, Etzel's court is a place of unequal equality. It is the counterpart to the Arthurian court, but clearly exclusive, based on high nobility. At Arthur's court, the kings' sons are only knights. In Etzel's court, differences of status are never discarded. Seen from the perspective of the Christian feudal world, this court is itself exile. The heroes there come from various *gentes* and hold their rank, not by the grace of Etzel, but by birth. There is no serious conflict over rule. The world around is peaceful. Everyone just seems to be waiting for a call to battle.[96] Unlike in the Arthurian court, Etzel and his warriors do not aim to propagate order in a chaotic world. Etzel's court has no mission. He merely offers the temporarily inactive heroes a home and support.[97]

This basic pattern can be recognized in *Biterolf*, which represents the unproblematic variant. Etzel is only the first among equals. He acts on behalf of his followers (who do not abuse his riches), but he remains dependent on them, whether to conquer a town (Bit 1468–72) or to save his life (Bit 1588–93). His power grows thanks to the guests (Bit 1788–89). The *geste* have left their identity in feudal society behind—in Biterolf's case, going all the way to keeping his name and his kingship secret:

> *er gedâhte im eines namen:*
> *er dorfte sichs niht enschamen;*
> *der in von wâren schulden truoc,*
> *biderbe was er genuoc;*
> *er was ein recke ûz Tenelant,*
> *Diete*[98] *sô was er genant.* (Bit 1905–10)
>
> [He thought up a name for himself:
> he would not be ashamed of it;
> the one who had it by right,
> was perfectly fine;
> he was a hero from Tenelant,
> he was called Diete.]

By choosing the Amelung name Diete, which is related to his son's, Biterolf opts for being a hero and against his inherited rank of king.[99]

Antagonism, which was such a determining factor in the first part of the *Nibelungenlied*, is dissolved at Etzel's court. Strength alone matters, but it does not in any way endanger rulership. An undisputed king rules over all strong heroes and guarantees their livelihood. The king himself is completely concentrated on his formal role as host. Former social positions have no concrete political meaning in exile. One "is" king, without ruling. Rank does not have to be performed. The inherited rank is only set aside for a time. The reasons for exile are blurred in the *Nibelungenlied*, unlike in *Waltharius*, the *Book of Bern*, and *Rabenschlacht*, and can only be gleaned from secondary references (tribute, banishment, blood debt). The consequences are disregarded.[100] There is no question of return (and if, as in the *Klage*, it is nonetheless undertaken, it seems to be based on the exiled Dietrich's decision alone). In this way, Etzel's extraterritorial court creates a laboratory environment in which political structures are ignored, so that everyone can just be a hero.

The prerequisite is not royal rank, but noble status. The hero is not an outsider, and even in exile, he is recognized as an equal. Unlike in the courtly epic, it seems that for the pre-courtly and heroic epic of the twelfth century, even a temporary suspension of ranking is impossible. Where doubts might arise, they are explicitly rectified. Volker is a musician, for example, but above all—and the narrator seems to want to make this point perfectly clear—he is a noble warrior and lord:

> *er was ein edel herre. im was ouch undertân*
> *vil der guoten recken in Burgonden lant.*
> *durch daz er videlen konde, was er der spilman genant.* (1477,2–4)
>
> [He was a noble lord. Many of the
> great heroes in Burgundy were subject to him.
> Because he could play the fiddle, he was called a minstrel.]

Heritage and status are not, as so often in the courtly romance, secondary and only subsequently validated by the individually gained rank,[101] but belong to the prerequisites for heroic action. The fact that status and personal strength are no longer in conflict in the second part of the epic only operates under the conditions of exile.

Rehter heldes muot

The only thing that matters in the final episodes is the single *helt, recke, herre.* Thus the tendency begun in the first part asserts itself. Already with Sivrit, what matters is being a lord.[102] The epithet *hêrlîch* denotes everything that distinguishes such a lord. This can be the appearance of women (786,3), the retinue (794,1: *Daz hêrlîche gesinde*), or a sword (2185,3). The hero Hagen, when he comes to identify Sivrit, is described thus: *man sach in hêrlîche mit recken hin ze hove gân* [he was seen going to court with heroes as a lord] (82,4). Sivrit is called this when he is seen for the first time in Worms: *daz ez sî der recke, der dort so hêrlîchen gât* [that it is the hero, who goes there in the manner of a lord] (86,4), and when he meets up with the hunting company's camp, *Wie rehte hêrlîchen er zen herbergen reit* [How he rode to the encampment the way a lord does] (951,1), *der hêrlîche jägere der was hôhe gemuot* [the hunter, behaving like a lord, was in high spirits] (955,4). Sivrit is still called the *hêrlîche gast* (977,4) before Hagen's spear hits him. *Hêrlîch* is the appearance in battle of the blood-smeared Dancwart (*man sach den Hagenen bruoder ze hove hêrlîchen gân* [Hagen's brother was seen going to court like a lord], 1947,4), also of Wolfprant (*dô sach man Wolfpranden in strîte hêrlîche gân* [Wolfprant was seen fighting like a lord], 2281,4), and of Gunther in his last battle (*ez het der künec Gunther einen hêrlîchen muot* [King Gunther had a spirit like a lord], 2359,4). Where the appearance of heroic superiority belies differences of special rank,[103] when Hagen and Volker refuse to greet Kriemhilt, it is stated: *Nu dûhten sich sô hêre die zwêne küene man* [The two bold men thought themselves to be like lords] (1786,1).

Hagen talks about Sivrit's *hêrschaft* (993,4) in the sense of a dangerous superiority:

> *wir vinden ir vil wênic, die türren uns bestân.*
> *wol mich deich sîner hêrschaft hân ze râte getân.* (993,3–4)
>
> [We find only few who will dare to stand up against us.
> I did well when I put an end to his lordlike status.]

Hêrschaft here must refer to another kind of lordly being, one which is opposed to Gunther's institutional rulership.[104] In the future, the Burgundians have nothing to fear from this kind of superiority. It will be dangerous for them again only in an environment where they meet their own kind: in exile at Etzel's court.

The downfall of the Burgundians appears to be a triumph of heroic identity. The actors become "themselves" (again). This reverberates in Hagen's decision, without consideration of the danger for himself and others, to accompany the kings to Etzel. Hagen wants to demonstrate [*erzeigen*][105] that there is no one *der getürre rîten mit iu ze hove baz* [who will have more courage to ride to court with you] (1464,3–4). The undertaking provides an opportunity to prove something to oneself. This continues in the fight against the Bavarians: *sie versuochten wer si wâren; dâ wart vil grimme gestriten* [they tested who they were: they fought with great determination] (1608,4). Helmut de Boor rationalizes this by translating it as "erprobten, was sie leisten konnten" [(they) sought to prove what they could do].[106] It is not what they "can do" that is at stake, but what or who they "are." It is about a heroic identity that ignores all other roles and is fought out in battle, man to man. The explication of the quoted sentence in the following strophe is therefore: *Wie möhten sich versuochen immer helde baz?* [How could heroes test themselves any better?] (1609,1). The *erzeigen* and *versuochen* refer to an audience. The only measure is honor, whether a move is tactically clever or not. Even when they anticipate an attack by the Bavarians, the Burgundians by no means want to hurry across the land, because the appearance of fear would be shameful:

> *diu ross diu sult ir lâzen deste sanfter gân,*
> *daz des iemen wæne, wir vliehen ûf den wegen.* (1593,2–3)

[Make your horses walk all the more slowly,
so that no one might think that we are running away down the roads.]

All that counts is proving oneself a *helt* [hero], and the story is only concerned with *helden*. The hostile ferryman *was ein helt zen handen* [was a brave hero] (1603,4), as is the Bavarian duke Gelpfrat (1613,3). Now Gunther also receives the standing that was previously denied him, and he is no longer just king: *er was ein helt zen handen* [he was a brave hero] (1968,4); *helt* means he who has *helde sin* [heroic intent] (2208,2). This is not a "break" in the "character" of Gunther, who has grown from the "weakling" to the hero who fights to the last drop of blood; rather, it is the consequence of a suspension of political order in Hunnish exile.

"To become a hero" is the only positive perspective for action. All that exists is the rating scale of superior strength. After he has witnessed Volker in battle, Hagen regrets that he—thanks to birth?—has taken a higher place (2005,1–2). The kings are also judged in comparison to other warriors:

doch sach man vor in allen Gîselheren stân
gegen den vîanden . . . . (1971,2–3)

[Giselher was seen standing in front of them all
against the enemies. . . .]

Giselher's counsel cannot be given higher praise than being called the counsel of a *degen*, because this means that it is not just the counsel of a king:

"Sô wol mich sölhes herren," sprach dô Hagene.
"der rât enzæme niemen wan einem degene,
den uns mîn junger herre hiute hât getân . . . ." (2012,1–3)

["Thank goodness for such a lord," said Hagen.
"This counsel, which my young lord has given today,
is suited only for a hero . . . ."]

The king is replaced by the hero.

When, at the festive meal, the hierarchy breaks down, whoever cannot fight is in a difficult spot. It is said of Etzel: *waz half in daz er künec was?* [what good did it do him that he was a king?] (1982,4). From now on, what counts is the claim *daz die herren væhten z'aller vorderôst* [that the lords fight in the front line] (2020,2). Etzel, too, does not want to be left behind, and must be prevented by force from rushing headlong into the melee: *daz von sô rîchen fürsten selten nu geschiht* [something that today occurs only rarely with powerful princes] (2022,2), as the narrator states with respect. The rank of king might only increase the luster of the hero, so that Wolfhart can be proud that a king gave him his mortal wound (2302,4). Rüedeger, too, only has to prove in the end that he is a hero:

> *dô lief er zuo den gesten einem degen gelîch.* (2206,3)
>
> [He rushed at the foreigners like a hero.]
>
> *dem tet des tages Rüedegêr harte wol gelîch,*
> *daz er ein recke wære . . . .* (2213,3–2)
>
> [Rüedeger acted like him (Gunther) that day,
> in order to show that he was a hero . . .]

The Burgundians let Rüedeger into the hall *durch mortræchen willen*, in order to kill him: *si heten helde sin* [they had a hero's intent] (2208,1–2).

In the lament of Rüedeger's death, the dissolution of hierarchies is evident: there rises a lament so *ungefuoge* [out of measure] (2234,4; 2237,4), *daz palas unde türne von dem wuofe erdôz* [that palace and towers resounded with the cry] (2235,2). This must, it is believed, refer to the king or the queen: *wie möhtens' anders alle haben solhe nôt* [how else could everyone be in such grief?] (2237,1). In reality, it is the *recke* Rüedeger who is lamented. This "mistake" is only related in order to highlight all the more effectively the true valuation. It is not the death of the king but of the hero that stirs such grief.

The Amelungen are also pulled into the fight, and once more structures of political order dissolve. King Dietrich had strictly forbidden his people to join in the battle and taken care until the very end that they were not involved in Kriemhilt's revenge. He had "divorced" them from the tournament [*bûhurt*] (1874–75), had desired *vride* from the Burgundians at the festival (1992,2), had kept himself and his men distant, and did not even let himself get involved as a go-between (2137). Even when asking for the circumstances surrounding Rüedeger's death, he seeks to avoid any provocation (2240). This forestalling is repeatedly questioned (1993; 2239; 2246), most vehemently by the young hero Wolfhart. And it is Wolfhart who sets the stage when the Amelungen go to the Burgundians to get more information.

In the mutual provocation of Wolfhart and Volker, King Gunther cannot prevent the outbreak of violence. When Wolfhart refers to his lord's prohibition of fighting, Volker answers in a provocative manner:

> *der vorhte is gar ze vil,*
> *swaz man im verbiutet, derz allez lâzen wil.*
> *daz kan ich niht geheizen rehten heldes muot.* (2268,1–3)

> That is too fearful,
> when a man leaves undone whatever was forbidden to him.
> I cannot call that a true heroic spirit.]

Rehte[r] heldes muot apparently does not have constraints placed on it from above, not even by the king. Negotiating is already derisively termed *vlêgen* (2265), and the threats escalate. Wolfhart's *tumber zorn* [unconscious wrath] can no longer be held back by considerations for the *herren hulde* [the grace of his lord] (cf. 2271,3–4). With the renunciation of *hulde*, social bonds are ripped apart.

After Dietrich's attempt to maintain peace has failed (2137) as well, the only alternative open to him is to fight, and this of course means:

> *Dô gewan er wider rehten heldes muot.* (2325,1)
>
> [Then he regained his true heroic spirit.]

He encounters the surviving Hagen and Gunther in single combat not as king but as a hero.[107]

In a duel of words with Hagen and Gunther, the dissolution of the political structure continues. Dietrich requires atonement for what the Burgundians have done to him by killing his men (*wider mich ellenden*, 2329,3), first from King Gunther (2336–37). Hagen answers, however, and turns the offer down (2238).[108] The *man* declares himself to be the subject of the action. Dietrich then turns to both, *Gunther unde Hagene* (2339,2), but again only Hagen answers. The word duel continues between Hagen and Hildebrant, both of them *man*, and Dietrich—the final vestige of kingly power?—forbids Hildebrant to continue speaking, but then directs his speech only to Hagen, speaking as an exiled hero himself:

> *mich ellenden recken twingent grœzlîchiu sêr.* (2345,4)
>
> [I, an exiled hero, am hard pressed by grief.]

Hagen is his equal (2346,1–2).

Now even Gunther may be a hero, so that the honor of the final battle remains his. He brings Dietrich to the edge of defeat and demonstrates *einen hêrlîchen muot,* namely, the *muot* of a hero (2359,4). In the climax of the final combat in this respect, there remains at least a remnant of ranking, but Hagen will be the one who is killed last, so that up until the final scene, the balance is precisely maintained. What is avenged in the end is not the death of the king, Gunther, whom his sister Kriemhilt has beheaded, but the death of the *man*

Hagen. Where King Etzel only complains of Kriemhilt's deed, even though he acknowledges the terrible Hagen in death (*swie vîent ich im wære, ez ist mir leide genuoc* [as much as I was his enemy, I am sorry for him], 2374,4), the *man* Hildebrant performs a kind of macabre poetic justice. No royal power reestablishes the law. Hildebrant may be as unconcerned about the consequences of his action (*swaz halt mir geschiht* [whatever may happen to me], 2375,2) as Hagen was before.

The rush in which the kings become heroes goes hand in hand with the radical destruction of the order whose peaceful stabilization is what they had been fighting for.[109] Those who had warned against "heroization" are degraded step by step, from Rumolt, the hero and holder of a high court office, who is degraded to an ordinary cook, to the border guard Eckewart, who sleeps through his role, to Dietrich, who at first only speaks and then sits around moping, until he, too, becomes a hero again. Only he, Hildebrant, and Etzel remain alive. The *Klage* conveniently allows new social and political units to be (re)established. Mercifully, there are no more heroes.

Frouwen ziehen

What appears besides the heroes does not amount to much. This is especially true of the groups to which the nobility around 1200 owed the most: women and the *clerici*. Women do not play an important part in heroic epic, and if they do, then it is often a fairly dubious one.[110] Heroic epic is about a man's world. This is so matter-of-fact that Gunther, in front of Prünhilt's castle can only imagine the Amazon-like Prünhilt and her ladies under the protection of a male lord:

> *swi ir herre heize, si sint vil hôhe gemuot.* (390,4)[111]
>
> [Whoever is their lord, they are full of spirit.]

Heroic epic is dominated by a negative image of women.[112] The *Rosengarten* especially sketches a distorted picture of female power that provokes punishment and violent reactions by men. In *Biterolf*, this image is pushed back, but Brünhilt has some traits of Kriemhilt in the *Rosengarten*, who takes delight in the bloody conflicts of men. The *Nibelungenlied* creates a completely different picture only at the beginning.

The *tugende* [virtues] of the young Kriemhilt (3,4) mirror ideal courtly harmony. These *tugende*, however, unlike what the falcon dream seems to announce, are not an incentive for the education of the man—as *Minnesang* declares again and again—but for heroic deeds. The woman is subjugated by the man's power and serves the honor of his court.[113] This is why the men watch over the women's *zuht* [education, upbringing]. They, not the men, are objects of education. Male power includes brute punishment. When Kriemhilt crosses the line, drawn by *fuoge*, with her insult of Prünhilt, Sivrit criticizes her behavior as *üppelîch* and *ungefüege*, that is, uncontrolled, giving in to spontaneous impulses, and therefore disruptive:

> *"Man sol sô vrouwen ziehen," sprach Sîfrit der degen,*
> *"daz si üppelîche sprüche lâzen under wegen.*
> *verbiut ez dînem wîbe, der mînen tuon ich sam.*
> *ir grôzen ungefüege ich mich wærlîchen scham."* (862)
>
> ["Women should be kept in such a way," said Sivrit the hero,
> "that they leave their dissolute speeches be.
> Forbid it of your wife, I shall do the same of mine.
> I am truly ashamed of their great immodesty."]

What *vrouwen ziehen* means is already made clear by the threatening undertone of the preceding strophe (861), and Kriemhilt later confirms:

> *"Daz hât mich sît gerouwen," sprach daz edel wîp.*
> *"ouch hât er sô zerblouwen dar umbe mînen lîp;*
> *daz ich iz ie geredet daz beswârte ir den muot,*
> *daz hât vil wol errochen der helt küene unde guot."* (894)
>
> ["I have since regretted that," said the noble woman.
> "He beat me soundly for it,
> that I ever spoke what weighed heavily on her (Prünhilt's) mind,
> the bold and great hero made me pay for it."]

Behind the courtly *zuht*, whose most perfect example is Kriemhilt, another kind of discipline comes to the fore that is richly attested in medieval narratives. The story of Sibote, where a woman is treated like a horse to tame her, shows what kind of education this is. As Sivrit is contemplating his rights to punishment, it is already too late. The calamity that is set in motion by two women takes its course. It becomes ever more clear that female power is dangerous and must therefore be eliminated.[114]

This lesson is first taught by Prünhilt's rule, which is associated with demonic powers. She turns a chivalrous contest into a game of life and death: *der ir dâ gert ze minnen, diu ist des tiuveles wîp* [the one you hope to love is the devil's wife] (438,4).[115] Prünhilt's strength endangers the patriarchal order:

> *suln uns in disen landen nu verderben diu wîp?* (443,4)[116]
>
> [Will the women in this land be our downfall?]

Prünhilt defends herself in vain against subjugation by a man, first in the contest, then when Dancwart begins to squander her wealth, and finally on the wedding night. When Sivrit is in danger of losing the fight in bed, he gains strength from the idea that his loss would fundamentally endanger male dominance:

> *"Owê," gedâht' der recke, "sol ich nu mînen lîp*
> *von einer magt verliesen, sô mugen elliu wîp*
> *her nâch immer mêre tragen gelpfen muot*
> *gegen ir manne, diu ez sus nimmer getuot."* (673)
>
> ["Oh no," thought the hero, "if I now lose my life
> at the hands of a woman, then all women will
> from now on be disrespectful
> to their husbands, who would otherwise never do so."]

Prünhilt's subjugation (by the wrong man) confirms who is the lord and who has to follow whom.

> *ich hân daz wol erfunden, daz du kanst vrouwen meister sîn.* (678,4)
>
> [I have seen very well that you can certainly handle a woman.]

Prünhilt is tamed. The first and third time she is thrown down; the second attempt does not result in any lasting conflict.[117] Kriemhilt, on the other hand, breaks the chains of male *zuht*. To the extent that she is given the possibility of independent action, the world spins out of control. Even the possession of property is dangerous in her case. When she uses the hoard she inherited from Sivrit to bring foreign warriors into the land, Hagen remarks:

> *ez solde ein frumer man*
> *deheinem einem wîbe niht des hordes lân.* (1130,1–2)
>
> [A wise man should
> not leave the hoard to any woman.]

Kriemhilt feels unsatisfied with what she gets from her new husband:

> *ez gewan küniges tohter nie rîcheite mêr*
> *danne der mich Hagen âne hât getân.* (1276,2–3)
>
> [A king's daughter never gained greater riches
> than those Hagen has stolen from me.]

The message is repeated over and over to the listener that the ruthless revenge is the work of a woman who sacrifices her closest relatives:

> *Z'einen sunewenden der grôz mort geschach,*
> *daz diu vrouwe Kriemhilt ir herzen leit errach*
> *an ir næhsten mâgen und ander manigem man,*
> *dâ von der künec Etzel vreude nimmer mêr gewan.* (2086)
>
> [At the solstice came the great slaughter,
> when Kriemhilt took vengeance for her grief
> on her nearest kin and many others.
> Because of this, King Etzel could never again be joyful.]

The revenge itself is less scandalous than is the fact that it is executed by a woman. When Kriemhilt herself kills Hagen, this is too much even for Etzel. He would otherwise have reason to want the murderer of his son dead, but it is a woman who slays him:

> *"Wâfen . . . wie ist nu tôt gelegen*
> *von eines wîbes handen der aller beste degen . . . ."* (2374,1–2)
>
> ["Alas . . . how the best of all warriors
> lies dead now by the hands of a woman . . . ."]

This is wrong, and it is why Hildebrant avenges his dead enemy (2375,1–2). It is an act of "discipline." Kriemhilt has dared to do something that she had no right to do and is therefore "punished." The *zuht* must make sure that the courtly *vrouwe* does not in fact become the lord. What seems at first to fit the culture of courtly love is reversed, with the approval of the narrator, step by step into a story about male power over women.

The fearfully fantasized, superior woman is a stereotype of heroic epic, as is her forceful punishment. The Kriemhilt of the *Rosengarten* subjugates herself to male strength, but she wants to view the mutual slaughter of men as entertainment, and this shows that something is lacking in her "discipline": *warumbe lât ir den willen ir? Warzuo hât ir sie gezogen?* [why do you let her have her way? What is the role you educated her for?] (Ro A 174,2). She is punished by the bloody defeat of everyone fighting for her, but also in that the reward for the winner is harmful: she had promised to each victorious hero a *helsen und küssen* [an embrace and kisses]. Now in kissing her, the combatants scratch her face until it bleeds. If in the Kriemhilt of the *Nibelungenlied* one can still recognize the image of a courtly *vrouwe*, despite its perversion, an image that spurs the knight to his highest achievements, then this image is twisted here into a caricature of female tyranny that gets what it deserves.

The same stereotype can even be found in *Kudrun*, where otherwise the political order relies on women. The raw and violent character of the phrase *vrouwen ziehen* is even more ruthless there. It refers to the bloodbath that is caused by the hero Wate against Kudrun's opponents. He comments on his slaughter of the women with the words:

> *Ich bin kamerære; sus kan ich frouwen ziehen.* (*K* 1528,3)
>
> [I am the chamberlain; I know how to discipline women.]

This kind of brutal "education" even here seems to be the price for the fact that the peace in *Kudrun* is in the end the work of a woman instead of a man. Normally this is pointless, according to Wate: *solte ich nu frouwen volgen, war tæte ich mînen sin?* [if I were to listen to women, where would my head be?] (K 1491,2).

Even the *Klage*, otherwise so concerned about harmonizing everything, does not change this estimation. A few words of regret from Hildebrant about Kriemhilt's death is as far as it goes. Sanctions, such as Hildebrant himself might fear (*swaz halt mir geschiht* [whatever happens to me], 2375,2), are absent. There is only one way to justify Kriemhilt, and that is to use the favorite cliché of female weakness: it was the limited insight of a woman (*kranke sinne*, Kl 243; cf. 1910) that caused such terrible results. Revenge fundamentally contradicts the female gender, but Kriemhilt had no choice, since no man would help her:

> *sine hete mit ir henden,*
> *ob si möhte sîn ein man,*
> *ir schaden, als ich mich verstân,*
> *errochen manege stunde.*
> *Geschehen ez nin kunde,*
> *wand si hete vrouwen lîp.* (Kl 128–133).
>
> [With her own hands,
> had she been a man,
> she would have avenged her wrongs,
> that's what I think, many times.
> It couldn't happen that way
> because she was a woman.]

The narrator calls the cause of the downfall of the Burgundians a *wunder*. Two kingdoms might be destroyed by the great pathos of heroes, but hardly by the *zorn* of a woman:

Für wunder sol manz immer sagen
daz sô vil helde wart erslagen
von eines wîbes zorne. (Kl 317–319)

[It should certainly always be considered a marvel
that so many heroes were killed
on account of a woman's wrath.]

The story is worth telling because such revenge lies well outside the ordinary:

des hât man immer genuoc
dâ von noch ze sagene,
wie daz kœm daz Hagene
sturbe von einem wîbe. (Kl 736–39)

[Even today people
have enough to tell about
how Hagen came
to die at the hands of a woman.]

This is so incredible that many believe it to be a *lüge* [lie], even though it is *wârheit* [truth] (Kl 743–43). The *Klage* does not justify Kriemhilt but rather excuses her because she was just a woman. Exemplary courtly *zuht*, as initially represented by her, is just the other side of weakness and, if this should be forgotten, requires male discipline.

Why is the pfaffe *the Hero's Victim?*

The role of the *clerici* is completely marginal.[118] Their assessment can be seen in the poor priest [*pfaffe*], whom Hagen first throws into the Danube and then reluctantly saves. Why is it the *pfaffe*, of whom we otherwise hear nothing, who is almost killed by Hagen and then is the only one saved?

To understand the scene, we need to consider the role of *pfaffen* in comparable texts. The *pfaffe* in the *Nibelungenlied* remains quite nondistinct, and is, for example, not characterized by the *wîsheit* that would otherwise distinguish his order. Thanks to this *wîsheit*, the *pfaffe* can act as a careful counselor in dangerous undertakings and as a counterpoint to heroic audacity. In Herbort's *Liet von Troye*, for example, one of the sons of Priamus, Elenus, warns in the king's council of the fatal consequences of the adventure advocated by Paris. His criticism is haughtily rejected, because it is well known what somebody like him has to say:

Armer bleiche wissage
Vnseliger cappelan
Ir soldet zv dem bethus gan
We uwern buchen. . . . (LvTr 2266–69)

[Poor pale prophet,
miserable chaplain,
you should go to church
to your books. . . .]

Someone who counsels caution is a *pfaffe.*

The *pfaffe* can prognosticate the future, especially the unhappy ending of heroic action. The *Liet von Troye* offers a number of prophets of doom, and they are all characterized by the fact that they have wisdom from books.[119] Prophesizing is rationalized as a book science. Those who know books are, according to the contemporary understanding, above all *clerici,* and consequently some of the forecasters of future ill fate are also described as such.

There is nothing of the kind in the *Nibelungenlied.* Neither bishop nor chaplain takes part in warning against the dangerous journey. This is a matter for the warriors themselves, at first Hagen and Rumolt, later Eckewart and Dietrich. Other voices are not heard. The role of the *wissagen,* too, belongs, not to the world of books, but to prophetically gifted wise women and dreams. Their interpretation does not require book learning. The *pfaffe* has no role to play.

In the *Nibelungenlied,* there are traces of a switch. The *pfaffe* is deliberately removed. He is neither really needed to be the object of the sprites' gloomy prophesy nor as a means to test their veracity. Anyone else in the army would do just as well. But the *pfaffe* must, where he is not in the know, at least be the victim of knowledge. It is another kind of knowledge represented by Hagen and the *merwîp. Gotes hant* (1579,3), however, saves its servant.

In Hagen's unfounded aggression (*zornec,* 1578,3) and the ridicule of the helplessness of the *pfaffe* (he can't swim, he flails about *genôte,* and shakes off his wet clothes on the other side of the river), there lies the remnant of a conflict as told by the *Liet von Troye,* the conflict between fearless warriors and cautious clerics. In the *Nibelungenlied,* this conflict is even pointedly blasphemous. Hagen grabs the priest *ob dem heilectuome* [near the altar] (1575,2) and tries to drown him. At the same time, the heart of the conflict is shifted to the disadvantage of the *pfaffe,* for he is completely passive, and not only can he not prophesy, he can't even swim. It is an image of a pitiful clown, a character who knows nothing except that the hero's mythic knowledge can test him. The boundary between knowledge and non-knowledge does not run between *miles* and *clericus*, but instead between the warriors themselves. The *pfaffe* is completely uninvolved. Even God, in saving him, confirms for the hero what he knows from the water sprites.[120]

Where the spiritual guide is absent for the rest of the journey, Hagen takes over. Hagen, who is no *pfaffe*, is from now on the prophet of doom who correctly gauges the situation, but who also prevents anyone from flinching. He prepares the Burgundians for their church visit (1850–56) not only by proposing functional, aggressive equipment but also by recommending appropriate prayers and a penitential state of mind:

> *ir sult vil willeclîchen zuo der kirchen gân,*
> *und klaget got dem rîchen sorge und iuwer nôt,*
> *und wizzet sicherlîchen daz uns nâhet der tôt.*
>
> *Ir'n sult ouch niht vergezzen,*
> *swaz ir habet getân, und sult vil vlîzelîche dâ gein gote stân.* (1855,2–1856,2)
>
> [You should want to go to church
> and pray to mighty God for your cares and your trouble,
> and be assured that we are close to the hour of death.
>
> You should also not forget all that you have done
> and stand before God with all zeal.]

How this can be reconciled with his "character" is a question that goes beyond the logic of substitution. If piety was a part of courtly life, then it now guides the heroic battle to the last drop of blood. There will be no church service after this scene in the epic—the *Klage* will make up for this—but it does refute the assertion that there is a contradiction between Christian piety and heroic self-assertion. Thus, the *pfaffe*'s responsibility for the care of souls also transfers to Hagen. The one who otherwise always knows best also knows best in the matter of last things—as far as these count at all in the world of heroes. For this reason, it cannot be just any warrior who becomes the proof of what Hagen has learned from the sprites. It can only be a *pfaffe*, because this will eliminate the knowledge that competed with and proved itself superior to the lay warrior society's knowledge. The scene stands for the attempt to incorporate a possible alternative position. This coincides with the heroic epic's tendency to parody and reinterpret "clerical" skills as warlike: Hagen as the "teacher" at court, Volker with his sword as a talented "musician," the pious exercises of the brutal monk Ilsung in the *Rosengarten* epics, or the newly "pious" Wolfdietrich, who proves his qualities as a warrior and even as a monk and, in the context of a Crusade, teaches the heathen bloody "letters":

> *gar übele buochstaben wil er iu vor lesen,*
> *Mit sînem swerte schrîben. daz sin wunden sêr.* (Wo D X, 35,4–5)
>
> [he wants to read you harsh letters,
> and write them with his sword. That means grave wounds.]

The letters and the well-tempered music of the clerics are "reinterpreted" in the warrior's world into bloody script inscribed on the enemy's body.[121]

The topical opposition of *chevalerie* and *clergie* does not play a role in heroic epic, because the only form of knowledge worth mentioning is on the side of the *chevalerie*. The heroic world disposes of a special kind of knowledge. The greatest heroes, Hagen and Sivrit, "know everything." Sivrit knows all about Prünhilt's world. Hagen is put aside for a time by the *starken Sivrit* not only as a warrior but also as someone who "knows," only to take back that role as soon as Sivrit is eliminated. He, for his part, knows about Sivrit; he knows Rüedeger, Dietrich and the Amelungen (1721,1–2); he knows their history, he can identify foreigners (1178,4), and he can correctly gauge danger:

> *het ir Etzeln künde, als ich sîn künde hân.* (1205,2)
>
> [If you knew Etzel the way that I do.]

Hagen "knows everything there is to know" because he represents the possibilities of the heroic world in its highest potency. Similarly, Dietrich knows "all about Kriemhilt." Rüedeger knows *bî Rîne die liute und ouch daz lant* [the people and the countryside on the Rhine] (1147,2). Volker must also be characterized by knowledge:

> *"Wer sol daz gesinde wîsen über lant?î*
> *si sprâchen: "daz tuo Volkêr, dem ist hie wol bekant*
> *stîge unde strâze . . . ."* (1594,1–3)
>
> ["Who will guide the warriors across the country?"
> They said: "Volker will do that, he knows well
> the ways and byways . . . ."]

Other heroic epics confirm this conclusion. Wate in *Kudrun* alone knows the paths on the sea (K 836,4) and is therefore the best counselor and also the best leader in war.[122] "Knowledge" is linked to other high values of feudal war craft.[123] The mightiest and strongest knows the most. The hero's knowledge is completely positive. It is not connected to deception (as is that of the dwarf in *Laurin*) or to weakness (as in the *Liet von Troye*). It is different from the knowledge of the clerics.

The *Nibelungenlied* does not give sacred institutions much space. Their absence has been taken as an indication of its non-Christian intent and a fundamental criticism of the godless world of heroic epic.[124] The state of the matter is more complex, however. It is neither possible to deny the Christianization of medieval lay society nor appropriate to assume a closed, homogeneous Christian horizon of understanding around 1200, one that had assimilated everything that was foreign, resistant, or deviant. Cultural systems are never free of contradictions, but always to a certain extent permit the existence of antagonistic tendencies. In the replacement of the "person in the know," one can see the attack of a lay world against the clerics, even though their usual place is not disputed. In the difficult process of acculturation,[125] the *Nibelungenlied* takes an extreme position of lay self-awareness.

The Nibelungian world is so matter-of-factly Christian that clerical institutions do not always need to be mentioned. Sacred rites have their regular place in the normal rhythm of life. In the interruptions of the everyday, one thinks of them: at a courtly marriage festival (*si giengen zuo dem münster dâ man die messe sanc* [they went to the church where mass was sung], 644,3), and at Sivrit's funeral (1050–65). After Sivrit's death, Kriemhilt leads the life of a pious widow who hardly leaves her cell near the church (1102). According to the redaction *C, she even wants to retreat to a *sedelhof* [hermitage] near the monastery of Lorsch (C 1158–64). The church is a normal part of courtly life, as are costly clothes or festive receptions. In this sense, the *Nibelungenlied* is far more explicitly Christianized than, for example, *Kudrun*.

But there is no Christian discussion of war as in moral theology before and during the Crusades. This would be the prerequisite for a religious justification of heroic poetry.[126] An "accommodation"[127] of heroic epic and Christian belief, as in the *Rolandslied*, lies outside the material's potential. The epic lacks a Christian perspective of salvation. The ritual expenditure of the *Klage* cannot make up for this, especially since the only decidedly Christian space is the spiritual court of Bishop Pilgrim in Passau. Since even the *Klage* cannot give a Christian meaning to the slaughter, it must time and again claim that the nexus of the story is a chain of missteps and misunderstandings.[128]

The epic discards a likely interpretation in that the opposition between pagan and Christian is downplayed. The positive image of Etzel may be old material from the southeast that sets it apart from the negative image of Atli in the north. Nonetheless, this appraisal of a heathen in the epic is unusual at the time of the Crusades, so that the composer of the *Klage* would rather give him a circuitous renegade career. Here, Etzel is less the peace-loving king of heroic legend than an apostate who is Christianized, relapses, and finally experiences his sad fate as God's punishment (Kl 4192–93).[129] He sinks into un-Christian *desperatio*. This interpretation is hardly reconcilable with the preceding story. The Etzel of the *Nibelungenlied* is presented in stark contrast. He is intent on peace, he supports the Christians at his court, he is a ruler who attempts to promote harmony between different faiths, and even has his own son baptized. This eliminates a possible justification for the battle between the Huns and the Burgundians, as it does in the chansons de geste. The marriage to a heathen serves only Kriemhilt, as a—questionable—pretext for a revenge that breaks all bounds. The *vâlant* works through her and not through the heathen. A Christian interpretation is imposed in the end with the devil, but it does not serve the polarization of Christian and non-Christian worlds. Instead, it is supposed to "explain" the incomprehensible action of a "Christian" queen. Hagen provides what is needed of Christianity. The *pfaffe* is excused.

4 *Nibelungian Anthropology*

Against Psychologizing

The turn of Nibelungian scholarship to psychology has had to connect seemingly disparate material in the transmitted texts and to make plausible what is seemingly contradictory.[1] The question most often not asked concerns the origin of the psychological categories that are employed. These categories are usually based on the critic's intuition, and they claim validity because of their seemingly timeless qualities: love, hate, envy, jealousy, loyalty, and so on are thought to be universal. They do not need to be directly addressed in the epic, but can, where they are absent on the surface of the text, be substituted intuitively by any reader. If there is still no conclusive view of the story or the "character" of a person, then one can try to create a psychological coherence, in the sense of modern expectations, at the cost of one of the contradictory components. Or one might point to the slight demands the Middle Ages made on psychological credibility. This would allow for "two" different Kriemhilts, Prünhilts, or Hagens, of whom each would satisfy modern demands for a consistent character.[2]

Is this really permissible? Historical anthropology has opened our eyes to the fact that the standards of modern, Western action, behaviors, and experiences in no way hold true everywhere and for every time. They are modeled differently according to different cultural contexts.[3] It is true that we are dealing with structures with longer longevity and greater reach than other cultural phenomena, such as, for example, architectural styles, a genre, or a drinking custom. The chance of discovering something comparable or even familiar to us is greater than elsewhere, but the assumption of anthropological constants in affects, habits, attitudes, and emotional mechanisms is based on unscholarly naïveté. This is also true of the European Middle Ages, where the conditions of our world first developed. Insight into the historical conditioning even of supposed anthropological universals is by no means new. However, a methodology that has long been the standard in ethnology or in the research on archaic societies has up to now only seldom been used in the investigation of medieval texts.[4]

This is what will be attempted here. Assumptions about psychologically plausible behavior, which are supposedly timeless, will be suspended. Instead, I assume that historically different concepts of emotional dispositions, patterns of behavior, motivations, and personal identity are possible. To determine these will involve considerable methodological difficulties, above all where the sources are concerned. Here, I shall proceed with a strictly text-based methodology. Literary texts, as with other kinds of texts, are more or less explicitly inscribed with anthropological models. These models are not independent of practically lived models of the same culture, but I shall set aside for the moment the question of the relationship between different types of discourse and the models inherent to each. The reconstruction of a "Nibelungian anthropology" will at first disregard whether it corresponds to common beliefs held around 1200 and to contemporary living (which would need to be reconstructed from other texts). To begin with a kind of fictitious world model has the advantage of not blurring the unavoidable (and much-demanded) distinction between different orders of signs. The anthropological conception inscribed in one text should not be understood as a direct "expression" of a historical mentality, but as a conception that is constituted by situationally dependent, pragmatic, linguistic, stylistic, and genre-specific conditions. These can all be more or less distant from everyday conditions.

My investigation must limit itself to a few, especially conspicuous examples. In this sense, the following considerations remain far behind what has been achieved for spatially or temporally distant cultures in anthropological terminology and specific behavioral stereotypes. The examples have been selected because they have been especially prone to dangerous confusion with unquestioned current assumptions, and because they have in fact determined the interpretation history of the *Nibelungenlied*.

Literary texts display the extraordinary, which they put into language, against the foil of the ordinary. We have to distinguish between fore- and background structures. What happens in the foreground depends on presumptions in the background that do not have to be made explicit, since they are considered to be self-evident. They only have to be brought to mind through allusion. With this backdrop, the events in the foreground can be recognized in their specialness, as something unusual, perhaps even unique, but also as something ordinary and unremarkable. The distinction between just two levels, a "foreground" and a "background" is already an impossible simplification, because in actuality there are structures at various levels that overlap and form a quilt of more or less explicit, more or less remarkable assumptions and conditions. Tacitly presupposed, unproblematized conditions must be distinguished from those that are controversial or that encourage alternatives, and finally from special constellations that refer to these but at the same time break them apart. What is not problematized, implicit or explicit knowledge is probably accepted by all and valid beyond the text. Problematic exaggeration and radical particularity are the farthest distant.

The kinds of expectations that the listeners brought to the *Nibelungenlied* are, of course, no longer reconstructible. The use of other texts promises approximations at best. It has certainly been shown what kinds of insight Latin chronicles can provide for medieval patterns of behavior and rituals, ways of experience, and orders of thought. It must also be remembered, however, that these distinguish themselves through the tradition and the constrictions of the genre with its referential claim—chronicles claim to say "how it was"—from a vernacular heroic epic that tells "old stories" of an extraordinary warrior world. This world is not identical to the everyday, even though its beliefs are also formed by it, as evidenced by formulations such as "this happened, as it tends to happen still today."

Zorn

I shall begin with some observations on expressions of feelings. The terms that I use are meant to be aids. They should be used in a way that leaves them relatively unburdened by later connotations.

The modern reader tends to gather from the "character" of the acting persons their affective reactions, their sudden mood swings, and their permanent temperament. The relationship should be reversed. Reactions, which we would ascribe to affects, are functions of the behavioral constellation in which the characters move. What is supposedly their character is nothing more than a successive bundling of these functions. Emotional drives, which are certainly recognizable, are not based in the core of the self, but in constellations and structures in which the individual character is placed.

This can be exemplified with the term pair *minne* and *haz*.[5] Both denote emotional impulses. Both are also legal terms: *minne* refers to a relationship of peaceful interactions and their legal protection; *haz* the opposite. A constellation of behavior (with certain legal implications) and an emotional phenomenon coincide; *minne* and *haz* signify the intact or broken relationship of two persons according to their legal relationship, their behavior, and their emotional attitudes about each other.

Emotional constellations do not result from interactions between the "internal world" and the "external world."[6] A level is missing where an impulse from the external world is processed according to a character's personal dispositions and is then expressed as an affect of this character. The affective reaction is directly dependent on the situation and does not require any special disposition of a character. On the other hand, certain characters like Wolfhart can be characterized throughout by an affective demeanor; no triggering situation, no impulse from the outside world is necessary in order for the corresponding affect to appear. A situation is governed by emotional habitus, whereas in the first case, emotional behavior depends on the situation. There is no in-between.

Both cases can be observed in a typical heroic reaction, that of *zorn. Zorn* and its consequence, a blind rage, have characterized the hero ever since the Homeric Ajax. Therefore *zorn* can be one of the characteristics of a specific hero. Wolfhart is not irascible in the sense that he falls into *zorn* at the drop of a hat; rather, he is always *zornig.* This says nothing about his particular emotional composure, but designates him as heroically prone to violence. *Biterolf* coins the phrase *in zornes siten* (Bit 8104): *zorn* is a disposition that steers behavior, as is every other *site.*

In Wolfhart, we have a one-sided version of what is appropriate for every hero if he is done *leit. Zorn* is expressed in violent raging.[7] When he faces off against Dietrich, who has beaten his last ally, *Gunther was sô sêre erzürnet und ertobt, wand er nâch starkem leide sîn herzevîent was* [Gunther was enraged and furious, since he was his fierce enemy on account of the grief he had experienced] (2358,2–3). Every situation of violent confrontation shows the actors to be *zornig.* The emotional impetus of *zorn* is completely secondary. When the Saxons challenge the Burgundians to war, the messengers "explain" this by the *zorn* of their kings for the Burgundian rulers: *Ir habt ir zorn verdienet* [you have earned their anger] (144,1). There is no reason to ask for the motivation of *zorn*, because *zorn* is not a cause, but a manifestation of a hostile condition that leads to war (*daz iu die herren beide tragent grôzen haz* [both men have a great hatred toward you], 144,2). The statement that *zorn* is earned is identical to the statement that war will begin. Attack and *zorn* are one and the same, and *zorn* is only seemingly the reason for the attack.[8]

The deferred effect of *zorn* and its decoupling from inner emotional attitudes is especially noticeable in Rüedeger's battle against his Burgundian relatives, whom he did not want to fight as enemies. After the battle has become inevitable, he rages on in wild anger, as if there had never been any gesture of reconciliation (*des muotes er ertobete* [he fell into a rage], 2206,2). The opponent, also just prepared to reconcile, resorts to *zorn*: *daz sach ein Burgonde* [Gernot]: *zornes gie im nôt* [a Burgundian saw this, and he was moved to anger] (2215,3). One might suppose Gernot's *zorn* to be motivated by the fact that he has seen his *vriunde* fall at Rüedeger's hand. But this does not seem to be the reason, because Hagen, who must have seen it too and who is always ready for revenge, remains passive. Since he has promised to stay clear of the fight against Rüedeger, Hagen is initially lacking any *zorn*. He only falls into *zorn* at the moment when he is freed from his promise, namely, when Rüedeger dies: *alrêrst erzurnde Hagene* [only then was Hagen most enraged] (2221,4). It is the action that calls forth the *zorn* and not the other way around.

The decoupling of *zorn* from its emotional foundation is common in medieval heroic epic.[9] This can have strange consequences, as seen in *haz*, an emotion related to *zorn*. In *Biterolf*, Etzel's messengers exchange long courtesies at Gunther's court before they present their message—the challenge to battle—with the words: *iu tregt vil hazlîchen sin/der künec von Hiunen rîche* [the mighty king of the Huns hates you] (Bit 4872–73). The friendly manners before and the *haz* of a declaration of war are not exclusionary, because they refer to different situations, first, to the courtly ritual of a messenger, second, to the military confrontation.

Of course, *zorn* often means the emotional reaction to a stimulus (insult, injury), but this is not the only possibility. The distinction from a constant angry demeanor is often difficult to make. Hagen attempts to refute the water sprite's prophesy that the entire army will perish at Etzel's court and that only the chaplain will return by trying to drown the chaplain while crossing the Danube. The characteristic that best befits a violent deed is *zorn*. This is why, when Hagen seeks to push the *pfaffen* under water, we read: *wan der starke Hagene vil zornec was gemuot* [because the bold Hagen was feeling very angry] (1578,3). Why should he be angry? Hagen's *muot* is identical with what is apparent to all in his deed. The deed "is" *zorn*. Hostile feelings for the *armen pfaffen* do not have to be justified separately. Giselher, on the other hand, reacts to what he sees: *zürnen erz began* [he began to be angry] (1576,3). Visible demeanor and spontaneous impulse go by the same name.

Here is another example. Prünhilt's contest with Gunther is fought bitterly. In the second contest, we read:

> *Dô gie si hin vil balde; zornec was ir muot.*
> *den stein huop vil hôhe diu edel maget guot.* (462,1–2)
>
> [She went there quickly, and she was very angry.
> The noble woman raised the stone up high.]

This could mean that Prünhilt is goaded by her defeat in the first test, although *zorn* here more likely signifies violent physical effort. Whoever wants to defeat an opponent "is" angry. Only when Prünhilt loses the contest does the momentary emotion come to the fore:

> *Prünhilt diu schoene wart in zorne rôt.* (465,3)
>
> [Prünhilt the beautiful became red with anger.]

Does Gunther speak *zorneclîchen* (1624,4) in the heat of the moment when, on the journey to Etzel, he hears of an attack on his army by the Bavarians, but only after the fighting is over, because he feels that he has been bypassed,[10] or do his angry words simply substitute for the demeanor that would have been appropriate in the case of hostile attack? The question is inappropriate to the narrative method of the epic.

The emotional component seems to move to the foreground more clearly if the affect cannot be acted out. After Hagen takes the hoard from Kriemhilt, it is said that

> *daz zurnde ir bruoder Gêrnôt, do er daz rehte bevant.* (1132,4)
>
> [Her brother Gernot was enraged when he found out the facts.]

There is no action that corresponds to this *zorn*. Giselher's reaction to the violent act against the priest is similar:

> *Gîselher der junge, zürnen erz began.*
> *er'n wold' iz doh niht lâzen er enhet im leide getân.* (1576,3–4)
>
> [The young Giselher became enraged.
> But he [Hagen] would not stop until he had hurt him.]

Even in these cases, *zorn* is more than an emotional outburst. It is the attitude appropriate to Hagen's lawbreaking, even though it cannot express itself in deed, because other legal obligations interfere. The *zorn* gets stuck and is to that extent deficient in comparison to usual expressions of heroic *zorn*.

If the deed is lacking, then *zorn* itself is missing something. In *Kudrun*, King Ludewic grabs Kudrun by the hair so as to drown her in the sea. His son Hartmuot intervenes and says:

> *tæte ez ander iemen, sô zurnte ich alsô sêre,*
> *dan Ludewîc der vater mîn, ich næme im beide lîb unde êre.* (K 964,3–4)
>
> [If anyone but Ludwig my father were to do this,
> I'd be so enraged I'd take his life and his honor.]

Restricted by familial ties, Hartmuot's indignation cannot rise to the appropriate level of *zorn*, which would have to express itself in action against his father.

Due to the close link between the expression of affect and deed, it is meaningless to ask about the emotional reality of *zorn*. Hagen takes advantage of the absence of the kings in Worms to rob Kriemhilt of the hoard. Upon the brothers' return, she presses charges, with the result that Hagen has to remove himself from the court for a time in order to avoid *der fürsten zorne* (1139,2). Why should the kings be angry, in that by their absence they permitted Hagen to steal the hoard? The question of whether this *zorn* of the kings is just playacting misses the point.[11] The word shows that Hagen's transgression is determined by the royal court and results in a judgment. A damaged legal relationship between king and vassal is called *zorn*. *Zorn* is identical to the loss of closeness and is publicly testified to by a legal act. The loss is temporary. When Hagen regains the *hulde* of the kings (1139,3), the *zorn* will seamlessly disappear as well. What the royal judges think in terms of the judgment is completely besides the point. Their attitude corresponds completely to the legal-social constellation.

Here is a similar case. Gunther's final offer to Etzel and the Huns to effect a *suone* [reconciliation] is presented in *zornes muot* (2094,1–2). This should be an inappropriate affect, one would think, if the suggestion is to be received by the opponent with an open mind. This is not what matters, however. *Zorn* corresponds to the enmity between the two parties, which Gunther wants to overcome not through capitulation but through *suone*—a just reconciliation. *Zorn* expresses his insistence on his legal position, which, until a reconciliation can take place, must be presented in a forceful manner.

Most enlightening is the variety of *zorn* in the scene where Etzel prohibits the outbreak of hostilities between the Burgundians and his men for the last time. This is the situation: Volker has slain a Hunnish knight in a sporting melee. This act of violence threatens to lead to a battle of all against all. Etzel intervenes, however. He knocks the weapon out of the hand of a relative of the deceased and declares the slaying an accident that cannot justify any action against the guests. Any expression of violence is nipped in the bud, and, in the words of the narrator, this means: *zorn er mêr deheinen dâ niht werden lie* [he would not allow others to show their anger] (1898,2).[12] Of course, Etzel cannot control the feelings of his men. He can prevent actions in which *zorn* is present. Seen from the outside, nothing else is distinguished that is "behind" the deed. *Zorn* marks a situation of violent confrontation that should be defused. In that Etzel is successful, he has also overcome what here is called *zorn*. There does not seem to be an affect beyond what is openly visible.

Trûren

Trûren [mourning, grieving] is also a reaction to a troubled state of the world. It is no more a subjective reaction than *zorn*, but it expresses attitudes that result from a conflict-laden situation and certain affiliated gestures, whether disingenuous or real.[13] *Zorn* and *trûren* are appropriate reactions to *leit*; one is active, the other passive, but the passive condition can switch to the active and vice versa. *Trûren* is semantically close to *leit*, and this suggests the meaning "to feel emotional pain." But this aspect is a typically modern restriction of meaning, because *leit* is more than this. This is not mean to limit *leit* to a predominantly legal aspect (*Be-leid-igung*), but to recognize that both aspects are indistinguishable. *Leit* generally refers to a "defective state" that is caused by someone else.[14] This certainly includes "pain" over the "death of loved ones" or "heartache,"[15] but that is not to say, conversely, that this is the only or even the dominant shade of meaning. In the *Nibelungenlied*, there is no distinct semantic boundary between external injury and internal hurt.

This touches upon the meaning of *trûren* as a reaction to *leit*. An insult (*leit*) puts Rüedeger in a *trûrige[n] muot* (2141,1). *Trûren* points to the defect in *êre*; *trûren* has symbolic character.[16] *Muot* expresses itself in a violent deed that eliminates the defect. *Trûren* turns to *zorn* when Rüedeger avenges his *leit* and slays the offender. Here *zorn* is not really a motivation for the deadly blow, but subsequently gives a name to what everyone has seen: *daz von des heldes zorne dem Hiunen was geschehen* [what happened to the Hun because of the hero's anger] (2147,2); *trûren* is the moment that precedes the deed (*zorn*).

When Dietrich beats down Hagen, we read: *Gunther der edele dar umbe trûren began* [the noble Gunther was pained by that] (2352,4). This is the paralysis of someone who can hardly help himself anymore,[17] before he pulls himself together one last time, now *erzürnet und ertobt* [angered and in a rage] (2358,2). From passivity (*trûren*), he motivates himself to action (*zorn*). Where this fails, what remains is *trûren*. Sivrit causes King Liudegast severe wounds; *des muose der künec Liudegast haben trûrigen muot* [Liudegast had to suffer because of that] (188,4). This is not simply defeat, but a sign that Liudegast must surrender (189).

What might appear harmless as a "dampening of spirit" is a disturbance of balance that can change to aggression. Dietrich considers how he can be informed of Rüedeger's fate without becoming involved in the fight: *ob ungefüegiu vrâge danne dâ geschiht, / daz betrüebet lîhte recken ir muot* [if an inappropriate question is asked, that will easily darken a hero's state of mind] (2240,2–3). Dietrich is not afraid that his men might spoil the Burgundians' mood, but he considers that an exchange of words might result in an irreparable insult. *Trûren* threatens to turn into violence. During the journey to Etzel, when the ferryman refuses to transfer Hagen across the Danube, Hagen answers: *trûrec ist mîn muot* [I'm in a dark frame of mind] (1559,1). This *trûrec* is not explained by the bad news that Hagen has just received, nor does it express a sour mood. It shows that Hagen, although he understands the words of the *vergen* to be an attack, at first remains passive. *Trûren* characterizes the conflict-laden situation, the consequences of which he tries to avert one more time by requesting, *ze minne* (1559,2), that the other party take the fare that is offered and transfer the army. Hagen is *be-leid-igt* and gives the other a chance to take back the insult. When this fails, the scene immediately turns violent, and this is followed by more violence.

Dietrich's "mournful" pose at the end of the epic is to be understood as a gesture of hesitation, as it becomes increasingly obvious that he can no longer keep out of the conflict with the Burgundians:

> *vil harte senelîche er in ein venster saz.* (2247,2)
>
> [He sat at a window feeling depressed.]
>
> *Dô sah er trûreclîche sitzen hie den man.* (2309,2)
>
> [He saw the man sitting there unhappily.]

Trûren is an expression of temporary paralysis, not only in the *Nibelungenlied*. In *Rother*, King Constantine has forbidden, upon pain of death, that anyone should court his daughter, but he nonetheless allows Rother's messengers to present their case. When it becomes apparent that the case is precisely about the forbidden courtship, we read:

> *Trorich sprach do Constantin—*
> *zurnich was der mot sin—*
> *"Daz ich die rede irlovbit han,*
> *des moz ich lange trorich stan . . . ."* (KR 324–27)
>
> [Constantine spoke gloomily—
> he was in an angry mood—
> "I shall long regret
> that I allowed such speech . . . ."]

Constantine regrets having unknowingly gotten himself into a position where he cannot act as required by *siete,* namely, to kill the messengers. He must lock up his *zorn* in *mot. Trorich* does not signal compassion for the messengers or indignation over the unsuitable speech that he had to hear; rather, it expresses the loss of options by prematurely restricting his room to maneuver.

At the conclave over Sivrit's murder, Gunther is at first undecided and points to Sivrit's innocence (868,1–2). The vassals (represented by Ortwin) are, however, prepared to sacrifice Sivrit. Then Hagen raises the question of power: he

> *riet in allen zîten Gunther dem degene,*
> *ob Sîfrit niht enlebte, sô wurde im undertân*
> *vil der künege lande. der helt des trûren began.* (870,2–4).
>
> [counseled Gunther time and again
> that once Sivrit was dead, he would possess
> many royal lands. The hero was saddened by that.]

What does *trûren* mean here and why (*des*) does Gunther begin to *trûren*? De Boor psychologizes *trûren* into "an expression of internal division and uncertainty" (p. 146). This scene is followed by a kind of suspension (871,1) in which Gunther continues to argue against the murderous plot, but finally gives in. In this sense, *trûren* again expresses the uncertain state of affairs before the outbreak of violence. There is another reason, however. Hagen points out a "defect" to the king. The realms that Sivrit possesses and that, according to Hagen, would fall to (*undertân*) Gunther after his death, are now lacking. The *êren* that characterize the Burgundian rule are incomplete, but Hagen suggests a way to change that. *Trûren* is a sign of indecisiveness and deficiency.

Trûren/trûrec signify objective defect, in which the individual is only a participant. They cannot be reduced to an emotional dimension. This is especially evident in zeugmatic phrases. When Rüedeger tells his wife that he is about to journey *nâch Kriemhilde* to ask for her hand on Etzel's behalf, we read:

> *dô wart diu marcgrâvinne trûrec unde hêr.* (1160,2)
>
> [then the margravine became sad and proud.]

The two predicates, *trûrec* and *hêr*,[18] seem to lie on different levels. De Boor tries to smooth this out by paraphrasing: "sad and at the same time glad, internally lifted."[19] This relates both statements to the margravine's internal mood,[20] but that is only one side of it. The basic meaning, around the word field *hêrre*, *hêrlîch*, should be kept in mind; *hêr* designates a positive condition and appropriate demeanor, such as would befit the status of a lord. A designation of status includes the attributes and attitudes appropriate to it. The word can therefore designate an emotion as well as the external appearance or certain objects, such as weapons.[21] In Gotelint's case as well these aspects go together, and this is why *hêr* can be the complement for *trûrec*.

The one epithet designates a deficiency, the other an uninjured condition. Neither applies to Gotelint alone, but to the whole land. In Etzel's realm, a gap resulted from the death of Helche (1143), and this gap must be closed (1144). The entire land is affected by this deficit: *sîn volc ist âne freude* [his people are without joy] (1194,2), *dâ von iz ime lande vil jâmerlîche stât* [on account of this there is much misery in our land] (1195,2). "Joy" depends on the condition of rule. Rüedeger's message brings hope that the defective condition will end (*ergetzen*, cf. 1170,3), a condition under which Gotelint[22] and the entire land suffer:

> *Dô diu marcgrâvinne die botschaft vernam,*
> *ein teil was ir leide, weinens si gezam,*
> *ob si gewinnen solde vrouwen alsam ê.*
> *sô si gedâht' an Helchen, daz tet ir inneclîche wê.* (1161)
>
> [As the margravine listened to the news
> she became sad on the one hand; she had to cry,
> whether she would gain a queen like the one before.
> As she thought of Helche, it pained her heart.]

The *leit* and the *weinen*, which is appropriate to the situation (*gezam*!), are for the queen and the ongoing defect that her death has caused. The predicates *trûrec unde hêr* do not show a contradictory mood, but rather a contradictory condition, which immediately turns to joy when Kriemhilt arrives (Gotelint: 1313,4; the land: 1379,2–4).

This tie between joy and sadness with extra-personal constellations seems to have no longer been obvious already in the late Middle Ages. In ms. D, the statement that the land is *âne freude* (1194,2 according to mss. AB) has been replaced with: the land is *ane vrouwen.*[23] The loss of the queen and of joy are no longer unquestionably the same. In ms. D, the statement is narrowed down to the public-political aspect and is no longer automatically assigned to a certain emotional state.

Tension Between "External" and "Internal"

The turn away from modern psychologizing in no way leads to a reduction to the political dimension of the story. This would, of course, assume a division into "private" and "public," "internal" and "external," "individual" and "social" components, which an anthropology that argues historically must eliminate.[24] Both are closely related; even where there is the hint of tension between the two poles, the link remains evident.

Gunther is, after his unsuccessful wedding night, *trûrec* in an environment in which joy dominates (*wol gebârte*), and this is so even though it would be appropriate for him, in view of the coronation, to show joy:

> *swie wol man dâ gebârte, trûrec was genuoc*
> *der herre von dem lande, swi er des tages krône truoc.* (643,3–4)
>
> [although everyone put on a smile, the lord of the land
> was distressed, wearing the crown that day.]

This contradiction between appearance and Gunther's damaged self-esteem is at first not evident upon arriving *under krône*. Ceremony and attitude are congruent; they express joy (*vrœlîchen*, 645,4). The predicate *vrœlîchen* is in only a few manuscripts; the rest concentrate only on the external appearance.[25] A "subjective" interpretation of the publicly manifest joy is explicitly excluded from these manuscripts—a sign of increasing disassociation.[26] Gunther's hidden *trûren* comes to light at the tournament, however, in that he excludes himself from the general joyousness (647,4). If his psychological fate were at stake—"to preserve the secret of his marriage"—then it would be unwise to stay away from the tournament. *Trûrende* has proved to be more than just a mood that can be suppressed, however. It is the expression of an objective state of affairs. Gunther's deficient status shows itself with a limited ability to represent kingship and is therefore visible to anyone who looks closely, such as Sivrit.[27]

The defect comes to light in a situation in which Gunther is bound more loosely in the collective ritual, when he is not only a king but also a knight. In a tournament, it is not inherited rank that counts but personal superiority. In the coronation ritual, Gunther was still able to show the joy required of him, but in the personal contest, his deficiency becomes visible. When Sivrit asks why, Gunther emphasizes the public consequences of his failure as a husband and the damage to his honor: *ich hân laster unde schaden* [I have shame and injury] (649,1). Sivrit promises to help him, and immediately he feels himself restored as lord and king:

> *der rede was dô Gunther nâch sînem arbeiten hêr.* (651,4)
>
> [the words sounded splendid to Gunther after his trouble.]

Again, the counterbalance of *trûrec* is *hêr*, which embraces internal condition and external status.

It is primarily the king who gains the upper hand in bed. Prünhilt speaks to her vanquisher, whom she believes to be Gunther, formally: *künic edele, du solt mich leben lân* [noble king, please let me live] (678,1). After this, nothing is left of Gunther's *trûren*. There is no personal relationship between the married couple that could be disturbed by the embarrassing memory of the first night, not even by the act of rape, which seems to have left hardly a mark on Prünhilt. The next morning, Gunther is no longer excluded from the common joy, and because his royal self-esteem has been restored, the entire land again lives in harmony:

> *Der wirt wart an dem morgen verrer baz gemuot*
> *danne er dâ vor wære. des* [!] *wart diu vreude guot*
> *in allem sînem lande* . . . . (685,1–3)
>
> [The king was in better spirits that morning
> than he had been before. Because of that the joy
> was restored in all his land . . . .]

Different perspectives on a formerly defective, but now intact, condition are distinguished, not "internal" and "external," "public" and "private."

Still it is not advisable to rely on the façade, as shown by two related scenes. The Saxons have declared war on the Burgundians. This is *leit* to Gunther (148,1; 153,1). He "complains" to his vassals, so that they, too, see the challenge as their own *leit* (*daz lât iu wesen leit* [(you) take this as a personal affront], 149,3). Until there is a solution in sight, Gunther walks around *trûrende* (153,2; cf. 158,1). The declaration of war damages the harmonious balance of Burgundian rule. Gunther provokes Sivrit's observation with his *trûren*:

> *wie ir sô habet verkêret die vrœlîchen sit*
> *der ir mit uns nu lange habt alher gepflegen.* (154,2–3)
>
> [how you have turned around the joyful manner
> that you have shown us for so long now.]

This questioning demonstrates that Sivrit is not focusing on Gunther's feelings, but the condition of the court (*sit*), which is mirrored in the king's demeanor.[28] He asks about the reason for the disruption and is told of the war. His offer to help frees the king from his *trûren* and restores both his joy (157,3) and the court's. Gunther can display *hôhen muot* (174,3).[29]

Gunther's *trûren* at the declaration of war was well-founded. But later, when he only simulates a war against the Saxons with Hagen, the talk is of *zorn* and *trûren*, too. Since he made up the cause himself, Gunther should have no reason to believe his own lie. When the false declaration of war is brought to him, however, a reaction similar to before sets in:

> *der künic begonde zürnen do er diu mære bevant.* (880,4)
>
> [the king became enraged when he heard the news.]

The *zorn* is a visible gesture. Ms. B does not allow a peek behind the façade. Only the redactor of *C works out the break between the behavior that is publicly displayed and what lies behind it:

> *do begunde zvrnen Gunther, als ob ez wære im vnbechant.* (*C* 888,4)
>
> [Gunther became enraged, as if it was unknown to him.]

In the vulgate version, on the other hand, Gunther's demeanor is simulated but indistinguishable from the first time, and as with the first time, Sivrit therefore asks:

> *wie gât sô trûreclîche der künic unt sîne man?* (883,3)
>
> [why are the king and his men so gloomy?]

Nothing is said about what Gunther feels, but instead about what he shows in front of the others. The gesture can be misinterpreted. When Gunther reacts to Sivrit's willingness to help with the fake Saxon war, he only acts

> *als ob er ernstlîche der helf wære vrô.*
> *in valsche neig im tiefe der ungetriuwe man.* (887,2–3)
>
> [as if he were actually glad of the help.
> The disloyal man bowed to him deceitfully.]

The separation of body language and signified affect can only be imagined as a perfidious act of deception. Gunther is *ungetriuwe.* The gesture of *trûren* cloaks a subversive intrigue.

The *als ob* splits "internal" and "external." This disconnection is a great discovery of vernacular literature around 1200. It is reflected in high *Minnesang* in songs, in which the courting "I" asserts the truth of his feelings—his lovesickness—against the body language that seems to belie it through the obligatory show of joy. The singer, who speaks to society of the *leit* of his *minne,* must preserve courtly form. He has to suffer in an exemplary manner, so that nobody sees through his simulated joy; to use Reinmar's terms, he must *schône . . . getragen* [properly . . . carry] (MF 163,9) his *leit.* If he upholds the form, then this could mean that he does not love passionately. So he must tirelessly say what he is not allowed to show. He must dissimulate and point out that he is dissimulating. To present this artistically in song is the achievement of courtly self-control and at the same time allows the articulation of *minne* as an experience that can never in the full sense be accounted for and internalized.[30]

Only the starting point in the *Nibelungenlied* is comparable. The answer to this dissociation is dissimilar, however, because what is here an insidious distortion appears in *Minnesang* under a positive sign. *Dissimulatio* is an achievement of courtly civilization, allowing the differentiation of an internal experience that is shielded from "others" and acts as a stimulus to a paradox artistic practice, but here it is deception. What shields itself from the outside is not a new "internal" dimension but something that seeks to avoid the spotlight.

Even Kriemhilt's pain for Sivrit is never just internal and physically conceived. It therefore never completely escapes perception:

> *man hôrte hie z'allen zîten Kriemhilde klagen,*
> *daz ir niemen trôste daz herze unt ouch den muot,*
> *ez entæte Gîselher . . . .* (1099,2–4)
>
> [Kriemhilt was heard crying all the time,
> and no one consoled her or encouraged her,
> except for Giselher . . .]

Assuming the normal convergence of affective gestures and situation, Kriemhilt's *leit* would have to disappear with the restoration of her *êren* after her marriage to Etzel, but this is not the case from the outset. At the wedding feast with Etzel, she has to hide her tears. What she is thinking secretly immediately comes out and must be hidden from others. This time, she does so successfully. Even though she has taken her magnificent place next to Etzel, Dietrich knows:

> *Kriemhilt noch sêre weinet den helt von Nibelunge lant.* (1724,4)
>
> [Kriemhilt still weeps often for the hero of Nibelungland.]

The kings can ask witnesses in order to learn about *der vrouwen Kriemhilde muot.* Dietrich warns:

> *ich hœre alle morgen weinen und klagen*
> *mit jâmerlîchen sinnen daz Etzelen wîp*
> *dem rîchen got von himile des starken Sîfrides lîp.* (1730,2–4)
>
> [I hear her crying and moaning every morning
> with pained emotion, the wife of Etzel,
> to almighty God in heaven for the death of Sivrit the Strong.]

This lament for Sivrit does not take place in front of others and for others, as with a funeral. Kriemhilt is alone with herself and God. Still, there is no "internal" that separates itself. Dietrich does not have to go to great pains to find out what Kriemhilt secretly feels. He can hear her. Deciphering dissimulating body language belongs, on the other hand, to one of the most important problem fields of courtly instruction and consequently to the constituting conditions of the modern novel. In the *Nibelungenlied*, however, *dissimulatio* is nothing but treason.

Kriemhilt's unsuccessful attempt to hide her pain is deception, just like Gunther's simulated *trûren*. Her invitation to her relatives openly makes use of deception. She orders the messenger: *den sult ir niht verjehen / daz ir noch ie gesæhet betrüebet mînen muot* [you should never reveal to them / that you ever saw me depressed] (1415,2–3). This assumes that the pain, which has not been driven away by all the *êren* with Etzel, was also visible to the messengers. The *muot* comes to the surface and is visible, but it should not be visible to all. What is done or said secretly is available to some and cunningly excludes others.

Herzen jâmer—herzeliebe

Strong emotions come out, as in the excessive gestures of mourning after Sivrit's death. The most expressive are Kriemhilt's: feinting, screaming, bleeding. Pain is not something just for the individual, however: *mit klage ir helfende manic vrouwe was* [many women helped her with lamentations] (1067,2).

Allez ir gesinde klagete unde schrê
mit ir lieben vrouwen, wande in was harte wê. . . . (1013,1–2)

[All her kin cried and screamed
with their beloved lady, because they were deeply hurt. . . .]

Sigemunt der herre den fürsten umbeslôz.
dô wart von sînen vriunden der jâmer alsô grôz,
daz von dem starken wuofe palas unde sal
und ouch di stat ze Wormze von ir weinen erschal. (1025)

[Lord Sigemunt embraced the prince.
Then the pain of his friends became so overwhelming
that the palace and hall were filled with a loud howl,
and the town of Worms resounded with their crying.]

Iu enkunde niemen daz wunder volsagen
von rittern unt von vrouwen, wie man die hôrte klagen,
sô daz man des wuofes wart in der stat gewar.
die edelen burgære die kômen gâhende dar. (1036)

[No one could adequately recount the miracle
of knights and ladies, how they cried aloud,
so that everyone heard the howling in the town.
The noble citizens came running to see.]

Vil lûte schrîende daz liut gie mit im dan [the crowd went along with him with loud cries] (1065,1) and: *mit ungefüegem leide vil des volkes ranc* [many people tried to control their unbearable grief] (1064,2). The pain is represented in the castigation of the body:

Ane ezzen und âne trinken beleip dâ manic man. (1058,1)

[Many people no longer ate and drank.]

This is why the body also sets limits for mourning. The three-day refusal of food and drink cannot be sustained:

doch mohten si dem lîbe sô gar geswîchen niht:
si nerten sich nâch sorgen, sô noch genuogen geschiht. (1072,3–4)

[but they were not able to ignore their physical needs:
they recuperated from their sorrow, as still happens often enough.]

The mourning is at an end when its public signs are removed. At least, this is generally true. Kriemhilt's pain, however, is something special in this world of collective and visible affects. This is first expressed when Kriemhilt rejects the cries by Sivrit's family for vengeance and justice. Her *leit* is called *herzen jâmer* on several occasions.[31] The *herzen jâmer* displaces the origin and the expression of the pain into (still thinking physically) the person's interior. As is true of the Kriemhilt character as a whole, it thus seems like a foreign body in the Nibelungian world. What distinguishes Kriemhilt from other characters seems to be closer to modern expectations, but that does not mean that it represents the "real," "deeper" meaning of the work.[32] Above all, it should be remembered that it is not until the loss, the murder of Sivrit, that the exclusive bond that scholarship wants to see as "love" is formed in a marriage made for dynastic convenience and courtly norms.[33]

The spectrum of *jâmer* covers, similarly to *leit*, personal as well as extrapersonal phenomena.[34] This is why the collective mourning for Sivrit (1025,2) or for Rüedeger (2241,4) can be called *jâmer*, too, and the condition of the land after the death of the queen is called *jâmerlîche* (1195,2). It is only in combination with *herze* that *jâmer* is related to internal pain. This and other related combinations cut a path through the second part of the epic that leads to Kriemhilt's motivation for her relentless revenge:

> *dô was ir daz herze sô grœzlîche wunt:*
> *ez kunde niht vervâhen, swaz man ir trôstes bôt.*
> *si hete nâch liebem vriunde die aller grœzisten nôt,*
>
> *Die nâch liebem manne ie mêr wîp gewan.* (1104,2–1105,1)

> [her heart was so deeply hurt:
> nothing was able to help, whatever consolation was offered.
> Above all she longed for her beloved
>
> More than any woman ever for her dear husband.]

The meaning attributed to *herze* was associated with the influence of contemporary courtly literature.[35] There, the interior with *herze* was conceived as a stage. Various drives contend with each other on this stage, such as service to ladies and to God, *minne* and honor. The *herz* is one of the instances of the I, counterpart to the *lîp*, with which it fights for primacy. And it is—at least for Walther von der Vogelweide—the embodiment and seat of all affective drives, bringing into question conventional values of courtly-feudal society like class, birth, beauty, and wealth. Even where the clash is not between personified instances of the I in scene or dialogue, the acting out of internal conflict is one of the great discoveries in the new vernacular literature.

It is not possible, however, simply to transfer this variety and depth of meaning to the *Nibelungenlied.* Vocabulary is often transferred, but this is not necessarily true of concepts. To be sure, it is *herzeliebe[] minne* that holds Sivrit in Worms (294,2), and he carries Kriemhilt *in herzen* (134,1). When it is said that he draws attention to himself *durch herzen liebe*, however, this in no way refers to Kriemhilt's love, but to the desires of other women (*manec frouwe*).

> *Swenn' er bî den helden uf dem hove stuont,*
> *alsô noch die liute durch kurzwîle tuont,*
> *sô stuont sô minneclîche daz Siglinde kint,*
> *daz in durch herzen liebe trûte manec frouwe sint.* (135)
>
> [Whenever he stood with the heroes in the court,
> as people still tend to do for enjoyment,
> Siglinde's child was so eye-catching
> that many women fell in love with him.]

This means that *herze liebe* is not—as in Walther—distinguished from conventional *minne*, this attraction from afar that is directed to extrapersonal values and that is based on the admiration of appearances.

Sivrit's service, which is exclusively directed to Kriemhilt and swings between hope and disheartenment, is much closer to the conventional opposing concept to *herzeliebe*, namely, desperate high *minne*, even though Sivrit himself claims that it comes *von herzen* (136,3). The course of his service (*diu ist mir noch vil vremde: des muoz ich trûric gestân* [she is still a stranger to me, therefore I have to be sad], 136,4; *er leit ouch von ir minne dicke michel arebeit* [he had many troubles on account of her love], 137,4) paradigmatically quotes the effects that are ascribed to high *minne.*[36] Kriemhilt, on the other hand, noticeably calls Etzel's relationship to Queen Helche *herzeliebe*, too. The narrator has presented this relationship as an ideal, if rather conventional, dynastic bond and as the collective affair of the entire realm. Kriemhilt asks: *waz sold' ich einem man, der ie herzeliebe von guotem wîbe gewan* [what am I worth to a man who had won true love from a good woman] (1218,3–4). Even if one sees in Kriemhilt's words a projection of her own love for Sivrit (cf. 1238,3–4) onto the Hunnish king, the impression of terminological carelessness remains. The *herze* is employed exactly where convention remains dominant.

If elements of courtly psychology can be found, a semantic differentiation is generally lacking. Its vocabulary is used in nonterminological ways. The meaning of *herze* can sometimes be so obliterated that it only replaces adverbs like *sêre* or *fast*, to emphasize a certain state of affairs or to mark a special intensity: *wand' er nâch starkem leide sîn herzevîent was* [he was his archenemy on account of his great grief] (2358,3). In a similar sense, *herzeleit* can designate a particularly painful condition, such as living a great distance away from close relatives (741,4). *Herze* can also metonymically stand for other instances of the I, without addressing an emotional intensification, for example, when it is said of the young knights and their enjoyment of knightly contests: *den ir tumbiu herze gâhen hôhen muot* [their young hearts gave them high spirits] (809,3). One should not weigh down courtly vocabulary too much with the connotations of courtly literature.

Beyond this, *herze* is not always positively defined. The interior is not the stage for a new sensibility, but a closed space in which treason can be prepared. What Prünhilt thinks about Kriemhilt's pride and the "serf" Sivrit's lack of attention to duty is the engine for a fateful intrigue: *truoc si in ir herzen unt wart ouch wol verdeit* [she kept this in her heart and it was concealed] (725,1). If what she is holding inside comes out, it will have catastrophic consequences.[37] Kriemhilt's desire for revenge is called *wille[] in ir herzen* [a yearning in her heart] (1396,1); *ir herzen leide . . . niht vertragen* [she doesn't want to get over her grief] (1960,2). The *herze* is the place for carefully kept secret plans. Thinking takes the form of a secret discussion with oneself (1397,4).[38] In version *C, which brings the interior marked by *herze* into play more often, *herze* is mentioned exactly where the vulgate version speaks of the influence from the *vâlant* [devil] (1394,1–2):

> *Sine chvnde ovch nie vergezzen, swie wol ir anders was,*
> *ir starchen hercen leide, in ir hercen si ez las*
> *mit iamer zallen stvnden, daz man sit wol bevant.*
> *do begvnde ir aber salwen von heizen trahen ir gewant.* (C 1421)
>
> [She also could not forget her heavy-hearted grief,
> how things had changed, in her heart she felt it
> painfully all the time, which has since been found out.
> Then she began to soil her dress with hot tears.]

In this passage, the *herze*, the internal authority that prevails against the many external dependencies, replaces the dark, I-remote determination with Satan (in ms. B). To be sure, this is a programmatic revaluation, but still it shows the original negative meaning of the place, to which the *herze* comes close. It denotes an eerie place for secret planning that leads to the destruction of social order (*triuwe*). Only the reviser of *C neutralizes this eeriness (cf. C 1421,3!), and the composer of the *Klage* changes the heart back to a seat of *triuwe*, certainly a *triuwe* that is largely bereft of its social implications.[39]

One of the problematic consequences of *herzen jâmer* is that Kriemhilt becomes isolated with her pain. She must bear it alone and against all others. This is first shown in her retreat to the proximity of the grave site, in the tireless service to the dead, and in the restriction of her association to a few relatives. With the tears of *suone* that are shed by Kriemhilt and Gunther along with their followers, the attempt to free Kriemhilt from the isolation of *herzen jâmer* seems to have been successful. Since there is no view into the interior of those involved, *suone* has to be seen as a binding reconciliation. There is nothing beyond ritual. Only the redactor of *C calls the *suone mit valsche gefvget* [poisoned with deceit] (C 1128,2). Here the *herze* remains excluded from the publicly concluded act: *min munt im giht der sv̂ne; im wirt daz herce nimmer holt* [my lips say that we are reconciled; my heart will never do the same] (C 1124,3–4). The vulgate version knows nothing about this. With the supposed reparations for the crimes by the marriage to Etzel, the *jâmer* is also pushed aside to the "interior," to the *herze*.

In the description of the beginning of the Burgundians' trek, the narrator inserts a foreshadowing of future misfortune:

> *die Sîfrides wunden tâten Kriemhilde wê* (1523,4)
>
> [Sivrit's wounds pained Kriemhilt.]

This is a paradoxical formulation, because no one can feel the physical pain of another. There must then be other injuries that are nonphysical. This discovery of courtly literature is adapted here to a warrior society. Nonphysical, but no less serious injuries—the mourning for Sivrit—are described with the metaphor of physical pain. This is inexplicable, to the point of provocation, in the heroic world. Hagen makes a brutal point when he reminds us of the temporary nature of physical pain and connects this with the persistence of feelings:

> *Si mac wol lange weinen . . .*
> *er lît vor manigem jâre ze tôde erslagene.*
> *den künec von den Hiunen sol si nu holden haben:*
> *Sîfrit kumt niht widere . . . .* (1725)

> [She may cry as long as she wishes . . .
> he lies dead, murdered, for several years already.
> Now she is to be beholden to the king of the Huns:
> Sivrit is gone forever . . . .]

Dietrich answers within the same worldview:

> *Die Sîfrides wunden lâzen wir nu stên.* (1726,1)
>
> [We should now just put aside Sivrit's wounds.]

Both, however, miss the point. *Sîfrides wunden* are also Kriemhilt's, and they cannot just be forgotten.

This kind of suffering must be made comprehensible in early feudal epic by way of the body metaphor. Eilhart's *Tristrant* is similar in its description of courtly intrigue: *dô wart âne wundin / Tristrant sêre vorsnitin* [Tristrant was sorely hurt, / but without physical wounds] (Trt 3082–83). Similarly, late medieval texts of ecstatic piety require of the believer that he experience Christ's passion on his own body, not just as a spiritual experience, not even in intensive imagination, but as a physical pain. In order truly to feel the wounds of Christ, it is sometimes recommended to actually wound one's self.[40] The somatic connection of *compassio* is not completely given up even in late medieval passion piety. In an analogous way, the bold metaphor of Kriemhilt's suffering of Sivrit's wounds circumscribes an emotional, but still physically experienced syndrome. In a world where pain is a concrete physical experience, Kriemhilt's love is very strange. In its diametric opposition to spiritual piety, this com-passion is, of course, destructive; it breaks down all expectations.

The narrator is able to work out a side of Kriemhilt that is completely improbable in the world of the *Nibelungenlied* and is therefore misconstrued by all. What has been thought, based on the constellation of events, to be an indestructible love for and faithfulness to Sivrit occupies a space that appears in the epic as a dark void. It is the *herze*, known from courtly literature as the locus of a new culture of interiority, but also as a closed place of secret thoughts and plans that apparently cannot be divulged. The difference between Gunther's lie and Kriemhilt's dissimulating *jâmer* is only one of degree.

The arme *Queen*

In the *Nibelungenlied* interior processes can only be taken up in a negative form. This is evident in the phrase *Kriemhilt diu arme* [Kriemhilt the poor] (1053,1). One is tempted to take *arm* as a statement about her *herzen jâmer*, but the epithet *arm* has a much richer meaning.[41] It includes subjective feelings and objective facts, without separating one from the other.

Kudrun can sharpen our sensibilities. Kudrun, too, is called *gotes armiu* in her captivity.[42] This refers to her situation as a whole. She is an orphan (K 1217,4), whose father was slain; she is separated from Herwic, whom she was supposed to marry; she has lost her possessions, is supposed to be forced to marry her kidnapper, and, because she refuses the marriage, performs the degrading services of a maid. God seems to have forsaken her (K 1036,3). All this means *arm,* but the loss of her royal position is especially emphasized. Upon her arrival in Ormanie, she accepts the service of Hartmuot, even though she still spurns him as her kidnapper:

> *jâ nam ouch diu arme den dienst von im durch êre* (*K* 975,3),
>
> [The poor woman accepted his service for the sake of her honor]

because Hartmuot's behavior restores, for just a moment, the position (*êre*) that she—*diu arme*—had lost. Synonymous with *armiu meit* (K 979,1) is *ellende meit* [exiled, estranged maiden] (K 989,1). Kudrun is *ellende* because she is separated from the social group in which she is recognized and that knows her status.[43] The force that Gerlint, Hartmuot's mother, uses against Kudrun is primarily meant to demean the princess:

> *von allen hôhen dingen wil ich dich swachen unde scheiden.* (K 999,4; cf. K 1062)
>
> [I am going to humiliate and divorce you from all that is noble.]

She succeeds: *jâ mohten si ir adeles niht geniezen* [they could not enjoy her nobility] (K 1007,4). The restoration (*ergetzen*) of her royal position can only be had at the price of marrying Hartmuot (K 1028,3). Because Kudrun refuses, she remains *armez ingesinde* (K 1190,3; K 1194,1).

How concretely this status is conceived and how little it can be understood as just demoralized despair is apparent when rescue is announced. Kudrun is prepared for the appearance of her rescuers—her fiancé and her brother—by an angel (K 1206,2). When the two at last come, however, she is not happy and first remarks how *arm* she is. She is ashamed and wants to flee:

> *Dô sprach diu jâmers rîche: "owê, ich armiu meit . . .*
>
> [Then she, full of despair, said: "Oh, I am a poor maiden . . .]
>
> *sint ez die boten Hilden, suln mich die sus hie vinden*
> *waschen ûf dem grieze, daz laster kunde ich nimmer überwinden.* (K 1208,1; 3–4)

> [If these are Hilde's messengers, and if they see me here
> Washing on the beach, I could never get over the shame.]

The disparity between the status of the former *vil edelen frouwen* and her present appearance as *arme[z] ingesinde* (K 1216,2–3) and *gotes armiu . . . in disen grôzen schanden* [wretched before God . . . in such great shame] (K 1209,1;4) is so intolerable for Kudrun that it almost botches the rescue. Rather than being seen in a condition of humiliation, she wants to stay where she is (*ê wolte ich immer heizen ingesinde* [I would rather be forever a servant], K 1209,4). Her companion does not dare give advice in such a risky matter (cf. K 1210,2). Only once, when the rescuers implore her to stay *durch ander magede êre* [for the sake of other young women's honor] (K 1215,3; cf. 1214,3), does Kudrun at least wait until they come closer.

In the ensuing conversation any recognition is again delayed, so that Kudrun's deficient status—poor clothing, separation from home and family (*diu vil armen weisen*, K 1217,4)—can be emphasized once again. She must be set up in her previous position before the rescue can begin. It is true that even in her current condition, her nobility and beauty are still evident. The rescuers do not recognize Kudrun, but they suspect, when they first see her, that she is of royal blood: *ir möhtet krône tragen . . . ir soltet landes frouwen sîn mit grôzer êre* [you could wear a crown . . . you should be the lady of a land with great honor] (K 1222,1;3). They address her and her companion as *schœne frouwen*—that is, as ladies (K 1224,3). They also take into consideration, however, a difference in status with the *armen* Kudrun, which is why both men, in order to lessen this difference, do not introduce themselves as kings but only as *eines küniges ingesinde* [servants of a king] (K 1228,4).

Kudrun's humiliation also affects her rescuers: *Kûdrûn diu arme* (K 1240,3), *diu arme meit* (K 1246,1), the *vil armiu* (K 1277,2) is not even recognized by her own brother. On the contrary, he thinks: *mîner swester nindert anelîch* [she's not at all like my sister], because she was a *sô schœne maget* [a beautiful young woman] like no one else in the world (K 1239,2; 4).[44] The psychologically correct explanation, that they have not seen each other for over a decade, is too cursory, because Herwic is not deformed by a humiliating servile role, and Kudrun positively recognizes the features of her fiancé: *dem sît ir anelîch* [you look like him] (K 1241,2). Kudrun is able to convince him, on the other hand, that she is dead, even though she is standing in front of him, and that the washerwoman he sees before him is not Kudrun.[45]

What is needed is a sign to establish Kudrun's identity: her ring. The sign represents Kudrun's real status, because it is gold. Herwic recognizes her rank more than he does the unrecognizable person in shabby clothing:

> *dich truog ouch anders niemen, ez <en>wære küniges künne.* (K 1250,3)
>
> [None but royalty could have borne you.]

The characterization *arm* stands primarily in opposition to noble, admired, and powerful and designates the alienation from the position that Kudrun has thanks to her birth, promise in marriage, and family.[46] Emotional *leit* is conveyed primarily through the loss of identity, the result of the kidnapping—isolation from her family and relatives—and humiliation—-the loss of royal rank.[47]

Influenced by characters of courtly romance like the mourning Enite and Sigune, this portrayal of a poor queen lamenting the loss of her throne along with the loss of her husband, and the loss of her identity along with the loss of her throne, later seems to have been found wanting, but it by no means disappears. In *Wolfdietrich D*, it becomes farcical: Liebgart, the widow of Emperor Ortnit, nightly laments the loss of her husband, whom half of Europe served, bewailing the great power and magnificent position she has lost with his death:

> *ich han es als verloren und mus es faren lan.* (Wo D 1477,4)
>
> [I have lost it all and must live without it.]
>
> *Di vor min diner waren, sin nu di herren min.* (Wo D 1478,1)
>
> [Those who were previously my servants are now my lords.]
>
> *Ach wer sol mich nu trosten, mich arm elendes wip.* (Wo D 1480,4)
>
> [Who will console me now, poor woman that I am.]

This may correspond to the image of a "poor" queen, but it cannot be justified by the story. Liebgart is still empress. No one has subjugated her or threatened her possessions. Her lament is parody. This is evident when the watchman only hears the material aspect of the lament of the *arme[n] frawe* (Wo D 1482,3). He advises her to make a living with what she has learned:

> *Sidt ir wol kunnet spynnen und wurcken an der ram:*
> *Dar mit ir wol gewynnet brot und den klaren win,*
> *Sidt ir von lant und luten sollend verstossen sin.* (Wo D 1483,2–4)
>
> [Since you know how to spin wool and can work at the loom,
> you can make a living and earn your bread and wine,
> because you have been ostracized by land and people.]

The words of the guard make fun of the double meaning of *arm* by reducing Liebgart's pain to a problem that, on the one hand, does not exist, and, on the other hand, seems solvable.[48] The late burlesque is a reply to the implicit notion that *arm* does not primarily concern something emotional, but is rather about position in society, property, *êren*, and its related privileges.

Kriemhilt, the gotes arme

The fact that *arm* cannot be restricted to this aspect alone is what makes the *Nibelungenlied* "modern."[49] It is not at all meaningless either. "Subjective" and "objective" components, for instance, are linked in Rüedeger's complaint:

> *Owê mir gotes armen, daz ich ditz gelebet hân.*
> *aller mîner êren der muoz ich abe stân,*
> *triuwen unde zühte, der got an mir gebôt.* (2153,1–3)
>
> [Oh, I am forsaken by God, that I have lived to experience this.
> I have to give up all my honors,
> loyalty and decency, which God required of me.]

Being forsaken by God brings not only the destruction of the ethical values that Rüedeger represented, but also the loss of their expression in terms of social status and general worth before God and mankind.

When Kriemhilt is called *diu arme*, one first thinks of her pain on account of Sivrit: *daz si des recken tôdes vergezzen kunde niht* [that she could not forget the hero's death] (1142,3). Sivrit's immeasurable wealth cannot make up for the loss of his person:

> *Und wære sîn tûsent stunde noch alse vil gewesen,*
> *und solt' der herre Sîfrit gesunder sîn gewesen,*
> *bî im wære Kriemhilt hendeblôz bestân.*
> *getriuwer wîbes künne ein helt nie mêre gewan.* (1126)[50]
>
> [Had there been a thousand times more wealth,
> if lord Sivrit were alive again,
> Kriemhilt would have stood by his side with nothing.
> A hero never had a more loyal wife.]

Other statements that point in the opposite direction should not be discounted, however, and statements like those just cited should not be taken out of context.[51] Strophe 1126 serves as heroic hyperbole. The tremendous size of the treasure is exceeded by the even more tremendous extent of pain. This is not to say that the treasure is unimportant. The two belong together:

> *Mit iteniuwen leiden beswæret was ir muot,*
> *umb ir mannes ende, unt dô si ir daz guot*
> *alsô gar genâmen. dône gestuont ir klage*
> *des lîbes nimmer mêre unz an ir jungesten tage.* (1141)
>
> [Her mind was laden with renewed grief
> for her husband's death, and then they stole all that
> she owned. She could never end her lament
> for the rest of her days.]

It is likewise wrong to reduce Kriemhilt to the quest for power or to deny her dependence on her royal position.[52]

From Sivrit's death on, Kriemhilt is called the *arme[] Kriemhilt* (1056,4), *diu gotes arme* (1080,4),[53] the *vil arme[] wîp*, who regrets her trust in Hagen (1112,2). The epithet *arm* brings aspects of the loss of status and the loss of the beloved together. To some extent, being *arm* can be compensated for materially. When Giselher offers: *nu zer mîn eines guot* [you can depend on my resources] (1079,2) and promises: *jâ wil ich dich ergetzen dînes mannes tôt* [I shall compensate you for your husband's death] (1080,3), the material aspect of the loss is in the foreground, and the narrator underlines this with the agreement of the *gotes arme[]: des wære Kriemhilde nôt* [I—the poor woman, Kriemhilt—do need it, indeed] (1080,4), or even more clearly in C 1091,4: *dô sprach diu küniginne: "des wær mir armen wîbe nôt."* [the queen answered, "That would be necessary for a poor woman like me"] With very similar words, Kriemhilt will later remind Rüedeger of his promise to help her with her revenge: *des wart mir armem wîbe nie sô grœzlîche nôt* [I, poor woman that I am, have never needed it so much] (2149,4). In each case, *arm* denotes a deficiency that could be remedied by Giselher's *guot* and by Rüedeger's military assistance. *Arm* is a counterconcept to a position of power (*rîche*), which includes property and status.[54]

The epithet equating Kriemhilt with the *armen* means her temporary exclusion from the circle of the rich and powerful.[55] This impairs her status only to a limited extent, because what counts for Etzel is what she was at Sivrit's side. If the greatest hero took her as his wife, she is therefore also desirable for the most powerful king:

> *Dô sprach der künic Etzel: "was si des recken wîp,*
> *sô was wol alsô tiure des edelen fürsten lîp,*
> *daz ich niht versmâhen die küneginne sol.*
> *durch ir grôzen schœne sô gevellet si mir wol."* (1158)

> [King Etzel spoke, "As she was the hero's wife,
> the noble prince was of such merit,
> that I should never denigrate the queen.
> She is pleasing to me on account of her great beauty."]

Etzel's desire (*gevellet*) is not for the person, whom he does not know, but for the beauty and the nobility she represents, which are a result of the value (*tiure*) of her first husband and forbid that she be held in low esteem (*versmâhen*). Kriemhilt is defined for him by the status she gained at Sivrit's side.

What is most important for Kriemhilt, on the other hand, is what she has lost through Sivrit's death. She therefore calls Etzel's courting *spot* [mockery], such as God should not allow, because it is addressed to an *arme* woman (1218,3). "Poverty" defines a state of powerlessness and material dependency that should require consideration, but in reality makes Kriemhilt subject to the whims of the powerful.

Because the elimination of Sivrit's power and the destruction of his person and beauty are two sides of the same coin,[56] his death not only causes Kriemhilt's loss of position but also makes her beauty worthless. When she is called the *schœne[] vreudelôse[]* (1009,2) after Sivrit's murder, this is actually a contradiction of her general status and current condition, the same contradiction evident in the phrase *Kriemhilt diu hêre und vil trûrec gemuot* [Kriemhilt, the ladylike and totally dejected] (1225,1).[57]

"Befitting" (*zemen*!) her disrupted social position is *weinen* (1242,4; 1245,2),[58] not what is expected of a queen, which is the display of beauty. Beauty is not a quality that attaches to a person, but one that requires a suitable rank. So Kriemhilt doubts whether she is still beautiful enough to present herself at Etzel's side:

> *wie sold' ich vor recken dâ ze hove gân?*[59]
> *wart mîn lîp ie schœne, des bin ich âne getân.* (1245,3–4)

> [How could I appear at court before heroes?
> If I was once beautiful, that is no longer so.]

No one should calculate how Kriemhilt's beauty may have faded after so many years, and it is inappropriate to see only the self-estimation of a careworn widow in these words. The verses say something else. Beauty is one of the usual qualities that go along with Kriemhilt's status. With the loss of status, beauty—as a publicly viewed value of representation—is lost as well. On the other hand, beauty is born to Kriemhilt by virtue of her origin. It is a potentiality that can immediately be restored in the proper social context. Rüedeger therefore counters Kriemhilt:

> *zwiu woldet ir verderben einen alsô schœnen lîp?* (1254,3)
>
> [why would you want to ruin a beauty like yours?]

Kriemhilt has hardly accepted Etzel's courtship when the magnificent clothes return. As the future wife of the king of the Huns, she appears *hêrlîchen* [like a lady] (1337,3), and when she lifts her veil in front of Etzel, her beauty shines as before: *ir varwe wol getân / diu lûht' ir ûz dem golde* [her beautiful color / shone through the gold] (1351,1–2), just as was the case with her appearance with Sivrit at Worms: *ir varwe gegen dem golde den glanz vil hêrlîchen truoc* [her color appeared to radiate against the gold] (799,4). She again has the setting that suits her.

The first dispute over Etzel's courtship is about Sivrit (*mir hât der tôt an einem sô rehte leit getân* [the death of the one man pained me greatly], 1238,3). But it is already about Kriemhilt's deficient status and the possibility of curing this defect, too. This continues when she thinks to herself about Etzel's courtship:

> *Dô bat si got vil dicke füegen ir den rât,*
> *daz si ze geben hête golt silber unde wât,*
> *sam ê bî ir manne, do er noch was gesunt.* (1247,1–3)
>
> [She asked God in earnest to give her advice,
> so that she could give gold, silver, and garments,
> as once when her husband was still alive.]

Kriemhilt does not ask God an open question, but instead asks him for help (*rât* also has the meaning of assistance), so that she might once again have property that she can give away. This possibility is opened up by Etzel's riches, as before with Sivrit's hoard. In the plan for revenge, the thought of material loss and the possibility of making it up is not forgotten. The one is a requirement for the other:

> *"waz ob noch wirt errochen des mînen lieben mannes lîp?"*
>
> *Si gedâhte: "sît daz Etzel der recken hât sô vil,*
> *sol ich den gebieten, sô tuon ich swaz ich wil.*
> *er ist ouch wol sô rîche, daz ich ze geben hân.*
> *mich hât der leide Hagene mînes guotes* [!] *âne getân."* (1259,4–1260,4)

["what if my dear husband's death might still be avenged?"

She thought: "Since Etzel has so many warriors,
if I command them, then I could accomplish anything I wanted.
He is also so wealthy that I can give freely.
That horrible Hagen took all my property."]

The narrator reminds us twice of the defect at the very moment it is remedied. He calls Kriemhilt *trûrec lîp* (1263,3) when she finally agrees to Etzel's wooing, and he has her say: *ich wil iu volgen, ich armiu künegîn* [I shall obey you, I am a poor queen] (1264,1).

It seems unimaginable to the protagonists that Kriemhilt would remain *unvrœlîche* once she lives in *vreuden* again. However, this kind of restoration is not enough. This becomes apparent in the ceremony of the rulers' *hôhzît* when her status is restored:

Sie wæn' in Niderlande dâ vor niene gesaz
mit sô manigem recken. dâ bî geloube ich daz,
was Sîfrit rîch des guotes, daz er nie gewan
sô manigen recken edele sô si sach vor Etzelen stân. (1368)

[I think she had never before lived in the Netherlands with
so many heroes. Therefore, I believe,
however rich Sivrit was, that he never had
as many noble warriors as she saw standing in front of Etzel.]

But "sitting" at the side of a ruler—a sign of happiness exclusive to class and a metonymy of rule—is devalued under another aspect:[60]

Wie si ze Rîne sæze, si gedâht' ane daz,
bî ir edelen manne. ir ougen wurden naz.
si hetes vaste hæle, daz ez iemen kunde sehen.
ir was nâch manigem leide sô vil der êren geschehen. (1371)

[She thought of her life on the Rhine,
with her noble husband. Her eyes teared up.
She tried hard to hide it so that no one could see.
She had received much honor after so much grief.]

As ruler, Kriemhilt has more than before. Her past *leit* is relieved by *êren*, but her condition remains deficient.

Here, dissimulated but still visible, (restorable) status and (irretrievably lost) bonds to Sivrit's person are split. With Kriemhilt's comeback at Etzel's side, the two sides are distinguishable and conflict with each other. The restoration of Kriemhilt as queen does not bring with it reconciliation, but stimulates revenge.

Kriemhilt grew up *In disen hôhen êren* [with these great honors] (13,1)—in the position provided by the Burgundian kings. This *êre*, her royal rank and nobility (*adelvrî*, cf. 828,1), was first contested by Prünhilt. The confrontation resulted in Sivrit's death and with it the destruction of all *êren*. After the intermezzo of the hoard, Etzel's marriage to Kriemhilt equipped her with *vil grôzen êren* (1387,1). The return to the original state is not real, however. Kriemhilt uses it for revenge, and as a result she will not only be destroyed, but so will the power to which she owes her restitution. In this way, the concrete background to the meaning of *arme Kriemhilt* is present to the very end.

Even the *Klage* does not initially emphasize the memory of Sivrit with regard to Kriemhilt's *leit*. Instead, it focuses on life in the (heathen) foreign land (*ellende*):

> *Iu ist wol geseit daz*
> *wie si zen Hiunen gesaz*
> *alsô diu edele Helche ê.*
> *doch tet ir zallen zîten wê*
> *daz si dâ ellende hiez,*
> *wand si der jâmer niht enliez*
> *geruowen selten keinen tac,*
> *wand ir an dem herzen lac*
> *wie si verlôs ir wünne.*
> *ir aller næhstez künne*
> *het ir ir lieben man benomen.* (Kl 71–81)
>
> [You have been told
> how she ruled over the Huns
> as once the noble Helche did.
> But she was always saddened by the fact
> that she was a foreigner there.
> The pain she felt
> was with her every day,
> for she remembered
> how she had lost all her happiness.
> Her closest family members
> had taken her dear husband from her.]

This lessens the scandal that Kriemhilt does not accept what is meant to be restoration. What Kriemhilt was offered as a ruler at Etzel's side was not reparation for the treason of the *næhste[n] künne* but exile among heathens.

Kriemhilt's continual *jâmer* is proper for an external situation that is itself deficient.

The epic juxtaposes the two sides of the *armen Kriemhilt.* This explains how contrary interpretations, each seeking to harmonize the whole, can offer plausible arguments based on the text, but from different parts of the text. Being at Etzel's side as queen, the *arme Kriemhilt* seems again to be what she once was, but it is evident that her *leit* was not centered on the loss of her position as queen. But the other side of personal identity, hidden from others, is discovered to be only destructive.

Emotional Complexity

The narrator does not content himself with a simple aggregation of different schemes of interpretation, however. Contradictory characterizations are employed in order to develop a complex web of contingency. This is especially noticeable in *Âventiure* 23, in which Kriemhilt's motivations become blurred,[61] when she, as uncontested ruler in control of Etzel's power, thinks of her Burgundian relations and her unfinished revenge. The narration tells of an only seemingly confused, but in reality highly artful sequence of considerations, recollections, internal dialogue, feelings, desires, dreams, gestures, all of which take on the concrete form of a plan, ending in the request to Etzel that he invite her Burgundian relatives. Narrator speech from personal and authoritarian perspectives, something like "perceived speech" (1392,4), and a character's direct speech take turns. Likewise the story and the main character's thoughts, desire, dream, and prescience are all interwoven in an erratic, alogical narrative style. The radiance of Kriemhilt's position and her past *leit,* her conflicted feelings, and her contradictory relationship to the Burgundians are placed squarely side by side.

The starting point is Kriemhilt's recognition of her own power (*daz ir niemen widerstuont* [that no one opposed her], 1391,1), then her memory of what happened earlier:

> *si gedâht' ouch maniger leide, der ir dâ heime geschach.*
>
> *Si gedâht' ouch maniger êren von Nibelunge lant,*
> *der si dâ was gewaltic unt die ir Hagenen hant*
> *mit Sîfrides tôde hete gar benomen,*
> *ob im daz noch immer von ir ze leide möhte komen.* (1391,4–1392,4)

[she remembered all the pains that she had endured at home.

She also remembered all the honors in Nibelungenland,
of which she had disposed and that Hagen
had taken completely from her with Sivrit's death,
if she might still be able to hurt him as well.]

The two things are still not connected. The memory of *maniger leide* (1391,4) immediately recalls *maniger êren* (1392,1). The anaphora (*si gedâht' ouch—si gedâht' ouch*) points to the "linkage" within the *memoria*, as described by contemporary theory.[62] The two are connected with each other by Hagen's crime (*die ir Hagenen hant / mit Sîfrides tôde hete gar benomen* [which Hagen had / taken completely from her with Sivrit's death] 1392,2–3). The conclusion from this is the desire for revenge:

ob im daz noch immer von ir ze leide möhte komen. (1392,4)

[whether she might still be able to hurt him as well.]

To accomplish this would mean that she could bring Hagen into her sphere of power: *Daz geschæhe ob ich in möhte bringen in ditz lant* [this could happen if I managed to get him to come to this land] (1393,1). Thus, a link to the recognition of her power (1391,1) is established. What remains incomplete is its realization. At first, her considerations stop: a standstill. The next verse seems to begin afresh with a dream, in other words, below the level of a conscious plan. However, the dream takes the very place left open in the wish (*Daz geschæhe . . .*):

ir troumte daz ir gienge vil dicke an der hant
Gîselher ir bruoder, si kuste'n z'aller stunt
vil ofte in senftem slâfe: sît wart in arbeiten kunt. (1393,2–4)

[She dreamed that she very often walked hand in hand
with her brother Giselher. She kissed him all the while
very frequently in her gentle sleep. Afterwards they experienced much travail.]

The dream seems on the surface to show the opposite of the desire for revenge. Instead of the recompense of hatred for Hagen, it shows the joy of being close to her brother. That both are connected is only shown by the narrator's forewarning in the fourth verse, which points to the fateful end for "them." Does this mean Kriemhilt and Giselher? Everyone? Again, the speech breaks off.

The narrator retains his voice in the following strophe, which starts afresh:

> *Ich wæne der übel vâlant Kriemhilde daz geriet,*
> *daz si sich mit friuntschefte von Gunthere schiet,*
> *den si durch suone kuste in burgonden lant.*
> *dô begonde ir aber salwen von heizen trehen ir gewant.* (1394)
>
> [I think that the evil devil counseled Kriemhilt
> to end her friendship with Gunther,
> whom she had kissed in reconciliation in Burgundy.
> She then began to soil her dress with her hot tears.]

The narrator attributes to the *übel vâlant,* a superhuman power, an event that has not yet been mentioned. What is the reference? Apparently, it is to a future event, that Kriemhilt *mit friuntschefte von Gunthere schiet,* that is, that after she has kissed him in reconciliation (*durch suone*), her *friuntschaft* with Gunther comes to an end.[63] And in fact, Kriemhilt will consummate her plan against her brother without regard for *friuntschaft* and *suone.*

What is at stake is shown by a variant in mss. A and B, which was corrected by Karl Bartsch according to the parallel manuscripts.[64] According to this variant, Kriemhilt separates herself not *von Gunthere,* but instead *von Giselhere,* her favorite brother. This is, based on the story line, "a mistake," because nowhere has Kriemhilt exchanged a kiss of reconciliation with Giselher as she did with Gunther.[65] How does Giselher's name get here? For a moment, the former story seems forgotten: Kriemhilt's positive and negative relationships are most clearly polarized in Giselher and Hagen, and so kiss and treason can be aimed at the beloved Giselher instead of the ambivalent Gunther. The "wrong" name strengthens the impression of a monstrosity for which the *übel vâlant* must be responsible, whether directed against Giselher or against Gunther.

The stanza anticipates the impending treason. This anticipation assumes an implicit link between the statements of strophes 1393 and 1394—the hatred for Hagen and the love for her brother. The impossibility of coaxing Hagen into the realm, since all ties to him have been cut, is opposed by the possibility of seeing her *friunde,* represented by Giselher or also by Gunther, with whom Kriemhilt has been reconciled. What was considered in the conditional (*Daz geschæhe . . .*) can be realized thanks to this link. This is not stated here but will be accomplished later.

Again the speech breaks off. Instead of a commentary on what has passed or a glimpse into what will happen, there are more tears from Kriemhilt. As always with *trûren,* they seem to indicate an open, still undetermined situation. And again there is a new beginning:

Ez lag ir an dem herzen spât' unde vruo,
wie man si âne schulde bræhte dar zuo
daz si muose minnen einen heidenischen man.
die nôt die het ir Hagene unde Gunther getân. (1395)

[She thought about it night and day,
how she had innocently been brought to the point
where she had to marry a heathen.
This had been done to her by Hagen and Gunther.].

Nothing before or after seems, in fact, to justify what de Boor calls the "foolish incorporation of a religious motif."[66] Only in the *Klage* and to some extent in *C does Etzel's heathenness become a problem. In the ups and downs of considerations and moods, however, the stanza contains a precise argument even without this background. The *suone*, which has reconstituted the family peace, has taken away the legal justification for revenge. The use of *vâlant* makes it clear that if Kriemhilt steps outside the bounds of the law, she will be in danger of leaving the Christian order. The response is more tears. But if others forced her into leaving this Christian order, a matter *an dem herzen*, then she is no longer at fault (and through her the *vâlant*) in separating herself from them. Instead, the fault lies with Gunther and Hagen. If Hagen and Gunther had taken up opposing positions under the aspect of *suone*, then they are now side by side responsible for the *nôt* (1395,4) of a marriage outside of Christianity. This may be a rather futile claim, but it can lead out of the aporia. If Gunther (like Hagen) is guilty, then the argument of *suone* is nullified.

The speech starts anew: *Des willen in ir herzen kom si vil selten abe* [she was almost always mindful of this intent] (1396,1). Why *willen* [intent]? On the surface, the preceding verses talk of feelings and thoughts, but not of *willen*. The narrator abruptly makes clear here what stood behind these seemingly so irregular feelings and thoughts: a *wille*, namely, the desire for revenge. Dream, expression of feelings, the devilish dilemma, the accusation of being handed over to a heathen, all this can be summarized under *wille*, because it is driven from the desire expressed at the beginning (1392,4) that is now taken up again: *daz ich mînen vîenden gefüege noch ein leit* [that I shall still hurt my enemies] (1396,3). Now revenge can be explicitly linked to the awareness of unlimited power (*ich bin sô rîche unt hân sô grôze habe* [I am so powerful and have such great possessions], 1396,2), with which the scene opened.

Turning back to the starting point, a clear connection has emerged between different motivations in a dense web. The following stanza formulates this succinctly:

> *"Nâch den getriuwen jâmert dicke daz herze mîn.*
> *die mir dâ leide tâten, möhte ich bî den sîn,*
> *sô würde wol errochen mînes vriundes lîp.*
> *des ich kûme erbeite," sprach daz Etzelen wîp.* (1397)
>
> ["My heart longs often for those who are faithful to me.
> Those who did harm to me, if I were close to them,
> then the death of my love would be avenged.
> I can hardly wait," spoke Etzel's wife.]

Now the emotions are ordered, and without waiting any longer, Kriemhilt puts her plan into action, inviting the *getriuwen* so that she can get at her enemies. The conversation with Etzel, in which she pushes through her agenda, plays with the constant exchange of the terms *vriunt* and *vîent.* Kriemhilt once thinks *vriunt* (1399,3), once *vîent* (1400,4), where Etzel always hears and says *vriunt* (1401,4; 1402,4; 1406,2; 1407,2). *Vriunt* is the official term, even where *vîent* is meant.

This narration contradicts the cause and effect explanations of a commonsense psychology. Complexity is created beyond breaks, in that memory, desire, dream, longing, and contemplation switch off and take each other's places. From this sequence the contours of the vengeance plan begin to take shape. The aporetic consideration that vengeance assumes the presence of Hagen in Etzel's land is "answered" by a dream of comfortable proximity to Giselher. This is in turn answered by the commentary that Satan is involved when Kriemhilt moves past the kiss and *suone.* The argument's basis in Christian law is answered by the claim that Gunther as well as Hagen have delivered her up to a heathen. These "answers" do not exactly follow the rules of narrative association or clear argumentation, but in their alogical sequence, the image develops of a queen who is about to sacrifice everything to her desire for vengeance.

The Name and "Identity" of the Hero

Modern ideas about "identity," it seems, don't take us very far in the characterization of Kriemhilt, and the outlining of the other characters corresponds to these ideas even less.[67] Attempts to interpret them have mostly gone awry.

The *Nibelungenlied* contains a great many names, and we are inclined to see the carriers of these names as identical to certain characters, to whom we then attribute certain qualities and traits. While their composition may change gradually over time ("The courtly young girl becomes a horrible avenger, because . . . "), not all of them can be changed at once. The story then becomes "unbelievable." In order to reduce this unbelievability, one looks for clues to what comes later, searches for at least symptoms of what is repressed that later becomes virulent. If, on the other hand, one sees how in the epic someone is recognized as himself, then the criteria are completely different from those of a consistent character.

The individual is defined by his origins. A character is not built up successively out of many individual traits, but is what he or she is from the beginning, based on clan, family, and surroundings. Sivrit is introduced as a young knight educated at court. Mentioned first are his origins (*in Niderlanden*), then his class (*eins edelen küneges kint*); third, he is defined through his father's name (*Sigemunt*) and his mother's (*Sigelint*), then by where he grew up (*ze Santen*), and lastly by his own name (*Sîvrit*, cf. 20,1–21,4).

This only describes the social role of Sivrit, the son of a king, not that of the dragon slayer. The identification as hero is added "aggregatively" after Sivrit's appearance at Worms. There his high rank is suspected on account of the magnificence of his appearance. In the courtly world, there are signs that make it possible to recognize the new arrival as someone who "belongs" (*hêrlîch gewant*, 72,4; weapons). No one knows him by name, however, until Hagen arrives.

Hagen also assesses the *geverte* and *gewant* of those who have arrived (84,3), but for him they remain *vremde* (84,4). Based on their appearance, he concludes that the foreigners are *fürsten oder fürsten boten* [princes or the emissaries of princes] (85,2). Then he continues that while he has never seen Sivrit, nevertheless he is certain—*gelouben* (86,3) oscillates between "being convinced" and "claim to be true"—that it is he, *der dort sô hêrlîchen gât* [who goes there so splendidly] (86,4). He immediately begins to tell of Sivrit's heroic deeds. The hero is known by his appearance and his deeds alone. This is why he can be greeted in Nibelungenland, even though he had never been there before, as someone known as the *starke Sîvrit* (90,3), as if he were the only one who could have ridden there. The hero has a special story that belongs only to him, one that identifies from the beginning what he is, the *starke Sîvrit.*

For courtly protocol, on the other hand, identification as a hero and the story of his deeds are not enough. When Gunther suggests, after hearing Hagen's story and seeing Sivrit's combative attitude, *wir sulen im engegene hin nider zuo dem recken gân* [we should go down to meet the hero] (102,4), Hagen agrees, but now because Sivrit's royal descent is known to him:

> *"Daz mugt ir," sprach dô Hagene, "wol mit êren tuon.*
> *er ist von edelem künne, eines rîchen küneges sun . . . ."* (103,1–2)
>
> ["You may do so," said Hagen, "with complete honor.
> He is of noble lineage, the son of a powerful king . . . "]

Identity is determined in three ways. First, the individual is defined in his native environment by rank, surroundings, and clan, and only lastly by name. He embodies a clan and the rule over a certain area. What he does, or is, is based on this. Second, "recognition" at court is based on the decipherable signs of clothing, weapons and equipment, and bearing and appearance. Sivrit carries the signs of his social stratum. They are not completely clear as to status (prince or the messenger of a prince) and do not yet make it possible to identify the stranger by name. Third, "familiarity" with the hero requires neither acquaintance nor deciphering signs. Hagen's knowledge results from Sivrit's appearance (*der dort sô hêrlîchen gât,* 86,4), which represents his deeds. Sivrit's appearance is such that all other possibilities are discounted, paradoxically, because there is nothing individual about him. He appears as a great hero, who certainly has a name of his own, but above all eminently embodies the qualities that distinguish a hero.[68]

These forms of identification are assigned different spaces: one's own social group, courtly society, and the space of legend. The young knight must still be raised to become what he is by virtue of his birth. With a stranger, membership in courtly society is recognized only little by little based on the signs of his bearing. The hero is from the beginning recognizable by what he does. In each case, Sivrit is representative of a generality: a clan, a way of life, a power.

The three ways of identification are not equally valid everywhere. In Nibelungenland and in Isenstein only the third way works. It is not possible in Isenstein to recognize Gunther and his companions based on their origins, but the courtly signs are not recognized either. Their appearance is carefully staged. The four Burgundians wear expensive clothing, two in white—*reht' in einer mâze . . . von snêblanker varwe* [in a uniform manner. . . of a snow white color] (399,1–2), and two in black—*von rabenswarzer varwe . . . rîchiu kleit* [rich garments of a raven black color] (402,3). They appear as members of a courtly society of virtual equals. Gunther, the suitor, and Sivrit, the suitor's assistant, are highlighted. Such an exclusive courtly equality plays no role in Isenstein, because there can be only one contestant. Sivrit playacts rein and stirrup service so that those watching should know who is the suitor and who is the assistant. The production misses the mark, however. Prünhilt and her ladies do not draw the desired conclusions with regard to the distribution of rank and roles in the contest. The signs mean nothing to them. What is told is a story of misinterpretation.[69]

Only Sivrit, the hero, is recognized:

> *Dô sprach ein ir gesinde: "vrouwe, ich mac wol jehen*
> *daz ich ir deheinen nie mêr habe gesehen,*
> *wan gelîche Sîfrîde einer darunder stât.*
> *den sult ir wol enpfâhen, daz ist mit triuwen mîn rât."* (411)
>
> [One of her household said: "Lady, I can truly say
> that I have never seen any one of them
> except that one being like Sivrit is standing among them.
> You should receive him well, this is my loyal counsel."]

It is not about physiognomic similarity in this *gelîche Sîfrîde*.[70] The conventional signs that normally work for co-, sub-, and superordination (clothing, rein and stirrup service) are countered by the automatic recognition of the hero. The knowing of what and who is "the hero" is sufficient to allow Sivrit to be recognized, even when he is dressed like Gunther and leads Gunther's horse like a servant. Because the hero is incomparable, someone who is *gelîche Sîfrîde* must also be Sivrit. Who Sivrit is, of whom *ein ir gesinde* speaks, is apparently so obvious that Prünhilt has no need to ask who is meant. Previously in Nibelungenland, the speaker recognizing Sivrit had to explain his statement.[71] The other three are assessed in the usual way.[72] For Prünhilt, none of the three has a name; only Sivrit has one. Prünhilt greets him matter-of-factly as the suitor (and is corrected). In Isenstein, the third way dominates.

Sivrit, for his part, recognizes the heroic queen and can assure Gunther, who appraises the women he sees in the castle in a courtly manner according to clothing, beauty (392,2–3), and proper behavior (*gebærde*) (393,4): *ez ist diu edel Prünhilt* [it is the noble Prünhilt] (393,2) whom Gunther has selected out of the crowd. Just as only one among the arrivals can be Sivrit, so only one among the throng of women can be Prünhilt. She is recognized by the one who knows how to navigate her world.

The "improbable" certainty with which the heroic persons are identified is connected to the spaces to which the dragon slayer and the heroic virgin belong. This knowledge is separated from other kinds of normally valid knowing: origin, family, courtly signs of rank, all appropriate to the characters of the second part. Thus different ways of identifying someone overlap. One is bound to the deciphering of conventional signs and dynastic relationships, the other is couched as a kind of epiphany, all signs and gestures are placed in the shadows and devalued. This second method can even be accomplished when the bearer of the name has never been seen before.

Übermuot

What is manifest in the epiphany of the hero? Its core seems to lie in superior strength. This characterizes not only a hero like Sivrit but to various degrees all actors of the epic. These are transpersonal traits that come to the fore in the hero. The characters of the *Nibelungenlied* can be described as bundles of energy that become effective in them and through them. They are decentralized in the sense that there is no center of gravity of the "person" to which everything moves, but only collective energies in which they take part.

This excess of energy is called *übermuot*. It has been known for a long time that *übermuot* should not be misunderstood as a character trait, because it refers to a power that is effective beyond character-specific specialties. The vernacular concept is sometimes taken as a translation of Latin *superbia*. This results in overburdening the term theologically and identifying it with Lucifer's original sin.[73] Even in early medieval Latin chronicles, it can be observed that the boundary, sharply drawn by the term *superbia* between positive and negative behavior, is uncertain. The difference between religious and feudal value systems becomes apparent in the pairing *superbia/übermuot*. When, for example, Hermann Billung, in a "ritual of protest" against Emperor Otto I, "usurps the royal reception ritual to the last detail," the Church chronicler calls this *superbia*, a clearly negative judgment. In doing so, however, he only gives us the perspective of a cleric in the service of the Saxon kings, not that of the nobles who supported Hermann Billung and his actions. *Superbia* is a fighting word. For those involved, Hermann's behavior expresses his claim to rule over Saxony and represents the legitimacy of this claim.[74] Whether or not this is usurpation depends on one's point of view. The act only becomes *superbia* based on clerical opinion. This is documented in writing—by Thietmar von Merseburg—but the competing positive assessment, from the viewpoint of the nobility that supported Hermann, can be deduced from the story. The theological disqualifying term *superbia* is anti-feudal and partisan in the sense of monarchic power, which was supported by the clergy.

The theological background, characterized by the discussion of the seven deadly sins, pales when it is shifted to the vernacular. *Übermuot* becomes available for other meanings, as an "ethically undifferentiated exuberant feeling of strength and joy," as already hinted at by Latin chronicles.[75] *Übermuot* is hardly unambiguously positive or even neutral at this time. Only in certain religious contexts does the term share a meaning with the theological concept of *superbia*.[76] It often only remains tinged by religiously influenced, negative, and partisan shading.[77]

In the *Nibelungenlied, übermuot* denotes the attitude behind aggression. In this sense, one speaks of the *übermuot* of the Saxon attacker (151,2). Sivrit's challenge to the court of Worms is called *übermüeten* (117,4), and Gernot prohibits the Burgundian warriors' hostile speech (*mit übermüete*, 123,3; cf. 175,4; 240,1). The question of right or wrong is usually ignored. One may still assume that the Saxons' *übermuot* means that their attack is illegitimate, but on the other side, the attacker Liudegast also calls the Burgundian defense *starkez übermüeten* (167,4). Finally, when peace is restored, the whole feud is called *übermüeten* (254,4). As with Hermann Billung, risk-taking and offensive spirit are taken by the other side to be *übermuot*.[78] The characterization is therefore based on perspective.[79]

Übermuot is by no means completely negative,[80] but its value is controversial. The term itself is most often not self-descriptive, but an attribution from outside. What is meant is a self-assertion and self-awareness seemingly dangerous to the potential opponent. The mutual attributions cancel each other out. Elfriede Stutz's observation of ethical indifference hits the mark for exactly this reason.[81] *Übermuot* does not refer to an all-encompassing moral order (as *superbia* in the group of venal sins) that would guarantee a binding valuation. It corresponds moreover exactly to the absence of an abstract state order that would harmonize the varied and partly contradictory legal relationships.

Übermuot determines the quality of the hero who knows his own strength and does not think to be concerned about that of others. The epithet *übermüete* can denote the neutral characteristics of a warrior without any specific justification from the situation: the *übermüete Hagen*, who meets the water sprites (1549,1), *die übermüeten degene*, as the Huns are still called when they hold back like cowards (1792,4). What is often meant is nothing more than audacity and strength.[82] Kriemhilt says that with Sivrit she did not have to fear, *daz im iemen næme in sturme sînen lîp, / ob er niht wolde volgen sîner übermuot* [that someone could kill him in an attack / unless he would follow his *übermuot*] (896,2–3).

Übermuot crosses the boundaries between smart and foolish, legitimate and illegitimate, ethically defensible and inconsiderate, egoistical behavior. Values are uncertain. This can be exemplified by the advice Sivrit gives his companions when they arrive in Isenstein to pretend that he is Gunther's *man*:

> *durh ir übermüete ir deheiner ez niht liez,*
> *si jâhen swes er wolde, dâ von in wol gescach* . . . . (387,2–3)

> [no one failed on account of their *übermuot,*
> they spoke as he had asked them, and therefore they succeeded . . .]

Sivrit's advice is correct, because it ensures success in Isenstein (*dâ von in wol gescach*). The fact that his companions do what he asks can be *übermüete* in the sense of a careless self-assuredness that does not bother with consequences—this meaning seems to be dominant here—but also in the sense of a fateful self-overestimation and lack of consideration for what other people think. Only in this way can *übermüete* paradoxically refer to a gesture of subordination instead of self-presumption.[83]

Übermuot is ambivalent. Self-confidence can turn into aggression, such as with the *übermüet[n] verge[n]* [ferryman], who challenges Hagen with his words (1553,4) and thereby loses his life, or with Hagen himself, the *übermüeten gast* (1561,1). *Übermuot* can be a thoughtless delusion that confuses caution with fear.[84] Why did no one make Etzel aware of the latent enmity between Kriemhilt and her relatives?

> *er het wol understanden daz doch sît dâ geschach.*
> *durch ir vil starken übermuot ir deheiner ims verjach.* (1865,3–4)

> [He might have been able to stop what happened afterwards.
> No one told him about it because of their great *übermuot.*]

Thus *übermuot* moves into the sphere of inconsiderate presumption that knows no bounds of law or custom. Prünhilt's *übermuot* (340,3; 446,4) threatens all suitors with death. Her *übermuot* must be overcome by force.[85] After Sivrit's death, *übermuot* is the prepotency of the victor, who could care less about her rival's *leit*:

> *Prünhilt diu schœne mit übermüete saz.*
> *swaz geweinte Kriemhilt, unmære was ir daz.*
> *sine wart ir guoter triuwe nimmer mê bereit.*
> *sît getet ouch ir vrou Kriemhilt diu vil herzenlîchen leit.* (1100)

> [Prünhilt the beautiful ruled with presumption.
> However much Kriemhilt cried, she cared little about that.
> She was not willing to offer her any empathy.
> Lady Kriemhilt would someday also cause her great grief.]

Finally, *übermuot* comes close to the criminal. The murder of Sivrit and the profaning of his body is a story *von grôzer übermüete . . . und von eislîcher râche* [of great presumption . . . and of terrible revenge] (1003,1–2).

These negative qualities are strengthened in some variants in the manuscripts. The *Klage* (B) traces Sivrit's downfall to his *übermuot* (Kl 39), and in the *C version, it is traced to the *übermuot* of his murderers. *Übermuot* is in one place incomprehensible thoughtlessness; in another place, it is criminal insolence. Since the connotation of the Luciferian is also present in the vernacular, the turn to the pejorative is possible at any time.[86]

Thus *übermuot* comes close to *hôchvart*, which is clearly negative in meaning,[87] and, at least in courtly epic, it is even closer still to *superbia*.[88] This nuance is also present in the *Nibelungenlied*. Sivrit's father Sigemunt cautions others about Hagen: *der kan mit übermüete der hôhverte pflegen* [he can be overbearing and arrogant] (54,2), that is, his heroic self-esteem becomes presumption.[89] In a similar sense, Sivrit remarks on the defeated Prünhilt, *daz iuwer hôhverte sint alsô hie gelegen* [that your presumption has been humbled] (474,2). Here, too, the negative assessment is not completely clear. *Hochvert[ig]e site* seems to be more a personal characteristic of heroes and characterizes all their actions, like *übermüete*. When the Burgundian kings jump into the fray, this is described as *si tâten daz si wolden in vil hôhvertigen siten* [they did what they wanted in an overbearing manner] (1891,4).[90]

The negative connotations of *übermuot* and *hôchvart* only become prevalent in the reception of the *Nibelungenlied*, as is evident in the Kriemhilt character of the *Rosengarten*. The king's daughter from Worms drives warriors into battle senselessly and with a lust for blood. The challenge to a tournament is presumption and is called *übermuot*. Dietrich announces with indignation: *daz ich ir hôchvart niht übersehen wil* [I shall not overlook her presumption], because the invitation of the *unsinnigen meit* [thoughtless maiden] to chivalrous sport is *affenheit* [stupidity].[91] This makes unambiguous what the epic leaves open.

With a more positive accent, the courtly *hôhe muot* is within the semantic sphere of *übermuot*, too. In courtly culture, the source of *hôhen muot* is an awareness of the superiority of an elite, but violent conflicts are surmounted peacefully, and the exuberant awareness of one's own strength is changed into the experience of communal joy at a courtly festivity.[92] In the *hôhen muot* of courtly culture, the excessive and hybrid are tamed and the self-reference of *übermuot* is socialized. With *hôhen muot*, the epochal shift in the nobility's self-image becomes apparent.

In the *Nibelungenlied*, the boundaries are still fluid. The causes are often the same as in courtly poetry; *hôhen muot* causes the exhilaration of service to a lady,[93] the festival, or the reception of messengers,[94] the enjoyment of luxury,[95] well-being, the harmony of ordered rulership.[96] The phrase designates the attitude of those who belong to courtly society: *si sint vil hôhe gemuot* [they are in high spirits] (390,4). *Hôher muot* can also be used in the positive sense of "battle-hardenedness, courage, *virtus*."[97]

In the *Nibelungenlied*, the concept starts to shift to the (positively connoted) *übermuot* with the joyous anticipation of battle (181,4), or at the victorious return from the war (243,4), with the spirit of the quest in an adventure (381,4), or the excitement of the hunt.[98] But it is not only the self-assured satisfaction at the sight of a numerically superior army that is so called—*Sîvrit in hôhem muote sach vil vrœlîchen daz* [Sivrit looked upon it gladly in high spirits] (181,4)—but also the presumption and overestimation approximating *hôchvart*. The ferryman on the Danube is so rich and courtly (*sô rîche*) that he refuses his services to the Burgundians. The additional reason is given as *ouch wâren sîne knehte vil hôhe gemuot* [his men were high-spirited] (1551,3). This certainly points to his high status, but it also points to the future confrontation, where everyone is obliged to not give in. Another example: the narrator has characterized the willingness to deceive Prünhilt about Sivrit's status as *übermüete*, and he then asks, when Sivrit takes ring and girdle from Prünhilt's bedroom: *ine weiz ob er daz tæte durh sînen hôhen muot* [I don't know if he did it out of high spirits] (680,2). Sivrit acts from a feeling of triumph, so far, so good, but he pays dearly for it in the end. Are *übermuot* and *hôher muot* still distinguishable here? Finally, when Sivrit wants to motivate himself to defeat Prünhilt in the bedroom contest, and so prevent women from *tragen gelpfen muot* [being boastful] (673,3), this formulation can be substituted in the *C group by *hohe tragen den muot* [being high-spirited] (C 678,3). This moderates the *gelpfen muot*, but still points to the latently negative connotations of the new courtly fashion in the Nibelungian context.

A clear separation between the (more negative) *übermuot* and (positive) *hôher muot* cannot be maintained.[99] *Übermuot* and *hôher muot* appear, unlike *hôchvart*, to be used more often in a neutral sense,[100] which does not exclude an occasional negative usage. They represent a scale of self-esteem—at its core noble—between the insistence on one's own strength that wants constantly to prove itself through force and an unaggressive self-assurance manifest in courtly *vreude*. Both express themselves in an overabundance of *muot*, which is not a characteristic of an individual, but a force that penetrates heroes.

This force is what defines the hero, but it often appears to be ambivalent. Its complement is the hero's physical appearance.

Personality as Surface

The conception of this appearance is strangely two-dimensional. Everyone "is" what his exterior shows. Where the cloak *hût* covers up the surface, the person disappears. What seems to be meant by *hût* (unlike the more common *vel*—"skin")[101] is a layer that covers the body, similar to a dress. It is said of the dragon-blood armor that gives Sivrit his invulnerability, *sîn hût wart hurnîn* [his skin became scaly] (100,3); at the hunt, his clothing is of *einer ludemes hiute* [an otter's skin] (954,1).[102] The *tarnhût,* alternating with *tarnkappe* (invisibility cloak),[103] is also such a layer.

What happens under the protection of the cloak is just as hidden as what happens in the *herze.* Both conceal a dark reality, and it proves itself portentous whether the physical or the nonphysical, like thoughts and emotions, is hidden from view. Sivrit retains speech and his great strength while under the cloak, he can even—is this invisible, but sensory?—bleed (458,1). Whoever comes close to him, like Gunther, can hear and feel him (453). The body is present and absent at the same time. It is present for Sivrit himself and for those who touch him, but absent to everyone else, because Sivrit at first is only a visible surface exterior.

In the second contest with Prünhilt, heroic strength and physical appearance are strangely disassociated.[104] The battle for the ring with Prünhilt can be felt and heard. Sivrit and Prünhilt throw each other against the furniture, Prünhilt's gown is torn (671,4), blood flows (675,2–3), Sivrit presses Prünhilt so hard, *daz ir diu lit erkrachten unt ouch al der lîp* [that her bones cracked along with the rest of her body] (677,3), but the strength of the hero does not have an identifiable body, because his exterior is concealed. The brutal rape scene is completely impersonal,[105] so that the narrator, when Sivrit finally forces Prünhilt down, comments: *dô wart si Guntheres wîp* [she then became Gunther's wife] (677,4). The names of the men are interchangeable, because the one is "not there at all." Sivrit's strength only gets its name from a visible exterior—Gunther.

In these scenes, the figure of Sivrit is divided into three components: his exterior (which disappears), his other physical signs (which can only be sensed by some), and his strength (which is present independent of visibility and sensibility). All three components are conceived of physically. What would represent the core of a person in modern terms, his self-awareness, is only a secondary effect of the awareness of superior strength.

The characters in the *Nibelungenlied* have no depth, something that is "behind" their appearance. Even their physicality is flat and reduced to the visible exterior. What remains the same under all these exteriors is something general, the exorbitant strength of the hero. Whether in hunting attire, under the *tarnhût*, even under the armor of the dragon blood, Sivrit remains *der starke Sivrit*, the hero superior to all. His skins make him invulnerable, invisible, or a splendid courtly knight. He appears different in every case, thanks to these layers.

In order to gain some clarity with regards to Sivrit, and in this fantasy world this means in order to overcome him, his opponents have to pierce all of his "skins."[106] This finally succeeds when Hagen, supposedly to protect him in a threatening war, finds out where the skin can be penetrated under his clothing and the *tarnhût*. This episode shows once more that what someone is depends on his surface.

Generations of readers have asked themselves how Hagen can use the secret of Sivrit's vulnerability in the decisive moment. Probability is stretched thin, as it is unclear how Hagen could protect the vulnerable spot in any case and why he needs it marked so precisely. Kriemhilt designates it on Sivrit's clothing. When they are supposedly setting off to war, Hagen rides so close to Sivrit, *daz er geschouwete diu kleit* [that he saw his clothing] (907,4). Once he has seen enough (*Als er gesach daz bilde* [once he saw the image], 908,1), he has messengers come *tougen* [secretly], who then call off the war. A hunt is organized. The fact that Sivrit does not ride to the hunt in his combat attire, and that the sign cannot be seen at all on his clothing, is one of the illuminations of Nibelungian philology.[107] It gets worse, when during the fateful footrace with Gunther, Sivrit is dressed only in a white shirt. Did Kriemhilt mark the underwear, too? Nevertheless it is stated of Hagen:

> *er sach nâch einem bilde an des küenen gewant.*
>
> *Dâ der herre Sîfrit ob dem brunnen tranc,*
> *er schôz in durch daz kriuze . . .* (980,4–981,2).
>
> [he looked for a sign on the hero's clothing.
>
> When lord Sivrit drank from the fountain,
> he shot him through the cross . . .]

Now the sign is apparently on the shirt, where Hagen could hardly have seen it before.

The main point is not the suitable arrangement of a prop, but the discovery of Sivrit's vulnerability. The strength of the hero can be overcome by removing one layer of protective covering after another. Thanks to Kriemhilt's trusting nature, something that was *tougen* can now be seen through all the layers of coverings. Once it has become visible, it can never again be hidden. Once it comes to the surface, it remains present. Sivrit carries the sign of vulnerability on his body.

To be someone else for others requires darkening the visible form or pulling a cover over it, a foreign shirt: Kriemhilt in her everyday clothes in the midst of a festively clothed court society (1225,3) is the *arme Kriemhilt*, who must first be properly attired in order to become queen again. This is, translated to courtly civilization (and rationalized accordingly), a final magical conception: pulling on a skin can transform a person, making him into a member of courtly society or a werewolf. The *tarnhût* is closer to magical concepts than the courtly rationalizations, but it belongs to the same set of ideas: although the clothing does not change Sivrit himself, it does change his image for others.

Medieval literature has a series of phantasms of identity transformations accomplished by changing clothes or even one's skin. When Eilhart's Tristrant has to disguise himself in order to escape Mark's officers, he puts on a pilgrim's robe, making himself unrecognizable. Under this pilgrim's robe, however, he wears normal courtly attire. When he comes upon a chivalric contest by chance, he is asked to participate and of course proves himself to be an outstanding knight. He is only recognized as Tristrant, however, when the pilgrim's robe is torn and the courtly clothing becomes visible underneath it (Trt 7811–13). What is concealed under the pilgrim's robe is shown through his deeds, but only his social "skin" can show the others who the pilgrim really is.[108]

This seemingly burlesque disguise episode comes at the beginning of a series of changes in form that Tristrant must go through to be near Isald. The final disguise is that of the fool. It is not a disguise anymore than Sivrit's skin of dragon blood. A wound had transfigured Tristrant to such an extent that his earlier appearance has vanished and no one can recognize him (Trt 8650–53). The formerly handsome knight seems to be an ugly jester. Protected by his new exterior, he can approach Isald and make himself known to her with a sign and words (Trt 8917–21). He can then remain close to her, unrecognized, for a longer time. The skin that was worn is now real, the false and projected social identity are now grown together. Even under the new exterior, Tristrant remains the superior hero that he was. This is why Isald loves the ugly fool, and this is why the fool, when others try to grab him, creates havoc with his club, just as Tristrant used to do. What is distinguished here is what one is for others and what one is for oneself (and in this case, for one's beloved). Social existence—bound not only to clothing, but also anchored in the body, a matter of the "skin,"—is not the be all and end all, and this seems typical of the Tristan legend.

A foreign skin is appropriated by the villain Ruhart in *Morant und Galie* (MuG 3031–3168), allowing him to appear unrecognized at Karl's court.[109] Here, skin is meant literally. Ruhart gets a pilgrim drunk, kills him, and pulls off his facial skin along with his long, black beard. The bloody face mask is then rubbed with salt and dried in the chimney:

> *mit sines scharpen metzes ort*
> *begunde he eme ritzen*
> *beneden sime antlitzen*
> *die hut mit deme barde*
> *inde eme ane scharde*
> *also bluodich, also ro*
> *mit deme hare ave zo.*
> *mit salze he si sprede,*
> *dar na he si erwede*
> *in me rouche inde machede si hart* . . . . (MaG 3076–85)
>
> [With the sharp tip of his knife
> he began to cut him,
> taking the skin beneath his face
> along with the beard,
> and without any lesion,
> all bloody and raw,
> he pulled it off by the hair.
> He rubbed it with salt,
> then he dried it in the smoke, making it hard.]

The tricks borrowed from leatherworking for the preparation of the face mask and the technical considerations—Ruhart has to pull on the chin when he wants to put on the mask (*vaste he ne ouch nochte / beneden sime kinne* [he had to grab / underneath the chin], 3126–27)—already point to a late period, when magical concepts about switching identities by using a new skin have to undergo scrutiny based on criteria of believability. To the face mask of skin, Ruhart adds the shabby clothing of the deceased. He wounds himself in the legs and pulls on the face and beard of the dead in order to become unrecognizable. Where mask, clothing, or cloak of invisibility are thought of as second skins, which must simply be worn to change identity, the real skin of another person can also serve as a mask. Of course, Ruhart is discovered in the end. The deceptive change of identity fails. What is lurking underneath the skin is discovered.

There is a scene in *Salman und Morolf* that is peerless in its metaphoric precision. Morolf puts on the skin of a stranger, not only his face, in order to appear as someone else. He kills an old Jew, flays him *oberhalb dem gurtel* [above the belt], and puts on the embalmed skin:

> *inn der hute ging der ritter lobesan*
> *in allen den geberden,*
> *als were sie im gewachssen an.* (SuM 163,3–5)
>
> [The praiseworthy knight walked in the skin,
> in all movements
> it seemed as if it were his own.]

Not even his own brother Salman recognizes him until he takes off the skin and his courtly exterior is visible once again. It immediately manifests itself as a new skin: *scharlach cleider* [scarlet clothing].[110]

As long as the covering is on, what happens underneath, whether it is the skin of a Jew or the *tarnhût*, does not exist for the outside world. Personal identity, bound up with corporeal appearance, is a kind of cloak, whether it is actually a piece of clothing or the surface of the body. Social existence is given a physical and natural basis. On the other hand, even Morolf, when he puts on a foreign skin, remains the swindler that he is, and this is why he can change skins. Underneath the surface, there is something else, even if it is not named.

Such phantasms are the backdrop for the game with Sivrit's skins. Sivrit remains Sivrit, not only for the audience, but also for himself. Even if his body is not in view, he is still the strongest. The strange thing is that this identity, which is disconnected from surface appearances, plays no role in the story line. What Sivrit is for himself is unimportant. The only thing that matters is what he is for others. The conflict ensues because Prünhilt does not accept what she sees after Sivrit has taken off the top layer: the *tarnhût*, and its constant pendant, the role as Gunther's *man*. Prünhilt sticks to what she has said first and doubts what is presented to her at the double wedding and what she is later shown by Kriemhilt at the tournament. Prünhilt cannot get around what Sivrit now evidently is. She tries "to get behind" what she sees and had seen. After the truth is not cleared up at the court, one layer of Sivrit's skin after another has to be penetrated, to include the invulnerable *hût* that Sivrit carries under his courtly clothing.[111]

The "skins" are linked more or less closely to the person of the hero and affect to varying degrees what he is for others. The *tarnhût*—Sivrit's possession alone, rarely worn, and not used by anyone else afterwards—increases his strength, so that he is more hero than before, and at the same time it makes his strength unapproachable. The hunting outfit that he can take off emphasizes his elevated stature at court. In a shirt, he is reduced to his physical strength, although he is still superior to everyone else. The *hurnîn hût* is finally the surface and at the same time the basis for his power. If it is penetrated, strength and life end. Step by step, each of these "skins" is more strongly "interwoven" with the one who wears them. Sivrit's "skinning" and his destruction are one and the same.

The character of Sivrit is made up of overlapping layers. The uppermost, the cloak of invisibility, is also the most powerful, but it is worn only on exceptional occasions, and it proves to be a powder keg for the courtly world at Worms. The second layer, the magnificent hunting outfit (951–57) is the exterior of his true status and, one last time for all to see, leads his stature at court to event greater heights, from which the fall is all the more precipitous. His death means that he has been literally "disrobed." First, Sivrit takes off his hunting clothes (976), and then, after he has won the footrace, he also lays down his weapons (977). Only now can Hagen's spear penetrate the hole in the armored skin, striking Sivrit's lifeblood. Without the armor—the cloak of invisibility, the splendid clothing, the weapons, and as a final layer the armored skin—Sivrit is nothing more than a target for Hagen's spear. When all skins have been penetrated, he dies. He is a cadaver and is left to be found in the dark (1004–6). There is nothing left underneath the visible layers of changing exteriors.

5 The Shrouding of Visibility

The Transparency of the Nibelungian World

The Nibelungian world is basically constructed in terms of visibility. Horst Wenzel has interpreted the "dramaturgy of visibility in the tension between orality and literality" as the adjustment of the *alten mæren* to the "poetics of courtly representation." Based on previous work by Hugo Kuhn, Wenzel identifies the progression of the story in a "tableau vivante" and the scenic form as the core of Nibelungian poetics.[1] A narration in a *tableau* is chosen over a linear coherence of syntagmatic linkages.[2]

Visibility is the immanent norm of the Nibelungian world. Where it is manipulated or counterfeited, conflicts are sown in the first part that come to fruition in the second part. The ever more brutal breakthrough of violence can be understood as the uncovering of a crime, and its preparation as a sneaky game with false appearances. The reestablishment of transparency in the open confrontation proves, however, to be a process of regression, in which, in the end, everything that was at all important to this world is destroyed. Once all deception is put aside and everything that can shroud visibility is removed, there is nothing left to see: *Diu vil michel êre was dâ gelegen tôt* [the great honor lay there in ruins] (2378,1).

This *êre* was manifest in the splendor of those who were gathered at court, first in Worms and later at Etzel's court, in the furbishing of the court and courtly society, in the material means for this furbishing, and finally in the luminescence of the hero. This *êre* expresses itself in the reputation of a court (*mære*). What is said about a court (*mære*) attracts foreigners who want to see the splendor for themselves (107,4) and who themselves in turn increase it.[3]

What is told is reflected in the perception of those who can later testify and tell others. Prünhilt's contests are paradigmatic:

> *Der rinc der was bezeiget, dâ solde daz spil geschehen*
> *vor manigem küenen recken, die daz solden sehen*
> *mêr danne siben hundert. die sah man wâfen tragen:*
> *swem an dem spil gelunge, daz ez di helde solden sagen.* (433)
>
> [The circle was drawn out, there the contest would take place
> in the presence of many bold warriors, who were supposed to observe,
> more than 700 in number. They were seen carrying weapons:
> in order that the heroes would proclaim whoever was the winner.]

There are several "circles" of observers. In the center is the contest in which Prünhilt and Gunther are supposed to engage. There is, of course, a blind spot in this center, namely, Sivrit, who is invisible underneath the cloak. Only Gunther is seen, and he moves according to what Sivrit does. Around this circle stand armed *recken*, who are supposed to verify the results. These are Prünhilt's men.[4] They are the weapon-carrying witnesses who are so important in the feudal world, and what they are about to see will be valid in heroic memory. This circle of 700 is also seen from the outside (*die sah man*), although it is not stated by whom. There are apparently people who do not belong to the inner ruling circle. Around these there is apparently another circle, to which "we" belong, narrator and audience, all of those addressed by what is said about these old heroes. What the 700 will see is then later told by *die helde*. The memory of legend will see with the eyes of these 700. The narrator is the instrument for what "one" can see and what is then recounted. The eyewitnesses at the scene give the listener a perspective on the narrated world.

The only thing that matters is what happens in such a forum. It must be visible and also audible; audibility is complementary to visibility. Events are therefore often characterized as "loud." Prünhilt admits her defeat in front of her followers *lûte* (466,2) and calls on them to submit to Gunther. When Hagen greets him *harte lûte* (1183,1) in front of everyone, Rüedeger is recognized as a guest in Worms. An insult cannot be taken back once it is proclaimed *ze lûte*, as against Rüedeger (2141,4). When Volker asks his lords *vil lûte* (1802,4) to go *ze hove* [to court] (1803,2), he wants everyone to stop beating around the bush and tell him how Etzel is disposed toward them.

Audibility and visibility represent a legal bond. Legitimate rule is established when the king proclaims his will *vor sînen vriunden* [in front of his friends] (713,1), and the new ruler carries *vor . . . recken . . . krône* [his crown in front of warriors] (713,3). When Kriemhilt *in heimlîche vil dicke güetlîchen sprach* [secretly often spoke pleasantly] (132,4) about Sivrit, then this still does not say anything about Sivrit's position at the court of Worms, for "good speech" must reach everyone and cannot be restricted to the women's chambers. Sivrit's wedding must therefore take place in front of all. This ensures the general recognition of the foreign *künec* as the husband of the king's daughter.

> *vor*[5] *helden wart geküsset diu schœne küniginne sint.* (616,4)
>
> [The beautiful queen was kissed in front of heroes.]

The word for public recognition is *jehen*, which means to speak what is generally true or passes for true—for example, the *êren* that Hagen earns *billîche* (1797,4), the bravery that one must recognize in followers (1478,4), and Kriemhilt's *milte* (1333,3),[6] but also the fraudulent announcement of a second war against the Saxons (875,1). Those proclamations do not refer to certain single persons, but to heroic Fama. *Jehen* is at once justified and justifying:

> *sô müese man von schulden dem edeln recken jehen*
> *daz er wære ein der beste, der ie ûf ors gesaz.* (723,2–3)
>
> [Thus, one would have to acknowledge of the noble warrior
> that he was one of the best who ever sat in the saddle.]

Kriemhilt, when she distinguishes Sivrit in front of the court with her greeting, does not say what she herself thinks of him or feels for him, but what she has heard *jehen* by others. What she does say is what everyone says and what therefore must always be said of Sivrit.

One acts for the eyes of a noble audience, anticipating remembrance in future legend. This is expressed by the narrator's favorite formula: *man sach* . . . ,[7] less commonly *man hôrt* . . . .[8] Eyewitnesses are the source of future stories and credible memory. The events never just run their course, instead "one sees" their progression. What happens is mirrored in the perception of onlookers and listeners. The formula *man sach/man hôrt* does not shift the narrative world into a perspective of subjective perception, instead the narrator declares the topic to be of general interest. Glances are followed with glances: *under wîlen blicken man Prünhilden sach* [people saw Prünhilt glancing] (799,2). When someone removes himself from the bright arena of everyone's gaze, like Gunther after his unfortunate wedding night, it is noticed:

> *swes iemen ander pflæge, man sah in trûrende gân.* (647,4)
>
> [Whatever others were doing, he was seen to be walking about glumly.]

This signifies that something is defective.

What is worth seeing and is seen by all is by no means limited to the heroic core of the story. On the contrary, here, decisive matters take place in the dark, without anyone seeing anything. The many scenes of courtly life, which the scholarship of legend has derided as "tailor strophes," whether these are receptions, processions, chivalric games, or festivals, are also worth seeing. In these scenes, the congruence of seeing and meaning is most completely maintained for those who are present and for the remembering audience. They are the positive backdrop in front of which dark intrigues stand out.

Hearing is inferior to seeing. After Rüedeger disappears from Kriemhilt's and Etzel's sight in the palace while fighting, both incorrectly interpret the silence that ensues after his death (2228–29). Volker has to proclaim what happened in front of everyone: *daz er und sîn gesinde ist hie gelegen tôt* [he and his followers lie here dead] (2231,1–2). To dispel any further doubts, one has to show Rüedeger's corpse:

> *Welt ir des niht gelouben, man solz iuch sehen lân.* (2232,1)
>
> [If you don't believe it, then you can see it for yourselves.]

Perception through hearing is more ambiguous. The lament for Rüedeger could be for different people:

> *Dô hôrt' man allenthalben jâmer alsô grôz,*
> *daz palas unde türne von dem wuofe erdôz.*
> *dô hôrt' ez ouch von Berne ein Dietrîches man.* (2235,1–3)
>
> [Then a great cry was heard all around,
> so that the palace and towers resounded with the wailing.
> Then one of Dietrich of Bern's men heard it also.]

Dietrich's messenger goes to "see" the *jâmer*, which was previously heard (*done het man von liuten sô grôzen jâmer nie gesehen* [such a great outcry from people had never been seen before], 2241,4), to ask questions and be sure.

Whether in the courtly world of Worms, the distant Isenstein, or the legendary Nibelungenland, everywhere the main concern is to be seen and heard by witnesses. Sivrit's warriors from Nibelungenland must dress themselves magnificently for their journey to Prünhilt, *want uns dâ sehen müezen vil minneclîchiu wîp* [because many lovely women will see us there] (506,3). It is a sign of the shock of Sivrit's death that his men forget for a moment how they must present themselves in front of ladies (1022,2–3). The beauty and rank of the two queens, already heard tell of, must be proven for all eyes to see:

> *Dô speheten mit den ougen di ê hôrten jehen*
> *daz si alsô schœnes heten niht gesehen*
> *sô die vrouwen beide: des jach man âne lüge.*
> *ouch kôs man an ir lîbe dâ deheiner slahte trüge.* (592)
>
> [They looked upon them with their eyes, those who had heard tell before
> that they had never seen anything more beautiful
> than those two ladies: that was certainly said without lying.
> One could not discover any falseness in them.]

What is told (*jehen*) is based on eyewitnesses, and eyewitnesses confirm what is told. It can then be recounted (*jehen*) *âne lüge*. There is no deception (*trüge*) in the visible qualities of the ladies.

It is conspicuous, however, that the possibility of *trüge* is even considered (592,4). Given the complete transparency of the courtly ideal, we are reminded of the limits of visibility. Crossing these boundaries has fateful consequences.

The Anticipated Memory of Legend

The characters base their actions on what can be seen of them and what will be said of them in the future. An embassy or an appearance at a foreign court has to present itself to the judgment of a present or future audience as much as combat. When Rüedeger travels to the Rhine as Etzel's emissary, he promises the king:

> *Swâ man zen Burgonden mich unt die mîne sehe,*
> *daz ir ietslîcher danne dir des jehe,*
> *daz nie künic deheiner alsô manigen man*
> *sô verre baz gesande danne du ze Rîne hâst getân.* (1156)
>
> [Wherever people in Burgundy see me and my men,
> everyone will then confirm to you
> that no king had ever before sent so many men
> in a better way so far as you have to the Rhine.]

The quest is supposed to become a memorable occasion by virtue of the splendor of his arrival. Even where such an appearance could seem to be out of place, as in the wild Isenstein, the anticipated memory of legend sets the standard for the splendid display:

des sulen wir rîchiu kleider vor der frouwen tragen,
daz wirs iht haben scande, sô man diu mære hœre sagen. (344,3–4)

[Therefore, we should be richly clothed in front of the women,
so that we need not be ashamed when others tell our story.]

The protagonists are what others say they are. They are their *mære*:

Mære z'allen zîten der wart vil geseit,
wie rehte lobelîchen die recken vil gemeit
lebten z'allen stunden in Sigemundes lant. (720,1–3)

[Many stories were told constantly,
about how laudably the joyful warriors
lived day in and day out in Sigemund's land.]

The narrator spreads the word of what is rightly said of Sivrit, his strength, his power, and his wealth, and likewise of the fame of Kriemhilt's beauty, the might of her brothers, and the immeasurable realm of Etzel. The facts are less interesting than how they are mirrored in the judgment of those who matter. There are basically no differences between the authorities in their judgments. What characters and narrator say is only an expression of what "one" can see and say and will always say. And even where a judgment is controversial, it is presented as if it were the only one possible. In contrast to what everyone in the Middle Ages says about Kriemhilt, it is claimed that:

si was im getriuwe, des ir diu meiste menige giht. (1142,4)

[she was loyal to him, and this was acknowledged by most everyone.]

What is determined by *diu meiste menige* ought to be correct.

The judgment of others is the standard for action. Kriemhilt asks herself, what will others say when she, a Christian, has to marry a heathen in order to participate in Etzel's power? She is afraid: *des muoz ich ze werlde immer schande hân* [I shall always be disgraced in the eyes of the entire world for that] (1248,3). Instead of *schande*, some manuscripts have *schade*.[9] *Schade* and *schande* are closely related, because the negative judgment of people damages [*be-schäd-igt*] the individual, and *schade* also means *schande*.

The esteem of the eyewitnesses, and through them future memory, determines behavior. All major scenes are constructed so that many can watch and judge.

Even Rüedeger's conflict—this is usually forgotten in the dispute over its content—is recounted as a fight for appropriate recognition. It is therefore open for all to judge. It takes place in words and deeds on an open stage, in dialogue with the royal couple and in monologues, in which the speaker is apparently only talking to himself but in actuality speaks for everyone to hear. Rüedeger anticipates what others will think of him and what will later be said of him: *Di liute* (2160,1), *elliu diet* (2154,3), and *diu werlt* (2156,4) all represent authorities that must be impressed, that can impose shame, hatred, or the allegation of cowardice.[10]

It would be dishonor in the eyes of the *liute[n]* to go against the Burgundians: *wie sol ich râten in den tôt?* [how can I intend their death?] (2159,4):

Di liute wænent lîhte daz ich sî verzaget.
deheinen mînen dienest hân ich in widersaget,
den vil edeln fürsten unde den ir man.
ouch riuwet mich diu vriuntschaft, die ich mit in geworben hân. (2160)

[People will perhaps think that I am a coward.
I have denied my service to none of them,
to the noble princes and their men.
Above all, I regret that we concluded a friendship.]

To leave *vriunde* in the lurch could be interpreted as cowardice. Whoever follows incorrect norms "is" a coward, no matter how he fights.[11] The option to avoid a decision is determined by the opinion of all:

Swelhez ich nu lâze unt daz ander begân,
sô hân ich bœslîche und vil übele getân:
lâze aber ich si beide, mich schiltet elliu diet.
nu ruoche mich bewîsen der mir ze leben geriet. (2154)

[Whichever I now leave undone and do the other,
I shall have chosen poorly and done the wrong thing.
If I do nothing, then people will blame me for that.
He who gave me life must counsel me now.]

Rüedeger appeals to God, not so that He might show him how to solve a conflict of conscience, but so that he might be accepted by others.

It is also not said what Rüedeger thinks of Etzel's and Kriemhilt's genuflexion, but only what everyone else can see: *den edelen marcgrâven unmuotes man dô sach* [people saw the noble margrave's displeasure] (2152,3), or even more clearly: *trvren man do sach* [people saw him mourning] (C 2209,3). The gesture of submission puts him under pressure in front of others.[12] The standard remains what he should be in the eyes of others:

. . . vil sêre vorhte er daz,
ob er ir einen slüege, daz im diu werlt trüege haz. (2156,3–4)

[. . . he was very much afraid,
that if he killed one of them, the world would hate him for it.]

What Rüedeger says and thinks anticipates possible judgments of his behavior and expresses the two mutually exclusive demands on him that will form the basis of this judgment. He cannot free himself from this entanglement, but he can display his motivations, so that any judgment of him will be indisputable. The authority of God, to which he appeals (*Dô liez er an die wâge sêle unde lîp* [he exposed his soul and body to chance], 2166,1), will ensure that in the end his honor is intact.

Once his decision has been made, each one of his reactions is reflected in the glances of the audience:

Man sah in von dem künege vil trûrelclîchen gên. (2167,1)

[He was seen walking away from the king in sadness.]

Dô sah man Rüedegêren under helme gân. (2170,1)

[Rüedeger was seen going fully armed.]

daz sach der videlære: ez was im grœzlîche leit. (2170,4)

[the minstrel saw that: it hurt him deeply.]

Dô sah der junge Gîselher sîn sweher gên. (2171,1)

[The young Giselher watched his father-in-law go.]

Bedaz der videlære die rede volsprach,
Rüedegêrn den edelen man vor dem hûse sach. (2174,1–2)

[While the minstrel finished speaking,
Rüedeger, the noble man, was seen in front of the hall.]

Rüedeger satisfies Hagen's plea for his shield in the knowledge that everyone is watching him, which is why he hesitates at first, but then fulfills the request all the more demonstratively:

torst' ich dir in bieten vor Kriemhilde.
doch nim du in hin, Hagene . . . . (2196,2–3)

[I don't dare offer it to you in front of Kriemhilt.
But take it anyway, Hagen . . . .]

The fact that Kriemhilt is a witness increases the value of the gesture considerably, since it takes back a part of Rüedeger's decision in front of an even larger audience and reestablishes the balance between competing obligations. The reaction of those present (*dô wart genuoger ougen von heizen trähen rôt* [plenty of eyes were red from hot tears], 2197,2; cf. 2198,4; 2202,2) anticipates how Rüedeger will be remembered from now on, and Hagen proclaims the judgment of future legend:

> *ez wirt iuwer gelîche deheiner nimmer mêr* (2199,2)
>
> [There will never be anyone to match you.]

This is seconded by the narrator: *vater aller tugende lag an Rüedegêre tôt* [the father of all virtues, Rüedeger, lay dead] (2202,4).

The other protagonists act according to what will later be told about them. Memory is an authority not only for an individual but for an entire clan. The mortally wounded Sivrit complains of his *zagen* murderers (since they have offended central values of the Nibelungian world) by saying that the treason is directed against the honor of their own families:

> *Die sint dâ von bescholten, swaz ir wirt geborn*
> *her nâch disen zîten.* (990,1–2)
>
> [They will be stained by this, every child that is born
> from now on.]

Even those who are seemingly uninvolved, like Sivrit's own son, are affected:

> *Nu müeze got erbarmen daz ich ie gewan den sun,*
> *dem man daz itewîzen sol nâh den zîten tuon,*
> *daz sîne mâgen iemen mortlîche hân erslagen.* (995,1–3)
>
> [May God have pity that I ever had a son,
> whom people will blame for all time to come
> because his kin were murderers.]

Decisions are scrutinized based on what will be said:

> *ez wîzent uns die liute, und ob wir si bestân.* (1887,2)
>
> [People will blame us, if we attack them.]

Hagen says that the death of a warrior should not be lamented. There is nothing terrible in this as long as it can be said that he fell at the hands of a hero:

> *Daz ist ein schade kleine, . . .*
> *dâ man saget mære von einem degene,*
> *ob er von recken henden verliuset sînen lîp.* (1954,1–3)
>
> [That is nothing to worry about, . . .
> if people tell the tale about a warrior,
> as long as he dies at the hands of a hero.]

The most astounding expression of self-stylization for future remembrance is in a stanza where the dying Wolfhart speaks. Wolfhart takes pleasure in his own death, proclaiming himself a memorial:

> *Unde ob mich mîne mâge nâch tôde wellen klagen,*
> *den næhsten unt den besten den sult ir von mir sagen,*
> *daz si nâch mir niht weinen. daz ist âne nôt.*
> *vor eines küneges handen lige ich hie hêrlîchen tôt.* (2302)
>
> [And if my family wants to mourn me after my death,
> those who are closest and most dear, you should tell them for me
> that they should not cry for me. There is no need.
> I am lying here gloriously slain by the hand of a king.]

As a *hêrlîchen* slain warrior, Wolfhart will live on in heroic memory. The anticipation of the legend prohibits any distance. Individual and collective consciousness are identical. Wolfhart celebrates his own death as an example for future generations.

In this kind of programmatic self-stylization, Wolfhart's awareness could already be exaggerated. In late medieval heroic epic, this can develop into a rather cold calculation of one's own reputation. In *Biterolf*, Wolfhart says:

> *zwiu sol der in hervart*
> *von dem man niht ze reden hât?* (Bit 7784–85)
>
> [Who would go to battle
> if people did not speak of him?]

The only reason to fight is if something can be gained for posterity.

The *Nibelungenlied* does not suppress the cost of thinking like this. Hagen understands his last fight with Dietrich to be a test of who will take first place in future legendary commemoration:

> *man sol daz hiute kiesen, wem man des besten müge jehen.* (2326,4)
>
> [Today people will realize who is proclaimed to be the best.]

This is why he declines Dietrich's offer to find a legal settlement, because one would then tell the wrong story about him, and this cannot be allowed to happen:

> *von uns enzimt daz mære niht wol ze sagene,*
> *daz sich iu ergæben zwêne alsô küene man.*
> *nu siht man bî iu niemen wan eine Hildebranden stân.* (2341,2–4)[13]

[It would not be fitting if the story were told of us,
that two such courageous men surrendered to you.
Only Hildebrant is seen standing next to you.]

Where posterity judges a warrior's esteem, there is no chance of *suone* [reconciliation], because it could be interpreted as weakness. Even proposing it is seen as an insult (2347,4).

Such explicit self-memorialization questions the validity of heroic values. Wolfhart celebrates his death in a battle into which he was drawn by his unthinking wildness, and that will result in the death of his *vriunde*. Hagen's fixation on his own reputation seems like murderous pigheadedness in light of Dietrich's generosity. The anticipated *memoria* illicits reflection neither from Wolfhart nor from Hagen, but rather an impersonal plot mechanism that ruthlessly looks to one's own martial honor and nothing else.

It is telling that the two most positively drawn figures of the epic, Rüedeger and Dietrich, go their separate ways on precisely this point. Rüedeger also seeks to base his choices for action on what will later be said of him, but he acknowledges that the authority to judge is in itself contradictory. He is unable to evade its norms in testing what might be required of him, but he can try to be true to both sides. In Dietrich's flexibility, which borders on the self-denial of the *vergezzen* of *leit*, future commemoration as a motivation for present action is conspicuously absent. He answers Hagen's challenge to fight for first place in *memoria* with even greater flexibility and only submits to doing so when there is no other choice left. When memory becomes the object of subjective calculation, it begins to be irrelevant.

Extinguishing Visibility

The hero acts in the light. His visible presence is the zero grade of his mythical brilliance, which heroic legend identifies in Dietrich's fiery breath and the streams of light that emanate from him and his opponent Ecke.[14] A remnant of this persist in the gleam of weapons (1761,3; 1841,3), and in the fact that the hero proves himself by being seen. When Rüedeger suggests to his king that he take the widow of the famous Sivrit as his wife, he also reminds him that Etzel already "knows" the hero: *den hâstu hie gesehen* [you saw him here] (1157,3). This has irritated scholars from the beginning. Was this just the "composer's impulsive idea?" "There is no literature that tells of a stay by

Sivrit at the Hunnish court."[15] It may be possible that this is a reference to a forgotten legend. What is more important, however, is that the principle of "being known" is linked to "seeing." The fame of the hero is so matter-of-factly bound to visibility that "knowing" brings with it the impression of "having seen."

This principle is undermined in the intrigue involving Prünhilt. Sivrit's appearance at Isenstein serves to cover up his identity. The concealment of identity is a favorite narrative motif. The hero maintains his incognito in order to win honor independent of his inherited rank. His honor then shines all the more brightly when he is finally forced to disclose his name. This type is twisted in the *Nibelungenlied* when Sivrit allows his deeds to be counted toward the honor of another, and so the incognito can never be lifted. Sivrit uses the courtly signs of equality (through dress), the feudal signs of subordination (through service), and his greeting to Prünhilt to make his heroic identity disappear and to step behind Gunther.

He is successful because he pulls his second skin, the cloak of invisibility, on over his clothes during the contests. For those present, the person disappears along with his exterior.[16] This is shown by the events surrounding the contest with Prünhilt. No reader or listener spends much time on the question of how Gunther's cheating in the contest actually functions. The scene in which Sivrit, invisible beneath his cloak, wins the contest, while everyone watching thinks that it was Gunther, stymied the illustrators of nineteenth-century deluxe editions. It is easier said than done that Gunther moves during the contest pretending to be doing what Sivrit is actually doing (*nu hab du die gebære, diu werc wil ich begân* [you make the motions, I'll do the work], 454,3). It might still be imaginable that Sivrit holds the shield for Gunther during the spear fight, and then throws the spear with such force that Prünhilt concedes defeat. How Gunther picks up the rock that Sivrit then throws is difficult to imagine, however. Based on our idea of physical being, Sivrit's carrying the king as he jumps would certainly seem suspect. A modern reader would ask whether an exchange of clothing that could fool those standing further away or, even better, some sort of magical switch of bodies would not be more believable.[17]

Physicality in the *Nibelungenlied* means visibility. If Sivrit's body is invisible, then the feats that Gunther achieves with the help of an invisible body are ascribed to Gunther, because no one else can be seen. Gunther's actual body movements obviously play no role at all. Sivrit pulls a skin or cloak over his body and is no longer present to the onlookers. This is expressed as a phenomenon of (visual) perception:

> *dar in slouf er vil schiere, dô was er niemen bekant.* (431,4)
>
> [He slipped it on quickly, then no one knew him.]
>
> *dar gie er tougenlîche (von listen daz geschach),*
> *alle die dâ wâren, daz in dâ niemen ensach.* (432,3–4)
>
> [He came upon them secretly (this was done by trickery),
> so that, out of all who were there, no one saw him.]

Invisibility is essential for someone "not to be present."

Sivrit's night combat in Nibelungenland is based on similar assumptions. In this battle, the gatekeeper and Alberich feel the force of his body, but they cannot recognize him, because they cannot see him. It is not explicitly stated if Sivrit wears the *tarnhût* in Nibelungenland. Departing on the journey, he travels *in sîner tarnkappen* to the sea (482,2) and boards the ship *vil tougen* (482,3): *Den schefmeister sach niemen* [no one saw the ship's master] (483,1). The great speed of the ship, *alsam ez wæte der wint* [as if a wind were blowing] (482,4), *ein sunderstarker wint* [an especially strong wind] (483,3), is explained *von Sîfrides kreften* [by Sivrit's strength] (483,2), which can be enhanced by the *tarnhût*. Upon his arriving in Nibelungenland, it plays no role at all. The *tarnhût* stands above all for the removal of visibility, and this can be accomplished in different ways. In Sivrit's fight with the guards of his castle, nothing can be seen on account of the darkness, and so it is unimportant if he wears the *tarnhût* or not. Sivrit literally fights "under the cloak of darkness," which surrounds him like the *tarnhût*.

He arrives unrecognized (*der unkunde man*, 486,3). By disguising his voice (487,4) when he introduces himself as *ein recke* (488,1), nobody can recognize him. Even after he has defeated a giant and Alberich, the steward of the treasury, he remains unknown. Admittedly, Alberich recognizes in the physical superiority of his opponent that he must be a lord. He calls out that he cannot serve this lord, because he already belongs to another—he means Sivrit. There is only one way out of this dilemma, and that is if the victor is also Sivrit, and of course, whoever is as strong as Sivrit must also be Sivrit. So he says who he is: *ich heize Sîfrit; ich wând ich wær' iu wol bekant* [my name is Sivrit, I would think that you know me] (499,4).

He could not be *bekannt*, because he was not seen. The possible conflict between what was happening in the dark and what is confirmed openly is immediately sidelined, since the winner in the fight and the ruler are the same. The name clears things up, light is brought (*vil kerzen . . .* [many candles] are *enzündet* [lit], 504,1), and everyone recognizes Sivrit.[18]

The next scene in which the cloak is used is Gunther's second wedding night, and it confirms the importance of visibility. The second deception and fight in the bedchamber occur because Prünhilt has discovered another Sivrit, under the courtly exterior—Sivrit's social "skin"—at the wedding feast. She cannot decide which of her observations are true, those in Isenstein, which showed Sivrit as Gunther's *man* in the disembarkation ritual, in words, and in the contest, or those at the wedding feast of the kings, when Sivrit sat across from them as an equal and as *kunic*. She tries to find out by asking questions about what she sees, but she does not get very far. At first, she tries in the dark (*Diu lieht begonde bergen des edeln küniges hant* [the noble king's hand began to hide the light], 633,1) to find clues as to Gunther's role in the bridal quest. What she finds out about his strength in bed, however, clearly contradicts what was visible in Isenstein (639,3). She ties him up and hangs him on the wall. The sight of a king hanging helplessly must be erased by Gunther by daybreak, first by seeming to give in, and then by robbing Prünhilt of her power. To accomplish this, Sivrit's strength has to once again act behind Gunther's person.

The deception is executed as a removal of visibility. The cloak of invisibility covers the person, removes it from sight, and suddenly the one underneath it is "no longer present." When Sivrit has to stand in for Gunther in bed, he suddenly removes himself from Kriemhilt without her noticing.[19] At first, he disappears from her sight, and then she is no longer able to feel him:

> *si trûte sîne hende mit ir vil wîzen hant,*
> *unz er ir vor den ougen sine wesse wenne verswant.*[20]
>
> *Dô si mit im spilte unt si sîn niht mêr ensach,*
> *zuo sînem gesinde diu küneginne sprach:*
> *"mich hât des michel wunder, war der künic sî komen.*
> *wer hat die sînen hende ûz den mînen genomen?"*
>
> *Die rede si lie belîben. Dô was er hin gegân . . .* (661,3–663,1)
>
> [She stroked his hands with her white hand,
> until he disappeared in front of her eyes, she knew not where.
>
> After she had enjoyed herself with him, and he had disappeared,
> the queen said to his household:

"I wondered much where the king went to.
Who took his hands from mine?"

She left it at that. He had gone from there . . .]

The sense of touch follows the sense of sight.

When Sivrit enters Prünhilt's room in place of Gunther, the absence of his person, which Prünhilt is supposed to feel but not see, has to be covered up a second time. The presence of Gunther, whom Prünhilt will see but not feel, is not supposed to be noticed either. Sivrit, already invisible, puts out the lights of the servants that escort Gunther to bed (663,3).[21] This is not all. Gunther sends Prünhilt's servants away, bars the door himself with two bolts, and makes the room completely dark:

Diu lieht verbarc er schiere under die bettewât. (665,1)

[He hid the light under the bed canopy.]

The threefold extinction of visibility multiplies the bridal quest deception. Only now in complete darkness can Sivrit use his physical strength against Prünhilt. Again it happens in such a way that he *gebârte sam ez wære Gunther der künic rîch* [acted as if he were Gunther the powerful king] (668,1), in that he makes no other sign that might betray him:

Dô hal er sîne stimme, daz er niht ensprah. (667,1)

[He hid his voice, so that he did not speak.]

Sivrit cannot be recognized, even though Prünhilt feels his physical presence. When he withdraws after his conquest, in order to make room for Gunther in bed, he still tries to maintain the impression, *sam er von im ziehen wolde sîniu kleit* [as if he wanted to take off his clothes] (679,2). The perception of these clothes through touch is not affected by the cloak. Touch provides a reliable sense, as before with Kriemhilt, but touch is ineffective without sight, because it does not allow the identification of a person.

In the struggle with Prünhilt in the darkness, in which Sivrit again suppresses all physical characteristics, he remains, as long as he is not seen, not present for Prünhilt. Gunther, who is eavesdropping intently, is put at ease by the noises *daz heimlîcher dinge von in dâ niht geschach* [that secret things were not going on between them] (667,3). Because Sivrit is present underneath his *tarnhût* and takes with him signs that prove this presence,[22] there are doubts about which reality corresponds to the truth. In Gunther's quest, Sivrit is a foreign body who must be made to disappear in an excessive way, at first, only visually, later, when the deception can no longer be kept secret, quite literally. At the heart of the intrigue is the battle for what is visible and what therefore has a claim to the truth.

The Politics of Viewing

What can be seen and what is seen can be manipulated. Visibility is an effect that is produced. The distribution of gazes results from a game of power. Looks are controlled, looks can be used for political purposes. Not everyone is allowed to see everything. The distribution of gazes reflects the rank of the protagonists and their relationships to one another.

The formula "wanting to see someone" gives the gaze a hierarchical relationship, because the one who "wants to see" determines whose presence is desired and why.[23] To have a say over viewing signals power. A powerful ruler is one who "sees before him" (1391,3) many warriors or even kings. The view from up close represents a closeness to power, for example, when Gotelint says to Kriemhilt at the reception in Hun land:

> *nu wol mich, liebiu vrouwe, daz ich iuwern schœnen lîp*
> *hân in disen landen mit ougen mîn gesehen.* (1313,2–3)
>
> [How fortunate for me, dear lady, that I have seen your beauty
> in this land with my own eyes.]
>
> *daz si ir vrouwen sâhen, dâ von engerten si niht mêr.* (1342,4)
>
> [to see their lady, they wanted nothing else.]

A gaze promises favor:

> *sol ich gesunt belîben und Botelunges kint,*
> *ez mag iu komen zu liebe daz ir mich habt gesehen.* (1314,2–3)
>
> [If I remain well, and so, too, Botelung's child,
> it may yet be to your advantage that you have seen me.]

"To want to see" each other demonstrates social integration: *die liute in sâhen gerne* [people were happy to see him] (24,2) means that Sivrit is a focal point of the Xanten court. The phrase refers to intact relationships.[24] This is why Sigemunt wants to go with Sivrit to Worms:

> *sît daz iuch mîn sun Sîfrit ze vriunde gewan,*
> *dô rieten mîne sinne, daz ich iuch solde sehen.* (790,2–3)

[Since my son Sivrit gained you all as friends,
my senses advised me that I should come see you.]

Etzel has the same desire:

ir'n kundet iuwer vriunde sô gerne niht gesehen
als ich si gesæhe, der edeln Uoten kint.
mich müet daz harte sêre, daz si uns sô lange vremde sint. (1406,2–4)

[You could not want to see your friends
more than I do, the noble Uote's children.
It is very hard for me that they have not been seen for so long.]

Not seeing raises the suspicion that relationships are not intact. According to his emissaries in Worms, Etzel asks himself:

ob ir iuch iuwer swester niht sehen woldet lân,
sô wold' er doch gerne wizzen waz er iu hête getân,

[If you do not want to be seen by your sister,
then he would like to know what he has done to offend you.]
Daz ir in alsô vremdet und ouch sîniu lant.
ob iu diu küneginne wære nie bekant,
sô möht' er doch verdienen daz ir in ruochet sehen. (1448,3–1449,3)[25]

[that you shun him and also his land.
If you never knew the queen,
then at least he deserves that you should want to see him.]

When Kriemhilt exposes her brothers to the view of their new subjects, her royal rank becomes visible. Otherwise, the Huns might *wænen daz ich âne vriunde sî* [think that I am without friends] (1416,3):

ich hân vil hôher mâge; dar umbe ist mir sô leit
daz mich die sô selten ruochent hie gesehen.
ich hœre mîn di liute niwan für ellende jehen. (1403,2–4)

[I have a noble kin. That is why I am so hurt
that they so seldom desire to see me here.
I hear that people say I am an exile.]

Being allowed to see, on the other hand, is a privilege that not everyone enjoys, for example, when Sivrit is taken in by the Worms court. He is simply an object of Kriemhilt's and her ladies' looks (133,3). The power play of viewing has begun. Sivrit is a "gladly seen" guest at court (128,4)—*in sach vil lützel iemen der im wære gehaz* [no one who saw him disliked him] (129,4)—but he is still subject to the good graces of those who have a say over Kriemhilt's viewing. Whoever is seen but not allowed to see himself is dependent on the gaze of others. The dependence of viewing brings other dependencies with it.

Sivrit's wish to see Kriemhilt remains unfulfilled *volleclîch ein jâr, daz er die minneclîchen die zîte niene gesach* [he was not allowed to see his love for an entire year] (138,2–3). Even her interested glances are unknown to him:

> *Wess' er daz in sæhe die er in herzen truoc,*
> *dâ het er kurzewîle immer von genuoc.*
> *sæhen si sîniu ougen, ich wil wol wizzen daz,*
> *daz im in dirre werlde kunde nimmer werden baz.* (134)
>
> [If only he knew that the one he loved was watching him,
> he would have enjoyed that a great deal.
> If his eyes would have met hers, of this I am sure,
> there could have been nothing better for him in the world.]

The question, *ob er si gesehen möhte* [if he could see her] (260,2) and the futile hope, *daz ich die maget edele mit ougen müge sehen* [that I might see the noble maiden with my own eyes] (136,2), put him into a typical *minne* state of *trûren* (136,4), which he must overcome through deeds for the kings and the court. After his victory in the Saxon war, at first the hierarchy of viewing remains the same. When Sivrit returns with the army:

> *dô gie an diu venster vil manec scœniu meit.*
> *si warten ûf die strâze . . . .* (243,2–3)
>
> [many a beautiful young woman went to the windows
> and looked out upon the road . . . .]

Kriemhilt can see the victor, but she remains hidden.

This only changes at the victory feast. Now the kings use viewing as an explicit instrument of power. The warriors are to be rewarded by being allowed to see the women, with Kriemhilt at the fore:

> *lâzet iuwer swester für iuwer geste gân.* (274,3)
>
> [Let your sister go before your guests.]

The *für* ("before, in front of") expresses the fact that the distance between onlookers and the precious objects of desire is upheld ("before").

> *Von einer kemenâten sah man si alle gân.* (280,1)
>
> [They were all seen coming from the women's chamber.]

When the women appear, an empty space is drawn around them, like an aureole:

> *Die mit den frouwen giengen, die hiezen von den wegen*
> *wîchen allenthalben. daz leiste manec degen.* (287,1–2)
>
> [Those who accompanied the women ordered the crowd
> to make room. All warriors readily did so.]

Kriemhilt is like a distant light:

> *Nu gie diu minneclîche alsô der morgenrôt*
> *tuot ûz den trüeben wolken . . . .* (281, 1)
>
> [Then the lovely woman arrived, like the sunrise
> appears from behind dark clouds . . . .]
>
> *Jâ lûhte ir von ir wæte vil manec edel stein.* (282, 1)
>
> [Her clothing shone with many jewels.]
>
> *Sam der liehte mâne vor den sternen stât,*
> *des scîn sô lûterlîche ab den wolken gât.* (283,1–2)
>
> [As the bright moon surpasses the stars,
> whose light so clearly spreads from the clouds.]

Such a cosmic apparition is admired with a gaze "from below":

> *si was dâ ze ougenweide vil manegem recken erkorn.* (300,4)
>
> [She was meant to be a treat for many a hero's eyes.]

Beyond the metaphor, there is a ranking between those who look and the object looked upon.

> *man sach in hôhen zühten manec hêrlîchez wîp.* (287,4)
>
> [They saw many splendid women in gracious form.]
>
> *er sach die minneclîchen nu vil hêrlîchen stân.* (281,4)
>
> [He saw the lovely young lady standing magnificently there.]
>
> *daz er ze dirre werlde het iht scœners gesehen.* (282,4)
>
> [that he had never seen anything more beautiful in the world]

Sivrit will have to be lifted up to Kriemhilt.

The viewing is still collective. Everyone presses *daz si die maget edele solden vrœlîche sehen* [so that they could happily see the noble young lady] (280,4), and everyone is concerned *daz er an ze sehenne den frouwen wære guot* [that he would be favorably seen by the women] (277,2). The onlookers want to be the object of interested gazes. The asymmetry must be lifted, but only Sivrit succeeds. His shift to Kriemhilt's proximity is prepared when he himself moves from the subject to the object of the gazes:

> *Dô stuont sô minneclîche daz Sigmundes kint,*
> *sam er entworfen wære an ein permint*
> *von guoten meisters listen, als man im jach,*
> *daz man helt deheinen ni sô scœnen gesach.* (286)
>
> [Sigmund's child stood there so lovely,
> as if he had been drawn on parchment
> by a great master's hand, as it was said of him
> that never had a more beautiful hero been seen.]

As before with the "lightness" of the *vrouwe*, the masterpiece of the young knight is also detached from others at court. One can "see" that Sivrit is of the same rank as Kriemhilt.

He is distinguished by being allowed to see close up. Up to now, everyone could see Kriemhilt. No one's view was privileged over another's, and no one was rewarded above another with a glance from the women *vor allen disen recken* [in front of all these warriors] (288,4). The greeting of Sivrit in front of all onlookers is a part of courtly ceremony. He is invited to *ze hove gân* (290,3).

> *Der herre in sînem muote was des vil gemeit . . .*
> *daz er sehen solde der scœnen Uoten kint.* (291,1;3)
>
> [The lord was very happy in his heart . . .
> that he would see the child of the beautiful Uote.]

This kind of seeing denotes proximity, an appropriate greeting, touching of the hands, a ceremonial kiss, and finally a formal speech.

Up to this point, looks and gestures are displayed in everyone's presence. Only now does a sphere open up to Sivrit that is off-limits to others. The gaze goes back and forth, instead of just one person looking at the other (*do begund' er minneclîche an froun Kriemhilden sehen* [he began to look lovingly at the lady Kriemhilt], 303,4):

> *mit lieben ougen blicken ein ander sâhen an*
> *der herre und ouch diu frouwe daz wart vil tougenlîch getân.* (293,3–4)
>
> [They looked at each other with loving glances,
> the lord and also the lady, it was done so that no one else could see.]

Along with the secret gaze comes a secret touch that no one else knows of. Even the narrator claims to have no knowledge of it:

> *Wart iht dâ friwentlîche getwungen wîziu hant*
> *von herzen lieber minne, daz ist mir niht bekant.*
> *doch enkan ich niht gelouben daz ez wurde lân.* (294,1–3)
>
> [If a white hand was pressed tenderly,
> out of heartfelt love, I do not know.
> But I can't believe that it was not done.]

Taking away the competence of the all-knowing narrator, the mouthpiece of the legend, expresses that a space is opened up that is beyond heroic transparency.[26]

The distinction through proximity separates Sivrit from the others and arouses their envy:

> *hey wær' mir sam gescehen,*
> *daz ich ir gienge enebene, sam ich in hân gesehen,*
> *ode bî ze ligene! daz liez' ich âne haz.* (296,1–3)
>
> [If only it would have happened to me,
> that I could walk side by side with her, as I have seen him do,
> or to sleep with her. I wouldn't mind that at all.]

The phrase *gienge enebene* means "next to," on the same level.[27] It is meant literarily. Sivrit has been lifted up to Kriemhilt and may now stand by her side. The vertical arrangement of the gaze is replaced by the horizontal, and this distinguishes Sivrit from the others. The closeness that is permitted him cannot be observed exactly by the court but can still be seen by everyone from afar. It is telling that the desires now directed at Kriemhilt do not concern just any kind of familiar proximity, such as Sivrit now enjoys, but progress further and imagine the forbidden "secret" closeness of intercourse.

The kings direct the view of others through Sivrit's distinction:

> *die nâmen al gelîche niwan ir zweier war.* (297,2)
>
> [They all only looked upon the two of them.]

The message that the distinction must have been "earned" is understood, or as the king of Tenemarke expresses it sarcastically:

> *diss vil hôhen gruozes lît maneger ungesunt*
> *(des ich vil wol enpfinde) von Sîvrides hant.* (298,2–3)

[This distinguished welcome was paid by many
(this I know too well) who were defeated by Sivrit's hand.]

Now it is not only Kriemhilt who appears to be at an unapproachable distance. The court gives way to both (299,1). For the rest of the celebration, Sivrit is at Kriemhilt's side and moves "in front of" the other Burgundians. He is lifted above the others:

Inre tagen zwelven, der tage al ieslîch,
sah man bî dem degene die maget lobelîch,
sô si ze hove solde vor ir vriwenden gân. (305,1–3)

[A whole twelve days, day after day,
the praiseworthy young lady was seen with the hero,
as she went to court in front of her friends.]

The politics of viewing have succeeded. When Sivrit, still despairing of his goal, wants to leave the court, Giselher points out to him:

hie ist vil scœner frouwen, die sol man iuch gerne sehen lân. (321,4)

[There are many beautiful women here, you will gladly be allowed to see them.]

The view is opened up. Sivrit stays, because *er nu tägelîche die scœnen Kriemhilden sach* [he saw the beautiful Kriemhilt every day] (323,4). Yet, an intermediary is still necessary when he wants to get closer to Kriemhilt. As he departs with Gunther for Isenstein, the king and his guest still have to request the privacy of a conversation:

Do enbôt er sîner swester daz er si wolde sehen [!]
und ouch der degen Sîvrit. (347,1–2)

[He notified his sister that he wanted to see her,
along with the hero Sivrit.]

Afterwards, when Sivrit as emissary wants to report the successful adventure in Worms, he must ask Giselher for permission to have access to Kriemhilt:

Ir sult daz ahten schiere, swie sô daz geschehe,
daz ich die küneginne unt iwer swester sehe [!] (546,1–2)

[You should make it happen any way you can,
that I can see the queen and your sister as well.]

Still the appearance *ze hove* (550,2; 551,2) is staged in a courtly fashion, with festive clothing (347,3; 348,1; 551,1) and ceremonial speech (349,1; 552,1), and it is dependent on formal permission: *diu magt siht iuch gerne: des wil ich iu-*

wer bürge sîn [the woman would gladly see you, I vouch for that] (547,4). The view from up close remains a privilege that must be earned.

In the framework of this officially licensed closeness, more private looks can be exchanged (*Friwentlîche blicke und güetlîchez sehen* [friendly glances and gracious looks], 353,1), and whatever is ceremonially prepared comes to have a personal meaning for those involved, *want er si gerne sach* [because he liked seeing her] (551,3).[28] Only after the public marriage is viewing no longer part of the power game, and it can be openly displayed:

> *Von lieber ougen blicke wart Sîfrides varwe rôt.* (614,1)
>
> [Sivrit turned red at the gaze of her loving eyes.]

The Confusion of Gazes

In Isenstein, politics depend on looks as well. Upon the arrival of Gunther and his companions there is a back and forth of who can see and who can be seen. In the beginning—as compared to Sivrit's arrival in Worms—the direction of gazes is reversed. Sivrit wants to conquer the foreign Worms by fighting Gunther. This fails, and the division of looks corresponds. At his appearance, he is assessed from above, whereas a glimpse of Kriemhilt, the goal of his journey, is denied him for a long time. Admittedly, Prünhilt and her women stand *oben in den venstern* [up in the windows] (389,3), and look *her nider* [down] (390,3), but the view is narrated from below to above, those who have just arrived look at the castle and its inhabitants. Gunther is able to see them *tougen*[29] [secretly] (391,1) and to make out his new wife from among them.

> *Sô sihe ich ir eine in jenem venster stân,*
> *in snêwîzer wœte, diu ist sô wol getân,*
> *die welent mîniu ougen durch ir scœnen lîp.* (392,1–3)
>
> [I see one of them standing alone in that window,
> in a snow white dress, she is so outstanding,
> my eyes pick her out for her beauty.]

Sivrit confirms this:

> *Dir hât erwelt vil rehte dîner ougen schîn.* (393,1)
>
> [The light of your eyes has made the right choice.]

This is the calculating eye of the Worms court society that will acquire the world of Isenstein in the person of the queen. Success and failure are configured in the distribution of viewing.

Prünhilt tries to interrupt the judging glances of the arrivals, and therefore the positions of seeing and being seen have to be switched explicitly (something that is completely irrelevant to the story). Prünhilt tries to establish the "correct" distribution of gazes by removing her retinue from view of the strangers. They are no longer be the targets of foreign gazes:

> *Dô hiez diu küneginne ûz den venstern gân*
> *ir hêrlîche mägede, sin' solden dâ niht stân*
> *den vremden an ze sehene.* (394,1–3)
>
> [The queen commanded her splendid maidens
> to quit the windows, they should not stand there
> to look at the strangers.]

Now, paradoxically, when they can no longer be seen, the women dress in festive clothing for the *unkunden* (395,1). They step *an diu engen venster* [up to the narrow windows], from where they can observe the strangers without being seen (395,3): *dâ si die helde sâhen; daz wart durh schouwen getân* [there they looked upon the heroes; this was done to observe them] (395,4). Why are this roundabout way and Prünhilt's order even necessary? Who should be able to observe whom is obviously a matter of dispute. Prünhilt tries to get out of her defensive posture.

Once the direction of viewing is reversed, the view into the interior of the strange world is denied those from Worms (404). They themselves become objects of gazes: *doch wart michel schouwen an die küenen getân* [the bold ones were well inspected] (408,4) by Prünhilt's female retinue: *ez wolden sehen die geste diu vil wætlîchen wîp* [the attractive women wanted to see the foreigners] (417,4).

For Prünhilt and her women, who, themselves unseen, watch the arrival of the strangers, a little drama is acted out with Sivrit's rein and stirrup service. This is supposed to inform them on the assignment of roles within the expedition. Sivrit's service to Gunther is meant to distinguish Gunther in front of the women (*daz sâhen durch diu venster die vrouwen schœn' unde hêr* [the beautiful and splendid women saw this through the windows], 398,4) as a king and as the suitor. He himself understands the scene the same way, even though he knows better (396,4): *des dûhte sich getiuret des künec Guntheres lîp* [King Gunther thought it made him all the more honorable] (396,4). The play places Gunther above Sivrit and increases his *êre*.

Even though *allez* [everything] can be observed from Isenstein (396,3; 398,4), including Prünhilt, the women do not see what is suggested, neither the performance of subordination nor the ceremony of equality that precedes it.[30] The courtly play's dual message—that there is a first among the exclusive equals of courtly society—is wasted on Prünhilt.[31] At first, when she determines who sees and who must let themselves be seen, she succeeds in establishing the usual order of viewing according to rank. But then the organization of viewing fails, in that she does not understand the meaning of the scene the Burgundians play out, despite the fact that it all takes place in plain view. Her mistake demonstrates a basic lack of understanding of the world into which she is supposed to be transplanted. What she sees remains incomprehensible and foreign to her.[32]

The initial direction of gazes is "wrong," in that the newcomers are not the objects of the gazes of the court; rather, Prünhilt and her retinue are watched by the strangers. Yet in another sense this is "fitting," because the foreigners will take over the land. After the correction of positions the seeing and interpretation of events still fails, and yet it succeeds in another sense. By not understanding the fiction of vassality, Prünhilt understands the situation and Sivrit's role correctly. The blindness of the one side challenges the deception of the other side, and the mutual sightlessness continues until the murder intrigue in Worms. When Sivrit comes from Nibelungenland with his chivalric retinue, the women (*diu minneclîchen kint*, 508,1) attribute his splendid appearance again to Gunther. They now see what they are supposed to see and what Gunther assures them of: *ez sint mîne man* [they are my vassals] (509,1). The whole arrangement of the fiction continues.

What everyone in Isenstein is finally forced to see and to recognize cannot be easily undone, as will be proven in Worms. The criterion of the evidence binds the truth to visible situations, but the individual situations are comparable. The presence of one is not affected by the presence of another. Prünhilt remembers, and this means that her look and that of others are out of sync.

At Prünhilt's and Gunther's wedding, everything is still fine. Gunther and Prünhilt present themselves with their crowns (604,2): *dô sach man* [people were watching]. The ceremony is interrupted, however, so that Sivrit can receive his reward, Kriemhilt's hand. Their wedding then proceeds properly for all to see (*vor helden*, 616,4), except for Prünhilt.[33] Prünhilt is explicitly removed as an eyewitness (611,4) when the couple appears before the royal retinue (*dâ stuonden ritter edele von maniger fürsten lant* [there stood noble knights from many princely lands], 611,2).

The general view (*an daz gegensidele man Sîfriden sah / mit Kriemhilde sitzen* [Sivrit was seen seated facing the king / along with Kriemhilt], 617,2–3) and

Prünhilt's view differ,[34] and this is accentuated by the almost word-for-word repetition:

> *dô sah si Kriemhilde (dô wart ir nie sô leit)*
> *bî Sîfride sitzen: weinen si began.* (618,2–3)
>
> [She saw Kriemhilt (she had never been so hurt)
> sitting with Sivrit, and she began to cry.]

Sivrit no longer sits next to his legitimate wife; instead, Kriemhilt sits next to a man whom Prünhilt believes to be inferior:

> *die sihe ich sitzen nâhen dem eigenholden dîn.*
> *daz muoz ich immer weinen, sol si alsô verderbet sîn.* (620,3–4)
>
> [I see her sitting next to your serf.
> It makes me cry to see her so disparaged.]

The ensuing conflict is announced in the shrouding of visibility, as observed by Gunther:

> *daz ir sô lâzet truoben vil liehter ougen schîn.* (619,2)
>
> [that you allow your bright eyes to become so gloomy]

The tears of the queen (620,1) make the disturbance public, but Gunther forbids any open comment on the conflict: *ir mügt wol stille dagen. / ich wil iu z'andern zîten disiu mære sagen* [please keep quiet / I'll tell you the whole story some other time] (621,1–2).

Prünhilt loses the power struggle regarding who decides who will get information from whom. The "other time" (*z'andern zîten*) with which Gunther consoles Prünhilt will never come. The following dispute remains hidden from view and takes place in the bedroom (635,4), where nothing is cleared up, and then later in a series of "secret" conversations with Gunther in an unknown place. They are "space-less" because they have no legitimate space: *si reitez heinlîche, des si dâ hete muot* [she spoke in confidence about what she had in mind] (726,3). The incident is removed from the transparent sphere of legitimate action.

The argument grows into a conflict over Gunther's honor as king. He only barely avoids open dishonor in front of his *kamerære* at the cost of giving up the entire expedition to Isenstein and possessing Prünhilt. At the coronation the next day, what is "seen" (645,4) is just a façade that is lifted at the ensuing celebration. It is a fateful solution that—with Sivrit's help—the battle over appearances is to be decided in the dark.

Words and Signs, I: Sivrit's Trophy

In connection with the deception of Prünhilt, Wenzel speaks of the "downfall of a reliable world of signs."[35] Signs are ambiguous, have always been malleable, and can be manipulated, but in the *Nibelungenlied*, there is no authority to decide what is valid and what is not. In situations of oral communication, signs are valid for the duration of their presentation and can only be replaced or supplanted by others, and this is how they are used in the *Nibelungenlied*. In the written text, however, the sign is removed from its primary context. It must be interpreted. This requires the "contextual description of the particular employment of signs." The sign appears in front of the background of the competing validity of other signs.[36] The *Nibelungenlied* reflects this different mode of using signs and expresses the confusion of signs in a world without writing, but in a way that the literality of the epic allows the recipient to see through the confusion.

The listener learns of Sivrit's service gesture in Isenstein, unlike the witnesses to the scene, with the background of what was previously recounted. He therefore knows that it is a lie. The same is true of those who are present in Worms and Isenstein, for Gunther and his companions,[37] whereas Prünhilt and her people are helplessly consigned to what they have seen and heard. At the contest with Prünhilt, no one sees *ander niemen wan Gunther den degen* [other than Gunther the hero] (465,2), and so the audience is presented with a different reality than the listener. Prünhilt and the other ear- and eyewitnesses of Sivrit's deception cannot see beyond the scene and so are confused by conflicting appearances.

This is especially true when what is seen is itself contradictory, as with Gunther's appearance after the wedding night,[38] or when signs and words contradict each other or are taken back at the first opportunity. Signs function only within a social framework with certain conventions, and they do so differently in Isenstein than in Worms.[39] It is what Prünhilt experiences when the one who showed himself to be subordinate now appears to be equal.

There are two realities after the deception in Isenstein. What Gunther assures her of and what Prünhilt is able to see collide with her knowledge of what she heard and saw in Isenstein. Words and signs correspond each time, but what they mean each time is different.

Prünhilt is prevented from gaining certainty through speech. Signs are what remain. What she sees is irreconcilable with what she and others have been told (*jehen*), and therefore with what she believes to be true. She clings to the Isenstein words. After comparing them with the signs that support Sivrit's status as lord, she has to make a choice. She chooses the only version that fits her role as queen and wife of Gunther, and she tests the truth of this version by once more putting the result, her subjugation by Gunther, to the test. This test (which would be senseless, if what she had heard in Isenstein were beyond doubt) results in a failing grade. The supposed winner at Isenstein is hung on a nail in the bedroom. This is hardly the king who was able to force Sivrit to undertake the dangerous expedition to Isenstein. The repetition of the test the following night disproves the first result, so that the conclusion is once again ambiguous. Since the deception is repeated, Prünhilt is unable to decipher the contradiction between signs and words.

Prünhilt, who is overcome a second time, confirms: *ich hân daz wol erfunden, daz du kanst vrouwen meister sîn* [I am now convinced that you can be the master of women] (678,4). She directs her words unknowingly at Sivrit, the wrong man. Gunther is not the *vrouwen meister*. For Prünhilt the false Isenstein version has been confirmed a second time, but Sivrit's strange status as husband of the king's sister remains a mystery.

This questions a fundamental principle about the validity of truth. What can be seen—Sivrit rules as a king—and what is said—he is Gunther's *man*—should be the same. The evidence is of the same kind. A decision seems impossible, however, because there is no authority that can reveal what lies behind speech and appearance. The discovery of the deception is not a process of decoding involuntary symptoms or refuted circumstantial evidence, pointing to hidden motivations and revealing the true meaning of openly communicated words and signs. There is no consistent text that dissimulates the true conditions more or less deftly. Rather, two irreconcilable pictures of reality confront each other. One of the two realities must be true, because there is an undeniable expectation that what everyone sees and what everyone hears should correspond to each other. Competing pictures of reality can only exist as a result of manifest deception.

What has happened in the darkness of the bedchamber between Prünhilt, Sivrit, and Gunther remains hidden and is therefore not subject to being tested. Not even the actors were able to see. Their perception was limited and unreliable. Gunther could hear that Sivrit was sticking to the bargain (667,2; 676,2), whereas Prünhilt had to believe that she was overpowered by Gunther. The visible signs, the ring and the belt that Sivrit took with him, again confront Prünhilt with her error.[40] Observation and signs vary. The sign points to Sivrit's conquest in the nocturnal battle and disproves his (personal and class) subordination. What Prünhilt believes herself to observe speaks for Gunther's superiority and consequently for the truth of the claim that Sivrit is his *man*. Ring and belt, however, say just the opposite.

The relationship between sign and reality is contrary to what it was in Isenstein. In Isenstein the sign (the gesture) spoke for Gunther, even though the action (*werc*) belonged to Sivrit. Now the gesture (*Er gebârte sam ez wære Gunther der künic rîch* [he acted as if he were Gunther, the powerful king], 668,1) and sign (the ring and the belt) speak for Sivrit, even though Gunther accomplishes the *werc*. Sivrit takes possession of the sign that does not correspond to reality, although he had previously refused the real trophy of his victory so that Gunther could have it instead. The situations are therefore symmetrical, the positions are reversed. Both times, what can be seen is objectively false, and both times, the context provides liability. When Kriemhilt displays Prünhilt's ring and belt publicly, their legal meaning is undeniable (Sivrit has "possessed" Prünhilt), although according to the narrator's commentary, this is incorrect. When Sivrit serves Gunther in front of everyone at court as a vassal, then he clearly determines his status within this circle, regardless of what the narrator and his characters otherwise know to be true.

The signs of ring and belt are paradoxical.[41] Why does Sivrit take a trophy from the dark chamber that he is not allowed to show in public? Above all, a sign would only signify something false.[42] The answer is cryptic: *ine weiz ob er daz tæte durh sînen hôhen muot* [I don't know if he did it out of his high spirits] (680,2).[43] Sivrit's *hôher muot* originates from a personal triumph in a fight that brings the honor of the queen and the king into question. So long as Sivrit alone is affected, the reaction based on *hôher muot* would be unproblematic. Since others are aware of it, however, it necessarily leads to conflict. Sivrit's *hôher muot* is not a courtly expression of common harmony—this distinguishes it from *minnesang* and Arthurian romance—but a completely self-referential knowledge of his superiority to Gunther.[44]

The trophy as a sign is by no means meant to, and in fact does not, remain hidden—a victory in battle only gains recognition through proof.[45] Sivrit does not "tattle, but the symbol itself spoke."[46] The fact that the trophies get into Kriemhilt's hands at an auspicious moment goes almost unnoticed.[47] Sivrit only hides them at first:

> *er hal si sît vil lange daz er ir hete brâht,*[48]
> *unz daz si under krône*[49] *in sînem lande gie.*
> *swaz er ir geben solde, wie lützel erz belîben lie!* (684,2–4)

> [He hid from her for a long time what he had brought for her,
> until she wore the crown in his own land.
> What he should give her, he did not hold back!]

Even if the time is not taken too precisely (he hid the trophy until the time of the coronation), it is true that the symbolic gift of ring and belt is linked to Sivrit's and Kriemhilt's royal rule, perhaps even to the ceremony of coronation, the public attestation of royal power. It is at least linked—if *under krône gie* is taken to be durative—to the exercise of power. In this way, Sivrit actually did take the signs *durh sînen hôhen muot*.

Both trophies can also heighten the festive joy and the self-esteem of Kriemhilt as ruler. Kriemhilt triumphs over her distant rival at the moment her royal status is conferred. This sign of triumph should not have been kept from her by Sivrit (*geben solde*). This is harmless, because the ceremony takes place *in sînem lande*, that is, at the "appropriate" court. The *êre* of another is not at stake there, and the sign can heighten the magnificence of the other coronation symbols. Only the new connection between the two courts—driven by Prünhilt's unease about the contradiction between words and signs—leads to conflict, in that Kriemhilt's trophies become evidence of Prünhilt's deception. That these trophies might be employed at the right moment is apparent from the fact that Kriemhilt takes them along in her travel baggage, although no one seems surprised at this.[50] Why would she do so if they could not be shown?

Again the removal of the sign from its original context endangers its validity or at least makes it unpredictable. What was valid in Isenstein is not valid in Worms and Xanten, and what can be shown in Xanten is better not shown in Worms. Medieval publicity requires presence. If the circle of onlookers changes, then it must be established anew. If signs and words do not correspond to each other in varying situations, then one can only decide what is "true" or "false" or "just faked" by once more introducing a situation in which evidence can be checked. The proof is general agreement. This is why Gunther's word alone at the wedding feast counts for nothing. Prünhilt must therefore invite Sivrit and Kriemhilt. Only in this way can she discover which appearance is valid, that of Isenstein or that of the coronation and wedding celebration. Therefore, the dispute of the queens—in contrast to the Nordic transmission—must be fought out in full view of everyone, at the tournament and then at the entry to the church. This is why Kriemhilt, when her self-esteem is questioned, must try out the sign that verifies it in the different court, too.

Signs can point in the wrong direction. Ring and belt make something visible that did not exist.[51] They refer indirectly to something that is unrecognizable, because it is pushed—multiple times and explicitly—into the darkness. The sign only seems like evidence.

The *Nibelungenlied* touches on a problem here that other narratives of the twelfth and thirteenth centuries treat problematically. Learned theological and juridical discussion had recourse to pleading the unreliability of visible signs and the unreliability of attested words. In the *Nibelungenlied*, the resulting entanglement is presented but not reflected upon. By contrast, tales of adultery in courtly epic focus on this problem. Adultery offers—as in the *Nibelungenlied*—a particularly well-suited context for doing so, because it lies beyond the limits where visibility counts as the criterion of truth. For Marke in Eilhart's *Tristrant*, for example, which is still relatively close to heroic epic, the indications of adultery—the traces on the floor and the blood in the bed—are counterindicated when Marke sees Tristrant and Isalde in bed with his own eyes, but with a sword between them. The visible sign as legal proof is stronger than indirect evidence. The sword has such undeniable validity for Marke that he proclaims the intactness of his marriage to the entire land and so gives Isalde renewed recognition as queen (Trt 4865–71). For the narrator and his audience, the contrary is clearly true. What Marke determines publicly is a lamentable mistake.

Gottfried von Straßburg sees reliance on visible signs—as opposed to the circumstantial evidence of facts—as so offensive that he has to explain Marke's decision in psychological terms as a delusional passion that does not want to accept whatever does not confirm it (Tr 17534ff.). Because of his depraved delusion, Marke is cut off from the interior space of *minne*. Because he does not know this space and because there seems to be nothing for him beyond what is visible in public, he misses the mark in the reverse situation, too. When he finds his Tristan and Isot in bed in the middle of the day, he wants to make their adultery public in front of the entire court, in order to grant the visible truth validity. This is crude and stupid and fails accordingly, discrediting Marke yet again.

King Arthur also suffers through the pains of reading contradictory signs in the *Prosa-Lancelot*, so that he hesitates again and again from drawing the logical conclusions of what he sees. He receives proof upon proof of the queen's adultery, but he continues to doubt, because he wants to see it for himself, not just hear the rumors, or the eyewitness accounts of others, not even the public presentation of the adultery in a picture, even though this is authorized by Lancelot—both perpetrator and painter—with the accompanying text recounting the adultery. So he attempts to bring matters to a head himself (*das ich sie by einander finden mag* [that I might find them together]), which both exposes the scandal and brings down his kingdom: the visible truth motivates him to self-destruction.[52] Arthur, like Marke, misses the truth of (even adulterous) love.

All of these cases concern the unreliability of signs when removed from the public space at court, in other words, the incommensurability of two different spheres, each with its own truth. In the *Nibelungenlied*, there is a sphere beyond visibility that is treason and intrigue. Therefore, the deception of Prünhilt, even though it does not involve adultery, has direct and catastrophic consequences. It attacks the social system as a whole. Whereas in the courtly romance, the criterion of visibility becomes dubious in that it misses the reality beyond these boundaries, in the *Nibelungenlied*, it claims its validity in a problematic way, even when what is said and done for all to see is ever more clearly exposed as false.

Words and Signs, II: The Fight for Appearances

Prünhilt goes about searching for Sivrit's real status in a test of rank.[53] At the marketplace of the court, the conflict over rank between Kriemhilt and Prünhilt was already negotiated before it began, that is, when Prünhilt came to Worms for the first time:

> *Die vrouwen spehen kunden unt minneclîchen lîp,*
> *die lobten durch ir schœne daz Guntheres wîp.*
> *dô sprâchen dâ die wîsen, die hetenz baz besehen,*
> *man möhte Kriemhilden wol für Prünhilden jehen.* (593)
>
> [Those who knew a thing or two about beautiful women
> praised Gunther's wife for her beauty.
> The wise ones, however, observing more thoroughly, said
> that Kriemhilt should be praised more highly than Prünhilt.]

Whoever can look closely (*besehen*) will discover differences, so that it can be agreed: Kriemhilt's reputation (*jehen*) is still superior to Prünhilt's. The conflict of rank is latently present from the beginning, but at first in the peaceful form that generally characterizes courtly society and that does not discredit the loser.

Of course, Kriemhilt's advantage of beauty would be erased by Sivrit's lower status. Prünhilt therefore sees Kriemhilt's *schœne* and *zuht* (622,1) *verderbet* [destroyed] (620,4) by the (supposed) misalliance with Sivrit. Because she is unable to get a clear picture, she wants to "see more": *daz si Kriemhilde solde noch gesehen* [that she should see Kriemhilt more] (726,2), and *daz wir si hie gesehen* [that we see her here] (729,2–3). When her messengers have returned from Nibelungenland, she asks them what they saw of Kriemhilt: *hât noch ir schœner lîp / behalten iht der zühte, der si wol kunde pflegen?* [has her beauty / retained the grace that she once exhibited?] (771,2–3). This aims at Kriemhilt's rank, expressed in her actions and appearance and indicated by what can be seen. Does she look like the wife of an *eigenholden* or like a queen?[54]

When Kriemhilt and Sivrit come to Worms, the comparison is no longer harmless. The splendor of both courts is no longer reflected in the disinterested recognition of a shared glance. Prünhilt's view is already different from others at the wedding feast. She is seen to be looking:

> *under wîlen blicken man Prünhilden sach*
> *an vroun Kriemhilde, diu schœne was genuoc.*
> *ir varwe gegen dem golde den glanz vil hêrlichen truoc.* (799,2–4)
>
> [Sometimes, Prünhilt was seen looking
> at Lady Kriemhilt, whose beauty was complete.
> Her color was of a splendid radiance against the gold.]

Prünhilt does not scrutinize, as modern readers might think, the looks of a relative who might have aged; instead, she observes the appearance of Kriemhilt's status. Her gaze probes the competition of rank.

In the dispute of the queens, it is the men who are judged, not the women, whose status depends on the men. This happens during a tournament. The contest begins according to the rules. Everyone wants to see who is the best:

> *dô liefen dar durch schouwen vil manic wîp unde man.* (814,4)
>
> [Many men and women ran to watch.]

Kriemhilt's first "proof" for Sivrit's superiority is again based on appearances. The dispute of the queens concerns the interpretation of an image:

> *nu sihestu wie er stât,*
> *wie rehte hêrlîche er vor den recken gât,*
> *alsam der liehte mâne vor den sternen tuot?* (817,1–3)
>
> [Now do you see how he stands,
> how magnificently he walks before the warriors,
> as does the bright moon before the stars?]

The exchange of argument and counterargument has often been analyzed. I want to sketch the scene from the point of view of signs, appearances, and words.

Kriemhilt opens the dispute by making an exaggerated comment on what everyone can see: Sivrit is so magnificent *daz elliu disiu rîche ze sînen handen solden stân* [that all these lands should be at his command] (815,4), which Prünhilt understands to be a claim to rule.[55] Kriemhilt points to Sivrit's brilliant appearance, but Prünhilt explicitly rejects this as a criterion. Gunther stands above all other kings: *swie wætlîch . . . swie biderbe . . . swie schœne* [how elegant . . . how capable . . . how beautiful] (818,1–2). Kriemhilt sticks with her judgment of Sivrit, but she does not infer any political superiority from it (819,4). Prünhilt, however, insists on making class matter, whereby she uses Sivrit's public claim (*jach*!), *er wære 'küneges man* [he said himself that he was the king's man]. From this she concludes: *des hân ich in für eigen, sît ihs in hôrte jehen* [I regard him as a serf, since I heard him say it myself] (821,2–3).

Sivrit's words, spoken in everyone's presence, stand in contrast to appearances. Since Prünhilt publicly repeats them (820,2), Kriemhilt has to expressly demand that she cease her discriminatory *rede* (822,4). Precisely because the words are legally binding, Prünhilt says: *ine mac ir niht gelâzen* [I can't let her repeat them], since the results would affect her own position as queen. Kriemhilt must dispute the claim just as well publicly. It is false speech (*verhehen*, 827,2; 831,4), which must be retracted (*lougen*, 831,4). Both women assume the obligation attached to publicly attended speech, and both want to ensure its validity in front of everyone. Prünhilt says:

> *nu wil ich sehen gerne [!], ob man den dînen lîp*
> *habe ze solhen êren sô man den mînen tuot.* (826,2–3)
>
> [Now I would like to see, if people honor you
> as much as they honor me.]

Kriemhilt, too, demands:

> *daz muoz et nû geschehen.*
> *sît du mînes mannes für eigen hâst verjehen,*
> *nu müezen hiute kiesen* [!] *der beider künige man,*
> *ob ich vor küniges wîbe zem münster turre gegân.* (827)
>
> [It has to happen now, indeed,
> Since you have claimed my husband to be a serf,
> now the two king's own men must decide today
> if I dare enter the church before the wife of the king.]

> *Du muost daz hiute schouwen [!], daz ich bin adelvrî,*
> *und daz mîn man ist tiwerr danne der dîne sî.* (828,1–2)
>
> [You must see today that I am noble and free,
> and that my husband is superior to yours.]

Since appearances are decisive, all visual means have to be employed to force Prünhilt to retract what she has said:

> *ez muoz âne schande belîben hie mîn lîp.*
> *ir sult wol lâzen schouwen, und habt ir rîche wât.*
> *sî mac s"n gerne lougen, des Prünhilt verjehen hât.* (831,2–4)[56]
>
> [I must not be humiliated here.
> You should let it be seen if you have fine clothes.
> Prünhilt will want to retract what she has said.]

So magnificent clothing is brought forward, which Kriemhilt is able to display (*erziugen*, 836,4), and which, in typical epic hyperbole, had never been seen this way before (837,2).

The dispute goes on in public declamations. Prünhilt brings in the class conflict for all to hear: *jâ sol vor küniges wîbe niht eigen diu gegân* [a maiden and serf shall never go before a king's wife] (838,4), and, for all to hear, Kriemhilt calls the queen a *mannes kebse* [a vassal's concubine] (839,4). In that Prünhilt is publicly *verkebset* [called a mistress] (840,1), Kriemhilt ensures for herself the precedence witnessed by the court (843,2).

Prünhilt attempts to make the words of Isenstein valid for everyone in Worms. Kriemhilt contests this with words, too. If these were valid, the queen would be dishonored, and her beauty would be devalued (*du hâst geschendet selbe den dînen schœnen lîp* [you yourself have dishonored your beauty], 839,3). Prünhilt breaks down in tears (843,1). She has lost the war of words, which Kriemhilt scornfully remonstrates to her (839,2; 849,2). Prünhilt now has to dispute Kriemhilt's word, her public accusation (*jehen*), if she is to restore her damaged honor:

> *mich muoz Kriemhilt mêre hœren [!] lân*
> *des mich sô lûte* [!] *zîhet daz wortræze wîp.* (845,2–3)
>
> [Kriemhilt must let me hear me more
> of what that sharp-tongued woman so loudly accused me.]
>
> *ir jâhet mîn ze kebesen: daz sult ir lâzen sehen [!].* (846,3)
>
> [You accused me of being his mistress: you will have to prove it!]

The usual forms of determining the truth are indicted and perverted.

The dispute continues. Instead of words, now signs claim to hold the truth: *Prünhilt mit ir frouwen* [Prünhilt along with her ladies] (845,1) demands and gets proof (*erziuge[n]*, 847,2; 849,3): the ring and the belt. She has nothing with which to counter these signs. She can still presume that the ring somehow improperly, that is, secretly,[57] came into Kriemhilt's possession, but with the second sign, the belt, this is not possible. Kriemhilt can assume from the possession of the belt: *jâ wart mîn Sîfrit dîn man* [indeed, my Sivrit slept with you] (849,4).

It is not possible to glean from the text what Kriemhilt knows,[58] and speculations about what Sivrit might have told Kriemhilt are pointless. What is important is the fact that words and signs diverge. Prünhilt is forced down to the level of signs, which she did not want to accept after what she had heard in Isenstein. With this her battle is lost. The signs, even though they are false, disprove what she thought she knew to be true.

Kriemhilt shows the proof of her superiority *offenlîche* [publicly] (851,4). Prünhilt's defeat is seen by all: *weinen si began. / daz muose vreischen Gunther und alle Burgonden man* [she began to cry. / Gunther and all Burgundian men must hear about that] (850,3–4). The king, too, sees that she is hurt (*weinen er so sach*, 851,1). Prünhilt's words to him, *ich muoz unvrœlîche stân* [I stand before you bereft of joy] (852,4), do not mean "I am incensed," or something similar, but rather: I have been forced to exclude myself from the *vreude*, that is, from the festive life of courtly society. This affects the queen's retinue as well. Gunther asks: *waz weinent dise vrouwen* [why are these women crying] (856,3)?

The attempt to settle the conflict remains in the sphere of public evidence, even if appearances have proved themselves to be misleading. Because this cannot be corrected, the attempt fails. The narrator makes it clear that Gunther is asked as a judge, not as Prünhilt's husband:

> *heizet here gân*
> *den fürsten vonme Rîne. ich wil in hœren lân*
> *wie mich hât gehœnet sîner swester lîp.* (851,1–3)

> [Ask him to come here,
> the prince from the Rhine. I want him to hear
> how his own sister has insulted me.]

Prünhilt appeals from the open lower court to higher authority, the royal judiciary. It is not about the truth of what happened, but instead about the insult.

In view of the importance of public demonstration, the handling of the accusation does not seem strange. Prünhilt's indignation at the allegations is already overshadowed by the fact that they were made public. So Gunther declares: *hât er sich es gerüemet, ez gêt an Sîfrides lîp* [if he boasted of this, it will cost him his life] (845,4). Not the facts, as many critics have believed, but the *offenlîche* (851,4) insulting speech about them is the important thing. Sivrit seems to be guilty of an error that the religious didacticism of the twelfth century would have criticized as much as the courtly didacticism of the thirteenth century, that of *ruom*. Bragging about one's sexual exploits was regarded as a serious crime. It was both an affront to Christian values and, above all, took advantage of a special aristocratic morality that permitted something the Church saw as a vice to enhance a man's reputation. This is also the background of the attacks of courtly *minne* didactics. Moreover, *rüemen* breaks the rules of courtly service to women, in that the man usurps his power over women without respect for their *êre*, thereby compromising them in society.[59]

Prünhilt is dishonored by Kriemhilt's words at the portal of the cathedral. Gunther is supposed to repair this dishonor publicly: *dune beredest, künic, mich / der vil grôzen schande* [if you cannot defend me, king / from this great disgrace] (854,3–4). The term *rede* belongs in the context of judicial proceedings,[60] and the following scene is to be understood as a legal action. The binding *rede* of the royal judge is supposed to eradicate Kriemhilt's false *rede*.

The conflict has up to now been played out on the level of what can be heard and seen, and it is only on this level that it continues.[61] What counts in an oral society is the publicly proclaimed word, and this is a prerequisite for Sivrit's oath. The "magic of the oath" comes into conflict with the "magic of the symbol," however.[62] Only from a modern point of view does Gunther cleverly maneuver the confrontation by means of the oath to an arena that is less dangerous for him and his miserable role in the wedding night. From the perspective of the epic, he acts consequently. There seems to be no reality for the participants beyond what has played out for everyone's eyes and ears. Gunther starts with the actual point of contention, the public dishonoring of the queen:

> *und hât er sihs gerüemet, daz sol er hœren lân,*
> *oder sîn muoz lougen der helt ûz Niderlant.* (855,2–3)
>
> [If he boasted of this, he should admit it here,
> or the hero from Netherland must deny it.]

Sivrit should repeat the *ruom* publicly or renounce it. Up to now, assertions have been based on assertions that in turn represent the assertions of a third party:

> *mir hât mîn vrouwe Prünhilt ein mære hie geseit,*
> *du habes dich des gerüemet daz du ir schœnen lîp*
> *allerêrst habes geminnet, daz sagt vrou Kriemhilt dîn wîp.* (857,2–4)

> [My wife Prünhilt has told me a story here,
> that you boasted of having been the first to make
> love to her, so claims your wife, Lady Kriemhilt.]

Sivrit offers to take an oath of purification that this assertion was never made, which means that he did not insult Prünhilt and that Kriemhilt's words have no foundation in what he himself said to her:

> *und wil dir daz enpfüeren vor allen dînen man*
> *mit mînen hôhen eiden, daz ich irs niht gesaget hân.* (858,3–4)

> [and I will deny it to you before all your men,
> with my solemn oath, that I did not tell her that.]

Since everyone hears him, the oath will make the truth evident; not the truth of the wedding night but rather the cause of the affront. It becomes apparent in the gesture of swearing:[63]

> *daz soltu lâzen sehen [!]*
> *den eit den du dâ biutest, unt mac der hie geschehen,*
> *aller valschen dinge wil ich dich ledic lân.* (859,1–3)

> [You must let us see
> the oath that you offer, and if you speak it here
> then I shall declare you innocent of all crimes.]

The phrase *aller valschen dinge* is a hysteron proteron: the accusations would be proven false by the oath, and Sivrit would be vindicated.

According to de Boor's Commentary, there is no reason to assume that Sivrit is exempted from the oath after Gunther's men have formed into a circle (*umbstand*).[64] The verse *Sîfrit der vil küene zem eide bôt die hant* [Sivrit the bold raised his hand for the oath] (860,1) refers to the gesture of swearing an oath.[65] There is a similar gesture when Gunther demands guarantees from his enemies in the Saxon war that the prisoners will not escape: *des bôt Liudegêr die hant* [Liudeger raised his hand for that] (251,4). Liudeger gives his word of honor, just as Sivrit proclaims his innocence. Accordingly, Gunther repeats his own formulation *ledic lân* (859,3) to indicate that the matter is settled:

mir ist sô wol bekant
iuwer grôz unschulde; ich wil iuch ledic lân. (860,2–3)

[your complete innocence
is well-proved to me; I declare you free of guilt.]

Sivrit's *unschulde* becomes apparent to all (*bekant*, 860,1–2) with the gesture (*sô*), above all to the king, who has been insulted along with Prünhilt. Gunther drops his accusation against Sivrit and proclaims: *des iuch mîn swester zîhet* [what my sister accuses you of]—and that means the *rüemen—daz ir des niene habt getân* [that you did not commit it] (860,4).[66] Sivrit's oath has turned Kriemhilt's speech into nothing more than stupid gossip. Without a man's support, the public word of a woman has no value. Sivrit suggests to Gunther that he should take the case out of the arena of public debate, which belongs to men alone, and where only what Sivrit says really counts, and confine it to the closed sphere of the house, where the husband has legal power over his wife, and where he can silence the opponent.

Gunther's verdict does not bring peace.[67] The contradiction between word and sign has not been resolved by Gunther's speech and Sivrit's oath. The back-and-forth between word and sign has gained another component. What is supposed to be true according to royal decree neither eliminates a public insult nor reconciles the contradictory evidence. There is a hierarchy of power that determines what is valid, but there is no hierarchy of criteria to decide what really happened.

Sivrit's words in Isenstein are called into question by a series of signs at Prünhilt's wedding. Other, more disturbing signs appear that cause even more consternation. It is determined in a formal trial that what the signs indicate was never asserted. This has nothing to do with the "truth" of Isenstein, however. Both can exist side by side. Sivrit can be a *man* and never have boasted of being Prünhilt's first lover. The troubling signs of rank remain unexplained, and belt and ring are there, no matter what Sivrit said. Prünhilt's question is not answered by the oath, and it can also not be answered by means of a public demonstration. Instead of leading out of the confusion, the oath just increases it. The contradiction cannot be resolved in a society that relies on words and signs.

Hagen and Sivrit take up complementary positions. There is no sphere where a woman can act independently for either one of them. The one wants to take the conflict back into the sphere of the house, "solve" it there with patriarchal force, and exclude the women from further discussions. The other acknowledges no sphere beyond the public, where only men act. Hagen continues to ascribe Kriemhilt's words to her husband Sivrit. *Suln wir gouche ziehen* [Shall we keep cuckoos?], he asks (867,1), and declares:

> *daz er sich hât gerüemet der lieben vrouwen mîn,*
> *dar umbe wil ich sterben, ez engê im an daz leben sîn.* (867,3–4)
>
> [That he has boasted of my dear lady,
> I am willing to die for that unless he pays with his life.]

By calling Sivrit a *gouch* [cuckoo],[68] he relies completely on the principle of visibility and follows what (thanks to ring and belt) can be seen and is therefore publicly valid.

False Appearances

The only thing that matters in the following intrigue is what happened in public: the dishonoring of the queen. Prünhilt's crying (850,3); 852,1) has forced the king to intervene, and after his attempt to solve the conflict fails, the weeping of the *vrouwe* becomes a matter of concern for the entire court (863,4). The entire kingdom has been insulted through Prünhilt:[69]

> *dô trûret' alsô sêre der Prünhilde lîp,*
> *daz ez erbarmen muose die Guntheres man.*
> *dô kom von Tronege Hagen zuo sîner vrouwen gegân.* (863,2–4)
>
> [Prünhilt was very depressed,
> so that Gunther's men felt pity for her.
> Then Hagen of Troneck went to see his lady.]
>
> *Er frâgete waz ir wære, weinende er si vant.*
> *dô sagte si im diu mære.* (864,1–2)
>
> [He asked her what the matter was when he found her crying.
> Then she told him the story.]

The defect forces Hagen the *man* to act, because the court's "joy" is destroyed along with the "joy" of the queen. This is also manifest in that Prünhilt is no longer seen at courtly feasts.

With the failure of the judicial hearing in Worms, the story descends into a fateful darkness where crimes are planned. The murder plot succeeds partly because the events are removed from perception and partly because a false picture is arranged for it (*lüge,* 877,4). Behind what happens *offenlîche* (874,4), Hagen can pursue his plan *heinlîche* (873,2): *Der künec mit sînen vriunden rûnende*[70] *gie* [the king spoke with his friends in hushed whispers] (882,1) and: *Eines tages Sîfrit si rûnende vant* [one day Sivrit found them whispering] (883,1). This is not the conclave about the supposed second declaration of war. What would there have been to consider if it were known that there was no war? *Rûnen* expresses the fact that the plan cannot be discussed openly or officially, even if everyone knows about it. Later on, *rûnen* refers to a hostile attitude (1959,2) that is not publicly admitted, before the Huns openly take up arms. The moral reprehensiveness of an action is designated by *rûnen. Rûnende* refers in the *Rolandslied* to the secretive councils of the heathens (Rl 1317). *Rûnen* is the suspicious murmuring between Neidhart's *dörpern* and the *vrouwe*. Beyond the control of courtly society, it leads to open conflict.[71] Like everything that happens in secret, *rûnen*, too, can be observed. Sivrit notices something, but he wrongly interprets it as a breakdown in the court's formal obligation to seem joyful and as signaling the threat of the supposed war.

Visibility becomes a façade in the preparations for the second Saxon war:

> *Sîfride und den sînen ze sehen ez was getân.* (888,2)
> [It was done for Sivrit and his men to see.]

The false façade is confronted once more by an exaggerated staging of Sivrit's visible superiority, where the principle of visibility triumphs for the last time: the splendid appearance (*in hêrlîchem site* [in a magnificent manner], 917,1), the hunt as a competition (*wer die besten jegere an dirre waltreise sîn* [who are the best hunters in this forest expedition], 930,4), which Sivrit wins in everyone's opinion (*dô wart sîn jaget daz rîche wol den Burgonden kunt* [the Burgundians learned of his success at the hunt], 939,4; 942,2–3), his magnificent outfit,[72] and the shining weapons (952–956). All agree, *die daz sâhen, er wære ein kreftec man* [all those who saw it vouched that he was a powerful man] (963,1): *man jah im grôzer êren swer iz ie gesach* [all who saw it gave him high praise] (971,3). Hagen's devious suggestion of a race with Gunther is supposed to affirm the splendid heroic world: *hey wolde er uns daz sehen lân!* [If only he would show us that] (972,4). The winner is supposed to glow in the fame of the present and future: *dem sol man jehen danne, den man sihet gewunnen hân* [everyone will then praise the one who is acclaimed the winner] (973,4). Everyone sees Sivrit's last victory: *dô sach man bî dem brunnen den küenen Sîfriden ê* [Sivrit was seen to be the first one at the spring] (976,4). He is literally extinguished by the murder: *Erblichen was sîn varwe* [His color faded away] (987,1).[73]

Sivrit's death will tear the web apart. Hagen wants to return immediately to openness (*mir ist vil unmære, und wirt ez ir bekant* [it's unimportant to me if it is found out], 1001,2), but again, as in Isenstein and in using the same words, it is agreed that the truth should be hidden and everyone should tell the same lie (*ir sult ez heln alle unt sult gelîche jehen* [you should keep it a secret and all claim the same thing], 1000,2).[74] The murder of the "shining" Sivrit is supposed to disappear in the darkness: *Do erbiten si der nahte* [they waited for nightfall] (1002,1). Kriemhilt is literally supposed to stumble across Sivrit's corpse, which has been *tougenlîchen* [secretly] (1004,1) laid on her doorstep. It is discovered by a *kameræe* [servant], who must first bring a light (1006,3).

The confusion of appearances is demonstrated by the condition of Sivrit's shield after his murder.[75] The *schilt* was Sivrit's last weapon after Hagen had cunningly removed the others. Up until the end, it remained uncertain whether or not the attack would succeed, because Hagen would not have been able to harm Sivrit had his weapons been within reach. The hero is defenseless, but not completely, because he is still dangerous even with his shield:

> *Swie wunt er was zem tôde, so krefteclîch er sluoc,*
> *daz ûz dem schilde dræte genuoc*
> *des edelen gesteines; der schilt vil gar zerbrast.*
> *sich hete gerne errochen der vil hêrlîche gast.* (985)
>
> [Mortally wounded though he was, he struck back so forcefully,
> that the jewels sprang
> from his shield; and the shield itself burst asunder.
> The magnificent foreigner wanted only to avenge himself.]

He knocks Hagen to the ground, the spear in his back—*sô sêre zurnt' der wunde* [the wounded man so raged] (986,4)—until his strength is gone.

This seems to be forgotten when Kriemhilt finds Sivrit dead:

> *Dô rief vil trûrecklîche diu küneggine milt:*
> *"owê mich mînes leides! nu ist dir dîn schilt*
> *mit swerten niht verhouwen; du lîst ermorderôt.*
> *wesse ich wer iz het getân, ich riet' im immer sînen tôt."* (1012)
>
> [The gentle queen then called out in grief:
> "Oh miserable me! Your shield
> has not been damaged by swords; you lie here murdered.
> If I knew who had done this, I would always aim at his death.]

One could argue whether or not in the first scene *vil gar zerbrast* really means that the shield was completely split apart or just damaged, or whether Kriemhilt's words refer only to a certain kind of damage done by swords in battle.

Each time the shield has a different meaning. In the first case, it makes Sivrit's strength visible once again at the moment in which it is destroyed, since even the defensive weapon serves him well in a dangerous attack. In the second case, the shield points to the fact that Sivrit did not die in an open fight but was killed from behind. Ambiguous as a sign, the shield brings two aspects of one and the same thing—treason—to the fore, even if people may debate to what extent it was destroyed or only scratched.

In the following episodes, new attempts are made to illuminate the darkness in which the story has lost itself. The uncovering of the crime and the criminals—the restoration of transparency—proceeds with agonizing sluggishness up to the confrontation at Etzel's court. To get at the truth is an arduous process; to have truth prevail is even more so. Admittedly, Kriemhilt "knows at once" who the dead man is at her door, and also who killed him:

> *Ê daz si reht' erfunde daz iz wære ir man,*
> *an die Hagenen vrâge denken si began . . .* (1008,1–2)
>
> [Before she really found out that it was her husband,
> she began to think of Hagen's question . . .]
>
> *dô sprach si: "ez is Sîfrit, der mîn vil lieber man:*
> *ez hât gerâten Prünhilt, daz ez hât Hagene getân."* (1010,3–4)
>
> [Then she said: "It is Sivrit, my beloved husband:
> Prünhilt instigated it, and Hagen carried it out."]

Intuition is not enough, however.[76] Kriemhilt states a bit later: *wesse ich wer iz het getân, ich riet' im immer sînen tôt* [If I knew who did this, I would wish his death more than anything] (1012,4). She needs proof for her revenge: *der mir in hât benomen, / wird' ich des bewîset, ich sol im schädelîche komen* [whoever took him from me, / once I have proof, I shall make him pay dearly] (1033,3–4). She seems to get proof when Gunther and Hagen come to the funeral with their retinue. The "bier test" can discover the murderer in full view of everyone:

> *Si buten vaste ir lougen. Kriemhilt begonde jehen:*
> *"swelher sî unschuldic, der lâze daz gesehen;*
> *der sol zuo der bâre vor den liuten gên.*
> *dâ bî mac man die wârheit harte schiere verstên."* (1043)
>
> [They maintained their lies. Kriemhilt began to speak:
> "Whoever is innocent, he should let it be seen;
> he should go to the bier for all to see.
> With this the truth will very quickly be manifest to all.]

The proof is given through a *michel wunder* [great wonder] (1044,1):

> *swâ man den mortmeilen bî dem tôten siht,*
> *sô bluotent im die wunden, als ouch dâ geschach.*
> *dâ von man die schulde dâ ze Hagene gesach.* (1044,2–4)
>
> [Where somebody stained with the murder is seen near the corpse,
> his wounds will bleed, as happened there.
> By this people saw that Hagen was guilty.]

Having demanded (*jehen*) the test, Kriemhilt is now able to determine:

> *Gunther unt Hagene, jâ habet ir iz getân.* (1046,3)
>
> [Gunther and Hagen, indeed you have done it.]

Why are there no consequences? The disassociation between truth and legitimacy first comes to light at the oath and returns under reversed conditions. It is clear what the truth is this time, but truth is not necessarily valid. Gunther refutes the accusation. The royal word, spoken in front of the court, stands against the sign, visible to all, and it is stronger. The *wunder* of the bleeding wound of the victim cannot match the public proclamation of the king and its attestation by his retinue (*Si buten vaste ir lougen* [they stuck to their lies], 1043,1). The intent for revenge remains (1046,4). The appearance of the bier test would have to be validated, and this is hopeless. Truth depends on power. Justice cannot prevail against the guarantors of justice, the king and his powerful vassals.

Kriemhilt has to pay with her *leit* because she *hât betrüebet den Prünhilde muot* [has made Prünhilt distraught] (1001,3). The same Hagen, however, who made the tears of his queen his own affair, now declares: *ez ahtet mich vil ringe, swaz si weinens getuot* [I don't care how much she cries] (1001,4). This is not a sign of his well-known coarseness or his role as a traitor, but it shows that Kriemhilt's crying is a matter for her alone, and unlike Prünhilt's, has no meaning for the Burgundian rulers. It is not a matter for public concern.[77] In that those from Xanten leave the story, the forum where Hagen's and Gunther's guilt had been manifest and Kriemhilt's tears should have had consequences has, for the time being, disappeared.

The conflict remains unresolved until *suone*, which in a curious deviation from what the test had shown, legally determines what is valid. Kriemhilt declares Gunther innocent of the murder (*des zîhet in niemen: in sluoc diu Hagenen hant* [no one accuses him of murder: Hagen killed him], 1111,1), including his retinue, with the exception of Hagen (1113,2). This is a prerequisite for the hoard coming to Worms. It allows Kriemhilt to return to the light of honor (*si pflac vil guoter tugende, des man der küneginne jach* [she exhibited many great virtues, and the queen was praised for this], 1127,4) but also serves to prepare a new intrigue. There is a new break between a shining façade and a secret plan, which provokes secret counteractions.

The new crime—the theft of the hoard—is hardly camouflaged; the forum in which it would have to be judged is just temporarily removed (1136). Hagen can only act "in the absence" of the king and "outside" the legal system that he guarantees. Concerning the moves and countermoves, the sequence of events is anything but transparent: inconsequential anger, ineffective promises, a pragmatic solution that harms Kriemhilt's legal rights (1134), and a dubious oath (1140).[78] Instead of transparency there is a clouded flurry of intrigue and counterintrigue.

Kriemhilt's lament after the return of the kings *mit meiden unt mit vrouwen* [with maidens and with women] in a public trial (1138) once again creates the semblance of order. She at least achieves a guilty verdict for Hagen. The verdict remains without consequences, however. It cannot restore the disrupted legal situation, and it cannot restore her rights against the offenders. The dark entanglement of the kings is not cleared up, however; the listener only hears of their *eiden* (1140,2) after the verdict that makes them co-conspirators.

With the first failed trial, the confrontation is pushed into the twilight of secret plots, which is the arena of treason. This is evident when Sivrit's corpse is laid before Kriemhilt's door in the dark. The display of his heroic body is denied him in death. According to medieval criminal codes, secrecy produces far worse crimes than even the most brutal public act of violence.[79] In retrospect, the secrecy of treason sheds an ambiguous light on the preceding scenes, even those that were connected to *minne.*[80] Secrecy does not necessarily always have negative connotations, but as the story progresses, it becomes more and more associated with dark events that are removed from visibility.

Betrayal grows out of the secrecy of *minne* in Isenstein. Sivrit sneaks to the ships, where the cloak of invisibility is kept (431,2–3), *ê iz iemen erfunde* [before someone discovers him], and *tougenlîche*, secretly—*von listen* [by trickery]—he returns to the site of the contest (432,3); *tougenlîche,* he touches Gunther (452,3) and asks him to *heln* [hide] the trick (455,1); according to ms. A, Gunther laments his miserable wedding night *tougen* (A 600,3);[81] and the second deception under the cloak is executed in the dark and *tougenlîche* (653,2).[82]

Above all the intrigues of the women are discredited as being *heimlîche.*

Prünhilt keeps her doubts concerning Sivrit's rank to herself (*verdeit*, 725,1) and executes her plan in secret (*heinlîche*, 726,3) in what is at first only an honest conversation with Gunther, but then becomes more and more hypocritical. The parallel discussions between Etzel and Kriemhilt about the invitation of her brothers (1400–1407) proceed explicitly in "secrecy," *Dô si eines nahtes bî dem künige lac* . . . [One night when she was lying with the king . . .] (1400,1).[83] Even more clearly than with Prünhilt and Gunther, all others are excluded, so that Kriemhilt can use the situation for her deceitful attack without Etzel realizing what he is doing.

While Etzel publicly orders the messengers to proceed with the invitation, Kriemhilt speaks with them secretly (*tougenlîche*, 1413,3). She tells them what they should and should not say in Worms (1414–1419), and orders them, according to some manuscripts,[84] to proceed with their mission undercover (*tovgenlichen*). She is playing a double game with them. She does not entrust them with her real plans, fakes concern for her relatives, and tries to prevent Hagen from getting wind of her intent for revenge (1420,1–3). The messengers, without knowing it, are misused as accomplices. There is, then, another intent behind the secret mission. In the triple sequence of the scene, secrecy is empowered as a site of treachery.[85]

Only once, when Rüedeger tells his wife of the bridal quest mission to Etzel (1168), is nocturnal intimacy not a means of treachery, and, tellingly, there is no mention of *tougen* or *heinlîche*. On the other hand, Rüedeger's fateful conversation with Kriemhilt, in which he promises his help for her *leit*, is *in heimlîche* (1255,2). This alone—more than the controversial content of the promise—is dubious.

The War of Looks and Violence

The metaphor of light and dark expresses the tension between apparent exterior and actual intrigue, and with the shift from one to the other, the catastrophe is unleashed. Seemingly, the transparency of the world is restored, but with fateful consequences. Kriemhilt's return to the light of the public sphere reflects the restoration of the façade. Her journey to Etzel is a succession of splendid images: *wie hêrlîchen Kriemhilt dâ kæme durch diu lant* [how magnificently Kriemhilt traveled across the country] (1337,3). The splendor of the courtly world is once more elaborately staged.[86] Etzel's power is *wît erkant* [widely recognized] (1334,1); his people proclaim (*jâhen*) Kriemhilt's honor (133,3); Kriemhilt seems to be again what she once was: *hey waz si grôzer êren sît dâ zen Hiunen gewan!* [what great honor she gained then with the Huns!] (1330,4). But when Kriemhilt begins to follow her *argen willen* [dreadful plan] (1399,4), this again occurs in the dark of night (1400,1).

The seemingly legitimate desire to see her relatives "with her" and to renew an intimate familiarity actually becomes a cunning pretext. Kriemhilt, unlike Prünhilt, not only wants to find out what she does not know, but wishes to set her revenge in motion based on what she knows all too well.

To "see" her brothers and Hagen means to control them. Kriemhilt's plan for revenge could fail, if her request would not seem to be perfectly ordinary and harmless. The principle of social cohesion is instrumentalized for revenge.

The Burgundians' expedition to Etzel is mostly cloaked in darkness. Darkness equals insecurity. Hagen creeps *tougen* to overpower the *merwîp* (1534,1). What is true and what is false proves to be uncertain. Hagen is at first handed a lie by the water sprites (1539,3). When they correct the lie, he considers the correction of the lie to be deceptive (1541,1). He has to put the truth to the test. The truth can only come out by way of a haphazard and violent act against the innocent priest.

Then, Hagen deceives his lords (*lougenlîche*, 1568,1) about the fact that he killed the ferryman, as his still steaming blood is discovered in the ship (1566–67). In crossing the Danube, the light, in which heroic action must be bathed, is completely extinguished. The battles against the Bavarians take place in darkness: *In was des tages zerunnen* [the day had come to an end for them] (1600,1). The ambush of the rearguard happens at night. At first the enemy can only be heard (*si hôrten hüeve klaffen* [they heard hooves clomping], 1602,2). Only when the battle is all over does the moon break out from behind the clouds (*Ein teil schein ûz den wolken des liehten mânen brehen* [Part of the bright moon broke out from behind the clouds], 1620,1), but the impending danger that lurks in the gloom is still present. The army is not allowed to rest before day breaks (1623,2). In addition, Hagen advises that the battle should be kept from the kings until daylight makes the blood on the armor visible (1624). Suddenly, the trial of warriors no longer belongs in the light of public observation.

The Burgundians seem to have temporarily left the darkness behind them in Passau and Bechelaren. At Etzel's court, however, the violent game of hide-and-seek begins anew.

Only when there is no turning back does Hagen tell the Burgundians what he heard from the *merwîp* (1589,1): nobody will return. From that point on the truth comes to light bit by bit. Kriemhilt's greeting already expresses a confrontation, and her look becomes a weapon: *wan daz si swinde blicke an ir vîande sach* [she threw sharp glances at her enemies] (1749,4).[87]

In the following scene, Volker and Hagen offer themselves to the Huns as objects for curious scrutiny from a distance:

> *Alsam tier diu wilden wurden gekapfet an*
> *die übermüeten helde von den Hiunen man.* (1762,1–2)
>
> [They were stared at as if they were all wild animals,
> the proud heroes next to the Huns.]

This is the reverse of the splendor that heroes exude: dread. The sight of Hagen alone is already hurtful to Kriemhilt. She breaks out in tears in front of her Hunnish retinue: *Ez mante si ir leide: weinen si began* [it reminded her of her grief: she began to cry] (1763,1). Her crying is a political act, as was Prünhilt's, and conjures up a similar reaction:

> *des het michel wunder die Etzelen man,*
> *waz ir sô schiere beswæret het ir muot.*
> *si sprach: "daz hât Hagene, ir helde küene unde guot."*
>
> *Si sprâchen zuo der vrouwen: "wie ist daz geschehen?*
> *wand' wir iuch niulîche haben vrô gesehen.*[88]
> *nie niemen wart sô küene, derz iu hât getân,*
> *heizet irz uns rechen, ez sol im an sîn leben gân."* (1763,2–1764,4)
>
> [Etzel's men were very astonished about
> what had so suddenly darkened her spirits.
> She said: "Hagen did it, you bold and great heroes."
>
> They spoke to the lady: "How did that happen?
> Not long ago we saw that you were happy.
> No one was ever so bold, whoever did this to you,
> if you have us avenge this, that he would remain living.]

The opportunity to shine some light on the darkness seems finally to have come. Kriemhilt declares the reason for her *leit.* She tries ceremoniously to stage the discovery of the truth about Sivrit's death and the theft of the hoard, so that sanctions can immediately be imposed. By strengthening her military retinue and appearing *under krône* (1770,4), that is with the insignias of her royal power, the appropriate frame is created for the triumph of the truth.

Kriemhilt provokes a confession in front of the entire court. She orders her people to listen well to Hagen's words (1771,1–2): *ich weiz in sô übermüeten daz er mir lougent niht* [I know that he is so proud that he will not deny it to me]. She designates him as the object of revenge: *sô ist ouch mir unmære, swaz im dar umbe geschiht* [it is unimportant to me whatever happens to him for this] (1771,3–4). The first objective succeeds, the second does not. Now words and signs correspond again. The truth comes out, but its validity is disputed.

The order reverses the dispute with Prünhilt in front of the church. Before a word is said, the *übermüete Hagene* openly displays the evidence of his guilt, Sivrit's sword: *wol erkandez Kriemhilt, daz ez Sîfrides was* [Kriemhilt knew well that it was Sivrit's] (1783,4–5), but he also shows the weapon so that Kriemhilt is unable to punish him. The sign offends Kriemhilt in two ways:

ez mante si ir leide: weinen si began.
ich wæne ez hete dar umbe der kuene Hagene getân. (1784,3–4)

[It reminded her of her grief: she began to cry.
I think that this is why the bold Hagen did it.]

The words confirm the gesture. Just as with a judicial proceeding, Kriemhilt asks Hagen the question not to determine the whether (this has already been determined) but the why of his deed:

zwiu tâtet ir daz,
daz ir daz habt verdienet, daz ich iu bin gehaz?
ir sluoget Sîfrîden, den mînen lieben man. (1789,1–3)

[why did you do this,
whereby you have earned my hatred?
You murdered Sivrit, my dear husband.]

She hears what she wants to hear, and Hagen declares in front of her retinue: *Der rede ist nu genuoc . . . ich binz aber Hagene, der Sîfriden sluoc . . . Ez ist âne lougen . . . ich hân es alles schulde . . . ich enwolde danne liegen* [Enough talking . . . I, Hagen, was in fact the one who killed Sivrit . . . It is the truth . . . I alone am guilty of all this. . . unless I were to lie] (1790–91). Kriemhilt repeats to her retinue what Hagen has confessed:

Sie sprach: "nu hœrt ir recken, wa er mir lougent niht . . . ." (1792,1)

[She said: "Now listen, warriors, he does not deny it . . . "]

She declares that he is a free target of vengeance (1792,3). There are weapons-carrying witnesses. Everything should normally be clear.

Hagen's words *nu rechez swer der welle . . .* [avenge it who will . . .] (1791,3) cut off the consequences and repeat the aggressive gesture.[89] With Sivrit's sword on his knees, he takes up the pose of judge in his own case and threatens Kriemhilt's retinue (1783; 1785).[90] He redefines the act of judgment to his own advantage. The judgment is no longer a matter for the queen, but for the one who can make his own right with the sword. Instead of avenging their queen, as the Burgundian vassals did formerly in Worms, the Huns retreat.

The defeat is reflected in viewing. The looks of the Hunnish retinue cannot withstand the aggressive acknowledgment of the truth and are thrown back:

die übermüeten degene ein ander sâhen an. (1792,4)

[The proud warriors looked at each other.]

A Hun asks: *wes sehet ir mich an?* [why are you looking at me?] (1794,1), another does not dare to attack Volker *durh sîne swinde blicke, die ich an im gesehen hân* [because of the sharp glances that I saw him casting] (1795,4). The war of gazes is lost, *die helde kêrten dannen* [the heroes turned to retreat] (1799,3).

It has turned out that the truth, which is uncontested and public, has no consequences, because it depends on power. The reestablishment of visibility does not equal the reestablishment of justice, but is a demonstration of pure might. As long as Kriemhilt has no one who can stand up for her, Hagen's position is unassailable.

If the scene throws light on the queen's attitude, it does nothing of the kind for Etzel's. Again, what matters is making public what most everyone already knows. Volker therefore requests, *vil lûte*, of his lords:

ir sult ze hove gên
und hœret an dem künege, wie der sî gemuot. (1803,2–3)

[you should go to the court
and hear from the king, what is his mind.]

The reception, however, does not bring about the desired resolution by the king. What the Burgundians experience in terms of friendliness at Etzel's greeting contradicts what the confrontation with Kriemhilt has produced (1808; 1811,4), and again it will be imperative to try to resolve the contradiction anew. Kriemhilt, Volker, and Hagen are intent on doing this in the following scenes. Etzel must choose his role.

Up until then, Kriemhilt has acted covertly, and this again represents treachery. Light and darkness stand for justice and injustice. After Hagen lays bare the brutal truth *âne lougen*, the light has turned to the Burgundian side, and the darkness is with Kriemhilt. The first attack on the guests occurs in the dark, as the Burgundians are sleeping. But what happens in the dark cannot be completely covered up. The attackers are noticed, because Volker, who is standing guard with Hagen, sees a helmet flashing (*schînen*) *verre ûz einer vinster* [from somewhere in the darkness] (1837,2–3). What was supposed to stay hidden in the dark is revealed only by accident in the light. The Burgundians are different. Volker shines in the bright light, whereby the nocturnal situation seems to have been forgotten:

> *Der treit ûf sînem houbte einen helm glanz*
> . . .
> *ouch lohent im die ringe sam daz fiwer tuot.* (1841,1–3)

> [On his head he wears a shining helmet,
> . . .
> His chain mail glows like fire.]

Heroic splendor on the one side and cowardly hide-and-seek games on the other correspond to the roles from here on out.

Volker wants to pull into the light what was started in the dark:

> *Dô sprach aber Volkêr: "sô lât doch daz geschehen,*
> *daz wir si bringen innen daz ich si habe gesehen.*
> *daz des iht haben lougen die Kriemhilde man,*
> *daz si ungetriwelîche vil gerne hêten getân."* (1845)

> [Then Volker spoke: "Make sure
> that we let them know that I saw them.
> This way Kriemhilt's men cannot deny
> that they would have liked to act disloyally."]

This time Volker tries unsuccessfully to force the opponents to come out of hiding and to give up their *lougen*.

At the procession to church, which is actually a show of arms, the war of viewing continues. Hagen's false explanation for the Burgundians' martial demonstration is answered by Kriemhilt with just a glance: *wie rehte fientlîche si im under diu ougen sach!* [how she gazed at him with hatred] (1864,2). The tournament [*bûhurt*] is also supposed to provoke looks:

> *lât die vrouwen schouwen und die degene,*
> *wie wir künnen rîten; daz ist guot getân.*
> *man gît doh lop deheinen des künec Guntheres man.* (1888,2–4)

[Let the ladies and the warriors watch,
how we can ride; that's the right thing to do.
King Gunther's men will not be praised anyway.]

The Hunnish court no longer stares at the foreigners like wild animals without them now returning the aggressive gazes. A Hunnish courtier provokes Volker's looks, and this is reason enough to kill him. The uninvolved onlookers of the courtly show become witnesses to a violent act (*Etzel unde Kriemhilt ez bescheidenlîchen sach* [Etzel and Kriemhilt clearly saw it], 1890,4). Etzel can once more prevent the open outbreak of general fighting by publicly certifying what he did not see (1896,3): it was an accident. One last time, a lie is able to fabricate legitimacy.

Etzel's gaze is now included in the conflict. When Hagen, at the feast, predicts the early death of the king's son:

Der künec an Hagene blihte; diu rede was im leit. (1919,1)

[The king looked at Hagen; the speech caused him grief.]

The look stands in for the answer to the provocation that Etzel's nobles desire.

The epic returns to the transparency of the heroic drama with Dancwart's appearance at the feast: *man sach den Hagenen bruoder ze hove hêrlîchen gân* [Hagen's brother was seen splendidly going to court] (1947,4). He reports *vil lûte* (1952,1) what happened with the servants. Finally, what was hidden now comes to light. The price for this breakthrough of truth is incomparable brutality and total destruction.

The slaughter only stops when almost everyone is dead. Kriemhilt's look, which had once seen many heroes, so it is said, no longer has a place to rest:

nu sehet al umbe, Kriemhilt, wem ir nu gebieten welt. (2231,3)

[Look all around, Kriemhilt, at whom you will now command.]

The end also represents the extinguishing of viewing. The window, in front of which courtly splendor unfolded in countless receptions, is now Dietrich's seat (2247,2). Having retreated to this spot, he had hoped to keep out of the fight. There is nothing left to see from this window. What is left is a melancholic gesture:

Dô sah er trûreclîche sitzen hie den man. (2309,1)

[There he saw the man sitting sadly.]

Hagen is removed from view after his defeat; he is brought

an sîn ungemach,
dâ er lac beslozzen unt dâ in niemen sach. (2356,1–2)

[to his miserable prison,
where he lay in chains and where no one saw him.]

The one who did everything so that it could be seen now disappears to a place where he is seen by no one—the greatest distance from his role. Viewing is no longer a means of social connection, and Gunther and Hagen have lost sight of each other:

Si lie si ligen sunder durch ir ungemach,
daz ir sît dewedere den andern nie gesach [!],
unz si ir bruoder houbet hin für Hagenen truoc (2366,1–3)

[She had them separated, to their displeasure,
that neither would ever see the other again,
until she carried her brother's head to Hagen.]

When Hagen returns to the stage for a final test of strength, Kriemhilt forces him to look upon his dead lord (2370,1) by carrying his head *bi dem hâre* [by the hair] (2369,3), and she makes Etzel a witness to her last act of cruelty (2373,4). This is all that remains to be seen. The splendor that presented itself to the views of participants and future generations alike is gone. The causes as well as the effects of the destruction of the Nibelungian world are encoded in the initial shrouding and final extinction of visibility.

6 Spaces

Open Versus Closed Space

Hagen's account of Sivrit's youth sketches a strange world with no reliable system of space-time coordinates.[1] In this it is distinguished from the normal Nibelungian world, which is again different from the everyday world. There are no clearly separated spaces, and none are closed off from each other. The actions normally take place on an open stage, to which in principle everyone has access. This basically open space explains the popularity of the "fight in the hall" motif in heroic epic, because the exclusion from outside allows the action to be concentrated.[2] Separation must always be explicitly indicated. It is, as was seen in the intrigues of Prünhilt and Kriemhilt, not always localized, but usually marked as *tougen, heimlîche,* and so on. It is sufficient to emphasize that no one is listening.

Space is not a continuum. It is a stage for action. All the required actors are on that stage, and whoever is not there has nothing to do with the current events. Often only those presently acting are named, and whoever is needed is suddenly there. It is not that somebody who enters a space takes part in the action. Instead, those who are to take part are always present. The appearances of protagonists depend on their function in the story. It is incorrect to assume the absence of a character if he or she is not named explicitly.[3]

One acts within eye- and earshot. What is said in a certain space—for example, in the hall of the Hun king—can be heard by those outside, if the story so requires, and vice versa.[4] What is said in a battle on one side is heard and acted upon the other side. After the Burgundians have driven the Huns from the hall and are forcefully holding them at bay, for example, it has just been said that the fighters have separated: *den Etzelen man / gab er herberge hôher von dem sal* [to Etzel's men / he assigned quarters further beyond the hall] (2018,2–3). Yet the Huns are still close enough to hear everything the Burgundians say. Hagen and Volker negotiate with Etzel (2019,2–3); Kriemhilt gets involved (2021,2–4); Hagen insults Etzel and Kriemhilt, who is *in unmuote* [angry] (2024,2), because this happens in front of *Etzelen man* (2024,3), that is, within earshot. When Kriemhilt promises great reward to Etzel's men, Volker the Burgundian answers her by mocking the Huns' cowardice (2026–7).

Irinc is among Kriemhilt's retinue when he calls for his weapons (2028). Then Hagen warns him (2029), and Irinc answers (2030). Only then does Volker see Irinc advancing with 1,000 men, apparently from a greater distance. In the closing scene, Dietrich leaves Kriemhilt *mit weinenden ougen* [with tearful eyes] (2365,2). Kriemhilt has Hagen and Gunther locked up separately *durch ir ungemach* [to their discomfort] (2366,1); then she leaves to see Hagen (*dâ si Hagenen sach* (2367,1)—in his prison cell?—and argues with him about the treasure; after Hagen's refusal she has—where?—Gunther beheaded and—has she left Hagen?—carries his head *bî dem hâre* [by the hair] (2369,3) to Hagen; another argument ensues; and when this breaks out in violence suddenly Etzel, Hildebrant, and again Dietrich are on the stage—but where? There is no mention of how they arrived and what has happened in the meantime.[5]

Because the space of the action is open, and spaces are not closed off from each other, changes in space do not generally have to be mentioned. Kriemhilt had just attempted in vain to draw Dietrich into the fight when she promises Blœdelin a reward for his help in getting her revenge (1903–4), without it needing to be said that she has just left the one to find the other. Blœdelin immediately orders his retinue to arm themselves (1910). Are they present during the discussion? When Kriemhilt leaves him and goes *ze tische* [to the dinner table] (1911,2), this demonstrates that she acts from the background in the following scenes.

Relationships of rank are expressed in spatial configurations, too. When the royal couple stand side by side, this makes an ordered rulership visible. The fact that Sivrit wears his crown in view of his warriors (*vor . . . recken . . . krône,* 713,3) means that they are his subordinates. Gunther's and Prünhilt's appearance under the crown does not occur in a specific place but "in the presence of the realm" (*in des küneges lande* 604,4). The subsequent coronation feast, the next part of the wedding ceremony, is distinguished from this representional act, and so it belongs in "another" space (even though it seems at first that the *gesidele* [retinue] is in the same room); one has "to go there" (*der künic wolde gân / ze tische mit den gesten* [the king wanted to go / to dinner with his guests], 604,1–2); where it takes place is not said. Prünhilt has to leave, because she will not take part in the wedding of Sivrit and Kriemhilt. Protagonists move seamlessly from one space to another. If Sivrit's marriage to Kriemhilt is supposed to be equivalent to that of Gunther to Prünhilt, then it has to take place in the same location. Kriemhilt then "replaces" Prünhilt. After that it is unnecessary to state that one goes into another room for the wedding meal, and of course Prünhilt is immediately there again.

In this male-dominated world, there is no space beyond the stage where heroes act and sometimes women join them. At best, there are spaces that are darkened or closed off, where *heimlîche* things take place. These spaces are not "private" in the modern sense, but only in the original sense of the word that "something is missing." That is the sphere where women act.

It is not so much spaces as spheres of legitimate and illegitimate action that are counterposed. When Kriemhilt talks Etzel into inviting her relatives, there is a sequence of three spaces: the matrimonial bedchamber (*Dô si eines nahtes bî dem künige lac* [when she lay with the king one night], 1400,1), the room in which Etzel prepares the messengers, and the *kemenate* [chamber] (1413,2,) in which Kriemhilt finally instructs the messengers separately. People have wondered why the nocturnal discussion transitions directly to the scene in which Etzel speaks to the messengers (*die guoten videlære hiez er bringen sâ zehant* [he ordered that the fine musicians be called for], 1407,4).[6] Kriemhilt at least orders them to another place. It is not the change from one room to another that is interesting, but rather the fact that one of the rooms is public and two are closed. The first scene does not represent a scene of spousal intimacy, but a situation removed from the public eye, and this allows for a double game: Kriemhilt can weave her deceitful plan, about which the players are only half informed. Etzel, on the other hand, can demonstrate the harmony of the clan, which concerns everyone and is thus essentially public. The continuation of the scene therefore takes place in different rooms: one according to Etzel's purpose, the other to Kriemhilt's. There is no need for secret exclusion for what Etzel understands Kriemhilt's suggestion to be. This is why the result of the discussion, the invitation of the Burgundians, can be made public directly. From the beginning, Etzel never leaves the sphere of rulership, not even in his discussion with Kriemhilt, and this is why the messengers find him immediately where he is normally (*dâ der künec saz* [where the king was seated], 1408,1) and not in bed with Kriemhilt. Kriemhilt, on the other hand, acts covertly and in closed spaces. This is why the messengers, after they have received their instructions from the king, have to leave the public space and look for her *in ir kemenâten.*

Such symbolically connoted space is well known from heroic epic representation. It is especially worth noting that space is more clearly defined in the *Nibelungenlied* than in a work like the *Rolandslied.*[7] Rather than space merely being treated as a prop, its separate segments denote fields of action and constellations of characters. In this sense, space is always more than just space.

Ze hove: *Space, Institution, and Constellations of Characters*

This is demonstrated by the phrase *ze hove,* which designates a space, a group of persons, an institution, and frequently all three at once. Usually, *hove* is an indeterminate space with indeterminate boundaries. It is the center of power. So we see the supposed messengers of the Saxons with the false declaration of war *ze hove rîten* (877,2), which probably means to the surroundings of the kings. There they are allowed (*urloup*) to appear before the king in person (878,1). The arrival of the Burgundians at Etzel's castle is called riding *hin ze hove,* that is, they leave the open fields (1719,3) where they have set up camp and approach Etzel's seat of power (1732,1). Only later do they go *ze hove* in the sense of "to the king" (1803,2; 1804,4). This time, what is meant is not the seat of the court, but instead more narrowly the ruler, wherever he may be at the time. In this sense, the Saxon messengers are escorted *ze hove für den künec* (141,4). The phrase *in was ze hove erloubet* therefore means "they were granted an audience with the king" (744,4).[8]

In addition, there is a purely spatial meaning. *Hof* can refer to the open space in the interior of the castle, where new arrivals can congregate, young knights can test their strength, or a *bûhurt* [tournament] can take place.[9] At the arrival of the Burgundians at Etzel's court, the lords at first stay in the courtyard (*die herren ûf dem hove stân,* 1760,1), while Volker and Hagen cross *über den hof vil verre für einen palas wît* [over the courtyard to a distant, spacious palace] (1760,3). Here *hof* is the space between various buildings.[10]

These different concepts are not always clearly differentiated, and the meaning can change within a single episode. When Hagen and Volker, after having gone *über den hof,* return to their kings, this is called going *hin ze hove* (1800,3). Here the court is again a constellation of persons. Shortly thereafter, the concept of space again pushes itself to the fore when we read:

> *si giengen dâ si funden die zieren degene*
> *in grôzen antpfange an dem hove stân.* (1802,2–3)
>
> [They went where they found the splendid warriors
> standing in a grand formation in the courtyard.]

Immediately thereafter, Volker suggests to his lords *ir sult ze hove gên* (1803,1–2). Now "court" is again somewhere else. It refers to neither the place where one stands nor the group around the Burgundian kings. The meaning is: to Etzel, in the proximity of the Hunnish king.[11]

Because *ze hove* is not clearly defined spatially or institutionally, the ruler can, if he wants to, gather his people, send *ze hove* [call them]: *hat ouch harte balde ze hove nâch Gêrnôte gân* [Gunther ordered men to go quickly for Gernot] (148,4). Most likely *ze hove* here means the direction in which someone is asked to come. We could then translate: "Gunther sent for Gernot, so that he might appear at court."[12]

Court is the assembly of those who rule over the land.[13] When Kriemhilt is supposed to appear in public, Gunther orders that she comes before him and his people:

> *daz si mit ir mage den hin ze hove solde gân* (275,4)
>
> [that she should go to the court with their relatives]

Similarly at the wedding with Sivrit:

> *dô hiez man Kriemhilde ze hove für den künic gân* (609,4)
>
> [Kriemhilt was told to go see the king at court.]

What happens or is made known *ze hove* is witnessed by the ruler's surroundings, that is, it is "public" and valid. This is the reason for Rüedger's revulsion and revenge for a Hun's disparaging speech, which was spoken *ze hove ze lûte* [too loudly at court] (2141,4).

Finally, *ze hove* can mean in the surrounding of ladies. Sivrit asks for permission to go *ze hove*, to see Kriemhilt and her mother (550,2). Going *ze hove* is a festive event in festive clothing. The women also change their clothes before asking Sivrit to visit. Even when the king goes there, it is called *ze hove*.[14] Centers of power and spaces where power is focused can take each other's places: *hie ze hove*, that is, in Worms near to King Gunther, is the place of the *Tronegære* (699,3). Besides the center of rulership in the proximity of the prince, there is another center with the *vrouwe* as its focal point. These centers coincide in Isenstein when the heroes go *ze hove*, or set out for Prünhilt (359,2;

359,4). Various concepts overlap that are integrated only in the courtly romance. In heroic epic, *ze hove* is rather unspecific. It generally does not imply a specific lifestyle.

Sometimes, *ze hove* means a place where women reside. Here the influence of contemporary courtly culture makes itself most clearly felt. But it is a space separated from the male world of feudal lords. Spatial separation represents the strict social separation of men and women. The male-dominated world can be observed by the women (133,2–3), but they generally remain excluded from it. In the opposite direction, view and access are blocked. The women can only be seen when they appear in the sphere of the (masculine) court—when, for example, Kriemhilt and her women appear in a festive procession in their finest clothing (276–80): *Mit ir vil schœnen mägeden si kom für den sal* [she entered the hall with her most beautiful maidens] (610,1).[15] The sphere of women is only accessible under very specific conditions. When Sivrit wants to announce Gunther's message to the women, he must obtain permission *ze hove gân* (551,2; cf. 550,2).

"Courtly life" is displayed only when the separation of the two spaces is temporarily lifted, but the transition from the male court to the women's chambers is ceremoniously formalized. It is prepared like a diplomatic reception (*Do enbôt er sîner swester daz er si wolde sehen* [he told his sister that he wanted to see her], 347,1).[16] Messengers are used as interlocutors.[17] The women, like the men, put on their best clothes; greeting, seating, speech and counterspeech, and departure take their formal course.[18] Here, where in a narrower sense "courtly" life is palpable, the forms of interaction are clearly distinguished from those in the courtly romance. There is no relaxed, exclusive social interaction that includes both men and women, only the highly formalized contact of two social realms that are normally separate.

Regionality and Foreignness

There are centers of courtly order and political power that are structured relatively similarly: Worms, Passau, Bechelaren, Etzelburg, and even Isenstein, insofar as it is the seat of Prünhilt's rule and the goal of the courtly Gunther's quest. The world between these points of political power is empty. The only thing that matters is what happens there. The known feudal world consists of a number of "islands" surrounded by a dangerous wilderness. On these islands, one has relatives, one is known, even if one has never been seen there before. Between the islands lies a space that must be crossed heavily armed and with great caution. This is especially true of the space that stretches between the Burgundian and Hunnish realms.

This geographic-social structure is based on "segmentary differentiation."[19] There is a series of equal units, but there are no, or hardly any, structures that go beyond these units. There is neither a binding legal system that has mediated local powers—this is why the need for revenge must be constantly proven anew—nor a rulership that subordinates smaller rulerships. There are only a few reliable standards of conduct that are valid everywhere. This explains the "misunderstandings" when strangers arrive with regard to regional *site* [custom].[20] Such a world already had an archaic character around 1200-especially in contrast to courtly culture.

Nevertheless, it closely approaches the known world. The names of places that normally localize the action in heroic epic "far away," whether in the "orient" or "Lamparten," an archaic "Bern" of legend or "in the mountains," are here connected to precise geographic ideas: *in Burgonden* (2,1), more specifically *ze Wormez bî dem Rîne* (6,1).[21] This is not just somewhere in a strange space of a special epic world, but a well-known town, although the old name *zen Burgonden* (21,4) might seem strange. Even if the geographic knowledge of the poet, who presumably came from the southeastern part of the Holy Roman Empire, is not all that good with regard to the upper Rhine, one would expect him to be able to distinguish the [ancient] Burgundian kingdom from contemporary Burgundy. Worms was surely a familiar name (as a center of royal power in the twelfth century). The names in the Danube area, whose detailed explication is in odd contrast to the meaninglessness of the events that occur there, are certainly well known. This nomenclature is a geographic counterpart to the "familialization" of dynastic clans with characters of heroic legend that became increasingly popular above all in the late Middle Ages. What is demonstrated is that heroic legend takes place "here."

The geographically fixed spaces are contrasted with those that float around in the darkness of legend.[22] There may be some notion of Iceland behind Isenstein, but it lies far away, *über sê* (326,1). It will disappear from the epic when Prünhilt's power is broken. As a place of the contest, it lies, along with her, "beyond" the known world. Once Prünhilt is overpowered, however, her realm proves itself to be fairly closely related to that of the Burgundians as a hereditary monarchy, especially when female rule is replaced by male rule, and Prünhilt's mother's brother takes her place. In this sense, Isenstein turns out to be, after the victory in the contest, a fairly "normally" structured land. It does not fall apart with Prünhilt's departure, as would be expected if the rule were based on her person alone. Isenstein is no longer foreign, but it then also becomes uninteresting for the narrator.

The land of the Nibelungen is different. Its location is shrouded in darkness.[23] Sivrit arrives there the first time by accident. Later, coming from Isenstein, he reaches it in a short time, *bî des tages zîte unt in der einen naht* [in a day and a night] (484,1). These two places are "next to each other" because they both lie beyond the normal world. There are giants and dwarves in Nibelungenland.

Only the *merwîp* still seem strange to the normal world. This, however, is a modern misconception. They are water sprites, and they can be found according to medieval beliefs in the known world, as here on the banks of the Danube. Water is inhabited by these kinds of beings.[24] To be sure, the *merwîp* inhabit a border area, where the Burgundians leave their own secure world forever and cross over to a dangerous space beyond their own sphere of influence.

The epic world seen as a whole is divided into two parts, into the courtly world of Worms, Xanten, Bechelaren, and even Etzelburg, and a foreign world, from which Prünhilt comes and where Sivrit wins his hoard. The border of the normal world is crossed at only two points. Isenstein is to a certain degree colonized, and Nibelungenland seems at first to share the same fate, until it then gains a strange power over the other space.[25]

Rules are basically valid on a "regional" basis. The subordination that is necessary in Isenstein is no longer required, in fact it is even offensive, in Worms. Sivrit's trophies can be shown at the court of Xanten, but not at the Burgundian court. The proof of Hagen's murder is shown only to the community of mourners in Worms. For the Huns, Hagen must repeat his confession of guilt. Behavior becomes plausible in reference to a specific context. Latent conflict escalates in the transition from one space to another, as when Prünhilt brings her knowledge from Isenstein to Worms, or when Kriemhilt uses the trophies of her victory over Prünhilt outside her own sphere. The *suone* [reconciliation] of Worms runs aground when the Burgundian clan drags the burden of an unatoned crime before Etzel.

Conflicts do not only arise because the foreign world "beyond" intrudes into the feudal world (Prünhilt, Sivrit's strength, his hoard). They become virulent as soon as the "sectors" of the feudal world are crossed, from Isenstein to Gunther's court, from Xanten to Worms, from Worms to Etzelburg. The segments of feudal society are only secure if kept separated.

The borders of the known world begin to become visible when one steps out of one's own social group but has not yet arrived at a similar place. An example of this in-between is when the Nibelungian army has to cross the Danube on the way to the Hunnish court.

The Danube marks a border. Kriemhilt's faithful followers accompany her this far on her expedition to Etzel (1291). A threatening world begins here. Hagen is now dependent on the advice of supernatural beings, the water sprites, whom he consults on the auspices for the journey to Etzel. Here special heroic conditions like those formerly encountered in the vicinity of the Nibelungen hoard set in again; the equivalent of the small boat used on the journey to Isenstein now suffices to ferry across a gigantic army.[26] Foreign places harbor a violence that requires no explanation.

What Hagen learns from the water sprites about the land he has to cross, and about the chances of bringing the entire army safely across the Danube, tells him that he has to confront a social group that closely resembles the Burgundians. There is a *herberge* and a ferryman upriver. This is the only place where the river can be crossed (1544,2–3); *dirre marc herre* [the lord of the march] is named Else (1545,4), his brother is Gelpfrat, the ferryman *ist Gelpfrâte holt* [is beholden to Gelpfrat] (1547,4), which means that he is his vassal. But for a foreigner like Hagen, this ferryman is life-threatening: he is *sô grimmes muotes, er lât iuch niht genesen, / ir enwelt mit guoten sinnen bî dem helde wesen* [so severe that he will not let you live, / unless you treat him with prudence and caution] (1547,1–2), that is, if you fail to react cleverly to the situation. This is why the sprites advise Hagen to use duplicity. He should pretend to be a certain Amelrich:

> *der was ein helt guot,*
> *der durch fientschefte rûmte ditze lant.*
> *sô kumt iu der verge, swenne im der name wirt genant.* (1548,2–4)
>
> [he was a great hero,
> who left this land on account of enmity.
> The ferryman will come when he hears that name.]

This is quite a complicated piece of information, a veritable sociogram of the foreign land. As in Worms, brothers rule together. As in Worms, they have in the ferryman an incredibly powerful vassal, who serves them, like Hagen, based on personal obligation (*holt*).[27] Then there is Amelrich, the fourth to be named, linked to the others in some dark way (cf. 1552,3). He has been exiled on account of a feud (as Hagen has likewise had to stay away from the court at Worms for a while), but he is nevertheless apparently so rooted to the land that he will be helped across the Danube.

Hagen follows this advice. The ferryman is on the opposite bank. Apparently, in this world, there is no way that a regular agreement for the crossing can be reached. Hagen calls: *nu hol mich hie, verge . . . , sô gib' sich dir ze miete einen bouc von golde rôt* [come get me here, ferryman . . . and I'll pay you with an armband of red gold] (1550,2–3). *Miete* alone will not suffice, however:

> *Der verge was sô rîche, daz im niht dienen zam,*
> *dâ von er lôn vil selten von iemen dâ genam.* (1551,1–2)
>
> [The ferryman was so wealthy that he did not need to serve,
> which is why he never took any payment from anyone.]

This, on the other hand, recalls the position attributed to Sivrit. He was also so *rîche* that he did not take a *lôn*. Unlike Sivrit, however, the ferryman is apparently a *man* of the duke of Bavaria, a loose dependency, but that will later cause the lord to avenge the murdered ferryman, who is called a *helt zen handen* [brave hero] (1603,4). This structure of rule is similar to the Burgundian one.

Hagen has to pretend to be this certain Amelrich, as *Elsen man, / der durch starke fientschaft von disem lande entran* [Else's vassal, / who had to leave the country because of strong enmity] (1552,3–4). With this he says more than he heard from the sprites. Hagen understands the foreign land according to the rules of the world known to him, and he formulates his ruse accordingly. He concludes that Amelrich must have been *Elsen man*, if his name is so well known. In this way, he can hope to obtain the other's help. Although apparently personal relationships count primarily, Hagen must additionally show the promised golden ring *vil hôhe an dem swerte* [high upon the tip of his sword] (1553,1) in order to succeed. This seems to disqualify the opponent, as it will later disqualify the Hunnish warriors from wanting to fight just for gold. He has *mvolich gesit* [bad manners],[28] and the *gir nâch grôzem guote* [greed for a great payment] (1554,2) persuades him to ferry Hagen across. This is a curious double motivation, but the priority is clear. The ferryman will only take someone (and this means: put himself in someone's dependence) from the group of persons known to him. Social relationships are doubly secured, personally and materially. Even Amelrich, the (supposed) brother, has to show the *vergen* a gold ring so that he will come over to the opposite bank to ferry him across.[29]

When he sees Hagen close up, the *verge* realizes, however, that he has been duped:

> *den er dâ nennen hôrte, do er des niht envant,*
> *dô zurnde er ernstlîchen. . . .* (1555,2–3)
>
> [since he did not find the one who was named,
> he became exceedingly angry. . . .]
>
> *des ich mich hie verwæne, dem sît ir ungelîch.*
> *von vater und von muoter was er der bruoder mîn.* (1556,2–3)
>
> [You are unlike the one I thought to find here.
> He was my brother—we shared a father and a mother.]

He immediately refuses to ferry him across. Hagen's suggestion to take him, the *vremde[n] recke[n]*, across the Danube as a friend (*vriuntlîche*) for payment, is rejected:

> *ez habent fîande die lieben herren mîn,*
> *dar umbe ich niemen vremden füere in ditze lant.* (1558,2–3)
>
> [My dear lords have enemies,
> and this is why I do not let strangers into this land.]

The fellowship of persons stabilizes itself against the outside through strict exclusion.

When Hagen insists, the ferryman gives him a good blow with the rudder. Hagen strikes back, and the ferryman is killed. The Burgundians then cross into *daz unkunde lant* [the unfamiliar land] (1572,4). The vengeance of the lords of the land, Else and Gelpfrat, brings along with it further battles and further victims.

The foreign land is both hostile and familiar. It makes itself known with names. By knowing the name of the exiled member of the fellowship, Hagen can hope to enter the foreign space, because then he would identify himself as a *vriunt*, as a member of the fellowship.[30] Rules—service based on payment—are only valid within one's own group, where one is *holt*, *liep*, and *vriunt*. Not even the desire for gold can bring the ferryman to cross these boundaries. Hagen's attempt to handle the crossing *ze minne* [on good terms] fails with the stranger's rejection. The alien starts beyond one's own social group, and agreements obviously do not hold there. Most important, even more than gold, are personal, at their core, familial relationships. The personal bonds to the ancestral social group are not broken through feud (*fîentschefte*, 1548,3), as a result of which Amelrich had to quit the country (was he exiled?), but instead prove themselves to be stronger than any *fîentschaft* within the group. Contractual relationships to a stranger, as Hagen suggests, cannot take their place. Hagen's trick would have almost succeeded had the bonds between the exile and the ferryman not been stronger than he could have known. Naturally, the *verge* would have recognized his own brother.

Once the deception has been uncovered, the only thing left is combat. Communication once again functions without problems at this level. The opponents belong to the same ruling class. The ferryman is also a powerful noble, who does not work for money. He is thus an opponent equal to Hagen, and there is also a mutual understanding between the two groups, even though this does not bring about a peaceful resolution. It is an intuitive understanding of enmity. The offensive spirit of the other is recognized and countered with deception and force.

Once more, the *Nibelungenlied* creates a segmentarily differentiated world.[31] The world is divided into different, equally structured units (segments) that have no relationship to one another and can therefore only come into contact through conflict. In the heroic epic, the story only deals with the top of each segment, the group of lords who base their rule on military superiority and who are connected to one another through familial or other personal relationships. All important tasks are concentrated in this group. The border guard therefore provides not only military security but also performs the functions of the *verge*, just as Hagen is not only a powerful army commander but also shows his kings the way or serves as an ambassador. The segments are so similar that intuitive understanding (not agreement, of course) between them is possible, first through accommodation (Hagen disguises himself and tries to lie his way into the foreign fellowship of persons by using the name Amelrich) and, if this fails, then at least by taking up arms.

Unlike in the courtly romance, there is no layer (*stratum*) extending beyond the single segments that is obligated to mutual rules of interaction that exclude violent conflict. The heroic world of the *Nibelungenlied* is the archaic countermodel to the "stratified" differentiation of courtly society,[32] as it is played out, for example, in Konrad von Würzburg's *Engelhart*.[33] Konrad asks what happens when a knight meets a stranger outside of the court and one cannot determine whether he is friend or foe. In this case, the courtly principle of reciprocal consideration has to prove itself. So the hero's father advises his son to give the stranger an apple. If he eats it himself, it is better to leave him alone. If he shares it by returning half of the apple, then he qualifies as a "friend." Engelhard tests the advice twice, with negative results. The third time, the stranger not only shares the apple, but gives it back peeled. This is a true friend. Members of the same stratum recognize one another (as potential "friends," that is, as fellow courtiers) under unlikely circumstances (on the *heide* [on the heath, i.e., removed from civilization]) by virtue of a mutual code of conduct. The test recommended by the father formulates a core requirement of the courtly code of conduct: reciprocity. The one who fulfills this condition adds something to it: the amiable form of the civilized gesture.

Here, unlike in the *Nibelungenlied*, there are no "strangers" within one's own stratum, and one is understood everywhere and can become friends under any circumstances. It is different in the Nibelungian world. There are no rules there that ensure safe interaction outside one's own social group when guarantees of power fail. People always encounter the same structures, but these do not guarantee peaceful contact. The "regionality" of the Nibelungian world corresponds to its point-to-point social relationships.

Presence/Absence

Proximity is loaded with social meaning. Presence and absence are signs of involvement in or distance from an event. They replace considerations of motivation and expression of emotional events. Presence and absence are therefore always explicitly established. When Sivrit appears at court for the first time, Hagen has to be absent, because knowledge of the newcomer's character is missing, and this knowledge is represented by Hagen. The absence of knowledge is noted, and Hagen is called for. His knowledge receives a festive reception: *man sach in hêrlîche mit recken hin ze hove gân* [he was seen going like a lord to court with other warriors] (82,4). When Hagen is present, it is revealed who Sivrit is. Just as heroic strength must be seen, so the absence or the availability of heroic knowledge must become noticeable. This is even true of secondary characters. When Rüedeger arrives, Hagen has to be absent, so that he can be called for: *der wirt nâch Hagene sande, ob si im kündec möhten sîn* [the host called for Hagen, wondering whether he knew who they were] (1177,4).[34]

Similarly, Prünhilt is missing at Sivrit's wedding, without any need to explain why she has left the room:

> *dô was diu vrouwe Prünhilt vol hin unz an den tisch gegân* (611,4)
>
> [Lady Prünhilt then went all the way up to the table.]

It is unimportant where this table is; what is important is Prünhilt's absence, which shows that she is excluded from the agreements about the marriage, with all their dark implications. Since she is "somewhere else," she lacks complicity with regard to what is happening.

There is analogous absence and presence with Rüedeger's conflict. A Hun, who speaks *zer küniginne* (2138,3), reproaches him for his uninvolvement in the fight. This means that the queen must be present somewhere close by. The Hun thus makes his rebuke where he will find some resonance. Rüedeger kills him on the spot. The king, without it needing to be said, was "standing nearby" and then questions his help as a vassal. This raises the reproach to the level on which it must be negotiated: as a conflict of vassality. It is a matter for the king, less so for the queen, who therefore has to enter the scene, even though she should have been present already, since the Hun had just spoken to her.

> *Dô kom diu kuniginne und het iz ouch gesehen.* (2147,1)
>
> [The queen arrived and had also seen it.]

Along with Kriemhilt, now a new obligation for *hilfe* comes to the fore, and that is Rüedeger's personal promise to her. The conflict is built up as the protagonists of the exchange come together.

The dramaturgy of the clash of the queens reflects the conflict's growing dimension. The argument begins in a dialogue with both retinues as witnesses. With its escalation Kriemhilt's retinue must be separated from Prünhilt's. Still, *die liute*, the observers who are just standing around, don't know what it all means (834,1). Kriemhilt, bedecked in jewels, returns with her ladies, now apparently also with Sivrit's retinue (*ir warten vor dem hûse alle Sîfrides man* [all of Sivrit's men were waiting in front of the house], 833,4).[35] This raises the argument well above the level of a dispute between women. Sivrit himself is not there, because he is not yet needed and must be summoned at a later time. Prünhilt is also surrounded by *ir frowen* [her ladies] (845,1) and *vil maniges ritters lîp* [many knights] (835,2), but also not accompanied by the most renowned men at court, because these must later come with Gunther.

After Kriemhilt's victory in the war of words, the circle is expanded once more. Prünhilt makes the insult stick in front of the *fürsten vonme Rîne* [the princes from the Rhine], she calls for Gunther (*heizet here gân*, 851,1–2), and Gunther gets his entrance: *Der künic kom mit recken* [the king arrived with his warriors] (852,1). Sivrit's appearance is also necessary to mediate the dispute: *er sol her für gân* [he must come forward] (855,1). In order to narrate his "joining," it is necessary that he not be part of Gunther's entourage. Sivrit takes his oath in front of the entire court, *vor allen dînen man* [in front of all your men] (858,3), who come together *zuo dem ringe* [to form a circle] (859,4). Now all seem to be assembled. Curiously, Hagen seems to be missing, because he has to appear and ask questions when Gunther's attempt at reconciliation fails and Prünhilt remains depressed. Is it possible that Hagen, who otherwise knows everything, has heard nothing of the scandal, has not been among the witnesses in the king's retinue, and must therefore get his information from Prünhilt?[36] This is the wrong question. Presence and absence apparently mean something else. Hagen is not mentioned in the preceding scene because he is "not responsible" for the failed reconciliation attempts. His time will come when the reconciliation fails and help must come from elsewhere. Then he can step in to take the queen's side, once more indicated by a movement in space *dô kom von Tronege Hagene zuo sîner vrouwen gegân* [then Hagen of Troneck went to his lady] (863,4).

Has the scene changed in the meantime? Are we still in the same place? The narrator does not provide the answers. It is only clear that something new is beginning, something different from the previous public judicial proceeding, namely, a secret intrigue. This is why those who were just assembled must be brought together again. Now, not "everyone" who was at the trial is present. Sivrit is absent above all. A conspiracy is growing that must be kept secret and from which others exclude themselves:

> *Zuo der rede kômen Ortwîn und Gêrnôt*
> *dâ die helde rieten den Sîfrides tôt.*
> *dar zuo kom ouch Gîselher* . . . . (865,1–3)
>
> [Ortwin and Gernot joined the discussion
> where the heroes were counseling Sivrit's death.
> Giselher joined them as well . . . .]

It is pointless to ask whether all those named were previously absent from the oath ceremony. What is starting to happen now is no longer public. This is why the circle of those in the know must be formed anew. Common action is replaced by single decisions. Hagen counsels murder. Ortwin, who has joined them, agrees. The other new arrival, Giselher, dissents. Nothing is heard of Gernot's reaction, but he later does not take part in the conspiracy. Suddenly, Gunther is also present (868,1), and then the group breaks up as quickly as it came together:

> *Sîn gevolgete niemen, niwan daz Hagene*
> *riet in allen zîten* . . . . (870,1)

[No one followed him, only Hagen
kept counseling him incessantly . . . .]

In what follows, only those who matter, namely, Gunther and Hagen, speak. Where? When? How often? The murder plot has no space, since it cannot show itself on the stage of courtly drama.

Participation in the deed is represented by presence, absence represents nonparticipation.[37] Giselher and Gernot do not ride along on the hunt, and consequently they are innocent of Sivrit's murder. *Gêrnôt und Gîselher die wâren dâ heime bestân* [Gernot and Giselher had stayed home] (926,4). The redactor of *C will ask why they did not warn Sivrit, because after all they were present at the murder conclave:[38]

Do die vil vngetriwen vf geleiten sinen tot,
si wistenz al gemeine. Giselher vnd Gernot
wolden niht iagen riten. ine weiz durch welhen nit,
daz si in niht en warenden; idoch erarneten siz sit. (C 923)

[When the traitors plotted his death,
they all knew about it. Giselher and Gernot
did not want to join the hunt. I don't know on account of what quarrel
they didn't warn him, but they paid for it afterwards.]

This is a Christian recipient's question concerning the laconism of the *alten mæren.* Gernot and Giselher get a conscience, obligating them to prevent a murder and assigning guilt if they keep their knowledge to themselves. Their destruction can then be interpreted as punishment.

The stanza certainly was inserted. The question of why the brothers keep silent remains disturbing, because both are considered to be innocent even in the *C group. Originally, absence was enough to clear them of all wrongdoing, but the principle that only presence means participation was retrofitted to a different moral code.[39] The change also shows that the previous understanding of responsibility was becoming obsolete. It is constitutive, however, of the symbolism of space, because in this way, guilt and innocence can be made visible in a spatial sense.

This no longer works in the case of the theft of the hoard. None of the kings is directly involved. Gunther disapproves of the plan as a bad idea; Giselher reacts angrily; Gernot, in order to end the argument, advises sinking the treasure in the Rhine. Only Hagen, who was excluded from the *suone*, is prepared to steal the hoard: *lât mich den schuldigen sîn* [let me assume the guilt] (1131,4). This is achieved by the absence of the kings. The kings have *rîtennes wân* [the desire to travel] (1135,4) and are out of the country when Hagen sinks the treasure. Giselher's protection of Kriemhilt is therefore temporarily abrogated (1135,34). What is created, in a literal sense, is a lawless space in which Hagen can be engaged. When the kings return, the prior judicial order is restored. Since they did not participate in the crime on account of their absence, they can now sit in judgment on Hagen, and Giselher can represent Kriemhilt's rights (*gerne wær ir Gîselher aller triuwen bereit* [Giselher wanted to serve her loyally in every way] , 1138,4).[40] Hagen is convicted.

Of course, if one considers how they are drawn into avenging the theft, such an interpretation might seem doubtful. Significantly, mss. C and a replace the verse about Giselher's *triuwe* by pointing out the farcical nature of the supposed nonparticipation of the kings: *do gebarten die degene sam si im heten widerseit* [the heroes acted as if they had declared a feud against him] (C 1154,4). The situation is more complicated than in the murder of Sivrit, when only Gunther was directly involved. Admittedly, Hagen is from now on dealt with as the one who steals the hoard, but the kings are also implicated by their secret transactions and by the fact that they left Hagen the room to maneuver. They temporarily abrogated their duty as kings to protect the law.

Generally, however, presence still indicates an intact relationship. Personal bounds are symbolized by spatial dimensions. Gunther accompanies Kriemhilt when she starts out for Etzel, *ein lützel für die stat* [just a bit out of town] (1288,4). This already expresses a certain distance to the one who was most involved in the murderous intrigue. Gernot and Giselher accompany their *swester* "very far," namely, all the way to the Danube,[41] as do Gere, Ortwin, and Rumolt. Why it is this group is not said. However, it is they who are missing at the final battle in Etzelburg. Rumolt is not there because he would rather stay at court; the two others are not mentioned.[42]

Permanent absence threatens the courtly order. When Prünhilt removes herself after the queens' dispute, this demonstrates that she is stepping off the courtly stage.[43] Initially, she is only excluded from the demonstration of courtly joy at the tournament, which is continued by Kriemhilt alone (871); then she continues agitating in the background; the encouragement of murder is ascribed to her (917,4; 1010,4); and her triumph is noted (1100). Then, however, she disappears from the story. There is no reconciliation with Kriemhilt. She is absent from the funeral and also from Etzel's embassies. When Rüedeger asks for Kriemhilt's hand, she is not even mentioned. Her absence is expressly marked when Kriemhilt's messengers appear. Werbel and Swemmel are supposed to greet Prünhilt (1426,1), and they even obtain permission to see her:

> *Der künic in erloubt, (des was noch niht geschehen)*
> *ob si wolden gerne froun Prünhilde sehen,*
> *daz si für si solden mit sînem willen gân.* (1485,1–3)
>
> [The king granted them (this had not yet happened),
> that if they wanted to see Lady Prünhilt,
> they should go to her with his permission.]

But then Volker prevents the meeting, *daz was ir liebe getân* [she was grateful for that] (1485,4):

> *"Jane is mîn vrouwe Prünhilt nu niht sô wol gemuot*
> *daz ir si müget schouwen," sprach der ritter guot.*
> *"bîtet unz morgen, sô lât mans' iuch sehen."*
> *dô si sie wânden schouwen, dône kund es niht geschehen.* (1486)
>
> ["My lady Prünhilt is not feeling well enough
> to see you, really," said the excellent knight.
> "Wait until morning, you can see her then.
> When they went to see her, it was not possible.]

Why is there a detour, when the messengers are not allowed to see Prünhilt in the end anyway?[44] Why *kund es niht geschehen*? If one considers that *vröude* and *leit* are not subjective emotions ("she doesn't feel like it"), then *niht sô wol gemuot* does not mean a temporary indisposition, but a permanent disturbance, visible for the first time in her *trûren* after her argument with Kriemhilt. Her relationship to Kriemhilt, who is represented by Etzel's messengers, is permanently damaged, as is her position at the court of Worms. She has received satisfaction through Sivrit's death (therefore her *übermuot*), but she could not realize her goals. This is why we have the contradictory and contrary disposition. Gunther allows her to see the messengers, but Volker prevents it. This is the Volker who, next to Hagen, will become Kriemhilt's bitterest enemy and who shows already here that familial bonds have been severed. Prünhilt has no further role to play, and this is made apparent by her absence. She is only mentioned one more time (1515,4), as Gunther's wife, not as queen, who spends the night with the king before his departure.[45] Only in the *Klage* does she once again play an important role, as the addressee of Swemmel's message, ruler of the land, and mother of the future king.

"To Come Close"

Spatial configurations and their corresponding patterns of action and behavior play a central role where the social order is no longer secured by institutions. Social relationships have to be constituted via personal ones. Where these are not stabilized by ancestral, cult, or clan groups or also by ties to place, they are threatened with decay—the "centrifugal" tendencies of feudalism are well known—and must therefore constantly be renewed. This can occur through special rituals, through regularly recurring festivals, through cooperation at trial, military expeditions, and also through extraordinary opportunities.

In the *Nibelungenlied,* we do not find as many official occasions as reported by medieval chronicles, but more informal opportunities to "come together" and to "see one another." "Coming together" fulfills the function taken over in later societies by the legal system and a system of institutions. Social cohesion is shown by closeness.[46] Being together in heroic epic can metaphorically express family, alliance, and peaceful coexistence. In *Kudrun,* for example, Hartmuot expresses his wish to marry Kudrun in the following way:

> *möhte daz geschehen,*
> *daz ich die Hilden tohter solte hie gesehen.* (K 740,1f.)
>
> [if it could be arranged
> that I could see Hilde's daughter here.]

The closeness of Kudrun would be a sign of an important political alliance, and it would increase the value of Hartmuot's rule and his own rank. This is why his own sister is happy about Kudrun's arrival: *daz si in ir vater lande / Kûdrûn gesæhe* [that she should see Kudrun in her own father's land] (K 971,3–4). In light of the difference in status, Kudrun declines the marriage as politically undesirable, however, refusing a publicly visible proximity:

> *ich wil des haben rât,*
> *daz der küene Hartmuot bî mir niht enstât*
> *vor unser beider friunden . . . .* (K 769,1–3)
>
> [I do not want
> the bold Hartmuot standing by my side
> in front of both our families . . . .]

Any closeness that would be visible to her followers would be an expression of a marriage alliance. "To be with someone" is therefore much more than a statement of the place of a character within a given space. The sentence: Ortrun *was ir [= Kudrun] gerne bî* [Ortrun was happy to be next to her] (K 983,2) expresses a connection between the kidnapped Kudrun and the kidnapper's sister that exists beyond the political conflict and on which Kudrun can rely even later, when she wants to secure peace between the opposing groups. These kinds of bonds are expressed in spatial terms: *Ortrûn saz zuo ir nâhen* [Ortrun sat close to her] (K 1046,2).

Spatial proximity as an abbreviation for personal relationships can lead to seemingly absurd consequences. In Eilhart's *Tristrant*, when it is supposed to be expressed that Marke wants to take Tristrant back into his trust, he has Tristrant's bed placed in his own bedroom—as we know, an apparently careless decision (Trt 3733–34). This emphasizes the symbolic meaning of space. Being close to the king is conceived of as "taking part in Marke's personal space" (Trt 3192).[47]

This kind of spatially concrete concept of "concord" continued until the late Middle Ages, when much more complex political structures had replaced the old personal alliances. In Maximilian I's *Weiskunig*, this is transferred to the relationship of territories. Military alliances are represented graphically when "kings" or lords of a territory come together in a space or in a ceremony, and the dissolution of alliances is shown by moving apart. In reality, there never was such an act, alliances were concluded over great distances and between different political systems—principalities, towns, cantons, the Church—and with the employment of many middlemen and diplomats. But this is irrelevant for the old medieval metaphor of closeness, even if it seems more and more inadequate to political theory and praxis.[48]

In the *Nibelungenlied*, the semantics of closeness are still matter-of-factly paramount. To create such a closeness where it does not yet exist is a complex affair. After Sivrit's death, Kriemhilt has broken with Gunther and Hagen, but her relationship to Gernot and Giselher, who did not participate in the murder, is still intact. This is expressed by Gunther in the following words: *mîne bruoder sint ir bî* [my brothers are with her] (1108,1). Gunther can use their "closeness" to Kriemhilt to prepare his own rapprochement. Representatives of both parties have to come together:

> *Dô hiez er Ortwînen hin ze hove gân*
> *unt den marcgrâven Gêren. dô das was getân,*
> *man brâht' ouch Gêrnôten und Gîselher daz kint.*
> *si versuochtenz vriuntlîche an vroun Kriemhilde sint.* (1109)

[He ordered Ortwin to go to court
along with Margrave Gere. After that was done,
then Gernot and the young Giselher were called for.
They tried to persuade Kriemhilt in a friendly manner.]

If the embassy is successful, then a ceremonial gathering will be agreed upon:

"Ich wil den künic grüezen," dô si im des verjach,
mit sînen besten vriunden man in vor ir sach.
dône torste Hagen für si niht gegân. (1113,1–3)

["I want to greet the king." When she had told him this,
he then came to her with his closest followers.
But Hagen did not dare to visit her.]

The range of the reconciliation ends at the boundary of the space in which the gathering takes place, because Hagen is not present. Kriemhilt's split with him is expressed by the fact that she did not see him (*in der zîte nie gesach* [she never saw him during that time], 1106,4), and Hagen also keeps his distance from her up until the confrontation at Etzel's court.

To make peace means to reestablish closeness. Chronicles offer examples,[49] as does heroic epic. The reconciliation rituals in *Kudrun* require that Hartmuot's clan is allowed to approach Kudrun's (*suone,* K 834,1):

dô giengen zuo einander die recken vil gemeit. (K 834,2)

[then the warriors joined together in cheerfulness.]

Kudrun must overcome the resistance of her mother, Hilde, who rejects a close relationship even to Hartmuot's sister Ortrun, who helped Kudrun in her distress. She says:

Ich wil hie niemen küssen, er<n> sî mir danne bekant. (K 1580,1)

[I don't want to kiss anyone here whom I don't know.]

The distance must be elaborately diminished through the intercession of those to whom one is "already close": Herwic, Hilde's future son-in-law and Kudrun's husband, leads Ortrun *an sîner hende* [by the hand] (K 1579,1). Later, Hartmuot receives permission to go *ungebunden ze hove* [unbound to court], that is, no longer as a captive of the queen (K 1599,2). The gift of courtly clothing incorporates him and his people into the court again (cf. K 1647,2–3). Kudrun allows Hartmuot to remain seated in her presence (K 1623,1). That way even the original opponents can come "together":

unz Ortrûn und Hartmuot für froun Hilden gê
und biete sich ze füezen der edelen küniginne. (K 1646,2–3)

[until Ortrun and Hartmuot go before Lady Hilde
and fall at the noble queen's feet.]

The *Nibelungenlied* problematizes this principle of establishing social order like many other things. Bringing people together is not necessarily the best way to resolve conflict, because the order expressed by closeness can also represent subordination and dependence. It should be understood in this sense when the *Tronegære*, as Hagen says, must *bî den künigen hie en hove bestân* [stay with the kings at the court] (699,3) and not near Kriemhilt and Sivrit. Distance implies independence, and closeness represents dependence. Sivrit's presence at the court of Worms can be mistaken, and the fact that the kings are interested in his presence (and use Kriemhilt to this end) makes "closeness" appear to be part of their power game. The counsel to

belîbet bî den recken, tuot des ich iuch bit,
bî Gunther dem künege und ouch bî sînen man (321,2–3)

[stay with the warriors, do what I ask of you,
with Gunther the king and also with his men]

is less harmless than it sounds. Sivrit's permanent incorporation into the court at Worms must always be explicitly excused with his *minne* to Kriemhilt, and so his decision to return *heim in mîniu lant* [home to my own land] (690,3) is again ambiguous: return to an ancestral position and the reestablishment of the independence of the *künec* (this is how almost everyone sees it), or forgetting his obligations as the *küneges man* and departing from the Burgundian ruling group (this is how Prünhilt sees it). She laments:

daz si ir vremde wâren, daz was ir harte leit,
daz man ir sô selten diente von Sîfrides lant. (725,2–3)

[that they became strangers to her, she found distressing,
that she was so seldom served by those from Sivrit's land]

This is why it is her goal to bring Sivrit back with an invitation to a festival. The reestablishment of closeness can express a familial concord as well as the actualization of a ruling bond. This is why Gunther and Prünhilt agree on the invitation. The distance between Worms and Nibelungenland, which could complicate the acceptance of the invitation,[50] actually makes a meeting necessary in order to renew the unity of the clan or to stabilize political dependence.

The spatial order is a potential for conflict. The harmless meaning—closeness as a sign of concord—is twice deceitfully misused in order to get distant relatives to enter the other's sphere. The treacherous invitations of the first and second part of the epic employ a fundamental principle of social order, and this is why the instigators are successful both times. "Coming together" is therefore ambivalent.

This can be seen especially in the misleading configurations of closeness that precede the violent confrontation. When Kriemhilt dreams

> *daz ir gienge vil dicke an der hant*
> *Gîselher ir bruoder; si kuste'n z'aller stunt* (1393,2–3)
>
> [that with her walked hand in hand
> Giselher her brother; she kissed him over and over again.]

this expresses the intact relationship to her youngest brother. But she can use this closeness to bring her enemies into her realm.

Before the conflict breaks out, configurations of closeness also develop between the Burgundians and the Germanic heroes at Etzel's court, which associate the later parties to the conflict:

> *Bî henden sich dô vîengen zwêne degene:*
> *daz eine was her Dietrîch, daz andere Hagene.* (1750,1–2)
>
> [The two warriors clasped each other's hands:
> the one was lord Dietrich, the other was Hagen.]

Other combinations follow:

> *Der fürste von Berne der nam an die hant*
> *Gunthern den vil rîchen von Burgonden lant,*
> *Irnfrit nam Gêrnôten, den vil küenen man.*
> *dô sach man Rüedegêren ze hove mit Gîselheren gân.* (1804)
>
> [The prince of Bern took by the hand
> the mighty Gunther, the lord of Burgundy,
> Irnfrit took Gernot, the very bold man.
> People saw Rüedeger going to court with Giselher.]

Hawart and Irinc *sach man geselleclîchen bî den künegen gân* [were seen escorting the king in a friendly manner], Dancwart with Wolfhart (1807). Concord, expressed in closeness, is also created with Etzel. When the Burgundians appear before him, he leaps to his feet and greets the kings, as well as Hagen and Volker, by name and seats them near him:

dô nam der wirt vil edele die lieben geste bî der hant.[51]
Er brâhte si zem sedele, dâ er ê selbe saz. (1811,4–5)

[Then the noble host took his dear guests by the hand.
He led them to where he himself was seated.]

These are, as will soon become evident, shaky alliances that feign bonds that will not hold. This, too, is represented spatially with the only configuration that does not go beyond party lines: Hagen and Volker, who at first "stand together" with the others but then immediately after their arrival separate themselves from them.

Dô schieden sich die zwêne recken lobelîch,
Hagen von Tronege unt ouch her Dietrîch. (1758,1–2)

[The two famous warriors separated then,
Hagen of Troneck and also lord Dietrich.]

Then Hagen detaches Volker from Giselher and calls him to his side:

Dô sah er Volkêren bî Gîselhere stên.
den spæhen videlære bat er mit im gên . . . . (1759,1–2)

[Then he saw Volker standing next to Giselher.
He asked the master fiddler to accompany him . . . .]

Hagen and Volker stay together, *niwan si zwêne aleine* [nobody but the two alone] (1760,2), and later both of them are the only ones who do not congregate with Etzel's heroes. The special role both play from then on is shown by their closeness, which distances them from the others:

Swie iemen sich gesellete und ouch ze hove gie,
Volkêr unde Hagene di geschieden sich nie,
niwan in einme sturme an ir endes zît. (1805,1–3)

[However they joined and went to court together,
Volker and Hagen were never parted,
except in a fight at the end of their days.]

Other close relationships will be doomed by the closeness of Hagen and Volker.

A Threatening Remoteness / A Violent Closeness

Where family is expressed by closeness, being distant implies enmity, and being separated hints at discord. Things are not this clear-cut, however. Basically, the bond of the social group, the ruling structure, familial bonds, and *vriuntschaft* between individuals generally are expressed in closeness. In this respect, spatial proximity can reactivate the bond between *vriunden*. But it can be misunderstood as dependence and is a means to stir up and engage in conflict.

When closeness and *vriuntschaft* on the one hand, and remoteness and foreignness on the other are incongruent, conflicts threaten. This explains what an extraordinary threat Hagen must see to himself and his lords when Kriemhilt calls *vil unkunder recken* [many unknown warriors] (1127,2) into her land with Sivrit's gold. She brings warriors in *ir dienst* [her service] (1128,4), who are obligated to her alone and not to the kings. Foreigners who are close by are suspected of violent intentions before there is any sign of intrigue or action.

The foreign is potentially violent:

> *Nu nâhten vremdiu mære in Guntheres lant,*
> *von boten die in verre wurden dar gesant*
> *von unkunden recken die in truogen haz.*
> *dô si die rede vernâmen, leit was in wærlîche daz.* (139)
>
> [Strange reports came into Gunther's lands at that time,
> from messengers sent from far away,
> of unknown warriors who were their enemies.
> When they heard the reports, they were truly distressed.]

The foreign, hence bad, message, sent by strangers through strangers from far away (141,3), announcing *vil manegen hêrlîchen gast* (140,4)—a multitude of weapon-bearing enemies[52]—means *haz* and causes *leit*. Force rules in the foreign affairs of the Burgundian kingdom. If one were to accept their conditions, the Saxons and Danes announce:

> *sone rîtent iu sô nâhen niht die manegen scar.* (146,2)
>
> [then the great army will not come so near to you.]

Keeping one's distance means being secure. Peace with foreigners requires distance. The reverse means taking up the challenge, moving in on the opponent and crossing the border:

> *wir sulen in gerîten sô nâhen in ir lant,*
> *daz in ir übermüeten werde in sorgen erwant.* (175,3–4)
>
> [We should attack them closely in their own lands,
> so that their pride turns into regret.]

Distance provides safety, which is why Sigemunt and Sivrit's men return home so quickly after the murder:

> *bî ir starken vîenden was in ze wesen leit.* (1076,3)
>
> [It was painful to them to stay amid their powerful enemies.]

Breaking off friendly relations is expressed in staying away:

> *man sol uns nimmer mêre hie zen Burgonden sehen.* (1092,4)
>
> [We shall never again be seen here in Burgundy.]

Gunther supports the plan of a marriage for Kriemhilt with the dangerous, powerful Etzel with the argument:

> *ich behüete vil wol daz,*
> *daz ich im kome sô nâhen daz ich deheinen haz*
> *von im dulden müese* . . . . (1206,1–3)
>
> [I shall take care
> that I do not come so close to him that I
> fall victim to his enmity . . . .]

Etzel's might is not threatening as long as Gunther is not close to it. Later, with Etzel's invitation, he mistakenly relies on the reconciliation with Kriemhilt as a sufficient guarantee (1460), so that the distance can be closed without danger, because Kriemhilt has reestablished familiar bonds. Hagen, on the other hand, fears: *welt ir Kriemhilde sehen, / ir muget dâ wol verliesen die êre und ouch den lîp* [if you want to see Kriemhilt, / you may well lose your honor and your life] (1461,2–3).

How literally order depends on the fact that bodies are kept apart is shown by the word *scheiden*, which means not only the quitting of a comfortable closeness but also the establishment of distance that prevents aggression. In the latter sense, it can express the peaceful resolution of a conflict.

Separation is at first harmless. After Sivrit's marriage to Kriemhilt, there are two centers of gravity, Gunther and Sivrit, each with his own following. This corresponds to Sivrit's return to his role as ruler: *Sich teilte daz gesinde* [the households separated] (617,1). Similarly, later: *sich teilten dô die recken, der zweier künige man, / dô sach man vil der degene danne mit Sîfride gân* [the two warriors then parted, the two king's men, / many warriors were seen leaving with Sivrit] (627,3–4). But the confrontation is prepared with the separation. When after the wedding Kriemhilt's and Prünhilt's retinues meet each other in front of a narrow stairway, it must be expressly remarked that this still occurs "peacefully":

vor des sales stiegen gesamenten sich dô sît
Kriemhilt und Prünhilt; noch was iz ân' ir beider nît. (626,3–4)[53]

[at the foot of the stairs they met,
Kriemhilt and Prünhilt; there was as yet no sign of malice.]

The question of precedence has not come up yet. The spatial arrangement, however, foreshadows the later scene. The narrowing of the space in front of the steps points to the narrowing in front of the church, and the peaceful separation of the retinues, to the hostile separation later.

At issue in the queen's dispute is priority. Priority can be decided by precedence, that is, through the occupation of space. This leads to conflict when two characters want to occupy the same space. In the courtly festival, precedence is a distinction given peacefully to the other, and in this spirit also the conversation between Prünhilt and Kriemhilt begins. Kriemhilt points to Sivrit, who literally "precedes":

nu sihestu wie er stât,
wie rehte hêrliche er vor [!] *den recken gât.* (817,1–2)

[Look at how he stands there,
how lordly he goes before the warriors.]

Prünhilt distinguishes between precedence of prowess and precedence of rank, expressing this in a spatial metaphor: *sô muost du vor im lân / Gunther den recken* [you have to let the hero / Gunther go ahead of him], because he *muoz vor allen künegen . . . sîn* [has to be first among all kings] (818,2–4).[54] After the first exchange of words fails to bring about a solution, the *scheiden* of the retinue makes the conflict visible. Prünhilt demands: *sô muostu dich scheiden mit den vrouwen dîn / von mînem ingesinde* [you must depart with your ladies / from my household] (830,2–3). The spatial separation shows that the accustomed familiarity is destroyed:

Die liute nam daz wunder, wâ von daz geschach,
daz man die küneginne alsô gescheiden sach,
daz si bî ein ander niht giengen alsam ê. (834,1–3)

[The people were astonished why that happened,
that the two queens were seen apart,
and that they did not walk together as they used to.]

Later when the divided groups collide with each other again, this represents an outbreak of violence. The portal of the church gives the collision an effective backdrop. The house of God as a space of peace is contrasted with the conflict that is building. The collision is provoked: *Hie stuont vor dem münster daz Guntheres wîp* [Gunther's wife stood in front of the church] (835,1) and *Ze samne si dô kômen vor dem münster wît* [they came together in front of the large church] (838,1). The narrow doorway forces the two opponents into a dangerous proximity. The argument will be decided by the test of precedence, in that all are supposed to see, *ob ich vor küniges wîbe zem münster türre gegân* [whether I dare enter the church ahead of a king's wife] (827,4), or as Kriemhilt ironically objects to Prünhilt: *wie diu eigene diu dîn / Ze hove gê vor recken in Burgonden lant* [how your maiden will / go to court before warriors in the land of Burgundy] (828,4–5). For Prünhilt, too, rank is mirrored in space: *jâ sol vor küneges wîbe niht eigen diu gegân* [a bondswoman should never go before a king's wife] (838,4). Kriemhilt counters that the *kebse* [mistress] does not go before the legitimate wife. The question is, who will prevail. Kriemhilt is able to go first: *vor des küniges wîbe inz münster si dô gie* [she went into the church before the king's wife] (843,2). In the continuation of the scene, closeness remains the flash point for conflict. Prünhilt blocks Kriemhilt's path at the end of Mass. The dispute escalates once again, this time resulting in a permanent separation: *Mit rede was gescheiden manic schœne wîp* [many beautiful women were separated by the dispute] (863,1).

The confrontation increases in the second part. Once more the opponent must be brought close. At Etzel's court, Kriemhilt makes sure from the outset that her guests are denied space. First, the Burgundians are separated from their servants:

> *Gunthers ingesinde daz wart gesundert dan.*
> *daz riet diu küneginne, diu im vil hazzes truoc.* (1735,2–3)
>
> [Gunther's household was separated from them.
> This was done on the advice of the queen, who hated him sorely.]

At the first greeting by the queen, the space is still open. Kriemhilt has the disadvantage in her exchange with Hagen and must retreat: *dô gie si vom im balde, daz si niht ensprach* [then she left them quickly and said nothing else] (1749,3). The guests and Etzel's heroes remain behind in harmony. The room to maneuver is not yet restricted. Hagen and Volker are able to go *über den hof vil verre für einen palas wît* [across the courtyard to a distant and large palace] (1760,3). Singled out in this way, they become the targets of Kriemhilt's attacks for the first time. Her attempt to press Hagen into a corner and force a confession out of him is expressed very concretely in the use of space. Kriemhilt "crowds his personal space" so that he has nowhere to run: *des gie in an den fuoz / diu edele küneginne und bôt in vîentlîchen gruoz* [she walked right up to them, / the noble queen, and greeted them as enemies] (1786,3–4). It was clear to see how her attempt failed and how her retinue withdrew from the confrontation with Hagen: *Dâ mit was gescheiden, daz niemen dâne streit* [with this the quarrel was decided, so that no one fought there] (1799,1). But this is only temporary; the separation (this includes *scheiden*) only delays the dispute.

It is possible to still move about freely and to go to the reception with Etzel *in den palas* [in the palace] (1808,1). To sleep at night, the guests are brought *in einen wîten sal* [into a spacious hall] (1824,1). But the accommodations already seem like a fortress, where a watch must be placed outside. Hagen and Volker *giengen ûz dem hûse für die tür stân* [left the building and stood in the doorway] (1832,3). Volker sits down *under die tür des hûses* [in the doorway of the house] (1834,1) and sings his companions to sleep, then he takes his shield and goes *ûz dem gademe für die tür stân* [out of the room to stand in front of the door] (1836,3). The lager is to be, according to Kriemhilt's plan, a trap. The guests who are shut up inside are to be set upon by the Huns, but the closed space also offers security, and so the Hunnish attackers avoid coming too close, as Hagen would like them to do (*lât se uns her nâher baz* [let them come closer to us], 1839,1). The Huns go out *von dem hûse* [away from the house] (1842,3). It is dangerous to follow them (1843–44). The room to maneuver has already grown smaller.

At daybreak, the space seems to grow larger once more: churchgoing, *bûhurt,* and the feast with the king. The proximity of the Huns becomes increasingly threatening. But the Burgundians do not retreat an inch (1866,2–3).[55] Where violence tends to erupt from being close, one has to try to get possible adversaries apart (*scheiden* in its second meaning) or to remove them from the center of the action. Dietrich and Rüedeger order their followers to stay away from the tournament [*bûhurt*].[56] Those left behind clash. Volker, who has provoked the clash, concludes that any mediation is pointless (*ez kunde nimen gescheiden; ez gât im an den lîp* [no one could stop it; it cost him his life], 1886,3). Etzel can separate them a last time only with great difficulty (*scheiden*, 1894,4).

At the king's feast, Dietrich and Rüedeger are present again, but they will have to leave the stage a second time, when violence breaks out, this time irrevocably. The attempt of the kings to *scheiden* the masses fails (1967,2).

Vertical Organization

The constellation of characters shifts along with the symbolic occupation of space. Order and hierarchy are expressed in the vertical arrangement of the protagonists.[57] The world is organized vertically above all in the first part of the epic, apparent especially in the arrival scenes. This arrangement cannot be explained by the epic situation alone (someone arrives and is observed—from above!—from the castle).

The distribution of above and below is clear when Sivrit first arrives in Worms. The narrator follows Sivrit and his companions (71–72) and describes their reception by *die hôhgemuoten recken, riter unde kneht* [the warriors in high spirits, knights, and squires] (75,1), but then the perspective changes from the arrivals to the surroundings of the king, where one tries to assess them. Hagen goes *zeinem venster* [to a window] (84,1) and recognizes Sivrit. The asymmetry of power is reflected in the distribution of above and below. Hagen's view decides how the arrivals are to be treated. He agrees with Gunther's suggestion to go down to them (*wir sulen im engegene hin nider zuo dem recken gân* [we should go down to meet the warrior], 102,4):

> *"Daz mugt ir," sprach dô Hagene, "wol mit êren tuon.*
> *er ist von edelem künne, eines rîchen küneges sun. . . ."* (103,1–2)
>
> ["This you may do," spoke Hagen, "with full honor.
> He is from a noble clan, and the son of a powerful king. . . ."]

Once he knows whom he faces, Gunther puts himself on the same level as Sivrit. Sivrit's rank is recognized in the courtly *gruoz*, but then his demand for a contest of arms on equal terms is refused. Sivrit's "equality" with Gunther is established and limited by the invitation to stay peacefully at the court, but this equality remains precarious. In the exchange of words, the legitimate king wins out.

This distribution of positions is dominant in the continuation: *Sivrit ûf dem hove* [Sivrit in the courtyard] (133,1; 135,1), at games of chivalry, Kriemhilt looking *durch diu venster* [through the windows] (133,3), observing him from above, herself unseen. In the same way the Burgundian warriors, returning from the Saxon war, are exposed to the gazes of the women, again from the windows (243,2). Finally, at the courtly celebration with the other warriors, Sivrit gazes at the entrance of Kriemhilt and her ladies, who seem to be a heavenly procession (281–83). The hierarchy of the knight suitor and the *vrouwe* is thus manifest. It is evened out only at the highpoint of the celebration. Sivrit is allowed to approach Kriemhilt, appears *enhende* [hand in hand] with her (295,4), and is then at her side for the remainder of the feast (305).[58]

Gunther's quest for Prünhilt does not display the same kind of unambiguous arrangement of gazes from above. First the arrivals study the women *oben in den venstern* [up in the windows] from below (389,3). Prünhilt has to establish the normal direction of gazes from above. It is not the strangers who seek out the queen, it is she who goes to where they have already sat down (418,4). These seem to be meaningless details, but they reflect the fact that in Isenstein the normal courtly structures do not apply and that the strangers will in the end make this world their own. The normal relationships are established with Gunther's "victory," and suddenly everything is as it should be. He stands above—with the queen—*in den zinnen* [on the ramparts] (508,1). They look down on Sivrit, who comes back from his expedition to Nibelungenland bringing "Gunther's" military retinue. Following the king's advice, Prünhilt goes down *für den palas* [in front of the palace] (511,1) to honor Sivrit by receiving him. The vertical order seems to be intact, but it is based on falsehood.

Up until the dispute of the queens, things seem to stay the same. The ladies observe the chivalric sport at the wedding festival (647). When Margrave Gere appears at Sivrit's and Kriemhilt's court to invite them to Gunther's celebration, Kriemhilt recognizes him from above, looking out a window. The situation is similar just before the conflict breaks out: *In diu venster sâzen diu hêrlîchen wîp / und vil der schœnen mägede* [In the windows sat the fine women / and many beautiful maidens] (810,1–2).

> *Ze samene dô gesâzen die küneginne rîch.* (815,1)
>
> [The powerful queens sat there together.]

But the gaze of the ladies—according to ms. C even more explicitly from above[59]—ends up in conflict. After Kriemhilt defeats Prünhilt, Prünhilt is removed from her previous position. Now Kriemhilt alone looks at the games:

> *spiln man dô sach.*
> *hey waz man starker schefte vor dem münster brach*
> *vor Sîfrides wîbe al zuo dem sale dan!* (871,1–3)
>
> [People were watching the games.
> Wow, what strong shafts were broken in front of the church
> Before Sivrit's wife, right up to the hall!]

The order that was demonstrated by the tournament is deficient now, because it excludes Prünhilt.

In *Biterolf*, the peacefully ending response to the *Nibelungenlied*, the inverse process is told. There, the confrontation between the Rhine heroes and Etzel's heroes begins as a war. But the war already takes place in front of a female audience, who have virtual box seats on the walls of Worms.[60] In their panoramic view of the battle, what began as a bloody fight is soon transformed into a tourney. The conflict can be settled. The structure of above and below is maintained. With the failing settlement in the *Nibelungenlied*, the tournament, which started peacefully, is only seemingly continued and will lead to complete destruction.

There is no interest in vertical structure in the episodes between the two great conflicts—the first leading to Sivrit's death, and the second, to the downfall of the Burgundians. It even seems to be avoided, so that neither an intact hierarchy nor its disruption is suggested. When Rüedeger woos [for Kriemhilt] in Etzel's place in Worms, there is no raised point from which his arrival can be observed, even though what is seen or not seen is told in an exaggerated manner. Rüedeger interacts on the same level with the Burgundians.

Etzel and Kriemhilt are both on horseback when they meet for the first time. They dismount and greet each other on foot: equality is demonstrated instead of hierarchy. Previously, at Kriemhilt's reception in Bechelaren, this level of equality first had to be established. The windows of the castle are open (1318,1), but no one is looking out, because the inhabitants have run out to greet their new queen. The view from above would be inappropriate. Kriemhilt's higher rank is shown in that she is on a horse when Gotelint sees her. She stops the horse and asks to be lifted down quickly, before she approaches Gotelint and kisses her (1311). The sign of her superiority in rank is corrected by a courtly gesture. The balance between hierarchical structure and courtly equality, as shown first in the greeting of Sivrit, has been successfully established. This remains an intermezzo, however.

At Etzel's court, the reestablishment of the hierarchy of above and below is only a façade. The reception of the Burgundians still seems conventional:

> *Kriemhilt diu vrouwe in ein venster stuont:*
> *si warte nâch den mâgen, sô friunt nâch friunden tuont.*
> *von ir vater lande sach si manigen man.*
> *der künic vriesc ouch diu mære; vor liebe er lachen began.* (1716)
>
> [Lady Kriemhilt stood in a window:
> She was waiting for her relatives, as family will do for family.
> She saw many men from her father's land.
> The king heard that they had arrived; he laughed out of joy.]

This well-known scene—the queen looks out at the arrivals from a raised point—is cited to make clear that everything is wrong. Kriemhilt's threat (1717) gives her joy—normally appropriate for the occasion—a sinister meaning. Her gaze is at enemies, not relatives, and Etzel's laughter is therefore clueless.

Kriemhilt will not be able to maintain the raised position from which she views the arrivals. There is no vertical in the greeting of the Burgundians by the Amelungen; they are on the same footing. Dietrich rides out onto the field toward the kings (1719,3). When Hagen sees him from afar (1720,1), he advises his lord to dismount. Dietrich sees them after he has also dismounted, *gegen im komen* [coming towards him] (1723,1) and welcomes them. But the ceremony of courtly equality anticipates the future confrontation on "the same footing." Later at the court, the relationship to king and queen proves itself even more clearly to be disturbed: Kriemhilt and the Burgundians already clash at the greeting (1737).

The scenes of peaceful or hostile equality are followed in *Âventiure* 29 by Kriemhilt's descent from her raised position. In this already much-discussed episode, where she openly provokes Hagen's confession of guilt, the vertical structure is rescinded in a conspicuous way. Hagen and Volker sit "down" in the court:

> *vor dem hûse gegen einem sal,*
> *(der was Kriemhilde) ûf eine banc zetal.* (1761,1–2)
>
> [in front of the house opposite a hall,
> (it was Kriemhilt's), down on a bench.]

They are exposed to the usual gaze from above to below and are stared at like animals (1762,1).[61] This seems to clear up the relationship between the queen and the foreigners, but only seemingly, as will become apparent. Kriemhilt also sees them from above, but she cannot observe them coolly from a distance:

> *si ersah ouch durch ein venster daz Etzelen wîp.*
> *des wart aber betrüebet der schœnen Kriemhilden lîp.* (1762,3–4)
>
> [Through a window Etzel's wife saw them, too.
> This darkened the mind of the beautiful Kriemhilt.]

What was set before is reversed: up and down, the subject and object of seeing, the distant and curiously watching court, and the "animal" that is subjected to gazes. Kriemhilt must give up her position on high and come down the stairway to Hagen and Volker. This is told from a perspective of below to above, that is, from the perspective of those who are being stared at:

Dô sach der videlære . . .
die edel küneginne ab einer stiege gân
nider ab einem hûse . . . . (1772,1–3)

[Then the fiddler saw . . .
the noble queen going down a staircase,
down from the house . . . .]

"On the same footing" with Hagen, Kriemhilt suffers a defeat despite the insignia of her royal power. There is no question of her return to "above."

The hierarchic order only seems to be reestablished when Etzel and Kriemhilt *mit ir vrouwen* [with her ladies] look out the window and observe the tumult of locals and guests in front of the church (1869,1–2). What is called *riterschaft* [tournament] (1879,3) and *kurzwîle* [entertainment] (1882,1) takes place in front of their eyes but becomes deadly serious, while the stage suggests a courtly and well-regulated game.[62] When violence breaks out a first time, it is Etzel who is forced to give up his observation post from above and step down in order to mediate:

der wirt ûz einem venster vil hart gâhen began. (1893,4)

[The host rushed out from where he was in the window.]

Neither he nor Kriemhilt will ever return to their distant place above.

The solemn meal is the last joint appearance of the opponents "above" in the hall. Dancwart, the only survivor of the attack on the servants, must fight his way through to reach this height. Each one who opposes him at the stairs (*im für die stiege spranc* 1950,1) is pushed back.[63] The hall becomes a graveyard for the Huns. Luckily, Etzel and Kriemhilt are able to leave the hall under Dietrich's protection, which means stepping down. From now on, the boundaries are clearly marked. The Burgundians are "above" in the hall, Etzel and his men run at them from "below," until almost no one is left. Above and below have been reversed with the melee at the feast.

A Shrinkage of Space

Order is narrated by the *Nibelungenlied* paradoxically as the order of destruction, and this order becomes more and more obvious up to the battles at the end. The hall is unassailable. Since the hall of the Hun king has been left to them, the Burgundians move into the center of the action and marginalize others. These must first find their way back to the center in order to accomplish something worth telling. Only a few succeed, and all of them lose their lives in the attempt.

The vertical gains another meaning. It no longer represents order but its destruction. The dead and wounded Huns are thrown down the stairs in order to gain space for maneuver in the hall (2011,1):

> *vor des sales stiegen vielen si zetal.* (2013,3)
>
> [They fell down in front of the hall stairs.]

Even the lightly wounded are killed *von dem hôhen valle* [by the high fall] (2014,3).

Etzel has been displaced from the center of his power. He must negotiate from outside with those who have occupied the *palas*:

> *Dô stuonden vor dem hûse vil manec tûsent man.* (2019,1)
>
> [Some thousand men were standing in front of the building then.]

A margrave who wants to cross the boundary in order to save his wounded relatives, who have been thrown onto a heap of corpses, is immediately killed (2016). With his spear, which he throws *über daz volc vil verre* [a great distance beyond the troops] (2018,2), Volker marks out the Burgundians' [defensive] perimeter, *hôher von dem sal* [further from the hall] (2018,3). Etzel is also prevented from surmounting this (*man muose in bî dem vezzel ziehen wider dan* [they had to pull him back by the straps], 2022,3).

A space is thus designated in which the slaughter will play out to the last man. Those from Düringen and Tenemarke have not been mentioned at Etzel's feast. They are neither "present" nor "uninvolved." But now they are the first of the foreign *recken* whom Kriemhilt throws into the battle and who cross the boundary. First, they rush all at once, *eine vol grôz[iu] schar* [a great army] (2032,1). The downfall takes place in its own good order, however. Irinc must push his people back behind the boundary in order to fight alone. He succeeds in making it up to the hall. His battle distinguishes itself from the well-ordered combats of the final scenes. It continues the chaotic violence of the fight of the servants and then at the feast. Irinc jumps up to Hagen, then to Volker, then to Gunther, and then further. He is attacked by Giselher, but still nobody is wounded, neither Hagen (cf. 2040,1), nor Volker, and even the fierce fight with Gunther *brâhte niht von wunden daz vliezende bluot* [does not cause any bleeding wounds] (2042,3). Irinc kills four men from the *edeln ingesinde* [noble household] (2044,3), Giselher's blow leaves him *âne wun-*

den [without wounds] (2046,4), too. Finally, in retreating, Irinc succeeds in wounding Hagen. After a hard fight he manages to reach the stairs:

> *hin nider von der stiegen Hagene im volgen began.* (2052,4)
>
> [Hagen began to follow him down the stairs.]

He is able to cross the demarcation line between the hostile forces in the opposite direction. But this unresolved fight is only a prelude to the coming battles. In his second attempt, Irinc fails even to get back up.[64] Hagen comes at him *die stiegen ûz an ein ende* [at the bottom of the stairs] *(*2061,3) and kills him. His death brings into the fight those from Düringen and Tenemark, who rush in [*sprungen für daz gadem (*2070,1)] to avenge him. They, too, fall, and a terrible battle begins *vor dem hûse* [in front of the building] (2074,2), until Volker suggests that they feign a withdrawal, that is, take up the superior position in the hall again: *lât si her in gân* [let them enter the hall] (2075,1); *si müezen drinne ersterben* [they will have to die inside] (2075,3), and so it happens. All those who flock back to the hall are killed (2076,1; 2077,1).

More and more, the place on high becomes a prison that the Burgundians can only leave during short pauses in the battle. This becomes especially clear after another terrible fight (2083–85), when the Burgundian kings ask for a decision in open combat to make a quick end of it (*daz lât kurz ergân* [let it happen quickly], 2097,1) and to all be allowed to go *hin nider an die wîte* [down to the open space] (2096,4):

> *die bluotvarwen helde und ouch harnaschvar*
> *trâten ûz dem hûse, die drîe künege hêr.* (2088,2–3)
>
> [The bloodstained heroes, their chainmail blackened,
> came out of the building, the three splendid kings.]

Kriemhilt makes sure that this does not happen:

> *Lât einen ûz dem hûse niht komen über al,*
> *sô heiz' ich viern enden zünden an den sal.* (2109,1f.)
>
> [Let no one come out of the building,
> I'll have the hall set on fire at all four corners.]

Those who are still standing outside are driven inside (2110,1–2). The *sal* is put to the torch. Yet even this devious attack fails. In any case, 600 Burgundians survive, but there is no longer any way out of the ruins of the *palas*.

"To be pulled into battle" is to be understood quite literally in spatial terms as an "arrival" at the epicenter of destruction: *Dô riefen ir genuoge: "nâher, helde, baz/. . . hie belîbet niemen wan der doh sterben sol*" [Many of them called: "come closer, you heroes/. . . only those fated to die will stay here!"] (2132,1; 2132,3).[65] Like a black hole, the hall devours one Hunnish contingent after another (2134,3). Even those who want to stay out are sucked into the vortex: *wine der Gotelinde kom ze hove gegân* [Gotelind's beloved came to the courtyard] (2135,2). Rüedeger had been able to get out of the melee in the hall along with Dietrich. His distance is expressed when he reappears on the stage, for then he simultaneously sends a message "somewhere else," namely, to Dietrich, who is still at bay:

> *Dô sande an Dietrîchen der guote Rüedegêr,*
> *ob siz noch kunden wenden an den küenegen hêr.* (2137,1–2)
>
> [The excellent Rüedeger sent for Dietrich then,
> to see if they could turn things in favor of the splendid kings.]

Rüedeger's position is between two places. He has already left Dietrich by "joining" the others. The attempt to *wenden* [turn, avert] the fight is likewise in vain.

Still he "stands" at the edge, undecided and "outside" *mit weinenden ougen* [with tearful eyes] (2138,2), but he is already with Etzel's party. Later, when he has made his decision, it is also expressed as a movement in space:

> *Man sah in von dem künege vil trûreclîchen gên.*
> *dô vant er sîne recken vil nâhen bî im stên.* (2167,1–2)
>
> [He was seen leaving the king with great distress,
> then he found his warriors standing close by his side.]

Rüedeger withdraws *von dem künege*, but not by much (*vil nâhen*) and only to arm himself.[66] He approaches the Burgundians *under helme* [in full armor] (2170,1; 2171,1–2), that is, with hostile intent. He is still on his side of the demarcation line, *vor dem hûse* [in front of the building] (2174,2), calling *in den sal* [into the hall] (2175,1). On the other side, Hagen answers *von der stiegen hin zetal* [from the stairs down below] (2192,4). Volker goes on speaking *von dem hûse*—that is, from above (2203,1). The Burgundians do not come out, and Rüedeger must fight them in the hall. He is let in *durch mortræchen willen* [with intent to kill] (2208,1) and is killed with his men, like all those before him: *die dô dar inne wâren, die muosen lîden nôt* [those who were inside had to suffer much] (2224,2).

In the final two battles, the Burgundians have to fight in a closed space against Rüedeger and the Amelungen. Even Dietrich can no longer stay away.

His reluctance to fight is narrated with even more detail than Rüedeger's. He is not allowed to see Rüedeger killed, because up till then he has to be "absent." Someone else hears the lament over Rüedeger's death without knowing the reason. Dietrich's distance from the focal point of the battle is doubled, but this is of no use. A scout is sent out, and Dietrich is informed and asks for more exact news. He tries to avoid anything that might anger the Burgundians. Dietrich turns down the first volunteer messenger, because he is afraid of becoming committed. The second volunteer, Helpfrich, is allowed *dar gân* [to go there] (2241,1) *und hiez in daz ervinden an Etzelen man / oder an den gesten selben* [and ordered to find out what he could from Etzel's men / or the guests themselves] (2241,2–3). Helpfrich remains on his side when he asks the Huns for information.[67] On hearing of Rüedeger's death, Dietrich still does not go himself:

> *Der vogt der Amelunge hiez ez ervinden baz.*
> *vil harte senecliche er in ein venster saz.* (2247,1–2)
>
> [The prince of the Amelungen asked for more information.
> He sat at a window in great distress.]

There are only a few spaces that grant a separation from the stage of heroic action. Sitting in the window seat, Dietrich expresses this distance. He sends others who are only allowed to go up to the boundary between the parties to find out more (2254,1–2). At first, it looks as if there might be a settlement, but no one is permitted to return *ûz dem sal*, with Rüedeger's corpse, which the Amelungen demand (2262,1). Consequently, Dietrich's men are lured inside: *nemt in in dem hûse dâ der degen lît* [come get the hero in the house where he lies] (2266,2). Only in the beginning is Hildebrant able to keep Wolfhart out of the vortex of the deadly hall for a moment, but then Wolfhart charges ahead *für des sales want* [up to the wall of the hall] (2274,1), but Hildebrant is even faster, reaching the steps and forcing his way into the hall. There the fight goes on;[68] *scheiden* now just means momentarily separating the fighters who are jammed together,[69] in order to recombine them anew in the slaughter. Only one man comes out alive—Hildebrant. He even fails to carry the dead Wolfhart out of the hall (*ûzem hûse mit im tragen dan*, (2300,1). Inside only two are left—Gunther and Hagen.

Each time the room to maneuver becomes smaller, and each time it includes fewer people. The wide-ranging Nibelungian world has shrunk to a battle in a hall, to the dimension of archaic heroic lays. For the final battle of the survivors, there is no longer any need to demarcate power blocs. There no longer seems to be any Hunnish contingent. Dietrich seems to be left alone with Hildebrant, and in the background are Etzel and Kriemhilt. Now the surviving Burgundians can leave their superior position in the hall a final time. Dietrich meets Hagen and Gunther *stênde . . . ûzen vor dem hûse, geleinet an den sal* [standing . . . outside the building, leaning against the hall] (2328,3). Later Hagen lurches into battle *von der stiege* [down from the stairs] (2348,3), and Gunther runs *für den sal* [in front of the hall] (2357,3). There is no longer any kind of hierarchically organized space in the two last fights.

The defeated are taken prisoner; they can no longer move. They lie *sunder durch ir ungemach* [separated to their own discomfort] (2366). In the final tableau, the stage is open again— it is not so clear to where it is opened and who is present on it—but there are hardly any survivors left.

Paths

The dissolution of organized space is prepared by the confusion of paths. The paths that lead through the known world are barely conspicuous. The route from Xanten to Worms, from Worms to Isenstein and back is a distance that can be measured in time. It takes seven days from Xanten to Worms, from the Rhine to Isenstein, twelve days. To overcome distance almost without effort is one of the stereotypes of a successful bridal quest. It is different with the path to Nibelungenland.

How one gets there is shrouded in mystery, and it is difficult to localize in relation to the courtly centers of Worms and Xanten. The path leads through a nowhere land that cannot be measured. In *Âventiure* 8, the remoteness is symbolized by the sea. Sivrit moves easily between the known and the foreign world, and he can lead others from the one to the other. He disposes over the empty space (the sea), and so he leads Gunther, Hagen, and Dancwart *ûf der fluot* [over the sea] and knows *die rehten wazzerstrâzen* [the right waterways] (378,1–3) where no paths seem to exist. This is shown again when he guides the ship quickly from Isenstein to *Nibelunge lant* as if *ein sunderstarker wint* [an especially strong wind] (483,1–3) were blowing.[70] Sivrit (and with his help Gunther) masters the space *in recken wîse* [in the manner of heroes], as the adventures there are also to be mastered.

The conception of space shifts when the Nibelungen hoard and Prünhilt are won and their areas of dominion have been taken over by the courtly centers. The distance between Gunther's and Sivrit's seat seems to have changed for the first time when Gunther invites his relatives to Worms (727,3; 758,4).

Now the narrator does not distinguish between the Netherlands, which can be reached in a few days, and the mythical *Nibelunge lant.* It is no longer accessible just to the hero, and it no longer lies in a distant nowhere, but seems to belong to the Netherlandish kingdom where Sivrit and Kriemhilt are supposed to be staying. It can be localized geographically (*ze Nibelunges bürge . . . ze Norwæge in der marke* [to Nibelungen Castle . . . to the march of Norway], 739,2). Mythical inaccessibility is turned into a difficult but finally surmountable distance. The space between the two courts of Burgundy and *Nibelunge lant* is measurable (*in drîn wochen* [in three weeks], 739,1). This *Norwæge* is certainly, unlike the place-names from the Danube region, something very far away, but it is reachable. It is such a natural part of Sivrit's royal lands that there is no need to explain why the messengers do not meet Sivrit in Xanten.

On Sivrit's and Kriemhilt's journey from Worms to Xanten, where they will be crowned, nothing worthy of epic happens, because the world in between belongs to Gunther's dominion:

> *man hiez in allenthalben ir nahtselde legen*
> *swâ sis gerne nâmen, al durch der künige lant.* (702,2–3)
>
> [They were told to get their accommodation for the night
> wherever they wanted to stay, anywhere in the king's land.]

But the journey in the other direction, from Nibelungenland to Worms, now on horseback and not with a ship (779–81), is even less worthy of note. It is an empty time. The narrator immediately goes over to the preparations for the reception in Worms. The boundary of the world of legend to the normal world is permeable. It is easily possible to travel *von Nibelunge lant* (778,3) to Worms. And later, when Sivrit is dead, even Gernot and Giselher can travel there and collect the treasure.

Just as the inaccessible becomes accessible, the paths through the known world start to change. This becomes clear with the Burgundian expedition to Etzel. During Kriemhilt's journey to the land of the Huns, there is nothing of note in this regard, even given the long way. The geographic space is again organized into seats of rule. Kriemhilt touches on a series of marked points: up to *Verge* (Pföring) in the company of her brothers; a stop in Passau at her uncle's; then in his company to Everding and *Ense* at the crossing of the Traun, where she meets Gotelint; then with her to Bechelaren, to Herzog Astolt in *Medelicke*, who shows her the way to *Mûtaren*, where the bishop leaves her, then to *Zeizenmûre* on the Treisen, where Etzel owns a castle, to the town of *Tuln*, where she meets Etzel, to Vienna, where she is married, and then via *Heimburc*, *Misenburc*, finally to *Etzelnburc*. Kriemhilt's journey leads through an ordered political world.[71] Her path passes a series of fixed points. She is taken in everywhere, first in the Burgundian sphere of influence, then in Passau and in the different stays in Rüedeger's and Etzel's realms. The night accommodation (*nahtselde*) is always secure, sometimes in *hütten und gezelt* (e.g., 1304,2) or at some noble seat.[72] Everywhere the topic is *gemach* [comfort], eating and drinking, and the regulated balance between journeying by day and sleeping at night: *die naht si heten ruowe bis an den morgen vruo* [they rested well during the night until the next morning] (1317,4). This makes the hardships bearable: *die wegemüeden vrouwen die heten senfte und ouch gemach* [the road-weary women had luxuries and comforts] (1377,4). At each station, the foreign space is converted into a familiar one. Kriemhilt, the foreigner,[73] is able to replace the deceased queen from the start.

Twelve days—apparently the normal time for a "long" journey—is what it takes for Rüedeger's ride to the Rhine when he asks for Kriemhilt's hand. Twelve days is what it takes the messengers when they go to invite the Burgundians. Time plays no part in Kriemhilt's journey; everything goes according to plan, and there is no danger. When the Burgundians travel to Etzel, everything is different. The same route is long and difficult. After twelve days, they just reach the Danube. Of course, one might say, it takes longer to travel with a large army than with a small group. Nevertheless, the journey to their doom seems endless. It is arduous. When Kriemhilt first reaches the Danube at *Verge*, *Verge* is just a place-name (Pföring). When the Burgundians reach the same Danube, they encounter a violent *verge* [ferryman] who blocks their progress. The homonymy, whether intentional or not, sharpens the impression of contrast.

The space between Worms and Passau stretches out, but after Passau (1630) it is empty, except for the *marke* at Bechelaren, a military post that Eckewart has occupied. After the enclave of Bechelaren, the route runs *nider über sant / zetal bî Tuonouwe ûz in daz hiunische lant* [down over the riverside, / down by the Danube, toward the land of the Huns] (1712,3–4). Although it is slower, this journey offers local historians far fewer references than Kriemhilt's preceding trip.

The space is suddenly dangerous. Etzel's repute protects Rüedeger's company (1174,4) just as it did the messengers Werbel and Swemmel (1429,3). Rüedeger himself protects Kriemhilt. It is different with the Burgundian expedition. Etzel's protection is apparently no longer sufficient for his guests, because they have to fight their way through. Three times, once with difficulty, they have to cross a river. The Burgundians begin their journey aboard ships (1514,4),[74] and it will be necessary to cross a river twice more, the rushing Danube at Möringen with a struggle, then the Inn (?) at Passau (1629,3). Does the crossing of the river have symbolic character? In the murder of Sivrit in the Wasken forest, one has to (incorrectly) cross the Rhine, whereas in the Saxon war, one does not.[75] There are two additional border crossings: to the duchy of Bavaria and the march that protects Rüedeger's land. Between the Danube and Etzel's castle, there are only two rest stops, in Passau and Bechelaren, which both contrast sharply with their surroundings.

Up to the Danube (*ze Mœringen*, 1591,1) the Burgundians pass geographically fixed spaces (even though these are no longer a dense series of ruling centers), the region of the Main River or East Franconia. Then a dangerous space opens up, through which the expedition travels without any precise direction. The dangers start at the rapids of the Danube. To cross them is laborious and leads to the first martial confrontation. After this, the space becomes diffuse and there are no stops; the Burgundians have to defend themselves *ûf der strâze* [on the road] against the attacks of the Bavarians (1602,4). They must then quickly ride on *ûf disen wegen* [on these paths] (1617,2). For three stanzas, it is told how there is no night camp for them, despite their exhaustion after the attack. At first, *manic man* is asking for accommodations, but Dancwart decides: *wir mugen niht herberge hân* [we can't make camp] (1621,3–4). Then Volker begs for a rest (1622,2–4), but again Dancwart's answer is:

> *"wir enmugen niht geruowen ê iz beginne tagen.*
> *swâ wirz danne vinden, dâ legen uns an ein gras."*
> *dô si diu mære hôrten, wie leit in sümelîchen was!* (1623,2–4)
>
> ["We can't rest until the beginning of day.
> Wherever we find ourselves then, let us lie down there in the grass."
> When they heard this, how depressed they all were!]

To be sure, this concerns the rear guard, Hagen, Dancwart, Volker, and their men. A little later, however, we see that the kings, along with all of the Burgundians, also have no place to rest in this hostile environment. They have fallen out of the known world: *Wir kunnen niht bescheiden wâ si sich leiten nider* [We don't know where they rested] (1627,1). On the way to Etzel, the Burgundian elite seem to become a band of nomads who must rest somewhere "in the grass," wherever they may find themselves.[76]

This is expressly contrasted with what would be "in order" and immediately occurs again when they approach a well-known seat of power like Passau: *si wurden wol enpfangen dâ ze Pazzouwe sint* [later they were well-received in Passau] (1627,4). Passau, however, is an exception. It is repeated when the Burgundians reach Rüedeger's march. The perfect hospitality shown by the margrave brings an end to a desolate situation in which Etzel's guests don't know where they will end up. Given their number, the Burgundian contingent should by no means be too weak to find their own accommodations and provisions, as was common in the Middle Ages. Nevertheless, the Burgundians are driven by the concerns of those who have no home at all.

If one listens to Hagen, they seem to be lacking everything in the meantime. Hagen complains to Eckewart about the *sorge* of his people *umb die herberge* [worry about their accommodation]. No one knows where to stay: *wâ wir in disem lande noch hînte nahtselde hân* [where we can still find a place for the night in this land]. He asks about a place "this evening," so that *die künige und ouch ir man* [the kings and their men] (1636,2–4) can rest. The resources of the army seem to be exhausted:

> *"Diu ross sint uns verdorben ûf den verren wegen,*
> *unt der spîse zerunnen," sprach Hagene der degen.*
> *"wir vinden'z ninder veile. uns wære wirtes nôt,*
> *der uns noch hînte gæbe durch sîne tugende sîn brôt."* (1637)
>
> ["Our horses have perished on this long journey,
> and our food has run out," said Hagen the warrior.
> "We can't find anything to buy. We need a host
> who will give us, out of generosity, his bread tonight.]

The contingent seems to have gone from a festive expedition to a downtrodden, half-starved band of mercenaries. Instead of impressing others with generous gifts, they are beholden to Rüedeger's *milte*.

This certainly has rhetorical functions as well. Their need provides the dark background for the perfect *wirt* Rüedeger, who takes in the guests, *daz ir ze hûse selten sô wol bekomen birt / in deheinem lande* [so that you will never be so well supplied in a house / in any land] (1638,2–3). Yet the delay and the retarding character of the stay in Bechelaren are recognizable in even sharper focus. The ruin has already begun with the leave-taking in Worms, and it continues unabated, interrupted only in Passau and Bechelaren. These seem to lie close to one another, given the short narrative time between the two locations.

The stay in Bechelaren is preceded by another obstacle. The border to Etzel's kingdom is guarded, even though it can apparently be crossed with ease.[77] When Kriemhilt passed this way before, there was no mention of this.

The border is characterized by contradictory signs. There is the guard Eckewart, but he is asleep. Eckewart is foreign, yet known at the same time. He is Kriemhilt's vassal, but also concerned about her potential enemies. He does not defend the frontier, instead, he warns the intruders. The crossing is peaceful, but Hagen takes the guard's weapons away. The Burgundians are received as guests, but they find out that *man ist iu hie gehaz* [you are considered enemies here] (1635,3).

They have entered an ambiguous space whose danger only gradually becomes apparent. With Rüedeger everything will change; he will bring them to Etzel safe and sound. As at the beginning of the journey, at the end, everything seems to be in order. The way to Etzel, however, is no longer either a space easily overcome by heroes or a string of princely courts. The journey isolates the Burgundians completely from their surroundings and puts them totally at risk.

The expedition is characterized by a strange sort of restlessness, and this unease continues at Etzel's court. Despite Etzel's friendly *gruoz* and in spite of his hospitality, *volleclîchen* and according to everyone's desires, the *sorge* [worry] about a place to rest returns:

> *die wegemueden recken, ir sorge si an vaht,*
> *wanne si solden ruowen und an ir bette gân.* (1818,2–3)
>
> [The weary warriors began to worry
> when they might rest and go to bed.]

Unlike on Kriemhilt's journey, the hardships are not compensated for by comfort. Even though everything seems to be going smoothly, and the camp is extensively described in its splendor and comfort (1824–26), Hagen's hope *lât uns ellenden hînt haben gemach* [let us foreigners have some comfort this night] (1823,3)[78] must be defended against the pushy Huns. Giselher complains *Owê der nahtselde* [beware of these accommodations] (1827,1) because he fears an attack by Kriemhilt. The Burgundians have been accompanied by tiredness since the beginning of their journey, from crossing the Danube (1571,4) to reaching the Hunnish border *Dô die wegemüeden ruowe genâmen* [when exhausted from the journey they took some rest] (1631,1).

It's hard to get a good night's sleep. During the first night at Etzel's court, only Volker and Hagen have to stay awake. Volker's music puts to sleep *vil manegen sorgenden man* [many worrying men] (1835,4). Thus the *sorgen* [cares] (1828,1) of the *stolzen ellenden* [proud foreigners] (1834,4) are once again assuaged. Afterwards, there is an end to *nahtsælde*. The next night, things change: *In was des tages zerunnen: dô gie in sorge nôt* [The day had passed for them: now they had to feel anxious] (2087,1). Not only are they no longer able to rest, but Kriemhilt attempts to burn the house down, and them along with it: *In sus getânen leiden in doch der naht zeran* [The night passed in such difficulties at last] (2120,1). At daybreak, the battle resumes: *Des tages wider morgen grüezen man in bôt / mit hertem urliuge* [People came to greet them in the morning / with tough battles all over again] (2128,1–2). Instead of rest, there is only exhaustion: *Den sitzen, disen leinen sah man manegen degen* [the one was seen to be sitting, the other leaning up] (2227,1). The way back *heim in iuwer lant* [home to your land] (2340,2) promised by Dietrich remains an empty illusion.

It is the *Klage* that will reverse the tendency to block paths and dispute space, when Swemmel spreads Etzel's message throughout the land. He moves unharmed, apparently under protection of Etzel's power (which is actually destroyed) from one ruling house to another: Vienna-Bechelaren-Passau-Worms. No one, not even the Bavarians, makes trouble, and so he is able to spread his message everywhere. The paths are open once again.

Proliferation of the Nibelungian World

On the way to their ruin, the Burgundians mutate into Nibelungen. The Nibelungen celebrate their resurrection in the company of warriors whose place in the world is more and more contested. In the beginning, Sivrit represents the force of the Nibelungen. Unlike other versions of the legend, the *Nibelungenlied* does not tell about a vagabond who comes from "outside." Instead, Sivrit is bound to a court. There are stories about him, however, according to which he is a hero who moves around: *durch sînes lîbes sterke er reit in menegiu lant* [with his strong body he rode to many lands] (21,3). He proves himself when he comes upon the Nibelungen and their legendary treasure, or later in Isenstein, thanks to his superiority. His story is partially rooted in the foreign world "out there." He alone can find the way there; he has an affinity to this world, but that is about it.

Only someone who reads carefully will notice that this affinity is shown in his stature. Sivrit is characterized as being very large, based on the size of his *gêr*: *Sîvrit der fuort' ir einen wol zweier spannen breit* [Sivrit carried a spear whose tip was two handspans wide] (73,3).[79] It is notable that this is not stated explicitly but only through an epic hyperbole. Prünhilt is also characterized as very tall based on the size of her weapons.[80] Yet, no conclusions are drawn from this in either case. External, physical clues that Sivrit and Prünhilt belong to a exorbitant heroic world are downplayed.

Once Sivrit is king, Nibelungenland shifts into reach of the court at Worms. After Sivrit's death, it comes even closer. Hagen's treason apparently destroys Sivrit's supposedly invincible armor and with it his strength, magnified by the magic *tarnhût*. Sivrit's weakening is also the weakening of his realm. When Gernot and Giselher pick up the *hort*, the symbol of Nibelungen might, Alberich complains about the loss of the *guoten tarnhût*, which leaves him and the *Nibelunge land* defenseless against the Burgundian kings:

> *"Doch wurdez nimmer" sprach Albrîch, "getân,*
> *niwan daz wir übele dâ verlorn hân*
> *mit samt Sîfrîde die guoten tarnhût,*
> *want die truoc alle zîte*[81] *der schœnen Kriemhilde trût.*
>
> ["This would never have happened," spoke Alberich,
> "if we had not wickedly lost
> along with Sivrit the good cloak of invisibility,
> because Kriemhilt's lover wore it all the time."]
>
> *Nu ist ez Sîfrîde leider übel komen,*
> *daz uns die tarnkappen het der helt benomen*
> *unt daz im muose dienen allez ditze lant."* (1119,1–1120,3)
>
> ["Now unfortunately it ended badly for Sivrit,
> that the hero took from us the cloak of invisibility
> and made the entire country serve him."]

Sivrit, the new owner of the *tarnhût*, guarantees the protection and secrecy of Nibelungenland. Just as the cloak is able to hide him, so the treasure and its guards remain out of reach of those from Worms. After the *tarnhût* is gone *mit samt Sîfrîde*, Gernot and Giselher are able to come to Nibelungenland with their eight thousand warriors, make good on their legal claims (*ze morgengâbe* [as a dowry], 1118,4), and then load and carry off the treasure. Although it is supposedly inexhaustible, it is transported in a finite number of wagons, if many.[82] Its mythical potency, materialized in a magic wand (*von golde ein rüetelîn* [a wand made of gold], 1124,1), by which the world can be dominated, remains unrecognized and unused. *C emphasizes this reduction of Nibelungenland to a normal scale by a supplementary stanza that tells of Gernot and Giselher:

> *do vnderwnden si sich sint*
> *des landes vnd der burge vnd maniges rechen balt.*
> *das mvos in sider dienen bediv durch vorht vnd gewalt.* (C 1138,2–4)

> [then they overcame
> the land and its castles and many a warrior.
> They had to serve them since then because of fear and their power.]

Nibelungenland has been incorporated.

The disempowerment of the hoard, and with it the Nibelungian world, continues. Hagen sinks the treasure in the Rhine because he fears its resources. Its once mythical dimensions must have become more manageable in the meantime. Only a portion remains, but it is still big enough so that even a hundred horses cannot carry it all (1271,3). It becomes comparable to Etzel's treasure, and lo and behold, the newly accumulated treasure of the Hunnish kingdom, a world fixed in time and space, is larger than the mythical hoard. The hoard—or at least what is left of it—can be quantified. The talk is of 30,000 marks, which Kriemhilt wants to distribute among the Hunnish guests (1277,3), and of *zwelf schrîn* [twelve cases] full of gold, which she takes with her (1280,1). Nibelungenland and its hoard are subject to the same fate as their lord. In this sense, they are indistinguishable, and not only for Kriemhilt.

Then something amazing happens. Nibelungenland begins to grow at precisely the same moment that it disappears from the story's horizon.[83] After the world beyond is incorporated, it begins to change the known world. It swallows the courtly world that was at first its opposite. *Nibelunge* is no longer connected to a specific place, but now stands for a group of people and their way of life. Ensconced in Etzel's *sal,* the *Nibelunge* will be destroyed.

First, the kings of a distant world were called *Nibelunge* (*Nibelunge lant,* 92,3; 94,4), and so, too, perhaps even their retinue (87,2; 90,4), who are otherwise known as *der Nibelunge man* (89,3) or *di Nibelunges man* (98,3). *Nibelunc* is also the name of one of their young princes (87,3; 91,1). The use of the word shifts from personal to family name. Sometimes in the singular, sometimes in the plural: *Nibelunges hor[t]* (88,3), *Nibelunges swert* (93,1), or *Nibelunges man* (98,3) as opposed to *Nibelunge lant* (92,3; 94,4) or *Nibelunge man* (89,3). Apparently, the distinction is not very important. The carrier of the name does so because he belongs to the *gens,* and the *gens* determines its identity through the personal name.[84] This corresponds to early medieval practice.

It is soon shown that the name does not only apply to an individual or to a dynasty or its vassals. It can be transferred first to Sivrit and his men, then eventually to the Burgundians. So named are not just groups of people, but a complex of people, their legal relationship, and their sources of power.

In *Âventiure* 8, things have not yet changed. The land is called *Nibelunge* (484,4);[85] in the *burc*, there is a *Nibelunges sal* (492,2); the occupants are the *Nibelunge* (501,3) or *Nibelunge man* (502,3)—the singular already would be inappropriate for them, because there is no longer a *Nibelunc*. Sivrit is served by *daz lant zen Nibelungen* (721,1);[86] the retinue is also called *Schilbunges recken* (721,3); Sivrit lives in *Nibelunges bürge* (739,2), and comes *von Nibelunge lant* to the festival at Worms (778,3). He and his retinue are only seldom called those *von Niderlant*,[87] for they take their name from the *Niblunge lant* even after the murder of Sivrit.[88] This, too, still corresponds to the usual name-giving based on titles or houses.

The name does not stick with Sivrit and those from Xanten, however, and this is why it does not disappear with Sigemunt, who leads Sivrit's men home. It does not even stick to the paternal dynasty. When Sigemunt replaces Sivrit, the use of names begins to vacillate again. First, his realm is still called *Nibelunge lant*; *zer Nibelunge lant* is where Sigemunt returns with Sivrit's retinue (1083,3).[89] Kriemhilt also declares, oddly enough, that she has no relatives *in Nibelunge lant* (1085,3)—and not in *Niderlant*.[90] Once the separation is completed, however, and Kriemhilt remains in Worms, *Sigemundes man* (1091,2)[91] journey *zuo Sigemundes lande* (1090,3). Once more, we find the term *Nibelunge* when the subject turns to defense against possible enemies with *der küenen Nibelunge hant* [the brave hands of the Nibelungen] (1095,4), but then they arrive unscathed *heim ze Niderlant* (1098,3).[92] They return to the normal world and are forgotten.

The name, however, remains latent and crops up when the Burgundians' attention is directed at *daz Nibelunges golt* (1107,3), when the hoard *von Nibelunges lande* (1116,3: now again in the singular!)[93] comes to Worms, and again later when Kriemhilt wants to take her property along to Etzel. Now the treasure is called *gol[t] von Nibelunge lant* (1271,1), and then *Sîfrides golt* (1272,2).

The name lives on in the remembrance of Sivrit, *den helt von Nibelunge lant*, as he is later referred to by Dietrich of Bern (1724,4).[94] The Huns, on the other hand, know him as *von Niderlande Sîfri[t]* (1733,2), and he is not the hero from the world of legend but the ruler of a well-known kingdom. Both aspects are distinct for Kriemhilt. At the wedding celebration with Etzel, her current wealth is compared to that *in Niderlande* (1368,1), and she thinks about *wie si ze Rîne sæze . . . bî ir edelen manne* [how she ruled on the Rhine . . . with her noble husband] (1371,1–2). Later, when planning her revenge, she remembers the *êren von Nibelunge lant* [honors of Nibelungenland] (1392,1). They are not the same thing.

Rules for the Endgame

When the Burgundians set out for Etzel, suddenly, without any narrative logic, *die Nibelunges helde* (1523,1) appear, one thousand in number, who ride with (!) the Burgundians.[95] As the hoard becomes available to feudal politics, so does the realm from which it originated, along with its inhabitants and subjects. Still the Burgundians are distinguished from them. Somewhat later, however, the name is applied to the expedition as a whole, when it is stated of Hagen, the leader of the Burgundians and their kings:

> *Dô reit von Tronege Hagen z'aller vorderôst.*
> *er was den Nibelungen ein helflîcher trôst.* (1526,1–2)[96]
>
> [Hagen of Troneck rode there at the head.
> He was a great consolation to the Nibelungen.]

This can no longer be explained with the transfer of rule to the Burgundians.[97] From now on they are often called *Nibelunge*. The name designates them as protagonists of the heroic narrative.[98]

First, the legendary "foreignness" is transformed into the political "neighborhood" of kingdoms (*Norwæge*) and then into a legal title. With the illegal appropriation of this title, the *Nibelunge* seem to associate themselves with the victors. But it goes one step further. During the journey to Etzel, association becomes identity.[99]

The downfall of the Burgundians is not localized in a threatening heroic counterworld, but in a world that, from the perspective of the original audience, seems to lie within reach, even if it was ruled "back then" by the legendary Etzel. The unfamiliar space of legend, as Hagen's story relates it in the beginning, as those from Worms experience it in Isenstein, and as Sivrit masters it once more in *Âventiure* 8, recedes further and further. The people and the objects that come from this space, however, pull the Burgundians as well as the Hunnish rulers to destruction.

The Burgundians become Nibelungen. This is connected to the gradual dissolution of political order.[100] The transition is hardly perceptible. The name Burgundians does not disappear completely by any means, but the designations are mostly carefully distributed. As a place of origin, *Burgonden* is mostly used to name themselves,[101] or where the framework of the courtly celebration remains intact, when they are Etzel's guests or relatives of the queen, or when the narrator neutrally remembers their dynastic origin,[102] and finally at the end, when Kriemhilt greets the defeated and bound Gunther, reduced to the status of a defenseless victim: *willekomen Gunther ûzer Burgonden lant* [welcome Gunther from Burgundy] (2362,4).[103] But when the enemies of the

Huns, who take them with them to their ruin, are concerned, they are called *Nibelunge.*

The designations change in a short time, and along with them, so does the perspective. The crossing of the Danube, the first occasion for violence, causes difficulties for the *Nibelungen* (1725,2). Rüedeger says *zen Burgonden* (1713,1). When the news of their arrival in Etzel's land is spread, however, it is stated *daz die Nibelunge zen Hiunen wæren* [the Nibelungen have arrived in the land of the Huns] (1715,2).[104] Dietrich's warning of Kriemhilt's treacherous intrigue is directed at Hagen as the *trôst der Nibelunge* [consolation of the Nibelungen] (1726,4), but it is *di Burgonden man* [men from Burgundy] (1735,1) who are given accommodations, and Dancwart, *der helt von Burgonden* (1736,4), takes care of the servants. For Kriemhilt, the arrivals are no longer members of her *gens* but instead *die Nibelunge* (1737,2).[105]

Different actions are associated with these names. People want to have *kurze wîle* with *den Burgonden* (1873,3); the *Nibelunge* are to be fought.[106] One time, the origin is maintained—Hagen expresses his disregard for the Huns with the remark that they will not prevent him from returning *in der Burgonden lant* (1776,4); another time, the new role is emphasized—Dancwart and the *ingesinde von Burgonden lant* [retinue from Burgundy] (1870,3), once they arm themselves, are called the *küenen Nibelungen* (1870,4). This is also their name when the bloody battle begins. Dietrich calls them *Nibelunge* (1900,2) as does Rüedeger, who disassociates himself from them: *ir küenen Nibelunge, nu wert iuch über al* [you bold Nibelungen, now defend yourselves everywhere] (2175,2).[107] *Nibelunge* is the name for the heroic opponent and at the same time signifies the pariah.

The previously constructed political system is destroyed in the battles of the heroes. In that the Burgundians "become Nibelungen," the destructive power that "comes from outside" is transferred to them. The danger does not originate with the Huns, as the history books claim. Etzel, the (historical) nomadic leader,[108] possesses an ordered kingdom. The courtly Gunther, on the other hand, becomes the leader of a troop that fights with the rage of berserkers. The direction of violence has been reversed.[109] In the first part, the threat to order comes "from outside"—from Sivrit and the Nibelungen. It might still be deflected. In the second part, the Burgundian ruling elite itself loses control and brings the Amelungen and Etzel's kingdom down with it. The space of legend, closed off by the narrator's strategy to let one of his characters speak for him, has incorporated the known world of kingdoms and vassality and destroyed it.

7 Disrupted Rules of Interaction

To describe rules of communication, behavior, and interaction in the *Nibelungenlied* would be a task well beyond the limits of this investigation.[1] The following considerations are therefore limited to a few significant phenomena. I shall discuss certain basic alternatives of action and certain ambiguous patterns of behavior on which the Nibelungian world depends, the changes they undergo, and the consequences of breaking through rule-based behavior. There have been many attempts to glean theories for this or that opinion, order, or way of thinking from the *Nibelungenlied*. These attempts have always been faced with contradictions that were supported by other parts of the texts. It therefore seems more appropriate to ask about fields of problematization, about the primary themes the narrator discusses, about the positions from which this occurs, and about the alternative solutions he suggests.

The Failure of Ritual

Rituals guarantee the existence of the world. Their failure results in its destruction. Normally only formal acts are conceived as rituals,[2] such as ceremonies, judicial customs, receptions, or the distribution of gifts. But beyond such prominent acts, everyday life in the Middle Ages was much more ritualized than it is today. Ritualization guarantees regular behavior in a world that is hardly institutionally secure. Demarcations between ritual and ceremony or ritual behavior are usually pointless.[3]

The character of ritual may be greater or weaker, and sometimes a process that only appears to be ritual from a historical perspective was just routine for its contemporaries.[4] In a literary text, however, the distinction does not matter, for both are loaded with meaning. In historical processes the question of whether or not and why a ritual fails depends on the standpoint of who describes and judges it. In this way, one and the same process can be narrated as a successful or failed ritual. This problem disappears in literary texts because the question is answered by the text itself. Unlike in the reality of everyday, contingency, as it endangers the success of every ritual, is eliminated in literature. What is claimed to be "contingent" and thus disruptive to ritual in a literary text is itself a result of literary selection. If rituals create meaning and their failure destroys it in historical reality, then in literature their disruption is meaningful, too. There are deviations on many different levels that can have serious consequences. The narrative world proves the ritual order to be problematic. Here the disruption of ritual is no less meaningful than its fulfillment.

Religious rituals are missing in the *Nibelungenlied*, or at least they seem to be mostly meaningless.[5] More meaningful are political rituals. It would be too narrow, however, to limit the concept of ritual to this area. Certainly, ritual plays an important role there, as reported in chronicles above all in the early Middle Ages. Ritual acts have to express, beyond their simple performance, social order and its underlying values.[6] In the *Nibelungenlied*, they become more and more disturbed as the epic progresses.

The narrative proves that rituals are contradictory. *Under krône* (684,3), that is, when demonstrating legitimate order, Kriemhilt receives from Sivrit the fatal trophies of his victory in Gunther's bedroom. The dispute of the queens takes place at a peaceful tournament. Gunther's attempt at reconciliation is the starting point of a conspiracy against Sivrit, the public reconciliation [*suone]* in the ruling family instigates a new crime. Rituals hide something else. When Prünhilt greets her Xanten relatives, she distrustfully observes them to discover signs of her status. Behind Kriemhilt's and Etzel's wedding celebration (*dâ diu schœne Kriemhilt bî Etzel under krône saz* [where the beautiful Kriemhilt sat enthroned alongside Etzel], 1374,4) lies the memory of past *leit* (1371). Kriemhilt's reception of her brothers and their men is a disguised call to battle. In the queens' dispute, it comes to light that the normal meaning of an event (chivalric games as a means to prove who is best without regard for status and as an affirmation of courtly order) can be distinct from the actual meaning (social rank) and the starting point of disastrous intrigue. Rituals are unreliable.[7]

Rather than integration, rituals cause separation (*scheiden*):[8] in the queens' procession to church (834,1–2); after the failed attempt at legal restitution (863,1); at Kriemhilt's reception of the Burgundians (1738,3). These turn into rituals of exclusion that foreshadow future aggression. Rituals fail as means to overcome conflict. They may do nothing more than reveal the state of affairs.[9] The *Nibelungenlied* narrates the shift from ritual to anomie.

This dysfunction can be observed not only in acts of state, but also in the para-ritual ways of life in courtly society. I call them para-ritual,[10] because they have a lesser degree of obligation than, for example, a coronation. They do, however, subject everyday events to stylization and thus allow them to be controlled.

The open failure of ritual guarantees and the breakdown of para-ritual forms lead to an outbreak of violence, but—and here the movement seems to reverse itself—also to a brutal openness that defeats all attempts at regulation, whether by law, by rule, or by good form. Rituals prove to be means to fight.[11] Instead of guaranteeing the security of the world, they make the breakdown of the world more evident. As rituals fail as a whole, so single acts make the whole more and more ambivalent.

Positions that at first seemed secure shift or dissolve at all levels of the story. The heterogeneity of the following examples makes this consistent tendency all the more impressive.

Milte *and Rulership*

Milte is a virtue of rulers. The words *die herren wâren milte, von arde hôh erborn* [the lords were generous and well-born] (5,1) introduce the Burgundian kings as ideal rulers. Gifts establish peaceful relations between foreign groups.[12] The excessive giving of gifts reflects the splendor of rule. Gifts are given apparently without intent or regard for a person's status. Giving is public and usually hierarchically structured; whoever gives is above whomever receives. Where gifts create or strengthen bonds of friendship between equals, they must be reciprocated with equal gifts. Giving can also be employed aggressively as a means of competition. One attempts to outdo the other in giving, until the opponent can no longer answer with another gift.[13]

The recognition of royal status depends on the ability to give. Bishop Pilgrim expresses this succinctly when he advises Kriemhilt *daz si ir êren koufte als Helche hete getân* [that she should buy honors as Helche did] (1330,3). Honor is something that can be exchanged for gifts,[14] gifts to strangers as well as one's own people. There is, however, no set price relationship between gift and reciprocal gift. Giving must be done without doing the math.

Generous gifts can be distinguished from *miete* or *lôn* that are intended for a specific purpose (such as an armed attack) or a certain service (such as military support) and therefore geared only toward the commissioned person. *Milte* on the other hand is undirected; it is limited neither to a goal nor to a specific recipient. It is expressed to one's own vassals in order to bind them more closely, and to others in order to make them more inclined to serve. It is self-referential, raises feelings of self-esteem, and the honor of those who give. Sigemunt and Sigelint, at Sivrit's knighting, give without distinction *den vremden und den kunden* [to strangers and to the well-known] (27,4) and thereby increase their own esteem:

> *Von der hôhgezîte man möhte wunder sagen.*
> *Sigmunt unde Siglint die mohten wol behagen*
> *mit guote michel êre; des teilte vil ir hant.* (29,1–3)
>
> [One could tell marvelous stories about the wedding celebration.
> Sigmunt and Siglint were able to gain much honor
> with their giving; they gave generously.]

Milte belongs to those virtues of leadership mentioned time and again. Thanks to its normalcy, it becomes an indicator of disruptions and conflicts. Overspending for the sake of *êre* also expresses Prünhilt's royal status. Her subordination to Gunther is apparent when her ability to give is endangered. At her leave-taking from Isenstein, she wants to exercise her royal munificence once more with *mîn silber unt mîn golt/mîn unt des küneges gesten* [my silver and my gold/to mine and the king's guests] (513,2–3). Dancwart is given the task of distribution. Dancwart distributes, but in such a way that Prünhilt, who wants to display her *milte*, disappears from sight: *daz er* [!] *milte wære, daz tet er* [!] *grœzlîchen schîn* [he proved clearly by his actions that he was generous] (514,4). Dancwart practices *milte* with someone else's property, and the consequence of the *milte* that the *man* exercises is the disempowerment of the queen,[15] who has to fear that she can no longer exercise *milte*. The excess of giving is too much for Prünhilt (*ez was ir wærlîche leit* [she was truly sorry about that], 516,4).

> *Er gît sô rîche gâbe, jâ wænet des der degen,*
> *ich habe gesant nâch tôde: ich wils noch lenger pflegen.*
> *ouch trûwe ichz wol verswenden, daz mir mîn vater lie.* (518,1–3)

[He gives such precious gifts, the warrior must believe
that I have sent for death: I want to hold on to it a while longer.
I might also just as well squander what my father left me.]

Giving everything away means death through the extinction of social existence. A *milte* that has to proceed economically, however, is no longer *milte*. Prünhilt's status, which has difficulty demonstrating itself, proves here to be already weakened. The *milte* is in danger of exhausting itself, precisely because she is already socially dead, even though she has not yet physically died. She is nothing more than an appendage of Gunther's power. Dancwart shows what the result of the contest is: Prünhilt's disempowerment. He demonstrates the loss of economic and political resources after physical defeat.[16]

Prünhilt's concerns are comical: *Gunther unt Hagene dar umb lachen began* [Gunther and Hagen began to laugh about that] (521,4), since her husband Gunther has much more to give away.[17] The laughter shows the irreversible shift of power. Before her defeat, it was Prünhilt who laughed (447,2). She wanted to take at least *zweinzec leitschrîn* [twenty large cases] of precious goods with her to Worms (520,2), with which she could show herself to be a rich queen. Her wealth is certainly significant and comparable to Gunther's, but it is brought down to size, to what can be tolerated in Worms.

Kriemhilt's status as queen is destroyed with the murder of Sivrit, manifest by the fact that she has nothing left to give.[18] The transport of the hoard to Worms reestablishes her ability to give for a short time, and she uses the opportunity perfectly:

daz man sô grôzer milte mêre nie gesach.
si pflac vil guoter tugende, des man der küneginne jach. (1127,3–4)

[that one has never seen such generosity since.
She practiced perfect virtues, for which people praised the queen.]

This incomparable *milte* is ambiguous, however, and politically dangerous. It is suspected of being calculating, rather than innocuous, like Prünhilt's. Hagen thinks she is misusing the hoard for the payment [*miete*] of future warriors against the Burgundian kings:

si bringet ez mit gâbe noch unz ûf den tac
dâ'z vil wol geriuwen die küenen Burgonden mac. (1130,3–4)

[She will go so far with her giving
that the bold Burgundians may regret it yet.]

Whereas Prünhilt's *milte* was, in the eyes of the Burgundians, excessive but harmless, one fears a threat here. There is no room for Kriemhilt's *milte* next to the *milte* of the king. The hoard as a means to recruit foreign troops and the hoard as a means of self-representation seem to be two different things. In that Hagen prevents *milte* from being used as a cover for revenge, he must prevent Kriemhilt from the exercise of *guoter tugende* [appropriate virtues], to which she owes her esteem. What would normally distinguish her in legend memory (*jach*) proves itself to be latently destructive and is therefore removed by another crime.

After accepting Etzel's suit, Kriemhilt's ability to exercise *milte* is reestablished, but its latently destructive character immediately moves to the foreground again. Kriemhilt wants to control the remaining parts of the dangerous *gol[t] von Nibelunge lant* [gold from Nibelungenland] (1271,1), and the dispute starts anew. Hagen fears that generosity is just an excuse for distributing the *golt ûf den mînen haz* [gold to my disadvantage] (1273,2). One could ask how anything of the sunken hoard is still left, but this is not the point. The repetition underscores the ambivalence of *milte* and again increases Hagen's crime.

Kriemhilt is supposed to limit herself to her husband Etzel's (and Rüedeger's) wealth.[19] Her legitimate claim seems to be finally fulfilled (1277), but its dangerous consequences for Hagen are diffused (1278–79), because Rüedeger "does not want to touch anything from the hoard."[20] What Kriemhilt finally takes with her is limited, even more so than what is left for Prünhilt: *zwelf schrîn* [twelve cases] (1280,1).

This back and forth highlights contradictory intentions: avoiding a repetition of the theft of the hoard and avoiding Hagen's threat, reestablishing harmony and rekindling a conflict.[21]

Kriemhilt's new power as queen of the Huns is expressed in what she can give away. In the beginning her resources are limited:

> *Swie ir genomen wære der Nibelunge golt,*
> *alle die si gesâhen, die machte si ir holt*
> *noch mit dem kleinem guote, daz si dâ mohte hân.* (1323,1–3)
>
> [Even if the Nibelungen gold was taken from her,
> all who saw her, these she made beholden to her
> with what little property was left to her.]

Then the restriction is soon forgotten. Kriemhilt can *geben* more perfectly than Helche (1331,1). She makes herself known *mit gâbe dem der si nie gesach* [with gifts to those who had never seen her before] (1366,1) and causes astonishment:

> *wir wânden daz vrou Kriemhilt niht guotes möhte hân:*
> *nu ist hie mit ir gâbe vil manic wunder getân.* (1366,3–4)
>
> [We thought that Lady Kriemhilt would have nothing left:
> now she has done marvelous things with her gifts.]

Her *milte* encourages everybody (1369–74) to equal her. As queen at Etzel's side, she exercises the excess of giving.

> *dô teilte diu küneginne golt unt ouch gewant,*
> *silber unt gesteine. swaz si des über Rîn*
> *mit ir ze Hiunen brâhte, daz muose gar zergeben sîn.* (1384,2–4)
>
> [The queen distributed gold and also clothing,
> silver and gems, all of this that she brought across the Rhine
> with her to the Huns, this all had to be given away.]

Secretly, however, *milte* transforms into something else. It is less and less an unintentional giving away for honor's sake alone and becomes more and more instrumentalized as *miete* for vengeance against Hagen. In Kriemhilt, uncontrolled voluntary giving leads to uncontrolled voluntary reciprocation, illustrating the perversion of the system. Etzel's court, whose paradigmatic *milte* in heroic legend is a magnet for the finest heroes (*Book of Bern*, *Rabenschlacht*, and *Biterolf*), thus becomes a deadly trap, into which the Burgundians fall.

This ambivalence is confronted by another kind of uncompromised *milte*: Rüedeger's.[22]

> *Rüedegêr der kunde vil wênic iht gesparn*
> *vor der sîner milte. swes iemen gerte nemen,*
> *daz versagete er niemen: ez muose in allen gezemen.* (1692,2–4)
>
> [Rüedeger was not able to withhold
> his generosity. Whatever anyone wanted,
> he denied them nothing. It had to suit them all.]

His *milte* is described as completely unselfish, in that he is *den ellenden holt* [favorable toward the exiles] (2245,4) and he gives *nâch . . . leide tagen* [after . . . difficult days] (2258,3) his wealth to those from whom he expects no reciprocal gift. In this way, he gains immeasurable honor. What does it mean, when he gives to the Burgundian kings, who come to him as Etzel's mighty guests? The hierarchy of *milte* has to be maintained. He exercises *milte* with the kings only after he has betrothed his daughter to the youngest Burgundian king and his concerns about the discrepancy in status have been allayed (1676–78). It is emphasized how unusual it is that King Gunther should receive a gift from a margrave *mit êren; swie selten er gâbe enpfienge* [with honor; however seldom he received gifts himself] (1695,2–3). Rüedeger's giving the kings gifts suggests that from now they will work on the same level, and that their status has begun to change. They are already, despite appearances, *ellende*,[23] just like the other exiles at Etzel's court. In the final dialogue with Rüedeger, the kings will memorialize once more *der hêrlîchen* [the magnificent] (2180,3), *der vil rîchen gâbe* [the many rich gifts] (2184,2), and Hagen will praise him for being generous to *ellende* warriors:

> *ez wirt iuwer gelîche deheiner nimmer mêr,*
> *der ellenden recken* [!] *sô hêrlîchen gebe.* (2199,2–3)
>
> [There will never be another like you,
> to give such splendid gifts to exiled warriors.]

As recipients of Rüedeger's *milte*, the Burgundians already belong to the *ellenden recken*. This *milte* is pure, a phantasm of unselfish help that is uncompromised by the demands of rule and therefore without the expectation of unrestricted obligation. In this sense, Rüedeger is praised after his death as *vröude ellender diete* [the joy of exiled people] (2258,4). With his death, the prospect of *gemach* (2258,2), that is, a rank-appropriate life at Etzel's court,[24] and the support of warriors in a *hervart* [campaign] (2260,2) is destroyed. The *schade* [harm] of his death therefore concerns everyone.

Rüedeger's gifts to the Burgundians prove to be ambivalent. Rüedeger stabilizes familial ties by bestowing his daughter on Giselher and anticipates enmity by giving weapons to his royal brothers. Gernot receives a sword, which will kill Rüedeger. Gunther receives *ein wâfenlîch gewant* [coat of mail], which he can use against Etzel's men (1695,3), but also against Rüedeger. Hagen receives a shield. What is meant to be a courteous gesture that presumes equality turns into a macabre exchange. It is further heightened when Rüedeger gives Hagen a second shield just before the outbreak of the battle, which would have to protect him from Rüedeger's own blows, if Hagen's reciprocal gift of staying out of the fight failed to prevent that.

Once Rüedeger has decided to fight, he gets back what he gave the Burgundians in a distorted form, in that they use the weapons against him, and he is killed by the sword he gave Gernot. Rüedeger receives enmity, and that is why his *milte* is the most complete, because it is the least calculating and includes the sacrifice of the giver. Its perfection is identical with the destruction of Rüedeger and the world that once depended on his *milte.*

Milte is decentralized in the political system. It is no longer a means of rulership and can even contradict feudal bonds. Rüedeger's last and biggest gift, the shield for his strongest foe, brings a tear to everyone's eye, because it is directed against his king. A direct conflict is avoided, but the obligation to the king has to be explicitly set aside: *torst' ich dir in bieten vor Kriemhilde* [if I would dare do that because of Kriemhilt] (2196,2). In that *milte* is perfected, it latently endangers the political order, because in the final analysis it proves to be asocial.

Milte is in any case disrupted. Rüedeger's *milte* anticipates the transformation of Etzel's royal *geste* into *ellende* and actually undermines Etzel's rule. Prünhilt's caution shows the loss of her independence, and Kriemhilt's excessive generosity foreshadows the unscrupulous employment of any and all means for the purpose of revenge.

Disrupted milte

Two scenes of gift-giving to messengers, seemingly marginal, show how *milte* becomes ambiguous. First, the messengers who bring the Saxons' declaration of war receive rich gifts from Gunther and accept them in spite of the impending enmities:

> *dine torsten hint versprechen die Liudegêres man.* (166,3)
> [Liudeger's men did not dare refuse them this time.]

Apparently, they are compelled by Gunther's power to accept. This power impresses them, even though aggression would be appropriate. But beyond the impending hostilities, it also creates a basis for a peace settlement. Gifts for these kinds of messengers seem to be unusual. In older societies, they were more commonly treated as enemies and, for example, hanged (Al 1003–28). Gifts are not exchanged when violence looms. In *Kudrun*, Hilde wants to give gifts to Hartmut's men, but they take nothing (K 772), because hostilities are immanent.[25] In that the *Nibelungenlied* deviates from this, it demonstrates the advantages of a courtly behavior that also treats a potential enemy *vil scône* (152,3). But that is true only in the first part.

The rejection of this order in the destruction at Etzel's court is prepared in a different but parallel context with Etzel's invitation to the Burgundian relatives.[26] To give gifts to the messengers who deliver this invitation means accepting Etzel's friendly gesture. Gunther is *den boten holt* [favorable to the messengers] (1487,1). He has costly gold brought to them, and others at court, including Margrave Gere and Ortwin, follow his lead. At first, the messengers refuse the gifts, however.[27] Several reasons are given for this, which indicates that none of them are really valid. First, the narrator explains:

> *alsô rîche gâbe si buten die boten an,*
> *daz si se vor ir herren niht getorsten enpfân.* (1488,3–4)
>
> [They offered the messengers such rich gifts,
> that they did not dare accept them because of their lord.]

Does the costliness of the gifts diminish the esteem of Etzel, to whom they are obligated? Or do they hesitate to accept a gift *vor ir herren,* because he will be unable to increase it as would be appropriate? In that case, *milte,* the exchange of gifts, would reflect a covert power struggle between Gunther and Etzel that started long before the Burgundians set off to Kriemhilt's celebration.[28] Then the messengers would correctly fear an obligation that might be directed against their lord. What is related on the surface points in the opposite direction, to *vriuntschaft* between Etzel and those from Worms. To accept gifts from the *mâgen* [relatives] of their lord should be unproblematic, because obligations within *mâgenschaft* are not supposed to be competitive. But here behind the competition for *milte,* there are hints of competition for power that anticipate a trial by military force.

The other reasons for rejection point even more clearly to a disruption. The messengers give transportation difficulties as their second reason: *wir mugen ir doch niht füeren* [we can't take them along] (1489,3). A third reason is a supposed prohibition from Etzel. The fourth is that they are not in need of gifts: *ouch ist es hart lützel nôt* [we hardly have need of them] (1489,4).

Considerations concerning transportation are at best ironic. When Kriemhilt asks Hagen what he brought her at Etzel's court (meaning Sivrit's hoard), Hagen counters that he had enough to carry with his own weapons. This is nothing more than a cynical excuse and answers a threat with a counterthreat. In view of the Nibelungen hoard, which is transported over long distances, the messengers' excuse apparently seems to be a sign that a regulated exchange of gifts between Etzel's and Gunther's people is actually no longer possible.

Why should Etzel have decreed a prohibition, mentioned here for the first time? In view of the friendly invitation to the *konemâgen* and the *vriuntschaft* to them, this seems to be inappropriate. In a parallel scene, Sivrit gives gifts to Gunther's messengers (764; 773), who invite him to Worms. Here any hidden hint of malice is missing. Gifts strengthen existing bonds. Only gifts from enemies are not accepted. It is therefore understandable that Gunther reacts *vil ungemuot* [very unhappily] (1490,1) to the rejection, since it contradicts the oft-bespoken *vriuntschaft*.

The last reason is all the more provokingly unbelievable. A wealth that allows them to reject the gifts of a king would be highly unusual for minstrels, even if Etzel's minstrels are rich.[29] Even the Bavarian ferryman, who is *ze riche* to be dependent on gifts from strangers, requires payment within his own personal alliances. Minstrels are expected to accept gifts, and it is an epic convention that powerful kings give minstrels gifts in unreasonable quantities. Werbel and Swemmel are no exception in a former situation:

> *Wärbel unde Swemmelîn, des küniges spilman,*
> *ich wæn' ir ieslîcher zer hôhgezît gewan*
> *wol ze tûsent marken oder dennoch baz,*
> *dâ diu schœne Kriemhilt bî Etzel under krône saz.* (1374)
>
> [Werbel and Swemmel, the king's musicians,
> I think each of them gained at the wedding
> at least a thousand marks or more,
> as the beautiful Kriemhilt sat with Etzel at their coronation.]

Still on the way to Worms—not a word about transportation difficulties!—they receive rich gifts from Rüedeger, as well as from the bishop of Passau:

> *Sine liezens' âne gâbe von in niht scheiden dan.* (1425,1)
>
> [They did not let them leave without gifts.]

> *niwan sîn golt alsô rôt*
> *Gap er den boten ze minne; rîten er si lie.* (1427,4–1428,1)
>
> [except he gave his red gold
> to the messengers; then he let them ride on.]

To not accept gifts would point to enmity. The geographic distance that the messengers claim to be an obstacle represents the deadly confrontation to which the attempted closeness will lead.[30]

None of these reasons is therefore acceptable. In the end, they play no role, since the messengers really do have to yield, and Gunther succeeds in giving them gifts, without any of the difficulties they had previously cited:

> *doch muosen si enpfâhen sîn golt und gewant,*
> *daz si mit in fuorten sît in Etzelen lant.* (1490,3–4)

[They had to receive his gold and clothing anyway,
which they took back with them to Etzel's land.]

So why then the detour via this refusal, when everything in the end seems to be in order? Gunther's gifts, unlike gifts normally, give offense. The messengers take Uote's gifts without problem a few verses later,[31] as they have done Rüedeger's, or—already in a foreign realm— Pilgrim's. This is different with Gunther's gifts. They feign relationships that are intact, where treason is already manifest.

Open hostility did not exclude the bestowing of gifts. Gunther's gifts to the Saxon messengers are not deceitful. In giving them despite the declaration of war, he seeks to recognize his enemies and asserts that beyond the armed conflict, orderly relationships will be possible. In giving to his enemies, he suspends any manifest interest. To give gifts to the messengers of his *vriunt* Etzel seems much less worthy of note, since mutual *vriuntschaft* has been pledged. In that the acceptance is at first refused, the peaceful relationship is called into question. The order of giving mirrors the order of society. Its disruption shows what is being prepared under the surface. An exemplary gesture represents an element in a hidden power struggle.

Acte gratuit, miete, lôn

As with *milte,* other forms of gift exchange can be threatened by misuse and misunderstanding. Giving is symmetrical and asymmetrical at the same time, because one gives and the other receives, but the one who gives hopes to exchange the gift for something else: *êre*. This exchange is cloaked in the concept of *milte,* because the prince who is *milte* does not receive a reciprocal material gift but only recognition, and there is no measurable relation, not even a cause-and-effect relationship, between gift and honor. Therefore the interconnection between "right and interests" seems to be nullified in the exchange of gifts. Receiving gifts is avoided, however, where the implicit connection is also to be avoided.[32]

Where unintentionally excessive, *milte* is the duty and distinction of the lord, all other forms of gift and reciprocity seem incomplete. They are guided by interests and always in danger of being misunderstood. The interested expectations that are wrapped up even in gestures of unintentional generosity should not be allowed to come to the fore. The point is demonstrative self-sacrifice, visible in Rüedeger's gifts of weapons to his later enemies. The peace that Gunther concludes with the Saxons by far exceeds the rules of politics in making peace with a defeated opponent, even if one of these rules says that "one should not exaggerate the compensation, but nonetheless be generous."[33] In the *Nibelungenlied,* however, absolutely nothing is demanded of the conquered foe, because it is expected that *vîentlîchez rîten her in iuwer lant* [enemy attacks in your land] (315,3) would cease in the future. One could be wrong about this, and this is why—despite this generosity—a new attack by the Saxons certainly lies within the realm of possibility. Such an attack, even if feigned to lure Sivrit into a trap, is therefore completely plausible. A treaty that sounds like a prudent political tactic is therefore primarily a demonstration of Gunther's power. He can certainly do without the huge reparations that have been offered (*swaz fünf hundert mære goldes möhten tragen* [the gold that five hundred horses can carry], 314,2). This demonstration continues with the generous gifts to the messengers. That Gunther can afford to generously give away this victory is a warning against any repetition of the attack, and still the demonstrative unintentionality is maintained.

Noble action must, if it is to be noble, appear disinterested. This is especially true when it is *dienest* to another lord. Such a relationship does not imply a fixed proportion of service and counterservice. In *Biterolf,* for example, Biterolf serves Etzel as if he were fighting in his own cause (*sam er ervehten wolt diu lant* [as if he wanted to conquer the land], Bit 1341), but without ever making himself dependent on any acceptance of *gâbe* (Bit 1369). Everyone suspects his royal rank, even though he does not openly insist on his status: *seht disen, der möhte künic sîn* [look at him, he could be a king] (Bit 1355). He is kinglike, *swiez umbe sîn geslehte stât* [without considering his family] (Bit 1358).

At first, the mutual services of Gunther and Sivrit are not calculated either.[34] At the end of the third *âventiure,* Gunther puts everything he owns at Sivrit's disposal, "on credit," as it were. The credit pays off when Sivrit, likewise without requiring any reciprocity, offers his assistance in the Saxon war. Sivrit, too, acts without reward. Then he receives something unexpected, however, something on which he could not count and that distinguishes him without making him dependent on the king: the symbolic gift of the ladies' *gruoz* in front of the entire court. The system, where performed service is without calculation and where only those who cannot afford to do so calculate, is maintained.

In the exchange of women between Gunther and Sivrit, a discriminating misunderstanding seems impossible, because it is narrated as a legal transaction that is secured with an oath (334). Sivrit provides an initial service and can then require a reciprocal service from Gunther (608–12). The deal seems to function as *do ut des*. Gunther and his brothers have control over Kriemhilt (this means: *hetens in ir pflegen* [had custody of her], 4,4), whom Sivrit desires. Sivrit has the knowledge and strength by which Prünhilt can be won, whom Gunther would like to have as his wife. This makes an exchange clearly desirable: *gistû mir dîne swester* [if you give me your sister] (333,2). Such an exchange assumes equality and rejects its interpretation as a service-payment relationship. If he were to have Kriemhilt, says Sivrit, *sô ger ich deheines lônes nâch mînen arbeiten mêr* [then I'll require no further reward for my trouble] (333,4). The word *lôn*,[35] however, could imply dependence. Sivrit sets the price for his gift, but the payment could also be meant for service. The opponents understand and follow the agreement to the letter, but Prünhilt will have a different interpretation—as a service-payment relationship, as Sivrit's words in Isenstein lead her to believe. With this, the entire exchange structure begins to crumble, admittedly from both sides. Prünhilt assumes Sivrit's dependence on the *lôn* from his lord, and Kriemhilt exaggerates Sivrit's independence, in that she suggests that Sivrit received a wife from Gunther as contractually stipulated, but also takes possession of the woman whom he had acquired for Gunther, that is, of his gift. Gunther would have been twice the loser in the exchange.

Free agreements with stipulated reciprocity and payment for service rendered cannot be separated with final clarity. Only under the exceptional conditions of *minne* is it correct to speak of a *dienest-lôn* relationship, which can imply material payment.[36] But even then *botenmiete* (557,4) could discriminate. In trying to avoid this, Sivrit immediately passes it on. The *verge* on the Danube also refuses to take the *lôn* that Hagen offers him for the crossing (1551,1–2). He would take it from a relative, because then equality would not be in question.

In contrast, the terms *lôn*, *solt*, and *miete* clearly presume dependence on reciprocal service.[37] The Hun Blœdelin lets himself be misled by *miete* in attacking the Burgundian baggage train. He is bribed with *silber unde golt* [silver and gold] (1906,2), *lant zuo den bürgen* [land along with castles] (1907,1), a *marke* [a border land] (1907,3), and a wife (1906,3). Death in the attempt to earn all this is cynically commented on as *brûtmiete* [dowry] (1928,2).

To do something only for payment is considered base. The Burgundians mock Etzel's men as not being worth the *fürsten brot* [princely bread] that they eat (2027,1). Kriemhilt employs huge amounts of gold in order to pursue her goal:

Daz wold' ich immer dienen, swer ræche mîniu leit.
allez des er gerte, des wær' ich im bereit. (1765,1–2)

[I would always repay whoever avenged the wrong done to me.
Whatever he wanted, I would be prepared to pay.]

. . . *der mir von Tronege Hagenen slüege*
unde mir sîn houbet her für mich trüege,
dem fult' ich rôtes goldes den Etzelen rant,
dar zuo gæbe ich im ze miete vil guote bürge unde lant. (2025)

[whoever kills Hagen of Troneck for me
and brings his head to me,
I'll fill Etzel's shield with red gold for him,
in addition I'd give him many grand castles and lands in payment.]

This has nothing to do with *milte*. What is otherwise exemplary is malice on Kriemhilt's part. This is why the mortally wounded Irinc warns his Thuringian and Danish followers of such dangerous *gâbe*:

die gâbe sol[38] *enpfâhen iwer deheines hant*
von der küneginne, ir liehtez golt vil rôt.
unt bestêt ir Hagene, ir müezet kiesen den tôt. (2068,2–4)

[None of you will get the gift
from the queen, her bright red gold.
And if you fight against Hagen, you will die.]

The further the destruction progresses, the greater Kriemhilt's offers become (*von geheize und ouch von gâbe* [of promises and of gifts] or *solt* [pay], 2130,1; 2130,4), and the more negative their estimation and the more unambiguous the recognition that Burgundian heroes cannot be bought. Material dependence stigmatizes the Huns. In this, Rüedeger is the perfect counterimage to them. In order to get out of his obligations as vassal, he is prepared to give up everything that he has received from Etzel.

Exchange is disrupted in two ways. It undermines the model of uncalculated *milte* and is corrupted by betrayal.

Honor

Êre is "bought" with *milte* (687,2) and is the concrete embodiment of inherited status and available power.[39] The term describes a corresponding "code of behavior" that is a "highly effective communicative system of rules."[40] As a regulator of social behavior, *êre* is ubiquitous. King Gunther can receive Sivrit in Worms *mit êren* (103,1), without harming the generally accepted hierarchy; the Burgundian dynasty rules the land *mit êren* (112,2), as the codex of legitimate rule requires; a courtly celebration that fits the general norm—*mit vollen êren*—is one that is distinguished by the appearance of the ladies (273,2); Rüedeger's oath to Kriemhilt binds him to this norm: *des si êre haben solde* [that she thus should have honor] (1258,4), and Dietrich promises his opponents: *ich leit' iuch nâch den êren* [I'll escort you in honor] (2340,3).

What looks like a generally binding norm is not clearly defined at all and is often a subject of conflicts. Paradoxically, as a rule based on consensus, *êre* is supposed to control antagonistic forces, which for their part are likewise striving for *êre*, but in the sense of primacy. What is conceived as *êre* must first be fought for. Anarchic and orderly tendencies clash in *êre*. When the *Nibelungenlied* ends: *Diu vil michel êre was dâ gelegen tôt* [the great honor lay there dead] (2378,1), the anarchic tendency has retained the upper hand.

Êre is bound to a group. When Gernot rejects Sivrit's challenge to single combat against the king of Worms: *wir hetens lützel êre und ir vil kleinen frum* [we would gain little honor, and it would do you little good] (124,3), he compares two negative and categorically different possible outcomes of the fight. In the case of the Burgundians, his gauge is *êre*, in the case of Sivrit, it is only benefit (even if Sivrit, too, bases his challenge on *êre*: *ich wil daz gerne füegen daz si von mir sagen . . .* [I want to make it so that men say of me . . .], 109,2). Sivrit is thereby verbally excluded from the Burgundian order of *êre*. His goal is reduced to a simple advantage. He is only later included in this order when Gunther puts everything at his disposal as a guest, with the proviso: *geruochet irs nâch êren* [if you observe honor] (127,2). This means, however, that he must acquiesce to the Burgundians' conditions .

The competition of *êre* and personal interest that first appears in Gernot's words is thus put to rest but not resolved. What generally counts as *êre* and what an individual sees as *êre* do not necessarily coincide. The conflict begins with the dispute of the queens. It is Kriemhilt who refers to Sivrit's *êre* (*an vil manigen dingen so ist sîn êre grôz* [his honor is great in many things], 819,3). *Êre* is a product of "self- and other perception."[41] Prünhilt refers to Sivrit's words in front of the court in Isenstein and contests his status. According to her, his *êre* is faulty and must be vindicated. Since the assessments diverge, it must be put to the test. Prünhilt demands that Kriemhilt consider *ob man den dînen lîp / habe ze solhen êren sô man den mînen tuot* [whether your person / is as honored as mine] (826,2–3), a challenge Kriemhilt accepts. *Êre* is antagonistic. Whereas Prünhilt is concerned with the range of the hierarchy of *êren*, at whose head she herself stands, Kriemhilt is concerned with her personal *êre:*[42] *ich wil selbe wesen tiwerr* [I intend to be more honored] (829,2). With this she jeopardizes the Burgundian balance of *êre.*

The forced precedence is an attack on the honor of the queen (*Von allen mînen êren mich diu swester dîn / gerne wolde scheiden* [Your sister / wishes to deprive me of all my honor], 853,1), and therefore on the entire court. Kriemhilt's and Sivrit's *êre* has publicly put itself in the place of the king's and the queen's *êre.* Gunther still holds to the earlier conditions when he votes against Sivrit's murder: *er'n hât uns niht getân / niwan guot und êre* [he has never done us anything but good and honor] (868,1–2), but Hagen counters with: *Suln wir gouche ziehen?* [Should we then tolerate fools?] (867,1)—someone who struts around here—and answers his own question: *des habent lützel êre sô guote degene* [such distinguished warriors would have little honor from that] (867,2), for there is not very much *êre* for them at Sivrit's side. He uses the same words that Gernot had used earlier to reject Sivrit's challenge to combat. Sivrit's *êre* is no longer integrated into the Burgundian system of *êre,* and so Hagen is able to advocate his murder as that of a foreigner.

From this point on, *êre* no longer means nonviolent recognition of an order to which all are obligated, even if appeals to it are still made. Above all, it means self-assertion in armed conflict: *sô wil ich iu daz râten, ir hüetet deste baz / des lîbes unt der êren* [I advise you to watch out / for your life and honor] (1774,2–3), says Hagen when the Burgundians arm themselves to go to church. Whoever attacks the other's honor will be liquidated. One has to refuse *êre* to someone who is hostile: (*zwiu sold' ich den êren, der mir ist gehaz* [why should I honor him who hates me], 1782,2). Kriemhilt is unconcerned that her plan for vengeance completely disregards *êre* in her relationship to her *mâgen* (1902,1). Everyone strives to prove his *êre* in the increasingly vicious fight—*ich hân ûf êre lâzen nu lange mîne dinc* [I have put all my efforts into honor] (2028,2), Irinc cries as he races into the desperate battle. His aim is *daz er warp nâch êren* [that he strived for honor] (2036,3), and so it goes until Hagen's and Gunther's refusal of a peaceful settlement that would endanger their future reputation as heroes (*von uns enzimt daz mære niht wol ze sagene* [it would not be fitting to have that story told about us], 2341,2). Even Dietrich's unwillingness to kill Hagen is above all self-referential (*ich hâns lützel êre* [I would gain little honor], 2351,2). In the end, the result of insisting on one's own *êre* is that *êre* as the embodiment of the courtly-feudal order is completely destroyed (2378,1).

Oaths

The oath is the most important kind of evidence in early medieval judicial proceedings.[43] Other ways of determining the truth, such as those that came into use in lay society after the eleventh century, do not exist in the *Nibelungenlied*. It is demonstrated, however, that this form of evidence cannot guarantee justice. Only in the beginning does the oath ensure the reliability of action. Sivrit obligates himself under oath to Gunther to help him in his bridal quest, and Gunther swears to give him Kriemhilt (335,1). After the successful quest (608,3), Sivrit demands fulfillment, and Gunther makes good on his obligations (612,2).

The oath guarantees the relationship between two contractors, but it is not a guarantee of law. The oaths of Gunther and Sivrit include deceit, and this is why they are doomed, for they injure Prünhilt's rights. What is supposed to ensure reliability actuality undermines order.

This ambiguous role is played by oaths throughout. Sivrit's oath of justification does not end the queens' dispute, but only serves to inflame its consequences. Whoever determines the formula of the oath determines the criteria for measuring the truth. Sivrit is able to disprove that he was the source of Kriemhilt's insulting speech, but this expunges neither the insult itself nor the evidence of other signs. What is true in Sivrit's oath is not decisive, and Gunther's power over truth by way of a formula proves to be fragile.[44] As a function of power, its legal meaning is compromised.

For the *suone* between Gunther and Kriemhilt, Gunther also proposes a formula that ignores the facts: *iu wil der künic rihten daz er sîn niht hât erslagen* [the king wants to affirm to you that he did not kill him] (1110,3), which Kriemhilt rejects: *des zîhet in niemen* [no one is accusing him of that] (1111,1). So the *suone* seems to take place without any guarantee. Gunther later summarizes its content this way: *ich swuor ir einen eit / daz ich ir getæte nimmer mêre leit* [I swore her an oath / that I would do her no more harm] (1131,1–2). He holds fast to this: *und wil es fürbaz hüeten: si ist diu swester mîn* [I mean to keep my word in the future: she is my sister] (1131,3). Yet another kind of manipulation is exposed by the oath. Since it is sworn among individuals, it is only worth as much as these people guarantee, and this requires that they be present. The line *ir sumelîcher eide wâren umbehuot* [all their oaths were broken] (1132,1) only means that those who swore the oath suspended their guarantees. Thus the oath is not "guarded," and someone who was excluded from the oath, such as Hagen, has a free hand: *lât mich den schuldigen sîn* [let me be the guilty one] (1131,4). Anyone whose hands are not tied by the oath can act unfettered and will do so. The oath provides a basis for a new crime.

Because oaths are considered to be precise and extremely personal, an additional oath, such as that by which Hagen and the kings agree to the consequences of the theft of the hoard, does not interfere with the reconciliation oath, since it concerns a completely different matter:

Ê daz von Tronege Hagene den schaz alsô verbarc,
dô heten siz gevestent mit eiden alsô starc,
daz er verholn wære unz ir einer möhte leben.
Sît enkunden sis in selben noch ander niemen gegeben. (1140)

[Before Hagen of Troneck thus hid the treasure,
they pledged with solemn oaths
that it should remain hidden as long as they lived.
Later they could neither keep the treasure nor give it away.]

The oath only states that no one should gain advantage from Hagen's deed. It therefore does not judge the deed (this occurs separately in a judicial hearing) and does not regard Kriemhilt's claim. The previous oath is not even explicitly linked to the later oath. Legal obligations are simply placed side by side. The judicial proceeding against Hagen is not based on a superior right; rather, judgment and oath are—as so often in the Middle Ages[45]—equally valid instruments of judicial order and equal means of conflict resolution (elimination of danger without sacrificing justified claims to brute force). The *Nibelungenlied* demonstrates how fragile this order is based on the ad hoc authority of an oath and its implicitly contradictory nature.

An oath can be directed against otherwise legitimate claims. Hagen refers to his oath
when he refuses to show Kriemhilt the hoard:

jâ hân ich des gesworn,
daz ich den hort iht zeige die wîle daz si leben,
deheiner mîner herren, sô sol ich in niemene geben. (2368,2–4)

[I have sworn an oath
that I shall not reveal the hoard as long as one of my lords
is still alive, and so I shall give it to no one.]

A consideration of whether these words would not better have been left unsaid, for the sake of the "greater" purpose of saving Gunther's life,[46] misses the precision of the oath. Hagen has to keep the promise he made, no more and no less. Given this, Kriemhilt's rights do not matter anyway.

Oaths can be ambiguous, their validity is debatable, and their content can be manipulated. Rüedeger's oath is not clear, and how it has to be upheld is controversial. It is given to one single person at the expense of all others. Kriemhilt demands:

> *Ich man' iuch der genâden und ir mir habt gesworn,*
> *do ir mir zuo Etzele rietet, ritter ûz erkorn,*
> *daz ir mir woldet dienen an unser eines tôt.*
> *des wart mir armem wîbe nie sô grœzlîche nôt.* (2149)
>
> [I remind you of the faith that you have sworn to me,
> when you counseled me to accept Etzel, best of knights,
> that you would serve me while we live.
> I, poor woman, have never been more in need of it than now.]

Rüedeger confirms the oath, but he adds a reservation, which has been much discussed:

> *Daz ist âne lougen, ich swuor iu, edel wîp,*
> *daz ich durch iuch wâgte êre und ouch den lîp:*
> *daz ich die sêle vliese, des enhân ich niht gesworn.* (2150,1–3)
>
> [That is the truth, I swore to you, noble woman,
> that I would risk honor and my life for you:
> but I did not pledge to lose my soul.]

This questions the obligation under such a single oath, which, of course, remains without consequences.[47]

The formula of the oath was unclear from the beginning, and it is described in various ways. Kriemhilt understands it to be encompassing:

> *Si sprach: "gedenke, Rüedegêr, der grôzen triuwe dîn,*
> *der stæte und ouch der eide, daz du den schaden mîn*
> *immer woldest rechen, und elliu mîniu leit."* (2151,1–3)
>
> [She spoke: "Think, Rüedeger, of your great loyalty,
> of constancy, and also of the oaths that you would always
> avenge the harm done to me and all my suffering."]

Around 1200, people began to pay close attention to the exact formulation of sworn declarations in order to avoid any undesirable self-obligation.[48] The oath that Rüedeger swears is not so much careless—like the unconsidered and therefore dangerous promises of King Arthur (which might cost him his wife, for example)—but its shifting formulations remain open to different interpretations.[49]

The oath is at first paraphrased by the narrator as an indirect promise to "comfort" Kriemhilt (*ergetzen*) if someone were to harm her. This promise refers explicitly to the past as well (*swaz ir ie geschach* [whatever had happened to her before], 1255,3). Rüedeger's own formulation (*er müeses sêr' engelten, unt het iu iemen iht getân* [he would pay dearly, if anyone should have done anything to you], 1256,4) also leans in this direction. Kriemhilt's version of the oath (*sô swert mir eide* [swear me an oath]) refers on the other hand more to the future (*swaz mir iemen getuot, / daz ir sît der næhste, der büeze mîniu leit* [whatever someone does to me, / that you will be the first to avenge the wrong done me], 1257,2–3). There are at least two versions, then. Rüedeger's words correspond to Kriemhilt's real intentions, but Kriemhilt's formula refers to Rüedeger's future intentions. The assignment of speech and person are exactly reversed, and this reversal underlines the ambiguity of the oath. The consensus of the protagonists is built on a shaky foundation.

The wording of the oath that Rüedeger then publicly repeats with his men deviates from the previous versions and therefore does not cause any suspicion. Rüedeger makes a general promise of service for himself and his vassals to their future queen:

> *Mit allen sînen mannen swuor ir dô Rüedegêr*
> *mit triuwen immer dienen, unt daz die recken hêr*
> *ir nimmer niht versageten ûz Etzelen lant,*
> *des si êre haben solde, des sichert' ir Rüedegêres hant.* (1258)
>
> [With all of his men, Rüedeger swore
> to serve loyally, and that the splendid warriors
> would never forsake her in Etzel's land,
> from this she would have honor, this Rüedeger swore.]

Three obligations with different content compete. The last version is both collective and public and therefore the most binding in form, but it is the least binding in content. In the phrase *mit triuwen* lies the usual proviso of every legitimate service, likewise in the consideration of Kriemhilt's *êre*. What Kriemhilt, on the other hand, concludes from this oath is not necessarily valid: *waz ob noch wirt errochen des mînen lieben mannes lîp* [what if my dear husband could someday be avenged] (1259,4). In short, Rüedeger's oath is ambiguous. In its publicly proclaimed form, it seems harmless; its secret form comes in two versions, oscillating between a promise regarding the past and one regarding the future. It opens up an interpretive space that allows the Burgundians to misunderstand the background, give Kriemhilt hope, and let Rüedeger deal in good faith.

The oath that should secure law and order through personal obligation is employed as a means of treason that can be manipulated. But is an exact comparison of the formulas not all too dependent on a culture of writing that can check the wording?[50] The text says one thing for certain: Rüedeger obligates himself to Kriemhilt by swearing an oath, and by doing so, he comes into conflict with other obligations. In an oral society, the sworn word must be considered binding. Loyalty to the pledge is a principal rule of medieval specula of nobility and the basis for endless epic conflicts when an impulsive promise brings with it seemingly insurmountable difficulties. Manipulation of an oath undermines the certainty of the world.

As a guarantee for the reliability of the world, oaths take on a dubious character both in terms of their interpretation and in their validity. Sivrit's and Gunther's sworn agreements are clear and are kept, but since they were meant to perpetrate deception, they create conflict. Gunther's obligation to Kriemhilt is also clear, but it is not upheld. The oath favored circumstances under which it could be broken. The oath between Hagen and the kings presumes breaking the law; it attempts to neutralize the consequences, but even graver consequences result. Hagen's loyalty to the oath undermines its goals. Finally, Rüedeger's oath, with whose help his realm again acquires a queen, seals its ruin. The means to secure order proves itself to be the instrument of lawlessness.

Truth-making Speech Acts

Valid is only what those who matter see, and what those who have a say publicly proclaim. This starts with Hagen, who recounts Sivrit's history at the Burgundian court and advises the king on how to receive this prominent guest. This continues with Gernot's prohibition to the Burgundian warriors against arguing with Sivrit (123,2), and with Gunther authoritatively putting an end to the dispute (137). Kriemhilt's words of greeting for Sivrit determine his esteem in the Burgundian court (303,2–3). The principle can be perverted, however, because what is publicly displayed as truth may be a lie, and what claims to be important in public speech may remain ineffective. At first, when he calls Gunther his lord, Sivrit abuses the expectation that what is stated in the presence of everyone is true and valid. Prünhilt relies on what all could hear: *ich hôrte si jehen beide . . . ; dô jach des selbe Sîvrit, er wære 'sküneges man* [I heard them both declare . . . Sivrit declared the same, that he was the king's vassal] (820,3; 821,2). One has to trust the publicly spoken word like an oath. By doing so Prünhilt is deceived, and by trying to clear up the deception, she puts the fateful events into motion.

It makes no difference that the king does not demand what he could demand after the events in Isenstein (*er'n jahes im niht ze dienste* [he did not demand Sivrit's service following his words], 728,4), and his attempt to dispute their consequences remains futile:

ich tuon ez iu wol bekant
er hât als wol bürge als ich unt wîtiu lant:
daz wizzet sicherlîche. Er ist ein künic rîch. (623,1–3)

[I'll tell you the truth,
he has castles as well as spacious lands:
this you may be sure of. He is a powerful king.]

The solemn declaration (*tuon . . . bekant; wizzet sicherlîche*) proves itself to be ineffective. It is the first time that the word of the king is supposed to diffuse a conflict yet remains fruitless. It is also often false.

In the dispute of the queens, Gunther declares Sivrit to be free of all guilt, but the king's words again fail to resolve the conflict. The declaratory gesture of the judgment (*mir is sô wol bekant/iuwer grôz unschulde* [I am well aware of/your complete innocence], 860,2–3) by no means empowers justice and truth; at best, it defers new injustices. The speech act strives in vain against the evidence of the sign.

On several occasions, speech that seems to vouch for justice and truth proves to be false, and the authority that proclaims it is corrupt or powerless. On the first occasion, Gunther makes an assertion (*sprach*) that is a plain contradiction to what the bier test has just disclosed about Sivrit's murderer:

ich wilz iu wizzen lân.
in sluogen schâchære, Hagene hât ez niht getân. (1045,3–4)

[I want you to know how it was.
He was struck down by robbers. Hagen did not do it.]

He is not taken seriously even for a moment (1046), and yet the truth is unable at first to win out against the word of the king. The matter remains undecided.

A formula for compromise seems to have been found in the *suone*: *iu wil der künic rihten daz er sîn niht hât erslagen* [the king wants to let you know that he did not kill him] (1110,3). This is undeniably true, but it only clouds the facts. The *suone* does not hold, however, inasmuch as it only creates the prerequisite for new, more or less secret, actions and counteractions, which lead to another crime. Again a declaratory act tries to reestablish the law in the kings' judgment of Hagen:

> *Dô sprâchen si gemeine: "er hât übele getân."* (1139,1)
>
> [They all said together: "He has done an evil deed."]

This judgment is legally binding but does not touch on the agreement of Hagen and the kings that was made in the background.[51] Hagen is punished only with temporary banishment, but the circumstances of the theft remain in the dark and no amends are made.

Finally, there is the way that Volker's murder of a Hun at the *bûhurt* [tournament] is handled, an act of violence that will prompt the Huns to strike back. Again, a king—this time, Etzel—tries to prevent further violence by declaring the crime to have been an accident:

> *ich sach vil wol sîn rîten, dô er den Hiunen stach,*
> *daz ez âne sîne schulde von eime strûche geschach.* (1896,3–4)
>
> [I saw the way he rode when he hit the Hun,
> it was not his fault, it happened because he stumbled.]

This is an obvious lie. A king's power to determine what is true once more overcomes the facts.[52]

The authorities that decide on justice and truth come into conflict with appearances, and their word is proven to be increasingly ineffective. The performative power of royal judgment is unable to erase the facts forever, as they are drawn into the light. Declaratory speech proves to be powerless once the battle is under way (1967,2). What counts as truth is then decided by force of arms. In the end, when Dietrich forbids Hiltebrant, the last surviving vassal, to speak, this is not done as in *Âventiure* 3 to secure the peace, but because he wants to fight.

Suone *and* ergetzen

Kriemhilt's revenge overcomes all alternatives, especially *suone* [reconciliation]. As a legal settlement, *suone* had been implemented since the early Middle Ages as a means to provide satisfaction and restitution.[53] Beyond the main story, the system functions effectively. There is *suone* with and without compensation (*ergetzen*), as, for example, at the end of the Saxon war. The defeated Saxons and Danes want a legal settlement of the damages that the two warring parties have caused each other, since this is something that might lead to a future war:

> *wir gern stæter suone. des ist uns recken nôt.*
> *wir hân von iuwern degenen manegen lieben vriwent tôt.* (311,3–4)
>
> [We want a lasting reconciliation. This is what we warriors need.
> We have lost many a dear friend to your warriors.]

The Burgundians reject their offer of rich treasures as compensation (314). Thus the justification for renewed enmity is eliminated.

This is a basic pattern in violent conflicts, and in this way, the need for vengeance after Sivrit's murder should be settled through *suone*. The legal procedure is reported with painstaking exactitude.[54] The royal brothers act as *mediatores* between Gunther and Kriemhilt, since they maintain intact relationships with both sides (*die sul wir'z biten werben, daz si unser vriunt sî* [we should ask them to advocate that she be kindly disposed to us], 1108,2). Taking Kriemhilt's side, they are especially qualified as mediators, along with Gere and Ortwin. The one is a follower of Kriemhilt, the other a vassal who is especially close to Gunther, but has not fallen out with Kriemhilt.[55] Thus the conditions for both sides can be adjusted accordingly. The *suone* (1113–15) is a legally binding ritual in which Kriemhilt agrees to the formula of reconciliation proposed by Gunther (1110,3; 1111,1). The king and his closest followers appear before her, she "greets" him and exchanges the kiss of peace, whereby she renounces her *haz* for him (*verkiesen,* 1114,1). Unlike *ergetzen, verkiesen* is not a "forgetting through settlement" but rather a renunciation of vengeance. The *suone* is so binding for Gunther that he does not want to participate in the theft of the hoard (1129; 1131) and later trusts in the authority of the kiss of peace when accepting Kriemhilt's invitation (1460). After the reconciliation, Kriemhilt's former position vis-à-vis the hoard is restored:

> *er was ir morgengâbe, er solt' ir billîche sîn.* (1116,4)
>
> [This was her dowry, it was hers to dispose of.]

But in that the *suone* provides the opportunity for a new crime, the judicial act becomes ambiguous. For Kriemhilt, as later for Gunther, it proves to be unreliable, and so it is replaced by another means of effecting conflict: revenge. From now on, *suone* is only mentioned as a cynical parody or as something to be rejected. During the journey to Etzel, when the Bavarians demand satisfaction for the ferryman, whom Hagen has killed, Hagen mocks:

> *"daz bringe ich iu ze suone swie iuch dunket guot."*
> *dô gie ez an ein strîten. Si wâren herte gemuot.* (1606,3–4)
>
> ["This I bring to you in reconciliation in a way that pleases you."
> Then a struggle began. They were staunchly determined.]

Later, Kriemhilt does not receive her due from Hagen, but only a confession of guilt and the refusal to pay for it: *nu rechez swer der welle* [now avenge it whoever will] (1791,3). The chance to eliminate the conflict through *suone* is present only on the margins, with Rüedeger (1997,2) or Dietrich, whom Gunther offers:

> *buoze und suone der bin ich iu bereit.*
> *swaz iu iemen tæte, daz wær' mir inneclîchen leit.* (1991,3–4)
>
> [I am willing to compensate and reconcile.
> Whatever was done to you, I am truly sorry for that.]

Suone is no longer possible between the main antagonists (2094,2), because an adequate settlement for the mutually inflicted *leit* is no longer imaginable: *mîn und iuwer leit / diu sint vil ungelîche* [my suffering and yours / weigh very differently] (2095,1–2), says Etzel. For Kriemhilt's *leit*, all that is left is vengeance:

> *"ez ist vil unversüenet, di wîle ich hân den lîp.*
> *ir müezet es alle engelden," sprach daz Etzelen wîp.* (2103,3–4)
>
> ["It will not be reconciled, as long as I shall live.
> All of you will have to pay," spoke Etzel's wife.]

At the very least, she says, Hagen should be handed over to her before she works for a reconciliation with Etzel: *sô rede ich ez nâch der suone mit disen helden die hie sint* [then I'll speak about reconciliation with the heroes who are here] (2104,4). After Etzel has rejected *suone*, this is a vague promise that aims more at provocation than at peaceful settlement. In Kriemhilt's opinion, to work toward *suone* instead of exacting vengeance borders on treason. She suspects Rüedeger (2228,2–4): *der wil der suone pflegen* [he wants to ask for reconciliation] (2229,2), until she hears from the Burgundians: *er unt die sînen degene sint an der suone gar betrogen* [he and his warriors have been deceived regarding a reconciliation] (2230,4). Hagen rejects the *suone* offered him by Dietrich in a similarly unreconciliatory manner.

Suone usually includes restitution, *ergetzen,* for damages suffered. However, *ergetzen* does not necessarily require a legally relevant conflict. The etymological connection with "forgetting" [*vergessen*] implies that the damage is made to disappear,[56] but *ergetzen* is not only aimed at material compensation.[57] *Ergetzen* includes restitution in a comprehensive sense and therefore includes the different attempts to make up for losses in nonviolent ways.

Loss can be meant quite neutrally, and *ergetzen* thus need not always have legal implications. The void that a person's death causes has to be filled. Helche's death provides such a void. It is manifest again and again in the Huns' mourning for their queen.[58] Etzel's *vriunde* want to repair the defect by advising the king to take a new wife. When Kriemhilt is chosen, the wife of the margrave Rüedeger hopes that *si ergazt' uns mîner vrouwen* [she may replace my lady for us] (1170,3). For the land and the people, compensation is possible. The reign is intact once again.

Ergetzen usually means compensation for damages, at least up to the final episode. Dietrich asks for reparations from Hagen and Gunther after the loss of his men: *ergetze mich der leide* [compensate my losses] (2336,3).[59] Here, *ergetzen* has legal implications. Dietrich calls his suggestion *suone* (2342,1).[60] In concrete terms. this means: *Ergip dich mir ze gîsel, du und ouch dîn man* [Surrender yourself as a hostage, you and also your man] (2337,1). The status of hostage means that Dietrich can secure his claim for restitution,[61] for Gunther and Hagen, it represents protection from the other attackers (*daz dir hie zen Hiunen niemen niht entuot* [that none here in the land of the Huns will harm you], 2337,3).

This kind of legal solution has no chance. Certainly, when Hagen refuses to give himself up, Dietrich reminds him of his claim for compensation:

> *ir habt beide mich*
> *sô sêre beswæret, daz herze und ouch den muot,*
> *welt ir mich ergetzen, daz irz billîchen tuot.* (2339,2–4)

> [You have both
> greatly burdened my heart and mind,
> should you compensate me, you would do so rightly and properly.]

Instead of the thought of compensation Dietrich now emphasizes the idea of security, and *ergetzen* is replaced by the softer *vergezzen*:

> *Ich gibe iu mîne triuwe und sicherlîche hant,*
> *daz ich mit iu rîte heim in iuwer lant.*

ich leit' iuch nâch den êren oder ich gelige tôt,
und wil durch iuch vergezzen der mînen grœzlîchen nôt. (2340)

[I give you my faith and my solemn pledge,
that I shall accompany you back home to your land.
I shall escort you in honor or give my life trying,
and I shall forget all my heavy losses for your sake.]

It is not entirely clear whether or not these words include a complete renunciation of compensation.[62] The material content of *ergetzen* is in any case softened in favor of the simple gesture of recognizing Dietrich's claim. Dietrich's readiness for *suone* has to be raised to the extreme so that Hagen's rejection appears all the more uncompromising. The price of heroic self-validation is driven to new heights. Once the battle seems unavoidable, the idea of securing claims through hostage-taking immediately returns:

ich wil ez sus versuochen, ob ich ertwingen kan
dich mir ze einem gîsel. (2351,3–4)

[I'll do my best, if I can manage it,
to capture you as my hostage.]

Dietrich's action is contrasted with Kriemhilt's. Dietrich turns over Hagen to her also to secure her claim for recompense:

ir sult in lân genesen,
edeliu küneginne. und mac daz noch gewesen,
wie wol er iuch ergetzet daz er iu hât getân!
er ensol ez niht engelten, daz ir in seht gebunden stân. (2355)

[You should let him live,
noble queen. And if this can still be done,
how well he will compensate you for what he has done to you!
He should not suffer in that you see him being bound before you.]

Dietrich apparently means the common kind of compensation,[63] which he distinguishes from the exploitation (*engelten*) of actual superiority. Kriemhilt at first seems to play along with the game of *ergetzen* as a restitution of damages (2367), but the ambiguity of the two antagonists, Hagen and Kriemhilt, dooms it to failure.[64] There is no need for clarification of whether there can be any *ergetzen* for Sivrit's death.

The attempts to recompense (*ergetzen*) Kriemhilt are the subject of the second part of the epic, and they all fail without exception. The different meanings of *ergetzen* do not agree. With the loss of Helche, only a void had to be filled. Later, *ergetzen* contains legal and material implications. For Kriemhilt, it means a compensation for the loss of her *holden vriedel. Ergetzen* seems to be unproblematic in the first sense. As Kriemhilt is supposed to replace Helche, so Etzel could replace Sivrit.[65] Apparently, the advice of the brothers Gernot and Giselher to accept Etzel's proposition lies on this level. It could compensate (*ergetzen)* Kriemhilt by reestablishing her previous position as queen:

> *ergetzet si der leide und ir ir habet getân*
> *an swiu ir wol gelunge, daz soldet ir ungevêhet lân.* (1208,3–4)
>
> [Compensate her for the sorrows you have caused her
> and if she succeeds in that, you should not fight against it.]

Support of this connection is supposed to compensate Kriemhilt for what has been done to her,[66] but the hope, *daz elliu dîniu leit/der künic Etzel swende* [that King Etzel will make all your suffering disappear] (1243,2–3) is dashed, because it is based solely on what Etzel has to offer: power and wealth.

> *"Er mac dich wol ergetzen," sprach aber Gîselher.*
> *"vom Rôten zuo dem Rîne, von der Elbe unz an daz mer,*
> *sô ist künec deheiner sô gewaltec niht.*
> *du maht dich vreun balde, sô er dîn ze konen giht."* (1244)
>
> ["He may well be able to compensate you," spoke Giselher.
> "From the Rhône to the Rhine, from the Elbe to the sea,
> no king is more powerful.
> You may soon rejoice if he makes you his wife."]

These components of *ergetzen* remain in the background, because the younger brother wants to compensate Kriemhilt for what she has lost with Sivrit's death:

> *nu trœste dich nâch tôde, als iz doch muoz sîn.*
> *wir wellen dich ergetzen die wîle wir geleben.* (1049,2–3)
>
> [Console yourself after his death, as it must be anyway.
> We'll compensate you as long as we live.]

This includes material support: *nu zer mîn eines guot* [you may rely on my resources] (1079,2), in addition to protection. Kriemhilt rejects neither of these when Giselher proposes:

> *"du solt bî dînem bruoder Gîselhere sîn.*
> *jâ wil ich dich ergetzen dînes mannes tôt."*
> *dô sprach diu gotes arme: "des wære Kriemhilde nôt."* (1080,2–4)

["You shall stay with your brother Giselher.
Really, I'll compensate you for your husband's death."
Then the forsaken woman said: "Kriemhilt truly needs it."]

"Being with Giselher" can in some ways replace the closeness of Sivrit.

From the beginning, however, *ergetzen* has only limited success as material compensation:

done kunde ir trôst deheinen zer werlde niemen gegeben. (1049,4)[67]

[But no one in the world could console her.]

Whereas no one else makes any distinction between the different aspects of *ergetzen*, there is no economy of lamentation for Kriemhilt that would correspond to the economy of material compensation, as Gernot expects it should when he tells Kriemhilt: *ir klaget ze lange den Sîfrides tôt* [you have been mourning the death of Sivrit too long] (1110,2). There is no adequate material substitute for Sivrit: *si klagete unz an ir ende* [she mourned the rest of her life] (1105,3). Gere advises that she should be pleased by Etzel (*wol behagen*, 1215,2), because he commands so many warriors,

er mac si wol ergetzen swaz si leides ie gewan (1215,4)

[He can well compensate her for whatever she has suffered]

but for Kriemhilt the first is related to the second only insofar as Etzel provides her with the means for vengeance.

After she has agreed to marry Etzel, Kriemhilt becomes *ergetzet* in the sense of her brothers, as is Etzel for his loss. How she takes Helche's place is described in detail. Helche can only be replaced by Kriemhilt (1333,1); in fact, the replacement exceeds the loss. Kriemhilt supersedes Helche (1383; 1385), and Sivrit's military might was never like Etzel's (1368). This is only one side of it, however.

Instead of replacing Helche, Kriemhilt in reality becomes a counterpart. That an exchange on the political level is not enough is shown by a seemingly meaningless detail. Despite her agreement with the new queen Kriemhilt, it is said of Helche's sister Herrat:

Diu hete tougenlîchen nâch Helchen grôzlîchiu leit. (1389,4)

[She secretly mourned for Helche.]

There is an aspect that is not included in *ergetzen*, and it is hidden (*tougenlîchen*), just as Kriemhilt's tears when she is thinking about *Wie si ze Rîne sæze* [how she lived on the Rhine] (1371,1): *si hetes vaste hæle* [she kept it a secret] (1371,3). *Ergetzen* seems to succeed so completely in the sense of material compensation because the loss seems to be more than made up. Everything is in order in the sense of "what people think," but the gap between what Kriemhilt thinks and what everyone else thinks is all the more stark.

The meaning of *ergetzen is o*nly seemingly the same for Kriemhilt as for Etzel. Etzel needs a queen, Kriemhilt needs a powerful ruler. Replacement in the ruling group apparently does not include that of personal bonds. The *Nibelungenlied* does not yet have a language for this, but the split is nevertheless clearly marked.[68] Where the personal component of the loss is meant, *ergetzen* proves itself to be insufficient. It is precisely this that is scandalous in the predominant perspective of the Nibelungian world and therefore finally unthinkable.

Rüedeger asks: *Waz mac ergetzen leides . . . / wan friuntlîche liebe . . . unt der dan einen kiuset, der im ze rehte kumt* [What can compensate for suffering . . . / except kind love . . . and if one chooses somebody who is right for one] (1234,1–3). How little individualized personal relationships are taken into account is shown in that this sober recommendation even neutralizes the gender difference: "one" has to choose someone, *der im ze rehte kumt.*[69] Hagen assumes the exchangeability of persons even more radically when he remembers Sivrit:

> *er lît vor manigem jâre ze tôde erslagene.*
> *den künec von den Hiunen sol si nu holden haben.* (1725,2–3)
>
> [He was slain many years ago.
> She ought to love the king of the Huns.]

Kriemhilt, on the other hand, questions the notion of so easily substituting one person for another. She starts by asking Rüedeger of Etzel:

> *waz sold' ich einem man,*
> *der ie herzeliebe von guotem wîbe gewan?* (1218,3–4)
>
> [What would I be to a man,
> who had ever gained the true love of a noble woman?]

When this notion is rejected, she speaks for herself:

> *wær' iemen der bekande miniu scharpfen sêr,*
> *der bœte mich niht triuten noch deheinen man.*
> *jâ verlôs ich ein den besten, den ie vrouwe gewan.* (1233,2–4)

[If anyone knew how much I still ache,
he would not ask me to love another man.
Really, I lost the best husband that a woman ever had.]

And against Rüedeger's objection:

wie möhte mînen lîp
immer des gelusten, daz ich wurde heldes wîp?
mir hât der tôt an einem sô rehte leit getân,
des ich unz an mîn ende muoz unvrœlîche stân. (1238)

[Why should I ever
desire to become a hero's wife?
The death of one hurt me so much,
that I must remain without joy until the end of my days.]

Rüedeger's rhetoric about *ergetzen* is thus lost on her. We have seen how other aspects of *ergetzen* surface in Kriemhilt's reflections: *ergetzen* through wealth is possible; *ergetzen* in the shape of a person is impossible; *ergetzen* through revenge remains (1259,4).[70] What external compensation cannot resolve comes together in the plan for vengeance.

Whereas satisfaction requires in principle that hatred (*haz*) comes to an end,[71] Kriemhilt's assertion of lifelong *leit* excludes this possibility. That the rules of *ergetzen* do not count for Kriemhilt as for others makes her unpredictable and allows her brothers to fall naïvely into the trap of the invitation. At the end of the battle, when Dietrich hands over the archenemy to Kriemhilt, she has achieved her goal, but in a sense that is different than the others' understanding of *ergetzen*:

immer sî dir sælic dîn herze und ouch dîn lîp.
du hâst mich wol ergetzet aller mîner nôt.
daz sol ich immer dienen, mich ensûmes der tôt. (2354,2–4)

[Blessed be your heart and person.
You have well compensated me for all my suffering.
For this I shall always serve you unless death prevents it.]

This *ergetzen* allows for the execution of Gunther and the beheading of Hagen.

The *Klage* restores the normalcy of recompense, as the others assume it to be. By enthroning a son, Gunther is replaced, and Prünhilt is compensated for her *leit*:

so ergetzet iuch daz kindelîn
und uns der grôzen leide. (Kl 3758–59)

[The child will compensate you
and us for that great suffering.]

This denies the validity of the *Nibelungenlied*'s position.

Gruoz

Formal greeting (*gruoz*) implies the promise of peaceful interaction.[72] The ritual of *gruoz* makes social order visible. It is staged in elaborate ways: *Wir suln den herren enpfâhen deste baz* [we should receive the lord all the better] (101,1), because the reception deflects aggression: *daz wir iht verdienen des jungen recken haz* [so that we do not earn the young warrior's enmity] (101,2).[73] Sivrit's martial attitude (*er stêt in strîtes vâr* [he is standing ready for combat], 102,2) is answered by a particularly honorable greeting. One goes toward the guest, as is appropriate to his royal rank, greets him (*nu sî uns willekomen* [you are welcome here], 104,1), and receives him with *zühten* [social grace] (105,2). Sivrit can be placated by the repetition of the *gruoz* and honorable reception at court: *Ir sult uns wesen willekomen* [you are welcome to us] (126,1).

Gruoz manages peaceful interaction, even where a violent conflict might loom on the horizon. Of the Saxon messengers who declare war, it is said: *Der künec si gruozte scône, er sprach: "sît willekomen . . ."* [The king greeted them courteously and said: "you are welcome . . . "] (142,1). Even more ceremonial is Kriemhilt's greeting of Sivrit after his victory over the Saxons, a celebratory ritual that is planned as a reward for his labor (*sîn swester sol iuch grüezen; daz ist zen êren iu getân* [his sister will greet you; this is done to honor you], 290,4) and executed formally: *"sît willekomen, her Sîvrit, ein edel riter guot"* [you are welcome, lord Sivrit, noble knight] (292,3). The political ritual also has a personal, but likewise conventional meaning for the participants. It is the *gruoz* of the beloved *vrouwe* for the questing knight: *dô wart im von dem gruoze vil wol gehœhet der muot* [by the greeting his spirits were lifted] (292,4).

The *gruoz* fails for the first time as a mirror of order at the arrival in Isenstein. Prünhilt greets—again formally—the wrong man and has to be set right; it is not Sivrit but Gunther who must be greeted. When Sivrit brings the Nibelungen, Prünhilt remains doubtful: *sol ich die geste enpfâhen oder sol ich grüezen si verdagen?* [should I receive the guests or should I refuse to greet them?] (510,4). Not until she is asked by Gunther to do so does she greet the new arrivals: *Sîfride mit dem gruoze si von den anderen schiet* [she greeted Sivrit separately from the others] (511,4), but Prünhilt's question shows that the order of greeting has become uncertain.

This continues in Worms. The *gruoz* (591,1) for Prünhilt is an endless succession of kisses and other honorifics between the women, but strangely enough Sivrit is absent.[74] Until Prünhilt's discovery that the *man* Sivrit has been married to the king's daughter, Sivrit's place in courtly society is not discussed. When Sivrit and Kriemhilt come to Gunther's festival, the *grüezen* (786,4) is already nothing more than a façade of harmony. It surpasses the previous greetings (787,2–3), but above all it provides an opportunity to assess the arrivals skeptically (799; 803).

The *suone* after Sivrit's death attempts to reinstate the order via the greeting ritual, as is evident in Kriemhilt's declaration: *Ich wil den künic grüezen* [I'll greet the king] (1113,1). After the theft of the hoard, the ritual of the *gruoz* becomes marginal. There are still models of perfect reception, such as the kings' *gruoz* for Rüedeger: *Dô nigen im die recken mit triuwen âne haz* [the warriors bowed to him with goodwill and loyalty] (1657,1), or Rüedeger's *gruoz* of the Burgundian retinue: *besunder gruozte er Hagenen: den het er ê bekant. / alsam tet er Volkêrn* [he greeted Hagen specially: he had known him before. / He did likewise to Volker] (1657,3–4), or that of the Amelungen for Etzel's guests (*si gruozten minneclîchen die von Burgonden lant* [they lovingly greeted those from Burgundy], 1722,4). Etzel's greeting also still points to a peaceful accord, even if he expresses a difference in rank to the Burgundian kings by not going toward them.[75] He honors them, however, with a staged spontaneity (*er spranc von sînem sedele . . . ein gruoz sô rehte schœne von künege nie mêr geschach* [he jumped up from his seat . . . there never was a more courteous greeting by a king], 1808,3–4). Otherwise, however, the greeting ritual is perverted.

In the first meeting with Kriemhilt, the *gruoz* barely masks the open hostility. Kriemhilt's *gruoz* is false (*mit valschem muote*, 1737,2). It offers the first occasion for presenting competing demands for payment. It does not unify, it divides, because only Giselher is distinguished. Hagen states:

> *man grüezet sunderlingen di künige und ir man.*
> *wir haben niht guoter reise zuo dirre hôchzît getân.* (1738,3–4)
>
> [The kings and their vassals are greeted differently.
> We were unwise to travel to this celebration.]

This is no longer the rank-based greeting of courtly ceremony (as, for example, in st. 1348), but instead the differentiation between friend and foe. The one king and brother is distinguished from his rank-equal relatives. With such a greeting (*sus getânen gruoze*, 1737,4), caution is the watchword. Kriemhilt's greeting formula does not welcome the Burgundians and denies them the title *vriunt*. She thereby revokes what the *gruoz* otherwise effects:

> *Si sprach: "nu sît willekomen swer iuch gerne siht.*
> *durch iuwer selbes friuntschaft grüeze ich iuch niht."* (1739,1–2)
>
> [She said: "Be welcomed by someone who is happy to see you.
> I do not greet you as friends."

The reversal of *gruoz* into aggression is repeated when Hagen and Volker refuse courteous respect to Kriemhilt (1780–82). Kriemhilt answers with her own provocation, with a *vîentlîchen gruoz* [a greeting as an enemy] (1786,4) that reverses the usual intent of a *gruoz*. The reception by the royal couple is still ambiguous. The intact hierarchical order reflected in Etzel's *gruoz* will not survive the upcoming battles. Kriemhilt's verbal aggression will turn into a direct one.

At the procession to the church, the *gruoz* becomes a measuring stick of violence: *und geltet ob iu iemen biete swachen gruoz* [strike back if anyone greets you poorly] (1858,2), retaliation instead of reciprocal esteem. Then the façade falls down altogether. Dancwart's greeting for Blœdelin: *willekomen her ze hûse* [welcome here in this house] (1922,3) already rests on a misunderstanding, because Blœdelin comes with hostile intent and rejects the greeting (*Jane darftu mich niht grüezen* [you should not greet me] 1923,1). Instead of greetings, there is a bloody battle.

Only when everything is over does Kriemhilt return to the greeting ritual, but in plain contempt, when she addresses the bound Gunther formally: *willekomen Gunther ûzer Burgonden lant* [welcome, Gunther, from Burgundy] (2362,4). The *gruoz* shows open aggression (*zornec gemuot*) instead of receptivity (*genædelîche[]*), and so Gunther does not return this insincere greeting (*swache[] grüezen*, 2363,4), but takes her words ironically: *ich solt' iu nîgen, vil liebiu swester mîn* [I should bow to you, dear sister] (2363,1).[76]

The gestures of familiar closeness that accompany the *gruoz* have also lost their meaning: holding hands expresses a recognition of equal status, friendship, and peace.[77] When Kriemhilt recognizes Sivrit in front of the court as victor, she takes him *bî der hende* [by the hand] (293,1). Her bond to Giselher is expressed in a dream. She imagines that he *gienge vil dicke an der hant* [very often walked hand in hand with her] (1393,2). Taking another's hand is a sign of respect: *dô nam der wirt vil edele die lieben geste bî der hant* [the noble host took his dear guests by the hand] (1811,4), or honors the guest in general:

Diu junge marcgrâvinne diu nam bî der hant
Gîselher den recken von Burgonden lant.
alsam tet ouch ir muoter Gunther den küenen man. (1667,1–3)

[The young margravine took Giselher
by the hand, the warrior from Burgundy.
Her mother did the same with Gunther, the bold man.]

Harmony between different groups is expressed in this gesture:

Daz hêrliche gesinde daz vie sich bi der hant. (794,1)

[The splendid companions took each other's hands.]

Bî henden sich dô viengen zwêne degene:
Daz eine was her Dietrîch, daz ander Hagene. (1750,1–2)

[Two warriors took each other's hands:
The one was Dietrich, the other Hagen.]

Der fürste von Berne der nam an die hant
Gunthern den vil rîchen von Burgonden lant,
Irnfrit nam Gêrnôten, den vil küenen man.
dô sach man Rüedegêren ze hove mit Gîselheren gân. (1804)

[The prince of Bern took by the hand
the mighty Gunther of Burgundy,
Irnfrit took Gernot's hand, the bold man.
Rüedeger was seen walking with Giselher to court.]

Once the conflict has broken out, these kinds of gestures disappear. They only return, like the *gruoz*, as a parody. Only at the very end, when Dietrich has bound the beaten Gunther (*swie künege niene solden lîden solhiu bant* [even if no king should ever be made to suffer such bonds], 2361,2), Dietrich takes Gunther *bî der hant*, but now in order to lead him as a prisoner to Kriemhilt (2362,1). The gesture of trust and friendship is belied by the shackles.

Carrying Arms

Weapons are assigned to certain spaces; in others, they are unwelcome. Weapons must be carried, as would be expected, "outside," at war, on dangerous journeys, and on the hunt. They are undesirable at court. Strangers are therefore relieved of their weapons as a sign that they are welcome and have nothing to fear. When, in *Âventiure* 3, the danger of confrontation is averted and Sivrit is taken in at the court, it is stated: *Dô hiez man in gehalten allez ir gewant* [all of their gear was put away] (128,1). This is what usually happens.

In two cases, it does not succeed so easily, and both times, a future conflict is indicated. At the reception of the Burgundians in Isenstein, a chamberlain tries to take the weapons away from the arrivals. Hagen refuses: *wir wellens' selbe tragen* [we'll carry them ourselves] (406,3) and only reluctantly gives in (407,4) when Sivrit, the only one who knows, tells him *diu rehten mære* [what is correct here] (406,4):

> *Man pfliget in dirre bürge, daz wil ich iu sagen,*
> *daz neheine geste hie wâfen sulen tragen* (407,1–2)
>
> [This is the custom in this castle, and so I should inform you,
> that no guests are allowed to carry weapons here.]

The laying down of weapons usually means that a space of peace is guaranteed in the court, but the prohibition on weapons at Isenstein apparently has another meaning. The court of Isenstein is the site of a deadly contest. The life of all arrivals is in danger. Carrying weapons would offer a chance for self-defense or revenge. The prohibition therefore expresses the opposite of what is normally the case: the goal is not to secure the peace but to disarm potential enemies.

Aside from this, weapons would be useless at this court. This becomes apparent when Dancwart and Hagen lament that they are without their weapons when their king is engaged in the dangerous contest (444–46), and Prünhilt derisively and contemptuously (*mit smielendem munde* and *über ahsel* [with a smile and over her shoulder], 447,2) orders that they be given back their weapons. It is the hero's advice that disarms the Burgundians, and it is the *vrouwe* who condescendingly gives them back their weapons. In Isenstein, the normal means of heroic self-assertion are useless. As it turns out, the weapons are not used, because Sivrit's victory and then later his men (477) make them unnecessary. Why then the back and forth? The disarming uncovers the latent violence, and the return of the weapons shows that any defense would be futile. This time, all trepidation is needless, because Sivrit, and he alone, is up to the task, albeit only in secret.

Isenstein shows the limited range of courtly pacification. Carrying arms or not in a world like Isenstein is simply irrelevant. Things are completely different at Etzel's court. The invitation of relatives to a celebration would normally be a peaceful event, and weapons should normally not be necessary. In reality, it turns into a fight to the death, and it is better to be cautious. The conflict over weapons reflects this ambiguity. The *vrouwe* of the court has to receive the guests, but the way Kriemhilt plays this role is purely contemptuous. Her demand for the weapons sounds like a command to disarm an enemy rather than courtly protocol:

> *"man sol deheiniu wâfen tragen in den sal.*
> *ir helde, ir sult mirs' ûf geben: ich wil si behalten lân."*
> *"entriuwen," sprach dô Hagene, "daz wirdet nimmer getân."* (1745,2–4)

> ["No one shall carry weapons into the hall.
> You heroes, you must give them to me: I'll order them to be kept."
> "I swear," spoke Hagen, " that will never happen."]

Hagen, like Kriemhilt, is not concerned with courtly interaction, but instead with an advantage in the upcoming battle. Hagen mocks the queen with his courtly correct, exaggerated refusal (1746).[78] Weapons have their place at this festivity [*hôhgezît*].

The break with convention is increased at the procession to the church, to which Hagen advises the Burgundians to carry heavy equipment: *sît daz wir wol erkennen der argen Kriemhilden muot* [since we know Kriemhilt's evil intent] (1853,4). The sign is unambiguous—normally, the church is a place of peace—and is immediately understood. Etzel surmises, when he sees his *friunde . . . under helme gân* [friends . . . completely armed] (1861,3), that they were treated as enemies. He claims that their *leit* is also his, and he wants to grant them satisfaction (1862). Hagen, however, explains this break with convention as a Burgundian custom:

> *es ist site mîner herren, daz si gewâfent gân*
> *z'allen hôhgezîten ze vollen drîen tagen.* (1863,2–3)

> [It is the custom of my lords that they go fully armed
> to all celebrations for a full three days.]

He manages to fool Etzel, but lets Kriemhilt—who has never heard about this custom—know that he has understood the true character of the *hôhgezît.*

Carrying arms is still one-sided. But after Volker has taken the *kurzewîle* [entertainment] at the play of the horses (1882,1) as an excuse for violence, the opposing side also wants to arm itself:

> *Nâch swerten und nâch schilden riefen dâ zehant*
> *des marcgrâven mâge von der Hiunen lant.*
> *si wolden Volkêren ze tôde erslagen hân.* (1893,1–3)

> [They shouted for their swords and shields,
> the kinsmen of the margrave in the Huns' land.
> They wanted to kill Volker.]

They can only be disarmed with force by the king one last time: *ein vil starkez wâfen brach er im ûz der hant* [he struck a heavy weapon out of his hand] (1895,2). Peace can only be maintained through the use of force.

Blœdelin disregards the king's prohibition on weapons: *Nu wâfent iuch . . . alle die ich hân* [now arm yourselves . . . all my men] (1910,1). At his attack of the servants, the attackers are armed, whereas the defenders have to, in part (*Die niht swert enhêten* [those who had no sword], 1931,1), defend themselves with stools and chairs. At the following feast, it is the reverse. The dining Huns are slaughtered by the armed Burgundians. No one helps them from outside, and their defense is futile.[79]

After the outbreak of the fighting, rules lose all authority. Men arm themselves openly (2028,4 and elsewhere). Only Rüedeger and Dietrich remain unarmed at first, in order to stay aloof from the conflict, but both do so in vain. Dietrich orders the Amelungen to approach the Burgundians without their weapons. Hildebrant, too, wants to go unarmed *in sînen zühten zuo den gesten* [as a courtesy to his guests] (2248,3). But this might collide with *êre* and the hero's need to prove himself. Wolfhart considers in an exchange of words that it might be dishonorable to be without arms:

> *sô müezet ir lasterlîchen tuon die widervart.*
> *komt ir dar gewâfent, daz etelîcher wol bewart.* (2249,3–4)

> [Then you will be forced to retreat in a shameful way
> If you go there fully armed, we'll all avoid this.]

Wolfhart's advice is unsound, but Hildebrant follows it anyway: *Dô garte sich der wîse durch des tumben rât* [then the experienced man armed himself following the young man's counsel] (2250,1). The armed entrance of the Amelungen is taken as an attack by the Burgundians (2252–3), and so the last remnants of courtly order fall apart.

Dringen *and* schal

The perversion of courtly forms of interaction is also evident in *dringen* [crowding]. In the first part of the epic, *dringen* is an expression of joyous excitement. The king, a guest or messenger, the lady: in the middle is the person on whom all eyes are set. *Dringen* expresses the worth of a person or the importance of an event.[80] Occasionally, crowding is explained by a large number of people (512), but then, too, it is an expression of courtly effusion. In the crowd at the *buhûrt*, for example, a feeling of excessive strength can play itself out (585,4). There is a *gedranc* at Mass (33,2; 644,4), at the reception (788,4: *dringen unde stouben kunde niemen dâ bewarn* [no one could prevent the crowding and the dust]), and at Sivrit's funeral, where it demonstrates great devotion:

> *Dô man daz gehôrte, daz man zem münster sanc,*
> *unt man in gesarket hête, dô huop sich grôz gedranc.* (1052,1–2)
>
> [When they heard the singing coming from the church,
> and he was put in a coffin, there was a great outcry.]

Of course, there is also crowding and noise in battle (204), but even then it expresses above all exorbitant heroic strength.

At first, the throng is controlled. Where ladies appear, crowds are waved aside, so as to let them pass unhindered:

> *Die mit den frouwen giengen, die hiezen von den wegen*
> *wîchen allenthalben. daz leiste manec degen.* (287,1–2)
>
> [Those who escorted the ladies told the others
> to open the way. All the warriors obeyed.]

At Kriemhilt's appearance in Passau, *wart vil michel wîchen an der selben stunt* [many gave way immediately] (1312,3). How large the crowd is is evident from the kind of control exercised. If the turbulence at a celebration becomes disruptive, then it is ended (598).

This changes in the second part of the epic. Newcomers are surrounded by crowds as objects of curiosity, as before, but the *dringen* is suspected to be merely a pretext for something else, namely, treason. Volker suddenly sees the crowd as something aggressive when *in grôzem antpfange* [at the solemn reception] (1802,3), he asks his lord: *wie lange welt ir stên, / daz ir iuch lâzet dringen* [how long are you going to stand there / and let yourself get pushed around?] (1803,1–2). It is dangerous and not a sign of friendly disposition.[81] Even after the friendly reception by Etzel, *dringen* is experienced as oppressive: *Dringen allenthalben die geste man dô sach* [the guests were seen to be crowded] (1820,1). Volker again states indignantly: *wie geturret ir den recken für die füeze gân?* [how dare you step on the warriors' toes] (1820,3) and *wan wîchet ir uns recken?* [why don't you give way to us warriors?] (1821,3). He threatens: *und welt irs iuch niht mîden, sô wirt iu leide getân* [if you won't refrain from doing so, you'll be struck] (1820,4). *Dringen* now represents a threat to life and limb.[82]

The throng at the church procession is latently violent. Honor is supposed to express itself through feats of arms and making way, not giving an inch: *Leget, mîne friunde, die schilde für den fuoz* [My friends, put down your shields at your feet] (1858,1). A clash is practically planned. Hagen and Volker go in front of the church:

> *daz si daz wolden wizzen,*[83] *daz des küneges wîp*
> *müese mit in dringen; jâ was vil grimmec ir lîp.* (1859,3–4)
>
> [For they wanted to make sure that the king's wife
> would have to crowd in with them; they were utterly furious.]

Actually, when the queen appears with her entourage, there is not only a noisy and impressive entrance, as has been often described before (*dô kôs man hôhe stouben von den Kriemhilde scharn* [a dust cloud rose above Kriemhilt's throng], 1860,4),[84] but almost a violent collision, since the procession meets resistance:

> *done wolden dise zwêne doch niht hôher stân*
> *zweier hande breite. daz was den Hiunen leit.*
> *jâ muose si sich dringen mit den helden gemeit.* (1866,2–4)
>
> [The two men were not about to stand aside
> even two breadths of a hand. This was distressful to the Huns.
> Really, they had to crowd in with the heroes.]

Dringen is no longer an expression of festive joy, but an opportunity for an unexpected collision (1867; cf. 1859,4). The narrator even seems a little disappointed when the violence latent in *dringen* fails to break out:

> *dâ was vil michel dringen unde doch niht anders mêr.* (1867,4)
>
> [They pushed and shoved but nothing more.]

When later someone must *wîchen* or *hôher stân*, then it is only under duress, namely, to avoid violence. Dancwart chases away the Huns by saying *nu lât daz dreuwen und wîchet hôher baz* [stop your threatening and move aside more] (1943,1), and of Volker it is told: *den Etzelen man / gab er herberge hôher von dem sal* [he forced Etzel's men / to withdraw themselves further away from the hall] (2018,2–3).

Similarly, *schal* no longer accompanies just courtly sport (*der bûhurt unt daz schallen*, 1872,2) as a sign of excessive self-esteem. The "representative *schal*" is "an expression of mighty rule; in battle, the claim to superior strength is expressed in *schal*; the *schal* represents rule."[85] Berhtunc in *Wolfdietrich*, for example, allows no one to act more conspicuously than he does (*nieman dâ überschallen*, Wo A 137,4; 141,3; 203,3), that is, his appearance at court must trump all others.[86] *Schal* expresses *kurzewîle* (947,1; 950,4), not only the courtly festival, with its clash of weapons and festive music (686,2; 807,2; 808,2), but the splendid reception (797; 800,1) and the relaxation of the hunt (941,2).

In the second part, the meaning changes gradually. At first, *schal* is just a joyous noise, but then a sense of regret is mixed in:

> *Swes iemen dâ pflæge, sô was ez niwan schal.* (1881,1)
>
> [Whatever they did, it was just a lot of noise.]

But what one moment is still "nothing more than *schal*" suddenly becomes the din of battle and cries of pain. When Blœdelin promises: *sô heb' ich einen schal* [then I'll raise the alarm] (1909,2), he announces a bloody attack that leads to further bloodshed: *Dô huop sich von den liuten allenthalben schal* [there a great noise was made by the people all around] (1894,1). The clash of weapons turns into the *schal* of crying: *von wuofe grœzlîchen schal* [a great sound of wailing] (1972,4).[87] Dietrich laments the loss of his men:

> *daz daz hûs erdiezen von sîner stimme began.* (2324,4)
>
> [The house began to echo with his voice.]

The *grœzlîche[] schal* [loud noise] (2357,4) of the fight between Dietrich and Gunther shakes the entire castle: *palas unde türne von den slegen dôz* [the palace and the towers resounded from the blows] (2359,2).

Once this *schal* comes to an end, it is followed, not by rest, but instead by an unnatural, deadly *stille*:

> *des was der schal geswiftet, daz iemen mit in streit.* (2008,3)
>
> [Therefore the noise had ceased, because nobody fought them anymore.]
>
> *Dar nâch wart ein stille, dô der schal verdôz.* (2078,1)
>
> [There followed a silence, since the noise had subsided.]
>
> *dâ wâren tôt gelegen*
> *die Rüedegêres helde. vergangen was der dôz.*
> *sô lange wert' diu stille daz sîn Etzeln verdrôz.* (2227,2–4)
>
> [There lay dead
> Rüedeger's heroes. The noise had subsided.
> The silence lasted so long that Etzel became concerned.]

There is no return to the joyous noise of the beginning. The only thing that is heard is *jâmer alsô grôz, / daz palas unde türne von dem wuofe erdôz* [a great lamenting, / so that the palace and the towers echoed with the wailing] (2235,1–2). Then it is all over.

Rest and gâhen

This gradual transition is accompanied by an acceleration of movements, both in narration and in the narrated events.[88] When at the beginning, the action accelerates in phases, starting in *Âventiure* 3, it always finds its way back to rest. The static, quiet, or quickly quieted movement of the epic's first part succumbs to the turbulence of the catastrophe.

At Sivrit's challenge of the Worms court, the antagonists stand as if frozen:

> *Mit grimmigem muote dâ stuonden friwende sîn.* (116,1)
>
> [His friends stood there with furious intent.]

Before the scene can lead to tumult (*Nâch swerten rief dô sêre von Metzen Ortwîn* [Ortwin of Metz called urgently for swords], 119,1), Gernot forbids his men their ever increasingly hot-headed speech. They seem paralyzed in their actions as well. Sivrit asks:

> *War umbe bîtet Hagene und ouch Ortwîn,*
> *daz er niht gâhet strîten mit den friwenden sîn . . . ?* (125,1–2)
>
> [Why are Hagen and Ortwin waiting,
> why don't they enter the battle with their friends . . . ?]

Raw impulse (*gâhet strîten*) is repressed, and the men wait tensely (*bîtet*). Sivrit is calmed by Gunther's courtliness and from now rests motionless in the melancholic pose of a seemingly hopeless *minne.* Time stands still:

> *Sus wont' er bî den herren, daz ist alwâr,*
> *in Gunthers lande volleclîch ein jâr.* (138,1–2)
>
> [Thus he lived with the lords, that is true,
> in Gunther's land for a full year.]

In the Saxon war, the movement quickens (*man hiez die boten balde . . .* [the messengers were quickly called for . . .], 141,4; *dô îlten si de friwende deste mêr bejagen* [they hurried to call more friends], 169,2), especially when the armies meet: *Zen rossen gâhte Gêrnôt unde sîne man* [Gernot and his men went quickly on horse] (196,1): noise, dust, large contingents, stroke and counter-stroke, weapons and pieces of armor flying all around, in short: a *sturm[]* (210,4), then again measured movements of courtly ceremony, with Sivrit frozen in an idyllic picture:

> *Dô stuont sô minneclîche daz Sigmundes kint,*
> *sam er entworfen wære an ein permint*
> *von guotes meisters listen* . . . . (286,1–3)
>
> [Sigmund's son stood there so handsomely,
> as if he had been painted on parchment
> by a great master's art . . .]

Again, a quiet time of unknown duration follows, until the rhythm picks up with the departure to see Prünhilt. The tempo quickens from the council of the heroes to the seven-week-long *unmuoze* of the women (366,2–3), the quick leave-taking and the fast journey, to the appearance before Prünhilt. Once the suitor has been determined, everything proceeds quickly: *der spile bat si gâhen* [she commanded that the games begin immediately] (428,2), so quickly, in fact, that Sivrit, who has *vil schiere* [quickly] (431,4–5) slipped on the cloak of invisibility, can claim to have missed the contest. The competition is described as a sequence of fast movements (461,1; 462,1; etc.). The highlight is Sivrit's swift journey to Nibelungenland (483,3). Then the movements slow down again until the uneventful, peaceful life in Worms and Xanten.[89] The new conflict, long and patiently prepared, only slowly emerges from the seemingly harmless duration of time (*z'allen zîten* [at all times], 720,1; *z'allen stunden* [at every hour], 720,3). The conflict of rank, the confrontation in front of the church, the judicial proceedings, all are developed out of the quiet of watching the tourney, all in the measured tempo of a ritualized test: an undecided state, during which the treachery can be planned.

For the first time, tempo and violence are connected in the murderous intrigue. The details of chronology become more precise the further the plan is developed: *An dem vierden morgen* [on the fourth morning] (877,1)—measured starting when?—; *Eines tages* [one day] (883,1); *dô gie von Tronege Hagene* [Hagen of Troneck went] (891,3); *Des andern morgens* [the next morning] (907,1); *vil vruo* [very early] (912,2). The movement forward only seems to halt when the fake war against the Saxons is replaced by the peaceful entertainment of a hunt. Sivrit surpasses everyone, even the prey, in speed. His successes at the hunt grow in an ever-increasing tempo until the footrace with Gunther, at the end of which he is killed.

The rapid movement continues in Kriemhilt's wild pain (1007,4; 1009,4), in the hurried reactions of those from Xanten (*spranc, zuhten, liefen* [jumped, jerked around, ran], 1021,103; *jane mohten si der sinne vor leide niht gehaben* [they had lost their senses from sorrow], 1022,3), in the *wuofe* [wailing] (1025,3), the hasty desire for revenge (*dô îlten nâch den wâfen alle Sîfrides man* [all of Sivrit's men ran to get their weapons], 1027,4) and Sigemunt's hasty departure (*dô wart ein michel gâhen nâch rossen getân* [many ran to get their horses], 1076,2).

After the reconciliation, the pace of events quickens only for a short while, then comes to a halt. Again there is a standstill: thirteen years of mourning after Sivrit's death (1142,2), seven and then again six years at Etzel's side. Kriemhilt's journey to Etzel's court proceeds quietly. Only the king is in a hurry: *der künic begonde gâhen da er di wolgetânen vant* [the king began to hurry to where he found the beautiful woman] (1337,4). Once again there is quiet after the marriage. Only in *Âventiure* 23 does the vortex of the downfall increase. Without any real reason, it is said of Kriemhilt's invitation and embassy to her relatives: *des man dô gâhen began* [therefore they hurried then] (1423,4). The departure of the messengers is delayed in Worms in order to stop what is then ultimately an inexorable development (1480). Then they quickly return (*îlten*, 1494,4; *gâhen*, 1497,1).

The quick, determined movement becomes unstoppable at Etzel's court. Before this, there are only single episodes that—as latent sources of conflict—disrupt the equilibrium of an ideal state. After crossing the boundary to open violence, these interruptions are more and more obviously in vain. Only when everything has been destroyed will a permanent quiet settle in.

From the beginning, control over movements is lost. The first confrontations are still restrained in their movement: Hagen and Volker in front of Kriemhilt, the night attack of the Huns that is stopped even before it can begin, and so on. With only the slightest reason for violence at the *bûhurt*, Hagen and his men dive into the fray *vil harte hurteclîche* [in a great rush] (1890,1). Etzel's quick intervention—*der wirt ûz einem venster vil harte gâhen began* [the host rushed from his place in the window] (1893,4)—imposes quiet once more. The next time, at the attack on the servants, this fails: *mit ûf erburten swerten si sprungen für diu kint* [with swords raised high they rushed toward the pages] (1929,3). At the feast, everyone jumps into the brawl, continuing this furious movement (*springen*).[90]

This goes on in the whirl of destruction. Etzel has to be pulled back by the strap of his shield to keep him out of the fight, a movement that can only be stopped from the outside (2022,3). Irinc's battle is a series of strong attacks, all of them broken off as quickly as they begin: he *lief . . . vaste* [he ran quickly] (2037,3); *gâhen er began* [he began to run] (2040,2); *dô lief er Guntheren . . . an* [he ran toward Gunther] (2041,4); *lief Gêrnôten an* [he ran toward Gernot] (2043,1). *Dô spranc er von dem fürsten* [he leaped in front of the princes] (2044,1); then Giselher attacks and wounds him: *Wie rehte tobelîche er ûz dem bluote spranc* [raving wildly he jumped out of the blood] (2050,1); *dô lief er ûz dem hûse da er aber Hagenen vant* [then he ran out of the building where he encountered Hagen again] (2050,3). The movements are all for naught: *Irinc der lie Hagenen unverwundet stân* [Irinc left Hagen without having wounded him] (2040,1); *den liez er dô belîben* [he left him standing there] (2041,3); *Gunthern er lie belîben* [he left Gunther there] (2043,1); *Dô spranc er von dem fürsten* [then he leaped away from the princes] (2044,1); *Wider zuo den sînen kom Irinc wol gesunt* [Irinc returned to his side quite unhurt] (2054,1). The battle escalates to mad raving (*tobelîche*, 2050,1), a wild tumult, which returns to its starting point, Hagen, but ultimately fails.[91]

Rüedeger's final battle also escalates from a standstill (*stân*, 2138,1) into a frenzy:

> *des muotes er ertobete, done beit er dâ niht mêr,*
> *dô lief er zuo den gesten einem degen gelîch.*
> *manegen slac vil swinden sluoc der marcgrâve rîch.* (2206,2–4)
>
> [his mind raged, then he could wait no longer there,
> he ran toward the guests like a hero should.
> The powerful margrave landed many swift blows.]

Abrupt movements characterize the battle: *sprungen* (2209,1); *brast* (2209,4); *sluogen . . . vaste* (2210,1–3); *sprungen* (2211,2); *spranc* (2212,2); *reis* (2213,3); *gie wider unde dan* (2213,1); *dô sprungen zuo ein ander* (2218,3). At the end, instead of quiet, there is only deadly silence and the complete exhaustion of the survivors. They can no longer stand upright once the battle is over—*müezec* [idle] is the word used by the narrator, in one of his rare touches of irony: *Den sitzen, disen leinen sah man manegen degen. / si wâren aber müezec* [some warriors were seen to be sitting, others leaning; / they were idle again] (2227,1–2).

When Rüedeger is lamented noisily, a *Dietrîches man* (2235,3) hurries to his lord: *wie balde er gâhen began* [he raced off immediately] (2235,4). The pace of destruction increases once more. Dietrich warns his men in vain about brusque reactions: *nu gâhet niht ze sêre* [don't rush off too quickly] (2238,2), but in the dispute between Burgundians and Amelungen, calm is lost. It escalates more and more, until finally, Wolfhart rushes in and all follow him.

> *Im wart ein gæhez volgen von sînen vriunden getân.* (2273,4)
>
> [His friends followed his lead in a great hurry.]

Even the old Hildebrant, on whose calmness Dietrich had counted, jumps in even faster than Wolfhart:

> *Swie wîter sprunge er pflæge für des sales want,*
> *doch ergâhte in vor der stiege der alte Hildebrant* (2274,1–2)
>
> [Even if he (Wolfhart) jumped far to come to the wall of the hall,
> the old Hildebrant reached the stairs first.]

not to hold him back, but to be the first one to start fighting.

There are two aspects combined in *gâhen*: the increase of tempo and unconscious recklessness. A fury breaks out (2280,4); 2282,1), and in the end only three fighters remain, one of them merely because he flees in time.

The raging continues to the final fight: *Gunther was sô sêre erzürnet und ertobt* [Gunther was completely furious and raging] (2358,2), and Hildebrant's last deed is sheer wild movement:

> *Hildebrant mit zorne zuo Kriemhilde spranc.* (2376,1)
>
> [Hildebrant jumped toward Kriemhilt in a rage.]

Gâhen becomes a senseless frenzy.

8 The Failure of the Courtly Alternative

The ambivalent norms, behavioral patterns, and social orders of the Nibelungian world make the epic seem out of place in the world around 1200. Most radically ambiguous is the courtly ideal as it is formed in the beginning and destroyed in the end. A conflict between different models of nobility is by no means foreign to the literature of the twelfth and thirteenth centuries. How the courtly world and untamed heroism relativize each other is demonstrated above all in the epics of Wolfram von Eschenbach, but also in the versions of the *Rosengarten* epic, here from a heroic perspective.[1] It would be too simple, however, to speak of the confrontation of two worlds, one critical of the other.[2] This would presume the homogeneity of these worlds. I shall show how heterogeneous ways of life permeate each other,[3] and how they view, contradict, and destroy each other, without the emergence of a single, clear message. There are alternatives at different levels that cross each other in many different ways, combining structural, sociological, and ideological elements and motifs.[4] Some elements point more in the one and some more in the other direction and comment on, question, or undermine each other. Along the way from the first to the last *âventiure,* the light in which they appear changes.[5]

Ze hove: *Ceremony and Displays of Grandeur*

The starting point is an idealized courtly world. What is meant by "courtly" in the *Nibelungenlied*? The court existed long before courtly society, and so there was already a vocabulary derived from the *hove* [court] without any connection to a "new," emphatically "courtly" way of life. The crux of the discussion of what is courtly and what is not lies mostly in the fact that the distinctions between normative and descriptive perspectives, and between the emphatic concept and single phenomena connected to the *curia regis* or *principis*, are not sufficiently drawn.[6]

From the story's first line, the court is the center of government and knightly actions. The power of the Burgundian court is indescribable, but we hear:

> *Von des hoves krefte und von ir wîten kraft,*
> *von ir vil hôhen werdekeit und von ir ritterscaft.* (12,1–2)
>
> [about the court's power and its own great strength,
> about its high esteem and its chivalry.]

Court offices (10–11), which originally related to tasks in the royal household, belong, as shown, to the complex courtly apparatus on which the Burgundian kingdom is based. From the twelfth century on (and in part already earlier), they were institutionalized as honorary offices.[7] In the *Nibelungenlied*, the officeholders—Sindolt, Hunolt, Rumolt, Ortwin—play their assigned roles in celebrations and their preparations, for example, in the receptions of Prünhilt (563; 564; 582; 583) and Sivrit (776; 777), while the *marscalch* Dancwart has to care for the entourage (178,1–2) and the baggage train (1921). The offices are not purely honorary titles, but are connected to actual functions in the royal household, even though the officeholders belong to the ruling elite of Worms. This is evident in the war against the Saxons.[8] Their significance, however, recedes more and more toward the end of the *Nibelungenlied*. In the first part, the distribution of the court offices functions well. In the second part, they disappear with the collapse of institutional guarantees.[9]

Courtly vocabulary is mostly used in unspecific ways. *Hovesite* can mean, as in ms. A, simply a custom that is common at court.[10] The narrator is above all fascinated by the display of courtly life.[11] The court is the place of festive receptions and grand celebrations. A great deal of attention is paid to courtly ceremonies like the greeting ritual. One is informed in great detail who had to kiss whom,[12] or who stands up before whom.[13]

The detail of courtly life is limited mostly to material culture, whose grandeur is endlessly tallied: rich clothes, horses, weapons, precious stones and metals. The much-derided "tailor strophes" are anything but unimportant insertions. They are meant to show courtly abundance and along with this, power and honor. Every adventure is prepared with great material logistics, and by no means just in the atmosphere of Worms. Sivrit even reports on the crude customs in Isenstein:

> *Wât die aller besten die ie man bevant,*
> *die treit man zallen zîten in Prünhilde lant.* (344,1–2)
>
> [The best attire that was ever seen,
> this is worn at all times in Prünhilt's land.]

This is not an inappropriate exaggeration, but a normal expression of the power and splendor of a ruling house.

In the courtly romance, these displays of grandeur recede into the background, because the ethos of an exclusive chivalry, the complex processes of identity formation, and the precarious relationship between individuals and society require greater attention. It is not less present, however. It belongs to the courtly culture of the Middle Ages.[14] In the *Nibelungenlied* that material culture is virtually the only aspect of courtly life.

This reduced concept of the court is typical of medieval heroic epic. "Court" means a distinguished way of life, but above all an amassing of and excessive distribution of wealth. Courtly life can easily receive an ambiguous tinge in this way. In the *Wormser Rosengarten*, for example, it culminates in the opulence of fashion. This is an expression of self-worth (Ro A 178–80) that, in the eyes of others, is in danger of turning into *hôchvart*, or the inconsiderate use of power. This is exactly what the loutish Wolfhart accuses Kriemhilt of when she orders her retinue to dress splendidly (*zieret iuch diu baz* [adorn yourselves], Ro A 178,2; cf. 181).[15]

This kind of grandeur, on the other hand, belongs to a great court and is not necessarily negative. In *Kudrun*, for example, costliness matters more than the concrete description of the luxury of clothing, weapons, equipment, and so on. Courtly standards are mostly determined quantitatively:

> *Hagene sîne frouwen niht unberuochet liez.*
> *baden ze allen zîten er si vlîziclîchen hiez.* (K 162,1–2)
>
> [Hagen did not leave his ladies unattended.
> He had them bathe often and regularly]

A court where people are incessantly bathing (actually, the lord allows the women to bathe) is more "courtly" than others. This display of courtly civilization is certainly connected to courtly peace, as is shown when Kudrun prepares the final alliances. At first, the antagonists have to take a bath and are properly dressed:

> *Kûdrun die helde tougen baden hiez*
> *unde schône kleiden und hin ze hove bringen.* (K 1600,2–3)
>
> [Kudrun secretly ordered that the heroes be bathed
> and dressed properly and brought to court.]

There is definitely an underlying connection between the elements of material culture and the programmatics of courtly ethics. The ethics itself, however, is not directly exhibited in the heroic epic, not even where there is a critique, as in *Kudrun*, of the heroic mechanisms of force.

A central courtly concept such as *fuoge* can be used in all kinds of proportions. For example, it is said of the Saxon army: *daz wider sîner helfe mit unfuoge wac* [it was disproportionately larger than his army] (181,2), that is, there is no relationship (numerically) between its size and that of the Burgundian contingent. It is vastly superior. This says nothing about either side's courtly behavior.[16] When Volker sings the *wegemüeden recken* [travel-weary heroes] (1818,2) to sleep, we read:

> *sîn ellen zuo der fuoge diu beidiu wâren grôz.* (1835,2)
>
> [His strength and delicate sensitivity were both great.]

Fuoge means nothing more than the musician's ability to control beautiful proportions, whereas *ellen* emphasizes his quality as a hero. Both go together, at least in the beginning.

Tournament and Violence

Feudal—heroic and courtly—epic is determined throughout by the principle of the agonal, and the *Nibelungenlied* is no exception.[17] The story runs—typical for a culture of nobility—between war games and military confrontations. Games of chivalry were not invented in the courtly culture of the twelfth and thirteenth centuries, but this is where they become a central pattern of culture. There is a set of rules that is supposed to control their latently violent character and make victory in battle nothing more than a beautiful and innocuous display of force. The *Nibelungenlied* takes part in this cultural pattern, but the controls and thereby the meaning and function of the war games gradually come into question.

In the first part of the epic, the games seem to dominate, whereas in the second part, the fight is to the death. Upon closer examination, however, the differences vanish. This blurs a boundary that is very important for the courtly epic: the distinction between direct and formalized violence,[18] which in turn is overlaid by the distinction between legitimate and illegitimate action.

In the opening scene of the *Nibelungenlied*, direct violence is excluded. Violence belongs to the prehistory of the epic. Burgundian power is firmly established:

> *Von des hoves krefte und von ir wîten kraft,*
> *von ir vil hôhen werdekeit und von ir ritterscaft,*
> *der di herren pflâgen mit vröuden al ir leben,*
> *des enkunde iu ze wâre niemen gar ein ende geben.* (12)
>
> [About the court's power and of their own great strength,
> about their high esteem and their chivalry,
> of whom the lords happily disposed all their lives,
> about all this no one could tell you the true extent completely.]

How that power was raised is in the past, as are the adventures of Sivrit's youth, when he killed the kings of a foreign land and won the crown along with its immense treasure. These events are not clearly situated temporally. They "happened back then" when the narrator begins to tell of the courtly harmony in Worms and Xanten.

Sivrit's first appearance in Worms is intended to force a violent confrontation over rule. Admittedly, it is not, as Sigemunt had suggested, a *hervart* [military campaign] (58,3), but it is already canalized as a duel with a foreign ruler. After a lengthy exchange of words, the tournament replaces the duel. Sivrit throws himself into the games, where he is allowed to display what he could not show in earnest: *sô was er ie der beste swes man dâ began . . . sô sî den stein wurfen oder schuzzen den scaft* [he was the best in whatever was tried . . . when they threw stones or cast spears] (130,2; 130,4).

His superiority has no consequences for the political order, but only increases his reputation. This playful form of agonal confrontation admittedly anticipates a less harmless game later on, because he excels precisely in two of the disciplines in which he must overcome Prünhilt in Isenstein: *sô si den stein wurfen oder schuzzen den scaft* [whenever they hurled stones or threw spears] (130,4). This time, it is still without risk and simply demonstrates strength and agility.

He also does not endanger the political order in Worms when he uses his strength externally in Gunther's service in the war against the Saxons.[19] There he can repeat what he was only allowed to do internally in the form of a regulated game: to be the best in battle. The war proves controllable and leads to a great festival of peace, and chivalric games are again part of it (308). The one conflict is as harmless as the other. The boundary between legitimate and illegitimate combat does not run between game and earnest.

This is confirmed, but now in a problematic way, at Prünhilt's court, where the *driu spil* [three games] that every suitor must play against the queen contain a high degree of risk: *gebrast im an dem einen, er hete daz houbet sîn verloren* [if he failed in any one of them, he lost his head] (327,4). What Prünhilt stages as *spil diu starken* [strong contests] (424,2) aims at real violence: *ez gât im an den lîp* [he will lose his life] (416,3). Such a *spil* is a life-threatening reality,[20] and it therefore causes real dread.[21] As with the combat to which Sivrit challenges Gunther in Worms, the contests are meant to decide who gets wife and rule, and so Prünhilt arms herself *sam ob si solde strîten umb elliu küneges lant* [as if she were fighting for all kingdoms at once] (434,2). Although it is a game, the contest is also a hostile confrontation: *Die zît was disen recken in gelfe vil gedreut* [the warriors were arrogantly threatened all the while] (430,1). In the end, Prünhilt has to become Gunther's wife and to order her people: *ir sult dem künic Gunther alle wesen undertân* [you must all be subjects of King Gunther] (466,4). Her *spil* blur the courtly distinction between real and playful violence. Sivrit is the only one who makes sure that the *spil* remain just a game:

> *Er dâhte: "ich wil niht schiezen daz schœne magedîn."*
> *er kêrte des gêres snîde hinder den rucke sîn.*
> *mit der gêrstangen er schôz ûf ir gewant.* (459,1–3)
>
> [He thought: "I do not want to shoot the pretty maiden."
> He turned the blade of the spear around.
> He threw the spear's shaft at her tunic.]

The boundaries between game and violence are kept intact only with the aid of the *tarnhût*, which is to say, by cheating.

In the bridal quest adventure's second battle in Nibelungenland, the boundaries between game and reality are not clear, but this time for the opposite reason. The combat is serious and is a struggle of life and death, but there is actually nothing at stake, because Sivrit is already the ruler of the land. His opponent threatens his life, but that does not prevent Sivrit from taxing his strength in a manifestly sporting manner:

> *ein teil begonde fürhten Sîfrit den tôt,*
> *dô der pôrtenære sô krefteclîche sluoc.*
> *dar umbe was im wæge sîn herre Sîfrit genuoc.* (491,2–4)

[Sivrit began to fear death a little,
since the gatekeeper hit back so powerfully.
His lord Sivrit was very well-disposed toward him for that.]

A deadly issue is not the attacker's intent: *er schônte sîner zühte al im diu tugent daz gebôt* [he held back because of his courtly behavior as his prowess demanded] (496,4), where sparing the enemy is notably tied to courtly qualities (*zuht, tugent*). Afterwards, everything is shown to have just been a playful contest of strength.

With the return to Worms, the mixing of game and earnest stops. Splendid tournaments (596–98; 646–47) are part of the kings' wedding celebration, as they are when Sivrit and Kriemhilt visit Worms (797; 808–10). But it is expressly on the occasion of *ritterschefte durch kurzewîle wân* [chivalric games for entertainment] (814,3) that the conflict between the queens starts. The situation actually should not permit a competition for rule and usually excludes questions of status, since all the fighters are seen as potentially equal. Nevertheless, the queens' dispute, first concerned with who proves to be the best knight at the tournament, escalates to who is subject to whom, and the nonviolent chivalric games turn into a struggle for power.

Unlike at the end of *Âventiure* 3, the games no longer canalize violence, but instigate it. The game makes it possible to engage in covert hostilities. This is continued in Sivrit's murder, where the frame is a hunt and the occasion is a footrace. The race serves as a pretext to disarm the opponent and so to dispose of him easily. Sivrit wins the race and loses his life; Gunther loses the race and is rid of a dangerous opponent:

ez hât nu allez ende unser sorge unt unser leit.
wir vinden ir vil wênic, die türren uns bestân. (993,2–3)

[Our cares and our suffering have now all come to an end.
We may find very few who dare fight against us.]

The meaning of *bestân* refers both to the (lost) footrace and the (won) power struggle.

In the long agony of Kriemhilt's suffering, chivalric games have no place. They only return at Etzel's court, but ever more overtly as a pretext for provocation. The departure to Etzel's celebration is already akin to a warlike expedition,[22] and as in a war, the Burgundians have to defend their lives. The peaceful contests of strength at Etzel's court become a pretext for violence, first at the tournament [*bûhurt*]. Usually, a *bûhurt* would serve as a demonstration of strength and agility in the cavorting of horses before the court, the ladies, and the king. It is *kurzewîle* [entertainment, fun] (1873,3; 1882,1), a nonviolent simulation of mounted warfare: *des wart von den helden sît vil hêrlîch geriten* [then the heroes demonstrated how magnificently they rode] (1871,4). A *bûhurt rîche[]* was part of the reception of Prünhilt in Worms (584,1; cf. 624). On that occasion, it was also loud with the clashing and din of weapons, and dusty, as if the countryside were in flames (596,3–4). It was under the control of the courtly celebration, however. It is said of Hagen:

den bûhurt minneclîche dô der helt geschiet,
daz si ungestoubet liezen diu vil schœnen kint.
des wart dô von den gesten gevolget güetlîche sint. (598,2–4)

[The hero asked that the tournament kindly be brought to an end,
so that the pretty girls would not all be covered in dust.
This was then amicably agreed to by the guests.]

Interrupting the fun to make room for other entertainment (*kurzewîlen*, 600,2) is easy (598,4), because the *bûhurt* is no more than a game. At Etzel's court, however, it is clear from the beginning that there is a propensity to violence. Everybody can see *daz in ummuote wæren die Guntheres man* [that Gunther's men were upset] (1876,3). The game that avoids violence by simulating violence invites a kind of covert violence.

The game seems to Volker to offer an opportune time to start the battle, an opportunity that is unfortunately missed:

ich wæn' uns dise recken türren niht bestân.
ich hôrt' ie sagen mære, si wæren uns gehaz.
nune kundez sich gefüegen zwâre nimmer mêre baz (1883,2–4)

[I believe that these warriors will not dare attack us.
I have always heard it said that they view us as enemies.
Really, it could not come at a better time than now.]

Again *bestân* oscillates between game and earnest. Shortly thereafter, just the sight of a Hunnish courtier is reason enough for Volker to misuse the playful ostentation as a pretext for violence. Hagen and his men immediately get involved in the *spil* (1890,3), which has already become a battle, and the kings follow suit.

The barriers between simulated and real violence are torn down. The game proves to be just a façade that cannot hold. Its rules are shown to be lies and a cover for intrigue. This blending of games and war is also present elsewhere in heroic parodies of courtly order. In *Rosengarten*,[23] Kriemhilt's invitation to a tournament is characterized as a shameless challenge.[24] Kriemhilt is a bloodthirsty, power-hungry woman—the usual negative image, which the *Klage* tries to correct—whose *hôchvart* (Ro A 173,4; 178,1) subjects itself to the will of men. The application of this image in the *Rosengarten* epic is all the more strange in that Kriemhilt does not hurl entire kingdoms to their doom there but instead simply suggests a test of strength between Rhenish and south-east German heroes. This is defamed as mean-spirited despotism, because Kriemhilt has not been the victim of *leit* (Ro A 188,2)—as if this were the point of a tournament! The difference between game and reality is missing completely. It is overlaid by legitimate and illegitimate violence.

The capriciousness of a woman endangers the lives of many men (Ro A 174,3–4). The impetus for heroic catastrophe is *übermuot* (Ro A 176,2).[25] To be sure, here heroic combat is parodied, in that the outcome is comical and grotesque,[26] instead of being catastrophic (although the battles against the giants are deadly). But the difference between game and bloody battle is ignored. It is a *hertez spil* [hard contest], which one engages in *zornlîche* [with anger] (Ro A 194,1), *griulîchen* [terrifyingly] (Ro A 199,2), *vreislîche* [terribly] (Ro A 210,3), *mit grimme* [mercilessly] (Ro A 222,1), and so on, and it is prepared as a martial campaign with sixty thousand men, even if the domestication of real battle remains obvious: it is a regulated sequence of combats in a bounded area (*garten*). The reward is only symbolic recognition from the ladies (a wreath, embrace, and kiss, Ro A 150,3). The replacement of war by a chivalric contest, however, is characterized as frivolous: *wir müezen iuwer gespötte sîn, / daz wir durch rôsen willen sîn komen an den Rîn* [we must bear your derision, / that we came all the way to the Rhine for the sake of roses] (Ro A 173,1–2). This kind of fight boils down to arbitrary murder (*ir seht gerne morden die recken unverzeit* [you gladly watch the murder of keen warriors], Ro A 187,3).[27] Since playful combat and violence are from the beginning indistinguishable, the slaughter can paradoxically establish eternal fame: *hernâch über tûsent jâr / man von uns seite und sünge* [hereafter for a thousand years / people would talk and sing of us] (Ro A 152,1–2). The attempt to peacefully canalize war, as attempted by the courtly tournament, is ridiculed.

A blurring of the boundaries also characterizes *Biterolf*, where the fatal movement of the *Nibelungenlied* from courtly order to catastrophe is reversed.[28] There is a huge campaign of Etzel's heroes to the Rhine against Gunther and the people of Worms. The motivation is not a woman's vengeance but revenge for an insult among men. Gunther counters Etzel's feud with an invitation to a celebration, to which he also invites his allies and their ladies.

This is apparently a treacherous invitation, as was Kriemhilt's—Gunther secretly wants to secure helpers against Etzel in this way, which is why he keeps his true intentions from his guests (Bit 5865).[29] The deception is clearly diminished, however, because Gunther, unlike Kriemhilt, does not seek to kill his guests. At first, there are dead and wounded, and the blood runs ankle-deep. But the battle is a show from the very beginning. Gradually, the threatened *hervart* (Bit 5011) turns into *hôchzîte* (Bit 5024), vengeance for a crime turns into a contest in the presence of the ladies for honor (Bit 5114–19).[30] In the end, a serious war has become a game, a parade of the greatest heroes:

> *ich tete ez niuwan umbe daz,*
> *als ez doch ist hie geschehen,*
> *daz wir die recken hân gesehen*
> *von den wir wunder hôrten sagen.* (Bit 12602–5)
>
> [I did it only for that,
> as it really happened here,
> that we could see the warriors
> of whom we heard marvelous tales.]

Finally, the battles lead to a feast for the former opponents. There, the warriors joke about the wounds they gave and received. The war, at first just camouflaged as *hôchzît*, actually becomes the noisy celebration at which Gunther's invitation at first only hinted: the inverse of the downfall of the Nibelungen. This is not a result that comes about by chance. The overlay of war and chivalric sport permits a peaceful ending.

The antagonism of courtly chivalric contests and heroic violence is played out differently in each of the three heroic poems: the tournament that is sponsored by the lady as a pretext for violence (*Rosengarten*), the transformation of war into tournament under the direction of the men, with the women as audience (*Biterolf*), and the perversion of peaceful competition into bloody combat (*Nibelungenlied*). In all three cases, the courtly control of violence is at stake. *Rosengarten* denounces the games as arrogance. In *Biterolf*, games and celebration are unintended consequences of war. The *Nibelungenlied* narrates the latent destructiveness of a playful contest that is used as a cover for deadly intrigue. Each time, the boundary between pacified sport and serious battle is blurred. Between the two simple solutions—strong criticism in *Rosengarten* and unproblematic transformation in *Biterolf*—lies the consistent ambiguity of serious fight and playful competition in the *Nibelungenlied*.

Service to a Lady: The Heroic Misunderstanding

Sivrit's *minne* is to blame for his death, since it causes him to play his fateful role in the deception of Prünhilt. Initially, however, his *minne* is idealized.[31] Service of a lady has an ambivalent value in the context of the story. At first, it is no more than a part of the courtly celebration and the material culture of the court. As such it is praised on all festive occasions in the *Nibelungenlied* far more than in other epics of heroic provenance. Service is, in a conventional sense, the knight's attention to the ladies:

> *dâ wart gedient vrouwen sô helde hôchgemuote tuont.* (602,4)
>
> [Ladies were served there as heroes of high spirits do.]
>
> *die vrouwen dienen kunden, die heten kleinen gemach.* (1308,4)[32]
>
> [Those who served ladies endured hardships.]

It is a part of courtly culture, even in Isenstein, and seems to be shorthand for the ideal courtly life.

The death of the *vrouwe* Helche makes her entire land miserable and undermines Etzel's rule. After Kriemhilt replaces Helche, the celebrations and chivalric games begin anew: *dâ wart vrouwen dienest mit grôzem vlîze getân* [service to ladies was practiced with great dedication] (1310,4). The desires of all men are directed at Gotelint (1669), as was previously the case with Kriemhilt at the court in Worms (296). Service of a lady as a courtly homage is an ornament, like splendid clothing and perfect manners.

The heroes are parts of this ornament, but there is no danger of ensuing conflicts. Etzel remembers, for example, how close Hagen's father Aldrian was to Queen Helche:

> *Helche diu getriuwe was im inneclîchen holt.* (1755,4)
>
> [Helche the loyal woman was lovingly devoted to him.]

Volker says farewell at the court of Bechelaren by playing the fiddle for Gotelint and performing *sîniu liet* [his songs] (1705). He is rewarded by the lady of the court with rings, which he promises to wear in her honor at Etzel's court. Upon his return, Gotelint wants to hear *wie ir mir habt gedienet dâ zer hôhgezît* [how you served me at the celebration] (1707,3). There is not a word about Volker's song containing any direct homage to Gotelint. He entertains her with music. The service that he promises the princess in no way refers to *minne*. *Dienen* does not even have to mean singing, but only that he will wear a sign from the lady at the courtly festival and will do everything for her honor. This will include the battles in which he excels, so that he can later challenge Rüedeger to be *geziuc* [witness] (2204,4) to the fact that he earned the rings and achieved honor for his lady.

Because beautiful women are the attraction of the court, service to women is also a political instrument that can be employed with the aim of keeping knights close to the seat of power. When Gunther considers *wi er lônte sînen man* [how he could reward his men] (256,3) at the victory celebration, he receives this advice:

> *sô sult ir lâzen scouwen diu wünneclîchen kint.* (273,3)
>
> [You should show them the beautiful young women.]

The plan works, when those who are rewarded with a view of the women ask:

> *Waz wære mannes wünne, des vreute sich sîn lîp,*
> *ez entæten scœne mägede und hêrlîchiu wîp?* (274,1–2)
>
> [What would be a man's pleasure, what would give him joy,
> if not beautiful girls and outstanding women?]

With this linkage to politics, service to women can turn to the negative when it is more than just a decorative element at court. In the beginning, the epic cites courtly love, as it is conceived in early *minnesang*. Kriemhilt's falcon dream develops the image of the *vrouwe* as the educator of men (*wie si züge einen valken, starc scœen' und wilde* [how she raised a falcon, strong, handsome, and untamed], 13,2). The "formative power of *minne*" is effected in the falcon, probably as a reference to Kürenberger's "Falkenlied," in whose strophic form the epic is composed.[33] This image is not confirmed, however. When Sivrit makes himself a part of the court at Worms, *minne* for Kriemhilt is at work in the background. The story is about his gradual integration into the ruling elite at Worms, not his education. This political meaning plays a part in the courtly concept of education, but it is overlaid with a program of noble behavior. "To raise the falcon" seems here to be an education for *dienest* at court.[34]

Sivrit's long and sacrificial quest for Kriemhilt seems to be only an epic version of the *arebeit* [travail] of high *minne* for an inaccessible *vrouwe*.[35] Upon closer examination, however, the analogy fails, because Sivrit's *arebeit* implies a political process. Sivrit's *minne* for the distant queen is a traditional motivation for a dangerous bridal quest, but not for courtly service. When called *hôh[iu] minne* (47,1), the concept is changed into a concretely political one, for *hôhiu minne* is not aimed at a *vrouwe* who is unapproachable because she represents all imaginable perfection, but means, here and later, love for a woman of superior status. This is the reason why Kriemhilt seems to be inaccessible. *Hôh[iu] minne* has to overcome the power of those who control the woman (str. 47: Kriemhilt) or the great distances and the especially difficult tests that are necessary to win her (544,4: Prünhilt). The concept of *hôhiu minne* is interpreted within the horizon of difficult bridal quests.

The considerations of Sivrit's parents and the court are aimed at avoiding such high (unattainable) *minne*, and so they press for a suitable marriage:

> *daz er dan eine wurbe diu im möhte zemen.* (48,3)
>
> [that he should court a woman who would be appropriate for him.]

Sivrit answers his parents' suggestion with the self-assurance of the hero who knows no difficulties. His answer rhymes with the line that recommends the search for a more suitable (*zemen*) woman: *sô wil ich Kriemhilden nemen* [So I want to take Kriemhilt] (48,4).

He relies on his overwhelming strength. When his mother and father complain of the *übermüete* and *hôhverte* (54,2) of the Wormsians, Sivrit counters:[36]

> *swaz ich friwentlîche niht ab in erbit,*
> *daz mac sus erwerben mit ellen dâ mîn hant* (55,2–3)
>
> [what I cannot obtain from them by asking in a friendly way,
> my own strength will get me (i.e., without an army).]

And when Sigemunt proposes to set out with an army (57) in order to overcome the Burgundian power, Sivrit answers:

> *Si mac wol sus erwerben dâ mîn eines hant.* (59,1)
>
> [I alone can win her without that.]

Such considerations go beyond the frame of courtly service to a lady. *Hôhiu minne* here requires overcoming nearly impossible difficulties through heroic deeds. Such difficulties are part of the courtly *minne* concept as an incentive for constant striving, but generally they do not consist of differences of status or sheer physical inaccessibility. Even the courtly romance, where *minne* depends on chivalric exploits, demands other qualities. In courtly lyric, the knight has to prove ethical perfection and endurance in an apparently vain service . *Hôch* is not understood in terms of class or rank.[37] Later on, Sivrit also becomes a model of courtly self-control and sacrifice in his quest, but at first, he is intent on heroic deeds.

In the confrontation with the court at Worms, Sivrit's wishes are redirected toward courtly *dienest.* His constant waiting for Kriemhilt, nearly despairing of success, transforms a lyrical situation into a narrative. But it is not the kind of *dienest* demanded by *hôhiu minne* that gets him ahead. He has to prove himself through deeds, by his help for Gunther in the Saxon war, and in the contests against Prünhilt.

A similar shift in the *minne* concept characterizes the second quest, that of Gunther for Prünhilt. Gunther, too, has to overcome external obstacles. Because she is afraid that he might fall short on account of them, Kriemhilt advises Gunther to woo another woman who is just as noble. She is interested in a suitable, but less risky marriage:

> *dâ iu sô sêre enwâge stüende niht der lîp.*
> *ir muget hie nâher vinden ein alsô hôchgeborn wîp.* (372,3–4)
>
> [where your life would not be so endangered.
> You can find a woman just as noble closer to home.]

This *minne* is difficult for external reasons alone. Gernot is afraid, as the mission has already been successfully accomplished, that his *hôhiu minne* (544,4)—and this means his dangerous journey to the dangerous Prünhilt—has cost Gunther his life. High *minne* has turned into high-risk *minne.* Thanks to this shift in meaning, *minne* becomes a part of the power game. It is no longer just a decoration of heroic action, but becomes part of it. With this, the service of ladies becomes ambiguous.

Hero and Servant of Ladies

Looking beyond Sivrit's own story then, the signals for the service of ladies are conspicuously concentrated where (heroic) efforts are avoided.[38] *Frauendienst* for Gunther means that he does not have to subject himself to the arduous Saxon war:

> *"Her künec, sît hie heime," sprach dô Sîvrit,*
> *"sît daz iuwer recken mir wellent volgen mit.*
> *belîbet bî den frouwen und traget hôhen muot."* (174,1–3)
>
> ["My lord, stay at home," said Sivrit then,
> "because your warriors will be under my command.
> Stay with the ladies and be of high spirits."]

Later some others exclude themselves from the noble sport of the hunt for the sake of courtly gallantry:

> *die aber hie bestân*
> *hövschen mit den vrouwen, daz sî mir liebe getân.* (912,3–4)
>
> [Those who stay here
> at court with the ladies, however, do so to please me.

Rumolt, who wants to dissuade the Burgundians from the dangerous journey to Etzel with the prospect of *gemach* [comfort], counsels: *minnet wætlîchiu wîp* [serve beautiful women] (1467,4). When Gunther hands over the affairs of state to him before departing Worms, this includes the charge: *diene wol den vrouwen* [serve the ladies well] (1519,2). Courtly service to ladies is for those who would rather stay at home than risk their lives in battle.

The replacement of *hôhe minne* by the dangerous love of a distant lady results in a series of misunderstandings. Gunther seems to speak in the horizon of heroic bridal quests when he says of Prünhilt: *ich wil durch ir minne wâgen mînen lîp* [I want to risk my life for the sake of her love] (329,3), but on the other hand he misjudges the undertaking as a gentleman's excursion, a *hovereise* [courtly journey] (530,4). He announces it to Kriemhilt with the words: *wir wellen höfschen rîten* [we want to ride out for courtship] (350,3), and *wir wellen kurzwîlen in Prünhilde lant* [we seek entertainment in Prünhilt's land] (354,3).[39] Kriemhilt understands that the object is *minne* (*der ir dâ gert mit minnen* [whom you desire to love], 351,3), and therefore Gunther's first concern is to find the right clothing (343,3). His and his men's astonishment is all the greater when he discovers what this *hovevart* (443,2) really means. He has undertaken anything but a pleasure trip. It is a journey where courtly devotion to a lady becomes life-threatening.

Gunther still speaks the language of courtly gallantry when he first sees Prünhilt: *die welent mîniu ougen durch ir scœnen lîp* [my eyes choose her for her beauty] (392,3). *Minne* as an emotion transmitted by sight competes with *minne* as a stimulus to heroic *arebeit.* Gunther is speaking the wrong language. A world where a woman is actually ruler and exceeds all the heroes in strength shatters the expectations of the male courtly world.[40] The essence of courtly *Frauendienst* is out of place in Isenstein.

The *Nibelungenlied* shares this assessment with many other heroic epics. The *Goldemar* fragment refers to the well-known type of the constantly fighting Dietrich von Bern, who, like his fellow heroes, knows only how to kill as many opponents as possible and never *gwan gên vrouwen hôhen muot* [acquired enthusiasm for women] (Go 2,5). This is the blueprint that makes it possible to tell about another Dietrich, a *hovelîch man* [a courtly man] (Go

2,7) who is conquered by a woman (Go 2,12).[41] Whereas *Frauendienst* is critically employed here against a heroic cliché, the *Virginal* version of the *Dresdner Heldenbuch* makes fun of the sexually inexperienced Dietrich loving the dwarf queen.[42] When *Frauendienst* is the reason for chivalric combat, as in *Rosengarten*, it is accentuated negatively.[43]

Even in *Kudrun*, which places women at the center of attention, and where a woman ends the escalation of heroic slaughter, courtly service is close to being comical. In the courtship of Hagen's daughter Hilde—actually, a regular bridal quest tale—the role of the assistant is split into two characters, a heroic and a courtly one: Wate and Horant. This split shows that two different cultural patterns were copied onto each other. Wate is above all a warrior, he must act, plan the kidnapping of Hilde, and stop the pursuers. Horant, otherwise a hero like Wate, is adept at courtly wooing, mostly through music. Wate, on the other hand, is foreign to the world of the court. Jokingly (K 343,1), Queen Hilte and her daughter of the same name ask him if he would rather fight or "sit" with beautiful ladies.[44] "To sit with beautiful ladies": this is, from a heroic perspective, the courtly alternative associated with inactivity. For someone like Wate, the decision is easy: he has never sat *bî schœnen frouwen sô sanfte* [with beautiful women so pleasantly] (K 344,2) that he would not rather have been in battle. In conversation with ladies, such an honest answer is a comical faux pas that is answered with laughter (345,1), but above all it shows the distance of the hero from the courtly world.

This world is represented by Horant. He is also primarily a warrior, but in this episode he is suddenly a minstrel. His songs enchant everyone. His singing is not, however, characterized as *minnesang*.[45] He is not bound to any sort of courtly "performance," since he apparently sings outside in the evening and for himself. Only because his singing is so pleasing to everyone is he invited to repeat it "inside" in front of the ladies. In any case, his songs open the doors to the ladies' chamber. There he can speak to Hilde and gain her acquiescence to marry his king Hetel. It is not mentioned that his song speaks of the king's love. The performance of the singer in front of the ladies is called *Frauendienst*, however.[46] Horant is less well suited for the kidnapping and therefore moves into the background. Only when the quest is completed after bloody battles is he again one of the most outstanding heroes. The transition to the courtly way of life, whose focal point is the women, means that the hero has temporarily changed his identity.[47]

In that Wate and Horant work well together, the bridal quest is successful. From the perspective of King Hetel's other warriors, however, Horant's change to a singing ladies' servant is comical. Fruote remarks:

> *mîn neve möhte lân*
> *sîn ungefüege dœne, die ich in hœre singen.*
> *wem mag er ze dienste als ungefüege tagewîse bringen?* (K 382,2–4)
>
> [My nephew should stop
> these unseemly songs I hear him singing.
> Whom is he serving with these unseemly lyrics?]

Unless one wants to assume that the uncivilized Fruote is here an arbiter of elegant manners who criticizes Horant for inappropriate singing, then we have a strange switch of paradigms, because *fuoge* [smoothness, appropriate behavior] is what actually distinguishes Horant's songs: *jâ kunde er sîner fuoge wol geniezen* [really he knew how to use his smoothness to his advantage] (K 389,4). *Fuoge* unites the ethical and aesthetic qualities of courtly *minnesang* and is the quintessence of appropriate behavior.[48] The beautiful song is *fuoge.* For Fruote, from the perspective of another world, this is precisely why the song seems *ungefüege.* In the cleavage of suitor roles and in the confusion of language, the disparity of different lifestyles becomes manifest.

Thanks to the employment of two characters, this does not lead to conflict. Horant's *minne* quest does him no harm. He can be a hero again later, and, conversely Wate's superior strength can be included in Kudrun's peaceful order. Fruote, the other archaic hero, also participates in the final peace negotiations. A character like King Hetel shows how easily the narrator relates the two types to each other. He only relates deeds of war for Hetel, but Horant knows to report of his virtues as a courtly knight. There are twelve singers at Hetel's court, all of them better than Horant, *doch singet aller beste mîn herre* [but my lord, King Hetel, sings better than all of them] (K 406,4). The perfect ruler must also master the courtly arts. In that the courtly singing only adorns the sociopolitical constellation, it can be integrated effortlessly. Nevertheless, the disparity with the dominant type of heroic action remains constantly present.

What is unproblematic in *Kudrun* becomes a major concern in the entanglements of the *Nibelungenlied.*

How to Serve the vrouwe*?*

As part of a power game, *Frauendienst* is linked to its other components. Already in Sivrit's decision for courtship, the *minne* desire is connected to fantasies of aggression. In preparation for the quest of Kriemhilt, he thinks about force (55,3–4; 57,1; 58), just as he conversely remembers his *minne* amid the aggressive dispute with the kings of Worms (123,4). The alternatives are played out. Sivrit is the challenger of the royal clan as in the bridal quest scheme, but then he falls into inactive waiting, as if in a courtly *dienest* for *minne. Minne* wins, Sivrit gives up his plans for attack, and the story runs into a dead end.

That means waiting for years and hoping without hope. The *maget* Kriemhilt is, like the courtly *vrouwe*, inaccessible. A solution is only possible when heroic deed and self-denial are combined in *minne* service. This happens when *Frauendienst* is instrumentalized by the kings in Worms. Sivrit's hope for Kriemhilt's favor is a means for the king to keep him in Worms:

> *er bat in minneclîche noch bî im bestân.*
> *niwan durch sîne swester, sone wærez nimmer getân.* (258,3–4)

> [He asked him courteously to remain with him.
> He would never have agreed had it not been for his sister.]

> *Durch der scœnen willen gedâht' er noch bestân,*
> *ob er si gesehen möhte.* (260,1–2)

> [He meant to stay on account of the beautiful woman,
> hoping to be able to see her]

The *gruoz* of the *vrouwe*, the goal of courtly *minne*, is employed by the kings as the victor's prize. Gernot proposes:

> *Ir heizet Sîvrîden zuo mîner swester kumen,*
> *daz in diu maget grüeze, des hab' wir immer frumen.*
> *diu nie gegruoste recken, diu sol in grüezen pflegen,*
> *dâ mit wir haben gewunnen den vil zierlîchen degen.* (289)

> [Tell Sivrit to come visit my sister,
> so that the maiden will greet him, thus we'll always have the advantage.
> She who has never greeted a warrior, she should do so to him,
> and then we'll have won the excellent warrior.]

Later, when Sivrit wants to leave Gunther's court, Giselher suggests:

> *belîbet bî den recken . . .*
> *hie ist vil scœner frouwen, die sol man iuch gerne sehen lân.* (321,2; 321,4)

> [Stay with the warriors . . .
> there are many beautiful women whom you'll be allowed to see.]

Frauendienst is a calculated way to keep the foreign lord at the court and in so doing make him available for one's own interests. This pays off in the Isenstein adventure.

Because Gunther himself is not able to withstand the danger, he needs the *dienest* of someone else, understood as *dienest* for the courted woman, even though it takes the form of service to a lord. Prünhilt does not need to be served, she must be overcome. Sivrit wins for Gunther, and in doing so, he "serves" him and at the same time also earns [*ver-dient*] Kriemhilt.

The cultural pattern of *Frauendienst* is politically interpreted so that service to ladies and service to lords can no longer be distinguished. Through the coupling of the two quests, the roles of the courtly suitor (Gunther) and the heroic assistant (Sivrit) and that of the heroic victor (Sivrit) and the *muntwalt* [guardian, warden] of the bride (Gunther) are so completely intertwined that only those directly involved even know the circumstances.[49]

In Sivrit's story, *minne* succeeds in integrating the warrior into the court, as is intended in lyric *Frauendienst.* This is not accomplished, however, in an act of virtual subordination to the lady, but in the actual subordination to the lord, even though this is done for the sake of *minne*, and even if only for a limited time and with the proviso that the royal status remains intact:

> *Jane lob' ihz niht sô verre durch die liebe dîn*
> *Sô durch dîne swester, daz scœne magedîn.* (388,1–2)
>
> [I promise this not so much for your sake
> as for your sister's, the beautiful maiden.]

After Sivrit has provided military assistance against the Saxons, this is still clearly distinct from the *helfe* to which Gunther's own vassals are obligated. Now in Isenstein, however, Sivrit explicitly subordinates himself to Gunther in a staging that all can see and by words that all can hear. The metaphor of *Frauendienst* is interpreted in concretely political terms.[50]

Different spheres are confused. Not even the *dienest* of a foreign king, "as if one were a vassal" (*recht als her sîn man wâre*, Trt 82) is discriminating,[51] especially not the virtual *Frauendienst*, which excludes political dependency. Here, on the other hand, the as-if character of this service is suppressed. The integration of the heroic deed into *hôhe minne* fails.

Gunther relies on the deeds of another, and Sivrit acts on behalf of foreign interests.[52] Sivrit's deeds are not directed against those who control his own beloved, that is, against Gunther and his *hôhferten man* (53,4). His intention when he sets out for Worms is that they should support him and subordinate themselves completely to his goals. There is no hostile father of the bride as usual in the scheme, but both women are nevertheless inaccessible. The father is replaced. Kriemhilt is under the *munt* [guardianship] of her brothers, and Prünhilt is protected by her Amazon-like position.[53] In both cases, the independent *vrouwe* of *hôhe minne* who decides over the acceptance or rejection of a suit is replaced: the *vrouwe* Kriemhilt has to fulfill what her brothers demand, and the *vrouwe* Prünhilt acts like a male hero. So *minne* and *Frauendienst* are distorted. By reinterpreting the *hôch* in *hôhe minne*, a potentially violent conflict takes the place of a model of courtly self-perfection.

The heroic world can apparently only integrate a part of the *minne* concept, and only at a high cost. This is demonstrated in *Kudrun*. The quest for Kudrun is similar to the quest for Kriemhilt in certain points at the outset. Three suitors "serve" the desired woman in different ways and meet with varying success. When Herwic is intent *ûf schœner frouwen lônen* [on a beautiful woman's reward] (K 646,4), he contrives a bloody war against the desired woman's clan, as Sivrit at first wants to do in Worms. This war is the "right" kind of *Frauendienst* and is therefore successful. Kudrun observes and assesses Herwic's accomplishments in battle:

> *Si sprach: "wer war diu frouwe, der versmâhte daz,*
> *der ein helt sô diente* [!], *daz si dem trüege haz?* . . .
> *holder danne ich iu wære ist dehein maget die ir ie gesâhet."*
> (K 657,1–2; 657,4)

> [She said, "What woman would scorn that
> a hero serve her so, that she would hate him? . . .
> I would be more devoted to you than any maiden you ever knew."]

Even if Herwic's aggression is directed against her own people, Kudrun can appreciate it as "service." For Herwic, service to a lady is also primarily about battle. Later, when he wants to free Kudrun from her kidnappers and has to fight standing in water up to his armpits, the narrator asserts:

> *herter frouwen dienest wart dâ <dem küenen> Herwîge künde.* (K 867,4)

> [The bold Herwic came to know the arduous service of ladies.]

It is the kind of heroic service that qualifies Herwic as a worthy suitor, despite his *lîhte[n] künne* [humble lineage] (K 656,3).

This aspect of *Frauendienst* is also primary for Sivrit of Morlant, Herwic's rival, who does not come as an aggressor but also seeks to overcome the lady's resistance and her courtly environment by demonstrating his strength, which he does by parading with his splendidly outfitted retinue in front of the court. This nonviolent show of force is not very effective. Admittedly, Sivrit's demonstration is successful to the extent that *si truog im holden willen* [she rather liked him] (K 583,2), but not enough for her to accept him as a suitor. When he is unable to get the better of Herwic, he abandons his earlier tactic and launches a war to achieve his goal, as Herwic did. This brings him close to defeat, which confirms Kudrun's choice of Herwic, but thanks to his courage, Sivrit remains a contender. Subsequently, in order to win back Kudrun from her kidnapper, the third suitor, Hartmuot, Sivrit allies himself with his rival Herwic, who is also in danger of losing the lady. Sivrit thus qualifies for a wife from the second tier of the epic cast.

In both cases the difference from the *Nibelungenlied* is obvious. Both suitors act just like Sivrit seems to intend in his first appearance at Worms. They seek the path of proving themselves in combat. Their cruel war for Kudrun is "service," but since this service is proof of (real or symbolic) strength, it not only does not endanger but even confirms their position as worthy spouses, first Herwic, then—somewhat less so—Sivrit.

The other, "modern" form of *Frauendienst*, however, is devalued in *Kudrun*. Kudrun's kidnapper Hartmuot displays the traits of a courtly suitor, and in this sense also shares some striking similarities with Sivrit. His father wants to dissuade him from the dangerous quest because of the *übermüete* (K 593,4) of Kudrun's relatives. The reason is made more explicit than in Sivrit's case.[54] Hartmuot is socially inferior, because his father was a vassal to Kudrun's grandfather. "High" *minne* is one that aims too high in terms of class. Rejected the first time, Hartmuot opts, unlike his rivals, not for the typical path of violent or cunning bridal quest, but like the Sivrit of the *Nibelungenlied*, for courtly service.

The gestures of *Frauendienst* are all present. There is talk of Hartmuot's *hôhen zühten* [courteous manners] (K 622,2), of his *gebære* [bearing] (K 622,3), *daz er edeler minne an hôhe frouwen gerte billîche* [that he strove accordingly for the noble love of high-born ladies] (K 622,4), of the desire of his heart, of *tougen ougen blicke* [secretive glances] (K 624,2), and of secret signs (K 624,3). Even a hidden reaction of the *vrouwe* is in the offing, when she shows herself *genædic* toward her admirer (K 626,3). This *genâde* of the *vrouwe*, however, does not necessarily mean affection, but simply a recognition of the labors of service and sympathy for the hopeless suitor. Hartmuot is recognized for his courtly service, but he is by no means rewarded.

Whereas Herwic is able to overcome a less distinguished origin with personal superiority, this does not succeed for Hartmuot, who goes down the wrong path of courtly *minne*. The paradoxical consequence is that the only courtly suitor becomes a kidnapper who does not respect the woman's will. The narrator makes this even more pointed. The same words, which seem to express the pain of his *minne*: *ez was nâch Kûdrûnen Hartmuoten wê* [Hartmuot ached for Kudrun] (K 748,2) are bound by rhyme to the verse that speaks of the preparations for kidnapping: *Mit drî und zweinzic tûsent si fuoren über sê* [with 23,000, they traveled across the sea] (K 748,1). *Minne* rhymes with crime. His courting, as his army already stands close to Kudrun's castle, is actually a camouflaged military ultimatum (K 753–59). The civilized form of wooing proves to be a mask for brutal violence, and this in a text that terminates the heroic mechanism of violence and counterviolence with a series of marriage alliances.

Courtly *Frauendienst* remains alien to heroic epic: ambiguous, discriminating, and discriminated.

Virtualizing Gestures

The solution to the threatening conflict in *Âventiure* 3—Sivrit's challenge of the Burgundian kings as a means of bridal quest—can be characterized as "courtly." The hero becomes a servant who teeters between hope and despair, one who recognizes the limits of his own strength. Instead of conquering the foreign realm, he serves it for Kriemhilt's favor. The challenge leads to an invitation to the *gast* (128,4).[55] The narrator "confronts the heroic directly with a contrary way of life."[56] The progress of the scene can be read as a model of the courtly pacification of the warrior.[57] Sivrit's contradictory nature is first clarified on the courtly side. Only on occasion, in Isenstein and in *Nibelungeland*, does the other Sivrit appear, and then always in the service of the people of Worms and their courtly kings. The *valke* is so completely domesticated that he behaves in an exemplary courtly manner up until his death.

The solution is made possible by a courtly gesture from Gunther. His words provide exactly what Sivrit wants, and yet again they do not. "Sigfrid's claim to the Burgundian kingdom is both accepted and nullified on a higher level by Gunther's formula of greeting," Walther Haug observes.[58]

> *wir sulen iu gerne dienen, ich und die mâge mîn.* (126,3)
>
> [We'll gladly serve you, I and my kin.]

and:

allez daz wir hân,
geruochet irs nâch êren, daz sî iu undertân,
und sî mit iu geteilet, lîp unde guot. (127,1–3)

[Everything we have,
if you will keep it honorably, will be yours,
it will be shared with you, both men and property.]

Gunther's words clearly pick up on Sivrit's initial demands: *dem sol ez allez dienen, die liute und ouch diu lant* [everything will serve him, the people and also the land] (114,3); *swaz ir muget hân: / lant unde bürge, daz sol mir werden undertân* [whatever you may have: land and castles, all will be subject to me] (110,3–4). Gunther succeeds in canalizing aggression into courtliness. It is expressly these words that calm Sivrit and make him retreat from the idea of a fight for rulership, and not the thought of Kriemhilt.[59]

It is a particular accomplishment of courtly speech that makes this solution possible. It can be called "virtualization": taking the pragmatic consequences of the speech act of subordination (which Sivrit demands) back to the simple verbal gesture, while suspending the literal meaning (Gunther gives up nothing by doing so) and arriving at a symbolic fulfillment of what the opponent demands. Gunther speaks the code of courtliness, according to which the "obedient servant" changes nothing in the social and political conditions to his disadvantage. The phrase, "everything is at your disposal," does not mean giving up any kind of property. What Gunther offers is neither real joint rule nor what he and his people have indignantly refused Sivrit,[60], but instead a courtly arrangement in which people act "as if," and the gesture feigns to concede what must actually be denied. By this, Sivrit's claim to rule everywhere where he is the strongest is both satisfied and shifted in a "courtly" way, and Sivrit—the courtly Sivrit—agrees by taking away from Gunther's offer, not a claim to rule, but hopes for his *minne.*

Such courtly forms of behavior characterize the first part of the epic, and they can still be found in the second while the peace holds. The threatening war with the Saxons is mitigated by Gunther's gifts to the enemy messengers. The perfect form makes the hostile character of the relationships disappear from the surface, so that a high-spirited mood, considered typical of courtliness, is established: *des stuont in hôhe der muot* [therefore they were in high spirits] (164,4). This means more than "they were happy about that," because *hôhe muot* is the epitome of a courtly harmony that allows the impending confrontation to be forgotten.

What these kinds of gestures can accomplish is shown by the outcome of the Saxon war. After the foreigners have been defeated, a celebration is held together with them. In place of peace negotiations, in which each side attempts to gain some advantage—the victors want to get the most possible, the vanquished try to give up as little as possible—we find gestures that aim at the advantage of the other side. The former enemies offer very generous reparations (314,1–3), yet for the sake of reconciliation (*suone*, 311,3; 313,3), Gunther requires no compensation. It is notably Sivrit—the courtier, the Sivrit who has subordinated himself to courtly pacification—who advises the rejection of reparations. Upon his return, he immediately exchanges the role of the superior warrior for that of the perfect knight. The seriousness of the dispute is suspended in the gestures of reciprocal "civility."

This "virtualization" also characterizes the service of a lady. It is a symbolic (and not factual) subordination of the stronger to the weaker. It does not change much in the legal and social position of women, as historical investigations have shown.[61] It offers an alternative model of social interaction at court. In this model, the woman is positioned as superior and the man as completely dependent on her. The required change in thought and emotion is continually practiced in high *minnesang*. How unfamiliar this rethinking and the "as if" really are, is constantly articulated by *minne* lyrics. It is recast in the epic in Ulrich von Liechtenstein's *Frauendienst*, where the courting man, who is one of the most important nobles in the land, must grotesquely enact his role as *minne* slave and victim of female arbitrariness in order to prove his love.

Sivrit's courtship of Kriemhilt tells the story of such a virtual reversal of the actual power relationship. Sivrit remains the strongest hero, is the bulwark of the Burgundian ruling elite, is the only guarantee for the success of the bridal quest for Prünhilt, and remains a lord [*kunic*]. But by his *dienest* for the lady, he subordinates himself to her kin and is forced into self-denial. The remarkable nature of such a subordination, along with its virtual character, is always emphasized in order to protect Sivrit's *dienest* from any misunderstanding.[62]

After the victory over the Saxons, Sivrit therefore renounces material rewards, unlike other warriors. *Dar zuo was er ze rîche, daz er iht næme solt* [He was too rich to take any reward] (259,1). He can only receive the *gruoz* of the court as a symbolic recompense. In her *gruoz* formula, Kriemhilt does not address Sivrit as *künec*—a *künec* cannot be rewarded—but as *riter*, that is, as what he is now: a member of the court.

> *sît willekomen, her Sîvrit, ein edel riter guot.* (292,3)
>
> [be welcome, Sir Sivrit, noble and excellent knight.]

The term *riter* expresses the virtual equality within courtly society. Gunther is similarly called *riter* at the beginning of his quest (328,2). Symbolic recognition replaces what Sivrit sought in rulership.

Courtly *minne* is even capable of turning the exchange of material gifts into a virtual gesture. When Sivrit announces to Kriemhilt the happy return of Gunther and Prünhilt from Isenstein, he must both subordinate himself to the *vrouwe* and yet remain a lord subordinate to no one. The contradictory requirements are met in a complicated sequence of actions. Sivrit asks Kriemhilt for *botenbrôt* (553,1), that is, for a material reward (*lôn*), even though he is actually *ze rîche* [too rich] (556,4) to need such a gift. Kriemhilt therefore wants to take back the *botenmiete* in a symbolic recognition, but Sivrit says:

> *"Ob ich nu eine hête," sprach er, "drîzec lant,*
> *so enpfienge ich doh gerne gâbe ûz iwer hant."* (557,1–2)
>
> ["If I alone," he said, "had thirty lands,
> I would still gladly accept gifts from your hand."]

The gift of twenty-four rings is a sign of *hulde* [recognition (cf. *holt*)] from his *vrouwe*, but also a rich reward for the messenger. Sivrit insists that both recognition and reward come together for a moment in his *minne* service, before he passes on Kriemhilt's rings to *næhstem ingesinde* [nearby servants] (558,4), to those who are used to receiving gifts based on their status.

The virtualizing effect of the courtly code is especially evident in gift-giving. In *Biterolf*, Rüedeger refuses, as Etzel's emissary, to receive gifts from the opposing King Gunther, which would put him under obligation and would discriminate against him as a lord (Bit 6722–42). He only agrees to a symbolic gift: permission to kiss the three most prominent ladies at court (Bit 6783). *Frauendienst* does not imply social or political concerns, and the symbolic gift is more valuable than any other present: *daz ein rîcher keiser möhte nemen* [even a powerful emperor would want to take a gift like that] (Bit 6748). The test is not at an end yet, however, because the ladies want to reward Rüedeger too. Rüedeger agrees to accept a costly gift from the queen—it is no longer the king's—, but, like Sivrit, he does not keep it;[63] instead, he passes it on to two of Gernot's men. In this way, he maintains his status as Etzel's emissary and as a challenger in battle. He may, however, keep the purely symbolic gift of a flag. In this he shows that he wants to excel at the imminent fight in front of the ladies, which is not compromised by the fact that these ladies are his enemies.[64] The rules of courtly service to ladies are binding beyond political alliances but do not obligate anyone to anything, which is why here, in the end, they work to resolve conflict.

The courtly code also implies a virtualizing suspension in *minnesang*. The *lôn* of the *vrouwe* in *Frauendienst* is not sexual intercourse but simply a sign of her favor. Subordination to her does not mean social inferiority but voluntary devotion "as if" the lord were a servant. In the *Nibelungenlied*, this code is perverted. In Isenstein, explicit lies and deceit replace symbolic subordination. What was courtly form becomes a false semblance. Real action and mere gesture are separate:

> *Nu hab du die gebære, diu werc wil ich begân.* (454,3)
>
> [Now you may make the gestures, I'll do the real task.]

Marked deception, in which Gunther simply simulates what Sivrit accomplishes, replaces the courtly virtualization, the "as if" of the courtly gesture gives way to masking reality. The courtly code is called into question with this shift. The *Nibelungenlied* takes up a classical motif of *Hofkritik* [criticism of the court] that does not thematize *dissimulatio* as a form of self-discipline, but instead as mean deception.[65]

The Breakdown of Courtly Virtualization

Back in Worms, Sivrit attempts to return to the virtualizing code of courtly behavior, as shown by his symbolic acceptance of *botenmiete*. His initial refusal even to undertake the task of messenger shows that the legitimate social order is supposed to be valid again after the end of the Isenstein adventure. Sivrit agrees one last time to suspend this order in favor of *minne*. Everything has changed with the deception, however, and the rules of Isenstein and Worms cannot be permanently kept apart.

The courtly world into which Sivrit incorporates himself, and to which Prünhilt has to submit, is shaken to the core when the virtualization of hierarchies and heroic rivalry fails. This is what happens when Prünhilt claims Sivrit for service as an *eigen man*. The dispute of the queens is based initially on the difference between courtly as-if speech and its literal, that is, feudal and legal, interpretation. The former holds true for Kriemhilt, the latter for Prünhilt.

In a society based on honor, the question of class cannot remain unresolved forever. Until the queens' dispute, it was possible to maintain form, for example, in that Gunther kept the question of class vague by transforming "the ultimatum to come to court into a friendly invitation to dear relatives to attend a celebration."[66]

The tournament eminently represents the courtly as-if. The best is crowned without those who actually carry crowns being in any way compromised. Power struggles are put aside. The death of the opponent is an accident that should be avoided. In the *Nibelungenlied*, on the other hand, the game is the starting point for a deadly misunderstanding. In the tournament, Sivrit is allowed to be the best after he as withdrawn his claim to rule (*Âventiure* 3). Now, as a guest and foreign king, he may demonstrate all the more that he is the best. Kriemhilt formulates this in the subjunctive:

ich hân einen man,
daz elliu disiu rîche ze sînen handen solden stân. (815,3–4)[67]

[If I had such a husband
all of these realms should be his.]

In courtly speech, this is not an attack on Gunther's rule. Prünhilt understands it as such, however. Notwithstanding that she rates Gunther above Sivrit as a knight, she rejects the political implications,[68] although these are not expressly articulated in Kriemhilt's remark:

wie kunde daz gesîn?
ob ander niemen lebte wan sîn unde dîn,
sô möhten im diu rîche wol wesen undertân,
die wîle lebt Gunther, sô kundez nimmer ergân. (816)

[How could this be?
If you and he were the only people left alive,
then these realms might well be subject to him,
but at long as Gunther is alive, that could never happen.]

Kriemhilt, on the other hand, continues to abide by the courtly code. She praises Sivrit's preeminence in the game (*wie rehte hêrlîche er vor den recken gât* [how splendidly he walks in front of the warriors) and his resplendent appearance (*alsam der liehte mâne vor den sternen tuot* [like the full moon in front of the stars], 817,2–3). Here, power is not even an issue, as in the courtly *minne* code where ruling conditions are set aside and the weaker—the *vrouwe*—appears to be strong and in command, while the stronger—even if a lord—has to serve her.

Prünhilt then forces Kriemhilt to accept her own code of class and feudal hierarchy. Given that her field of comparison is not the tournament but rulership, she says of Gunther:

> *der muoz vor allen künegen, daz wizzest wærlîche, sîn.* (818,4)
>
> [He must be above all kings, be assured.]

Kriemhilt's formula for consensus: *er ist wol Gunthers genôz* [he is Gunther's equal] (819,4) accepts Prünhilt's understanding and is therefore rejected by Prünhilt with the argument of Sivrit's vassality, which is then inflated to serfdom. In this code, Kriemhilt refutes Prünhilt with her insult. If she, Kriemhilt, is an *eigene diu* [bondswoman] (838,4), then Prünhilt is a *mannes kebse* [the concubine of a vassal] (839,4). Kriemhilt turns Prünhilt's understanding of Sivrit's status against her with an even stronger insult. She definitely leaves the courtly as-if; from now on all courtly gestures of conciliation are lacking (820,1–2; 822,3–4). Predicates that can be interpreted two ways, like *tiwerr* (824,2), which refers to class as well as individual rank, are reduced to their legal and political meanings.

The foundations of courtly socialization are destroyed. If up to this point the "courtly perspective" has prevailed over the heroic,[69] now the relationship is reversed. The breakdown is narrated as a breakdown of conventions of speaking and interacting. There is no room left for glossing speech. Hagen says of Sivrit's murder (1001,2): *mir is vil unmære, und wirt ez bekant* [it doesn't matter to me if it gets out]. A common ground of understanding is renounced, indirect speech no longer serves to diffuse conflicts, but instead to slight the opponent.

The consequences come to light when Kriemhilt has regained her former power. In her first encounter with the Burgundians at Etzel's court, the code of courtly speech that was able to appease Sivrit at his arrival in Worms is violated. Kriemhilt does not cover anything up and says what she thinks. In place of a courtly greeting, there is a direct affront (1739,1–2), and instead of giving gifts to the guests, as would be the courtly custom, Kriemhilt demands the return of her possessions:

> *saget waz ir mir bringet von Wormez über Rîn,*
> *dar umb ir mir sô grôze soldet willekomen sîn.* (1739,3–4)
>
> [Tell me what you bring me from Worms across the Rhine,
> that you should be so greatly welcome here to me.]

Hagen ironically deflects this break with convention by seeming to go along. He pretends not to understand. So he continues the courtly play on the one hand, and on the other he undermines it: *Het ich gewest diu mære . . . daz iu gâbe solden bringen degene* [Had I but known . . . that warriors should bring you gifts] (1740,1–2). He acts as if Kriemhilt has been talking about the courtly exchange of gifts and not a legal claim for the return of her property. As he continues to speak, he takes Kriemhilt's question literally and turns it into an insult: had he known that the queen was dependent on gifts from her guests instead of giving herself, then he would have used his property. With this, he forces Kriemhilt to say outright what she means:

> *hort der Nibelunge, war habt ir den getân?*
> *der was doh mîn eigen, daz is iu wol bekant.*
> *den soldet ir mir füeren in daz Etzelen lant.* (1741,2–4)
>
> [Where have you put the hoard of the Nibelungen?
> It was my property indeed, you know that well.
> You should have brought it to me in Etzel's land.]

She is forced to a level where demands, whether justified or not, are only seemingly wrapped in a courtly manner (form of address!):

> *Entriuwen, mîn vrou Kriemhilt, des ist vil manec tac*
> *daz ich hort der Nibelunge nine gepflac.*
> *den hiezen mîne herren senken in den rîn,*
> *dâ muoz er wærlîche unz an daz jungeste sîn.* (1742)
>
> [Truly, my lady Kriemhilt, it has been many days
> since I cared for the Nibelungen hoard.
> My lords ordered it sunk in the Rhine,
> really there it will stay until the end of time.]

When Kriemhilt asks once more about her property, Hagen replies again ironically: "Bringing back the stolen property" is basically a question of transportation. How could he have brought the treasure, when just carrying his weapons was trouble enough? Symbols of peaceful exchange are replaced by instruments of aggression.[70]

With this Hagen gives Kriemhilt the cue to continue her role as hostess and (seemingly) to reestablish the sphere of courtly and peaceful interaction. Part of this would be the voluntary disarming of the arrivals:

> *Dô sprach diu küneginne zen recken über al:*
> *"man sol deheiniu wâfen tragen in den sal.*
> *ir helde, ir sult mirs' ûf geben: ich wil si behalten lân."* (1745,1–3)

[Then the queen spoke to all of the warriors:
"One should not carry weapons into the hall.
You heroes, you should give them up to me: I'll have them kept for you."]

Again, Kriemhilt's words give Hagen the opportunity to reject a consensus on the virtual validity of courtly speech. Hagen disguises his refusal as a further "misunderstanding" that outdoes the courtly gesture by a seemingly more courtly one. He refuses to give up his weapons by playing the courtier who knows what is proper, and by referring to the difference in rank between him and the queen, rejecting Kriemhilt's request for both reasons:

Jane ger ich niht der êren, fürsten wine milt,
daz ir zen herbergen trüeget mînen schilt
und ander mîn gewæfen: ir sît ein künegîn.
daz enlêrte mich mîn vater niht: ich wil selbe kameræere sin. (1746)

[I do not covet such honor, fair friend of the prince,
that you should carry my shield to the storeroom
along with my other weapons: you are a queen.
My father taught me otherwise. I'll be my own chamberlain.]

Of course, Kriemhilt's speech does not mean that she herself would carry the weapons, just as Gunther does not actually offer Sivrit the rule of his lands. By turning the words back to their literal meaning, Hagen (ironically emphasizing his courtly upbringing and his courtly office) announces the return to verbal aggression that was abandoned with Sivrit's integration into the court of Worms and that courtly discourse had rejected. Kriemhilt understands the supposed courtesy in the way in which Hagen had understood hers: as an open threat:

war umbe wil mîn bruoder und Hagene sînen schilt
niht lâzen behalten? Si sint gewarnôt. (1747,2–3)

[Why will my brother and Hagen not allow
their shields to be held for them? They must have been warned.]

The rules of courtly convention are only cited in order to hide aggressive intentions. Until the very last scene, Hagen will use his encounters with Kriemhilt to escalate the confrontation through sarcastic misunderstandings. The courtly form is only regained when Kriemhilt has her opponents where she wants them. Her scornful greeting of Gunther is a parody of courtly form. It does not suspend violence, but instead announces it.[71] This is the opposite pole of an as-if courtly speech: no conflict-solving gesture, no conflict-dissimulating façade, no conflict-escalating game with conventions, but only cynicism. As the story progresses, courtly form changes its appearance. It is reduced to false semblance.

The Destruction of Courtly Form

At the beginning of the *Nibelungenlied*, there is only "a single figure, Hagen, who places himself directly into a seemingly obsolete heroic constellation," a figure initially so isolated that he remains unimportant to the story.[72] Only in the terrible ending does this figure prevail. The question remains of whether this constellation is already "something foreign and archaic," as Haug believes,[73] or perhaps, from the beginning, the secret measure of the epic, to which the courtly world gradually succumbs.

The perversion of courtly order and the outbreak of violence are closely connected. This is already true in the first part for Sivrit's death scene. Hagen's attack can only succeed because Sivrit wants to quench his thirst after the footrace, but allows Gunther to drink first at the fountain, even though he was the first to arrive:

> *Die Sîfrides tugende wâren harte grôz. . . .*
> *swie harte sô in durste, der helt doch nine tranc*
> *ê dez der künic getrunke.* (978,1; 978,3–4)
>
> [Sivrit's virtues were extraordinary . . .
> as thirsty as he was, the hero did not drink
> until the king had drunk first.]

Hagen thus gains time to carry away the weapons and to strike. The narrator comments: *Do engalt er sîner zühte* (980,1): "He had to pay for his courtly behavior there."[74]

Sivrit's gesture is the same as courtly speech. Precedence says nothing about the actual order of rank between Sivrit and Gunther. On the contrary, the courtly gesture to an equal distinguishes the one who makes it more than the same gesture to a person of superior rank. Sivrit shows also that he is not ruled by his physical needs. He demonstrates what courtly *zuht* can accomplish, sublimating desire and its fulfillment, as with *minne*. In this double sense, the gesture can be seen as courtly, and this is precisely what costs Sivrit his life.

The courtly order is again cast in an unflattering light when the Burgundians consult about how they should react to Etzel's invitation. The *kuchenmeister*, representative of one of the "modern" court offices (10,1), warns against the journey. But *Rûmoldes rât* is a caricature of courtly comfort:

> *Wie kunde iu in der werlde immer sanfter wesen?*
> *ir muget vor iuwern vîenden harte wol genesen.*
> *ir sult mit guoten kleidern zieren wol den lîp:*
> *trinket wîn den besten unt minnet wætlîchiu wîp.*
>
> *Dar zuo gît man iu spîse, die besten di ie gewan* (1467–68,1)
>
> [How could anything in the world be more pleasant to you?
> You can be safe from your enemies.
> You should dress in the finest clothing,
> drink the best wine, and serve beautiful women.
>
> In addition, you are served the finest food ever made.]

Elegant clothes, good wine, and service to ladies are the courtly alternatives to the dangerous heroic undertaking. These are the classic points of the criticism of the court.[75] The redactor of the *C group parodistically expanded this image of happiness. Rumolt wants to make staying at home particularly appetizing for them with a special recipe, *sniten in öl gebrouwen* [cuts (of meat?) roasted in oil] (according to ms. a[76] 1497,3). Court life is made banal here.[77] But Rumolt tempts them with exactly those things that up to then were the essence of a refined lifestyle. If *Rûmoldes rât* is an old retarding motif of being funny in a heroic context,[78] then it is certainly reformed in the *Nibelungenlied* by the associations with what is typically courtly. Rumolt's advice is sensible and agrees in its aim even with Hagen's. It does not alter the decision to undertake the dangerous journey, however, and only succeeds in making Gunther angry, because the courtier's advice means for him: *daz die hie heime wolden schaffen ir gemach* [that those at home here want only comfort] (a 1503,2). A peaceful life, which is still recognizable as courtly in this caricature, is characterized with the word that has the least value on the scale of goods: *gemach*.[79] The advice that would have prevented the revenge is therefore denounced with a derision of the objects of courtly life.

Courtly conduct is still binding. Hagen receives Etzel's emissaries *zühteclîche*.[80] Courtly *Frauendienst*, the veneration of a lady from afar, is still part of the festival in Bechelaren (1669). But then the assessment changes. Starting with the first direct confrontation with Kriemhilt, courtly form is questioned.

A key scene is the clash between Hagen and Volker and Kriemhilt, in which

Hagen admits *âne lougen* [without lying] (1791,1) that he killed Sivrit. The brutal directness and the refusal to continue to *liegen* [lie] (1791,4) amounts to a mockery of the courtly code. The courtly ceremony of the *gruoz* is the occasion for an ever-increasing aggression.[81] Hagen's open admission of guilt is introduced with an explicit break in manners. Hagen and Volker show the queen disrespect by not standing up in her presence. Volker, who has otherwise recognized her aggressiveness (1773–75), realizes what is at stake:

> *"Nu stê wir von dem sedele," sprach der spilman:*
> *"si ist ein küneginne; und lât si für gân.*
> *bieten ir die êre: si ist ein edel wîp.*
> *dâ mit ist ouch getiuret*[82] *unser ietweders lîp."* (1780)
>
> ["We should get up from our seat," spoke the minstrel:
> "She is a queen; let her come here.
> We should honor her, she is a noble woman.
> We thus also enhance our own standing."]

Hagen refuses: *zwiu sold' ich den êren, der mir ist gehaz?* [why should I honor someone who is loathsome to me?] (1782,2). A show of respect might be misunderstood as *vorhte* [fear] (1781,3).[83] No one had such doubts when the emissaries of the Saxons and Danes were shown respect despite their declaration of war. Hagen shoves aside the code of honor that has characterized the court of Worms since Sivrit's provocative appearance, and that has since withstood all challenges. He does away with the reciprocity of courtly recognition, where honor is shown to the one who shows honor. He reduces interaction to the alternatives of *vriuntschaft* or *haz*. The argument of *vorhte* will be raised again, when the aim is to reject Dietrich's offer of peace (2268,1). A more basic code of honor begins to prevail over courtly rules of behavior.

> *Nu dûhten sich sô hêre die zwêne küene man*
> *daz si niht enwolden von dem sedel stân*
> *durch nimannes vorhte des gie in an den fuoz*
> *diu edele küneginne und bôt in vîentlîchen gruoz.* (1786)
>
> [Now the two bold men considered themselves to be so lordly
> that they would not rise from their seats
> for fear of anyone. The noble queen walked up very close to them
> and greeted them with enmity.]

The recognition of law, which does not concern the stronger party if there is no one who can enforce it, falls at the same time as the code of courtesy (1782,4).

The importance of such an affront is emphasized by the narrator. Hagen's disregard of courtly rules is in any case the subject of an entire *âventiure* and is put front and center by the title of at least one manuscript: *Wie Kriemhilt Hagenen verweiz unt wie er niht gên ir ûf stuont* [How Kriemhilt rebuked Hagen and how he refused to rise in her presence].[84] This is without precedence in the rejection of courtly form. It is a necessary link in the chain of those actions that lead to the heroic ending. What is clear from here on between Hagen and Kriemhilt must now be clarified between the others. The outbreak of ever more bloody violence is therefore also narrated as the breakthrough of "truth."

This importance of courtly form is problematic only for modern understanding. For the Middle Ages, the connection between external form and the avoidance of conflict seems to have played a central role. Scenes of this kind are not limited to heroic epic. In the *Prose Lancelot,* for example, the rejection of chivalric forms becomes the motivation for a catastrophe of universal dimensions, the collapse of the Arthurian kingdom. In this text, which reflects like no other the endangerment of courtly chivalry, *Âventiure* 29 has a pendant in an encounter between Lancelot and Gawein that seals the final destruction of Arthurian order. Lancelot must defend himself in a duel against an unjustified accusation by Gawein. He does not want to fight against Gawein's *byderbkeit* [uprightness] on account of the *großen gesellschafft* [great camaraderie] that bound the two together, and he certainly does not want to kill Gawein (Lc III, pp. 658–59). When it comes to the trial by combat, and Arthur, who stands on Gawein's side, appears, the hatred does not—and this corresponds to the initial situation in the *Nibelungenlied*—at first invalidate mutual courtly recognition. Lancelot says to his men:

> *"Laßent uns abstan gein mynem herren dem konig, wann er ist von den biederbesten in der welt." Und sie sprachen, si wolten gein yren dotfinden nit abestan, ob got wil! Und er sprach, wie wol das er syn fynt were, so wolt er doch gein im abestan, wann er hett im men ere gethan dann im keyn man ye getet in der welt* ["Let us dismount in front of my lord the king, because he is one of the most proper in the world." And they said that they would not dismount for their mortal enemies, by God! And he said that even though he was his mortal enemy, he would still dismount in his presence, because he had honored him more than any other man in the world.] (Lc III, p. 664).

Lancelot's men argue like Hagen. Why should they honor Arthur, when he is the enemy? Unlike in the *Nibelungenlied,* they do follow Lancelot in the end, so that the king confirms: *an ynen ist hubschkeit und frúmekeit men dann an keinen in der welt* [they demonstrate more courtesy and proper behavior than any other men in the world]. Arthur takes this as a sign of hope for a satisfactory resolution. This is why he answers Lancelot's gesture, even if not completely:

> *Da saß er abe von synem roß, also daten auch die andern. Und Lanczlot, als bald als er nahe by yn kam, da gruoßt er den konig sere hoch, und mit dem so was er doch vol scham, wann der konig gruoßt yn nit wiedder, darumb das er wust das herre Gawin sich des sere betrubet hett* [Then he dismounted from his horse, and the others did likewise. And Lancelot, as soon as he approached him, greeted the king with great courtesy, but he was greatly ashamed because the king did not return the greeting, because he knew that Sir Gawein would have been very upset if he had.] (Lc III, p. 665).

Arthur returns the greeting—out of fear for Gawein—only half-heartedly. Gawein does not return it at all. This shows that Lancelot's gesture remains unsuccessful, that courtly interaction is no longer a basis for agreement, and that the destruction of the Arthurian kingdom is inevitable. Upon Lancelot's address of the king, Gawein "leaps" forward and demands the duel, which will end up being fatal for him.

In the *Prose Lancelot*, unlike in the *Nibelungenlied*, there is still an alternative that is divided between two characters. Lancelot demonstrates with his courtly respect for the king that he is the best knight in the world, and not only because of his physical strength, and that in any case, the disintegration of the Arthurian world is not his fault. Gawein, on the other hand, accepts, like Hagen, that the destruction of courtliness entails the complete downfall of his world. Volker, who wanted to react like Lancelot, ends up following Hagen. What is lacking in the *Nibelungenlied* is the courtly counterweight. From this break in courtly decorum, the *dissimulatio* on Kriemhilt's side escalates to intrigue and betrayal, and the Burgundians answer with a violence that scorns all form.

The procession to church is abused to demonstrate military might. This, too, is indicated by a perversion of courtly symbols. Hagen advises: *nu traget für die rôsen diu wâfen an der hant* [instead of roses, now carry weapons in your hand] (1853,2). Why roses? Roses are a sign of courtly joy and celebration. They belong to the realm of love service. The procession is a part of the *hôchgezît*, where people are festively crowned in wreaths. Roses belong to the courtly festival.[85] This is why they would be out of place if an armed confrontation is immanent. In Etzel's *hôchgezît*, weapons are more appropriate. In this way, heroic epics take roses as symbols of a peaceful foreign world.[86]

The destruction of a courtly way of life is expressed even in the playful cavorting of the horses in the *bûhurt*. At this occasion, latent *haz* is unloaded on a Hunnish knight, who is deprecated as a *trût der vrouwen* [a favorite of the ladies] (1886,2). He does nothing other than catch Volker's eye, because he rides around *sô weigerlîchen* [so pompously] (1885,1). The elegant Hun is not only characterized as a servant of the ladies. In his dress, he is *sam eines edeln ritters brût* [just like a noble knight's bride] (1885,4), in other words like a woman.[87] This is reason enough to strike him down. *Frauendienst* is no better than an exchange of gender roles: "men" are made into "women." Here the epic joins religious critiques of courtliness.[88] Courtly gallantry is not condemned from a moral standpoint, however. The Hun deserves hatred because he is not a real man. In Volker's unmotivated act of violence, we see coming to the surface what courtly decorum always kept under control, and it apparently comes up to the delight of the narrator and his audience. The "foppish" Hun has always been the object of German Nibelungen philology's disdain.[89] What is his real offense other than that he is a servant of ladies, as Sivrit was once? The epithet *weigerlîch* has not only negative connotations. It is used positively, for example, of Sivrit and the retinue of Nibelungen warriors he leads to Isenstein (507,4).[90] Then, the courtly order, which now arouses the antipathy of the Burgundian heroes, was still intact. A cultural refinement, projected onto the foreign, is quashed in this way. Such refinement shows itself ever more clearly to be a counterpart to the unrestrained raving of heroes.

One other time bloody violence grows out of *Frauendienst* (hardly stylized as courtly). Blœdelin, Etzel's brother, the first person Kriemhilt seeks to arouse against her relatives, has his head chopped off by Dancwart with the words:

> *daz sî dîn morgengâbe . . .*
> *zuo Nuodunges briute, der du mit minnen woldest pflegen.* (1927,3–4)
>
> [Let this be your dowry . . .
> for Nuodung's bride, whom you hoped to love.]

Dancwart's cursing denigrates the servant of ladies again as effeminate, because the dowry is to be paid by the man to the woman, not the other way around. Blœdelin receives from Dancwart what his wife would have coming to her, and Dancwart offers to pay other suitors of *Nuodunges briute* the *brûtmiete* [bridal payment] (1928,2) the same way. Controlled by women, the women's slave Blœdelin literally loses his head. Even the *Klage* still says of him:

> *er viengez bôslîchen an*
> *durh eines wîbes lêre.* (Kl 334–5)

> [He started the whole debacle badly
> on account of a woman's orders.]

Frauendienst in the *Nibelungenlied* is the stigma of those who are not up to being heroes.

The Meal

In archaic societies, the meal is the place of primal communality. It accompanies the conclusion of treaties and alliances and symbolically represents social order.[91] The communal meal metonymically stands for close bonds. When he refuses do battle with the Burgundians, Rüedeger thus proposes communal eating and drinking: *trinken unde spîse ich in güetlîchen bôt* [I kindly offered them drink and food] (2159,3). The older tradition of ritual meals continued in the courtly world, producing one of its most powerful visual images in Arthur's Round Table.

Communal eating is a sign of an intact society. The alternative to the Burgundians' heroic expedition is thus provided by Rumolt, the master of the kitchen, who would be responsible for organizing the meal. Its ritual power is disregarded with the quick rejection of Rumolt's advice. His suggestion is reduced to something that heroes can never accept: caring for their own physical well-being. The discriminating ridicule of a man who—if one follows *C or even Wolfram's parody—has nothing but new recipes in his head obscures the notion of the meal as a peaceful alternative, since Rumolt is by no means an outsider.[92] He is also called, like the others, *ein helt zer hant* [a real hero] (1518,1) and employed by Gunther as the administrator of his kingdom: *Daz lant sî dir bevolhen unt mîn kindelîn* [the land and my son are commended to you] (1519,1). He is the one who, according to the *Klage*, makes sure that the court in Worms is not completely at an end after the general destruction. The kitchen master stays back as the guarantor of the continuation of rule.[93]

The meaning of the meal as a ritual of fostering and securing peace makes it particularly susceptible to disruption.[94] In satirical poems like *Neidharts Gefräß*, the perversion of the meal entails the outbreak of chaos.[95] The connection between nuptials and collective destruction in Wittenwiler's *Ring* is similar.

In the *Nibelungenlied*, the meal and the outbreak of violence are intertwined in various ways. The first conflict becomes manifest at a festive meal at Prünhilt's wedding (and not at the previous marriage ceremony). The meal is prepared, as it should be, *mit guoten tavelen breit / vol spîse* [with fine wide tables / filled with food] (605,1), and it is supposed to follow the coronation act (604,3): *der künic wolde gân / ze tische mit den gesten* [the king wanted to go / to table with his guests] (604,1–2), but Gunther is held up once more, in order to wed Sivrit and Kriemhilt.[96] The fulfillment of his oath is considered to be a break—and it will later prove to be a continuing disturbance. Afterwards, when guests are sitting at the table, the seating order is meant to express the harmony between the royal couples Gunther-Prünhilt and Sivrit-Kriemhilt. Prünhilt, however, sees instead a scandal and attempts to find out more about what she thinks is the collapse of the hierarchical order.

A disruption of the meal precedes Sivrit's murder. The symbolism of peaceful interaction is multiplied in the hunt. Hunts are organized to strengthen friendships or possible alliances. In the hunt, violence is directed outward against an opposing, but basically inferior, nature, and it is at the same time defined as a game. Enmity is thereby barred. Here the hunt should replace a (supposedly cancelled) war with a peaceful celebration, and the communal meal should crown the entertainment. But the signs increase that everything is happening *in valsche* [with deceit] (966,2).[97]

The meal is disrupted before it begins. After Sivrit has demonstrated his strength one last time, he drives a bear through the royal camp just as people are beginning to sit down for dinner. The bear gets into the kitchen, scatters the kitchen help in all directions, and knocks everything over:

> *hey waz man guoter spîse in der aschen ligen vant!* (959,4)
>
> [Oh, what fine foods were found lying in the ashes!]

The victuals in the dirt are comical and symbolic at the same time. Sivrit jokingly mixes up the community of those feasting, a community that has already been destroyed by murderous intrigue (969,4). The defective meal illustrates the breakdown of social relationships.

The reaction to Sivrit's joke by the kings and their retinue is strikingly similar to their reaction at the banquet at Etzel's court, when Dancwart reports the attack of the servants, and Hagen answers with an act of violence against Etzel's son. At first, we hear:

> *Dô sprungen von dem sedele die herren und ir man.* (960,1)
>
> [The lords and their men jumped up from their seats.]

And later:

> *Ouch sprungen von den tischen die drîe künege hêr.* (1967,1)
>
> [The three great kings also leaped up from the tables.]

This may be an epic formula that is appropriate to the situation,[98] but it also links related occasions: the disruption of the meal as the outbreak of a (comical or gruesome) chaos. The first time the incident seems to be quickly forgotten:

> *hey waz man rîcher spîse den edeln jegeren dô truoc.* (963,4)
>
> [Ah, what fine foods were set before the noble hunters.]

The meal is spoiled, however:

> *ez enkunde baz gedienet nimmer helden sîn,*[99]
> *heten si dar under niht sô valschen muot.* (964,2–3)
>
> [Heroes could not have been better served
> if they had not had such dishonest intentions.]

This is illustrated in the meal itself. The *schenken* [servers] *die tragen solden wîn* [who were supposed to bring in the wine] are missing (964,1); *daz ist von Hagenen schulden; der wil uns gerne erdürsten lân* [that is Hagen's fault; he would have us die of thirst] (966,4), as Gunther says *in valsche* [dishonestly] (966,2). The murderer is he who has spoiled the meal. Hagen takes responsibility for the errors (967), just as he does later for Sivrit's death and for the theft of the hoard: *lât mich den schuldigen sîn* [let me bear the guilt] (1131.4). Sending away the servers is part of his deceit, but it means much more than that. The hunting company is no longer a drinking fraternity.

The physical need (*Sîvrit den recken twanc des durstes nôt* [Sivrit the warrior was compelled by thirst], 970,1) is all that is left of the social ritual of drinking,[100] and Sivrit hyperbolizes:

> *man solde mir siben soume met und lûtertranc*
> *haben her gefüeret.* (968,2–3)
>
> [They should have brought me seven horses loaded with
> mead and spiced wine.]

Quenching one's thirst in the *brunnen* is stylized into an agon in the footrace with Gunther. *Der brunne der was küele, lûter unde guot* [the fountain was cool, clear, and excellent] (979,1), it is said, but when Sivrit, for the last time together with Gunther, drinks from the spring, he is murdered.

Kriemhilden hôchgezît is both a celebration and an orgy of violence.[101] Kriemhilt literally carries the conflict to the diners. After she has provoked Blœdelin into making a surreptitious attack, she goes *ze tische* [to table] (1911,2), as Prünhilt previously went *unz an den tisch* (611,4) before the conflict about Sivrit's wedding had begun. Kriemhilt has her and Etzel's son carried *ze tische* (1912,3), *zuo der fürsten tische, dâ ouch Hagene saz* [to the table of nobles, where Hagen also sat] (1913,3), as is stated with more precision. The table metonymically stands for the order that is destroyed. At the same time, Blœdelin ambushes Dancwart and his men *ob dem tische* (1921,3). He goes *für die tische* (1922,1) and provokes Dancwart, until Dancwart jumps up *von dem tische* (1926,3) and kills him. The furnishings of the dining hall—*schamel, swære[] stüele[]*— are used as weapons (1931).

Despite the tensions, the meal with Etzel is supposed to complete the harmony of the *künne* [kin] ritualistically one last time. The beginning, when people are still sitting together peacefully and conversing, is already characterized by latent violence. When Etzel tells *lieben friunde mîn* [my dear friends] (1916,1) that he would like to entrust his son to their care (*ziehet in zen êren* [educate him to be honorable], 1917,1), Hagen responds with offensive jokes about the short future of the doomed (*veiclîch[en]*) Hunnish prince (1918,3): *man sol mich sehen selten ze hove nâch Ortliebe gân* [I'll seldom be seen going to court to visit Ortlieb] (1918,4). Instead of education, there is a death threat. The meal fails from the beginning. Etzel's men find it hard not to respond to the insult:

> *daz siz vertragen solden, daz was in ungemach.* (1920,3)
>
> [They were distressed that they had to bear it.]

The Different Celebration

What is needed is an impulse from the outside. It is associated with the disruption of the royal meal and a parody of the arrival of a courtly messenger. When Dancwart's opponents boast that he will only be able to report their attack as a corpse (1942,1–2), he counters: *ich wil diu mære selbe hin ze hove sagen* [I'll make the report at court myself] (1943,3), and in fact he gives a "courtly" performance: *man sach den Hagenen bruoder ze hove hêrlîchen gân* [Hagen's brother was seen going to court in splendid/lordly fashion] (1947,4). He has, as it is sarcastically put, a *hovemære* [a courtly tale] to deliver (1959,4). As he makes his way to the great hall, covered in blood, he interrupts the choreography of the courtly servants by mixing up *truhsæzen und schenken* [stewards and servers]:

> *vil maneger dô daz trinken von der hende swanc,*
> *und eteslîche spîse, die man ze hove truoc.* (1948,2–3)

> [Many of them let their drinks fall
> along with some food, all that was brought in to court.]

Again, food and drink fall to the ground (1948,2–3).[102] The chaos of the disrupted meal is apparently funny. It seems to be a special joke that Dancwart chides the *truhsæzen* to be more conscientious in the exercise of their office, instead of dropping everything, and to let him make his report calmly:

> *jâ soldet ir der geste güetlîche pflegen,*
> *und soldet den herren guote spîse tragen,*
> *und liezet mich diu mære mînen lieben herren sagen.* (1949,2–4)

> [You should take care of your guests,
> and should take fine foods to the lords,
> and let me give the report to my dear lords.]

When he bursts into the hall where the kings are dining with his news, courtly behavior becomes a bloody caricature. Dancwart plays the *kamerære* as a caricature of a court office.[103] He bars the door and allows no one to leave the hall alive, which he ironically celebrates as the epitome of royal service:

> *alsô rîchen künegen ich wol gedienen kan.*
> *sô pflige ich der stiegen nâch den êren mîn.* (1958,2–3)

> [I know how to serve such rich kings.
> So I supervise the stairs according to my honor.]

Hagen transforms the meal into an orgy of violence by seeming to continue with a toast to Etzel and his hospitality, but actually redefining it cynically as a funeral for Sivrit in a parody of *minne* memorial,[104] and then beheading Etzel's son:

> *Dô sluoc daz kint Ortlieben Hagen der helt guot,*
> *daz im gegen der hende ame swerte vlôz daz bluot*
> *und daz der küneginne daz houbet spranc in die schôz.*[105] (1961,1–3)

> [Then Hagen, the great hero, struck the boy Ortlieb,
> so that the blood ran down the sword to his hands,
> and the head flew into the queen's lap.]

The diners scatter. Volker and then the kings jump up *von dem tische* (1966,1; cf. 1967,1). Benches and tables now serve as podiums, helping those in the melee gain the attention of others (1981,3; 1989,1). The hosting Huns are cut down in the hall, with the exception of the king and queen.

The first victims of Hagen's violence metonymically stand for courtly society. The aggression is directed against Kriemhilt, the *vrouwe* of the court, whom he attacks in her son. Next, he strikes at the *magezogen . . . der des kindes pflac* [the teacher . . . who cared for the boy] (1962,1–2), whose head he lays at his feet, or—more precisely and symbolically—*vor tische* (1962,3). If there was ever a scene in which the Hunnish prince had insulted Hagen, and he and his teacher had to be punished,[106] then its memory is now completely erased. Ortlieb did not break any rule. This is exactly why he is the first victim. The *magezoge* must also pay the price because he is responsible for courtly *zuht*, which Hagen now smashes.

Next in line is the minstrel, and Hagen chops off his right hand *ûf der videlen* [upon the fiddle] (1963,3). He thereby brands him as having broken an oath, because Werbel brought the invitation to the bloody festival as a messenger. Werbel rejects this, however, and accuses Hagen of a breach of trust: *ich kom ûf grôze triuwe in iuwer herren lant* [I came in good faith to your lord's lands] (1964,3). Insofar as the motif of treachery is expressly avoided,[107] another explanation offers itself: Hagen mutilates the one who is responsible for the embellishment of the courtly celebration. Werbel complains:

> *wie klenke ich nu die dœne, sît ich verlorn hân die hant?* (1964,4)
>
> [How shall I play music, now that I have lost my hand?]

Hagen couldn't care less (*Hagene ahtet' ringe, gevidelte er nimmer mêr* [Hagen paid little attention to the fact that he could no longer play the fiddle], 1965,1), because the fight is about to begin, and it is also music to his ears:

> *dô frumt' er in dem hûse diu verchgrimmen sêr*
> *an den Etzeln recken, der er sô vil ersluoc.*
> *dô brâht' er in dem hûse liutes ze tôde genuoc.* (1965,2–4)
>
> [Then in the house he gave ruthless and bloody wounds
> to Etzel's warriors, of whom he slew a lot.
> He killed many people there in that house.]

The role of the courtly minstrel at the festival is over, now the "fiddling" is of a different sort. Volker is the new *spilman.*

> *sîn videlboge im lûte an sîner hende erklanc.*
> *dô videlte ungefuoge Guntheres spilman.* (1966,2–3)
>
> [The bow rang out loud in his hand.
> Gunther's minstrel played harshly then.]
>
> *er begonde videlende durch den palas gân;*
> *ein hertez swert im ofte an sîner hende erklanc.* (1976,2–3)

[He began to go through the hall fiddling;
a solid sword always rang out in his hand.]

The narrator hardly gets enough of the joke that the real celebration is just getting started, and finally with better music. The fight in the hall is a wild orgy of sound: Giselher's *wâfen hêrlîchen durch die helme erklanc* [weapon splendidly resounded cutting the helmets] (1970,2). There is a noise (*grœzlîche[r] schal*) of wailing (*von wuofe*) (1972,4),[108] or *grôzer helmklanc* [the great ringing of helmets] (1974,2) and *wâfen hellen* [weapons resonating] (1978,3). The narrator revels in metaphors of a courtly *hôhgezîte* to illustrate the slaughter:[109]

"Ach wê der hôhgezîte," sprach der künec hêr.
"dâ vihtet einer inne, der heizet Volkêr,
also ein eber wilde, und ist ein spilman.
ich dankes mînem heile, daz ich dem tiuvel entran.

Sîne leiche lûtent übele, sîne züge die sint rôt:
jâ vellent sîne dœne vil manigen helt tôt." (2001,1–2002,2)

["Curse this celebration," said the great king.
"There is one inside, by the name of Volker,
he fights like a wild boar, and he is a minstrel.
I thank my good fortune that I was able to escape from this devil.

His tunes are sinister, and his strokes are red:
His melodies strike many a hero dead."]

Gunther comments on the *schal* (2004,1):

hôrt ir die dœne, Hagene, die dort Volkêr
videlt mit den Hiunen, swer zuo den türn gât?
ez ist ein rôter anstrich, den er zem videlbogen hât. (2004,2–4)

[Hagen, do you hear the tunes that Volker
is playing there with the Huns if somebody tries to reach the door?
The strings of his bow are red.]

This is more than an expertly constructed metaphor. The blood music of the "real" *spilman* silences the courtly dance music: *die sînen leiche hellent durch helm unde rant* [his dancing melodies ring through helmet and shield] (2007,3).[110]

"Greeting" is from now on another word for attack:

Des tages wider morgen grüezen man in bôt
mit hertem urliuge; des kômen helde in nôt. (2128,1–2)

[This day in the morning they greeted them
with hard battle; by this heroes were hard pressed.]

Even in Kriemhilt's last words to Gunther (2364,4), the courtly vocabulary (*grüezen*) is the portmanteau of brutal violence; *hovemære* has become the story of an ever more horrible bloodletting.

Courtly *zuht* [self containment] cannot stand up forever to this force. Dietrich declines to fight *in sînen zühten* for a long time (1901,1). Hildebrant *wolde in sînen zühten zuo den gesten gân* [wanted to go to the guests out in a courtly manner] (2248,3). Both are finally pulled into the turmoil of the fight. The break with courtly rules of interaction seems to be staged almost as a joyous liberation from troublesome constraints that had dampened the vengeance from station to station: courtly speech, communal meals, and royal law and order. The story is now of bloody counterrituals reversing forms of peaceful interaction.

Blood and Wine

Drinking wine together was a sign of peace: *dô hiez man den gesten scenken den Guntheres wîn* [the guests were invited to drink Gunther's wine] (126,4) is what we read after Sivrit's challenge to the king has been rebuffed. Rejecting the fellowship of drinking is an act of aggression that replaces the peace drink with blood. This kind of "substitution" is recounted in *Kudrun*. The messengers, who reject hospitality to underline their threat to Kudrun and her relatives, are told:

ob si niht wolten trinken des küniges Hetelen wîn,
man schankte mit dem bluote im und <ouch> den recken sîn (K 773,3–4)[111]

[If they didn't want to drink King Hetel's wine,
then they and their warriors will be served blood.]

In the *Nibelungenlied*, wine is literally replaced by blood. Bloodshed had initially been avoided. Only the battle against outside opponents had been bloody: *daz swert an sînen ecken brâht ûz wunden bluot* [the edge of the sword brought blood from their wounds] (188,3). There is much blood spilled during the Saxon war.[112] Even before the peace is settled, the enemy is accepted into the drinking fellowship. The wounded are cared for, and *man schancte den gesunden met und guoten wîn* [those who were well were served mead and fine wine] (252,3). Instead of blood there is wine; the war concludes with a celebration, whose *wirtscaft* [service] (270,1) lets the wounded *vergezzen* [forget] (269,2) the slaughter, and peace and integrity are reestablished: *Liudegast geheilet sîner wunden was* [Liudegast was healed of his wounds] (312,1).

The next dangerous adventure also seems to be relatively harmless. Blood is spilled during the contest for Prünhilt: *Sîfride dem vil küenen vom munde brast daz bluot* [the blood spurted out of Sivrit the bold's mouth] (458,1) when he encounters Prünhilt's spear. Sivrit is invisible, however, and so the wound goes unnoticed. It is not possible to make any formal amends, because then everything would be divulged. Sivrit is also wounded in his nocturnal struggle with Prünhilt: *daz ûz den nageln spranc / daz bluot im von ir krefte* [her strength made the blood / spurt out of his fingers] (675,2–3).[113] This bloodletting also remains without consequences, because it is covered up by darkness and the cloak of invisibility. Blood is the sign of a crime that has not been atoned for.

In *Âventiure* 16, the underlying connection between the betrayal of the drinking fraternity and the murder comes to light in the contrafactual link between *brunne* [fountain] and blood. For several strophes, the story moves toward the *brunne* from which Sivrit drinks and where he will be murdered. The *brunne* is mentioned nine times within a short space.[114] It is supposed to make up for the disappointment of the meal: *Der brunne der was küele, lûter unde guot* [the fountain was cool, clear, and excellent] (979,1). Instead, blood spurts:

> *Dâ der herre Sîvrit ob dem brunnen tranc,*
> *er schôz in durch daz kriuze, daz von der wunden spranc*
> *daz bluot im von dem herzen vaste an die Hagenen wât.* (981,1–3)
>
> [As lord Sivrit drank from the fountain,
> Hagen shot him through the cross on his shirt, so that blood sprang from the wound
> in his chest and spattered Hagen's clothing.]

Sivrit's blood spatters Hagen, and from this point on, the trail of blood winds its way through the story.[115]

Sivrit's wounds begin to bleed again as the murderers approach the corpse (1044,3): *Die wunden vluzzen sêre alsam si tâten ê* [the wound flowed with blood as it did the first time] (1045,1). This is at first repressed. Sivrit's *wunden* only pain Kriemhilt (1523,4). This repression comes to an end with the journey to Etzel, and again there is blood all over. At first, the trail of blood is denied and hidden. When the Burgundians board the ship that will carry them across the Danube, the murdered ferryman's blood is still steaming:

> *dô sâhen s' in dem schiffe riechen daz bluot*
> *von einer starken wunden, die er dem vergen sluoc.* (1566,2–3)

[In the ship they saw the stream of blood
from the deep wound that he had given the ferryman.]

The questions of the *degene* and Gunther, who *daz heize bluot ersach / sweben in dem schiffe* [saw the hot blood / flowing in the ship] (1567,1–2), are answered by Hagen *lougenlîche* [with lies] (1568,1). Where the blood came from and what happened to the ferryman is covered up. The fight with the ferryman's men, which leaves *ir schilde trüebe und bluotes naz* [the Burgundians' shields dark and wet with blood] (1619,4; cf. 1617,3) is at first supposed to be kept from the kings:

Si beliben unvermeldet des heizen bluotes rôt,
unz daz diu sunne ir liehtez schînen bôt
dem morgen über berge. (1624,1–3)

[They were unaware of the hot red blood
until the sun began to rise
over the mountains in the morning.]

Only then do the kings discover why *die ringe naz / sus wurden von dem bluote* [the chainmail / was drenched in blood] (1625,2–3).

In Bechelaren, there is again wine instead of blood: *dô hiez man balde scenken den gesten guoten wîn* [the guests were quickly ordered to be served fine wine] (1668,3), and then once more at Etzel's reception:

dô schanct man den gesten (mit vlîze tet man daz)
in wîten goldes schâlen met, môraz unde wîn, (1812,2–4)

[The guests were served (this was done with great diligence)
mead, mulberry and clear wine.]

und bat die ellenden grôze willekomen sîn.
man gab in vollelîchen trinken unde maz.
alles des si gerten des was man in bereit. (1817,2–3)

[The great foreigners were welcomed.
They were given plenty to drink and eat.
Anything that they wanted was provided them.]

At the encampment the next day with Etzel, blood flows instead of wine, first, with Blœdelin's attack on the baggage train: the *ingesinde* [servant], who wanted to eat, is *von bluote rôt unde naz* [red and wet with blood] (1932,4); Dancwart makes *vil der ringe mit bluote vliezende naz* [many coats of mail drenched with flowing blood] (1938,4); his path is *von heizem bluote naz* [soaked with hot blood] (1947,1), and *mit bluote was berunnen allez sîn gewant* [all his clothing was drenched in blood] (1951,3).[116]

The trail of blood reaches the feast of the kings with Dancwart: *wie sît ir sô rôt* [why are you all red?] (1955,1), Hagen asks and finds out, to his relief: *Du sihest mich wol gesunden: mîn wât ist bluotes naz. / von der ander manne wunden ist mir geschehen daz* [You see that I am unhurt: my shirt is soaked with blood; / other men's wounds did this to me] (1956,1–2). This is the signal for Hagen to turn wine into blood: *nu trinken wir die minne und gelten's küneges wîn. / der junge vogt der Hiunen, der muoz der aller êrste sîn* [now we drink in loving memory and honor the king's wine / the young Hunnish prince must be the first] (1960,3–4). Hagen's toast, which costs the king's son his life, is the start of a new kind of hospitality with Hagen as sommelier: *hie schenket Hagene daz aller wirseste tranc* [here Hagen served the worst drink] (1981,4). He does not spill wine in the *minne* drink;[117] instead, he spills blood: *daz im gegen der hende ame swerte vlôz daz bluot* [blood flowed down to his hands from his sword] (1961,2). The king's wine is "paid for" with the blood of the king's son; blood springs from the swords (1986,4); many will *vallen in daz bluot* [die in their blood] (1971,4) struck down by Giselher, the most courtly of the royal brothers.

Then the Huns are driven out of the hall, and once again a climax of blood frenzy is staged. In the first attack, that by Irinc, the heroes—four anonymous Burgundians who evidently don't count here—do not yet shed their blood (2039–47). Only with Hagen's wounding (*Daz ir von mîner wunden die ringe sehet rôt* [you see my mail is red with my own blood], 2057,1) does the blood of the Burgundians begin to flow. This only stokes their anger for the second battle, *daz iz lougen began / von fiwerrôten winden* [there began a roar / as if from fiery red winds] (2062,1–2). This costs Irinc his life and pulls his men into the deadly battle until blood runs out of their chainmail (*daz bluot allenthalben durch diu löcher vlôz* [the blood flowed through the many holes], 2078,2).

The exchange of wine and blood is radicalized one more time in a pause just before the final destruction. Hagen advises the thirsty warriors:

> *swen twinge durstes nôt, der trinke hie daz bluot.*
> *daz ist in solher hitze noch bezzer danne wîn.* (2114,2–3)
>
> [Whoever is thirsty should drink blood.
> This is better than wine in such a fever.]

The Burgundians, who are choked by all the smoke, rationalize the magical practice of drinking one's enemy's blood as a survival strategy, but it retains its original meaning: *dâ von gewan vil krefte ir eteslîches lîp* [they gained much strength from that] (2117,3).[118] Such a drink revives the courtly encampment; blood is much better than wine:

> *dô begonde er trinken daz vliezende bluot.*
> *swie ungewon ers wære, ez dûhte in grœzlîchen guot.* (2115,3–4)
>
> [He began to drink the flowing blood.
> As unaccustomed as he was to it, it seemed to him to be quite good.]
>
> *mir ist noch vil selten geschenket bezzer wîn.* (2116,3)
>
> [I have seldom been served a better wine.]

Again, Hagen is the server. The speaker thanks him, *daz ich von iuwer lêre sô wol getrunken hân* [that I have drunk so well from your fountain of knowledge] (2116,2). The substitution can be seen as a blasphemous ritual. The religious connotations are weaker than in Hagen's *minne* drink at Etzel's feast,[119] but the provocation is increased. The eucharistic content seems to be at least implicitly present in a black, blood mass.[120]

Toward the end, the epic descends into a stream of blood. The warriors are covered with blood.[121] Blood runs out of their armor, it drips into the helmets:[122] *si holten ûz den helmen den heize vliezenden bach* [they poured from their helmets the hot, flowing stream] (2288,4). In order to rest, the Burgundians sit down on corpses, in their blood (*ûf die wunden, die vor in in daz bluot/wâren zuo dem tôde von ir handen komen* [on the wounded, whom they in that blood/ had dispatched with their hands], 2082,2–3). *Sigestap der küene den bluotegen bach/hiu ûz herten ringen* [Sigestap the bold carved a blood stream/out of the hard mail] (2284,2–3). The blood in which Wolfhart wades spurts *al über daz houbet* [all over his head] (2294,4). Men fight in blood and fall *nider in daz bluot* [down into the blood] (2299,3),[123] jump *ûz dem bluote* [up out of the blood] (2050,1), and put out fires in the hall with blood (*tret si mit den füezen tiefer in daz bluot* [kick them with your feet into deeper blood], 2119,3). The dying Wolfhart *blihte ouch ûz dem bluote* [looked up from the blood] (2300,3). Men no longer drink blood, they drown in it.[124] Hildebrant saves himself from the fight covered in blood.[125]

Then there is Hagen's deep wound (2350,4), Gunther's defeat (*daz bluot man durch die ringe dem helde vliezen sach* [blood was seen streaming through the hero's chainmail], 2360,2), and the decapitation of Gunther, then Hagen, single-handedly by Kriemhilt, who herself ends up *ze stücken . . . gehouwen* [hacked . . . to pieces] (2377,2). With a horrible scream—*waz mohte si gehelfen daz si sô grœzlîchen schrê?* [how could her loud shriek help her] (2376,4)—*ze stücken was gehouwen dô daz edele wîp* [the noble woman was hacked to pieces] (2377,2).

Heroic epics are usually full of blood, and it runs even more freely sometimes, for example, in the *Book of Bern*. In the *Nibelungenlied*, however, the trail of blood runs through a story that was at first laid out much differently. The courtly order does not just collapse, its destruction is celebrated as a bloody counterfeast.

9 *Deconstructing the Nibelungian World*

Disappointment that the *Nibelungenlied* does not yield a guiding concept faded when such concepts were questioned in other works of art, medieval as well as modern. It has long been the consensus that the *liebe-leit* formula was not the guiding concept. However, there have been attempts again and again, based on the Kriemhilt character, to provide the legend of destruction with a consistent and meaningful paradigm.

An epic like the *Nibelungenlied* mocked these attempts from the beginning, with the result that after one and a half centuries of interpretive history, scholars have given up, claiming that any interpretation of such a legendary conglomerate is impossible. The failure of so-called holistic interpretations, however, does not mean that all hermeneutic approaches to the epic must fail. It is more likely that the desire for wholeness and consistency, which the epic continues to frustrate, is based on a modern concept of literature that fails to understand medieval textuality between orality and literality and follows an older metaphysics of art.

The preceding approach has sought to show what insights the text offers by considering individual aspects of it without assuming that all elements can be put together in a global synthesis. A complex work of art consists of bringing together heterogeneous, incomplete, dissonant, and even contradictory material. The focus should be on this tension and the forces that it must withstand. An epic is a dynamic work of art. "Tension" does not refer to something static, or to an equilibrium, but realizes itself in movement. Within this movement, accents shift and appearances change. The aim of the movement in the *Nibe-*

lungenlied is not a solution but a dissolution. The *Nibelungenlied* deconstructs its own premises, and it is the *Klage* that tries to save some of them.

The term "deconstruction" is frequently used as a modern catchall. For many, it represents the quintessence of the postmodern sellout of the text to arbitrary interpretation. By the way, this has nothing to do with poststructural analysis of the rhetorical nature of texts. But here "deconstruction" is still understood in a more conventional sense. It should not be portrayed as the ceaseless "play of significants," a deferment of meaning that never achieves its goal. Deconstruction here is meant as a process that is accomplished within the text. In this process, the text simultaneously affirms and subverts, and ultimately destroys, the assumptions on which it is built. The world that it playfully creates and its values and norms, which it propagates, prove to lead into irreconcilable aporias.

Every attempt to determine some kind of positive "meaning" of the text immediately generates a competing interpretation equally capable of arguing from within the text. This should not be understood as an aesthetic deficit, however, but as a special aesthetic concept, which includes dissonances and ambiguities that also determine the precarious relationship of the *Nibelungenlied* to its contemporary culture, a culture characterized by a courtly worldview. The unproblematic stereotypes and patterns of interaction of this imaginary world progressively become ambiguous and are eventually perverted. Similarities dissolve as they are played out and transformed in barely recognizable ways. The collapse of this world is complete. Its deconstruction cannot be reduced to the critique of single social groups.

Criticism from a Clerical Point of View?

There is, therefore, no single standpoint from which the slide to anomy can be judged. Can the *Nibelungenlied* be interpreted as a "clerical rebellion" against a worldly, courtly culture, as C. Stephen Jaeger does?[1] Is it a courtly model of society that is being destroyed?[2] Is an archaic heroic order being dismissed? It seems more likely to me that the *Nibelungenlied* undermines the positions from which such interpretations can be made.

To be sure there are certain motifs of clerical criticism of the court—above all, of luxurious lifestyles and service to women—that are related to the negative representation of the court in the *Nibelungenlied*.[3] But the goals of the anticourtly "conservative clerics" and those of the nobility who are likewise critical of courtliness only seemingly converge in the *mos maiorum*. What the clerics mean by the traditions of the *patres antiqui* is Christian simplicity and modesty, resisting the temptations of the world. What is fascinating for the nobility about the *alten mæren*, on the other hand, is a warrior ethic that is not concerned with Christian values such as compassion, forgiveness, and goodness. Instead, it is an ethic "of self-assertion and revenge,"[4] which is diametrically opposed to the Christian commandments to be humble and to love your enemy.

Clerical criticism of the court is stimulated either by monasticism or by the *schola*, whose rational lifestyle is counterposed to its tumultuous confusion.[5] It is confronted by a "philosophical" lifestyle aimed at self-control.[6] Clerics criticized the moral perversion of courts, especially the courts of clerical princes, and the vices of court clergy in general. Laypeople are involved, too, insofar as they fail to live up to Christian values. A sober, Christian life in princely courts that is without malice and cunning can also be projected into the past, but it is not identical with the heroic portrayal of "ancient" nobility. Religious and heroic criticism only have some things in common, for example, a criticism of certain typical courtly behavior, such as flattery, slander, corruptibility, ambition, and intrigue. But clerical criticism goes beyond this and is directed against the secular ethic of a warrior class. This is not only where the rights of the Church come into conflict with the lay nobility. Its lifestyle as a whole is questioned: hunting, music, entertainment, gallantry, competition, and feuds.[7] Both groups might find themselves in the *laudatio temporis acti*, as Jaeger shows,[8] and heterogeneous elements of criticism can be taken up in counterexamples to courtly perversion, as, for instance, with a certain Starcatherus in Saxo Grammaticus, who, according to Jaeger, "combines the spirit of a viking with the moral sense of a reform monk."[9] However, this prehistoric hero, a positively portrayed critic of courtly softness, represents a pagan ethic in his proclivity to violence.[10] In clerical chronicles "Viking" was the embodiment of terrible and criminal roughness. This heroic type is, on the contrary, himself a target of clerically influenced historiography.[11]

Since the twelfth century, clerical *militia* in the sense of Saint Paul's Letter to the Ephesians is confronted with the combative spirit of a feudal nobility bent on physical destruction.[12] Heinrich von Melk offers just one voice:

swâ aber von sumlîchen
der manhäit wirt gidâcht,
dâ wirt vil selten fur brâcht,
wie gitâner sterche der sul phlegen,
der wider den tievel mûze streben.

dâ nennent si genûge
vil manic ungefûge.
si bringent sich mêr ze schanden,
swenne si sprechent "den mac man in allen landen
ze einem guotem chnecht wol haben:
der hât sô manigen erslagen." (HvM 362–72)

[but where people
talk about manhood,
it is very rarely considered
what kind of force should be used
by those who have to fight the devil.
Instead, they mention a lot
of bad things.
They bring shame on themselves
when they say: "this one should universally
be held up as a good knight:
he struck many dead.]

At stake here is the alternative between the ascetics of clerical *militia* and the unbridled violence of the warrior society.

Even if the conception and writing of the epic around 1200 could only be accomplished by a *clericus*, this writer is not a protagonist of clerical criticism of the court. Rather, he articulates the position of a noble lay society that only rarely found itself drawn to writing, because it was still predominantly illiterate. In this respect, the *Nibelungenlied* cannot be included in the tradition of European court criticism, which was at first mostly clerical, then later academic, and in the Middle Ages and the early modern period was still primarily religious and moralistic.[13]

Unlike the clerical criticism that dealt discursively with the problem of a new court culture, the epic has no "message." Instead, it plays through contrary positions, remaining open to different evaluations.[14] The reactions to its ending remain ambivalent up to the present. Is it really the case that one is "simply relieved that Kriemhild has finally been eliminated,"[15] or does disgust at the heroic blood orgy predominate? Can the ambiguity of courtly order be seen as a point for criticism,[16] if what replaces it is bloody chaos? On the other hand, is the outbreak of heroic-anarchic action criticized if it tears apart the web of lies spun by false speech and gestures? The epic refuses to answer.

Not even the *Klage*, so much closer to clerical norms in its attempts to simplify such openness, is based on a monastic counterpart to the *mundus perversus.* Rather, it is rooted in a well-tempered courtly ethic with Christian overtones. It laments the excesses of the heroic world without questioning its rules. It is constantly stated that things did not have to get this bad. By putting the blame on Hagen's meanness, the others are mostly left with the fault of going too far and not keeping each other informed. Even when the *Klage* presents this or that evidence for Kriemhilt's innocence, it does not correct the basically sound logic that requires Kriemhilt's death. Sanctions against Hildebrant, who kills her, are never discussed. The *Klage* does not fundamentally criticize the mechanisms of feudal ethics. It reacts to the brutal break in the story without questioning its foundation.

As determined by its dreadful end, the Nibelungian world is kept alive in memory.[17] It appears from the beginning to be split between courtliness, which can include deception, and heroism, which leads to ruthless destruction. What is told is how the one turns into the other, without offering any sort of constructive perspective. Pleasing courtly form and betrayal conclude an unholy alliance, and truth's heroic coming into the light is identical to complete extinction. The downfall of the Burgundians is not presented as a moral victory that eclipses the political defeat, as in the *Atlilied.*[18] There is no victor. Gunther disappears without a word. Hagen does not triumph morally (as does Gunnar of the *Atlilied*, who keeps what belongs to him). He wins by insisting on his crime and the impossibility of atoning for it. The best of all heroes who ever fought in battle or carried a shield (*der aller beste degen, / der ie kom ze sturme oder ie schilt getruoc*, 2374,2–3) does not die an undefeated warrior fighting against a superior enemy, like Roland, but as the weak victim of a woman. He has to leave his opponent the final word and has to rely on the revenge of his enemy Hildebrant, whom he previously mocked. Etzel retains the upper hand over his guests, but at the cost of his power and thanks to a deed he condemns (2374). Dietrich, who has the honor of the last victory, is nothing more than a tearful onlooker. Kriemhilt, the courtly *vrouwe* of the first part, has no time to enjoy her revenge; she is cut to pieces in a spontaneous act of violence. Nothing makes sense. The definitive end of the epic remains ambivalent, and its attempt to give meaning is incomplete. The question of a continuation remains open.

A Distancing from Heroic Patterns?

The *Nibelungenlied* cancels the complex order it had built up in the beginning and replaces it with single combat. A civilized lifestyle degenerates into the negative foil for heroic intractability. This links the text to other late medieval heroic epics that also articulate criticism and disdain for what was perhaps a finer, but also less warlike courtly world, as is practiced in *Frauendienst.*[19] The amazing popularity of anti-courtly resentment in the late Middle Ages is a reaction to the expansion of an elite courtly culture, although often the reaction is nothing more than a simple regressive fantasy.

The *Nibelungenlied* is different. It gleans its *aristeiai,* or heroics, from a courtly world that allows undomesticated violence only at its margins, not its core, but in the end succumbs to it nonetheless. The making of a hero is ambivalent: it represents timeless honor, but leads straight to destruction. It creates a social bond between individual warriors, but eliminates any more developed sociality. It cannot be consistently founded in ethics, but can only be told. In that the *Nibelungenlied* does not turn away from the aporias of its worldview, critique as well as fascination remain ambiguous.

The usual means with whose help late medieval literature would incorporate archaic heroics are therefore missing. In the *Nibelungenlied,* comedy is only seldom the answer to the ambivalence of heroic violence. Traces of such comedy are limited to the first part of the epic, where they concentrate, as usual, on characters who seem to originate from an archaic world. In the second part, on the other hand, only those characters who oppose the heroic rapture into destruction seem ridiculous.

The way in which the strong Prünhilt ends her marital conflict with Gunther is funny, in that she hangs him on a hook. Funny is also the force with which Sivrit chases a bear through the hunting party's dining area. Sivrit's second battle with Alberich also has comical elements. The disguise, the fight in the dark, the idea that the result has already been decided, all of these are comical. It may also be funny when the young margravine is repulsed by the thought of kissing the dreadful Hagen in greeting (1665,4). The background to all this is a civilized lifestyle as found in Worms, on a courtly hunt, or in Bechelaren. These conditions are never threatened by such exceptional figures. The representatives of heroic power prove harmless in the end.

Comedy grows out of the disparity between narrative worlds and their personnel. Where this disparity becomes too great—as in the terrible Prünhilt in Isenstein—men associate it with the devil.[20] Seen from Worms, Prünhilt is monstrous, but from the perspective of Isenstein, the Burgundians, including Hagen, offer a pitiful picture and provoke laughter (447,2). Back in Worms, Gunther complains again: *ich hân den übeln tiuvel heim ze hûse geladen* [I have brought the cursed devil home with me] (649,2), but this house devil, the domesticated version of the Amazon, rules only in the bedroom, and even there not for very long.

The heroic world is no longer funny in the downfall of the Burgundians in the second part of the epic. The *tiuvel* Prünhilt and the *vâlandinne* Kriemhilt can no longer be compared in their deeds.[21] The one becomes finally integrated into the court at Worms, the other cuts off all social ties. The difference between the courtly world at the beginning and the heroic world at the end can be seen in Hagen. In Isenstein, he cuts a rather poor figure; later, in Bechelaren, he scares a little girl, but at Etzel's court, he becomes a bloodthirsty warrior, whose jokes only comment on his own violence.

The comedy shifts from heroic to courtly objects. Rumolt, the gourmet who is concerned with people's well-being, is supposed to be funny. So are the Hun who has dressed himself to the nines in service to a lady, whom Volker brusquely kills, and Hagen's toast to the Hunnish prince before he chops off his head. Funny, too, is the commentary on the maimed minstrel Werbel, who can no longer draw sounds from his fiddle. The victims of this comedy are denounced as cowards or weak, like Etzel's son, who, according to Hagen, is *veiclîch getân* [marked to die young] (1918,3). This proves to be a self-fulfilling prophecy. Someone who is already marked for death is no great loss—if this is still supposed to be funny.[22] This kind of comedy is based on the fascination with barbarism, whose opponents are supposed to appear pitiful.

The *Nibelungenlied* stands apart from the late medieval reception of heroic epic in that it rejects a comic distancing.[23] The monstrosity of the *rehten heldes muot* [the mind of a true hero] is not softened by grim jokes about giants who have to be chained up, deformed creatures who must be bloodily eliminated, magical beings, and bullies, who all inhabit the heroic world, as in *König Rother*, *Wolfdietrich D*, or Wittenwiler's *Ring*.

In *Kudrun*, which is seen as a correction to the tale the downfall of the Nibelungen,[24] the gruesome comedy is clearer. The gruff Wate causes a young girl's consternation at the kiss of greeting (K 1641,2), just as Hagen does. But he seems comical when acting as a hero. His strength occasionally becomes animalistic. He works himself into a blind rage that mows everything down:

> *er begunde limmen. sam ein âbentrôt*
> *sach man helme schînen von sînen slegen swinden.* (K 882,2–3)
>
> [He began to growl. Like the red of sunset,
> helmets were seen to shine from his swift blows.]

The verb *limmen* is used of animals.[25] It is not a person who is fighting, but a force of nature let loose. Wate's thirst for blood does not stop for women and children. Attempts to calm him are answered with violence and threats. He grinds his teeth (*mit grisgramenden zenden*, K 1508,2), his eyes throw off sparks (K 1508,3), and he rages.[26] His own King Herwig, who tries to persuade him to spare an enemy, is thrown to the floor (K 1493,) and his plea is rejected as the counsel of women (K 1491,2). He cuts down women and does not spare even children in their cribs (K 1503).

Once the victory has been won, there is nothing more about this side of Wate. He remains one of the pillars of the court and is integrated into the new courtly, peaceful order, but he is no longer required in its establishment. His brutality in battle is accepted with only weak criticism. In the end, it is no longer needed.[27] Many of the traits of Hagen and other raging heroes in the *Nibelungenlied* can be seen in Wate. Unlike Hagen, however, he becomes less and less important to the story line. Even if there are no sanctions against the indiscriminate butcher Wate, he is removed from the core of the epic. In this way, *Kudrun* avoids the ambivalent fascination with the orgies of violence that characterize the *alten mæren*.

The *Nibelungenlied*'s criteria are partly emended by the *Klage*, which as evidence of reception, probably drawn from a clerical context, shows how horrifying the Christian world around 1200 must have found the ghastly downfall of the Burgundians. No comical ambivalences are to be found in the *Klage* poet, but the immoderate nature of the Nibelungian world is apparent everywhere, even in the way that this world mourns its own destruction: in *unbesceidenheit* [without measure] (Kl 641). Etzel's lament sounds like *ein wisentes horn* [a bison's horn] (Kl 625). He no longer roars like a noble animal but bleats and *mit wintender hant / stêt als ein blœde wîp* [stands around wringing his hands like a brainless woman] (Kl 1020–21) until the narrator plunges him into hopeless desperation.[28]

The heroic world is petrified in its overblown affects. Wolfhart lies there *mit durchpizzenen zanden* [with clenched teeth] (Kl 1704), and his sword must be removed *mit zangen / ûz sînen vingern langen* [with tongs / from his long fingers] (Kl 1689–90). The dimensions are already exaggerated into the gigantic, as in the later *Heldenbücher*. Giselher, Gernot, and Rüedeger can hardly be overcome even as corpses. Giselher's corpse *was ein teil ze swære, / er enpfiel in wider in daz wal* [was too heavy / and fell down on the battleground] (Kl 1834–5). Gernot is so *wol gewahsen . . . an grœze und an lenge* [large . . . in weight and height], that he can't fit through the door (*diu tür wart in ze enge, / dâ man die tôten ûz truoc* [the door was too narrow / where one wanted to carry out the dead], Kl 1928–31). Even Hildebrant breaks down under Rüedeger's weight (Kl 2099–2101). To get him out, a hole has to be made in the wall:

Hildebrant der bat dô lân
wîter offen den sal. (Kl 2126–27)

[Hildebrant commanded that
a wider opening be made in the hall.]

The bodies of heroes are obstinate, perhaps magnificent, but in any case monstrous representatives of a monstrous prehistoric world. The narrator of the *Klage* cannot reestablish Etzel's court, but he views its ruins with estrangement. The heroic passion for violence in the *Nibelungenlied* must have had an erratic effect, and yet was still fascinating enough that the epic (together with the *Klage*) was copied again and again.

There has been a reassuring conviction in more recent Nibelungen philology that nothing in the epic justifies its use for nationalistic or militaristic purposes,[29] and that this is based on a gross misreading. That is certainly right. But it is seldom questioned how such massive misunderstandings could have come about. The perversion of courtly forms of interaction and the destruction of the courtly world and the feudal order make such receptions seem not unreasonable. The passion for violence that disrupts all attempts at peaceful settlement, the denunciation of a few counterfigures, the unbelievable brutality of the battles, the uncompromising meanness of the plot for revenge, which is only "corrected" by another violent act—all of this is all too easily taken in by regressive and violent fantasies, at least as long as the ambivalences that the epic itself creates are not taken seriously.

An Epidemic of Violence

The *Nibelungenlied* tells about unleashing violence in what is a seemingly completely pacified world. The courtiers of Worms, first and foremost Gunther, become the *Nibelunge*, and the courtly *maget* Kriemhilt becomes the queen of the Huns, hell-bent on revenge. Once she has established herself with Etzel, she determines her old identity through the *Nibelunge* and not through the kingdom of the Netherlands. As with Sivrit himself and his dangerous strength, the Nibelungian power potential is at first useful to the kingdom at Worms. Gunther is able to make use of it through his stand-in, Sivrit, in Isenstein. It might be said, with Gilles Deleuze, that the "state" (in the medieval sense, the Burgundian kingdom) has appropriated a "war machine."[30] This is short-lived, however. Sivrit alone masters the Nibelungian might. As long as he is alive, it will be controlled, but after his murder, this power becomes too much for the survivors to handle.

Nibelungian power seems to be destroyed along with Sivrit's murder. It can be transferred to Worms, but it cannot be permanently incorporated into the political structure. Opposing interests are linked to the hoard. The gold lures the Burgundians with its immense power potential, but for Kriemhilt it represents the means to revenge. Both are rebuffed, and the hoard is withdrawn from both sides. Sunk in the Rhine, the Nibelungian potential seems finally to have been banished from the epic world. Inexplicable circumstances make it available again, first only in part, right after Kriemhilt has accepted Etzel's proposal. It causes the first conflict, which is quickly resolved. Then it appears again with the Nibelungen warriors, who link up with the Burgundians upon departing for Etzel's court, and shortly thereafter, it begins to transform the Burgundians who had tried in vain to control it.

The Burgundian power, which at first was introduced as a static and hierarchical order, is set in motion, and hierarchical structures lose their meaning. This transformation is much more basic than the supposed fact that the vassals put themselves in place of the kings. "Statehood" as a whole, as it was known in the Middle Ages, is destroyed. What arrives at Etzel's court is no longer an organized political group, but rather a motley crew of *ellenden* [homeless] warriors. This expedition breaks into the most powerful of all courts, the refuge of famous heroes, apparently to celebrate a festive occasion, but in reality to pull Etzel's court into a bloody battle of revenge for the ruler of the Nibelungen and owner of the Nibelungian gold.

Destruction does not result from an uprising against legitimate rule, but from an exceptional concentration of force and counterforce that takes no account of structures of rulership, vassality, or family.

New configurations result from the outbreak of the battle and replace the political order. On the one side is the faceless horde of Huns, apparently unlimited in number, which Kriemhilt and Etzel again and again launch against the Burgundians in the thousands, always in vain. Along with these is the only effective group of exiled heroes, who stand on Etzel's side but are not simply subject to his control and therefore only fight according to their own will. The Hunnish kingdom tends to dissolution, because it falls apart on the one side in an anonymous mass that fights on Etzel's command to be slaughtered, and on the other in a collection of single heroes, for whom Etzel's command means relatively little. They likewise fall victim to the Nibelungen, with the exception of Dietrich and Hildebrant.

Fighting on the Burgundian side is a contingent of heroes (*helde*) inextricably linked to one another, and only at first organized into a hierarchical order. It mutates more and more into a gang or pack, Deleuze's concept of which, it seems to me, best describes the strange social structure that evolves ever more clearly after crossing the Danube.[31] It is not defined by heritage and origin, does not represent any social formation in the normal sense, and rejects any kind of institutionalization. This applies to the Burgundian ruling elite at Etzel's festival. At first, Hagen and the kings are bound by family (1925,2)[32] and vassality, but these relationships lose their meaning. The Nibelungen warriors have their leader, but this is not the king who rules as in Worms. There are reminders of former condition, but now only single heroes count. In the lead is Hagen, not Gunther. The leading character is an "extraordinary individual," who is at first marginal but then forces his "eccentricities" on others.[33] Hagen is "eccentric" inasmuch as he is stigmatized by murder and theft and is the principal target of Kriemhilt's revenge. His position as an outsider gradually becomes everyone's position. Hagen is the outcast, the only one excluded from the *suone*, whose interests are different from those of the others from the beginning. By his linking himself to the others—or they to him—his menace extends to all. Through him, the entire group is changed. The fate of the outcast becomes the fate of everyone.

This is a process in slow motion that seems inevitable only from the perspective of its outcome. Deleuze calls the "gang" a simple "becoming." It "becomes" through "infection."[34] The metaphor of "infection" describes exactly what happens in the *Nibelungenlied*. The blood lust of general destruction spreads like an epidemic, which finally infects even those who try to keep clear of the contagion. "Infection" gives a name to the irrationality of events, to which alternatives always seem possible, but are never realized.

There is a good reason why the majority of interpretations of the *Nibelungenlied* are in the form of narratives and usually follow the chronology of the plot. They adjust themselves to the form of the epic. It is mostly only possible to say, "this is the way it was, this is what the narrator said," but not "this is why it is this way."

The second part of the epic can be read as the spreading of a pandemic. The tension gradually builds: with Kriemhilt's invitation, with the counsel concerning it, on the way to Etzel, with the reception, in Hagen's and Volker's provocation, with the nighttime raid, going to church, and the tournament [*bûhurt]*. But the crisis is put on hold. Up to this point, Kriemhilt's purposeful action, intent on revenge, governs the different incidents, only to be answered by Hagen's and Volker's equally purposeful attempts to ignite the conflict. This works until Kriemhilt persuades Blœdelin to attack the servants. From now on, purposeful action proves to be less and less important. The fact that Ortliep is carried to the feast—*Dô der strît niht anders kunde sîn erhaben* [since the battle could not otherwise be initiated] (1912,1)—can no longer strictly be viewed as a calculation of objective and means. What can Kriemhilt count on if she acts this way?[35] Nevertheless it is successful. Since Ortliep is present at the meal, he becomes the first victim, and because there can be no *suone* for his murder, there can be no retreat for Etzel. Since Kriemhilt cannot have a plan she can control, whether this is the elimination of an original motivational chain or not, it becomes obvious that the action exceeds all intentions.

In fact, all subsequent planned actions fail. None of Kriemhilt's various attacks—in the open, in the dark, with military means, with fire—work. The suggestions by the Burgundians to force a decisive battle are rejected. The attempts by Rüedeger and Dietrich to stay out of the conflict or to arbitrate fail to prevent them from being sucked in. The destruction cannot be stopped, and Kriemhilt achieves her aim, not with cool calculation, and not even by her own efforts, but to a certain extent by chance, because Dietrich becomes involved in the battle through an unfortunate chain of events.

An incredibly aggressive energy has built up. Ortliep acts as the catalyst that has the effect of freeing this energy. It can no longer be controlled; it just "happens." When Dancwart bursts into the hall with the news that the servants have been killed, reasonable intent (*sinne*) and will have no place:

> *sine mohtenz mit ir sinnen dô niht understân.* (1967,3)
>
> [They were unable to stop it with their intentions.]

Those who have up to now been uninvolved gradually become instruments of Kriemhilt's revenge in the following scenes. Irinc still does so willingly—he even succeeds in preventing his men from becoming engaged, and he comes back safely once. But when he is killed, those from Düringen and Tenemark fight despite explicit instructions to the contrary. There seems to be no choice left: *dô muost'ez* [!] *an ein strîten von den von Tenemarke gân* [then a battle had to be [!] started by those of Denmark] (2069,4). Deliberation and will play ever smaller roles. The initial desire to avoid the fight has no chance. Rüedeger still expresses his resistance. He fights under protest, but he fights, and does so with no holds barred.

The most spectacular victims of the epidemic are the Amelungen. Dietrich wants to avoid any provocation. He holds the hot-headed Wolfhart back and at first sends Helfrich, then the rational Hildebrant, just to get news from the Burgundians. But then Hildebrant arms himself, and before he knows what has happened (*ê daz ers innen wurde*, 2250,2), he is standing at the head of an armed company of men. Still an agreement seems within reach, but the dispute over the corpse of the dead Rüedeger gets out of control. Wolfhart and Volker work themselves into a rage—and everybody else is incited along with them: *im wart* [!] *ein gæhez volgen von sînen vriunden getân* [literally: a hasty following was provided to him by his friends; i.e., his friends followed him quickly] (2273,4).

When Dietrich asks *Wie kunde ez sich gefüegen* [how could this come about?] (2320,1), he is questioning an anonymous process controlled by no one. His attempt to clear up the responsibility for the slaughter fails. He gives up: *ez muos' et alsô sîn* [all right, it must be so] (2336,1). There is no alternative, and even his last plan to take Gunther and Hagen hostage in order to end the conflict by judicial means is destroyed by Hagen's fury (*zorn*, 2347,4). His request of Kriemhilt that she spare the lives of the foreigners (*die ellenden*, 2364,4; cf. 2355) is forgotten when the main antagonists come together. In the end, Hildebrant strikes Kriemhilt explicitly without regard for the consequences (*swaz halt mir geschiht* [regardless of what happens to me], 2375,2). One after the other is infected by murdering, until in the end almost everyone lies dead.

Dehumanization

This is not a revitalization of some unfortunate relic of a metaphysics of fate or even the remnants of an archaic Germanic religiosity,[36] and it is not about some dark power that makes human will and planning futile.[37] At the core is a simple narrative principle: in its last third, the *Nibelungenlied* narrates the contrariness of plans and events, tied to the dissolution of ethical responsibility and political order. A vortex comes into being that is beyond anyone's control and devours everything. This vortex cannot be explained, but it is also not mythologized.

Deleuze calls the "gang" the "reality of men becoming animals."[38] This does not refer to a regression to an "archaic," pagan barbarism, but instead describes an alternative that lies under the surface of every order. How heroes develop into animals is told first in Sivrit's downfall, then in that of the Nibelungen. The actors become one with the affect and, regardless of what was mentioned about them before in terms of considerateness, rationality, deliberation, or conscience, dissolve in the raging of the battle, Rüedeger and Giselher as much as Hagen and Volker. This "becoming animals" is first sketched by the narrator in the metaphors of battle, but then more and more literally, up to drinking the enemy's blood.

Animals belong to the Nibelungian world in which Sivrit proved himself as a *helt*. He and Alberich fight *alsam die lewen wilde* [like wild lions] (97,2). Wild animals rend everything that comes in their path, but they are themselves hunted and killed in the end. It starts when Sivrit, the best of all hunters, faster than any prey, himself becomes a hunted animal. The supposed prey, the animal, is replaced by the real prey, Sivrit. This is foreshadowed in Kriemhilt's second dream. The first, the falcon dream, is based on a courtly metaphor: the weaker, but more noble falcon is killed by the stronger eagle. Kriemhilt's second dream announcing Sivrit's death no longer places the perpetrator and the victim on the same level. It shows the reverse of the hunting situation. Sivrit, the hunter, becomes the prey of the animals to be hunted. The wild boars represent nonhuman violence (921,2–3). Gunther and Hagen are dehumanized by this metaphor. The following dream *wie ob dir zetal/vielen zwêne berge* [as if two mountains came crashing down upon you] (924,2–3) removes Sivrit's murder still further from intentional human action. He becomes a victim of raw natural forces.

In the narration of the hunt, Sivrit shares and then trumps the characteristics of the hunted animals. He is superior to all of them in strength and above all in speed, he has the fastest hound and the fastest horse (934,1; 937,3). He hunts a *halpful* (?), a *lewen* [lion], a *wisent* [bison], an *elch* [elk], four *ûre* [oxen], a *schelch, hirze oder hinden* [deer, stag], and finally an *eber* [boar] (935–38), the animal in which physical strength is most crudely manifest and which in the dream kills him.[39] When he can get no further on horseback, he runs on foot to catch a bear (949), ties it up, and then chases it through the camp. He is the only one who can reach the running animal and then kill it (962,3). The excess of speed peaks in the prey, on whose account the whole hunt was held to begin with: Sivrit himself. In his footrace with Gunther, which Sivrit naturally wins, both race off *sam zwei wildiu pantel* [like two wild panthers] (976,3), and even after Hagen has stabbed him, Sivrit is almost able to avenge himself on Hagen (982,2–986,4), *tobelîchen* [raging] (983,1), like a mortally wounded animal. In Sivrit's playful "becoming animal," it becomes evident what a dangerous force the Burgundians have eliminated.

As Nibelungen, the Burgundians encounter the same fate. In the chaos of the battle, Dancwart fights *als ein eberswîn / ze walde tuot vor hunden* [like a wild boar / in the forest, chased by hounds] (1946,3–4), and Volker *alsam ein eber wilde* [like a wild boar] (2001,3). Taunted by the mocking talk of the *übermueten* [arrogant] Volker (2269,4), Wolfhart becomes a wild animal that has to be held back by force. Volker ridicules Hildebrant: *Lât abe den lewen, meister, er ist sô grimme gemuot* [Let the lion go, master, he is so furious] (2272,1). Once Wolfhart has freed himself, he springs on the opponents *alsam ein lewe wilder* [like a wild lion] (2273,3). Becoming animal leads to the extermination of nearly all heroes, but also raises the fighting spirit to its highest degree.[40]

"To become a hero" means a finding back to oneself and at the same time "becoming an animal." The penultimate strophe formulates this conclusion:

> *Diu vil michel êre was dâ gelegen tôt.* (2378,1)
>
> [All that was great and honorable was now lying there dead.]

Êre is the epitome of a social order that rests on the stratified distance and mutual recognition of its members. Seen from a later perspective, this ending might seem barbaric and, from the perspective of courtly civilization around 1200, regressive, but it is, according to the narrator, the consequence of *rehten heldes muot* [the proper heroic spirit]. The narrator refuses to make any unambiguous assessment, because even the anti-character Hagen is finally called *der aller beste degen* [the best of all warriors] (2374), and the *getriuwe* Kriemhilt cannot avoid her horrible end.

The dynastic-genealogical principle that is dominant in Worms and works in Bechelaren to continue the Burgundian genealogical line is eliminated with the outbreak of the embittered fighting.[41] Where Prünhilt is far away and practically forgotten, a genealogically based order would have to end with Dancrat's youngest son, Giselher. With the elimination of the three kings by Rüedeger, Wolfhart, and Dietrich, the dynastic principle is finished. The epic fate of the second Gunther ends with his birth. The second Sivrit is long forgotten. Only the *Klage* will pull him out of anonymity and by doing so attempt to reestablish the dynastic principle.

Seen in this light, the Burgundians' change of name to *Nibelunge* makes sense. The *Nibelunge* are from the beginning located outside of the hierarchical courtly world. At first, they are extraterritorial. Through Sivrit, who forcefully breaks into the court of Worms "from outside," they to a certain extent become "statelike," as does Sivrit's own strength. With Sivrit's death, this unity breaks down. When the revenge for his murder enters its decisive phase, the *Nibelunge* are there again, at first at the Burgundians' side, then within them. At the departure from Worms, the Burgundians leave behind the order that they had represented up until then, and they are forced to be nothing but *helden*. They, like Sivrit before them, carry the war from outside into the ordered world of the Huns and destroy it.

Perspective?

The *Klage* was not satisfied with this result. It spends many words restoring the shattered order, and it does so in terms of royal power, whose powerlessness is demonstrated by the *Nibelungenlied*, without questioning the loyalty of the vassals. The protagonists of the *Klage* are Etzel and Dietrich, one of whom loses his rule through exaggerated mourning, while the other founds it anew elsewhere.

The actual continuation of the story,[42] however, takes place far, far away at the court of Worms and with characters who were made a mockery of in the epic. The minstrel Swemmel spreads the news of the downfall of the Burgundians from court to court, but the grief over the news does not last long. Then Gunther's young successor is installed. The court is built up again, and this time it is based on justice and tradition and not on the strength of the rulers. Heroes are not needed. The survivors of court office, the forgotten cellarer Sindolt and the disparaged kitchen master Rumolt, are leaders in the reestablishment of the Burgundian dominion (Kl 3747–64, 4074–81) through the assembly of the nobility (*lantschaft*, Kl 3723; *des landes êre*, Kl 3728). Rumolt is no longer a ridiculous cook, but rather an intelligent politician, who is proven right in his assessment that it was a mistake to follow Hagen's *übermuot* (Kl 4031) instead of his own advice:

> *dâ von daz lant nu âne stât*
> *freude und maneger êre.* (Kl 4076–77)
>
> [Therefore the land is now bereft
> of joy and many honors.]

As the royal administrator, he ensures the continuation of the court at Worms (Kl 4074–75), and the king's cupbearer (*des künges schenke Sindolt*), of whom it is said: *der diente dicke triuwen solt* [he had always served loyally what he was given] (Kl 3743–44) counsels a return to courtly *vuoge* and the restraint of exaggerated lamenting (*der klage diu ungefüege kraft* [the immoderation of this lamenting], Kl 3752). The end of the story in Worms is a *grôziu hôhgezît* [great celebration] (Kl 4089) with the coronation of the young king:

> *der hof unt daz gesinde*
> *wârn ein teil in freude komen.* (Kl 4098–99)
>
> [The court and the household
> had returned a bit to joy.]

Although damaged, in the end, courtly joy is restored, the joy from which the destruction had begun. This is the goal of the courtly romance, allegorized in the "Joie de la curt" episode in *Erec*. It cannot be achieved with the central characters of heroic epic. The *Klage* therefore places more weight on marginal characters. The head of the reestablished Burgundian kingdom is represented as weakly as possible, by a *kindelîn* [child] (Kl 3758, 4012), who is the legitimate heir, and by a woman (Kl 3754–57), but this does not diminish the rule:

> *si enpfiengen gemeinlîche*
> *ir lêhen von dem kinde.* (Kl 4096–97)
>
> [They all received together
> their fiefs from the child.]

With the exception of Dietrich, the type of the ruler-hero disappears elsewhere as well. What is left are those kinds of nobles who were marginalized in the heroic intoxication: the prince of Passau, the margravines, and one more who shows up quite surprisingly, a Viennese duchess bearing a name from courtly romance: Isolde. If the role of Rüedeger's widow and daughter can be derived from the epic's plot, then the completely irrelevant Isolde reveals the intended principle: to stylize rule as unheroically as possible.

It should have become clear by now that the *Nibelungenlied*, at least in conjunction with the *Klage*, can no longer be assumed to be an epic in the sense of classical epic theory. The *Nibelungenlied* not only repeats, but reflects the constellations, behaviors, patterns of action, and norms of a world that might be called "heroic" as transmitted to us primarily through (heroic) epics and songs. It reflects the end of its world without being able to construct its transformation. This kind of reflection is still not "novel-like," however.[43] Genres are constituted in a "familial similarity" that spans all transformations, and in this the *Nibelungenlied* is closer to other (certainly more straightforward) heroic epics than, for example, the Arthurian romance. The *Klage* also tries to bring the events closer to contemporary concepts and values, but leaves the story intact in its core.

The experiment that the *Nibelungenlied* undertakes is open-ended. The *Klage* was unable completely to allay irritation over this. The medieval recipients seem to have considered this work, as unloved as it is by modern philology, a prerequisite for the reception of the epic. It guarantees that the monstrous will be corrected by what is right and normal. Modern reception up until recent times ignored this frame and was interested in the epic alone. This manifests an ahistorical concept of art. The normalcy that the *Klage* reestablishes is foreign to the epic view. In the meantime, too, the epic perspective had itself become foreign and could therefore no longer function unproblematically, as in the Middle Ages, as the basis for a worldview that sought to assimilate even the most alien and monstrous. This aging of the *Klage* was probably already perceptible in the fifteenth century. In any case, this would explain why interest in it receded around that time.[44]

By this time at the latest, the discrepancy between epic and *Klage* had become obvious, a discrepancy that no reference to the medieval reception can argue away. Where the epic breaks off its memorial (2379,1), the *Klage* continues it. In doing so, it simply leaves the dissonances of the epic world behind. Modern critics have generally reacted mostly selectively, deciding for the one or the other. The *Nibelungenlied* was interpreted either as a celebration of Germanic heroes (the courtly is simply an added layer); a story of the *herzen jâmer* [the grief of the heart] of a woman (the bloody battles of annihilation are typical add-ons of the time); an accolade to *triuwe* (with the treachery as its shadow side, which makes it shine all the more brightly); or as a *civitas diaboli* (the praise of heroic deeds as blatant pride). The attempt here has been to understand the meaning of the obvious antagonisms of the text as the defeat of an ideal courtly world by a heroic one that was at first marginalized. The epic refuses to comment on how the two poles are related to each other and what perspective the process takes, critical or affirmative.

Attempts to distinguish between morally good and bad, politically appropriate or inappropriate, legitimate and illegitimate, psychologically plausible or implausible must fail, because the alternatives confront each other aporetically. The resignation of many critics and the attempts to seek refuge in the intact world of a hypothetical legend is an understandable reaction to this aporetic structure. The epic has refused clear decisions, not only in the sense that it contains neither a heroic critique of courtly optimism nor a courtly criticism of heroic combativeness. It narrates the antagonisms and ambivalences of the Nibelungian world without ever explicitly questioning the validity of its order. Its rules function, but they are rules for the endgame, for destruction.

Early on—from the third *âventiure* on—contradictions in the world initially constructed become evident. They can still be resolved at first, but at an ever-increasing price. These contradictions are irresolvable: between the self-assuredness of the hero and the institutionalization of rulership; the claim to and actual administration of justice; the unintentional demonstration and interest-motivated instrumentalization of nobility; the virtualization of power struggles and hidden intrigues; rituals as a means of order and ritualized disorder; the legitimacy of collective norms and the likewise legitimate but fateful rejection of them. The courtly form can divert and integrate aggression, but its "as-if" can also lead to distortion and lies. The *triuwe* toward *vriunden* is worthy of the greatest admiration, but it opens up the opportunity for betrayal. Admirable *stæte* proves itself in Kriemhilt's bond to her beloved (*holden vriedel*), but the price is irreconcilability and the end of all other *triuwe* bonds. A weakened hierarchy collapses, and the result is not only new solidarities but chaos. Heroic willpower tears through the web of duplicity and intrigue, but it expresses itself in bloody devastation. *Heldes muot* pushes aside the faux value of *gemach*, but this means drinking blood instead of wine.

The list of contradictions and ambivalences could easily be continued. The helpless commentaries of the *Klage* demonstrate what price clarity would cost. The epic is satisfied with the symbolic representation of constellations that in the long run cannot coincide. Medieval narration is meant to be heard successively. Writing makes it possible to create relationships between two stations that lie far apart, but in the *Nibelungenlied*, writing does not yet force everything into the tectonics of a structure that must be experienced simultaneously, as in the courtly romances. Constellations are summoned, disappear, reappear, and make room for others, to appear another time, but in a completely different form. What was true the first time is now ineffective, what was positively charged is now negative. Changing constellations with only a few related elements take each other's place and relativize each other. There is an initially unnoticeable, later ever more rapid restructuring of what was valid just before. Characters move from the light into darkness and vice versa, flawless actions prove themselves to be disastrous and questionable dispositions are praiseworthy, help is deception, betrayal guarantees the stability of the kingdom for a time, unquestioned values are perverted, and others take their place, one social order disintegrates, and the one that takes its place collapses immediately.

This is precisely what is meant by deconstruction: a movement of situating and dissolving that only comes to rest when there is nothing left to situate and dissolve. The *Nibelungenlied*, unlike most chansons de geste, does not weave a homogeneous world. There is no invitation to an almost endless continuation, but rather a brusque ending. The memories that the *alten mæren* conjure up are brought to a conclusion: *hie hât daz mære ein ende: daz ist der Nibelunge nôt* [here the story has an end: this is the destruction of the Nibelungen] (2379,4). This verse should actually prohibit the stammering beginning of the *Klage*. The fact that it continues nonetheless shows that the way in which the end is accomplished was felt to be unbearable. In the *Klage*, only Etzel, the heathen king, and his world are allowed to end irrevocably.

The epic brings together and relates motif, plot element, development, and interpretive perspective from a (to us mostly incomprehensible) tradition and social experience, which are only accessible in outline. It then plays through the alternatives. Its mode of representation is distortion and, with this, the uncovering of what had previously been covered up. This progressive distortion is not aimless (the goal is complete destruction), but it is without result or message. What has confused the critics as contradiction is the result of an impetus of narration that only fixes positions in order to confront them. The *Nibelungenlied* is, given the radical nature of this process, one of the greatest works of art of the Middle Ages.

Notes

For abbreviations used in citation of medieval texts, see Works Cited.

Preface

1. Althoff (1990b), trans. Christopher Carroll as *Family, Friends and Followers: Political and Social Bonds in Medieval Europe* (New York, 2004).

2. The question of how Kriemhilt became a villain ("Wie nun ward Kriemhild zur Unholdin?") serves here as a metaphor for how the complexity of the *Nibelungenlied* can be (mis)understood. What was once a simple composition question, with its lack of moral ambiguity and antiquated language intact, exemplifies how a complex and seemingly contradictory narrative epic should or should not be approached: not only is the crux of the question—Kriemhilt's good or evil character—not helpful in understanding the work, but investigation of the narrative principle behind a character "becoming" something else provides only a limited appreciation of the epic's intent. The *Nibelungenlied* resists and even undermines such a question, because its internal set of rules aims at the destruction of its own world rather than at answers.—TRANS.

Introduction

Jorge Luis Borges, "Ulrica," in id., *Obras completas: El libro de arena* (Buenos Aires, 1975), p. 30.

1. See the contributions in *Die Nibelungen* (1991), esp. the introduction by Heinzle and the article by von See; and also see Brackert (1971).

2. See, e.g., *Der Schatz des Drachentödters* (1977), p. 63.

3. On their actual dimension, usually overestimated, see von See (1991).

4. Schröder (1981) rightly comments that the concept of the "national epic" does not necessarily have to include an affirmative or glorifying understanding, and he intimates that the history of reception is more than just a sign of collective madness without any basis in the text (pp. 12–13).

5. See, e.g., Heinzle (1987a, 1991); Andersson (1978).

6. Documented in Ehrismann (1975).

7. *Schatz des Drachentödters* (1977), p. 96.

8. Kolk (1990), pp. 22–75.

9. See, e.g., Maurer (1951), pp. 13–38, esp. pp. 15, 20–33, on the concept of *leit* in the *Nibelungenlied.*

10. See esp. Schröder (1968), pp. 48–156, and also, with a bit of sociopolitical flourish, Spiewok (1989).

11. Schröder (1968), pp. 3–4, and elsewhere, refers to the different aesthetic conditions of medieval and modern literature but bases the "unity of the work" on a timeless "central theme: Kriemhilt's love, suffering, and revenge" (p. 7). Falk's (1974) interpretation of the epic "in its own time" combines global concepts of epoch with assumptions about general human experiences of crisis (e.g., pp. 65–71, 72–99, 240–58).

12. See even Haug (1981), pp. 39, 49n9.

13. Falk (1974), p. 123.

14. Ibid., p. 159. Similar interpretations produce daring deep thoughts such as: "Through the heroic acts of High Minne, Siegfried first had to overcome the inner Kriemhild before winning the external as his wife" (ibid.); "The main position of the young Siegfried was that of ruler in the dream world. He also had another role in the region of honor, which was at first, however, very weak" (ibid., p. 176); and Siegfried's "downfall will be the final consequence of the high, the arrogant Minne" (ibid., p. 181).

15. See, e.g., Beyschlag ([1952] 1961); Ihlenburg (1969).

16. See the controversy between Beyschlag and Schröder documented by Schröder (1968), pp. 82, 87–91; see also on this Müller (1974), pp. 112–13.

17. See, e.g., Beyschlag ([1952] 1961); Ihlenburg (1969); and cf. Müller (1974), pp. 112, 116.

18. The message is then necessarily somewhat general, for example, an appeal against egotism, pride, and hubris (see Bostock 1960); cf., on the other hand, Wehrli (1972), p. 99, on such moralizing attempts at interpretation.

19. See Ernst Jünger, *In Stahlgewittern: Aus dem Tagebuch eines Stosstruppführers* (Leisnig, 1920), trans. Michael Hofmann as *Storm of Steel* (London, 2003).

20. One is referred, e.g., to writings on ancient Greece or ethnology by Bruno Snell, E. R. Dodds, or Clifford Geertz.

21. Müller (1974); cf. id. (1987, 1992a, 1993b, 1996a).

22. See Ehrismann (1987), p. 89, on my 1974 attempt.

23. Fromm (1974).

24. Wachinger (1960), pp. 140–45; cf. pp. 103–4.

25. See, e.g., Haug ([1974] 1989), p. 293; Pérennec (1987), pp. 214, 219; fundamentally Heinzle (1987b). How these holistic interpretations lay a new text, supplemented with Middle High German tidbits, over the epic, is shown by Schröder's (1968) construction of the "Tragedy of Kriemhilt" (pp. 48–156).

26. Lugowski ([1932] 1976); cf. *Formaler Mythos*, ed. Martinez (1996).

27. Heinzle (1987a), pp. 88–89, and elsewhere; id. (1987b, 1991).

28. Müller (1987), p. 225.

29. Heinzle (1987a), p. 92; developed in the analysis of the final scene (1987b), in the subtitle of Heinzle's contribution (1991); finally (1997), p. 85.

30. See already Heinzle's (1978) critique of the scholarly speculations concerning the Dietrich epic.

31. Heinzle (1978), p. 6; similarly, Schröder (1968), p. 32; cf. also pp. 38–39. Schröder proposes as an alternative the *Nibelungenlied* as a "unique creation" of "a great poet" vs. "a plurality of equal redactors." But the writing of a book epic based on past stories does not have to be "unique"; it might, as otherwise evident in medieval textuality, invite augmentation, expansion, improvement, and so on. Moreover, if several authors were involved, these would not by any means have to be "equal."

32. Heinzle relates this to Iser's discussion of "empty spaces" in literary texts, but understands them completely differently (1987b, pp. 265–67). Iser wants to demonstrate that every reception of a literary text requires the productivity of the recipient, which is engaged at so-called places of uncertainty (1976, pp. 257ff.). This productivity is not basically constrained by any rules, but it must be disciplined in the process of reading. Where it attempts to make legitimate, intersubjectively relatable statements, it therefore remains constrained by the instructions of the text. If this work of the reader is absent, then the text remains mute. Heinzle, on the contrary, defines his "insinuation of meaning" as an activity of the recipient that necessarily leads to false results. He restricts that activity to uncontrolled interpolations of the reader's associations. Where Iser is concerned with a necessary assumption of every literary understanding ("empty spaces are necessary and they must necessarily be filled in"), Heinzle sees a methodologically faulty process that misses the meaning of the text. For him, "empty spaces" become "holes" in the text that are based on "structural deficiencies" (1987b, pp. 266–66), but this is something completely different.

33. Stech (1993, pp. 40–51) thus misunderstands Iser's concept. "The reader must motivate the action himself, must put himself in the character's shoes" (ibid., p. 85). This encourages exactly the kind of naïve speculations that Heinzle rightly criticized.

34. Heinzle (1997), p. 94.

35. Heinzle (1987a), p. 32; on the discussion of the "sources" debate "post Heusler," see Andersson (1987), pp. 105–17.

36. Trt 131–34. It is necessary to distance oneself from the tempting proximity to the poststructural concept of *lecture: lesen* here means to gather together (*colligere*) the many elements of a story that are in circulation and harmoniously unite them. For Gottfried, there is therefore a "correct" *lesen*, as opposed to the many incorrect versions.

37. Haug (1992), pp. 91–118.

38. Heinzle (1978) demonstrates this for the Dietrich epic.

39. And exactly this is the consequence: "This Nibelungen poet was simply

no genius" (Heinzle, 1987b, p. 268)—as if any author in the Middle Ages can be defined by the terminology of the eighteenth century. Likewise Andersson (1978). Alois Wolf (1995) characterizes the whole as a "splendid trunk," but he sees single "irregularities," "awkwardness," "weak points," "helplessness," and more, at least in the details (see pp. 297–300).

40. Heusler ([1921] 1965); affirmative still is Andersson (1980, 1987); for a basic critique see Haug ([1975] 1989) and ([1981] 1989).

41. Andersson (1987), pp. 109–10. Of course, if the *Thidreks saga* were a translation or reworking of a book that had been written on the continent at the end of the twelfth century (Andersson 1987, pp. 51–52), then it was most certainly circulating independently and competing with the *Nibelungenlied.* But it does not necessarily provide evidence for the story that the *Nibelungenlied* is supposed to tell.

42. See the jibe of Fromm (1990), p. 6, to the effect that the *Ältere Not* seems so real that students might look for it in vain in the library. Andersson (1987), pp. 118–19, in fact recounts the content of the *Ältere Not* in order to distinguish it from "original" additions to the *Nibelungenlied* (pp. 119–20). See on the other hand, Heinzle (1997), pp. 83–84.

43. Störmer (1973), pp. 491–96, and (1974, 1987); Meves (1980, 1981); Wenskus (1973), passim, summarized pp. 447–48.

44. Schröder (1968), p. 40.

45. Heusler ([1921] 1965), p. 316; but see Schnyder in *Biterolf,* pp. 61–62.

46. Beck (1990), p. 6 (with literature on the Nordist discussion).

47. Kuhn (1965), e.g., speaks of "serious disturbances" in the old hoard scene (p. 287), a "material that has become irregular and ragged through many interventions" (p. 280).

48. What right does Schröder (1968) have to call the scene of the demanding of the hoard "poetic primitive bedrock . . . that cannot be given up," a "foreign body that stands in the way of a linear execution of the new theme, Kriemhilt's revenge for Sivrit's murder" (p. 93)? Would not the "new theme" have to prove itself in the encounter with the tradition?

49. Wenskus (1973), p. 394.

50. See Klebel (1957) on the secondary characters of the epic; Birkhan (1977), pp. 4–11, on the early medieval history of the eastern alpine region and the supposed origin in Passau; generally, Voorwinden (1987), p. 31.

51. Andersson (1986), p. 6; cf. p. 4. The metaphor "layer" from Neumann ([1924] 1967), pp. 9–34, where he speaks of the "layers of ethics."

52. See Andersson (1987), p. 82; p. 84. The term "source" is inappropriate, regardless of whether it describes material or structural relationships or the recurrence of single poetic elements, because it is conceived in the horizon of writing and includes an unsuitable valuation: the "source" is "purer" than what flows from it, and one has to find one's way back if one wants to know what is "really" true. The (unanswerable) question of the "source" brings with it the equally unanswerable question of the "original" and "originality" (ibid., pp. 109, 118–43).

53. Andersson (1986) demonstrates this very effectively in the case of the "Sigurdarquiða in meiri." Just as the dialogue between Sigurd and Brynhild here represents an (unsuccessful in terms of genre history) transition to the novel, so, too, the *Nibelungenlied* brings different literary traditions together.

54. See Göhler (1996), p. 219, on the speculative argumentation on the "rule of the matter."

55. Haug ([1974] 1989), p. 295; Haug ([1975] 1989), pp. 279–80.

56. Alois Wolf (1988), pp. 168, 170.

57. Haug ([1975] 1989), p. 291, speaks of the "development of a specific heroic-historical knowledge" and deems the heroic epic more open than other genres.

58. Höfler ([1955] 1961), pp. 389–90.

59. Bumke (1960) sees "joints and seams," "rough spots and internal contradictions" (p. 1), "contradictions that cannot be argued away . . . , where traditions mix" (p. 5), he attempts to "separate the individual parts of the source" (p. 19); some things appear to be an "unworked slab" (p. 23), other things have been "slowly filed down in a centuries-old tradition" (p. 2), while others are only "seemingly connected to each other" (p. 12) or explained by the "convergence of two traditions" (p. 8).

60. Curschmann (1989), p. 383.

61. See comments by W. Grimm ([1929] 1957) on Kriemhilt; on the concept of "knowledge of legend," see Curschmann (1989), pp. 385, 387.

62. See Curschmann (1989), pp. 395–97, on the sometimes proverbial view of Kriemhilt against which the epic operates. Cf. Saxo Grammaticus and his judgment of Kriemhilt's *erga fratres perfidia* (reprint in English in Andersson 1987, pp. 252–55).

63. Beck (1990), p. 5; this leads to a "circular argument" in the evaluation of what is transmitted. Historical overviews of myth tend to describe the changes in the core of the myth as a process leading in only one direction. In this view, there are only single adaptations, whose transmission has depended up to the present on chance alone, and these adaptations are not necessarily coordinated.

64. Klaus von See has made this plausible for the flaming ride of the Nordic Brünhild saga. It is undisputed that the Eddic poems of the thirteenth century go back to a centuries-old oral tradition (von See 1993, p. 26), so that certainly a mutual influence is possible with continental tradition.

65. Paul Zumthor's concept of *vocalité* (Zumthor 1983, 1987) was introduced in Germany by Ursula Schaefer (1992) as *Vokalität.*

66. E. R. Haymes notably revised his earlier answer to the critique of an all-too-direct translation of the theories of Albert Lord and Milman Parry. Bäuml (1978, 1980, 1984–85) also considers the critique and approaches the "vocality" concept of Zumthor and Schaefer.

67. See Schaefer (1992), pp. 7–20, on the terminological fuzziness of the dichotomy orality/literality, especially the chapter "The Approach to Literality in Vocality," pp. 30–34.

68. Schaefer (1992), p. 17, speaks of the "intrusion" of orality in literacy and of its "fusion"; see pp. 21–29 for a description of the interferences in the early medieval culture of England. Surely the circumstances there cannot simply be transferred to the continent 400 years later; but it is the proportions of the two cultures, not the tensions between them, that are most different.

69. In semi-oral societies, oral communication has "changed its ritual status from that of a culturally necessary ritual in a preliterate society to a subculturally distinctive ritual in an illiterate subculture of a literate society" (Bäuml 1984–85, p. 39; cf. 1980, p. 243).

70. Individual abilities of writing therefore play a subordinate role. What is important is the possible collaboration between literacy and illiteracy in different social strata (see Bäuml 1978, p. 43; 1980, pp. 244, 246–47).

71. This distinction between "primary" and "secondary" orality is important; see Bäuml (1980), pp. 237, 239; (1984–85), p. 34, whose use of the terms is different from that of Ong ([1982] 1987).

72. Curschmann (1989), p. 384, also distances himself from the "absolute distinction—here 'pure' orality, there 'pure' literacy." Curschmann distinguishes between "literacy only in a technical sense" (the chance occurrence of a written record of an oral text, which can in later reception be reversed at any time) and "literary" literacy (p. 385).

73. For an overview of the mixed culture of nobility, see Grünkorn (1994), p. 29. Rösler (1980) has shown something similar for Greece in the case of the "discovery of fictionality"; on early medieval Ireland, see Richter (1994).

74. Richter (1994), p. 232; examples in Müller (1994a, b).

75. *Reallexikon der deutschen Literaturwissenschaft*, vol. 1 (1997), pp. 619–20 (Schmid-Cadalbert); Foley (1991), p. 38. According to the discussions of the more recent scholarship, "formulaicness" can no longer be understood as an aesthetically inferior collection of precoined set pieces: it is the framework that makes poetic production and reception possible in the first place.

76. Beck (1990), p. 15.

77. Bäuml (1984–85), p. 37, distinguishes between the formula as a technical means used in the creation of a text and the formula as an element of a particular literary type ("means of composition or technique" vs. "compositional type").

78. Heinzle (1978), p. 69.

79. On the consequences when "the process of production and the process of transmission . . . are impacted by literacy," see Rösler (1980), pp. 303–4; cf. Mertens (1996a), p. 62, on the use of elements of an oral poetic in the interest of the book epic.

80. The problem should not be approached only from this angle, says Curschmann (1979), pp. 93–94; similarly, Beck (1990), pp. 15–16.

81. Bäuml (1984–85), pp. 35–36; Schaefer (1992), p. 44.

82. Assmann (1992). This concept is still very broad, in that it includes very different types of texts and functions, verbal and nonverbal phenomena. It would

have to be differentiated for medieval culture. Institutions of mere preservation, such as the archive, that do not have a claim to the production of meaning, would have to be separated from institutions of cultural memory as places of preserving and transmitting meaning.

83. Bäuml (1981), p. 115.

84. This situational knowledge is fairly unspecific in the performance of an epic text and therefore of little importance. It can, for example, refer to the occasion for the recitation, to a commonly known current situation, to genealogical relationships between the narrative and the everyday world, and so on. This kind of knowledge cannot be reconstructed and is therefore unimportant for scholarly analysis.

85. See Goody, Watt, and Gough (1997), pp. 61–73.

86. Bäuml (1981), p. 119, says that in the "writing of oral texts, gaps develop where their former mimetic function, i.e., their reference to extratextual reality, is no longer recognizable" (cf. Bäuml 1984–85, p. 39).

87. The courtly romance, which is conceptionally much more strongly influenced by the clerical culture of literacy than heroic poetry, opens itself up in the area of the *âventiure* to the unexpected and new, but at the same time captures it in a net of obligatory patterns of signification.

88. See Bäuml (1980), pp. 251–52; Schaefer (1992), pp. 57, 71–87. Alois Wolf's frequent recommendation (1995, pp. 297, 397, and elsewhere) that we not take the details too seriously is thus justified.

89. Bäuml (1981), pp. 123–24; Fromm (1974) and Wachinger (1981), p. 90, have already pointed to the "high medieval oral-literate mixed culture" as a prerequisite for the *Nibelungenlied.*

90. Schaefer (1992), p. 44.

91. Heinzle (1987b), pp. 265–67, 275.

92. The "danger of missing the historical character of a work" (Heinzle 1987b, p. 275) is most present if one only refers to the ensemble of symbols that are fixed in writing, which the philologist concentrates on.

93. Brackert (1963), pp. 165–73; Bäuml (1978), p. 42; cf. the example in Heinzle (1997), p. 97.

94. Bäuml (1980), pp. 239ff.; on the resulting types, see Curschmann (1989), pp. 384–85, 410; cf. Bäuml (1984–85), pp. 37–38.

95. If this is not considered, then the reconstruction of different conditions of acting and behavior in a historic world remain without consequence, as can be observed with Grenzler (1992), who on the premise of radical cultural alterity, reads the text like a nineteenth-century novel, presuming a strictly linear and logical plot coherence, taking formulaic epithets to be situationally specific commentaries (e.g., p. 377), distinguishing between narrator and character perspectives (e.g., p. 378), and so on.

96. Criticism of this "narrative model" that is a priori assumed by the critics also in Stein (1987), p. 85.

97. Bumke (1996c), p. 32.

98. The last danger in Heinzle (1987b), pp. 264, 272, and elsewhere. "I believe this to be an insubstantial and inconsequential figure of speech" (p. 264) is a characteristic sentence.

99. It "may be assumed that it took some time, even after writing and the written word had been introduced, until ways and structures of thinking, forms and organization of discourse, that were typical of *primary* orality were completely pushed aside in writing by their literary counterparts" (Schaefer [1994], pp. 364–65).

100. Schaefer (1992), pp. 43–58; cf. Ong ([1982] 1987), p. 39: "An oral culture does not have texts."

101. Schaefer's explication (ibid.) remains indeterminate: "of course, *we* are dealing with *texts* (narrowly defined) when we speak of Old English poems. What a contemporary audience would have received in vocality were for them *énonciations* that were distinguished from other, everyday verbal discourses by certain signals." Here again is the dichotomy that should be overcome. An orally performed poem is sharply distinct from everyday utterances, as well as everyday "recurrent speech," and is therefore "text."

102. Ehlich (1994), pp. 18–19, calls oral texting the first step of a "making permanent" that is distinct from "the transitory nature of single speech acts"; cf. Ehlich (1989), p. 88.

103. Ehlich (1989), p. 90.

104. See the change of fixed texts under the influence of cultural change in Goody, Watt, and Gough (1997), p. 70.

105. Schaefer (1992), p. 54; she is nonetheless aware of its intermediate status; cf. p. 86, where she maintains "that this discourse is *different* from everyday discourse." "Even where nonfictional texts are concerned, these kinds of discourses are more autonomous in their approach to the world than are oral discourses" (p. 55). These distinctions are made less clear by the adoption of a term that was created for genuinely oral communication.

106. Schaefer differs (1992), p. 115, in line with a dictum of Zumthor's: "l'écrit nomme; le dit montre."

107. Schaefer (1992), p. 52, on the other hand, questions whether "the vocally transmitted poetry of the Middle Ages really appeared to the recipients as a text . . . these recipients knew it was 'fixed,' but did not receive the poetry as something written." The question must be negated only in terms of the author's concept of text.

108. See Curschmann (1979), p. 93; Grünkorn (1994), pp. 32–33; Mertens (1996b), pp. 360–61.

109. See Bäuml (1978), pp. 45–46; (1980), pp. 252–53.

110. Bäuml (1984–85), pp. 39, 44. Bäuml therefore sees every written epic based on oral tradition as a commentary on this tradition; cf. Rösler (1980) on early Greek poetry.

111. Summarized in Panzer (1945), pp. 5–86; most pronounced in several articles by Alois Wolf, who assumes a strong literary influence from the chansons de geste.

112. See Alois Wolf (1995), pp. 117–44 on the *Waltharius* epic.

113. See Andersson (1987), p. 30 and elsewhere.

114. Heinzle (1987b), pp. 269–70. On p. 272, the conjecture that the poet "took on a bookish interpretation of the matter with the Trojan formula" becomes certainty.

115. Wolfram's introduction to *Willehalm* is cautionary concerning the familiarity in Germany with the chansons de geste.

116. It can hardly be limited to the country from which the most texts come and that thematize them (cf. Alois Wolf 1981; 1987, p. 175; a contrary view in Splett 1968, p. 106).

117. See Alois Wolf's (first 1981) attempts to prove Hagen's, Rüedeger's, or even Kriemhilt's gestures as dependent on the *Wilhelmsgeste*, as Wynn (1961) had already demonstrated in the case of Hagen's charade as a judge in front of Kriemhilt. These are typical scenes that presume certain personnel, social, and legal constellations.

118. Panzer (1945), pp. 55–58.

119. Alois Wolf (1980); (1995), pp. 254, 374, 398–99, or 377 (epics of antiquity as a model for the motif of an attack on someone sleeping).

120. See Andersson (1987), pp. 56–60, on the bridal quest scheme in early medieval historiography and pp. 81–89 on the variations in the *Nibelungenlied.*

121. On this program and its reference to the *nouvelle histoire* of the Annales school, see Müller (1986a).

122. Esp. Alois Wolf (1981), p. 53.

123. This is true also for research on sagas that argues without any transmitted texts. Lohse (1959, pp. 298–99, 345) assumes an entire manuscript library in possession of the author of the *Thidreks saga,* especially a "lost" version of the Nibelungen legend with all the characteristics that connect the *Thidreks saga* with various Nibelungen manuscripts.

124. Jauß (1977), esp. the introduction.

125. This misunderstands Heinzle's polemic against the concept of alterity (1994, pp. 10ff.)

126. As in Grenzler (1992), who wants to relate everything, including constellations of persons, thought, and behavioral schemes, to the alien nature of the feudal structure of rule.

127. Geertz (1973), p. 14, has criticized the "famous anthropological absorption with the (to us) exotic" as a "device for displacing the dulling sense of familiarity." This corresponds with my own reservations.

128. Geertz (1973), p. 16 and elsewhere. "It shifts the analysis of cultural forms from an endeavor in general parallel to dissecting an organism, diagnosing a symptom, deciphering a code, or ordering a system . . . to one in general parallel with penetrating a literary text" (ibid., p. 448).

129. "Like any art form . . . the cockfight renders ordinary, everyday experience comprehensible by presenting it in terms of acts and objects which have had their practical consequences removed and been reduced (or, if you prefer, raised) to the level of sheer appearances" (ibid., p. 443).

130. Ibid., p. 14.

131. "As interworked systems of signs . . . culture is not a power, something to which social events, behaviors, institutions, or processes can be causally attributed; it is a context, something within which they can be intelligibly—that is, thickly—described" (ibid., p. 14).

132. Müller (1974), pp. 118–24.

133. "There is little profit in clearing a concept from the defects of psychologism only to plunge it immediately into those of schematicism" (Geertz 1973, p. 17).

134. Ibid., pp. 17–18.

135. The "ethnologization of literary studies" answers the discourse analysis within social sciences, the "anthropological turn" here and the "literary turn" there (Bachmann-Medick 1992, p. 2f.); cf. Clifford (1986), p. 102.

136. If "a cultural-politically inspired poetics is developing" that recognizes "literature as a cultural medium of presentation" (Bachmann-Medick 1992, p. 17), then the particular literary text can be examined with regard to its participation in general symbolic orders. "'Writing culture' finally means that the study of literature and ethnology become the 'cornerstones' of the new interdisciplinary field" (ibid., p. 18). Just as the literary text can be read "ethnologically," so ethnological material can be read "literarily" as a series of signs that is the carrier of "meaning" and not part of the reported facts (Clifford 1986, pp. 98–99); cf. on "culture as text" and "cultural poetics," above all the different efforts of new historicism (overview in Baßler 1995; cf. Thomas 1991).

137. Bachmann-Medick (1992), pp. 11–12, 19.

138. See the studies of Jacques le Goff in *L'imaginaire médiéval* (1985).

139. On this critique, see Müller (1986a), pp. 63–64.

140. Bachmann-Medick (1992), pp. 18–19; Thomas (1991), pp. 180–82 and elsewhere; Baßler (1995), pp. 17–20; cf. Greenblatt, pp. 39–40, 48–59; Kaes, pp. 256–60.

141. Adler (1975), p. 21. Literature radicalizes the possibilities inherent in every culture: "Every form of expression acts (if it acts) by bringing semantic connections out of order, in that it assigns characteristics, which are normally ascribed to certain things, in unusual ways to other things, whose characteristics these are then seen to be" (Geertz 1987, p. 251).

142. In this sense, literary configurations are in a way related to crisis situations in a society. Geertz (1973) asserts "the view that social conflict is not something that happens when, out of weakness, indefiniteness, obsolescence, or neglect, cultural forms cease to operate, but rather something which happens when . . . such forms are pressed by unusual situations or unusual intentions to operate in unusual ways" (p. 28).

143. Von See ([1978] 1981), pp. 184–88; (1993), p. 22.

144. Von See (1993), pp. 24–25, 27; cf. the considerations of G. W. Weber (1990) on archaic ethics.

145. Gerhard Neumann on the literary text at a culture studies colloquium in Ascona, October 1996.

146. Geertz (1973), p. 35, goes so far as to claim: "There is no reason why the conceptual structure of a cultural interpretation should be any less formulable, and thus less susceptible to explicit canons of appraisal, than that of, say, a biological observation or a physical experiment—no reason except that the terms in which such formulations can be cast are, if not wholly nonexistent, very nearly so" (p. 24).

147. I do not subscribe to the meaning given to the term by A. Assmann (1995), in which she confronts the collective obligations of the cultural text, its identifying activity, and its timeless topicality with respect to the openness and historicity of the "literary text" (pp. 241–43). It seems to me that both types can be distinguished only by the perspective under which the two kinds of text are thematized (cf. pp. 234–35): Every "literary" text can be read as a "cultural" text—as a configuration of a (possible) world,—and every "cultural" text can be received as a "literary" one (i.e., disregarding its original claim to validity).

148. Lugowski ([1932] 1976), esp. introduction by Schlaffer; cf. *Formaler Mythos*, ed. Martinez (1996).

149. See *Formaler Mythos*, ed. Martinez (1996), pp. 20–21, and Schlaffer in ibid., pp. 27–36.

150. On the relationship with the debate on alterity, see *Formaler Mythos*, ed. Martinez (1996), pp. 14–17.

151. See also Haug (1981), pp. 40–41.

152. Material in Alois Wolf (1981), pp. 60–64, where the interpretive aim is "the essential" (p. 62): "the human-sentimental" (p. 61), "humanization" (p. 64), "inner-human connections" (p. 63), centered on "spousal *minne,*" "friendship" (pp. 63–64), etc. Once issues have been so watered down, the *Nibelungenlied* seems downright "modern" (p. 63).

153. Neumann ([1924] 1967), pp. 9–34.

154. Ehrismann (1981), pp. 164–65.

155. Müller (1974), pp. 95–96.

156. Jaeger (1983); cf. Jaeger (1985), pp. 176–94.

157. Haug (1974).

158. Ehrismann (1981) corrupts the opposition "archaic-modern" with Elias's opposition "uncontrolled-controlled" and "pre/extra-civilized" and "cultural"; cf. Ehrismann (1987), pp. 116, 180. Put in such a framework, the concept to a certain extent prejudices the results to be expected based on its own premises.

159. Symptomatic for this is a sentence from Ehrismann (1981): "Siegfried is the personified suspension between the present and the past" (p. 113); cf. the characterization on p. 167.

160. Critical: von See (1993), pp. 5–6; on the problem of supposed linguistic archaisms, see Splett (1987), who posits several out-of-date words around 1200 (p. 117) but rejects as a whole the thesis of an archaizing speech gesture.

161. See von See ([1978] 1981), pp. 176–83, esp. 182.

162. Jaeger (1983); (1985), pp. 192–93.

163. On this discussion in detail, see pp. 427–30 above.

164. Haug (1974) and in reference to the conditions of reception (1994); see the discussion on pp. 377–80 above.

165. See Brackert's (1963), pp. 170–71, formulations; Schröder (1968), p. 38, criticizes, I believe correctly, Brackert's idea of the genesis of the text as a "fusing" together of the *Nibelungenlied* from divergent versions.

166. Fromm (1974); cf. Schröder (1968), p. 41.

167. Brackert (1963), pp. 169–70; on the *Sondergut* [special material], see Schröder (1968), pp. 33–37. Positive proof that a variant is based on *Sondergut* is hard to provide, but—and this is important to emphasize to Brackert's critics—the opposite is just as unprovable. Why would a manuscript diverge from a substantial point otherwise?

168. Bumke (1996c), pp. 11–30. Bumke does not completely exclude the possibility of contamination, but he makes it clear that these are special cases that need to be explained precisely. Whoever assumes contamination has to make a case for it and should not use it as an easy excuse.

169. See Müller (1998b), pp. 79–80, 85, 91–94.

170. Bumke (1996c), p. 82; Palmer (1997).

171. In this sense, it is wrong to speak of the failure of the *Notfassung* (= ms. B), contrary to Heinzle, 1997, p. 94. On the contrary, the variants and supposed corrections of ms. C (= *Liedfassung*) have not been very successful (complete correspondence only with ms. a!). The success of each version, independent of Braune's stemma, should be reviewed again based on the compilation in Batts.

172. Bumke (1996c), pp. 390–455, created a catalog of these variants for the *Klage*. This would have to be expanded for other works so that the variant options for vernacular writing in the thirteenth century could be determined more accurately.

173. In order to make the following discussions comparable to earlier works on the *Nibelungenlied*, I cite de Boor using simple strophe and line numbers. The numbering in B can be as much as 3 strophes off from the Bartsch–de Boor edition. With C, the critical edition by Ursula Hennig has also been consulted.

174. The *C-group is less homogeneous than editions suggest. When single variant readings of later fragments correspond with C, this does not mean that they were following C in all its additions. It is, on the contrary, very seldom the case (up to str. 270 in Db, later all the way through only in a).

175. Bumke writes that it is not "a priority task . . . to develop a program of investigation for the interpretation of epic parallel versions as long as the questions of transmission remain unanswered and as long as there are no critical edi-

tions that can form the basis for a comparative interpretation of parallel versions" (1996c, p. 88). What such a "critical edition" might look like remains an open question.

Chapter 1. Variations of the Legend

1. The concepts come from Assmann (1992), p. 79. In the Nordic world, at least, the stories' connection to the "heroic age" is established: von See (1991), pp. 50–51.

2. Ruh (1979), p. 20, points to the independence of the *Nibelungenlied*'s transmission from imperial history.

3. Assmann (1992), p. 79. The rediscovery of the *Nibelungenlied* in the eighteenth century as the "German *Iliad*" is a misunderstanding even in this sense and can only be explained by the primary role the epic played in the contemporary genre hierarchy, which required a national equivalent of the *Iliad* or *Aeneid.*

4. Bender (1967).

5. Maximilian I has Dietrich of Bern appear next to King Arthur on his Innsbruck tomb, not Siegfried or Gunther. His historical research was only concerned with Dietrich's connection toHabsburg and Merovingian genealogy (Müller 1982, p. 196).

6. Müller (1982), pp. 190, 346n8; recently Graf (1993a), pp. 57–58.

7. Störmer (1973), pp. 491–96; (1974, 1987); Meves (1981); Wenskus (1973).

8. On the relationship between Pilgrim, Wolfger von Passau, Wolfger's political plans, and the possible context of the Passau connection, see Meves (1981). It is certainly possible that behind the Kuonrat of the *Klage*, there might have been a Kuonrat at the time of Bishop Wolfger. Concerning this problem fundamentally, see Graf (1993b).

9. See the contrary attempts by Müller (1974) and Jaeger (1985).

10. Even if the historical background of its creation can be reconstructed with greater certainty, the results are of limited use for the understanding of the literary text (cf. Müller 1993a).

11. On the link between both texts in mss. A, B, and C, see Bumke (1996c), pp. 239–53. Even if one has to admit that the two texts are clearly distinct from each other, it seems that the scribes were concerned about showing their connection, binding them together to form one "work" (cf. p. 237). That the *Klage* is still secondary can be shown not so much in certain differences in detail as in concept.

12. With the exception of mss. n and k (the latter can hardly be seen as a manuscript of the same text).

13. On the priority of *Nibelungenlied* and *Klage,* see the discussion in Curschmann (1979), pp. 116–19; Wachinger (1981), pp. 265–66.; Schröder (1989), pp. 13–21; and Bumke (1996c), pp. 106–12. Lachmann already assumed the temporal

priority of the *Klage;* Voorwinden (1981) asks whether at least the written version of the *Nibelungenlied* followed the composition of the *Klage* poem. I do not consider Schröder's idea (based on Leitzmann) of a supposed borrowing of the *Klage* from Wolfram's *Parzival* to be convincing, but I do believe that his suggestions for dating (the *Klage* as the younger text) are correct, even though it must be admitted that the literary-typologically younger *Klage* was not necessarily preceded by the archaicizing epic.

14. See Klaus Graf's contribution to *Literarische Interessenbildung im Mittelalter* (Heinzle 1993).

15. See Ulrich v. d. Türlin, *Willehalm* 103,5, and the citations in Grimm ([1889] 1957), pp. 162, 165, 172, 289.

16. See von See ([1978] 1981), pp. 187–88.

17. "The author of the Kl obviously considers the NL to be inadequate, and he intends to dispel the uneasiness of the public by completing the narration of the life histories of the survivors of the "Destruction of the Burgundians" in a satisfactory manner" (Gillespie 1972, p. 155).

18. Curschmann (1989), p. 382. Since there are two different interpretations of the material, the *Klage*'s assessments, for example, of Hagen's killing of Kriemhilt (Frakes 1994, p. 178), should not be unquestioningly transferred to the epic.

19. Wachinger (1981), p. 95; cf. Voorwinden (1981), p. 102.

20. Curschmann (1979), pp. 101, 104; Mertens (1996b), pp. 360, 363.

21. That this is a problem for courtly romance authors is shown by the narrator *Hartmann* in Hartmann's *Iwein,* who allows himself to be corrected by a superior narrator figure, namely, *Minne.* Together, Hartmann and *Minne* ground the authority of the author Hartmann von Aue, who invented both.

22. I follow my arguments from a paper (Müller 1996c) in *Erzählungen in Erzählungen,* ed. Haferland and Mecklenburg. which I shall make more precise in certain points concerning the dialogue with Bumke's book on the *Klage* (Bumke 1996c).

23. It is not always clear whether the statements refer to concurrent legends, the epic, or the actual text. Scholarship mostly discusses how the reference to sources at the beginning fits the information about the author Kuonrat (cf. Bumke 1996c, pp. 111, 461–68: in the *Klage* recension *C, they fit best, but even *B contains no manifest contradictions).

24. See the variants taken up by Bartsch, especially in the opening part: *Iu ist gesaget dicke daz and Iu ist gesaget daz* (Kl p. 7).

25. Especially early in the *C-version (Bartsch, p. 4): *die sol ich iu nennen, / daz ir si müget erkennen, / als uns daz buoch gesaget hât* [I shall name them for you / so that you might know them, / as the book has told us] (Kl C 33–35).

26. The deictic signals in the beginning and the clumsy transition exclude the possibility that the symbiosis of *Nibelungenlied* and *Klage* is original. The *Klage* must have been conceived as an independent work and then appended to the epic as a correction and commentary.

27. This would also explain the missing first seventy verses in some manuscripts. They are redundant given the preceding text.

28. See Voorwinden (1981), p. 107, on the various indications of a diffuse oral transmission.

29. Bumke (1996c), p. 467, sees "no notable difference" between *schrîbære* (C) and the *tihtære* who appears in ms. B. It seems to me, however, that at least the mechanical process of writing should be distinguished from "dictation" (which can be the work of a scholar, someone of a higher position than the ordinary copier, or *scriba.* On the other hand *tihtære* is not clearly the *dictator* in the sense of the scholarly chancellor. Kl 4316–17 (*getihtet man ez sît hât/dicke in tiuscher zungen*) makes it clear that *tihten* is not necessarily the same as conceiving of a Latin written work, but can instead denote the composition of a vernacular, not even necessarily written, work.

30. Curschmann (1984); cf. p. 143 on the legend's transmission outside of poetically formed texts.

31. Wyss (1990), p. 169–70.

32. Meves (1981), pp. 76–83, is working on an identification of Kuonrat. This aspect is not included in what follows.

33. Again, it is a question whether this refers only to writing or to the Latin language. The latter seems more likely. In no way does it refer to an epic version in Latin, in other words a *Nibelungias.*

34. Bumke (1996c), p. 462, indicates that *schrîbære* can also mean *notarius* and *cancellarius,* in any case, a high episcopal official.

35. Even stronger in Kl C 4417: *allez an sach: adtestatio rei visae.*

36. I therefore agree with Voorwinden (1981), p. 105, in general, if not in the details, that the *Klage* brings the "singer" into play.

37. The meaning of *prieven* (to test, to consider) is not easy to determine. It should be questioned whether the rounded or unrounded form (*prüeven/prieven*) is the root. The form *prüeven* in the *C group, "to bring forth," "to put right" makes good sense. It seems to me, though, that the nuance of critical revision (*prüeven,* to consider) is worth thinking about. Bumke (1996c), p. 463, argues against this, as Ranft did before him, and for *brieven* "to finish in writing" (according to ms. B).

38. Kl C 4421 has *getichtet manig ez sît hât*; the preceding *meister chvnrat* cannot be the subject of the syntagma. This version in no way claims that Pilgrim directed Kuonrat "to write down the *Nibelungenlied*" (as in Spiewok, 1989, pp. 180–81). Hauck (1961) correctly speaks of "Bishop Pilgrim's Nibelungian domestic version" as the cornerstone of "all Nibelungen composition" (p. 170).

39. Earlier scholarship is reviewed by Bumke (1996c), p. 463: "a direct correlation . . . cannot be proven."

40. See the terms used in the prologue: *rede, sagen, horen,* etc. (HE 1–30).

41. Ms. b has instead: *Vnd lewchtet als ain liecht* (on the choice of the Nürnberger ms. a as the *Leithandschrift,* see HE, ed. Cornelia Weber, pp. 16–17).

42. The punctuation is problematic. It seems to me to make more sense to read HE 4470–74 as a unit, that is, to associate *von dem meister* with the preceding and the following syntagmas *apo koinou*. The scholar (*magister*) is the author of the authentic (Latin) written text, which is still in Bamberg.

43. This can be understood causally (therefore) as well as in the sense of "derived from this Latin work."

44. How each stage of this fictitious tradition is connected remains unclear. What did the *meister* put together? The written text that came from the emperor's decree? What does *tihten* mean? (Latin) dictation? In any case, here, too, the Latin book is distinguished from the *liet*. In ms. b the claim of HE 4474, that the work of the master was written in Latin, is missing (HE, ed. Cornelia Weber, Apparatus, pp. 385–86). The link to scholarly tradition is weaker there.

45. The following remarks are based on a debate at the 14th Anglo-German Medievalist Conference in Meißen in 1995 with Sebastian Coxon, who has since published a dissertation on the concept of authorship in *Ortnit und Wolfdietrich* (Coxon 2001).

46. I do not translate *finden* with "to invent" [*erfinden*]. The book is clearly conceived as a material object that can be "found."

47. On the relationship to history, see Müller (1985), pp. 76–77.

48. For an overview, see Curschmann (1985–87), col. 933.

49. Bumke (1996c), pp. 590–94.

50. Bumke calculates "five or six different versions of text" for the *Klage*, already "in the first phase of the textual tradition," which may have been written on the basis of a "constant working contact" in the framework of a "Nibelungen workshop" (ibid., pp. 591–92).

51. As has been emphasized by different scholars, the remarkable uniformity of the text in the manuscripts should be stressed, especially after the "variance" of the *Nibelungenlied* has made the idea of an "original" and an "archetype" illusory.

52. See the so-called composer fragment of the *Jüngerer Titurel* that refers to the construction of St. Mark's Cathedral in Venice [completed c. 1071]:

Venezær vil riche ein tempel hant erbouwen.
von den die meisterliche gestein künden graben und erhouwen.
der nam ein ende vil und muosten sterben:
ir werc daz edel tiure liezen sie dar umbe niht verderben.

Ander si do namen ze meister disem tempel.
die muosten eben ramen. Ir wage mæz gaben si exempel
uf elliu ort und worhten sam die erren.
ist witze, swer daz minner lobt, swenn er hat gebrechen an den merren?

[The Venetians built a very beautiful church.
Of those who were able masterfully to quarry and build with rock

Many came to an end and died.
They did not allow that noble and dear work of theirs to perish on that account.

They hired others as master builders for this church.
They aimed to achieve the same goal. They proved their worth as exemplary
In all places, and they worked as well as their predecessors.
Is it not wise to praise the lesser, if the greater has failed?]
(Albrecht [von Scharfenberg], *Jüngerer Titurel: Heidelberger Verfasserfragment*, str. 2–3)

53. See Curschmann (1985–87), cols. 927–29.

54. Curschmann (1979). To what extent ms. A can be seen as a "version" is debatable. It is more so for the bridal quest of Prünhilt, less so for the continuation.

55. Hoffmann (1967).

56. Bumke (1996c) underestimates the extent to which the *C version, and most especially the *Klage,* attempted to correct the *B version. The attempts at clarification and valuation should not be understood as a simple "effort to improve the master's work" (p. 593). They aim at a completely different work. Bumke's evaluation of *C goes back and forth: on p. 45, he denies that *C has the character of a "revision"; on p. 46, we read: "The *C-revision [!] . . . has all the characteristics of a version," and also on pp. 257 and 258, he speaks of *C as a "revision." I believe that *C in fact is secondary. Bumke (p. 46) emphasizes that "it has not been possible with the methods of textual criticism to demonstrate the secondary character of this version." "Methods of textual criticism" seem to me to be defined too narrowly, because they should include conceptual changes. Most of the changes of *C answer questions that remain open in ms. B and related manuscripts. According to the logic of question and answer, this sets the priorities.

57. Braune (1900). The following comments try to sketch only a few basic tendencies of Nibelungen scholarship. Detailed discussion of this point would warrant an entire project in itself.

58. On the terminological difference, see Oesterreicher (1993); cf. Schaefer (1994), p. 367.

59. On the epic's need for commentary, see Bumke (1996c), p. 532. I fail to see how, if it has different authors, the commentary can be "the product of one and the same work process," let alone a fundamentally different concept. Would it not be more reasonable to think in terms of a question that invokes—more or less compatible—answers?

60. See Bumke (1996c), p. 259. On account of this mutual orientation on *C, there are then, according to Bumke, several *Klage* versions, but not an independent *Klage* "revision" *C.

61. According to Masser (1981), p. 135, there are strophes in the *Nibelungenlied* that should be seen as performance alternatives. Concrete proof is hardly possible in individual cases.

62. Masser (1981), p. 135.

63. Since Brackert's critique of Braune, not much has happened in editorial philology aside from the basic discussions of the stemma problem and of "Lachmannian" philology. Only a few scholars attempt, like Schröder (1968), pp. 19–47, to reach an archetype from the manuscripts and to see variants as results of a single and therefore correctable transmission process (cf. Schröder, 1996).

64. Bumke (1996c), p. 54; cf. pp. 60–84. Bumke puts together the types for the *Klage.* The variants are conspicuously limited to certain classes. Generally on similar *ad libitum* elements, see Müller (1999).

65. Andersson (1980), p. 151: "Stern surgery [!] is required to separate the layers and expose the tradition that underlies the new growth." He is looking to uncover sources for the most important episodes of the first part, but thinks that the poet combined them differently, transferring motifs from one protagonist to another (cf. p. 159).

66. "Siegfried's youthful deeds were heavily abridged, Waberlohe and the exchange of forms became superfluous" (Ehrismann 1987, p. 126). How does he know this?

67. As in, e.g., Dinckelacker (1990): "We know from the legend" that Sivrit has seen Prünhilt before, so this does not need to be explicitly stated in the *Nibelungenlied.* Every listener will already presume this in the encounter in Isenstein (pp. 87–90). How obvious is such a claim? The hypothetical plot connection is then supposed to support modernizing abstractions, for example, that Prünhilt "has been robbed of her chosen self-image." Her questioning of her suitor's identity attempts "to realize her life's goal, or at least to discover the exact reason why it has failed" (p. 91).

68. This seems to me to be somewhat the case in an example from Heinzle (1997, pp. 82–83). At the reception of the Burgundians at Etzel's court, Dietrich's reply, *Die Sîfrides wunden lâzen wir nu stên* [let us forget about Sivrit's wounds] (1726,1), does not fit "with Hagen's [preceding] speech," in which there is no mention of Sivrit's wounds. This is different in the *Thidreks saga,* where the dialogue partner is already speaking of them. I cannot find anything here that does not fit. Dietrich speaks metonymically of Sivrit's death. To refer this to Hagen's preceding words about this death is possible, thanks to the rhetorical function of metonymic speech (and it is not "characteristic of the psychologizing Nibelungen criticism"). Even if one assumes that the remark really originated in an earlier source, it becomes an element of a more complex rhetorical presentation in the *Nibelungenlied.* The *Thidreks saga,* on the other hand, is satisfied with telling of a simple "prosaic" exchange of speech and counterspeech.

69. See Haug (1987), p. 286. The "*Nibelungenlied* does not have the character of a work in the modern sense. It is not a whole in itself. It is a whole only in combination with its intertextual horizon, to which it constantly refers anew, which it awakens, whose motif elements are playfully employed . . . . Many of the well-known inconsistencies and contradictions then just go up in smoke."

70. Haug (1987), p. 285. "The break with tradition, which is manifested in this, is of such a fundamental nature that the legendary material is incapable of making anything understandable. At the same time, however, it gains a secondary meaning as an intertextual horizon, without which nothing can be understood."

71. See Bernreuther (1994), pp. 26–27, on variants of this conflict.

72. It is strophe 1909 in ms. B, 1849 in ms. A, and strophe 1963 (revised) in ms. C. It has been assumed until very recently that it is a remnant of an older version of the story. Even so, one must question its meaning in a different context, where it seems to stand "incongruously" (Flood 1994, p. 181).

73. The next edition, after de Boor's death, has "poem" instead of *Älteren Not,* replacing a debatable but still precise term with an only seemingly more careful one, which is actually vaguer and evidently false.

74. De Boor, Commentary, in *Das Nibelungenlied*^{15}, p. 300. Several critics argue similarly, the most detailed being Heusler (1965^{6}), p. 99; Falk (1974), p. 206, is especially apodictic.

75. Falk (1974), p. 206; cf. HPr S. CXXV.

76. See Fischer and Völker (1975), pp. 88–89. The distribution of roles in the conflict (HvK 50–158) is completely changed, however, in the *Nibelungenlied.* Killing the tutor is also in Ulrich von Etzenbach's *Alexander* (ed. Toischer), 18913–57. De Boor, Commentary, in *Das Nibelungenlied*^{15}, p. 308: "Hagen's deed is only understandable based on the older version in st. 1912. Only there is the boy 'disrespectful,' so that the tutor deserved the punishment."

77. For example, the *Völsunga saga* reports that Gudrun does not love Atli and that the liaison is an unhappy one from the beginning. This is precisely what the *Nibelungenlied* does not say—nor does it claim the opposite to be true—and it is therefore improper simply to assume this circumstance, regardless of intuition.

78. On the term *Motivation von hinten,* see Lugowski (1932/1976), pp. 25–27, 66–81, showing that "from the back" motivation is intrinsic to premodern narration.

79. Kriemhilt is in fact morally "guilty," in the sense of liability for success, that Ortliep is present when her deceit comes to light. On the legal controversy about such "guilt," see *Handwörterbuch zur deutschen Rechtsgeschichte* 1, cols. 989–1001 (E. Kaufmann). Here, as is often the case elsewhere in the *Nibelungenlied,* we may be dealing with a case of extralegal concepts.

80. Hagen's prediction that Ortliep won't live long may be inspired by an old motive (Haug, 1981, pp. 43, 47), but this is also not played out.

81. Introduced by Genette 1982.

82. "The written form makes it possible for the variants to relate to each other. What is new does not replace what has been superseded, making it disappear [as in orality]. It layers itself on top and creates literary history. . . . One must assume that the time that preceded the written text of the epic, when its contents and forms were created, was considerably longer than the bit of written tradition that followed. But it is more important that this unwritten tradition must have caused

a much more dense and intensive test of all contents in terms of their certain impact" (Blumenberg 1979, p. 168).

83. Mixed forms are evident in mss. Jh and n, a milder form in ms. Q (Rosenfeld 1991, pp. 85–87). In ms. n, Kriemhilt tries to save Ortliep (ibid., p. 88). On the variants, see Batts, p. 583.

84. Ms. n (n 375,4) at first also follows the tone of *C and then closes similarly to the *AB group: *Wye kont ein wip dorch roch vmber mortlicher gethon* [How could a woman have acted more cruelly for the sake of vengeance?] (Göhler 1995, p. 74).

85. The *Straßburger Alexander* can also be placed in the genealogy of the courtly romance under this aspect.

86. Pérennec (1975) notes ironically that "some liberties are taken with the logic" (p. 1). It is logic that is presumed to be a matter of course for modern narrations.

87. Bumke (1960); Andersson (1980), pp. 170–77.

88. See Bumke (1960). The *Thidreks saga,* chap. 205, relates an earlier engagement.

89. I cannot agree with Strohschneider (1997), who concludes from Sivrit's knowledge of the circumstances in Isenstein (str. 382; 384; 407) that he had been there once before (p. 48). This is only true under the conditions of a normal world, in which "knowledge" assumes "having gained knowledge."

90. See on the other hand the *Völsunga saga* (*Heldenepen,* pp. 7–102); on the incongruities that would follow in the *Nibelungenlied* with the assumption of a similar story line, see Bischoff (1970), pp. 10–11.

91. See Strohschneider (1997).

92. On the irregularities of the system, see ibid.

93. Safety *vor slegen und vor stichen*—but where does this come into play?—the ability to see and hear while invisible—is this all that unexpected (C 342, 4–343, 3)?

94. If the structural connection between these statements is ignored, then one can come to certain conclusions with regard to Hagen's character and his habitual cowardice, in surprising contrast to the usual image of Hagen. That way, questions are asked that can lead to contradictory and hardly verifiable results (cf. Thelen 1997).

95. Whoever advises against something might be a traitor (Genelun in the *Rolandslied*). He can stay behind without abdicating his responsibility (*Rother*), or he can overcome his doubts (Sivrit and Hagen in the first and second part of the *Nibelungenlied*). Sivrit masters the adventure; Hagen is proven right in the downfall of the Burgundians.

96. Differently, Strohschneider (1997), p. 50. He sees in the episode an attempt to diffuse the complications of the scheme break, namely, the Tristan solution of the confusion of suitor and quest helper. He therefore emphasizes Hagen's role in ensuring that the marriage is not consummated beforehand. Sivrit has to be removed.

97. Missing is the emphasis of the dual resistance to the substitution of the *man* Hagen by the *künec* Sivrit (lacunae after A 497 and A 499).

98. This corresponds to the observation by Curschmann (1979), p. 97, that ms. A is more interested in individual episodes than in the story line as a whole.

99. In B 338–39; C 348–49.

100. Ms. C has no deviation.

101. On the phrase "syntagmatic and paradigmatic integration" used as a subheading to this section, see Titzmann ([1977] 1993), pp. 61–63, 149–164.

102. Curschmann (1979), p. 96 (following earlier considerations).

103. This is shown in the three manuscripts as follows: A 324–25 corresponds to B 323–24 and C 327–29. The inserted strophe in ms. C connects to the changed ending of C 327 and formulates the decision for a new undertaking:

do sprach der chunic riche: ine wil niht langer biten me.
Des wil ich beraten, wa ich die mvge nemen,
div mir vnd mime riche ze frowen mvge zemen
an edel vnd ovch an schone; der gib ich miniv lant.
als ich die reht ervinde, si sol iv werden wol bekant. (C 327, 4–328, 4)

[Then the powerful king spoke: I do not want to wait any longer.
I shall consider where I might find
the one who will suit me and my kingdom as a wife
in nobility and beauty. I shall give her my lands.
When I find her, I shall tell you.]

104. Not in the way "that A contains the original text here, which was conceived more carelessly in the stream of the source" (Curschmann 1979, p. 96).

105. "The redactor of *A does not only know, as supposedly everyone does in this circle, the story used from *Âventiure* 6 on, he also has it in mind as a still current oral episodic poem, so that he can sometimes shorten the corresponding passages accordingly" (ibid.).

106. There seems to be a "tendency toward the bridal quest scheme as such . . . , in that Sigfrid plays the standard role of the knowledgeable and cunning hero without the special complications that the further context of the *Nibelungenlied* brings to the story line and its motivation" (ibid.).

107. See the class terminology investigated by Hennig (1981), pp. 180–82, and on the basis of charter material, critically Schulze (1997b).

108. On the political implications of this model, see pp. 147–48 above.

109. I assume, along with Panzer (1945), that around 1200 the meaning of the rein and stirrup service is clear to everyone, along with its controversial political meaning (cf. pp. 100–108). There is no doubt that Sivrit performs the "normal service of a vassal" (p. 101); cf. Hennig (1981), p. 180; *Sachsenspiegel: Lehnrecht* 66.3; on this, see Wenzel (1992), p. 337.

110. On this misattribution, see p. 251 above.

111. Different but similar is C 431, 4. Haustein (1993) believes: "Siegfried would have won Kriemhild's hand even without the stirrup service" (p. 18). This contradicts the context of rules in Isenstein.

112. Gaps between A 383 and A 384 (three strophes = 396–98) and between A 385 and 386 (= 401).

113. Gap between A 392 and A 393 (=409).

114. Gap between A 394 and A 395 (four strophes = 412–15).

115. Peeters (1986), p. 9–10, calls Sivrit "originally an 'exiled nobleman'"; "probably an exiled, wandering hero."

116. See Curschmann (1979), p. 96.

117. Gap between A 376 and A 377 (=388).

118. Gap between A 442 and A 443 (three strophes = 471–73) as opposed to B 469–71 and C 482–84.

119. The hyperdramatization shows that the deceit is by no means meant to be seen as an acceptable alternative (as in Czerwinski, 1979, p. 71), but is something peculiar that is supposed to be hammered into the listener.

120. Gap of four strophes between A 348 and A 349 (= 354–57).

121. See A 361.

122. Even more sparsely narrated are the preparations for the wedding after returning to Worms, and the cooperation of secondary characters like Rumolt is not mentioned at all. There are gaps after A 526, A 529, A 531, A 532, A 551, A 559, and A 583.

123. Gaps after A 358 (= 368) and A 359 (= 370); missing in the following sequence are the third and fifth links: the clothing is ordered—prepared—is ready—is tried on—everyone sees that it fits.

124. Gaps between A 428 and A 429 (= 453), A 429 and A 430 (= 455).

125. Gap between A 432 and A 433 (= 459).

126. Ms. B, in a supplemental strophe, already emphasizes Gunther's fear more than ms. A (442). Ms. C inserts one more strophe.

127. Prünhilt's superior strength is called *vbermvot* (C 435,4). The long jump, in which Sivrit carries Gunther, is difficult to imagine, and the narrator states: *daz was ein michel wvnder vnd kunsteklich genvoch* [that was a great marvel and quite a trick] (C 475,3).

128. On the semantic shift of terms for dependence, see Wachinger (1960), p. 111; Hennig (1981), pp. 181–82; Schulze (1997b); on interpretations, see p. 178.

129. Differently, Schulze (1997b), pp. 44–45, who thinks that "the interpretation of vassal is removed from the beginning" by the switch; "a ministerial as a companion of the king . . . would also make sense." This is correct, but it would differ from the social constellation in the rest of the epic.

130. The process had not come to an end with ms. C, as shown by later manuscripts, for example, when a strophe is added behind C 336 in the *Ambraser Heldenbuch* (d) in the context discussed above. This supplemental strophe expresses Gunther's chivalric determination to risk his life for Prünhilt's sake (Batts, p. 101).

131. On this scene, see pp. 118–19 above.

132. See p. 333 above.

133. Str. 511 and 512 are replaced; 513–16 are missing (gap of four strophes between C 527 and C 528).

134. Gap between C 529 and C 530. In ms. A only one strophe (518) is missing, the gap between A 486 and A 487; this intensifies Prünhilt's protest against her disempowerment.

135. Ms. a here represents the *C group; the strophe is also in ms. d.

136. Fromm (1990), p. 8, observes: "It is inconceivable that the storyteller was not aware of this absurdity, that Hagen could carry an army with close to 10,000 men in a small boat in one day across the currents of the Danube. It is equally inconceivable that the poet could not have changed this detail with the stroke of a pen." That he does not do so is the consequence of a peculiar narrative principle.

137. Heinzle (1978), p. 262: "contemporaries of this work [in version B] were just as baffled as are German philologists. Its imprecision, along with version C and the *Klage,* but also with the *Rosengarten,* led to the commentaries that we have observed in the redaction of our texts: reception was accomplished as reworking."

138. Wehrli (1972), p. 101, describes the *Klage* as "a forceful and systematic liquidation of the downfall of the Nibelungs."

139. Bumke (1996c), p. 289; cf. pp. 282–97; for a list of gaps, see pp. 282–83; and see pp. 283–84 on the peculiarities of the *J *Klage,* which are not the result of "sloppiness and inattentiveness"; a "redactor with a plan is at work" (p. 284), and verses have been added "to bridge the gaps that occur [in comparison with the complete version]" (p. 285).

140. Reproduced in Bumke (1996c), pp. 306–39.

141. Curschmann (1989), p. 381: "The break is intentional." "A lack of space could not be the reason (since empty parchment leaves follow) that the scribe broke off the *Klage* text at this point, while describing how the news of the death of all the heroes in Bechelaren was received." The text ends in mid-sentence, but it is also possible to " supply a full stop, if what follows is disregarded" (Bumke, 1996c, pp. 170–71).

142. Break after Kl 3957, but as a result of page loss, so that observations on following passages are not possible (Bumke, 1996c, p. 185).

143. Some of the preceding epic is missing as well in that manuscript, namely, *Âventiure* 30, 32–34, and 37–39 (the end), but space has been left in the manuscript in each case.

144. Curschmann (1989), p. 381; Bumke (1996c), pp. 188–89. Even here it is not possible to speak of an "incomplete" text (p. 186; cf. mss. D and a); d ends where the story ends in mss. J and h, and only the epilogue is appended (Pilgrim, Master Kuonrat, and the first written version). In comparison with mss. ABCa, above all, the continuation of the Dietrich story is missing (up to Kl 4294), as are the passages on the writing of the story and Etzel's end.

145. Batts, pp. 98–103.

146. After 1718 (B 1715); cf. Batts, pp. 175–76.

147. Again ms. b after 2376 (Batts, p. 723): Kriemhilt's dismemberment.

148. On changes in the first two verses of 1568, see Abeling, p. 169; the proposition that the omission was "intentional" is difficult to support, above all given the point at which the narration continues (right after the battle of the rear guard, but clearly before the arrival in Passau). The subsequent smoothing of the transition (after erasure) more likely indicates that a gap in the source was noticed and a correction attempted.

149. On the gaps in the opening part, see Batts, pp. 105–21.

150. Batts, p. 795.

151. I would like to thank Peter Göhler for leaving me his (preliminary) transcription of the introductory strophes; for his characterization, see Göhler (1995), pp. 73–77; Vorderstemann (1976), pp. 116–19, gives an overview of the strophes.

152. It is presumed that Sivrit has saved Kriemhilt from a dragon (n 8, 3–4). An unthematized knowledge of the myth is evident in the background.

153. This programmatic strophe is by no means a redactional supplement only in ms. C or the *C group; it is also in the manuscripts closely related to ms. B as well.

154. Three strophes in mss. ABCDd, only two in ms. J (str. 6 is missing); cf. Batts, p. 3, on the alternate sequence in ms. D.

155. Namely, strophes 16 and 17; cf. Batts, p. 7.

156. See the mother-daughter conversation in Heinrich von Veldeke's *Eneit* (Wolf, 1995, pp. 271, 283, and more). In Veldeke, Lavinia believes that she can escape the power of *minne,* and here, too, this will prove to be impossible.

157. Another manuscript (b) starts with the (second) *Abentewr von Seyfrid dem Starcken* due to the loss of two leaves (cf. Bumke, 1996c, p. 184); the beginning of ms. h is also defective.

158. With an additional strophe of heroic praise in ms. A (A 21); cf. Batts, pp. 8–9.

159. Curschmann (1989), pp. 393–95; on the concurrence of the legends, see pp. 398–99; and see also Alois Wolf (1995), pp. 315–42, 401–2, 407–8.

160. According to Batts, p. 795; cf. Curschmann (1989), p. 406.

161. Curschmann (1989), pp. 406–7.

162. Curschmann (1989), p. 395. But these remain vague impulses. The chronological connection of the four battles in the Dietrich epics of the *Ambraser Heldenbuch* to the *Nibelungenlied* and *Klage* is not clear at all (cf. p. 394). And the conclusion of the *Klage* in ms. a, *dô her Dietrich dan gereit* [Lord Dietrich then rode off] (Kl 4206), is not very convincing at all as the end to a "Life of Dietrich."

163. Curschmann (1989), pp. 396–98. On the legend and cultural traditions, see pp. 398–404; esp. pp. 401–2; Heinzle (1978), pp. 247–54.

164. Curschmann (1989), pp. 389–89. In the *Nibelungenlied,* Kriemhilt is not yet portrayed as a "dangerous interloper" from the perspective of the Dietrich legend (p. 388), in my opinion. The justification of the *Klage* would otherwise not

be possible, since according to Curschmann, it also seeks to connect up with the Amelung legend and mourns from its perspective (pp. 390–94).

165. Curschmann (1989), pp. 408–9.

Chapter 2. Heroic Narration and Epic Composition

1. The stanza is present in mss. A and C in both the *nôt* and the *liet* versions. Of course, it is also possible that it was left out in ms. B. The strophe is generally considered to be relatively young, and not only on account of its internal rhyme; cf. Haubrichs (1995), pp. 44–46, on its meaning; Curschmann (1992); Strohschneider (1996), pp. 7–9.

2. Assmann (1992), p. 100.

3. Curschmann (1992), pp. 63–64, has shown how clever the narrator is in recalling an anonymous narrative tradition for the production of his—the poet's—entrance: "a poet presents a metaphor for a singer's entrance" (p. 64).

4. On the meaning of the personal pronoun for "cultural memory," see Assmann (1992), p. 16.

5. Ehlich (1989), p. 91. A "stretching out" of the communications situation is already present in oral texts, as soon as they remove themselves from oral communication's reference to a present situation. The distance is increased even more in the literate situation.

6. Schaefer (1992), p. 18, with reference to Vollrath (1981) and Clanchy (1970); Bäuml (1980), p. 249; Rösler (1980), p. 291; cf. the differentiation in Assmann (1992).

7. Rösler (1980) has shown with early Greek poetry that the preconditions of an oral culture and its expectations, as opposed to poetry, reach far into literate culture.

8. Bäuml (1980), p. 249.

9. Haug ([1974] 1989), p. 298, speaks of "alienation . . . to the inexplicable and inconceivable."

10. On typical initial formulae, see Masser (1981), pp. 127–28.

11. In this case—emphasizing the character of the book form—two strophes precede this one, which attempt to situate the narration in the context of literate tradition. As in the *Nibelungenlied*, the formula no longer designates the first beginning.

12. It is also evident as an epic introductory formula in other kinds of texts; cf. e.g., WvO: *Ain her in Francriche saz* (133).

13. The branching off of French heroic epic, and the creation of new branches, is examined by Adler (1971).

14.

> *Von dem man hie gesprochen hât*
> *des wil ich niht haben rât*
> *ich enkünde iu sînen namen.* (Bit 29–31)

[As for the person just spoken oft,
I'll certainly not agree to
tell you his name.]

15. Metaphorically also *rede, tihte.*

16. On the choices available from the repertoire of prologue strophes used by the manuscripts in different ways, see pp. 78–79 above.

17. I am following observations made by Haug ([1974] 1989), esp. pp. 299–303, who shows the slackening of the action at the striking turning points to be a (futile) attempt to repress heroic fatalism.

18. Kriemhilt is surely warned and emphasizes in 46,3: *daz si deheinen wolde ze eime trûte hân* [that she did not want to have a lover], but the pledge called forth by the dream plays no role in relation to Sivrit.

19. The action that began with the *wuohs* formula has reached its destination.

20. Haug ([1974] 1989), p. 302.

21. Thelen (1984), p. 146, refers *iteniuwe* to the narrator, who announces "the originality, the 'newness' of the story that is to follow." According to the text, however, what is new is addressed to the Burgundian court.

22. Czerwinski (1979), pp. 72–74, 78–79, postulates the "failure of the festival" as the key to the epic.

23. The *âventiure* ends between str. 1386 and 1387.

24. A variation of the *sitzen* formula; cf. 1142,2.

25. Similarly, Walther Haug sees a substitution of the purely "subjectively justified" will of the protagonists for "heroic fatalism" (Haug [1974] 1989, pp. 303–5; and summarizing Haug [1987] 1989). This subjective moment seems to me to be secondary to the impression of contingency.

26. See Göhler (1989), pp. 124–27: "But the author is unable to follow any of these possibilities seriously, since any one of them would have meant contravening the established plot."

27. Taken as an accusative object ("nothing") specified by the *wan* clause.

28. It is clearer in the *C group—*der Niblelunge liet*—that we are dealing with the title of a text, whereas *nôt* also signifies its object.

29. Haubrichs (1994), pp. 27, 44.

30. What is meant by *redebære:* "worth talking about," "worth being told or retold," or perhaps "full of speech" or "speech provoking"? (cf. Kl C: *daz ist vil redebære*, p. 3). This would fit what follows in the *Klage*'s: "endless talking."

31. Haubrichs (1995), pp. 44, 36; the contemplation of Kriemhilt's end or of the painful deaths of Gotelint and Uote manifests an attempt to "accommodate *labor sanctorum* and *labor heroum*" (ibid., p. 37).

32. See pp. 75–76 above.

33. Müller (1985), pp. 75–77; McConnell (1986b).

34. Similarly, Kl 912–13, 944–45, 1115–17, 1214–15, 1248, 1256–59.

35. See Gillespie (1972): "commentary, not only on the text which we have, but also on the story of the Nibelungen" (p. 154).

36. Kl *C has another order again, but it is also more the norm: the kings, their land, their family (*die in diu erbe liezen*, Kl C 32), Dancrat and Uote, then (once again) their three sons (= the kings), then the daughter (Kl C 41–42).

37. Curschmann (1992), p. 65: the author offers "different hypotheses to choose from."

38. The question of Christianity is different for the joint transmission of epic and *Klage* than it is for the epic alone (cf. Knapp 1987, p. 166).

39. Note Curschmann's (1979) thoughts on ms. A.

40. In *Kudrun,* as well as in heroic epic generally, quantity is often a means of hyperbole. The number of those executed is a criterion of successful jurisprudence.

41. See also the reference to the generally accepted opinion that heroic memory takes for granted (*daz helden wol gezam*, K 165,1).

42. Haug ([1974] 1989), p. 297, on the calculated relationship between the two stories of Sivrit's youth. Seitter (1987), pp. 81–82, is to my knowledge the only one who has pointed to the completely different narrative presentation.

43. "Legend" is meant here primarily as a narrative type. There does not need to be a reference to a story that was actually told orally. That there were such stories is evidenced by stories from northern Europe and also the *Hürnen Seifried*, which was not fixed in writing until the early modern period.

44. Curschmann (1992), p. 68, remarks correctly concerning the story of Sivrit's youth that it "was so powerfully anchored in common knowledge that it could be independently put into writing even two hundred years later."

45. G. Müller (1975), p. 96, sees one function of the second *âventiure* in cutting off "the memory, probably still alive, of a landless fighter of dubious origins." For a summary, see Schulze (1997a), pp. 136–41.

46. Mertens (1996a), p. 62, has recognized this doubling as an "epic book form's structural means," used paradoxically with a "reference to orality."

47. Göhler (1989), p. 14, points to the *âventiuren* register ms. m, where the narrator's decision is corrected. This had already struck a reviser of the late Middle Ages as curious. Göhler also mentions the many gaps in Hagen's story.

48. Of course, it would otherwise be "unlikely," based on normal life experiences, that the story of Sivrit's youth was told only to Hagen (see Dinkelacker 1990, p. 87).

49. Grubmüller (1994), p. 61, who does not see the importance of the scene: "this entire background, played down as a literary commonplace, is told in only sixteen stanzas (86–101), in a retrospective aside by Hagen in order to give Siegfried a modicum of respect."

50. The content of these verses could, but does not have to, refer to what Hagen is telling. This is commonly taken as their meaning (cf. Schulze 1997a, p. 138).

Eifler's (1989) thesis, which allows the story of Sivrit's youth to be inserted "in the time opened up between the end of the second and the beginning of the third *âventiure,*" interprets the text as a historic source that refers back to a reality, so that gaps and contradictions in the representation of this reality have to be filled in. In a referenceless literary text, such an interpolation is methodologically inappropriate (p. 285, cf. Falk 1974, p. 118; Andersson 1980, pp. 157–58; to the contrary, Schulze 1997a, p. 139: "But actually these kinds of speculations are out of place.")

51. A courtly turnaround of the *wuohs* formula.

52. Later, with the return to the land of the Nibelungs, we read: *Der helt der fuor aleine* [the hero traveled alone] (485,1).

53. See Göhler (1996), p. 217. To interpret the attempt, "to ride out alone" as a literary code for communal action (the hero as representative of the entire group, Peeters 1986, p. 7), rests on an (euhemeristic) interpretation scheme that is imposed on the text from the outside.

54. Curschmann (1992), p. 68, characterizes Hagen's story as "incomplete." "The hearer must fill in his own knowledge of the legend—or remain unsatisfied."

55. This is the solution offered by Stech (1993), pp. 71–80. Bäuml (1981), p. 119, sees a parallel—unfortunately without any further explanation—in the doubling of the narrator role with the complicated narrative fiction in the courtly romance.

56. Because he is equipped with the narrator's knowledge, Dietrich can later call Kriemhilt *vâlandinne* (1748,4), whereas the reproach based on what Dietrich can know as an individual would be pointless. It would be a "stylistic error of the most recent poet" (de Boor, p. 276) only in the poetological context of the modern novel.

57. This kind of statement is different from the appeals to the indulgence of the modern reader for inaccuracies in older texts first introduced in Homeric scholarship ("Even Homer sometimes nods"!). It is not about discounting a narrative logic that is valid everywhere and for all time, but rather the recognition of a historically distinct narrative method.

58. No one adopted Walter Falk's (1974) bizarre idea that Sivrit's youthful experiences are of a "dreamlike, psychic nature" (p. 120), "adventure in the realm of the psyche" (p. 121) or "in fantasy" (p. 123), rather than real. "It is true that Hagen did not want to give the imaginary any power over life in the world of honor," Falk concludes in true German philological style (p. 120).

59. Andersson (1978), p. 38.

60. See, e.g., Fromm (1990), p. 8.

61. Also in mss. Db; cf. Batts, pp. 8–9; Schulze (1997a), p. 138, concludes that B 21–22 was understood by the redactor as a "placeholder" for a rejected story variant.

62. Also in ms. D, but not in ms. b (Batts, pp. 14–15). As explained above, there were already various attempts to create everyday plausibility in the manuscripts.

63. See C 24,1. Left out, on the other hand, in ms. C is str. 24 of the vulgate version. This has Sivrit's upbringing end with his appearance at court.

64. Cf., to the contrary, Andersson (1980), p. 158. The reviser is the first to open up "a free space for his hero, which he can then fill in later according to need, whenever he needs the trappings of mythic tradition and of the unbelievable" (Ehrismann 1987, p. 113). The inference that "Siegfried might have become lord of the land *zen Nibelungen* (484) on one of his youthful travels" argues from the standpoint of a historian who uses the best source to establish a past "fact."

65. De Boor (1959), pp. 176, 187. The fight with the dragon is separated from this story (on its possible place in the narrative structure, see ibid. pp. 189–91).

66. See Alois Wolf (1987), p. 180. This is an intentionally developed counter-concept, just as with Kriemhilt.

67. Presuming a significant clarifying expansion for the Darmstadt *âventiuren* register, de Boor (1959), p. 185, speaks of "not very clear indications" and argues that Hagen "simply created vagueness."

68. Reichert (1990), p. 308.

69. Ehrismann (1987), pp. 115–16.

70. Göhler (1996), p. 218, also sees no connection between the dragon and the Nibelungen kings, Nibelunc and Schildunc; cf. Stutz (1990), p. 412.

71. This is paraphrased by Eifler (1989), p. 280, with the sense of "probable" linkage: "as Siegfried comes closer, he is recognized by one of the participants"—as if he had already been seen by someone and as if everyone knew afterwards who was meant. None of this is in the text.

72. Hagen is also immediately recognized and called by name by the water sprites, also inhabitants of this other world (1535,2). This is understood among heroes.

73. Where is it written: "they offer up their supporters against Siegfried, including twelve fearless men, *daz starke risen wâren*" (Eifler 1989, p. 280)? This or in some similar fashion is how it could be imagined if this were a report of fact. The epic says nothing of the kind. In Hagen's alogical presentation, it states: *Si heten dâ ir friunde zwelf küene man* [They had twelve bold men as their friends] (94,1).

74. As one must obviously conclude, it is the just-won sword that is feared by the *jungen recken.* This is not explicitly stated.

75. *Formaler Mythos*, ed. Martinez (1996), p. 18; Gabriel in ibid., pp. 49–61; and see on causality, space, time, and process structure, Cassirer ([1925] 1997), 2: 55–77.

76. Lugowski's "backwards motivation" describes a figure eliminating a clear chronological progression that constitutes an if-then relationship. This is called a "mythical analog" (cf. *Formaler Mythos*, ed. Martinez, 1996, p. 19).

77. Similarly, mss. Db. Correspondingly later in *C, str. 95, which recounts that Sivrit vanquishes his opponent with Balmunc, must be deleted (B 93; also in mss. AJdh). The progression in mss. CDb is more plausible, the other is the *lectio difficilior* (cf. Batts, pp. 30–31).

78. Eifler (1989, pp. 280–81) writes: "The ms. B text was not interested in this kind of assignment of responsibility. It was not necessary when it only concerned Siegfried's victory against a large superior force and thereby a description of his strength. It was also impossible since Hagen was not an eyewitness to the events" (as if, concerning the last point, an epic narrator ever took such doubts into consideration).

79. Instead of *die wâren im ê vremde, unz er ir künde dâ gewan* [they were strangers to him until he came to know them] (88,4).

80. "Siegfried does something here that is not right. He literally steals the treasure" (Peeters, 1986, p. 7). This is a conclusion that refers to this text and not to the vulgate text.

81. Taking possession of the treasure here means *hin furen* [take away] (*Das Nibelungenlied nach der Piaristenhandschrift*, ed. von Keller, 97,2), whereas in *ΛB it is brought back to its original location (98,2), where it still is later in *Âventiure* 19. The plausibility of the scene falls victim, as usual, to the context of the whole; de Boor (1959), p. 182, suspects another version of the conquest of the hoard (Seifrid takes the hoard away) for the Darmstadt *âventiuren* register (m). This would exclude the later theft of the hoard.

82. Some scholars at least assume different stylistic registers between the first and the second parts, whereby the second one is more archaic (cf. Voorwinden 1990, pp. 438, 441–42, on the description and motivation of fighting).

83. Curschmann (1979), p. 94; (1985–87), cols. 955–56; (1992), p. 60; Wachinger (1981), p. 93: "Literalization of an oral narrative style."

84. "The 'lay' transposes and stylizes traditional orality into a grand narrative of epic inventory 'in the old style,'" Curschmann writes (1989, p. 382). One has to be clear about the metaphorical status of this idiom. Attempts like Reichert's (1990) to nail it down in detail end in fuzziness. (Reichert, by the way, always refers to the *Klage* as the "*Clâge.*")

85. Ong ([1982] 1987), p. 43; Haug (1996), p. 194.

86. Assmann (1992), p. 97. "The audience expects the accustomed from the bard, the unaccustomed from the author" (Assmann, 1992, p. 98). Haug (1996) somewhat differently: varying repetition in book form is a means of wide-ranging integration: "doubling of the plot under changing signals" as a "means of constituting meaning" (pp. 194–95): "With the insecure text of improvisational poetry the meaning lies in the identical, in the secured text of written poetry it lies in the difference" (p. 195).

87. Haug has proposed taking the second part of the *Nibelungenlied* as a varying resumption of the first part, "but now as a subjective conscious act" (cf. 1994, pp. 396–97). This is the attempt that goes the farthest in understanding doubling as a commentary, but in my opinion this brings the *Nibelungenlied* too close to the literary doubling of the courtly romance. Its structure, however, has no support in the text.

88. See Haug (1979), esp. pp. 119–25; Müller (1980), p. 231.

89. Czerwinski (1989), pp. 14, 45, 79, 90, and elsewhere for examples from the courtly romance; on the discussion of the concept, see Strohschneider (1995), pp. 177–78.

90. Bumke (1958), pp. 258, 266–67; cf. also Mertens (1996a), p. 65.

91. Strohschneider (1997), p. 51, in whose interpretation the "political" purpose of the scheme is less important than structural variants. I thus interpret the sequence of the scene somewhat differently (cf. pp. 147–51 above).

92. Haymes (1975), p. 164: "The progress of narration in oral poetry can be understood as the result of interaction between the themes belonging to the tradition as a whole and the events belonging to the specific song being sung."

93. See pp. 72–73 above. Frakes (1994), p. 68, sees in these scenes an attempt of the men, typical of this era, to prevent the women from controlling any property. It seems to me that the strategic narrative effect—harmony is supposed to be demonstrated—gets short shrift.

94. In the *Thidreks saga*, the inheritance is to be divided between Sigfrid and Kriemhilt's brothers fifty-fifty. This narrates a conceivable conflict (c. 204; 321).

95. See p. 132 above.

96. This is not exactly clear, as shown in Kriemhilt's subsequent accusation of Hagen in a supplemental strophe in C 1785.

97. After str. 1744 of the vulgate version; cf. Göhler (1996), pp. 224–25.

98. Lexer ([1872–78] 1979), vol. 3, cols. 145–46, allows for both meanings; cf. de Boor, p. 213; mss. DJ have understood "to rush" [*eilen*], giving *zaute.* Both are equally illogical.

99. See pp. 206 and 360 above.

100. "Nuodung's death, caused by Witege, belongs to the *Dietrich* cycle. The poet leaves it unclear how he is related to Gotelind. According to the *Thidreks saga,* he was Gotelind's brother, according to German epics (*Biterolf, Rosengarten*), he was her son" (de Boor, Commentary, in *Das Nibelungenlied*[15], p. 268, footnote to 1699,2).

101. The gifts of woman and land are also linked with Nuodung later on. Kriemhilt offers them to Blœdelin (1906–7), and they lead him to his doom.

102. Strohschneider (1997), p. 58, has pointed out the structural approach of the "rejected narrative alternative." See also further examples there.

103. The *immer*—"always," "permanently"—makes the other meaning perhaps more likely, but it can also refer to Sivrit: "whenever, at some point in time."

104. Mss. Db have the more precise *wurd euch,* that is, "you," informal plural. On *gewinnen,* see Lexer ([1872–78] 1979), vol. 1, cols. 991–92: either "to gain control over" or "to gain advantage from" is possible.

105. See Müller (1987), p. 242.

106. Its double meaning is also noticeable in the variation with which Gunther's reaction is described in the manuscripts: if Kriemhilt, *von sînem râte* (1114,3)

would not have gained *leit, so moeht er vnzwifellichen zv Criemhilde gan* (B 1111,4); or instead of *vnzwifellichen: vreveliche* (A 1054,4, similarly, mss. Dod), *friuntlich* (mss. Jh), *freylichen* (ms. b); mss. Ca diverge (cf. Batts, pp. 336–37).

107. See already C 1142,4.

108. As far as I can see, Göhler (1996), p. 228, has recognized this most clearly; Schröder (1968), p. 149, also speaks of a "primary" and "secondary" meaning, emphasizing on p. 163 that Kriemhilt's question of Hagen does not necessarily have to refer to the hoard. He describes a series of intentional misunderstandings (esp. pp. 165–68, 173–79). His aim, however, is to establish a clear hierarchy (not present in the text) and to reduce the demand for the hoard "actually" (p. 178) into just a symbol for the love for Sivrit. In general, revenge and the demand for the hoard are understood as alternatives (Kuhn 1965, pp. 283, 293); only the tradition of the legend seems to promise a convenient way out of the related "imputations of meaning" and "contradictions."

109. Heinzle (1987b), p. 259, calls the linkage "illogical." He rightly criticizes the attempt by Schröder, Beyschlag, and others to simplify the sequence of the plot in terms of the motivation either by love or power (p. 260). He correctly determines that such interpretations all presume "that the text is coherent in the sense of a psychological or logical consistency" (p. 262), but he does not ask about the criteria for such consistency and about the basis of the controversy in the narrative style of the text.

110. The first demand for the hoard was already similarly doubled at the reception (Hennig 1981, p. 76).

111. Heinzle (1987b), p. 264.

112. Most critics believe that the composer of the epic is wrong in this conflict with the legend's tradition, and that sometimes even explicit changes in the material's meaning are nothing more than "polemics against the source," which create more chaos than connection (Bumke 1960, p. 8).

113. On the meaning of *ergetzen*, see pp. 355–62 above.

114. Schröder (1968), p. 162. The "making public" of Hagen's guilt is a major impetus to the plot, at least until the fight breaks out (pp. 285–86, 291–92).

115. Schröder (1968), pp. 174–76; cf. p. 168; on p. 95, he points to Hagen's intentional misunderstanding in an earlier scene. The tension between the demand for the hoard and for vengeance (pp. 93–99), which is presented as drawing on Hans Kuhn (1948), should not be prematurely resolved by reducing the material to a simple symbol for the spiritual (pp. 95–96); cf. Hennig (1981), p. 76.

Chapter 3. Nibelungian Society

1. I summarize the most important aspects of my 1987 article "Motivationsstrukturen und personale Identität im 'Nibelungenlied'" here. Inasmuch as the social relationships the *Nibelungenlied* presupposes are sometimes best under-

stood in light of much older circumstances (on early medieval concepts of *vriunt*, see ibid.), we dealing with considerable asynchrony. The goal of the discussion in this chapter is not, however, to identify the social conditions of the *Nibelungenlied* in any given historical period: they are fictional.

2. On the criticism of modern concepts of the state, see Keller (1989).

3. Müller (1987), p. 251.

4. Schröder (1968), pp. 60–66, mainly emphasizes the ethical aspects of the term; generally, see Gentry (1975).

5. For more exact references, see Müller (1987), pp. 234–35. The cognatic relationships play a special role; cf. Nolte (1995).

6. Hennig (1981), p. 179.

7. Althoff (1997), p. 185.

8. In the manuscripts of the *Nibelungenlied, mâgen* and *vriunt* seem interchangeable (cf. the variants of 1077,2 and 3 in A 1017, B 1074, C 1088, and Batts, pp. 324–25). In other texts, the distinction between relatives and vassals is more closely drawn, e.g., in the *Rolandslied* when Karl asks: *wanu frunt und man* [where are friends and vassals] (Rl 8811).

9. Bloch (1986), p. 144, with reference to Georges Duby, Marc Bloch, and Karl Schmid (pp. 30–63). The question debated by historians with regard to a restructuring of the open association of the early Middle Ages into the agnatically organized family of the High Middle Ages (Schmid) can be disregarded here, since statements of extraliterary relationships are not at issue.

10. Fundamentally, Althoff (1991b); id. (1997), pp. 199–228; and cf. (1997), pp. 202–3.

11. See Müller (1987), p. 236.

12. Peters (1994); cf. id. (1990); Bertau (1983), pp. 190–240; Bloch (1986), pp. 30–37.

13. E.g., 2106, 4; in this context of rulership alternating with *man* (2105,3).

14. See Müller (1980), pp. 228–29.

15. Tristrant's death would also threaten the livelihood of the *arme[n] lûte* Kurneval and Brangäne (*vorlise wir unser hêrschaft, / sô werde wir sêre schadehaft* [if we lost our rulers, we would be in great trouble] Trt 2624–26). In order not to complicate quotations with parallel versions, I cite the *Tristrant* according to the—basically problematic—edition of Lichtenstein.

16. The vassal Kurneval requires this of him to punish Isalde for the slight to his honor, or he will quit his service (Trt 7063–64). The promise given to the *man* remains valid even after Tristrant and Isalde are again reconciled.

17. Hagen resists a status such as that of the ministerial, who can simply be given away, but he remains devoted to the kings. Czerwinski (1979) emphasizes the contradiction of this constellation: "The best, that is, the strongest, vassal is he on whom the lord can no longer impose his will" (p. 74). In that Hagen orients his will solely to the benefit and honor of his lords, even against their explicitly announced wishes, he already represents "the different, firm constraint of modern

character. That is to say, what is new cannot be openly expressed as such, but must instead appear as the perfection of the principle which it dissolves" (ibid., p. 75).

18. See Kl 238–40; Kl C 1321–23.

19. Althoff (1997) has shown in many examples how difficult it was "to harmonize the different horizons of obligation" (p. 186) and that the obligation of rule by no means always wins out.

20. On the material prerequisites of feudalism, see Ganshof ([1957] 1967), pp. 162–63, 167–68.

21. See Hennig (1981), pp. 178–79, on the divergent ruling structure of the Hun kingdom.

22. Cf. 1339–47. Twelve *recken* among them are rewarded by Kriemhilt's kiss; twelve kings live at her court (1391,3).

23. The attempts to discuss away these unambiguous judgments (e.g., Grenzler, 1992, pp. 375–79) are therefore inexplicable.

24. Hennig (1981), p. 179, points out that the familial component in the Burgundian ruling clan is deemphasized in favor of vassality.

25. See in summary Splett (1968), pp. 70–106; most recently—again heavily psychologizing—Campbell (1996).

26. Thus, convincingly, contrary to Wapnewski (1960), Splett (1968), p. 87, and before him Harms (1963), pp. 40–41; on the legal obligations to the Burgundians, see also Bernreuther (1994), pp. 76–79; on the insolubility of the conflict, pp. 96–100.

27. In typical modern fashion, Wapnewski (1960) presupposes an opposition here between "legal" and "moral" obligations, of which only the latter can be seen as personal (pp. 384–88, 391–93). This kind of distinction is inappropriate to medieval ideas of law, which is understand as realized in personal relationships, rather than being seen as something abstract.

28. Panzer (1945), p. 178; cf. Althoff (1992); id. (1997), p. 71.

29. About this possibility, see Althoff (1993); id. (1997), p. 254.

30. On the ambiguity of the oath, see pp. 348–50 above; that it is the reason for the decision (Kuhn 1965, p. 295) is not to be gleaned from the text. The later formulation *ich muoz mit iu strîten, wande ihz gelobt hân* [I must fight you because I swore to do so] (2178,2) does not necessarily refer to the oath to Kriemhilt alone (otherwise, H. Naumann 1932, p. 390). The oath to Kriemhilt, by the way, is seen by Rüedeger as valid only if it does not endanger his soul (2150,3). Bernreuther (1994), p. 97, posits that the "maintenance of positive legal bonds" to which Rüedeger refers, "no longer refers naturally to the recognition before God and courtly society."

31. I do not see a "legal judgment" in this fight. Nothing support the legitimacy of Rüedeger's death as punishment for breaking the law (thus Splett 1968, pp. 87–89, and elsewhere, based on Hermann Nottarp's work).

32. See Splett (1968), p. 91.

33. Ibid., pp. 78, 84–86. Kuhn (1965), pp. 296–97, emphasizes that these du-

ties are exaggerated far beyond the legal norm. This is typical for the heroic representation of legal conflicts (Schmidt-Wiegand 1982a).

34. Wapnewski (1960), p. 396; cf. Bernreuther (1994), p. 100.

35. Bachorski (1996), pp. 9–10. "It remains . . . unimportant whether Rüedeger's vassal bond is really so much more compelling than the bond that results from the betrothal of Giselher and Gotelint . . . ; it is more important . . . that alongside all the already extant bonds a new, likewise compelling bond is created by the exchange of gifts [the gift of the shield to Hagen]."

36. Wapnewski (1960), p. 398.

37. Gillespie (1972), p. 163. He calculates that almost a fifth of the *Klage* is devoted to Rüedeger.

38. Gentry (1989), p. 305, speaks of a "message" of the *Nibelungenlied:* a critique of *untriuwe.*

39. Not thematized is the *triuwe* of mankind to God and of God to mankind.

40. This is why *triuwe* cannot be restricted to aspects of class or rule, as when Czerwinski (1979), pp. 76–77, understands Kriemhilt's bond to Sivrit only as "a bond to the strongest body, the mightiest and wealthiest."

41. The medium of reflection is mostly *Minnesang* and courtly romance, less so the heroic epic; cf. Zimmermann (1990), p. 523, on the ethical component.

42. Lexer ([1872–78] 1979), vol. 3, cols. 513–14. The spectrum of meaning spans from marriage to illegitimate love.

43. The competing statement, *daz si deheinen wolde ze eime trûte hân* [that she wanted no relationship with a man] (46,3), which places Kriemhilt's decision about marriage in the forefront, never becomes relevant to the plot. On differences from courtly *Minnedienst,* see pp. 387–95 above.

44. Althoff (1991b); id. (1997), p. 206: "Loss of favor marginalized and made living together in a group, where mutual favor was dominant, impossible." See Müller (1987), p. 242.

45. On the switch of names and on the web of motivation in this scene, see p. 210 above.

46. Similarly, Kuhn (1965), p. 291; McConnell (1986a), p. 47. Rupp (1985), p. 172, recognizes that "at this instant the destruction of all political and human order becomes clear"; cf. Müller (1987), pp. 250, 233.

47. Splett (1968), p. 86; on the motif of the treacherous invitation, see Hennig (1987).

48. Wynn (1965), p. 114, nn. 16, 20, 22; Haug (1987), p. 14; Müller (1987), p. 251. Kriemhilt's deed cannot be seen as a legally obligated blood revenge (Schmidt-Wiegand 1982a, p. 381).

49. The core family is made up of *næhsten mâgen* out of the extensive group of relatives, as was common in the early Middle Ages.

50. Ohly ([1989] 1995), p. 428.

51. Kuhn (1965), p. 302; Flood (1994), pp. 186–87; to the contrary, Bumke

(1996c), p. 475, who assumes that the *Klage* poet understood the dismemberment as a decapitation.

52. Voorwinden (1981), p. 105; on a similar statement by Reinmar, see Gillespie (1972), p. 162.

53. The narrator turns this around and accuses those who judge others to have sinned against God of not being without sin themselves (Kl 578–86), indicating that the discussion is played out in the religious sphere.

54. Ihlenburg (1969); on the criticism, see Hennig (1981), p. 175.

55. Gottzmann (1987), pp. 19–72.

56. Müller (1974).

57. I am repeating several arguments I formulated for the first time over thirty years ago (Müller 1974).

58. There is an ideal cooperation between the lord and his nobles so that any exception is made explicit, for instance, when Gunther permits Rüedeger *âne vriunde rât* to deliver his message.

59. Thomas Grenzler argues uniquely (1992, pp. 160–61) that there is "an agreement on the appropriate means to 'legitimize rule'" between Gunther and Sivrit. He can explain neither the scene itself nor Gunther's subsequent role, and he must therefore assume that some of the protagonists are uninformed (pp. 160–62). Sivrit's superiority to Gunther is confirmed again and again.

60. Czerwinski (1979), p. 71, whom I follow in his characterization of Gunther's rule, has overestimated the differences between Worms and Xanten as between an archaic world of direct force and a world of advanced courtly regulation of force, as "two stages in the process of the organization of governance" (p. 72). Xanten is still tailored "completely to a single representative" and rests "on the personal force and direct ability of the hero to rule" (p. 54). This seems exaggerated to me. Czerwinski relies mostly on arguments *e silentio* and underestimates the "courtly" side of Sivrit's heroic role.

61. On this episode, see pp. 68–70 above.

62. See Panzer (1945), pp. 105–6, following Gerhoh von Reichersberg, *De investigatione Antichristi* 1.72, in *Monumenta Germaniae historica. . . . Libelli de lite* (Hannover, 1891–97), 3: 393.

63. On the inconsistencies of this episode, see Pérennec (1975), p. 1.

64. The contradictions seemed so apparent that Bumke (1958) suspects this episode to be a mangled version of the winning of the hoard, completely misplaced here.

65. Pérennec (1975), p. 5, works out the connection between *Âventiuren* 3 and 7. As in *Âventiure* 3, Sivrit is not interested in being received as the lord; he would rather present himself as a *gast*, so as to show his strength.

66. Ibid., p. 9.

67. This is a stereotype that announces the future hero, who wants to accomplish chivalric deeds before he becomes king (cf. Al 398–420).

68. De Boor, Commentary, in *Das Nibelungenlied*, p. 12.

69. Otherwise, Gottzmann (1987), who blurs the semantic particularity of the canonical *idoneitas* when she claims that the principle of idoneity goes back "to the Germanic tribes," received "a Christian meaning" from the Carolingians, was taken up by the curia and used in the investiture conflict by Gregory VII against Henry IV ("since he [the pope] did not see the religious concerns of the king adequately represented"), and was finally employed in the battle for the throne in 1198 against "claimants inimical to the Church" who asserted the right of blood (pp. 63–64). The *Nibelungenlied* would then have "stripped the principle of idoneity of its clerical reinterpretation" (p. 65). Serious historical semantics should distinguish between the right of lineage and religious, ethical, and political legitimacy.

70. Therefore, Sivrit's challenge is not told in terms of feud, but Gernot recognizes in it the core of feud violence:

> *Wir hân des niht gedingen . . .*
> *Daz wir iht lande ertwingen, daz iemen drumbe tôt*
> *Gelige vor heldes handen.* (115,1–3)
>
> *[We have no intent . . .*
> of invading lands, so that people lie dead
> at the feet of heroes.]

71. Cf. G. W. Weber (1990), pp. 457–58, on the *Cid.*

72. *Handwörterbuch zur deutschen Rechtsgeschichte* 2, cols. 36–37 (G. Köbler); generally described under the aspect of the preservation of the place of judgment, but in heroic legend expanded to legal conditions of different kinds (cf. *Laurin*).

73. To this extent—and only to this extent—Newman (1981) is right when she speaks of "two Brunhilds" and contends that Prünhild changes after she gets to Worms (pp. 72–73).

74. Hennig disputes my 1974 contention that the *man* qualified as *eigen* (unfree) is to be understood as a ministerial (Hennig 1981, p. 182). She argues that *eigen man* is not a precise legal term of status, but rather an "expressive neologism of the poet's, which, just like *eigen diu,* is only supposed to demonstrate the outlandishness of the person so termed" (p. 185). Conversely, Schulze emphasizes that *eigen man* can in certain contexts be seen as the counterpart of *adelvrî,* that is, it can denote a ministerial status, and that *eigenholt* is cognate with *eigen man*, without necessarily having negative connotations (Schulze 1997b, pp. 46–47). In each case, the neutral term *man* is qualified as *eigen* (*eigen man/eigenholt*), with *dienest* serving as a modifier.

75. On the *Book of Bern,* cf. Müller (1980).

76. As an example, Czerwinski (1979) emphasizes the paradoxical role of Hagen, who, by being the perfect vassal, undermines the principle of vassality, that is, the independence of those who subordinate themselves.

77. Unlike in 1974, I would no longer link such a consideration to experiences

in a certain place, such as the area around Passau. Nevertheless, in an epic that thematizes questions of rule and legitimacy in such great detail, sensitivity to a contemporary process is likely.

78. This can hardly speak directly to Sivrit's rulership in Niderlant, which the Burgundian kings in no way usurp, and which continues after his death. Gephardt (1994) correctly remarks: "The Burgundians can in the end only destroy Siegfried's power—they are incapable of gaining it for themselves" (p. 77).

79. Questions of rank play an important role in the relationship of Tristrant to Isalde of the White Hands: *sie ist als edele als ir* [she is as nobly born as you are]) (Trt 6225).

80. Otherwise, Gephardt (1994), p. 46.

81. Rupp (1985), p. 168.

82. Seitter (1995), p. 149, following Georges Dumézil; cf. p. 152. The concept seems problematic to me, since Seitter silently assumes the monopolizing power of the modern state, whose "sovereignty" is only a modern result of different components of power and governance.

83. See Seitter (1995), p. 152; the many moralizing jeremiads about the weak king confuse the person with the institution; cf., to the contrary, Czerwinski (1979), p. 67.

84. Rupp (1985) has described this as a logical story line. What is problematic are his judgments as to what is "political" and "apolitical" in this regard.

85. Gephardt (1994), pp. 75–77.

86. 1524,4; cf. Seitter (1987), pp. 128, 202.

87. See p. 408 above.

88. This has become a firm part of tradition: Ortwin is the one who "is not present" at the decisive battle, according to another version, because he dies young (Bit 6001–3).

89. Ihlenburg (1969), pp. 141–42. His chief witness is the verse *Der künic gevolgete übele Hagenen sînem man* [the king wrongly followed Hagen his vassal] (876,1), but this lacks any programmatic political character, since it says no more than that the better discernment of the lord bows to the worse judgment of the vassal.

90. Similarly in the *Book of Bern;* cf. Müller (1980). Only a few supplemental stanzas of *C suggest Hagen's selfishness and betrayal of Gunther.

91. Only in mss. BC; the strophe is missing in ms. A. Ms. A is throughout principally less interested in questions of rank (cf. pp. 67–68 above).

92. He also refers to the *hôhe[n] mâge[n]* of the margravine (1678,2) and her inherited rank, which is reflected in the beauty of the daughter.

93. See also Splett (1968), p. 87, on 2164,4, where *ellende* is explicitly expanded to the people in Bechelaren.

94. 1823,3; 1834,4; 1836,4; 1935,2; 2135,1; 2222,4; 2238,3 (*die ellenden recken*); 2245,4 (only mss. AB; mss. Ca replaced by *Burgônden;* cf. Batts, pp. 682–83); 2253,4 (only mss. AB; another idea in mss. Ca; Batts, pp. 686–87); 2274,4.

95. The characterization *ellende [] rechen* in ms. C 1915,4 can be put in place of *Nibelungen,* also in ms. a; cf. Batts, p. 569.

96. This is also the premise in *Biterolf,* where one seems to be waiting for someone to attack from somewhere outside, or to become active in the war in eastern Europe or in the tournament war on the Rhine. On the relationship between the exile situation and the founding tribal legends, see Weddige (1989), pp. 99–103.

97. See *Biterolf, Book of Bern,* and *Rabenschlacht.*

98. The editor Oskar Jänicke put *Fruote* throughout for what the ms. transmits as *Diete,* which is unnecessary and has been completely rejected by later scholarship.

99. See Bit 1938–39, 2000; crowns have to be earned, not just inherited.

100. The historically confirmed practice of holding prominent hostages of tribute-paying peoples in the vicinity of Attila is only seldom still recognizable, e.g., in *Waltharius.*

101. Paradigmatic, for example, is *Wigamur,* in which the hero is a longtime, recognized member of courtly society based on his deeds, and the question of his royal blood is only raised at a trial by battle (ed. Buschinger, 4147).

102. Stutz (1990), p. 419, has observed that Sivrit only seldom receives the title *künic.* His exact social rank is secondary, based on his being a hero and a lord.

103. Walther von der Vogelweide has this same point in the phrase *ich vil hêrscher man* [I—a lord, and a *man*] (Lachmann 49,18).

104. This may be a genetic remnant of an older motivation, according to which Sivrit's power threatens Gunther, but here *hêrschaft* means something else. De Boor's Commentary again attempts here to uncover "layers," where a polar opposition in the concept of rule is concerned: "The age-old motif of increased power through Siegfried's death; cf. 870. Hagen's wild outcry archaically breaks through the courtly crust" (p. 164). It is still occasionally asserted that the first part is about a power struggle (Spiewok, 1989, pp. 193–94).

105. Ms. a has *versuochen,* "to risk everything, including oneself."

106. De Boor, p. 255.

107.The "heroic level" is finally reached with this and the following events, according to Heinzle (1995a, p. 229; cf. pp. 230, 233, 235), which refutes the cliché of Dietrich as a "new" man who trusts in peace (pp. 225–26), actually already to be found in Hebbel.

108. The fact that the king is excluded from the dialogue seems to be a heroic tradition. See Alois Wolf (1976), p. 180, on *Waltharius.*

109. "In destruction, the defeated feudal world rules again, its orgy of violence sweeps away the new, peaceful forms of intercourse and makes them seem silly" (Czerwinski, 1979, p. 79).

110. The Amazon-like traits of Kriemhilt and Prünhilt—who are certainly demonized throughout the epic—are emphasized by Frakes (1994, pp. 137–69), for whom the negative status accorded women is key.

111. The more courtly version *C has instead: *si gebarent dem geliche daz si hohe sint gemvuot* [they act as if they were in high spirits] (C 399,4).

112. An exception is *Kudrun*. Although theologically based misogyny is absent from the *Nibelungenlied*, women's dangerous independent action is condemned and corrected, especially in the *C redaction, Bennewitz notes (1995, p. 48). On criticism of so-called feminist interpretations, see ibid., pp. 34–45.

113. Czerwinski (1979), pp. 55–56.

114. On the ideological background, see Frakes (1994), pp. 161–62.

115. Similarly, the reference to the devil 442,2–4; 450,4; essential is Kuhn (1965); cf. Frakes (1994), pp. 157–68; Frakes sees the characterization as *tiuvel* as bound only to the perspective of the figure involved, but this contradicts the narrative practice of the epic.

116. On Kriemhilt and Prünhilt as "targets for male projections of fear," see Bennewitz (1995), p. 50.

117. Ibid., p. 46.

118. This is somewhat lessened in the *C group. Strophe 1523, in which the Nibelungs appear again for the first time, is replaced by the mention of a spiritual assistant for the journey to Etzel: *In der selben tzeiten was der gelaube nach chranckch* [in those days religion was still weak] (a 1559,1). This is a sign that the redactor had already noticed the deficit.

119. *Herbort's von Fritslâr liet von Troye*, ed. Frommann, 543ff., 2231ff., 2327ff.

120. Wyss (1990), p. 172, points out that Hagen "gets rid of the only witness who could write."

121. See pp. 417–20 above. This is true, mutatis mutandis, also of the chansons de geste, in which clerics like Bishop Turpin play an important part, but primarily as warriors.

122. See McConnell (1978), p. 43.

123. This belongs to the widespread stereotypes in early medieval historiography of great feudal lords; cf. also Widukind of Corvey's tenth-century *Sachsengeschichte* [Saxon History] 2.44 on Wichmann.

124. See G. Weber (1963); Willson (1963); Moser (1992).

125. The difficulties in the Christianization of heroic ideals are described by Huppé (1975). Clerical and knightly ideals are combined in the figure of the holy hero in the chansons de geste, who is not found in the *Nibelungenlied*. From the perspective of the early medieval Church, the heroic is "self-reliant, proud," and is a sign of fallen humanity and a condition without grace (ibid., p. 13). Huppé considers whether or not even Christian heroes like Beowulf must fail where their heroic superiority is no longer just an instrument of divine Providence. Bloomfield (1975) points to the ambiguity of the heroic in late medieval texts, in which it never appears as simply positive (p. 31).

126. Haubrichs (1994), pp. 39–43. The "legitimized emotion and solace" (p. 39) that heroic poetry can achieve require a spiritual framework. As the object of heroic poetry, even *gesta principum* must grant *utilia* in a spiritual sense (p. 40).

Examples of *gesta heroum et antiquorum patrum* include both stories of martyrs and the *historia regis Karoli* (p. 42).

127. Haubrichs (1995), p. 37.

128. See p. 97 above.

129. *C already has early traces of this.

Chapter 4. Nibelungian Anthropology

1. The argument against naïve psychologizing of heroic epic is beginning to prevail; see, e.g., G. W. Weber (1990), pp. 462–63, on the *Atlilied.* Nevertheless, the epics always invite psychological reconstruction, even with reference to the insights of psychoanalysis (McConnell 1978). Individual psychological characterizations have been attempted as recently as Thelen 1997.

2. Newman (1981).

3. On the discussion of medieval scholarship, cf. the report from Kiening (1996).

4. For the Greek epic, Snell (1948) has shown the way. Considerations by von See (1981) on the exorbitant and by G. W. Weber (1990) on the ethics of Germanic heroics take similar directions.

5. *Handwörterbuch zur deutschen Rechtsgeschichte* 3, cols. 582–88 (H. Krause); Hattenhauer (1963).

6. Czerwinski (1979), p. 68, has pointed out, that "already the conceptual opposition of 'internal/external' is false."

7. See *wüeten* 1967,4 (on Hagen and Volker in battle); *tobelîche* 2050,1 (on Irinc); 2280,4 (on Dancwart); *alsam er wuote* 2282,1 (on Hildebrant); *des muotes er ertobete* 2206,2 (on Rüedeger). Spontaneous anger as a heroic convention is parodied in *Orlando furioso,* the "furious Roland."

8. It is telling that in this passage a medieval manuscript (D) had already made a change. Here the messengers say that Gunther had *vernomen* the *zorn* of their lords, instead of *verdienet.* This creates the causal relationship more familiar to us, that a (previously known) hostile attitude causes a hostile act (Batts, p. 45).

9. Throughout in *Wolfdietrich* A, where *mit zorne* characterizes tense situations and only secondarily refers to an emotional condition (Wo A 134,1; 154,1; 173,1).

10. *Iu wæn' versmâhet daz/daz ich bî iu wære* [it seems that you disapproved that I should be with you] (1625,1–2).

11. De Boor, Commentary, in *Das Nibelungenlied*[15], p. 186. Symbolic punishments of a demonstrative character were widespread in making peace in the Middle Ages (Althoff 1989; id. 1997, pp. 31, 34, 36–37). They make it possible to represent the strength of the king and the legal order that he guarantees, and at the same time to reach a politically necessary compromise. They are by no means farcical. In the same way, the common interpretation of the trial against Hagen is wrong.

12. A perfect scene for Norbert Elias's thesis ([1936] 1969) that in the course of the Middle Ages, external obligations were transformed into self-imposed obligations.

13. Althoff (1989); id. (1997), pp. 29–30.

14. Maurer (1951); critique: Schröder (1968), pp. 10–11, 57–60, 67–70, 74–79, 127–33. Schröder discovers that a purely legal interpretation is unsatisfactory wherever *leit* appears in the *Nibelungenlied.* But no one claims that *leit* has only a legal dimension. Schröder sees alternatives where connections existed for the Middle Ages, and so he argues in circles: whatever cannot be satisfactorily explained proves the opposite of Maurer's thesis for him.

15. Schröder (1968), pp. 127–28. Schröder is able to prove his thesis most convincingly with the *Klage* (pp. 191–201), but the *Klage* is already quite distant from the epic in this point. The assumption of "basic similarity and purpose" (p. 225) of the *Klage* is wrong for both texts.

16. Althoff (1997), pp. 258–81, has shown the demonstrative character of expressions of emotion in medieval texts. This does not necessarily entail an opposition to "spontaneity" (cf. p. 274 and elsewhere). Only if demonstrative expression of emotion would necessarily include a calculated use of signs, would the emotional reaction become an intentionally presented, possibly deceptive production (not "real," cf. p. 276). Rüedeger's reaction indicates a wounding of honor, and this is discharged in a violent act.

17. In this sense, in Eilhart's *Tristrant,* Mark is called "trûrig" when he is unable to avert the threat to his land by Morolt (Trt 444).

18. Not like this in mss. Ca; similar, however, is 1222,1 (according to ms. B), *Criemhilt div here vnd vil trvrech gemvt,* as opposed to C 1249,1, *arme* (Batts, pp. 372–73; cf. 1225,1).

19. De Boor, p. 189. Exactly what the "internally lifted" is supposed to refer to remains unclear.

20. Actually, *hêr* does allow this connotation: Lexer ([1872–78] 1979), vol. 1, col. 251; cf. *hêr* = glad 1534, 3: the sprites; 1538,1: Hagen on the opportune prophecy.

21. 86,4; 409,2; 1337,3; 1595,2.

22. The connection is made in the same strophe: *si gedâhte minneclîche an der schœnen Helchen lîp* [she thought affectionately of the beautiful Helche] (1160,4).

23. According to Batts, pp. 362–63.

24. Some critics of "bourgeois" psychology continue to assume this division when they base their interpretation only on the sociopolitical "roles" of the characters and reduce them to "personifications of the noble ruler type" (Grenzler 1992, p. 178). Such interpretations are one-dimensional. Up to the final scene, Grenzler is concerned only with the political, like the maintenance of ruling status; cf. formulations like "the potential for rule contained in the magic cloak" (p. 188). Even sexual intercourse is seen as a "non-public act of rulership" (p. 197).

25. Only in mss. BDbd (for the following, see also Batts, p. 195). In ms. A, it

reads that one shows oneself *schone*, in mss. Ca, *lobeliche*, and in mss. IQh, *herlichen.*

26. See the antonym *unvrœlîche* (852,4), referring to Prünhilt's public insult. Both instances concern the intactness or insult of status in the public arena of the court.

27. "Accordingly, Siegfried, even in this case, was clear about Brünhild and her strength and had foreseen Gunther's failure," de Boor writes (p. 112), but it is not necessary to assume this.

28. See Czerwinski (1979), p. 66.

29. De Boor misunderstands this request when he again relates it only to Gunther's being "here only 'to be confident,' without any courtly implications" (p. 35).

30. On the paradox of believability in Reinmar, see, e.g., MF, 165,10; 170,36, and elsewhere.

31. A central concept in Alois Wolf's (1995) interpretation of the *Nibelungenlied,* pp. 400, 422.

32. Above all in Schröder (1968), pp. 113, 204–10. The argumentation is often circular. Schröder generally first defines *riuwe, smerze,* and similar concepts as spiritual, only then to "discover" a spiritual dimension in the relevant passages, while alternative meanings are marginalized.

33. Frakes (1994), pp. 133–35, 152, 156, is critical.

34. There is a tendency in scholarship to translate *jâmer* as "heartache" and to explain it as being at the core of Kriemhilt's acts of revenge (see Schröder, 1968, p. 204).

35. Alois Wolf (1987), p. 188, has pointed to Kriemhilt's closeness to the "modern" women characters of the courtly romance.

36. This is confirmed, by the way, by a variant to 137,4 in three manuscripts (mss. CDb) that replaces *minne* with *hohe minne* (Batts, pp. 42–43).

37. Two supplemental strophes, C 821 (also mss. Jad) and 822 (also mss. Jadh), make it even clearer that the *herze* is a hiding place, where it is difficult to hold in what wants to come out: *ine mac niht langer dagn* [I cannot keep silent any longer] (C 821,1) and *daz ir lach amme hercen ze lieht ez mvse chomen* [what was in her heart had to come to light] (C 822,3; cf. Batts, pp. 244–47).

38. *Si [ge]dâht[e]* (1391,4; 1392,1; 1396,2; 1399,1; 1400,4).

39. The first three verses are different in the vulgate version. They begin with: *Ich wæne der übel vâlant Kriemhilde daz geriet* [I think that the evil devil advised Kriemhilt]. On the interpretation of this scene, see pp. 210; 144–46 above. On the reinterpretation of *triuwe* in the *Klage,* see pp. 000–00 above.

40. Schuppisser (1993), pp. 189–91.

41. See the documentation in the *Frühneuhochdeutsches Wörterbuch,* vol. 2, cols. 100–119, whose outlines can already be seen in Middle High German.

42. K 1171,1; K 1209,1; also Hilde, after she has lost her daughter Kudrun (K 929,4).

43. This is why a formulation like *doch müejet mich mîn ellende sêre* [my exile is a great burden to me] (K 1040,4) means more than a "feeling of being a stranger" (K, p. 209).

44. Earlier she was *Kûdrûn diu schœne* (K 1243,4), *diu edele Kûdrûn* from the clan of heroes (K 1244,4), and *diu maget hêre* (K 1277,1).

45. When Kudrun speaks of the rumor that Herwic is dead (K 1246,2), this has another meaning: Herwic has just identified himself, and Kudrun blames him by saying that the real Herwic would have acted much sooner to rescue her. In reality, Kudrun knows from the angel that Herwic is alive (K 1174,2). The accusation also makes it possible to delay the recognition a bit longer.

46. When Kudrun's mother Hilde finds out about the death of her husband King Hetel, she cries out: *wie swindet mîn êre* [how my honor is lost] (K 926,3). The death of the king means above all a loss of power and respect.

47. When emotional consequences are at issue, then paradox phrases like *arme[] küniginne* (K 797,4; 941,4) or *arme[] frouwe[]* (K 1606,4) are fitting.

48. Wolfdietrich also hears the lament, and he will make up for the loss of Ortnit. A few strophes later, Liebgart can offer him Bern and Garda, over which she apparently still has complete control, along with herself and her crown (*Ortnit und Wolfdietrich*, ed. Lunzer, 1498).

49. Haug (1987), p. 293.

50. See Schröder (1968), pp. 11, 86. "Kriemhilt's hoard question . . . does not make str. 1126 go away" (Alois Wolf 1987, pp. 191–92); the many strophes that concern power and property do not just "go away" either.

51. Only in isolation can one claim that "external honor" means little to Kriemhilt, that the narrator conceived of her as a "one-dimensional lover," or, in a typically modern distinction, that "Kriemhilt loves Sivrit not for his power but as a person" (Schröder, 1968, pp. 80, 82, 87).

52. Beyschlag ([1952] 1961, 1957–58) vs. Schröder (1968); cf. Schröder (1968), pp. 87–91: Schröder calls the inclusion of sociopolitical aspects mere "fashion" (p. 87), but it was once also "fashionable" to tear apart the historical connection between social and political aspects.

53. Mss. Jh have *frævden arme* instead; mss. Ca, have *kuniginne* (Batts, pp. 326–27).

54. *Arm* and *rîche* correspond to the conceptual pair *potens* and *pauper* investigated by Bosl (1963).

55. In this meaning, Kurneval and Brangäne in *Tristrant* call themselves *arme liute* (Trt 5643). It is said of Isalde's self-castigation: *si gehabet sich als ein arm wîp* [she acted like a poor woman] (Trt 7223).

56. *Dô was gelegen ringe sîn grôziu schœne und ouch sîn leben* [there his great beauty was wasted, as was his life] (1063,4; cf. 1068,2; 1112,1).

57. Thus in ms. B; mss. A and C smooth out this contradiction to one side or the other. Ms. A "forgets" the current situation: *Criemhilt div schoene vnd vil reine gemuot* [Kriemhilt the beautiful and pure of spirit] (A 1165,1); ms. C, on the other

hand, harmonizes in the sense of the contemporary state of affairs: *Chriemh' div vil arme, div trurich gemvot* [Kriemhilt the poor, and sad of spirit] (C 1249,1).

58. Weeping is the appropriate expression of a defect; it should not be taken as referring only to Kriemhilt's feelings for Sivrit (Schröder, 1968, p. 108).

59. This is the formula that shows the representation and practice of rule: *dar zuo er gekrúnet vor vriunden solde gân* [there he was to walk before his clan with his crown] (706,3). Mss. Ca have *fvrsten* instead of *vriunden* (cf. Batts, pp. 214–15).

60. See Fromm (1990), p. 12.

61. On this masterpiece of telling a complex emotional situation, see Müller (1987), p. 250. It is irrelevant whether these thoughts of Kriemhilt's in *Âventiure* 23 are "during the sexual act" and whether the conversation with Etzel is "post- (or intra?) coital" (Frakes 1994, p. 128); asking these questions again treats the literary construct as if it were a real scene.

62. Carruthers (1990), pp. 61–64.

63. I follow de Boor in understanding the difficult *mit friuntschefte.* He glosses "separated in reference to her friendship, 'quitting the friendship.'" Brackert, on the other hand, translates: "separated in friendship with Gunther" (p. 59). Then it would make sense to take the verb to be past tense: "that (in becoming reconciled with him) she had separated herself from Gunther as a *friunt.*" It still seems more plausible to me to see the verse pointing to Kriemhilt's future attitude toward Gunther, which is so atrocious that it must have come from the *vâlant* (Kuhn 1965, pp. 281, 290–91, 294).

64. I accept Bartsch's conjecture based on mss. DJbdh (cf. Batts, p. 423). The *C group knows nothing about a seduction by Satan (C 1421), which is explained by the fact that the *suone* itself was not sincere (Kuhn 1965, pp. 297–98).

65. Giselher offers Kriemhilt his service even in Etzel's realm (1292), and Kriemhilt kissed her relatives upon her leave-taking without any *suone* (*Die ir mâge wâren, kustes' an den munt* [she kissed those who were her relatives on the mouth], 1293,1). In the passage in question, the kiss in her dream may have motivated the insertion of Giselher's name.

66. De Boor, p. 224.

67. The basic argumentation in this section is advanced in greater detail in Müller (1992b).

68. The components are the same, but there is a different hierarchy in the courtly romance. Greater attention is given to the problem in *Wigamur.* There the hero is at first introduced without name and family, and he must make himself known as the knight *mit dem ar* [with the eagle] (*das auch der nam mein / under andern rittern werd gezalt* [that my name also / be counted among those who are knights], 3444–45). At court, he is recognized as such, however, and as a *kempffer*, he must prove his heritage, which he cannot (*der fragt, wer ich seye; / das ist mir laÿder unkundt* [he wants to know who I am; / unfortunately I don't know myself], 4060–61). This is why he tells his story (4144ff.) so that others recognize him, and from then on he has a name. Here the sequence is: deed–courtly ac-

ceptance–clan name. The courtly social component is emphasized over origin and name.

69. To the contrary, Ehrismann (1987), pp. 125–26, who bases the misunderstanding on different perceptions: "If the words have been carefully chosen, then the women behind the parapets [!?] see Siegfried's service (396, 398), but the queen sees only the procession to the hall . . . . When she goes up to Siegfried and greets him first, this is because the vassal has named only him and because she did not see the service he rendered." I cannot see this distinction in the text.

70. The formulation is not completely clear. The *wan*-clause ("only one, who looks like Sivrit, is among them") is only loosely connected to the preceding statement. I believe that it does not express a special exception in this case (as in: "I haven't seen anyone yet, except for the one who looks like Sivrit"), but rather starts again and relativizes the criterion "knowing based on having seen": "I don't know any of them, but one of them looks like Sivrit."

71. Also in the *Thidreks saga*, chap. 148. Brunhild immediately knows that it can only be Sigfrid who has killed her watchmen, because only the greatest hero could have done so. Here she immediately knows his identity, which is still unknown to himself.

72. With Gunther, the ladies suspect that he is a *künic rîch* (412,2). Hagen is described as a ferocious, fearsome warrior, Dancwart as a courtly young knight. Digressing from the sequence (Sivrit-Gunther-Hagen-Dancwart), Peeters (1982) assumes the order Sivrit-Dancwart-Hagen-Gunther. The advantage is that then the king and not the secondary character Dancwart is given two strophes (414–15), but the disadvantage is that the anticlimax would be destroyed (from the standout Sivrit to the king, then to the hero-assistant, then to another vassal). The text follows the rule of "growing portions" (the one named last receives two stanzas). Aside from this, the verses *ob er gewalt des hête, wol wær' er künic rîch / ob wîten fürsten landen* [if he had the power over great princely lands, he would be a mighty king]) (412,2–3) fits Gunther the best. It is confirmed that the stranger looks like a king.

73. Hempel (1970), for example, talks of a "guilt" of the actors (pp. 221–22), and defines *übermuot* in a Christian sense as a vice provoked by the devil (*vâlant*) (pp. 220–22). The heroes are representatives "of the archaic Germanic *Virtus.*" They appear "to the poet of the Christian courtly world as impressive titans and heroes, but, subjected to the views of the times, unavoidably stand in the light of *superbia*" (pp. 223–24).

74. Leyser (1992), p. 11.

75. Stutz (1990), p. 417, based on the method in Heusler, Neumann, and others. See Grenzler (1992), p. 148.

76. Thus in *Heinrich von Melk* (ed. Heinzel), "Von des todes gehügede," 343–45: *zwêne geverten hât diu übermuot, / die setzent die rîter an die gluot / der êwigen viures vanchen* [such pride has two companions / that put the knights / into hell's fires]; cf. the material in Hempel (1970), pp. 122–30.

77. See the *Rolandslied,* where the heroes are characterized by *übermuot* and related designations (*uber muot,* e.g., 3361, 3478, 3510, 4604, 4611, 4743; *hochuart,* 3468, 3506, 4704, 7363). The usurpation of the traitors is more clearly theologically burdened (Rl 8844). The core of the vice is expressed in the verse: *si uersahen sich zu ir chrefte* [they counted only on their strength] (Rl 3479).

78. Gelpfrat C 1647,3 (on Hagen); cf. other heroic epics: in Bit 5047, 6447, and 6505, *übermuot* refers to the challenge of the Huns, in 6421, also to Dietrich's will to fight (in the words of Sivrit!), and in 6651, to the willingness of the Wormsians to accept the challenge. Roland and his followers' thirst for blood is condemned as *hôchvart* and *übermuot* (Rl 1842, 1879, 2440), but this is done by their enemies.

79. This is overlooked by the moralizing interpretations of the Sivrit character (to the contrary, Bumke 1996c, pp. 384–86).

80. Hempel (1970), p. 218, believes conversely that he can quantify the "relationship 1:4 negative." He does not, however, consider the partisanship of the assessments.

81. Stutz (1990), p. 417.

82. Also in Bit 7193 (Sifrit counsels for war, as do others); Bit 9837 (Sifrit's willingness to fight).

83. The latent conflict seems to me to have lost its point if Sivrit's lie in Isenstein (it is a lie) is reduced to a "sign of sovereign self-satisfaction" (Stutz 1990, p. 419).

84. This assessment is clear in the *Klage: die von Burgonden lant/liezenz durch ir übermuot* [those from Burgundy let/it be because of their recklessness] (Kl 288–89), but also in Kriemhilt's judgment of Sivrit (896,2) cited above.

85. In *C this is stronger: C 435,4; 466,2; Prünhilt's people are also characterized by *übermuot* (444,4).

86. See the summary in Göhler (1989), pp. 127–35. The religious component is missing, but the events characterized by *übermuot* are throughout "conflict-causing or conflict-intensifying" (p. 134). The negative connotations are also in the majority in Ehrismann (1987), pp. 114–15.

87. See in *Biterolf: Dort halt daz Sigelinde kint,/dem alle sîne sache sint/wan ûf hôchvart gewant* [there Sigelinde's child stands,/who had focused all/of his attention on arrogance] (Bit 9833–9835); *in einem hôchvertigen sit* [in an arrogant manner] (Bit 11696); or the contents as paraphrased by Hildebrant: *Sîfride . . . /dunket daz er alliu lant/mit sîner kraft ertwinge wol* [Sivrit . . . /believes that he all lands/could conquer with his strength] (Bit 7615–17).

88. See Trt 460 and 926, *hômût* (concerning Morolt's illegal usurpation). Parzival believes that he so distinguished himself in knightly deeds that God must nominate him to the Grail, if He knows anything about knighthood. Trevrizent call this *hôchvart* (Pa 472,13 and 17). Also called *hôchvart* is the transgression of Anfortas (Pa 472,26), who is seduced by *jugent, rîcheit* and *minne* (Pa 472,27–29). The Grail demands Christian *diemmuot* [humility] (Pa 473,4).

89. See 53,4: *doch hât der künec Gunther vil manegen hôhferten man* [but King Gunther had many presumptuous men].

90. *Hochvart* is so much associated with Prünhilt that ms. A talks of her *hochuerten siten* (A 670) when she wants to know about Sivrit's status, whereas mss. B and C emphasize, more in line with the situation, the deception with which she causes Gunther to invite relatives to Worms.

91. Ro A 11,2 (similar to Ro A 176,2); Ro A 81,2 (cf. 88,2); Ro A 111,3f. In Ro D, however, *hochvart* and *übermuot* are occasionally transferred to positive characters (cf. Heinzle 1978, p. 254).

92. On the concept, cf. Ehrismann (1995), pp. 245–48.

93. 174,3; 292,1; 292,4; 325,4; 350,2.

94. 283,4; 284,2; 543,1; 578,3; 602,2; 602,4; 787,4; 789,4; 809,3, etc.

95. 1171,4; 1347,4 (when Kriemhilt sees Etzel's magnificent company): *des wart dô vroun Kriemhilde vil wol gehœhet der muot* [Lady Kriemhilt's spirits were raised by this]. Brackert defines this in his commentary on 1171,4 as: the confluence "of external presentation, social representation, and personal existence" (cf. Grenzler 1992, p. 201).

96. For example, when Sivrit's and Gunther's rules seem to be secure (e.g., 721,4; 748,4; 750,2).

97. Hempel (1970), pp. 218–19.

98. 955,4: *der hêrlîche jägere der was hôhe gemuot* [the magnificent hunter was in good spirits].

99. Hempel (1970), p. 219.

100. The characterization is also positive for the *hochmuot, uobermuot,* or *hôchvart* of Roland or Karl (Rl 3689; 4038; 1842; 7627).

101. In the meaning of "naked skin," *hût* can also be found in Trt 1673; 7172; cf. Wh 447,28: *manic verhouwen hût* (reference from Christian Kiening); cf. on the "skins" of Sivrit: Seitter (1987), pp. 83–84.

102. In the *Straßburger Alexander,* the hero has a scaly armor (Al 1300–1305).

103. In closest proximity in 337 and 338; ms. D has *helkappe* and also *torenkappe.*

104. On the confusion of the senses, see Frakes (1994), pp. 115–16.

105. On this aspect, see Frakes (1994), pp. 113–21.

106. Seitter (1987), p. 83.

107. De Boor's Commentary, in *Das Nibelungenlied*[15], p. 153, turns the problem into a matter of legend history: "Here is one of the clearest seams between the older and younger parts. Leaving for the hunt is old, Hagen's trick with the sham war and the sign on the clothing are new. Of course, Siegfried does not ride to the hunt in his combat attire, and his hunting attire is described in detail 951ff. The silk cross is located on a piece of clothing that is not even present at the decisive moment."

108. Isalde also puts on a *hêrin hemede* (Trt 7175) over her *cleine edele hût* (Trt 7172), after which she lives *als ein arm wip* (Trt 7223). The queen temporarily becomes a penitent.

109. I thank Helmut Birkhan for the reference.

110. SuM, 169,5; cf. 161–69.

111. Seitter (1987), p. 83, speaks of Sivrit's special skin which his clothing hides and makes seem ordinary, whereby both skin and clothing can be made invisible by the cloak: an involution of concealment.

Chapter 5. The Shrouding of Visibility

1. Wenzel (1992), p. 323; Hugo Kuhn (1959); and see Heinzle (1987a), pp. 81–84; on the connection between orality and scenic construction, see also G. Müller (1975), p. 101.

2. G. Müller (1975), pp. 105, 112; on examples of falling out of the narrative progression, pp. 105–6.

3. The motif is widespread in heroic epic: Biterolf, for example, hears of Etzel's might and wants to see it for himself (Bit 464): *daz wir die grôzen êre/hie zen Hiunen wolden sehen* [that we the great honor/here with the Huns might see for ourselves] (Bit 1198–99). He stays at Etzel's court and serves him because *er die recken gerne sach* [he enjoyed seeing the heroes] (Bit 1353).

4. Hagen and Dancwart are without weapons (cf. 446–48).

5. Thus in mss. ADbd; B 613,4 has *von helden.* The kiss for Kriemhilt could express a recognition of the marriage by Gunther's followers (cf. the supplemental strophe C 616); more neutral are mss. Ca, *nach siten,* mss. Ih, *von im* (cf. Batts, pp. 186–87).

6. Further examples: determined by explicit proclamation are Sivrit's *grôze[] êren* (971,3), the winner of the footrace (973,4, missing in ms. C), Kriemhilt's *milte* (1127,4), her *triuwe* for Sivrit (1142,4), her beauty (1351,3), her role as exemplary queen (1390,2), the splendor of Etzel's messenger party (1156,2), etc.

7. E.g., 131,3; 133,2; 579,1; 584,1; 587,3; 590,4; 594,2; 788,2; 793,4; 799,2, etc. Sometimes also *man vant* (580,4; 795,4).

8. 585,3; 797,1; cf. 589,4.

9. The edition follows mss. ADJdh. Mss. B and g have *schaden.* In C 1272,3 we read: *groz itewize* (similar to ms. a; cf. Batts, pp. 378–79).

10. See Splett (1968), pp. 89–90, on the meaning of courtly opinion in Rüedeger's decision.

11. De Boor's suggested translation leans in this direction: "to have become faint-hearted, miserable" (p. 338).

12. See p. 137 above.

13. This argument occurs twice. In the parallel passage, (*daz sich dir ergæben zwêne degene/die noch werlîche gewâfent gegen dir stânt/und noch sô ledeclîche vor ir vîanden gânt* [that two warriors surrender to you/who are still armed and ready to fight/and still oppose their enemies freely] (2338,2–4), ms. C has as a variant for the fourth verse: *daz hiez ein michel schande und hiez ouch übele getân* [this would

be a great disgrace and would be wickedly done] (C 2397,4). Whatever could be called *schande* is unacceptable.

14. On the metaphor of shining in the *Eckenliet,* cf. Müller (1992b), pp. 105–7. Dietrich's and Ecke's appearance there is staged as an epiphany of heroic strength.

15. De Boor, p. 189.

16. See pp. 221–26 above.

17. The distance from modern concepts of individuality is recognizable in the retelling of this deception in Wagner's *Götterdämmerung,* where the failure to recognize the real winner—as already in the Edda—requires the exchange of bodies between Gunther and Siegfried. Brünhilde nevertheless recognizes the eyes of her beloved, which "flash" through the false personage. Siegfried's individuality cannot be hidden under a shell. *Thidreks saga,* chap. 207, is satisfied with the exchange of clothing.

18. Up until then, the intruder was only perceived acoustically (492,2; 492,4; 493,1; cf. 498).

19. Andersson's (1987) interpretation that Sivrit's exchange of identity is "parodistic," that Kriemhilt takes part in a "joke," and that Sivrit acts out "dramatic charades for his own amusement" has no basis in the text.

20. The redactor of *C smoothes out the sequence by substituting a verse that suggest Sivrit's obligation to Gunther for this one. The following strophe (662) is left out completely, and he continues, without concerning himself with the circumstances of the disappearance: *Er stal sich von den frowen. Vil tovgen chom er dan* [he snuck away from the women, he then came in secret]; cf. C 668,1 instead of 663,1 (according to mss. AB).

21. This is also agreed upon as a sign with Gunther.

22. See pp. 254–55 above.

23. See Müller (1987), pp. 232–38.

24. 750,4; cf. 794,4; up to and including love: 547,4; cf. p. 298 above and Althoff (1997), p. 296.

25. Etzel makes use of a generally accepted rule. His message to the Burgundians does not resemble a "summons" (cf. Schröder, 1989, p. 22) Had they refused, what sanction would there have been anyway?

26. Grenzler (1992), who extensively paraphrases the scene, speaks of "a further form of ceremonial exchange," that remains "hidden from the courtly public" (p. 179). But what is decisive is that these gazes are no long ceremonial. They belong to another sphere.

27. De Boor, Commentary, in *Das Nibelungenlied*[15], p. 55.

28. See the *güetlîche[]* speech (551,4), the expression of the face (561,4), the desire for the (ceremonial) kiss.

29. In C 400,2, *tougen,* which does not fit the situation very well (because the passage concerns *minne*) is replaced by *von hinnen.*

30. Panzer (1945), p. 101, writes what remains up to this day *communis opinio:* "The women draw the conclusion from what they see that Gunther is the *herre* and Siegfried is *sin man.* Siegfried's deception is therefore a success. The retinue in the castle know what the hero wants them to know." None of this is in the text, however, where one is only told that Prünhilt knows nothing, and there is no mention of her retinue's conclusions.

31. See, to the contrary, Wenzel (1992), pp. 337–38.

32. See p. 309 above on the disposition of space.

33. It is approved by everyone in a supplemental strophe in ms. C: *do sprachens al geliche: "si mag in wol mit eren han"* [they all said the same thing: "she may have him with honor] (C 616,4).

34. Salmon (1976), pp. 316–17, points correctly to the fact that Prünhilt alone is mistaken about Sivrit's rank, because the Burgundian witnesses of the scene in Isenstein know better. In C 626,1, this is made explicit. She does not know about the agreement (*Sine wesse niht der mære waz man da wolde tuon* [she did not know what they wanted to do]).

35. Wenzel (1992), p. 341.

36. Ibid., p. 329: writing makes possible "along with the continuation of oral traditions . . . , not only the conservation of the pre-literary repertoire of signs . . . , but also the contextual description of the individual employment of signs."

37. Sivrit is also "for the Nibelungian public" (this means the court at Worms) "neither *eigen* nor *man*" (Dinkelacker 1990, p. 88).

38. See pp. 188–89 above.

39. Wenzel (1992), p. 335.

40. "Ring and belt [function] as memorial signs in the sense of evidence of a legal claim: the ring as a sign of binding, the belt as a sign of loosing; the two together are signs of the extramarital surrender of Brünhild to Siegfried" (Wenzel, 1992, p. 332). Gunther is bound by Prünhilt with the belt. It is a sign of who retains the upper hand in the battle of the sexes.

41. Ibid., p. 334.

42. H. Naumann (1933), p. 47, points to the parallel case of the young Parzival at Jeschute, where what really happened does not matter. What matters is what the signs say.

43. On the meaning of *hôher muot,* cf. pp. 219–20 above.

44. See Grenzler (1992), pp. 201–2. In that the signs identify Prünhilt as a *kebse,* Sivrit takes evidence for his own status that disproves Prünhilt's claim (the *hôhe muot* is thus an expression of noble self-esteem).

45. Gephardt (1994), p. 36. The fight between Iwein and Ascalon is famous.

46. H. Naumann (1933), p. 47; he also criticizes the "garrulous" Sivrit's schoolmasters. As Naumann correctly remarks, there is nothing in the text to the effect that Sivrit includes Kriemhilt "in the dangerous secret" (de Boor, p. 117). He gives her the signs, and this is enough.

47. Grenzler (1992), p. 203, is an exception in surmising that this is a chess move in the power play over Sivrit's status, Kriemhilt's publicly stated doubts (?) about which Sivrit relieves with the trophies.

48. What Sivrit hides, according to this formulation, is not the answer to Kriemhilt's *vrâge, der si hete gedâht* (684,1), presumably also the question of his absence (thus G. Müller 1975, p. 111), but must refer to the object that "was meant for Kriemhilt" (*swaz er ir geben solde*), which is initially kept from her (reference of the *daz*!). I assume that *heln* is to be taken with a double accusative (Lexer ([1872–78] 1979), vol. 1, cols. 1242–43). The first object contains the subordinate clause, the second is *si*.

49. In ms. C has instead *da heime* (C 693,3; in ms. a, even this is missing). In both of these mss., the nexus between proof and rule is left out. Correspondingly, the remark that Sivrit *geben solde* (684,4) the trophies is replaced by a vague foreshadowing (cf. Batts, pp. 206–7).

50. Conversely, see Bachorski (1996).

51. Bischoff (1970), p. 19, remarks: "Kriemhild fell victim to the language of symbols."

52. Lc, 3: 470. The confrontation takes up over eighty printed pages. It is especially noteworthy that the kind of evidence that prevails in the history of jurisprudence—the written word—is here the basis for only one suspicion among many.

53. On variants of the contest of queens in the Nordic transmission, see Andersson (1980), pp. 186–204.

54. Ehrismann (1987), p. 138.

55. On the "virtualization" of competition for rule in the area of courtly norms, see pp. 398–402 above.

56. To interpret "public ostentation as a . . . conscious provocation" (Heinzle 1978, p. 253) is wrong in my opinion, since the splendor is evidence of social and political superiority. Not until *Rosengarten* is Kriemhilt's ostentation worthy of criticism (cf. p. 228 above), since in that case, any rationale for the demonstration of status is missing.

57. *Verstoln* (848,1), *diep* (849,1), *verholn* (848,2); D adds: *tougen* (Batts, p. 257).

58. It is unimportant in this scene whether Kriemhilt "consciously lies to the public with the convincing evidence of a symbol," that is, whether she knows the true circumstances surrounding the ring and the belt (G. Müller 1975, p. 110).

59. Wenzel (1974), p. 115).

60. See the scene after the murder of the servants, when Hagen wants to *reden* with the Huns (1957,3): "a confrontation on account of an illegal action."

61. It is possible to translate E. R. Dodds's (1991, p. 17), concept of "culture of shame" (as opposed to a "culture of guilt") in a way that addresses this case. It is unimportant what personal responsibility one has, but rather what seems to be obvious in the eyes of others. According to Dodds "the distinction is relative," since "many behaviors that are characteristic of a culture of shame" are maintained under the conditions of an ethic that is based on personal guilt (p. 19).

62. H. Naumann (1933), p. 47.

63. The oath reassures Gunther about something he really could not know (Salmon 1976, p. 318), whereas he does know that Sivrit is innocent in the matter itself, according to the narrator. The oath is devised to satisfy Gunther's ignorance, not Prünhilt's. On the meaning of the motif of the oath generally in the Siegfried legend, see Salmon (1976), pp. 321–25.

64. On the discussion, see Salmon (1976), p. 318; Bischoff (1970), pp. 20–21.

65. Thus Wachinger (1960), p. 112; Grenzler (1992), p. 290; differently, for example, Beyschlag ([1952] 1961), p. 199; Bumke (1960), p. 18.

66. De Boor (p. 145), supports his doubts about the oath on 861,4: *dô sâhen zuo zein ander die guoten ritter gemeit* [the chivalrous knights looked at each other]. He pictures these glances as being "disconcerted." This is not in the text (Bischoff 1970, p. 20). The meaning is anything but clear. If one does not want to take *gemeit* as a purely formulaic epithet, then it might indicate that the knights who are present can again be joyful (*gemeit*) after the (seeming) restoration of the peace. Aside from this, *ritter* could refer just to Sivrit and Gunther, who are happy about the outcome (cf. Salmon 1976, p. 319). De Boor (p. 145) introduces a category with Gunther's "bad conscience" that is alien to the epic (as before him G. Weber 1963, p. 69).

67. Where the actual deception is played out against the "façade" of the oath, one presumes a "culture of guilt" in the sense of Dodds (1991) as opposed to a "culture of shame." This goes against the text. It is demonstrated here, however, that the rules of a "culture of shame" are useless in solving conflict in this case.

68. If it refers to the fact that the cuckoo lays its eggs in other birds' nests, and is not just an empty word, *gouche* expresses the assumption that Sivrit has destroyed the king's marriage. Brackert (1970, 1: 193) translates: "Should we just put up with it?" The core of the metaphor is "acting in secret," of which Hagen accuses Sivrit.

69. Rupp (1985), p. 170, emphasizes that Hagen's actions, however one judges them in legal or moral terms, are necessary.

70. Mss. Jh have *trvrende* instead (Batts, p. 267).

71. Müller (1986b), p. 445; cf. Lexer ([1872–78] 1979), vol. 2, cols. 538–39

72. *Den sach man in tragen* [he was seen wearing it] (952,2); *in sâhen zuo in komende di Guntheres man* [Gunther's men saw him coming at them] (957,1).

73. This was expressed with a similar metaphor in a "more harmless" situation of the Saxon war: the Burgundian heroes *die lascten ime strîte vil maneges helmes schîn* [extinguished the shining of many helmets in the battle] (201,2).

74. As a reminder, as Sivrit had recommended, in order to betray Prünhilt: *ir habt einen muot. / ir jehet gelîche* [you should stick together / you all say the same] (385,1–2).

75. It seems to me (contra Grubmüller 1994, p. 66) that the inconsistent state of Sivrit's shield is not a "careless mistake" but rather a calculated signal.

76. "A certainty of intuition is not enough for revenge. It requires proof, which is provided by the test at the bier str. 1043ff." (de Boor, p. 167).

77. On tears as a sign of injustice, see Bernreuther (1994), p. 36.

78. On the competing legal institutions of the Nibelungian world, see pp. 347–48 above. In ms. C, the last stanza is missing. In its place after 1136 another is inserted (C 1151) that emphasizes the *giteklichen muot* [greed] of Hagen and the kings (C 1151,4).

79. See *Handwörterbuch zur deutschen Rechtsgeschichte* 1, cols. 731, on theft (R. Lieberwirth). This should be considered with Althoff's (1990a, 1997) thesis that medieval acts of representation were just "productions," and that they only publicly demonstrated what was previously agreed upon in secret negotiations (p. 167). It is surely to be assumed that there were preparatory discussions, but these hardly degrade the public act to simple theater. On the contrary, this act frees them from the odium of the secret and is constitutive of their legal legitimacy.

80. See Müller (1998).

81. To the contrary, 650,3; according to mss. BC, *ûf genâde* [trusting in Sivrit's discretion]; similar to ms. A, on the other hand, *heinlichen* in mss. JhQ.

82. Missing in ms. C.

83. The Darmstadt *Aventiurenverzeichnis* has deliberately paralleled Kriemhilt's intrigue with Prünhilt's invitation to Sivrit. It is explicitly stated: *also det brunhild vor* [as Prünhilt had done before] (p. 178). Both invitations are attributed to the *bose[n] fint* [devil] (de Boor, 1959, p. 177).

84. Thus in mss. CJKhla a variant of verse 1414,2 *daz ir mînen willen vil güetlîchen tuot* [that you willingly carry out my orders] (according to mss. AB); *güetlîchen* is replaced in the variant by *tovgenlichen* (cf. Batts, pp. 428–29); *tugentlich* (ms. d) also assumes this variant.

85. Secret action becomes a negative trait of the literary character, as when in *Rosengarten*, Kriemhilt *heimlîche* rejoices over the acceptance of her challenge by the Amelungs (Ro, A 83,2).

86. See the magnificent entrance in Passau (1297); the journey to Gotelint (1301; 1304); the reception with chivalric games (1306, 1307); the meeting of Kriemhilt with Gotelint (1311, 1313, 1314); the celebration in the castle (1318ff.); the demonstration of *milte* (1323; 1366; 1369; 1372; 1373); the assembly of Etzel's people (1339–47); the reception by Etzel himself (1349); Kriemhilt's shining appearance (1351,2); games of chivalry and the meal (1353–59); and the wedding in Vienna (1362–67).

87. I am following de Boor's translation ("hurled sharp glances at their enemies," p. 276), since it emphasizes the active-aggressive characteristic of looking ("to reciprocate a glance").

88. De Boor (p. 279) refers the words to "Kriemhild's outbreak of joy at the approach of the Burgundians." But the exclamation *Nu wol mich mîner vreuden* [how great is my joy] (1717,1) only continues the courtly harmony that Kriemhilt has feigned all these years. I think that *niuliche* means "some moments before."

89. Wynn (1969) recognized the presentation of symbolic gestures as a struc-

tural principle of the epic: "At crucial points of the plot he allows the gesture to take over the dialogue and detailed description" (p. 111).

90. Wynn (1965), p. 107. The gesture is in no way decoupled from its legal meaning (Alois Wolf 1981, pp. 59–60). The legal meaning emphasizes the incredible provocation.

Chapter 6. Spaces

1. On the historical space of the legend, cf. Brunner (1990); he will not be considered further.

2. Alois Wolf (1995), pp. 383–84.

3. One can therefore never know whether only those who are specifically named are present, or who is witness to a scene and who is not (contra Grenzler 1992, pp. 160, 371). The narrator is never concerned with complete situational protocols, which is implicitly suggested whenever a "realistic" sequence of events is cobbled together out of the text.

4. See 2034, 2230.

5. Schröder (1968), p. 162, proposes the "more likely" solution that Kriemhilt has Hagen "brought before her," and that "the whole exchange of words takes place in front of witnesses." This is certainly more plausible, but it has nothing to do with the concept of space in the text.

6. See 1407–13; Masser (1981) assumes performance variants here, because "the minstrels who are chosen as messengers would hardly burst into the king's bedchamber in the middle of the night" (p. 130). Andersson (1987), p. 134, also sees a mistake.

7. In the *Rolandslied*, King Marsilie does not at first participate in the initial battle, but he receives several messages about it, to which he can then react directly. Only after all of these actions fail does he intervene personally. A reader schooled in the realistic novel would have to assume that he must have been nearby and would ask where, and how this was possible, but we are told only that "he is involved in the battle" first through his army, then through others whom he commands directly, and finally in person.

8. This is common to heroic epic. In *Kudrun*, Hartmuot's messengers appear only after they have arrived at the castle, *ze hove* (K 766,1), that is, in front of the queens. Later, Hilde permits Hartmuot to appear *ze hove,* that is, before her, without being shackled (K 1599,2).

9. 133,1: *ûf dem hove;* 741,2: *an dem hove;* 742,2; 1869,4; 1872,3: *ûf dem hove,* etc.

10. The same in *Kudrun* 1618,4: Kudrun goes *des hoves an ein ende.*

11. Also in 1805,1 and 1806,1.

12. The syntactic order, however, also allows for the following meaning: "He

sent to the court for Gernot," which would mean that the other king's environment was also called *ze hove.*

13. Also, e.g., Rl 8674, 8681.

14. 290,3; 349,3; 550,2; 551,2; cf. 1109,1.

15. See 581, 582.

16. See 546, 549, 550; later again in the *suone* ritual.

17. Before the journey to Isenstein, when Kriemhilt wants to communicate with her brother:

> *Nâch den hergesellen wart ein bot gesant,*
> *ob si wolden scouwen niuwez ir gewant* (369,1–2)
>
> *[A messenger was sent out to the heroes*
> to ask if they wanted to see their new attire]

18. 348–61; 552–62; cf. Rüedeger's appearance before Kriemhilt (1225,3–4).

19. Luhmann (1980), 1: 25.

20. Segmentary differentiation is, of course, already consciously manipulated if one invents a *site,* as Hagen does, for one's own advantage (1863,2).

21. See Alois Wolf (1995), pp. 315ff.

22. Gillespie (1987) points out the different "mythical" and "realistic" concepts of space in the epic.

23. When Peeters (1986) tries to draw conclusions about the location of Nibelungenland from some geographic details (p. 6), he overlooks the fact that this information is only available later, after the land's foggy remoteness has passed into part of the Burgundian or Netherlandish sphere of influence.

24. Lecouteux (1978), p. 295, and (1979), p. 76.

25. See pp. 324–29 above.

26. Fromm (1990), p. 8

27. In 1591,2, he is also called *Elsen verge.*

28. This variant according to A 1494,1 (also in mss. CDla) seems to me to be preferable, despite the rhyme difficulty, to the *nivlich gehit* [newly wed] in ms. B (the first word miswritten? Misread?). Ms. b has—with a false diphthong of the long vowel *î* required in ms. A for the rhyme—*mulich gesait.* Ms. d (*newlich geschicht*) is closer to ms. B (Batts, pp. 472–73). De Boor follows, in line with the *Thidreks saga,* ms. B: just "newly wed"—an isolated, strangely private detail. De Boor wants to conclude from this—without any support in the text or even indirectly from the character of the *verge*—that the ferryman wanted "to give the ring to his young wife" (p. 247). If one accepts the variant of ms. B, the main point should be to anchor the ferryman even more closely to the land through marriage.

29. The scene also points to the negotiations of the German King Henry I with the French king, described by Althoff, in which each of the parties was positioned on one bank of the Rhine and they first became acquainted by gazing

across the river at each other before the actual negotiations began. "Seeing" from a safe distance can create trust (Althoff 1997, p. 246).

30. With a knowledge of names, Hiltibrant also tries to gain the friendship of his son Hadubrant in the *Hildebrandslied.*

31. On the terminology, cf. Luhmann (1980), 1: 25–27; with a different theoretical basis, Czerwinski (1979), p. 62.

32. Luhmann (1980), 1: 44.

33. Müller (1984–85), pp. 299–300.

34. Likewise, at the arrival of Etzel's messengers, Gunther is at a loss and has to ask who they are. No one knows anything *unze daz si sach / Hagene von Tronege* [until Hagen of Troneck / saw them] (1431,3–4).

35. See 846,1: Kriemhilt comes out of the church *mit manigem küenen man* [with many bold men].

36. Salmon (1976), p. 320. It is pointless to speculate who all is present at the oath.

37. See *Handwörterbuch zur deutschen Rechtsgeschichte* 1, cols. 989–1001, on the medieval discussion of liability for success (E. Kaufmann). On presence as a criterion for participation or support, cf. Althoff (1997), p. 296.

38. The supplemental strophe follows B 912 (915), and this not only in mss. C and a, which mostly correspond, but also in mss. Jdh, and in ms. d even a second time after C 913 (Batts, pp. 273, 277).

39. It is also worth considering the obligations within the fellowship (pp. 134–36 above). Because of their bond to their brother and his *vriunde,* it would have been improper if they were to betray these in favor of the foreigner Sivrit.

40. De Boor, Commentary, in *Das Nibelungenlied*[15], p. 186; cf. Müller (1987).

41. The Danube is twelve days' distant (1525,1). In comparison: Sigemunt has to leave Worms *ân' geleite* (1095,1) until Gernot and Giselher come to him. Gernot assures him of his innocence *an Sîfrides tôt* (1097,2), and only Giselher gives him *guot geleite ûz dem lande* [adequate escort out of the land] (1098,1–2.). Herein is the limit of their bonds.

42. This occurred to the redactor of *C, and he explicitly leaves Ortwin at home, to Gunther's chagrin (cf. pp. 156–57); ms. k has him die (as in Bit 6001–6003).

43. Ehrismann (1987), p. 147.

44. De Boor (p. 237), again sees a lapse in the legend: "Brünhild, unknown to the *ältere Not,* is once again allowed by the most recent poet to surface here—although in a fairly unsophisticated way."

45. This at least is the sequence in mss. AB; *C (represented by ms. a) has a tearful goodbye for the king and the army as it leaves for Etzel (a 1555–56). The woman who warns against the expedition to Etzel is not Prünhilt but again the old queen Uote.

46. See Althoff (1997), p. 296, on the relationship between consensus and spatial proximity; cf. p. 262.

47. This is why direct access to the ruler is contested and must be regulated (Althoff 1997, pp. 185–98).

48. Müller (1982), p. 138; examples on p. 330.

49. Althoff (1990b), pp. 195–203; cf. on the *mediatores*, Althoff (1997), pp. 177, 179.

50. 727,3; 758,4; cf. 752,4.

51. On the meaning of the handshake, see *Handwörterbuch zur deutschen Rechtsgeschichte* 1, cols. 1974–75 (A. Erler).

52. On *gast,* cf. Pérennec (1975).

53. In C 632, the reference to the latent disruption is deleted. Instead we read: *die frowen schieden sich / in zvehten minnekliche, als ich wol verwæne mich* [the ladies separated themselves / in harmony, I believe].

54. C 827 adds *mit lobe* [with praise], which spoils the point concerning class and misses the concrete conception of space.

55. See pp. 368–71 above on the change in meaning of *dringen.*

56. *Gescheiden,* "to go away": 1875,1; 1877,1.

57. See Wenzel (1995), pp. 131–35, on the hierarchical structuring of space.

58. See pp. 246–49 above.

59. The disposition of space in a tournament seems so ordinary that it is not even mentioned. Only ms. C. makes the framework more precise:

> . . . . *hvsir und dach*
> *was allez vol durch schowen von luten vber al* (C 823, 2–3).
>
> . . . . *houses and rooftops*
> were filled with people looking out everywhere]

60. Bit 10050–51; 11326–29; 11834–39.

61. See p. 274 above.

62. 1887,4; 1888,2; 1890,4.

63. See 1948,4; he wants to play Etzel's *kameræere,* who wants to guard the stairs in his way; on the meaning of the *stiegen,* see Alois Wolf (1995), pp. 395, 399, 411.

64. Wolf (1995), p. 395.

65. I take the sentence to refer to the Burgundians, who "pull" their opponents in.

66. The movement is only seemingly motivated by the story (such as: he has to go to get his weapons), because this would be a matter for the *ingesinde* (2168).

67. This is evident from the words of his informants: *dô ist vil gar zergân / swaz wir vreuden hêten in der Hiunen lant* [much has been lost / of the joy we had, here in the land of the Huns] (2242, 2–3).

68. 2287,2; 2292,3.

69. 2276,1; 2278,3.

70. On this passage, see Pérennec (1975), p. 2.

71. It is not true that Bechelaren is the last outpost of civilization (Frakes 1994, p. 163).

72. See 1316,3–1317,1.

73. In Tuln, e.g., Kriemhilt becomes acquainted with *vil manic site vremede* [many foreign customs] (1341,3).

74. As de Boor, p. 242, comments, that they set out in boats is, in fact, not noteworthy, because from Worms, one has to cross the Rhine (if headed east, as they were). It is worth considering, however, that the position of Worms is ignored previously (de Boor, p. 152).

75. On the meaning of river crossings, cf. Strohschneider and Vögel (1989).

76. It seems to me that this "becoming nomads" is important for the role that the Burgundians-Nibelungs will play at Etzel's court as destroyers of his kingdom (pp. 436–37 above). On nomads, see Deleuze and Guattari ([1980] 1992), pp. 552–26.

77. On Kriemhilt's character as "disruptive," see pp. 119–21 above.

78. See previously 1819,2; 1822,4.

79. Joachim Heinzle brought my attention to the fact that, given the size of this spear, Sivrit would have to be of gigantic height.

80. 437,4; 441,2–3; 449,4.

81. This can only mean that Sivrit "always had possession of" the cloak, because it is never said that he kept it "constantly." The formulation in ms. C is more precise in this regard: *trůch von allem rehten* [wore by right] (C 1132,4); ms. a interprets even further: *trueg vor allenn rekchenn* [wore in front of all warriors] (Batts, p. 339). This does not make sense, however, inasmuch as the *tarnhût* is not exactly an object to be displayed publicly. Alberich emphasizes that it belongs among Sivrit's instruments of power.

82. On the symbolism of numbers, see Brunner (1990), pp. 45–48.

83. Seitter (1990), pp. 23–24, above all, has pointed to the Burgundians "becoming Nibelungs." I am following his lead, but with some different accents.

84. *Nibelunc* is therefore not just the name of a young prince (who, by the way, is only due half of the hoard), but of the head of the clan. The certainty with which de Boor calls him the "father of the young kings" (p. 388) admittedly has no basis in the text.

85. This is to be taken as genitive plural, as also in 492,4.

86. The name of the Nibelungen land is now regularly formed as *Franken.*

87. 888,3; 934,2; 1018,4: in the words of a messenger.

88. We find references to *Sîfrit . . . von Nibelunge lant* (1003,3); *der helt von Nibelunge lant* (1011,4; here ms. A has *Niderlant,* mss. Cab have other formulations); *die Sîfrides helde von Nibelunge lant* (1015,2; 1027,1; 1071,3); and *Nibelunge* (1030,2; 1058,4).

89. Contrary is C 1094,3, *heim in Niderlant* (also a: Batts, pp. 326–27).

90. So, too, the other manuscripts.

91. Also *Sîfrides man* (1093,1).

92. According to mss. Jh: *hein ze sinem rich den kvnc von Niderlant* [home to his kingdom, the king of Netherlands] (Batts, p. 331).

93. C 1131,1 (corresponds to 1118) adds again for emphasis *in Nibelunge lant* (also ms. a).

94. In mss. Jbh, however, also *von Niderlant* (Batts, p. 525).

95. The late ms. a, which has to represent ms. C here on account of a lacuna, has expunged this senseless remark (not ms. C, as Seitter 1990, p. 23, claims). It tells of the chaplain, who was taken along to conduct Mass despite the lamentable state of faith at the time, and who is the only survivor. This seems to be another later smoothing out. A change in the other direction is inconceivable.

96. The title of *Âventiure* 25 "Wie die Nibelunge zen Hiunen fuoren" [How the Nibelungs Traveled to the Huns], which de Boor uses in his edition, is based on mss. b and d. In the others, a neutral formulation (e.g., "the kings") is used.

97. The Burgundians are able to take possession of Sivrit's instruments of power only in a supplemental stanza in *C.

98. In ms. k, this characterization, which is inexplicable based on the plot, is consistently expunged.

99. "The 'and' joining the Burgundians and Nibelungs is the hitch presented by the poem in order to make the new 'as,' that is, the Burgundians as Nibelungs, all the more noticeable" (Seitter 1990, p. 24).

100. See pp. 161–66 above.

101. 1989,2; 2012,4; 2201,4.

102. 1873,3; 1880,3; 1884,4; 1931,3; 1940,4; 2070,4; 2076,4; 2188,1; 2215,3; 2228, 4; 2242,4; 2244,4; 2317,4.

103. This is the tendency of all manuscripts, inasmuch as they add the name of the land. Ms. C adds *chunic* to the name Gunther, but the designation of origin is missing.

104. The perspective changes quickly, however. It can also vary in the manuscripts. When mss. ABDJh speak about *die Burgonden* coming into Etzel's land (1718,1), then mss. Ca have *Nibelunge* (cf. C 1758,1).

105. Thus also, of course, 1741,2 and 1742,2: *hort der Nibelunge.*

106. It is also noteworthy that in the *C group, 1870,4, the name is replaced by *ellenden rechen*—strangers who have lost the protection of home; and, in 1873,3, by *gesten*—strangers who have come to a celebration (Batts, pp. 568–69).

107. Contra, C 2233,2: *edeln rechen von Burgonden lant* [noble warriors from Burgundy], likewise ms. a. Only at the end does the name *Nibelunge* recede again. As long as Dietrich still believes in a peaceful settlement, he uses the more neutral *held ûz Burgonden lant* (2317,4). The name is from then on reserved for *Nibelunges swert* (2347,3; 2348,4).

108. This would be an epic countermodel, the incursion of a horde of "nomads." On this, see Deleuze and Guattari ([1980] 1992), pp. 481–585.

109. This is true geographically as well as structurally. The *Rosengarten* and

Biterolf stories reverse this and go back to the original constellation, in that they have hordes from the southeast of Europe appear as opponents on the Rhine.

Chapter 7. Disrupted Rules of Interaction

1. Störmer (1973), pp. 462–507, has worked out basic characteristics of "early nobility" based on literary sources. The ethos of early nobility is very closely related to the characters in the *Nibelungenlied.*
2. See Koziol (1992), pp. 289–324.
3. Karl Leyser (who otherwise works with a broad concept of ritual) posits as a criterion: "Ceremony is conservative. Ritual, on the other hand, creates a transition." He proposes: "going under the crown was ceremony, the coronation itself was ritual" (1993, pp. 2–3). Here, apparently, Arnold van Gennep's *rites de passage* are in the background, but they are a special case in themselves. Leyser also leaves any distinction out when he characterizes the hand-holding, the meal, the pre-combat boasting demonstrations of social demarcation, etc., as rituals. See Koziol (1992), pp. 298–99.
4. On the distinction, see Soeffner (1992), p. 107.
5. Unlike what is otherwise the case in early medieval culture.
6. Koziol (1992), p. 294.
7. Ritual acts are ambiguous (ibid., pp. 307–11).
8. See pp. 305–8 above.
9. Koziol writes: "rituals cannot create harmony where a basis for it does not exist. They will only reveal what is already present" (p. 311).
10. See Müller (1996b), pp. 45–46.
11. Rituals were not "an ideal as opposed to a chaotic reality. They were a vehicle for competition as well as for consensus" (Koziol 1992, p. 305).
12. Mauss (1975), pp. 145–279. On the political background of giving as a substitute for military action in the early Middle Ages, see Hannig (1986).
13. Hannig (1986), pp. 153–54, 155–56: the Amerindian potlatch.
14. On the relationship of "honor capital" and "economic capital," see Schreiner and Schwerthoff (1995), pp. 10–11.
15. See pp. 72–73 above. On the underlying problems of economic and social dispossession of women, see Frakes (1994), pp. 67–68, 73–76.
16. I thus see less of a fear of the future in this (Frakes 1994, p. 175).
17. See Pérennec (1975), pp. 10–12. Such comparisons of resources at the bride's departure are common, but the scene here is instrumentalized in its connection to the conflict. Koneczny's assertion (1977, p. 110) with regard to Kriemhilt that, here as later, "wealth belonging to the foreign bride alone is not really desirable" models epic constellations too directly on historically reality. Frakes (1994), pp. 70–71, also tries to find the key to the scene exclusively in explanations that pertain to historical (and not fictionalized) characters under the social conditions of the time.

18. The gifts given on account of Sivrit's death have nothing to do with *milte,* because they are *Seelgerät,* donations made to ensure salvation in the afterlife (1059,4; 1060; 1061,2–3).

19. Frakes (1994), pp. 82–83, stretches the text a bit in suggesting transportation difficulties in taking the hoard along or Rüedeger's satisfaction about the loss of the hoard.

20. The resistance of the kings to Hagen's new crime (*sie woltenz gerne wenden; dô des niht geschach . . .* [they wanted to avert it; but when this did not happen . . .], 1274,3) is corrected by Gernot (*Mit gewalt des küniges den slüzzel stiez er an die tür. / golt daz Kriemhilde reichte man darfür* [he put the key in the door by the king's authority, / and Kriemhilt's gold was passed out], 1277,1–2). The fact that he gives it to *die geste* (that is, to Rüedeger's entourage, 1277,4) does not yet run contrary to Kriemhilt's intentions. It remains unclear whether Rüedeger's orders (*Nu heizet ez behalten, wand' ich sîn niht enwil* [tell them to keep it, because I don't want any of it], 1279,1) are followed or whether the gold that was packed up "before" is a part of Kriemhilt's remaining possessions. De Boor understands *Dâvor in aller wîle* (1280,1) as "in the entire time (of the conflicts)" (p. 207; similarly, Frakes 1994, p. 83). Independent of this, Kriemhilt donates another *tûsent marc* (1281,2) for Sivrit's salvation.

21. See p. 119 above.

22. Gephardt (1994), pp. 55–61, underestimates, however, the unintentionality of *milte* and, for example, assumes a political agenda behind Giselher's engagement (p. 56). In my opinion, this is contradicted by the events. Hagen at first suspects some hidden agenda, but he then seems to be convinced by Rüedeger's *acte gratuit* and takes a gift, too.

23. See p. 323 above.

24. De Boor's interpretation, p. 353, seems to me too narrow: "the pleasant existence (like 2246,4) plays on Rüedeger's intercession."

25. In Rudolf von Ems's exemplary courtly *Willehalm von Orlens,* the messengers are offered rich gifts, but *Uf ir ere und uf ir leben / Versprach ir ait die gabe da* [by their honor and their life, / their oath then forbade the gifts] (WvO 1076–77).

26. On this scene, see also Gephardt (1994), pp. 31–32.

27. Walles (1982), pp. 268–69, surmises that this is an old motif of legend, where the messengers are included in the treacherous plot, and that the narrator compromised between the legend constellation and his continuous attempts to leave Etzel unscathed as a peaceful king (1479,1; 1482,4), which is corrected in ms. C.

28. This seems to be de Boor's interpretation (p. 238): "*vor ir herren,* that is, in consideration of their lord. Receiving gifts is normal for the minstrel, but at this point, they are representatives of their lord, whose respect would be diminished by their acceptance of gifts"; similarly, Gephardt (1994), p. 32.

29. This is expressed in that they distribute expensive travel clothing upon their arrival in Worms, whereas they are normally the ones who receive clothing (de Boor, p. 230; cf. 1434–35; Gephardt, 1994, p. 31).

30. This corresponds to Hagen's distrust, when he advises holding the messengers and giving them only seven days' head start on the Burgundians (1480).

31. According to Gephardt (1994), p. 32, "the *minne* gesture certainly plays a role . . . , which makes it possible for a highly regarded man to accept gifts from a *frouwe.*" In *Biterolf* as well, the gifts from the women are harmless in comparison to those from the king.

32. Hannig (1986), pp. 151–52, 156–57.

33. Althoff (1994), p. 254.

34. See Müller (1974). The way in which such a relationship of voluntary service functions smoothly is also shown in Eilhart's *Tristrant* in the example of Tristrant's father.

35. C 339 has instead *miete;* the same in ms. a (Batts, pp. 102–3).

36. On the special conditions, see pp. 400–401 above.

37. The fact that heroes are also rewarded by kings is certainly correct (Frakes 1994, p. 91), but this is far less frequently stated and is not referred to as *miete.*

38. To be taken as future tense.

39. See p. 206 above on Kriemhilt's concept of her own *êren.*

40. Schreiner and Schwerthoff (1995), p. 9.

41. Ibid., p. 5.

42. See *ob ich vor küneges wîbe zem münster türre gegân* [if I dare enter the church before the king's wife] (827,4), or, formulated negatively, *âne schande* [without disgrace] (831,2).

43. See *Handwörterbuch zur deutschen Rechtsgeschichte* 1, cols. 861–70 (A. Erler, Kornblum, G. Dilcher). The oath of purification is an archaic legal institution that was repressed more and more after the early Middle Ages by the prosecutorial oath and the evidence of witnesses (col. 863).

44. This is the theme of many manipulated formulas of oath-taking in medieval epic.

45. Althoff (1990a); id. (1997), p. 180. He shows with the example of the Carolingian capitularies how little even laws can be understood to be part of a unified legal structure that regulates legal relations fundamentally, and how foreign the concept of such a structure was to the Middle Ages (1997, pp. 283–84).

46. The attempts of the *C redactor to put Hagen in a bad light in this affair require a changed concept of oath and law.

47. Reference to the *sêle* was a key to the Christian interpretation of the Rüedeger character (cf. Splett 1968, p. 59; also on the following). It is notable, however, that the reservation plays no part in the following dispute, and that the oath generally recedes in importance, whereas the different legal-social obligations move to the foreground.

48. Gerd Althoff, orally on October 10, 1997, at the Berlin Colloquium "Medieval Literature and Art Between Court and Cloister." His presentation there, published in the conference papers, touches on this phenomenon.

49. It seems to me that the differences in the formulation of the oath are more striking than the concurrences (contra Schmidt-Wiegand 1982a, p. 378).

50. Bumke (1996a), pp. 125–26, on the compassion question in *Parzival.*

51. See pp. 183; 348 above.

52. See p. 184 above.

53. See E. Kaufmann in *Handwörterbuch zur deutschen Rechtsgeschichte* 5, pp. 73–76: *suone* is the (permanent) settlement of a dispute and the resulting condition of peace. It is legally binding. In the *Nibelungenlied,* it is validated by Gunther's oath (1131,1); see Althoff (1992); id. (1997), pp. 57–94.

54. Althoff (1994), pp. 250–51; id. (1990b); id. (1997), pp. 177, 179.

55. Gere is a relative of the royal house (754,1). He is Gunther's messenger to Kriemhilt and Sivrit. He is Kriemhilt's advisor (1215). Gere and Ortwin will accompany Kriemhilt on her journey to Etzel up to the Danube. On the legal bond of the kiss, see Schmidt-Wiegand (1982b), p. 372; id. (1982a), p. 379.

56. On the legal and the material aspects of *ergetzen,* see *Deutsches Rechtswörterbuch* 3, col. 196; cf. Lexer ([1872–78] 1979), vol. 1, col. 630; Kluge-Seebold, p. 185; Maurer p. 23; pp. 25–27; Czerwinski (1979), p. 77. Schröder (1968), p. 110, reduces the meaning to "causing severe harm to be forgotten," a healing of "deep emotional injury": "Who can forget heartbreak?"

57. This is overlooked by Grenzler (1992), who up to the end only sees the attempt to compensate for material damages (p. 367), whereas the epic narrates the impossibility of *ergetzen.* "Kriemhild's actions" seem to him "a model for legal action to compensate for damages according to medieval concepts."

58. 1160,4; 1161,4; 1389,4.

59. See 2339,4. This is neither "conscious of fate" nor "noble-minded" (de Boor, p. 365), but accepts the mechanism, as explained by Gunther, of strike and counterstrike. The scene is interpreted in detail by Heinzle (1995a).

60. See *süene iz* (2336,4).

61. *Handwörterbuch zur deutschen Rechtsgeschichte* 1, cols. 1445–51 (W. Ogris); Heinzle (1995a), pp. 228–29; the procedure varies, but hostages are usually treated honorably. The shackles (here only after the battle) are supposed to maintain Dietrich's claims.

62. This depends on whether the lines can be understood as an explication of the preceding stanza or as a continuation of the ideas there, but toward another goal. Heinzle (1995a), p. 229, argues in view of the following stanzas that "the demand is in no way taken back," but to do this he must paraphrase *durch iuch* [for your sake] with "through the compensation that you give me," which stretches the wording quite a bit. One could also argue that the rejection of Dietrich's offer again reestablishes the original claim.

63. The reproaches against Dietrich's carelessness go beyond the text. Dietri-

ch's words are differentiated with regard to Hagen and Gunther. He hands over Hagen to secure a legal title. As he hands over Gunther, he asks Kriemhilt to be lenient to her brother and to let them (the *ellenden*) live for his sake (cf. 2364,4).

64. See pp. 125–29 above.

65. This is also the meaning in the *Rolandslied.* Karl offers his own son Ludewic to Alda for the loss of Roland: *ich irgetze dich sin gerne* [I'll gladly compensate you for him] (Rl 8702). Alda, too, declines and dies.

66.

> *Jâ habet ir mîner swester getân sô manegiu leit*
> . . .
> *daz si des hete schulde, ob si iu wære gram.*
> *nie man deheiner vrouwen noch mêre freuden benam.* (1209,1; 3–4)
>
> *[You have done my sister so much wrong*
> . . .
> that she would have cause if she hated you.
> Never has more joy been taken from a woman.]

See Giselher 1213,3–4: *swaz êren ir geschæhe, vrô solten wir des sîn* [whatever honor she would obtain, we should be glad of that]; Gernot and Giselher primarily, then Gunther, support the connection to Etzel (1214,2–3).

67. *Trôst,* too, has legal connotations (Lexer ([1872–78] 1979), vol. 2, col. 1527: protection, aid), that are only in the background here.

68. This is missed by Czerwinski (1979), p. 77, when he limits *ergetzen* to the social and political component alone. Kriemhilt steps out of this framework, and this is why her behavior is unpredictable and monstrous. Czerwinski's criticism of the psychological interpolation of more recent critics is correct in that they try to fill positively what the narrator leaves open as empty space.

69. What might seem to be "Ovidian" or even cynical about this argument is probably just random. Rüedeger takes a middle position between the kings' ideas of compensation and those of Kriemhilt.

70. See pp. 203–4 above.

71. This is the basis for the multiform medieval rituals of conflict resolution. See Althoff (1994), p. 249, and elsewhere.

72. Czerwinski (1979), p. 68, sees *gruoz* connected to *minne* as a "form of nonviolent recognition of other nobility."

73. On the tradition of these kinds of arrival scenes, cf. Haymes (1975), p. 161.

74. He is not mentioned at all at the reception ritual; it is said only at 582,2–3 that he continues to serve Kriemhilt, and later (597,2–3) how he shines in the tournament.

75. Instead, they have to go *ze hove in den palas* [to court in the palace]. This corresponds to the reception for Rüedeger in Worms. Coming toward him are only *des küniges næhsten mâge* [the nearest relatives of the king] (1184,1). The king awaits him in the hall and honors him with a particularly respectful greeting:

der herre stuont von sedele. daz was durch grôze zuht getân. (1185,4)

[The lord rose from his seat. This was done as a great courtesy.]

den guoten Rüedegêren er bî der hende genam. (1186,4)

[He took the noble Rüedeger by the hands.]

76. Bowing the head is a gesture of subordination, which, in a courtly context where the subordination is only symbolic (see pp. 398–402 above), presumes a similar gesture from the other side (*genædelîche*); cf. Schmidt-Wiegand (1982b), p. 372.

77. See *Handwörterbuch zur deutschen Rechtsgeschichte* 1, cols. 1974–75 (A. Erler); cf. Leyser (1993), p. 3: "Between lords and servants, the gesture was impossible, even if the latter were free men."

78. See p. 405 above.

79. *Ouch werten sich vil sêre die Etzelen man* [Etzel's men also defended themselves well] (1972,1). The formulae that describe the melee are not entirely clear. There is no mention of those who are in the hall bearing offensive weapons, only of the Huns' armor: *Dô sluoc der fürste selbe vil manige wunde wît / durch die liehten ringe* [the prince himself cut many deep wounds / through the light chain mail (that is, of the Huns)], 1968–69; *sîn wâfen hêrlîchen durch die helme erklanc* [his weapon rang splendidly through the helmets], 1970,2; 1986,4; 2006,4.

80. This is similar in other heroic epics. For example, at the reception of the young Dietleib by Etzel: *vil helde stuont bedrungen dâ* [many heroes were crowded around] (Bit 3299); likewise at the arrival of Dietrich of Bern (Bit 5704; 5709). When, in the *Rolandslied,* Tirrich's combat against Binabel begins, Karl's supporters gather around him: *uil michel was daz gedranc* [the crush was great] (Rl 8899).

81. This is also de Boor's understanding, p. 284.

82. On the restriction of space, see pp. 309–10; 313–18 above.

83. de Boor suggests as a translation: "believed to know" (p. 293). This is imprecise, because Hagen and Volker are intent (*wolden wizzen*) on bringing out the true character of the *dringen.*

84. The *stouben* (1860,4) was also a sign of festive joy at the courtly celebration in Worms and demonstrated the excess of joy at Etzel's first encounter with Kriemhilt. This is different now.

85. Wenzel (1995), pp. 143–45. On the ambivalence of *schal* in a courtly context, cf. Müller (1986b), pp. 445–47.

86. This is not negative as in the *Rolandslied,* where the heathens' appearance is arrogant and violent (Rl 839; 3538; 7995; 8540).

87. See 1937,1; 2003,2; 2110,2.

88. See pp. 92–94 above.

89. See pp. 89–90 above, as well as the verbs of duration in this passage. One could ask whether Sigelint's death is built in as a signal of disruption to interrupt the standstill through some sort of important event.

90. *Springen:* 1940,1; 1940,4; 1946,1; 1950,1; 1966,1; 1967,1; 1970,1; etc. Dancwart's raving: 1946,3. On the vocabulary of the "description of unbridled fighting frenzy" see Alois Wolf (1995), p. 409.

91. Other verbs that express brisk movements are in 2029,3 and later 2061,2; 2070,1; and 2071,1.

Chapter 8. The Failure of the Courtly Alternative

1. On *Rosengarten D,* see Heinzle (1978), pp. 256–57; cf. on version F, pp. 259–61.

2. In my opinion, the *Nibelungenlied* neither recounts the "disillusionment of the courtly world" (Ihlenburg 1969, p. 51) and uncovers the "illusory optimism" of Arthurian epic, a thesis that Alois Wolf (1987), p. 199, rightly criticizes in investigations that compare heroic and Arthurian epic, nor do the *alten mæren* fall prey to the critique of the new courtly humanity.

3. Hansen (1990), p. 132, emphasizes that a strict distinction between courtly and heroic ethics is not possible.

4. Generally, Dürrenmatt (1945); Andersson (1980), p. 151: "old elements are obscured in new romantic and chivalric details;" Hoffmann (1974), p. 79, writes that the *Nibelungenlied* wanted to demonstrate the fragility of courtly norms; cf., to the contrary, the summary by Haug (1979), p. 371. Haug's thesis goes far beyond the usual assumptions that "courtly life" was only a "deceptive, flimsy façade" (Spiewok, 1989, p. 193) and that "illusion" was confronted by "reality." He presumes a conflicting interaction that impels the plot to its terrifying end. I am following his lead.

5. In the question of evaluation, however, I disagree with Haug (above all 1974, 1989), for whom the courtly world is implicitly the norm, against which an archaic heroic schema wins out. His thesis that in the *Nibelungenlied,* the heroic schema is no longer conceived of as objective necessity, but is interpreted as an intentional act of the protagonists, seems moreover to be oriented on anthropological positions on the courtly romance.

6. Ganz (1977, 1986); on the meaning of the phrase *ze hove,* see pp. 283–85 above.

7. Overview by W. Rösener in the *Lexikon des Mittelalters,* ed. Robert Auty et al. (Munich, 1977–98), vol. 5, cols. 67–68; cf. the court offices in *Kudrun* or *Tristrant,* where it is explicitly explained that such an office does not entail menial services, what kinds of important tasks it is responsible for, and how it is linked to noble rank (Trt 316–28); and cf. (also on the problems of dating) Bumke (1996c), p. 563.

8. See 162, 173, 200–201, and 235, where the officeholders are spoken of as superb warriors.

9. See p. 157 above.

10. Sivrit explains to his companions that it is *hovesite* in Isenstein to hand over one's weapons (A 390,4); similarly neutral, but without the catchword *hovesite,* is the vulgate version according to ms. B: *dô begonde im Sîvrit dâ von diu rehten mære sagen* (406,4; cf. C 415,4).

11. Jaeger (1983), pp. 194–95; cf. pp. 178–79, in agreement with contemporary chronicles.

12. E.g., in Bechelaren, 1651–52 and 1665–66.

13. For instance, at the receptions of Rüedeger or the minstrels in Worms or of the Burgundian kings by Etzel.

14. Bumke (1986), 1: 137–275.

15. Ro A uses this characterization not just for Kriemhilt but also for Dietrich (Ro A 170,4), whose *hochvârt* has to be compensated by splendid clothing from the Wormsians—a fact that is usually overlooked when the failure of the Rosengarten tournament is blamed entirely on Kriemhilt's arrogance.

16. De Boor's commentary is of another opinion: "The chosen Burgundians, schooled in chivalry, encounter the Saxons with their culturally and technologically inferior masses" (p. 36).

17. Pérennec (1975), p. 13, has pointed to the omnipresence of the agonal, and to the absence (better, perhaps, the quick crossing) of the boundaries between game and real violence.

18. See *Wigalois* 10183: *hie enist niht âventiure* [this is not adventure], when a feud with a large military contingent takes the place of adventurous accomplishments in a chivalric duel.

19. Seitter (1995), pp. 152–53, points out that this is the only war in the *Nibelungenlied.*

20. *Spil* is life-threatening: 432,2; 433,1; 467,4; 471,1.

21. *Spil* causes real dread: 425, 430, 441–45, 450.

22. Seitter (1995), p. 155.

23. According to Ro A. On the focus of terms like *übermuot, hôchvart,* etc. in this text, see pp. 216–21 above.

24. Heinzle (1978) thinks that it is not the challenge itself but its insulting exaggeration by Kriemhilt that is worthy of criticism and thus punished (pp. 247–52). In *Rosengarten,* this is the only form of challenge, and it is not the form that is criticized, but rather the event itself.

25. The entire vocabulary of *Rosengarten* corresponds to heroic self-appraisal, starting with the *stolzen Nibelunge* (Ro A 177,3). This is "wrong," because a woman's *hochvârt* is behind it; see p. 170 above.

26. Comical aspects include the refusal of Eckehart or Hiltebrant to accept the reward, the queen's kiss, or Kriemhilt's punishment of having to kiss the scratchy, bearded Ilsan (Ro A 376; on the parodistic character, see Heinzle, 1978, p. 254), or the bloodied monks on whose heads Ilsan presses rosebush wreaths; and perhaps so, too, is Dietrich's refusal to take over the last fight with Sivrit: *ir vehtet niht vor*

vrouwen, dâ man prîs bejagen sol [you do not fight in front of women, from whom the prize should be won] (Ro A 341,4) or his scuffle with Hiltebrant.

27. See *morden* (Ro A 19,2). The tournament inspires violence and counter-violence (*rechen,* Ro A 205,2) and is introduced like a feud (Ro A 314,4).

28. That *Biterolf* is conceived of as an "answer" is demonstrated in the fact that it reverses the movement of the *Nibenlungenlied:* from Etzel to the Rhine. As in the Nibelungenlied, the solstice is the time of the confrontation (Bit 4667, 5022), but with the opposite result.

29. Only the widow of the only important victim, the duke of *Püllelant,* condemns the invitation as treacherous (Bit 9388–89).

30. See Curschmann (1978), pp. 86–87.

31. Contrary to what Jaeger thinks (1983), p. 195, it seems to me that courtly *minne* is not negatively tinged.

32. Over and over it is said that one serves *schœnen wîben* (599,3; 710,4; 792,2; 1310; 1315; and elsewhere).

33. G. Müller (1975), pp. 97, 102.

34. On the background of the training that also ennobles the falconer, see Wapnewski (1979), pp. 41–42.

35. On the differences that are covered up by this terminology, see Achauer (1967), pp. 108ff.

36. See 51,3; 53,4; on these concepts, see pp. 216–21 above.

37. This is how Walther von der Vogelweide can delineate his *minne* concept from ideas of status (cf. Walther von der Vogelweide, *Gedichte,* Lachmann and Kuhn, 74,20 and elsewhere).

38. This corresponds again to the spiritual criticism of courtliness, which is directed against courtly love. See Jaeger (1983), p. 191.

39. On the courtly misinterpretation of the journey, see Newman (1981), p. 72. The concern for rich clothing corresponds, of course, to the image of the court as a place of grandeur (cf. pp. 378–79 above).

40. On the fraternal character of the Nibelungian world, see Bennewitz (1995), pp. 46–47.

41. See Heinzle (1978), pp. 241–42.

42. "Virginal," ed. von der Hagen and Primisser (1825), str. 125–28.

43. Heinzle (1978), pp. 247–59; principally p. 267, where Heinzle speaks of the "immanent tension between heroic literature and the courtly romance." This is especially true of *Rosengarten* A. In other versions, the criticism of *Frauendienst* is blurred. The prologue in Ro D *2-*7, for example, attempts to integrate *Frauendienst* and heroic combat. The challenge to Dietrich's heroes to fight in a tournament comes from a man, King Gibeche (Ro D 13; 18), as well as from a woman, Kriemhilt (Ro D 23ff.). Here, the conflict that A recounts can only be surmised in some circumstances and consequences of the battles (cf. a formulation like *den mort hât gebrûwen Kriemhilt* [Kriemhilt planned the murder], Ro D 604,4).

44. *Ob in daz diuht guot, / swann er bî schœnen frouwen <alsô> sitzen sollte* [whether it seemed satisfactory to him / that he should sit with beautiful women] (K 343,2–3).

45. It is called *tageliet* or *tagewîse* (K 382,4). Is this supposed to be an allusion to a dawn song, as usual in the *Tagelied* (*alba*) genre? It is in any case not a courtly performance of *minnesang.*

46. K 378,1; 378,4; 396,4; 397,4. This service of the vassal never impairs his status, unlike Sivrit's service.

47. His closeness to court is evident once again when he later guarantees the safety of the courtly suitor Hartmuot.

48. See, e.g., Walther 47,36: *Zwô fuoge hân ich doch* [I have two talents].

49. On the mix-up, see Strohschneider (1997).

50. Herein lies "Siegfried's guilt," according to Haustein (1993), who elaborates how different schemata are layered and lead to the contradictory plot constellation (pp. 382–83).

51. In *Tristrant,* there is a whole series of service relationships like this.

52. Strohschneider (1997) has interpreted the contradictory configuration of roles within the background of the bridal quest scheme.

53. On the Amazon motif, see Frakes (1994), pp. 137–69.

54. Sigemunt's and Sigelint's warnings against the *übermuot* of the Burgundians and the hopelessness of Sivrit's undertaking are not explained based on social inferiority. Where there were stories about the hero's doubtful origins, this is a conspicuous reinterpretation.

55. See 126,4; 127. On the ambiguous term *gast,* see Pérennec (1975), p. 3, and elsewhere. In *Âventiure* 3, *gast* is used in correlation with *wirt* in the sense of Latin *hospes* (cf. 105,1; 106,4), but Sivrit's behavior also corresponds to the aggressive connotations of *gast* in the sense of *hostis,* which Pérennec has worked out and that prevails when the Saxons are called *geste* or when the Burgundians are Etzel's *leide[n] geste[n].* See on the following also Müller (1974).

56. Haug (1974); id. (1989), p. 299; cf. 296–99.

57. Ehrismann (1981), pp. 165–66, with reference to Elias's civilization theory ([1936] 1969). Ehrismann sees the plot of the *Nibelungenlied* running between the poles "controlled/uncontrolled," whereby the "modern" control mechanisms are nullified by "archaic" modes of behavior. Ehrismann's interpretation shares elements of my own, even if his opposition, its evolutionary interpretation ("archaic" vs. "modern"), and its evaluation (cf. p. 169) seem to be in need of further discussion.

58. Haug (1974); id. (1989), p. 299.

59. To the contrary, G. Müller (1975), p. 100; only in 131,4 and 132,2 does the thought of *minne* come back to the foreground.

60. As Göhler (1989), pp. 21, 199–200, seems to believe. What makes Gunther's acquiescence a "real dependency," if it is never mentioned again?

61. Bumke (1983), p. 40.

62. Müller (1974), pp. 100–104; on the ambiguities of the service concept, see also G. Müller (1975), pp. 103–4.

63. The explicit reason for his rejection blurs the political context. The hunting birds that Prünhilt gives are supposedly of no use in the land of the Huns.

64. Bit 7112–14; 7529–31; 7534–38.

65. *Dissimulatio* is primarily thematized under rhetorical aspects in the *Historisches Wörterbuch der Rhetorik*, ed. Gert Ueding et al. (Tübingen, 1992–), vol. 2 (1994), cols. 886–88 (N. Népote-Desmares, T. Tröger).

66. Bachorski (1996), p. 3.

67. On the discussion in scholarship, see Bernreuther (1994), pp. 40–42. Unlike von See ([1958–59] 1981), 214–23, I take the words with which Kriemhilt opens the dispute not as "a claim to political rule" (p. 171). I also do not see in them, as in the following scene, "traces of arrogance" that connect the Kriemhilt of the *Nibelungenlied* with that of *Rosengarten* (Heinzle, 1978, pp. 252–53). The *Rosengarten* epic can at most be seen as a radicalizing interpretation of this scene.

68. C 821–22 makes Prünhilt guilty of escalation by making it clear that she was intent all along on provoking Kriemhilt and insisting on her claim.

69. Haug (1974); id. (1989), p. 300.

70. See de Boor's Commentary, in *Das Nibelungenlied*[15], p. 275.

71. See pp. 364–65 above,

72. Haug (1974); id. (1989), p. 302.

73. Haug (1974); id. (1989), p. 302.Courtly order is the determining factor for Haug, from an *ex post* perspective. I am skeptical in regard to the epic (cf. also Haug in the following on Hagen).

74. On this gesture, see G. Müller (1975), pp. 114–15. These verses seem to me to be neither mocking nor critical of Sivrit (Jaeger 1983, p. 195). A typical mechanism in the courtly code of behavior is uncovered. The mention of Sivrit's *tugende* is explicit.

75. Jaeger (1983), pp. 193–94.

76. This formulation is a conjecture supported by *Parzival* 420,29. It is not necessarily required. Ms. a has: *ich wolde ew ain speizze den vollen immer geben sieden in öl geprawen* (on a possible meaning, see Bumke 1996c, p. 575; cf. his translation according to Schröder 1989, who puts a period after *geben,* and a comma after *öl:* "cooking in oil, brewing; this is Rumolt's advice"). In any case, Rumolt confirms his advice with the prospect of a good meal. In this way, the advice is depicted as in a caricature in *C, although in ms. B, it is already discredited by *Frauendienst,* food, and *gemach* (contra Schröder 1989, p. 27).

77. It becomes perfectly clear with Pa 421,6. Schröder (1989), p. 28, sees in this passage a Wolfram-type joke in the denigration of Rumolt, which he thinks "uncharacteristic of the epic narrator." It seems to me on the contrary that the disdain of the easy life is already obvious in the *Nibelungenlied.* On the mockery of Rumolt, see also Bumke (1996c), pp. 578–79.

78. Wachinger (1981), p. 96, questions whether Rumolt's advice isn't a kind

of "skit" that was expected with the Nibelungian material. In this case, problems of dating the *C-version of the *Nibelungenlied* in relation to Wolfram's *Parzival* would be easier to solve.

79. The denigration of *gemach* is also known to courtly romances (*Erec, Iwein*), which are concerned about the proper relationship between competing demands. As one of the *bona corporis, gemach* is by no means just negative. It is the third of four goods of happiness, ahead of property (*guot*) in Ulrich von Liechtenstein's *Frauendienst.* It is only in the explication of the goods where *gemach* is criticized as the goal of those who are *swîn gemuot* [swinishly minded]. The other goods are criticized as well, with the exception only of *gotes hulde* (ed. Bechstein, 1829–34). Noble living only succumbs to criticism when compared to religious considerations.

80. Sivrit's first appearance at Gunther's court—*hêrlîche* (AB 82,4)—is called *zvhtekliche* in C 82 (also in mss. Db).

81. The threefold challenge to and insult of Kriemhilt has been examined by Wynn (1965), p. 112. The aggression is aimed at the queen, the relative and the wife of Sivrit, when Hagen presents her with Sivrit's sword. On the war of glances, cf. pp. 274–75 above.

82. C 1821 completes the courtly vocabulary: *an zvhten* (Batts, p. 540).

83. The mighty Morolt is characterized in *Tristrant* by a similar canon of virtues (Trt 841).

84. The formulation in de Boor's edition follows that in ms. d; in ms. B, titles are lacking; the title in ms. A is corrupted; in the other manuscripts the emphasis is: the alliance between Hagen and Volker (mss. Jh); Kriemhilt's appearance with an army (ms. D); the collective sitting in front of Kriemhilt's *sal* (mss. Ca); the accusation of murder (ms. b) (according to Batts, p. 535).

85. See Wh 144,2–3: in Monleun, masses of dewy roses (*touwec rôsen*) are strewn on the floor. Expressly on this motif, see Schwab (1992), pp. 189–200, who mainly emphasizes religious connotations, however.

86. The four-year old Wolfdietrich, for example, proves himself as a future hero, and even avoids death, by not grasping for roses, as one would expect of a child (Wo A 93,2–3; 208,3).

87. Unlike Seitter (1987), p. 41, I above all see in this an act of defamation. Courtiers are not real men!

88. Jaeger (1983), pp. 180–84, 190, 192, and 193 (on the Hunnish servant to ladies).

89. "The Hun appears as a modern *Frauendiener.* But the elegance of the Hunnish land is also barbaric; it lacks the assurance of good taste, of *mâze*" (de Boor, p. 296). How nice that the bloody Volker is distinguished by a fashionable *savoir*!

90. In C 959,1, *weigerlich* replaces the epithet *herlich* in A 892 and B 948 (in the edition 951); it is positively crafted for Sivrit's appearance.

91. On the meal as a ritual act, see *Handwörterbuch zur deutschen Rechtsgeschichte* 3, pp. 154–56 (S. Kramer); Leyser (1993), pp. 13–16; Hauck (1950); Oexle (1984), pp. 401–2; Hannig (1986), p. 153; Althoff (1987, 1991a).

92. It seems to me that Rumolt's achievements in the *Nibelungenlied* up to the departure to Etzel's court are in no way ironically portrayed as an "overlordship over an army of pots, pans, and cauldrons" (Jaeger 1983, p. 194). The evidence for such an appraisal, strophe 777, expresses approval of the splendid festival that Gunther organizes to honor his relatives and to which Rumolt contributes. Schröder (1989), pp. 27–28, concludes that only Wolfram makes Rumolt a comical character (Pa 206,28ff.), and that evaluations of him in the *Nibelungenlied are* wholly positive. This does not seem to me to exclude the criticism of Rumolt at the departure for Etzel's court (see notes 76 and 77 above).

93. On the affinity of kitchen and statecraft, see Deleuze and Guattari ([1980] 1992), p. 556.

94. The disruption of the meal is an especially well-liked joke in descriptions of battle. In the *Huge Scheppel,* the late epic adaptation of Elisabeth von Nassau-Saarbrücken, a decapitated head lands on a serving plate. On "kitchen humor" in Latin literature, see Curtius (1948), pp. 431–34.

95. Orgies of overeating are latently always full of potential conflict.

96. See pp. 154; 292–93 above.

97. See 964,3; 970,4; 971,4.

98. Schwab (1990), p. 63.

99. The edition places a period here. It seems to me that the conditional in 964,3 refers to the preceding as well as to the following verse. I therefore use a comma.

100. Althoff (1993); id., (1997), p. 243.

101. See Ulrich v. d. Türlin, *Willehalm* 103,5, and the citations in Grimm ([1889] 1957), pp. 162, 165, 172, 289.; cf. 2119,4: *übel hôchzît.*

102. The scene goes beyond the ritual "spilling of wine," which Schwab (1990), p. 75, has made the likely background of the reference.

103. Hagen also occasionally performs the duties of chamberlain. His chamberlain role is latently linked to violence, too, for example, in the theft of the hoard (1132; Seitter 1987, p. 138; Schwab, 1990, p. 75).

104. Schwab (1990), pp. 77–83, 86–87, 91–93.

105. In B 1958,3, however, Ortlieb's head lands in the king's lap, not the queen's; on this situational topos, see n. 94 above.

106. As in HvK; see Chapter 1, n. 76, above.

107. The epic seems to reject the supposition that the minstrels were originally in on the plot, as Wailes, 1982, pp. 268–69, believes.

108. Ms. C has *von strite*; ms. b, *von waffen.*

109. Similarly, Hansen (1990), p. 115.

110. On this tradition in heroic poetry, see Schwab (1991).

111. Schwab (1990), p. 97; id. (1992), pp. 200ff.

112. Cf. *des tages wart in sturme vil manec bluotige hant* [there was many a bloody hand in the battle that day] (199,4); *die lascten ime strîte vil maneges helmen schîn / mit vliezendem bluote* [they extinguished the glint of many helmets / with

streams of blood] (201,2–3); *dô sah man über sätele fliezen daz bluot* [they saw the blood streaming over the saddles] (203,3); *man mohte kiesen vliezen den bluotigen bach / durch die liehten helme von Sîvrides hant* [anyone could see the bloody streams / made from Sivrit's blows flowing through the bright helmets] (205,2–3); *man sach dâ var nâch bluote vil mangene hêrlîchen rant* [they saw there many battle shields reddened by blood] (212,4); *die truogen bluotes varwe von der Burgonden hant* [they were all made red from blood by the Burgundians' blows] (218,4); cf. 230,3; 253,2.

113. Frakes (1994), p. 121, points out that the rape scene and male and female roles are simultaneously reversed.

114. The *brunne* is mentioned at 969,2; 970,3; 976,4; 977,4; 979,1; 981,1; 983,1; and 984,3.

115. Cf. *daz bluot von sîner wunden sach man vil vaste gân* [they saw the blood from his wounds flowing swiftly] (988,2); *Die bluomen allenthalben von bluote wurden naz* [the flowers were made moist with blood] (998,1); *Er sah in bluotes rôten, sîn wât was elliu naz* [he saw him red with blood, his clothing was completely soaked] (1006,1); Kriemhilt's reaction: *daz bluot ir ûz dem munde von herzen jâmer brast* [blood burst from her mouth as her heart broke] (1010,2); she lifts Sivrit's head: *swie rôt ez was von bluote* [it was all red with blood] (1011,3); on the connection between fountain water and blood, see Schwab (1992), pp. 214, 234.

116. Taken up in 1955,1 and 1956,1.

117. As the ritual was meant to be: Schwab (1990), p. 75.

118. Parallels in Schwab (1990), pp. 73–74. There is more to this than just a practical measure for protection against a sneak attack by Kriemhilt.

119. Schwab is able to show examples of *minne* drinking in its material context from the monastic sector, but hardly (and much less specifically) from the lay sector. If the narrator consciously referred to the religious model, then it becomes a "sarcastic joke." Any analogy between Christian saints and the quasi "martyred, innocently murdered *minne* hero Siegfried" is redundant (p. 93), because Sivrit evades such an interpretation.

120. Wilson (1960); Hoffmann (1974), p. 91. Schwab (1992), p. 210, is critical.

121. Once the fighting has started: 1938,4; 1947,1; 1951,3; 1956,1 (luckily *von ander manne wunden*); 1961,2; 2055,3; 2078,2; 2279,4; 2296,2; 2308,3; 2310,1–2.

122. 2219,3; 2284,2–3; 2288,4; 2360,2; (already 1986,4; 2020,4).

123. 1971,4; 2016,2; 2046,1; 208,2–3; 2266,3; 2283,3; 2212,3; C 2359,3–4; *schiltgesteine* [shield ornaments, gemstones] are knocked off and fall into the blood; where, in 2299,3 (according to mss. A and B), Wolfhart falls into the blood, ms. C 2358,3 states instead that Gunther and Hagen wade *in dem blvote tief unz an div knie* [in blood up to their knees].

124. In a supplemental strophe in C: *ob im wart solch gedranch, / swie gesunt er anders wære, der in dem blvot doch ertranch* [around him was such a press, / that no matter how able-bodied he was, he would still drown in blood] (C 2280,3–4; also in ms. a).

125. Hildebrant: 2308,3; 2309,3; 2310,1–2.

Chapter 9. Deconstructing the Nibelungian World

1. On the following, see Jaeger (1983).
2. Haug (1974, 1989).
3. Jaeger (1983); Jaeger (1985), pp. 192–93.
4. Jaeger (1983), p. 192.
5. Uhlig (1973), p. 60.
6. Uhlig (1973), pp. 36–37; p. 41.
7. See the motifs in Uhlig (1973), pp. 28–136.
8. Jaeger (1983), pp. 188–92.
9. Jaeger (1983), p. 192.
10. See Jaeger (1983), p. 199.
11. For example, in the depiction of the Viking campaigns in Adam von Bremen's *Gesta Hamburgensis ecclesiae Pontificum* 1.47–48, 31–33.
12. Wenzel (1974), pp. 32–54.
13. Kiesel (1979), pp. 15–16.
14. On "amorality" and "moral indifference," see Wyss (1990), pp. 172–73; Pérennec (1987), pp. 218–19.
15. Wyss (1990), p. 172.
16. Ibid., p. 173, is skeptical.
17. G. W. Weber (1990), p. 462, writes in a similar fashion about the Iring saga: "The story may lead to the fact that the Thuringians disappear from the "screen." They do not disappear from its memory, however. They live on as long as how they were destroyed is in accord with the ethical norms of the society that carries on their remembrance, and as long as this society extends this memory backwards into a prehistoric and mythical darkness."
18. Ibid., p. 463.
19. Ruh (1979), p. 23, sees in the feudal epic of the thirteenth century advocacy of a more "pragmatic," less violent heroism (cf. pp. 24–26).
20. Association of comedy with the devil: 438,4; 442,2; cf. Frakes (1994), pp. 137–69.
21. Hans Kuhn (1965); contra Frakes (1994), p. 165.
22. This kind of disdainful comedy also includes the well-known joke in ms. b that Kriemhilt hardly notices when Hildebrant's stroke cuts her in two—his sword is that sharp—and she only falls apart when she bends over (Batts, p. 723).
23. See Ruh (1979), pp. 26–27.
24. See McConnell (1978), pp. 54–55; contra Frakes (1994).
25. Stackmann on K 882,2; Lexer ([1872–78] 1979), vol. 2, cols. 1922–23.
26. Wate's appearance in battle is described with the words *zorn, zürnen, tobeheit* (K 1520–23). His opponents also literally burst into flames and gleam bloodred in their final moments.
27. Frakes (1994), pp. 187–88; pp. 207–9.

28. In the epic, Etzel still laments with a lion's voice (*als eines lewen stimme,* 2234,2).

29. Von See (1991) has most clearly worked out the initial marginality of this type of reception.

30. Deleuze and Guattari ([1980] 1992), p. 548.

31. See ibid., pp. 326–39.

32. Gernot even uses his relationship with Kriemhilt (*der sippen dîner* [!] *mâge* [from your family's kin]) at 2105,3.

33. Deleuze and Guattari ([1980] 1992) call such forcing of one's eccentricities on others the "anomalous" (pp. 333–32) and assign it to "a peripheral position that results from no longer knowing whether the anomalous one still belongs to the band, stands outside of it, or is located at the band's movable boundary" (p. 335).

34. Ibid., pp. 329–32.

35. See pp. 56–61 above.

36. These supposed remnants of an archaic Germanic religiosity were exploited by National Socialist interpretations.

37. This still in G. Weber (1963), who, in view of these dark powers, declares all human beings to be *recken.*

38. Deleuze and Guattari ([1980] 1992), p. 331; cf. the entire section.

39. It is worth remembering the boar metaphor in Gottfried's *Tristan.*

40. Udo Friedrich discusses medieval animal metaphors in *Naturgeschichte zwischen Artes liberales und frühneuzeitlicher Wissenschaft: Conrad Gessners "Historia animalium" und ihre volkssprachliche Rezeption,* Frühe Neuzeit 21 (Tübingen, 1995). They embody a conflict between—grosso modo—noble feudal and learned clerical perspectives, the one promulgating the taming of raw animal power by human intelligence, and the other celebrating this same natural force in animals.

41. The "genealogical lines of state rule" and "hierarchy" are contrapositions to the exteriority of the "war machinery"; see Deleuze and Guattari ([1980] 1992), pp. 486, 492.

42. Lukács's concept of *Perspektive* (perspective) means the hint at a continuation of the history beyond the end of the story. His example is the end of Tolstoy's *War and Peace. See* Georg Lukács, "Das Problem der Perspektive" [1956], in id., *Schriften zur Literatursoziologie,* ed. Peter Ludz (Frankfurt/M., 1985). It remains to be shown that this historical-philosophical construct is inappropriate to the *Nibelungenlied.*

43. See Müller (1987), p. 256, on the "Kriemhild novel."

44. With two exceptions, all the manuscripts link the two texts. Only in the late Middle Ages does the connection no longer seem to have been the norm.

Works Cited

The abbreviations used in citation of medieval texts are shown in brackets following the relevant entries. The following abbreviations appear with secondary sources:

AbäG	Amsterdamer Beiträge zur älteren Germanistik
ATB	Altdeutsche Textbibliothek
BLV	Bibliothek des Litterarischen Vereins in Stuttgart.
DTM	Deutsche Texte des Mittelalters
EHS	Europäische Hochschulschriften
FMSt	Frühmittelalterliche Studien
GAG	Göppinger Arbeiten zur Germanistik
GRMLA	*Grundriss der romanischen Literaturen des Mittelalters*
HZ	*Historische Zeitschrift*
IASL	*Internationales Archiv für Sozialgeschichte*
JEGP	*Journal of English and Germanic Philology*
MLR	*Modern Language Review*
PBB	Hermann Paul und Wilhelm Braune: *Beiträge zur Geschichte der deutschen Sprache und Literatur* (Tübingen and Halle editions)
WdF	Wege der Forschung
WW	*Wirkendes Wort: Deutsche Sprache und Literatur in Forschung und Lehre*
ZfdA	*Zeitschrift für deutsches Altertum und deutsche Literatur*
ZfdPh	*Zeitschrift für deutsche Philologie*
ZRG	*Zeitschrift der Savigny-Stiftung für Rechtsgeschichte, Germanistische Abteilung*

Medieval Texts

Albrecht von Kemenaten. "Goldemar." In *Dietrichs Abenteuer.* Ed. Julius Zupitza. 201–4. Berlin, 1870.

Albrecht [von Scharfenberg]. *Der Jüngere Titurel: Heidelberger Verfasserfragment.* Ed. Werner Wolf. Altdeutsche Übungstexte 14. 78–80. Bern, 1952.

Alexanderlied des Pfaffen Lamprecht (Strassburger Alexander): Text, Nacherzählung, Wörterklärungen. Ed. Irene Ruttmann. Darmstadt, 1974. [Al]

Biterolf und Dietleib." Deutsches Heldenbuch 1. 1–197. Berlin, 1866. Ed. Oskar Jänicke. Reprint, Berlin, 1963. [Bit]

Biterolf und Dietleib. Ed. André Schnyder. Sprache und Dichtung 31. Bern, 1980.

Eilhart von Oberge. Ed. Franz Lichtenstein. Quellen und Forschungen zur Sprach- und Kulturgeschichte der germanischen Völker 19. Strasbourg, 1877. [Trt]

Gottfried von Straßburg. *Tristan und Isold.* Ed. Friedrich Ranke. Berlin, 1963. [Tr]

Heinrich von Melk. Ed. Richard Heinzel. Berlin, 1867. Reprint, Hildesheim, 1983. [HvM]

Heldenbuch aus dem Sagenkreise Dietrichs von Bern und der Nibelungen. Ed. Friedrich Heinrich von der Hagen. 2 vols. Leipzig, 1855. Contains "Heldenbuchprosa," vol. 1. cix–cxxvi.

Heldenbuch nach dem ältesten Druck in Abbildung. Ed. Joachim Heinzle. Litterae: Göppinger Beiträge zur Textgeschichte, 75. 2 vols. Göppingen, 1987.

Herbort's von Fritslâr liet von Troye. Ed. Ge. Karl Frommann. Bibl. d. gesammten dt. National-Literatur 5. Leipzig, 1837. [LvTr]

Untersuchung und überlieferungskritische Edition des Herzog Ernst B mit einem Abdruck der Fragmente von Fassung A. Ed. Cornelia Weber. GAG 616. Göppingen, 1994. [HE]

Der Huge Scheppel: Nach der Handschrift der Hamburger Staatsbibliothek. Mit einer Einleitung von Hermann Urtel. Ed. Elisabeth von Nassau-Saarbrücken. Hamburg, 1905.

Diu Klage: Mit den Lesarten sämtlicher Handschriften. Ed. Karl Bartsch. Leipzig, 1875. [Kl]

*Div Klage: Kritische Ausgabe der Bearbeitung *C.* Ed. Brigitte Ranft. Diss. Marburg, 1971.

Konrad von Würzburg. *Engelhard.* Ed. Paul Gereke. ATB 17. Halle, 1912.

———. "Heinrich von Kempten." In *Kleinere Dichtungen Konrads von Würzburg.* Ed. Edward Schröder. 41–68. Berlin, 1924. [HvK]

Kudrun. Ed. Karl Bartsch and Karl Stackmann. Deutsche Klassiker des Mittelalters. Wiesbaden, 1980. [K]

Lancelot. Ed. Reinhold Kluge. 3 vols. DTM 42, 47, 63. Berlin, 1948, 1963, 1974. [Lc]

"Laurin und Walberan mit Benutzung der von Franz Roth gesammelten Abschriften und Vergleichungen." Ed. Oskar Jänicke. In *Deutsches Heldenbuch* 1. 201–57. Berlin, 1866.[La]

Map, Walter. *De nugis curialium (Courtiers' Trifles).* Ed. and trans. M. R. James, revised by C. N. L. Brooke and R. A. B. Mynors. Oxford Medieval Texts. Oxford, 1983.

Des Minnesangs Frühling. Ed. Hugo Moser and Helmuth Tervooren. Stuttgart, 1977–82. [MF]

Morant und Galie. Ed. Theodor Frings and Elisabeth Linke. DTM 69. Berlin, 1976. [MuG]

Der Nibelunge Noth und die Klage[5]. Ed. Karl Lachmann. 1878. Reprint, Hamburg, 1948.
Das Nibelungenlied[15]. Ed. Karl Bartsch and Helmut de Boor. Deutsche Klassiker des Mittelalters. Wiesbaden, 1959.
Das Nibelungenlied: Paralleldruck der Handschriften A, B und C nebst Lesarten der übrigen Handschriften. Ed. Michael S. Batts. Tübingen, 1971. [Batts]
Das Nibelungenlied nach der Piaristenhandschrift. Ed. Adelbert von Keller. BLV 142. Stuttgart, 1979. [k]
Das Nibelungenlied. Ed. Siegfried Grosse. Stuttgart, 1997.
Orendel. Ed. Hans Steinger. ATB 36. Halle, 1935. [Or]
"Ortnit." In *Ortnit und die Wolfdietriche.* Ed. Arthur Amelung and Oskar Jänicke. Vol. 1. Deutsches Heldenbuch 3. 1–77. Berlin, 1871, 1873. Reprint. Hildesheim, 2004.
Ortnit und Wolfdietrich nach der Wiener Piaristenhandschrift. Ed. Justus Lunzer. BLV 239. Tübingen, 1908. [Wo D]
Der Münchner Oswald mit einem Anhang: Die ostschwäbische Prosabearbeitung des 15. Jhs. Ed. Michael Curschmann. ATB 76. Tübingen, 1974.
Das Rolandslied des Pfaffen Konrad[2]. Ed. Carl Wesle and Peter Wapnewski. ATB 69. Tübingen, 1967. [Rl]
Die Gedichte vom Rosengarten zu Worms. Ed. Georg Holz. Halle, 1893. [Ro]
Rother[2]. Ed. Jan de Vries. Germanische Bibliothek 2.13. Heidelberg, 1974. [KR]
Rudolf von Ems. *Willehalm von Orlens.* Ed. Victor Junk. DTM 2. Berlin, 1905. [WvO]
Der Sachsenspiegel: Land- und Lehnrecht. 1933. Ed. Karl August Eckhardt. MGH Nova series 1. Hannover. Reprinted in 2 vols., 1989, 1995.
Salman und Morolf. Ed. Alfred Karnein. ATB 85. Tübingen, 1979. [SuM]
Thidrikssaga af Bern. Ed. Henrik Bertelsen. 2 vols. Copenhagen, 1908–11.
Die Geschichte Thidreks von Bern. Ed. Fine Erichsen. Thule 22. Darmstadt, 1967.
Ulrich von Etzenbach. *Alexander.* Ed. Wendelin Toischer. BLV 183. Tübingen, 1888.
Ulrich von Lichtenstein. *Frauendienst.* Ed. Reinhold Bechstein. Leipzig, 1888.
"Virginal." Deutsches Heldenbuch 5. 1–200. Berlin, 1870. Reprint. Hildesheim, 2004. [Vi]
"Virginal." Ed. Friedrich Heinrich von der Hagen and Alois Primisser. In *Der Helden Buch in der Ursprache* 2. 143–59. Berlin, 1825.
Walther von der Vogelweide. *Die Gedichte*[13]. Ed. Karl Lachmann and Hugo Kuhn. Berlin, 1965.
Wigamur. Ed. Danielle Buschinger. GAG 320. Göppingen, 1987.
Wolfdietrich, vol. 1: *Der echte Teil des Wolfdietrich der Ambraser Handschrift (Wolfdietrich A).* Ed. Hermann Schneider. ATB 28. Halle, 1931. [Wo A]
Wolfram von Eschenbach. *Parzival*[6]. Ed. Karl Lachmann.11–388. Berlin, 1926. Reprint, 1965. [Pa]
———. *Willehalm*[6]. Ed. Karl Lachmann. 421–640. Berlin, 1926. Reprint, 1965. [Wh]

Works Cited

Secondary Literature

Abeling, Theodor. 1907. *Das Nibelungenlied und seine Literatur: Eine Bibliographie und vier Abhandlungen.* Leipzig.

Achauer, Heinz. 1967. *Minne im Nibelungenlied.* Munich.

Adelsherrschaft und Literatur. 1980. Ed. Horst Wenzel. Bern.

Adler, Alfred. 1975. *Epische Spekulanten: Versuch einer synchronen Geschichte des altfranzösischen Epos.* Munich.

Althoff, Gerd. 1987. "Der frieden-, bündnis- und gemeinschaftstiftende Charakter des Mahles im früheren Mittelalter." *Essen und Trinken in Mittelalter und Neuzeit.* Ed. Irmgard Bitsch. 13–26. Sigmaringen.

———. 1989. "Königsherrschaft und Konfliktbewältigung im 10. und 11. Jahrhundert." *FMSt* 23: 265–90.

———. 1990a. "Colloquium familiare, colloquium secretum, colloquium publicum: Beratung im politischen Leben des früheren Mittelalters." *FMSt* 24: 145–67.

———. 1990b. *Verwandte, Freunde und Getreue: Zum politischen Stellenwert der Gruppenbildungen im früheren Mittelalter.* Darmstadt.

———. 1991a. "Fest und Bündnis." *Feste und Feiern* (1991): 29–38.

———. 1991b. "Huld: Überlegungen zu einem Zentralbegriff der mittelalterlichen Herrschaftsordnung." *FMSt* 25 (1991): 259–82.

———. 1992. "Konfliktverhalten und Rechtsbewußtsein: Die Welfen im 12. Jahrhundert." *FMSt* 26: 331–52.

———. 1993. "Demonstration und Inszenierung: Spielregeln der Kommunikation in mittelalterlicher Öffentlichkeit." *FMSt* 27: 27–50.

———. 1994. "Genugtuung (satisfactio): Zur Eigenart gütlicher Konfliktbeilegung im Mittelalter." In *Modernes Mittelalter: Neue Bilder einer populären Epoche.* Ed. Joachim Heinzle. 247–65. Frankfurt.

———. 1996. "Empörung, Tränen, Zerknirschung: Emotionen in der öffentlichen Kommunikation des Mittelalters." *FMSt* 30: 60–79.

———. 1997. *Spielregeln der Politik im Mittelalter: Kommunikation in Frieden und Fehde.* Darmstadt.

Anderson, Philip N. 1985. "Kriemhild's Quest." *Euphorion* 78: 3–12.

Andersson, Theodore. 1978. "Why Does Siegfried Die?" In *Germanic Studies in Honor of Otto Springer.* Ed. Stephen J. Kaplowitt. 29–39. Pittsburgh.

———. 1980. *The Legend of Brynhild.* Ithaca, N.Y.

———. 1986. "Beyond Epic and Romance. Sigurðarquiða in meiri." In *Sagnashemmtun: Studies in Honour of Hermann Pálsson.* Ed. Rudolf Simek. 1–11. Vienna.

———. 1987. *A Preface to the Nibelungenlied.* Stanford.

Assmann, Aleida. 1995. "Was sind kulturelle Texte?" In *LiterturkanonñMedienereignisñkultureller Text: Formen interkultureller Kommunikation und Übersetzung.* Ed. Andreas Poltermann. 232–44. Berlin.

Bachmann-Medick, Doris. 1992. "Writing Culture: Ein Diskurs zwischen Ethnologie und Literaturwissenschaft." *Kea. Zeitschrift für Kulturwissenschaften* 4: 1–20.

Bachorski, Hans-Jürgen. N.d. [?]. "Kriemhilt verschenkt Sifrits Leben: Habitus und Kalkül im 'Nibelungenlied.' Ms.

Bäuml, Franz H. 1968. "Der Übergang mündlicher zur artes-bestimmten Literatur des Mittelalters: Gedanken und Bedenken." In *Fachliteratur des Mittelalters.* Ed. Gundolf Keil. 1–10. Stuttgart.

———. 1978. "Medieval Literacy and Illiteracy: An Essay Toward the Construction of a Model." In *Germanic Studies in Honor of Otto Springer.* Ed. Stephen J. Kaplowitt. 41–54. Pittsburgh.

———. 1980. "Varieties and Consequences of Medieval Literacy and Illiteracy." *Speculum* 55: 237–65.

———. 1981. "Zum Verständnis mittelalterlicher Mitteilungen." In *Hohenemser Studien zum Nibelungenlied: Unter Mitarbeit von Irmtraud Albrecht.* Ed. Achim Masser. 237–65. Dornbirn.

———. 1984–85. "Medieval Texts and the Two Theories of Oral-Formulaic Composition: A Proposal for a Third Theory." *New Literary History* 16: 31–49.

———. 1986. "The Oral Tradition and Middle High German Literature." *Oral Tradition* 1: 398–445.

Beck, Heinrich. 1990. "Eddaliedforschung heute: Bemerkungen zur Heldenlied-Diskussion." In *Helden und Heldensage: Otto Gschwantler zum 60. Geburtstag.* Ed. Hermann Reichert and Günter Zimmermann. Philologica Germanica 11. 1–23. Vienna.

Bender, Karl-Heinz. 1967. *König und Vasall: Untersuchungen zur Chanson de geste des XII. Jahrhunderts.* Heidelberg.

Bennewitz, Ingrid. 1995. "Das Nibelungenlied-ein 'Puech von Chrimhilt?': Ein geschlechtergeschichtlicher Versuch zum 'Nibelungenlied' und seiner Rezeption." In *3. Pöchlarner Heldenliedgespräch: Die Rezeption des Nibelungenliedes.* Ed. Klaus Zatloukal. Philologica Germanica 16. 33–52. Vienna.

Berges, Wilhelm. [1938] 1952. *Die Fürstenspiegel des hohen und späten Mittelalters.* Stuttgart.

Bernreuther, Marie-Luise. 1994. *Motivationsstruktur und Erzählstrategie im "Nibelungenlied" und in der "Klage."* Greifswald.

Bertau, Karl. 1983. *Wolfram von Eschenbach: Neun Versuche über Subjektivität und Ursprünglichkeit in der Geschichte.* Munich.

Beyschlag, Siegfried. [1952] 1961. "Das Motiv der Macht bei Siegfrieds Tod." Reprinted in *Zur germanisch-deutschen Heldensage: Sechzehn Aufsätze zum neuen Forschungsstand.* Ed. Karl Hauck. WdF 14. 195–213. Darmstadt.

———. 1957–58. "Überlieferung und Neuschöpfung: Erörtert an der Nibelungendichtung." *WW* 8: 205–18.

Birkhan, Helmut. 1977. "Zur Enstehung und Absicht des Nibelungenliedes." In *Österreichische Literatur zur Zeit der Babenberger: Vorträge der Lilienfelder Tagung 1976.* Ed. Alfred Ebenbauer et al. 1–24. Vienna.

Bischoff, Karl. 1970. *Die 14. Aventiure des Nibelungenliedes: Zur Frage des Dichters und der dichterischen Gestaltung.* Akademie der Wissenschaften und der Literatur: Abhandlungen der Geistes- und Sozialwissenschaftlichen Klasse 9. Mainz.

Bloch, Howard R. 1983. *Etymologies and Genealogies: A Literary Anthropology of the French Middle Ages.* Chicago.

———. 1986. "Genealogy as a Medieval Mental Structure and Textual Form." *La littérature historiographique des origines à 1500.* Ed. Hans Ulrich Gumbrecht, Ursula Link-Heer, and Peter-Michael Spangenberg. 135–56. Heidelberg.

Bloomfield, Morton W. 1975. "The Problem of the Hero in the Later Middle Ages." In *Concepts of the Hero in the Middle Ages and the Renaissance.* Ed. Norman T. Burns and Christopher J. Reagan. 27–48. Albany, N.Y.

Blumenberg, Hans. 1979. *Arbeit am Mythos.* Frankfurt.

De Boor, Helmut. 1959. "Die Bearbeitung m des Nibelungenliedes." *PBB* 81: 343–64.

Bosl, Karl. 1963. *Potens und Pauper: Begriffsgeschichtliche Studien zur gesellschaftlichen Differenzierung im frühen Mittelalter und zum "Pauperismus" des Hochmittelalters.* Göttingen.

Bostock, J. K. 1960. "The Message of the 'Nibelungenlied.'" *MLR* 55: 200–212.

Brackert, Helmut. 1963. *Beiträge zur Handschriftenkritik des Nibelungenliedes.* Berlin.

———. 1971. "Nibelungenlied und Nationalgedanke: Zur Geschichte einer deutschen Ideologie." *Mediævalia litteraria.* Ed. Ursula Hennig and Herbert Kolb. 343–64. Munich.

Braune, Wilhelm. 1900. "Die handschriftenverhältnisse des Nibelungenliedes." *PBB* 25: 1–222.

Brüggen, Elke. 1989. *Kleidung und Mode in der höfischen Epik des 12. und 13. Jhs.* Heidelberg.

Brunner, Karl. 1990. "Ein 'Land' den 'Nibelungen.'" In *Helden und Heldensage: Otto Gschwantler zum 60. Geburtstag.* Ed. Hermann Reichert and Günter Zimmermann. Philologica Germanica 11. 45–56. Vienna.

Bumke, Joachim. 1958. "Sigfrids Fahrt ins Nibelungenland: Zur achten Aventiure des Nibelungenliedes." *PBB* 80: 253–68.

———. 1960. "Die Quellen der Brünhildfabel im 'Nibelungenlied.'" *Euphorion* 54: 1–38.

———. 1983. "Liebe und Ehebruch in der höfischen Gesellschaft." In *Liebe als Literatur: Aufsätze zur erotischen Dichtung in Deutschland.* Ed. Rüdiger Krohn. 25–45. Munich.

———. 1986. *Höfische Kultur: Literatur und Gesellschaft im hohen Mittelalter.* Munich.

———. 1996a. "Der unfeste Text: Überlegungen zur Überlieferungsgeschichte und Textstruktur der höfischen Epik im 13. Jahrhundert." In Jan-Dirk Müller, ed., *"Aufführung" und "Schrift" in Mittelalter und früher Neuzeit.* DFG-Symposium 1994. 118–29. Stuttgart.

———. 1996b. "Die Erzählung vom Untergang der Burgunder in der 'Nibelungenklage': Ein Fall von variierender Überlieferung." In *Erzählungen in Erzählungen: Phänomene der Narration in Mittelalter und Früher Neuzeit.* Ed. Harald Haferland and Michael Mecklenburg. 71–83. Munich.

———. 1996c. *Die vier Fassungen der "Nibelungenklage": Untersuchungen zur Überlieferungsgeschichte und Textkritik der höfischen Epik im 13. Jahrhundert.* Berlin.

Campbell, Ian R. 1996. "Hagen's Shield Request: 'Das Nibelungenlied,' 37th *Aventiure.*" *Germanic Review* 71: 23–34.

Carruthers, Mary J. 1990. *The Book of Memory: A Study of Memory in Medieval Culture.* New York.

Cassirer, Ernst. [1925] 1997. *Philosophie der symbolischen Formen*, vol. 2: *Das mythische Denken.* Darmstadt. Translated by Ralph Manheim as *The Philosophy of Symbolic Forms* (New Haven, Conn., 1953–57), vol. 2: *Mythical Thought.*

Clanchy, Michael. 1970. *From Memory to Written Record: England, 1066–1307.* Oxford.

Classen, Albrecht. 1991. "Matriarchalische Strukturen und Apokalypse des Matriarchats im 'Nibelungenlied.'" *IASL* 16: 1–31.

Clifford, James. 1986. "On Ethnographic Allegory." In *Writing Culture: The Poetics and Politics of Ethnography.* Ed. James Clifford and George E. Marcus. 98–121. Berkeley, Calif.

———. 1988. *The Predicament of Culture: Twentieth-Century Ethnography, Literature, and Art.* Cambridge, Mass..

Colloquio italo-germanico sul tema I Nibelunghi organizzato d'intesa con la Bayerische Akademie der Wissenschaften (Roma, 14–15 maggio 1973). 1974. Atti Convegni Lincei 1. Rome.

Coxon, Stephen. 2001. *The Presentation of Authorship in Medieval German Narrative Literature, 1220–1290.* Oxford, 2001.

Curschmann, Michael. 1967. "Oral Poetry in Mediaeval English, French, and German Literature: Some Notes on Recent Research." *Speculum* 42: 36–52.

———. 1977. "The Concept of the Oral Formula as Impediment of Our Understanding of Medieval Oral Poetry." *Mediaevalia et Humanistica* 8: 63–76.

———. 1978. "Biterolf und Dietleib: A Play upon Heroic Themes." In *Germanic Studies in Honor of Otto Springer.* Ed. Stephen J. Kaplowitt. 77–91. Pittsburgh.

———. 1979. "Nibelungenlied und Nibelungenklage: Über Mündlichkeit und Schriftlichkeit im Prozeß der Episierung." In *Deutsche Literatur im Mittelalter.* 85–119. Stuttgart.

———. 1984. "The Prologue of Thidreks Saga: Thirteenth-Century Reflections on Oral Traditional Literature." *Scandinavian Studies* 56: 140–51.

———. 1985–87. "'Nibelungenlied' und 'Klage.'" In *Die deutsche Literatur des Mittelalters: Verfasserlexikon*², ed. Wolfgang Stammler et al. (Berlin, 1977–), 6, cols. 926–69.

———. 1989. "Zur Wechselwirkung von Literatur und Sage: Das 'Buch von Kriemhild' und Dietrich von Bern." *PBB* 111: 380–410.

———. 1992. "Dichter *alter maere:* Zur Prologstrophe des 'Nibelungenliedes' im Spannungsfeld von mündlicher Erzähltradition und laikaler Schriftkultur." In *Grundlagen des Verstehens mittelalterlicher Literatur: Literarische Texte und ihr historischer Erkenntniswert.* Ed. Gerhard Hahn and Hedda Rogotzky. 55–71. Stuttgart.

Curtius, Ernst Robert. 1948. *Europäische Literatur und lateinisches Mittelalter.* Bern.

Czerwinski, Peter. 1979. "Das Nibelungenlied: Widersprüche höfischer Gewaltreglementierung." In *Einführung in die deutsche Literatur des 12. bis 16. Jahrhunderts.* Ed. Winfried Frey et al. Vol. 1, Grundkurs Literaturgeschichte. 49–87. Opladen.

———. 1989. *Der Glanz der Abstraktion: Frühe Formen von Reflexivität im Mittelalter. Exempel einer Geschichte der Wahrnehmung.* Frankfurt.

Deck, Monika. 1996. *Die Nibelungenklage in der Forschung: Bericht und Kritik.* EHS, ser. 1, 1564. Frankfurt.

Deleuze, Gilles, and Félix Guattari. 1992. *Kapitalismus und Schizophrenie: Tausend Plateaus.* Trans. Gabriele Ricke and Roland Voullié. Originally published as *Mille plateaux*, vol. 2 of *Capitalisme et schizophrénie* (Paris, 1980).

Deutsche Heldenepik in Tirol: König Laurin und Dietrich von Bern in der Dichtung des Mittelalters. Beiträge der Neustifter Tagung 1977 des Südtiroler Kulturinstitutes. 1979. Ed. Egon Kühebacher. Schriftenreihe des Südtiroler Kulturinstituts 7. Bolzano.

Deutsches Rechtswörterbuch: Wörterbuch der älteren deutschen Rechtssprache. 1914–. Ed. Heidelberger Akademie der Wissenschaften. Weimar.

Dinkelacker, Wolfgang. 1990. "Nibelungendichtung außerhalb des 'Nibelungenliedes': Zum Verstehen aus der Tradition." In J*a muz ich sunder riuwe sin: Festschrift für Karl Stackmann zum 15. Februar 1990.* Ed. Wolfgang Dinkelacker, Ludger Grenzmann, and Werner Höver. 83–96. Göttingen.

Dodds, Eric Robertson. 1991. *Die Griechen und das Irrationale*². Darmstadt. Originally published as *The Greeks and the Irrational* (Berkeley, Calif., 1951, 1963).

Duggan, Joseph J. 1986. "Medieval Epic as Popular Historiography: Appropriation of Historical Knowledge in the Vernacular Epic." In *Grundriss der Romanischen Literaturen des Mittelalters, vol. 11: La Littérature historiographique des origines à 1500, 1: Partie historique*, ed. Hans Ulrich Gumbrecht, Ursula Link-Heer, and Peter-Michael Spangenberg, 285–311. Heidelberg.

Dürrenmatt, Nelly. 1945. *Das Nibelungenlied im Kreis der höfischen Dichtung.* Bern.

Ehlich, Konrad. 1989. "Zur Genese von Textformen: Prolegomena zu einer pragmatischen Texttypologie." *Textproduktion: Ein interdisziplinarer Forschungsüberblick.* Ed. Gerd Antos and Hans P. Krings. 84–99. Tübingen.

———. 1993. "Rom, Reformation, Restauration: Transformationen von Mündlichkeit und Schriftlichkeit im Übergang vom Mittelalter zur Neuzeit." *Homo scribens: Perspektiven der Schriflichkeitsforschung.* Ed. Jürgen Baurmann et al. 177–215. Tübingen.

———. 1994. "Funktion und Struktur schriftlicher Kommunikation." In *Schrift und Schriftlichkeit; Writing and Its Use: Ein interdisziplinäres Handbuch internationaler Forschung; An Interdisciplinary Handbook of International Research.* Ed. Hartmut Günther and Otto Ludwig. 18–41. Berlin.

Ehrismann, Otfrid.1975. *Das Nibelungenlied in Deutschland: Studien zur Rezeption des Nibelungenlieds von der Mitte des 18. Jhs. bis zum Ersten Weltkrieg.* Munich.

———. 1981. "Archaisches und Modernes im Nibelungelied: Pathos und Abwehr." In *Hohenemser Studien zum Nibelungenlied: Unter Mitarbeit von Irmtraud Albrecht.* Ed. Achim Masser. 164–74. Dornbirn.

———. 1987. *Nibelungenlied: Epoche, Werk, Wirkung.* Münchner Germanistische Beiträge 14. Munich.

———. 1991. "Der Fremde am Hof: Brünhild und die Philosphie der Geschichte." In *Begegnung mit dem "Fremden": Grenzen, Traditionen, Vergleiche.* Ed. Eijirô Iwasaki. Vol. 10. Akten des 8. Internationalen Germanisten-Kongresses Tokyo 1990. 320–31. Munich.

———. 1995. *Ehre und Mut, Aventiure und Minne: Höfische Wortgeschichten aus dem Mittelalter.* Munich.

Eifler, Günter. 1989. "Siegfried zwischen Xanten und Worms." In *Sprache, Literatur, Kultur: Studien zu ihrer Geschichte im deutschen Süden und Westen: Wolfgang Kleiber zu seinem 60. Geburtstag gewidmet.* Ed. Albrecht Greule and Uwe Ruberg. 277–90. Stuttgart.

Elias, Norbert. 1969. *Über den Prozeß der Zivilisation: Soziogenetische und psychogenetische Untersuchungen.* Bern.

Ertzdorff, Xenja von. 1972. "Linhart Scheubels Heldenbuch." In *Festschrift für Siegfried Gutenbrunner: zum 65. Geburtstag am 26. Mai 1971.* Ed. Oscar Bandle, Heinz Klingenberg, and Friedrich Maurer. 33–46. Heidelberg.

Erzählungen in Erzählungen: Phänomene der Narration in Mittelalter und Früher Neuzeit. 1996. Ed. Harald Haferland and Michael Mecklenburg. Munich.

Falk, Walter. 1974. *Das Nibelungenlied in seiner Epoche: Revision eines romantischen Mythos.* Heidelberg.

Feste und Feiern im Mittelalter: Paderborner Symposion des Mediävistenverbandes. 1991. Ed. Detlef Altenburg, Jörg Jarnut, and Hans-Hugo Steinhoff. Sigmaringen.

Fichte, Joerg O. 1991. "Das Fest als Testsituation in der mittelenglischen Artusromanze." In *Feste und Feiern im Mittelalter: Paderborner Symposion des Mediävistenverbandes.* Ed. Detlef Altenburg, Jörg Jarnut, and Hans-Hugo Steinhoff. 449–59. Sigmaringen.

Fischer, Hubertus, and Paul-Gerhard Völker. 1975. "Konrad von Würzburg 'Heinrich von Kempten': Individuum und feudale Anarchie." In *Literatur im Feudalismus.* Ed. Dieter Richter. Literatur-und Sozialwissenschaften 5. 83–130. Stuttgart.

Fleckenstein, Josef, ed. 1990. *Curialitas: Studien zu Grundfragen der höfisch-ritterlichen Kultur.* Göttingen.

Flood, John L. 1994. "The Severed Heads: On the Deaths of Gunther and Hagen." In *German Narrative Literature of the Twelfth and Thirteenth Centuries: Studies Presented to Roy Wisbey on His Sixty-fifth Birthday.* Ed. Volker Honemann et al. 173–91. Tübingen.

Foley, John Miles. 1991. "Orality, Textuality, and Interpretation." In *Vox intexta: Orality and Textuality in the Middle Ages.* Ed. A. N. Doane and Carol Braun Pasternack. 34–45. Madison, Wisc. *Formaler Mythos: Beiträge zu einer Theorie ästhetischer Formen. 1996.* Ed. Matias Martinez. Paderborn.

Frakes, Jerold C. 1984. "Kriemhild's Three Dreams: A Structural Interpretation." *ZfdA* 113: 173–87.

———. 1994. *Brides and Doom: Gender, Property, and Power in Medieval German Women's Epic.* Middle Ages Series. Philadelphia.

Fromm, Hans. 1974. "Der oder die Dichter des Nibelungenliedes." *Colloquio*: 63–74.

———. 1990. "Das Nibelungenlied und seine literarische Umwelt." In *Pöchlarner Heldenliedgespräch: Das Nibelungenlied und der mittlere Donauraum.* Ed. Klaus Zatloukal. Philologica Germanica 12. 3–19. Vienna.

Frühneuhochdeutsches Wörterbuch. 1986–. Ed. Robert R. Anderson, Ulrich Goebel, and Oskar Reichmann. Berlin.

Ganshof, François Louis. [1957] 1967. *Was ist das Lehnswesen?* Darmstadt. Trans. Ruth and Dieter Groh. Originally published as *Qu'est-ce que la féodalité?* (Brussels, 1944). Trans. Philip Grierson as *Feudalism* (New York, 1952).

Ganz, Peter. 1977. "Der Begriff des 'Höfischen' bei den Germanisten." *Wolfram-Studien* 4: 16–32.

———. "Curialis/hövesch." 1986. In *Höfische Literatur, Hofgesellschaft, höfische Lebensformen um 1200: Kolloquium am Zentrum für Interdisziplinäre Forschung der Universität Bielefeld (3. bis 5. November 1983).* Ed. Gert Kaiser and Jan-Dirk Müller. Studia humaniora 6. 39–56. Düsseldorf.

Geertz, Clifford. 1973. "Thick Description: Toward an Interpretive Theory of Culture." In id., *The Interpretation of Culture.* 3–30. New York.

Genette, Gérard. 1982. *Palimpsestes: La littérature au second degré.* Paris. Trans. Channa Newman and Claude Doubinsky as *Palimpsests: Literature in the Second Degree* (Lincoln, Neb., 1997).

Gentry, Francis G. 1975. *"Triuwe" and "vriunt" in the Nibelungenlied.* Amsterdam.

———. 1989. "*Mort* oder *Untriuwe: Nibelungenliet* und *Nibelungenôt.*" In *Ergebnisse und Aufgaben der Germanistik am Ende des 20. Jahrhunderts: Festschrift für Ludwig Erich Schmitt zum 80. Geburtstag.* Ed. Elisabeth Feldbusch. 302–16. Hildesheim.

Gephardt, Irmgard. 1994. *Geben und Nehmen im "Nibelungenlied" und in Wolframs "Parzival."* Studien zur Germanistik, Anglistik und Komparatistik 122. Bonn.

German Narrative Literature of the Twelfth and Thirteenth Centuries: Studies Presented to Roy Wisbey on His Sixty-fifth Birthday. 1994. Ed. Volker Honemann et al. Tübingen.

Germanic Studies in Honor of Otto Springer. 1978. Ed. Stephen J. Kaplowitt. Pittsburgh.

Zur germanisch-deutschen Heldensage: Sechzehn Aufsätze zum neuen Forschungsstand. 1961. Ed. Karl Hauck. WdF 14. Darmstadt.

Gillespie, George T. 1972. "'Die Klage' as a Commentary on 'Das Nibelungenlied.'" In *Probleme mittelhochdeutscher Erzählformen: Marburger Colloquium 1969.* Ed. Peter F. Ganz and Werner Schröder. 153–77. Berlin.

———. 1987. "Das Mythische und das Reale in der Zeit-und Ortsauffassung des 'Nibelungenliedes.'" In *Nibelungenlied und Klage: Sage und Geschichte, Struktur und Gattung.* Passauer Nibelungengespräche 1985. Ed. Fritz Peter Knapp. 43–60. Heidelberg.

Göhler, Peter. 1989. *Das Nibelungenlied: Erzählweise, Figuren, Weltanschauung, literaturgeschichtliches Umfeld.* Literatur und Gesellschaft. Berlin.

———. 1995. "Bemerkungen zur Überlieferung des Nibelungenliedes." In *3. Pöchlarner Heldenliedgespräch: Die Rezeption des Nibelungenliedes.* Ed. Klaus Zatloukal. Philologica Germanica 16. 67–79. Vienna.

———. 1996. "Überlegungen zur Funktion des Hortes im 'Nibelungenlied.'" *Hansische Literaturbeziehungen: Das Beispiel der Þidreks saga und verwandter Literatur.* Ed. Susanne Kramarz-Bein. 215–35. Berlin.

Goody, Jack, Ian Watt, and Kathleen Gough. 1997. *Entstehung und Folgen der-Schriftkultur.* Suhrkamp-Taschenbuch Wissenschaft 600. Frankfurt. Originally published as *Literacy in Traditional Societies*, ed. Jack Goody (Cambridge, 1968).

Gottzmann, Carola L. 1987. *Heldendichtung des 13. Jahrhunderts: Siegfried, Dietrich, Ortnit.* Information und Interpretation 4. Frankfurt.

Graf, Klaus. 1993a. "Heroisches Herkommen: Überlegungen zum Begriff der 'historischen Überlieferung' am Beispiel heroischer Traditionen." In *Das Bild der Welt in der Volkserzählung.* Ed. Leander Petzoldt et al. Beiträge zur europäischen Ethnologie und Folklore, ser. B, vol. 4. 45–64. Frankfurt.

———. 1993b. "Literatur als adelige Hausüberlieferung?" In *Literarische Interessenbildung im Mittelalter.* Ed. Joachim Heinzle. 126–44. Stuttgart.

Greenblatt, Stephen. 1990. *Verhandlungen mit Shakespeare: Innenansichten der englischen Renaissance.* Berlin.

Grenzler, Thomas. 1992. *Erotisierte Politik, politisierte Erotik? Die politisch-ständische Begründung der Ehe-Minne in Wolframs "Willehalm," im "Nibelungenlied" und in der "Kudrun."* Göppingen.

Grimm, Jacob. 1829. *Rechtsalterthümer.* Göttingen.

Grimm, Wilhelm. [1867] 1957. *Die deutsche Heldensage: Zweite vermehrte und verbesserte Ausgabe*[4]. Ed. Karl Müllenhoff and Oskar Jänicke. Darmstadt.

Grubmüller, Klaus. 1994. "Nibelungenlied." In *Ein Text und ein Leser: Weltliteratur für Liebhaber.* Ed. Wilfried Barner. 60–75. Göttingen.

Grünkorn, Gertrud. 1994. *Die Fiktionalitat des höfischen Romans um 1200.* Philologische Studien und Quellen 129. Berlin.

Gumbrecht, Hans Ulrich. 1972. *Funktionswandel und Rezeption: Studien zur Hyperbolik in literarischen Texten des romanischen Mittelalters.* Theorie und Geschichte der Literatur und der schönen Künste 28. Munich.

Haferland, Harald. 1989. *Höfische Interaktion: Interpretationen zur höfischen Epik und Didaktik um 1200.* Forschungen zur Geschichte der älteren dt. Literatur 10. Munich.

Das Handwörterbuch zur deutschen Rechtsgeschichte. 1964–98. Ed. Adalbert Erler and Ekkehard Kaufmann, with Wolfgang Stammler. 5 vols. Berlin.

Hannig, Jürgen. 1986. "Ars donandi: Zur Ökonomie des Schenkens im früheren Mittelalter." *Geschichte in Wissenschaft und Unterricht* 37: 149–62.

Hansen, Hilde E. 1990. *"Das ist Harnäckigkeit in einer verwerflichen Sache; sie selbst nennen es Treue": Literatursoziologische Untersuchungen zum Nibelungenlied.* EHS, ser. 1, 1195. Frankfurt.

Harms, Wolfgang. 1963. *Der Kampf mit dem Freund oder Verwandten in der deutschen Literatur bis um 1300.* Medium aevum 1. Munich.

Hattenhauer, Hans. 1963. "'Minne und recht' als Ordnungsprinzipien des mittelalterlichen Rechts." *ZRG* 80: 325–43.

Hatto, A. T. 1994. "The Secular Foe and the 'Nibelungenlied.'" In *German Narrative Literature of the Twelfth and Thirteenth Centuries: Studies Presented to Roy Wisbey on His Sixty-fifth Birthday.* Ed. Volker Honemann et al. 157–71. Tübingen.

Haubrichs, Wolfgang. 1994. "'Labor sanctorum' und 'labor heroum': Zur konsolatorischen Funktion von Legende und Heldenlied." In *Die Funktion außer- und innerliterarischer Faktoren für die Entstehung deutscher Literatur des Mittelalters und der frühen Neuzeit.* Ed. Christa Baufeld. 27–49. Göppingen.

Hauck, Karl. 1950. "Rituelle Speisegemeinschaft im 10. und 11. Jahrhundert." *Studium generale* 3: 611–621.

———. 1961. "Haus- und sippengebundene Literatur mittelalterlicher Adelsgeschlechter von Adelssatiren des 11. und 12. Jahrhunderts her erläutert." In *Geschichtsdenken und Geschichtsbild im Mittelalter: Ausgewählte Aufsätze und Arbeiten aus den Jahren 1933–1954.* Ed. Walther Lammers. WdF 21. 165–99. Darmstadt.

Haug, Walther. 1974. "Höfische Idealität und heroische Tradition im Nibelungenlied." *Colloquio*: 273–92. Reprinted in *Strukturen als Schlüssel zur Welt: Kleine Schriften zur Erzählliteratur des Mittelalters* (Tübingen, 1989), 293–307.

———. 1975. "Andreas Heuslers Heldensagenmodell: Prämissen, Kritik und Gegenentwurf." *ZfdA* 104: 273–92. Reprinted in *Strukturen als Schlüssel zur Welt: Kleine Schriften zur Erzählliteratur des Mittelalters* (Tübingen, 1989), 277–92.

———. 1979. Hyperbolik und Zeremonialität: Zu Struktur und Welt von 'Dietrichs Flucht' und 'Rabenschlacht.'" In *Deutsche Heldenepik in Tirol: König Laurin und Dietrich von Bern in der Dichtung des Mittelalters. Beiträge der Neustifter Tagung 1977 des Südtiroler Kulturinstitutes.* Ed. Egon Kühebacher.

Schriftenreihe des Südtiroler Kulturinstituts 7. 116–34. Bolzano. Reprinted in *Strukturen als Schlüssel zur Welt: Kleine Schriften zur Erzählliteratur des Mittelalters* (Tübingen, 1989), 364–76.

———. 1981. "Normatives Modell oder hermeneutisches Experiment: Überlegungen zu einer grundsätzlichen Revision des Heuslerschen Nibelungen-Modells." In *Hohenemser Studien zum Nibelungenlied: Unter Mitarbeit von Irmtraud Albrecht.* Ed. Achim Masser. 38–52. Dornbirn. Reprinted in *Strukturen als Schlüssel zur Welt: Kleine Schriften zur Erzählliteratur des Mittelalters* (Tübingen, 1989), 308–25.

———. [1987] 1989. "Montage und Individualität im 'Nibelungenlied.'" In *Nibelungenlied und Klage: Sage und Geschichte, Struktur und Gattung.* Passauer Nibelungengespräche 1985. Ed. Fritz Peter Knapp. Heidelberg. 277–293. Reprinted in *Strukturen als Schlüssel zur Welt: Kleine Schriften zur Erzählliteratur des Mittelalters* (Tübingen, *1989).* 326–38.

———. 1989. *Strukturen als Schlüssel zur Welt: Kleine Schriften zur Erzählliteratur des Mittelalters.* Tübingen.

———. 1992. *Literaturtheorie im deutschen Mittelalter von den Anfängen bis zum Ende des 13. Jhs*[2]. Darmstadt.

———. 1994. "Mündlichkeit, Schriftlichkeit und Fiktionalität." In *Modernes Mittelalter: Neue Bilder einer populären Epoche.* Ed. Joachim Heinzle. 376–97. Frankfurt.

———. 1996. "Die Verwandlungen des Körpers zwischen 'Aufführung' und 'Schrift.'" In Jan-Dirk Müller, ed., *"Aufführung" und "Schrift" in Mittelalter und früher Neuzeit.* DFG-Symposium 1994. 190–204. Stuttgart.

Haustein, Jens. 1993. "Siegfrieds Schuld." *ZfdA* 122: 373–87.

Havelock, Eric. 1963. *Preface to Plato.* Cambridge, Mass.

———. 1986. *The Muse Learns to Write: Reflections on Orality and Literacy from Antiquity to the Present.* New Haven, Conn.

Haymes, Edward R. 1975. "The Oral Theme of Arrival in the Nibelungenlied." *Colloquia Germanica,* 159–66.

———. 1977. *Das mündliche Epos: Eine Einführung in die "Oral Poetry" Forschung.* Sammlung Metzler 151. Stuttgart.

———. 1985. "Dietrich von Bern im Nibelungenlied." *ZfdA* 114: 159–65.

———. 1986. *The Nibelungenlied: History and Interpretation.* Urbana, Ill.

Heinrichs, Anne. 1985. "Brynhild als Typ der präpatriarchalen Frau." In *Arbeiten zur Skandinavistik: 6. Arbeitstagung der Skandinavisten des deutschen Sprachgebietes, 26.9.–1.10. 1983 in Bonn.* Ed. Heinrich Beck. Texte u. Untersuchungen zur Germanistik und Skandinavistik 11. 45–66. Frankfurt.

Heinzle, Joachim. 1978. *Mittelhochdeutsche Dietrichepik: Untersuchungen zur Tradierungsweise, Überlieferungskritik und Gattungsgeschichte später Heldendichtung.* Münchener Texte und Untersuchungen zur deutschen Literatur des Mittelalters 62. Munich.

———. 1987a. *Das Nibelungenlied.* Artemis-Einführungen 35. Munich.

———. 1987b. "Gnade für Hagen? Die epische Struktur des 'Nibelungenliedes' und das Dilemma der Interpreten." In *Nibelungenlied und Klage: Sage und Geschichte, Struktur und Gattung.* Passauer Nibelungengespräche 1985. Ed. Fritz Peter Knapp. 257–76. Heidelberg.

———. 1991. "Zweimal Hagen oder: Rezeption als Sinnunterstellung." In *Die Nibelungen: Ein deutscher Wahn, ein deutscher Alptraum. Studien und Dokumente zur Rezeption des Nibelungenstoffs im 19. und 20. Jahrhundert.* Ed. Joachim Heinzle and Anneliese Waldschmidt. Suhrkamp-Taschenbuch Wissenschaft 2110. 21–40. Frankfurt.

———. 1995a. "*Heldes muot:* Zur Rolle Dietrichs von Bern im Nibelungenlied." In *Bickelwort* und *wildiu maere: Festschrift für Eberhard Nellmann zum 65. Geburtstag.* Ed. Dorothee Lindemann, Berndt Volkmann, and Klaus-Peter Wegera. GAG 618. 225–36. Göppingen.

———. 1995b. "Konstanten der Nibelungenrezeption in Mittelalter und Neuzeit: Mit einer Nachschrift: Das Subjekt der Literaturgeschichte." In *3. Pöchlarner Heldenliedgespräch: Die Rezeption des Nibelungenliedes.* Ed. Klaus Zatloukal. Philologica Germanica 16. 81–107. Vienna.

Helden und Heldensage: Otto Gschwantler zum 60. Geburtstag. 1990. Ed. Hermann Reichert and Günter Zimmermann. Philologica Germanica 11. Vienna.

Hempel, Heinrich. 1952. "Sächsische Nibelungendichtung und sächsischer Ursprung der Thidrikssaga." *Edda, Skalden, Saga: Festschrift zum 70. Geburtstag von Felix Genzmer.* Ed. Hermann Schneider. 138–56. Heidelberg.

Hempel, Wolfgang. 1970. *Übermuot diu alte: Der Superbia-Gedanke und seine Rolle in der deutschen Literatur des Mittelalters.* Studien zur Germanistik, Anglistik und Komparatistik. Bonn.

Hennig, Ursula. 1981. "Herr und Mann: Zur Ständegliederung im Nibelungenlied." In *Hohenemser Studien zum Nibelungenlied: Unter Mitarbeit von Irmtraud Albrecht.* Ed. Achim Masser. Dornbirn. 175–85.

———. 1987. "Hinterlistige Einladungen in Geschichte und Heldensage." In *Nibelungenlied und Klage: Sage und Geschichte, Struktur und Gattung.* Passauer Nibelungengespräche 1985. Ed. Fritz Peter Knapp. 61–77. Heidelberg.

Heusler, Andreas. [1920] 1965. *Nibelungensage und Nibelungenlied: Die Stoffgeschichte des deutschen Heldenepos*[6]. Dortmund.

Höfische Literatur, Hofgesellschaft, höfische Lebensformen um 1200: Kolloquium am Zentrum für Interdisziplinäre Forschung der Universität Bielefeld (3. bis 5. November 1983). 1986. Ed. Gert Kaiser and Jan-Dirk Müller. Studia humaniora 6. Düsseldorf.

Höfische Repräsentation: Das Zeremoniell und die Zeichen. 1990. Ed. Hedda Ragotzky and Horst Wenzel. Tübingen.

Höfler, Otto. [1955] 1961. "Die Anonymität des Nibelungenliedes." In *Zur germanisch-deutschen Heldensage: Sechzehn Aufsätze zum neuen Forschungsstand.* Ed. Karl Hauck. WdF 14. 330–92. Darmstadt.

Hoffmann, Werner. 1967. "Die Fassung *C des Nibelungenliedes und die 'Klage.'"

In *Festschrift Gottfried Weber. Zu seinem 70. Geburtstag überreicht von frankfurter Kollegen und Schülern.* Ed. Heinz Otto Burger and Klaus von See. 109–43. Bad Homburg.

———. 1974. *Mittelhochdeutsche Heldendichtung.* Grundlagen der Germanistik 14. Berlin.

Hohenemser Studien zum Nibelungenlied: Unter Mitarbeit von Irmtraud Albrecht. 1981. Ed. Achim Masser. Montfort, vol. 3–4. Dornbirn.

Huot, Sylvia. 1987. *From Song to Book: The Poetics of Writing in Old French Lyric and Lyrical Narrative Poetry.* Ithaca, N.Y.

Huppé, Bernard. 1975. "The Concept of the Hero in the Early Middle Ages." In *Concepts of the Hero in the Middle Ages and the Renaissance.* Ed. Norman T. Burns and Christopher J. Reagan. 1–26. Albany, N.Y..

Ihlenburg, Karl-Heinz. 1969. *Das Nibelungenlied: Problem und Gehalt.* Berlin.

Iser, Wolfgang. 1976. *Der Akt des Lesens: Theorie ästhetischer Wirkung.* Uni-Taschenbücher 636. Munich.

Jaeger, C. Stephen. 1983. "The Nibelungen Poet and the Clerical Rebellion Against Courtesy." In *Spectrum Medii Aevi: Essays in Early German Literature in Honor of George Fenwick Jones.* Ed. William C. McDonald. GAG 362. 177–205. Göppingen.

———. 1985. *The Origins of Courtliness: Civilizing Trends and the Formation of Courtly Ideals, 939–1210.* Philadelphia.

Jauß, Hans Robert. 1977. *Alterität und Modernität der mittelalterlichen Literatur: Gesammelte Aufsätze.* Munich.

Keller, Hagen. 1989. "Zum Charakter der 'Staatlichkeit' zwischen karolingischer Reichsreform und hochmittelalterlichem Herrschaftsausbau." *FMSt* 23: 248–64.

Kiening, Christian. 1996. "Anthropologische Zugänge zur mittelalterlichen Literatur: Konzepte, Ansätze, Perspektiven." In *Forschungsberichte zur Germanistischen Mediävistik.* Jahrbuch für Internationale Germanistik, C, vol. 5, 1. 11–129. Bern.

Kiesel, Helmuth. 1979. "*Bei Hof, bei Höllî: Untersuchungen zur literarischen Hofkritik von Sebastian Brant bis Friedrich Schiller.* Studien zur deutschen Literatur 60. Tübingen.

Klebel, Ernst. 1957. "Baiern und das Nibelungenlied." *Probleme der Bayerischen Verfassungsgeschichte, Gesammelte Aufsätze.* Schriftenreihe zur bayerischen Landesgeschichte 57. 90–94. Munich.

Knapp, Fritz Peter. 1987. "*Tragoedia* und *Planctus:* Der Eintritt des 'Nibelungenliedes' in die Welt der *litterati.*" In *Nibelungenlied und Klage: Sage und Geschichte, Struktur und Gattung.* Passauer Nibelungengespräche 1985. Ed. Fritz Peter Knapp. 152–70. Heidelberg.

Koch, Peter, and Wulf Oesterreicher. 1985. "Sprache der Nähe, Sprache der Distanz: Mündlichkeit und Schriftlichkeit im Spannungsfeld von Sprachtheorie und Sprachgeschichte." *Romanistisches Jahrbuch* 36: 15–43.

Kolk, Rainer. 1990. *Berlin oder Leipzig? Eine Studie zur sozialen Organisation der Germanistik im "Nibelungenstreit."* Studien und Texte zur Sozialgeschichte der Literatur 30. Tübingen.
Konecny, Syvia. 1977. "Das Sozialgefüge am Burgundenhof." In *Österreichische Literatur zur Zeit der Babenberger: Vorträge der Lilienfelder Tagung 1976.* Ed. Alfred Ebenbauer et al. 97–116. Vienna.
Konziol, Geoffrey. 1992. *Begging Pardon and Favor: Ritual and Political Order in Early Medieval France.* Ithaca, N.Y.
Kuhn, Hans. 1948. "Kriemhilds Hort und Rache." In *Festschrift Paul Kluckhohn und Hermann Schneider gewidmet zu ihrem 60. Geburtstag herausgegeben von ihren Tübinger Schülern.* 84–100. Tübingen.
———. 1965. "Der Teufel im Nibelungenlied: Zu Gunthers und Kriemhilds Tod." *ZfdA* 94: 280–306.
Kuhn, Hugo. 1959. "Über nordische und deutsche Szenenregie in der Nibelungendichtung." In id., *Dichtung und Welt im Mittelalter.* 196–219, 277–83. Stuttgart.
Lecouteux, Claude. 1978. "La structure des légendes Mélusiennes." *Annales E.S.C.* 33: 294–306.
———. 1979. "Zur Entstehung der Melusinensage." *ZfdA* 98: 73–84.
Le Goff, Jacques. 1985. *L'imaginaire médiéval: Essais.* Paris.
Lexer, Matthias. [1872–78] 1979. *Mittelhochdeutsches Handwörterbuch.* 3 vols. Reprint. Stuttgart.
Leyser, Karl. 1993. "Ritual, Zeremonie und Gestik: Das ottonische Reich." *Frühmittelalterliche Studien* 27: 1–26.
Literarische Interessenbildung im Mittelalter. 1993. Ed. Joachim Heinzle. Stuttgart.
Lohse, Gerhart. 1959. "Die Beziehungen zwischen der Thidrekssaga und den Handschriften des Nibelungenliedes." *PBB* 81 (Tübingen): 295–347.
Lugowski, Clemens. [1932] 1976. *Die Form der Individualität im Roman: Studien zur inneren Struktur der frühen deutschen Prosaerzählung.* New ed. Suhrkamp-Taschenbuch Wissenschaft 151. Frankfurt.
Luhmann, Niklas. 1980. *Gesellschaftsstruktur und Semantik: Studien zur Wissenssoziologie der modernen Gesellschaft.* Frankfurt.
Lunzer, Justus. 1895. "Die Nibelungenbearbeitung k." *PBB* 20: 345–505.
Mahlendorf, Ursula R., and Frank Tobin. 1974. "Legality and Formality in the 'Nibelungenlied.'" *Monatshefte* 66: 225–38.
Masser, Achim. 1981. "Von Alternativstrophen und Vortragsvarianten im Nibelungenlied." In *Hohenemser Studien zum Nibelungenlied: Unter Mitarbeit von Irmtraud Albrecht.* Ed. Achim Masser. 125–37. Dornbirn.
Maurer, Friedrich. 1951. *Leid: Studien zur Bedeutungs- und Problemgeschichte, besonders in den großen Epen der staufischen Zeit.* Bibliotheca Germanica 1. Munich.
Mauss, Marcel. 1975. *Soziologie und Anthropologie 2: Gabentausche, Soziologie und Psychologie.* Munich. Originally published as *Sociologie et anthropologie* (Paris, 1950).

McConnell, Winder. 1978. *The Wate Figure in Medieval Tradition.* Stanford German Studies 13. Bern.

———. 1983. "Marriage in the 'Nibelungenlied' and 'Kudrun.'" In *Spectrum Medii aevi: Essays in Early German Literature in Honor of George Fenwick Jones.* Ed. William C. McDonald. GAG 382. 299–317. Göppingen.

———. 1986a. "Kriemhild and Gerlind: Some Observations on the *vâlandinne*-Concept in the 'Nibelungenlied' and 'Kudrun.'" In *The Dark Figure in Medieval German and Germanic Literature.* Ed. Edward R. Haymes et al. GAG 448. 42–53. Göppingen.

———. 1986b. "The Problem of Continuity in 'Diu Klage.'" *Neophilologus* 70: 248–55.

———. 1995. "Repression and Denial in the 'Nibelungenlied.'" In *Sô wold ich in fröiden singen: Festgabe für Antonius H. Touber.* Ed. Carla Dauven-van Knippenberg and Helmut Birkhan. Amsterdamer Beiträge zur älteren Germanistik 43–44. 361–74. Amsterdam.

Mertens, Volker. 1996a. "Hagens Wissen, Siegfrieds Tod: Zu Hagens Erzählung von Jungsiegfrieds Abenteuern." In *Erzählungen in Erzählungen: Phänomene der Narration in Mittelalter und Früher Neuzeit.* Ed. Harald Haferland and Michael Mecklenburg. 59–69. Munich.

———. 1996b. "Konstruktion und Dekonstruktion heldenepischen Erzählens: 'Nibelungenlied,' 'Klage,' 'Titurel.'" *PBB* 118: 358–87.

Meves, Uwe. 1980. "Zur Rolle der Sieghardinger für die Adelsliteratur im Südosten des Reiches (10.–11. Jh.)." In *Adelsherrschaft und Literatur.* Ed. Horst Wenzel. 115–80. Bern.

———. 1981. "Bischof Wolfger von Passau, *sîn schrîber, meister Kuonrât* und die Nibelungenüberlieferung." In *Hohenemser Studien zum Nibelungenlied: Unter Mitarbeit von Irmtraud Albrecht.* Ed. Achim Masser. 72–89. Dornbirn.

Modernes Mittelalter: Neue Bilder einer populären Epoche. 1994. Ed. Joachim Heinzle. Frankfurt.

Moser, Dietz-Rüdiger. 1992. "Vom Untergang der Nibelungen." *Literatur in Bayern* 30: 2–19.

———. 1995. "Zeit des Unheils im 'Nibelungenlied.'" In *Rhythmus und Saisonalität: Kongreßakten des 5. Symposions des Mediävistenverbandes in Göttingen 1993.* Ed. Peter Dilg et al. 161–70. Sigmaringen.

Müller, Gernot. 1975. "Zur sinnbildlichen Repräsentation der Siegriedgestalt im Nibelungenlied." *Studia neophilologica* 47: 88–119.

Müller, Jan-Dirk. 1974. "Sivrit: *künec, man, eigenholt:* Zur sozialen Problematik des 'Nibelungenliedes.'" *AbäG* 7: 85–124.

———. 1980. "Heroische Vorwelt, feudaladeliges Krisenbewußtsein und das Ende der Heldenepik: Zur Funtion des 'Buchs von Bern.'" In *Adelsherrschaft und Literatur.* Ed. Horst Wenzel. 209–57. Bern.

———. 1982. *Gedechtnus: Literatur und Hofgesellschaft um Maximilian I.* Forschungen zur Geschichte der älteren deutschen Literatur 2. Munich.

———. 1984. "Lachen, Spiel, Fiktion: Zum Verhältnis von literarischem Diskurs und historischer Realität im 'Frauendienst' des Ulrich von Lichtenstein." *Deutsche Vierteljahrsschrift* 58: 38–73.

———. 1985. "Wandel von Geschichtserfahrung in spätmittelalterlicher Heldenepik." In *Geschichtsbewußtsein in der deutschen Literatur des Mittelalters: Tübinger Colloquium 1983*. Ed. Christoph Gerhardt et al. 72–87. Tübingen.

———. 1984–85. "Die *hovezuht* und ihr Preis: Zum Problem höfischer Verhaltenregulierung in Ps.-Konrads 'Halber Birne.'" *Jahrbuch der Oswald von Wolkenstein Gesellschaft* 3: 281–311.

———. 1986a. "Aporien und Perspektiven einer Sozialgeschichte mittelalterlicher Literatur: Zu einigen neueren Forschungsansätzen." In *Kontroversen, alte und neue: Akten des VII. Internationalen Germanisten-Kongresses Göttingen 1985*. Vol. 11. 55–66. Tübingen.

———. 1986b. "Strukturen gegenhöfischer Welt: Höfisches und nicht-höfisches Sprechen bei Neidhart." In *Höfische Literatur, Hofgesellschaft, höfische Lebensformen um 1200: Kolloquium am Zentrum für Interdisziplinäre Forschung der Universität Bielefeld (3. bis 5. November 1983)*. Ed. Gert Kaiser and Jan-Dirk Müller. Studia humaniora 6. 409–51. Düsseldorf.

———. 1987. "Motivationsstrukturen und personale Identität im 'Nibelungenlied': Zur Gattungsdiskussion um 'Epos' oder 'Roman.'" In *Nibelungenlied und Klage: Sage und Geschichte, Struktur und Gattung*. Passauer Nibelungengespräche 1985. Ed. Fritz Peter Knapp. 221–56. Heidelberg.

———. 1990. "Die Destruktion des Heros oder wie erzählt Eilhart von passionierter Liebe?" In *Il romanzo di Tristano nella letteratura del Medioevo; Der "Tristan" in der Literatur des Mittelalters*. Ed. Paola Schulze-Belli and Michael Dallapiazza. Beiträge der Triester Tagung 1989. 19–37. Trieste.

———. 1992a. "Tristans Rückkehr: Zu den Fortsetzern Gottfrieds von Straßburg." In *Festschrift Walter Haug und Burghart Wachinger*. Ed. Johannes Janota et al. 529–48. 2 vols. Tübingen.

———. 1992b. "Woran erkennt man einander im Heldenepos? Beobachtungen an Wolframs 'Willehalm,' dem 'Nibelungenlied,' dem 'Wormser Rosengarten A' und dem 'Eckenlied.'" In *Symbole des Alltags, Alltag der Symbole: Festschrift für Harry Kühnel zum 65. Geburtstag*. Ed. Gertrud Blaschitz et al. 87–111. Graz.

———. 1993a. "Zu einigen Problemen des Konzepts 'Literarische Interessenbildung.'" In *Literarische Interessenbildung im Mittelalter*. Ed. Joachim Heinzle. 365–84. Stuttgart.

———. 1993b. "Ratgeber und Wissende in heroischer Epik." *FMSt* 27: 124–46.

———. 1994a. "*Ir sult sprechen willekomen:* Sänger, Sprecherrolle und die Anfänge volkssprachlicher Lyrik. *IASL* 19: 1–21.

———. 1994b. "Texte aus Texten: Zu intertextuellen Verfahren in frühneuzeitlicher Literatur, am Beispiel von Fischarts Ehzuchtbüchlein und Geschichtklitterung." In *Intertextualität in der Frühen Neuzeit*. Ed. Vilhelm Kühlmann and Wolfgang Neuber. Frühneuzeitliche Studien 2. 63–109. Frankfurt.

———, ed. 1996a. *"Aufführung" und "Schrift" in Mittelalter und früher Neuzeit.* DFG-Symposium 1994. Stuttgart, 1996.

———. 1996b. "Ritual, Sprecherfiktion, Literarisierungstendenzen im späteren Minnegesang." In *Wechselspiele, Kommunikationsformen und Gattungsinterferenzen mittelhochdeutscher Lyrik.* Ed. Michael Schillung and Peter Strohschneider. GRM-Beiheft 13. 49–76. Heidelberg.

———. 1996c. "Der Spielman erzählt: Wie denkt man sich das Entstehen eines Epos?" In *Erzählungen in Erzählungen: Phänomene der Narration in Mittelalter und Früher Neuzeit.* Ed. Harald Haferland and Michael Mecklenburg. 85–98. Munich.

———. 1998a. "Öffentlichkeit und Heimlichkeit im 'Nibelungenlied': Wahrnehmung und Wahrnehmungsstörung im Heldenepos." In *Das Öffentliche und Private in der Vormoderne.* Ed. Gert Melville and Peter von Moos. Norm und Struktur 10. 239–59. Cologne.

———. 1998b. *Spielregeln für den Untergang: Die Welt des Nibelungenliedes.* Tübingen.

———. 1999. "Aufführung, Autor, Werk: Zu einigen blinden Stellen gegenwärtiger Diskussion." In *Mittelalterliche Literatur und Kunst im Spannungsfeld von Hof und Kloster.* Ed. Nigel Palmer and Hans-Jochen Schiewer. Tübingen. 149–66.

Nagel, Bert. 1965. *Das Nibelungenlied: Stoff, Form, Ethos.* Frankfurt.

Naumann, Hans. 1932. "Höfische Symbolik, I: Rüdegers Tod." *Deutsche Vierteljahrsschrift* 10: 387–403.

———. 1933. "Brünhilds Gürtel." *ZfdA* 70: 46–48.

Neumann, Friedrich. 1967. *Das Nibelungenlied in seiner Zeit.* Kleine Vandenhoeck-Reihe 253. Göttingen.

New Historicism: Literaturgeschichte als Poetik der Kultur. 1995. Ed. Moritz Baßler. Frankfurt.

Newman, Gail. 1981. "The Two Brunhilds?" *AbäG* 16: 69–78.

Die Nibelungen: Ein deutscher Wahn, ein deutscher Alptraum. Studien und Dokumente zur Rezeption des Nibelungenstoffs im 19. und 20. Jahrhundert. 1991. Ed. Joachim Heinzle and Anneliese Waldschmidt. Suhrkamp-Taschenbuch Wissenschaft 2110. Frankfurt.

Nibelungenlied und Klage: Sage und Geschichte, Struktur und Gattung. 1987. Passauer Nibelungengespräche 1985. Ed. Fritz Peter Knapp. Heidelberg.

Nibelungenlied und Kudrun. 1976. Ed. Heinz Rupp. WdF 54. Darmstadt.

Nolte, Theodor. 1995. "Das Avunkulat in der deutschen Literatur des Mittelalters." *Poetica* 27: 225–53.

Oesterreicher, Wulf. 1993. "Verschriftung und Verschriftlichung im Kontext medialer und konzeptioneller Schriftlichkeit." In *Schriftlichkeit im frühen Mittelalter.* Ed. Ursula Schaefer. Script-Oralia 53. 265–90. Tübingen.

Österreichische Literatur zur Zeit der Babenberger: Vorträge der Lilienfelder Tagung 1976. 1977. Ed. Alfred Ebenbauer et al. Vienna.

Oexle, Otto Gerhard. 1984. "Mahl und Spende im mittelalterlichen Totenkult." *FMSt* 18: 400–420.

———. 1995. "Memoria als Kultur." In *Memoria als Kultur.* Veröffentlichungen des Max-Planck-Instituts für Geschichte 121. 9–78. Göttingen.

Ohly, Friedrich. [1989] 1995. "Der Tod des Verräters durch Zerreißung in der mittelalterlichen Literatur." In *Ausgewählte und neue Schriften zur Literaturgeschichte und zur Bedeutungsforschung.* Ed. Uwe Ruberg and Dietmar Peil. 423–35. Stuttgart.

Ong, Walter J. 1982. *Orality and Literacy: The Technologizing of the Word.* New York.

Panzer, Friedrich. 1945. *Studien zum Nibelungenliede.* Frankfurt.

Peeters, Joachim. 1982. "*Der jungeste darunder:* Zu den Strophen 411–415 des Nibelungenliedes." *PBB* 104: 44–47.

———. 1986. "Siegfried *von Niderlant* und die Wikinger am Niederrhein." *ZfdA* 115: 1–21.

Pérennec, René. 1975. "La huitième aventure de la Chanson des Nibelungen." *Études germaniques* 30: 1–13.

———. 1987. "Epische Kontinuität, Psychologie und Säkularisierung christlicher Denkschemata im 'Nibelungenlied.'" In *Nibelungenlied und Klage: Sage und Geschichte, Struktur und Gattung.* Passauer Nibelungengespräche 1985. Ed. Fritz Peter Knapp. 202–20. Heidelberg.

Peters, Ursula. 1990. "Von der Sozialgeschichte zur Familienhistorie: Georges Dubys Aufsatz über die Jeunes und seine Bedeutung für ein funktionsgeschichtliches Verständnis der höfischen Literatur." *PBB* 112: 404–36.

———. 1994. "Familienhistorie als neues Paradigma der mittelalterlichen Literaturgeschichte?" In *Modernes Mittelalter: Neue Bilder einer populären Epoche.* Ed. Joachim Heinzle. 134–62. Frankfurt.

Pöchlarner Heldenliedgespräch: Das Nibelungenlied und der mittlere Donauraum. 1990. Ed. Klaus Zatloukal. Philologica Germanica 12. Vienna.

3. Pöchlarner Heldenliedgespräch: Die Rezeption des Nibelungenliedes. 1995. Ed. Klaus Zatloukal. Philologica Germanica 16. Vienna.

Reichert, Hermann. 1990. "Autor und Erzähler im Nibelungenlied: Seine Mündlichkeit, Schriftlichkeit, Bildung, Trinkgewohnheiten und sonstigen Charakteristika." In *Helden und Heldensage: Otto Gschwantler zum 60. Geburtstag.* Ed. Hermann Reichert and Günter Zimmermann. Philologica Germanica 11. 287–327. Vienna.

Richter, Michael. 1994. *The Formation of the Medieval West: Studies in the Early Culture of the Barbarians.* Dublin.

Rings, Lana. 1987. "Kriemhilt's Face Work: A Sociolinguistical Analysis of Social Behavior in the 'Nibelungenlied.'" *Semiotica* 65: 317–25.

Rosenfeld, Hans-Friedrich. 1991. "Ortliebs Tod: Mit einer Einleitung zur Überlieferung des 'Nibelungenliedes.'" In *Uf der mâze pfat: Festschrift für Werner Hoffmann zum 60. Geburtstag.* Ed. Waltraud Fritsch-Rößler. GAG 555. 71–91. Göppingen.

Rößler, Wolfgang. 1980. "Die Entdeckung der Fiktionalität in der Antike." *Poetica* 12: 283–319.

Ruh, Kurt. 1979. "Verständnisperspektiven von Heldendichtung im Spätmittelalter und heute." In *Deutsche Heldenepik in Tirol: König Laurin und Dietrich von Bern in der Dichtung des Mittelalters. Beiträge der Neustifter Tagung 1977 des Südtiroler Kulturinstitutes.* Ed. Egon Kühebacher. Schriftenreihe des Südtiroler Kulturinstituts 7. 15–31. Bolzano.

Rupp, Heinz. 1979. "'Der Ortnit': Heldendichtung oder?" In *Deutsche Heldenepik in Tirol: König Laurin und Dietrich von Bern in der Dichtung des Mittelalters. Beiträge der Neustifter Tagung 1977 des Südtiroler Kulturinstitutes.* Ed. Egon Kühebacher. Schriftenreihe des Südtiroler Kulturinstituts 7. 231–52. Bolzano.

———. 1985. "Das 'Nibelungenlied': Eine politische Dichtung." *WW* 35: 166–76.

Sacker, Hugh. 1961. "On Irony and Symbolism in the 'Nibelungenlied': Two Preliminary Notes." *German Life and Letters* 14: 271–81.

Sacker, Hugh, and D. G. Mowatt. 1967. *The Nibelungenlied: An Interpretative Commentary.* Toronto.

Salmon, Paul. 1976. "Sivrit's Oath of Innocence." *MLR* 71: 315–326.

Schaefer, Ursula. 1991. "Hearing from Books: The Rise of Fictionality in Old English Poetry." In *Vox intexta: Orality and Textuality in the Middle Ages.* Ed. A. N. Doane and Carol Braun Pasternack. 117–36. Madison, Wisc.

———. 1992. *Vokalität: Altenglische Dichtung zwischen Mündlichkeit und Schriftlichkeit.* Script-Oralia 39. Tübingen.

———. 1994. "Zum Problem der Mündlichkeit." In *Modernes Mittelalter: Neue Bilder einer populären Epoche.* Ed. Joachim Heinzle. 357–75. Frankfurt.

Der Schatz des Drachentödters: Materialien zur Wirkungsgeschichte des Nibelungenliedes. 1977. Ed. Werner Wunderlich. Literaturwissenschaft, Gesellschaftswissenschaft 30. Stuttgart.

Schmid, Elisabeth. 1980. "Über Verwandtschaft und Blutsverwandtschaft im Mittelalter." *Acta Germanica* 13: 31–46.

Schmid-Cadalbert, Christian. 1985. *Der Ortnit AW als Brautwerbungsdichtung: Ein Beitrag zum Verständnis mittelhochdeutscher Schemaliteratur.* Bibliotheca Germanica 28. Bern.

———. "Formel." 1997. In *Reallexikon der deutschen Literaturwissenschaft,* 1: 619–20. Berlin.

Schmidt-Wiegand, Ruth. 1982a. "Kriemhilds Rache: Zu Funktion und Wertung des Rechts im Nibelungenlied." In *Tradition als historische Kraft: Interdisziplinäre Forschungen zur Geschichte des früheren Mittelalters.* Ed. Norbert Kamp and Joachim Wollasch. 372–87. Berlin.

———. 1982b. "Gebärdensprache im mittelalterlichen Recht." *FMSt* 18: 363–72.

———. 1984. "Nibelungenlied." In *Das Handwörterbuch zur deutschen Rechtsgeschichte,* ed. Adalbert Erler et al., vol. 3, cols. 965–74. Berlin.

Schreiner, Klaus. 1990, "'Er küsse mich mit dem Kuß seines Mundes' (*Osculetur me osculo oris sui,* Cant 1,1): Metaphorik, kommunikative und herrschaftliche

Funktionen einer symbolischen Handlung." In *Höfische Repräsentation: Das Zeremoniell und die Zeichen.* Ed. Hedda Ragotzky and Horst Wenzel. 89–132. Tübingen.

Schreiner, Klaus, and Gerd Schwerhoff. 1995. "Verletzte Ehre: Überlegungen zu einem Forschungskonzept." In *Verletzte Ehre: Ehrkonflikte in Gesellschaften des Mittelalters und in der Frühen Neuzeit.* Ed. Klaus Schreiner and Gerd Schwerhoff. Norm und Struktur 5.1–28. Cologne.

Schröder, Werner. 1968. *Nibelungenstudien.* Stuttgart.

———. 1981. "Das Nibelungenlied in unserer Zeit." In *Hohenemser Studien zum Nibelungenlied: Unter Mitarbeit von Irmtraud Albrecht.* Ed. Achim Masser. 9–18. Dornbirn.

———. 1989. *Wolfram von Eschenbach, das Nibelungenlied und "Die Klage."* Akademie der Wissenschaften und der Literatur Mainz, Abhandlungen der Geistes- und Sozialwissenschaftlichen Klasse Jahrg. 1989, 5. Wiesbaden.

———. 1996. "Die 'Neue Philologie' und das 'Moderne Mittelalter.'" In *Germanistik in Jena.* Jenaer Universitätsreden 1. 33–50. Jena.

Schulze, Ursula. 1997a. *Das Nibelungenlied.* Stuttgart.

———. 1997b. "*Gunther sî mîn herre, und ich sî sîn man:* Bedeutung und Deutung der Standeslüge und die Interpretierbarkeit des 'Nibelungenliedes.'" *ZfdA* 126: 32–52.

Schuppisser, Fritz Oskar. 1993. "Schauen mit den Augen des Herzen: Zur Methodik der spätmittelalterlichen Passionsmeditation, besonders in der Devotio Moderna und bei den Augustinern." In *Die Passion Christi in Literatur und Kunst des Spätmittelalters.* Ed. Walter Haug and Burghart Wachinger. Fortuna vitrea 12. 169–210. Tübingen.

Schwab, Ute. 1988. "Mancherlei Totendienst im 'Nibelungenlied': *si dienten im nach tode also man lieben vriunden sol.*" In *Festschrift für Ingo Reiffenstein zum 60. Geburtstag.* GAG 478. 353–96. Göppingen.

———. 1989. "Sigune, Kriemhilt, Maria und der geliebte Tote." In *Zwei Frauen vor dem Tode: Verhandelingen van de Koninklijke Academie voor Wetenschapen.* Letteren en Schone Kunsten van Belgie, Klasse der Letteren 51, no. 132. 75–143. Brussels.

———. 1990. "Weinverschütten und Minnetrinken: Verwendung und Umwandlung metaphorischer Hallentopik im 'Nibelungenlied.'" In *Pöchlarner Heldenliedgespräch: Das Nibelungenlied und der mittlere Donauraum.* Ed. Klaus Zatloukal. Philologica Germanica 12. 59–101. Vienna.

———. 1991. "Tötende Töne: Zur Fiedelmetaphorik im 'Nibelungenlied.'" In *Geist und Zeit: Wirkungen des Mittelalters in Literatur und Sprache: Festschrift für Roswitha Wisniewski zu ihrem 65. Geburtstag.* Ed. Carola L. Gottzmann und Herbert Kolb. 77–122. Frankfurt.

———. 1992. "Hagens praktische Todesregie." In *Triuwe: Studien zur Sprachgeschichte und Literaturwissenschaft: Gedächtnisschrift für Elfriede Stutz.* Ed. Karl-Friedrich Kraft et al. 187–241. Heidelberg.

See, Klaus von. 1981. *Edda, Saga, Skaldendichtung: Aufsätze zur skandinavischen Literatur des Mittelalters.* Skandinavistische Arbeiten 6. Heidelberg. Containing: "Germanische Heldensage" (1966), 107–153; "Was ist Heldendichtung?" (1978), 154–193; "Die Werbung um Brünhild" (1957), 194–213; and "Freierprobe und Königinnenzank in der Sigfridsage" (1958–59), 214–23.

———. Seitter, Walter. 1987. *Das politische Wissen im Nibelungenlied: Vorlesungen.* Merve-Titel 141. Berlin.

———. 1990. *Versprechen, versagen: Frauenmacht und Frauenästhetik in den Kriemhild-Diskussionen des 13. Jhs.* Merve-Titel 154. Berlin.

———. 1995. "Von heimlichen Pazifismus im Nibelungenlied." In *Übertragung und Gesetz: Gründungsmythen, Kriegstheater und Unterwerfungstechniken von Institutionen.* Ed. Armin Adam and Martin Stingelin. 149–57. Berlin.

Semmler, Hartmut. 1991. *Listmotive in der mittelhochdeutschen Epik: Zum Wandel ethischer Normen im Spiegel der Literatur.* Philologische Studien u. Quellen 122. Bielefeld.

Snell, Bruno. 1948. *Die Entdeckung des Geistes: Studien zur Entstehung des europäischen Denkens bei den Griechen.* Hamburg.

Soeffner, Hans-Georg. 1989. *Auslegung des Alltags, der Alltag der Auslegung: Zur wissenssoziologischen Konzeption einer sozialwissenschaftlichen Hermeneutik.* Suhrkamp-Taschenbuch Wissenschaft 785. Frankfurt.

———. 1992. *Die Ordnung der Rituale: Auslegung des Alltags.* 2. Suhrkamp-Taschenbuch Wissenschaft 993. Frankfurt.

Speckenbach, Klaus. 1981. "Der Reichsuntergang im 'Reinhart Fuchs' und in der Nibelungendichtung." In *Third International Beast Epic, Fables and Fabliau Colloquium, Münster, 1979: Proceedings.* Ed. Jan Goossens and Timothy Sodman. Niederdt. Studien 30. 404–34. Cologne.

Spiewok, Wolfgang. 1989. "Das Nibelungenlied: Eine Modellinterpretation." In *Mittelalter-Studien II.* Ed. Danielle Buschinger. 174–201. Göppingen.

Splett, Jochen. 1968. *Rüdiger von Bechelaren: Studien zum zweiten Teil des Nibelungenliedes.* Germanische Bibliothek Reihe 3. Heidelberg.

———. 1987. "Das Wortschatzargument im Rahmen der Gatungsproblematik des 'Nibelungenliedes.'" In *Nibelungenlied und Klage: Sage und Geschichte, Struktur und Gattung.* Passauer Nibelungengespräche 1985. Ed. Fritz Peter Knapp. 107–23. Heidelberg.

Stech, Julian. 1993. *Das Nibelungenlied: Appellstrukturen und Mythosthematik in der mittelhochdeutschen Dichtung.* EHS, ser. 1, 1410. Frankfurt.

Stein, Peter K. 1987. "Dietrich von Bern im 'Nibelungenlied': Bemerkungen zur Frage der 'historisch-zeitgeschichtlichen' Betrachtung hochmittelalterlicher Erzähldichtung am Beispiel des 'Nibelungenliedes.'" In *Nibelungenlied und Klage: Sage und Geschichte, Struktur und Gattung.* Passauer Nibelungengespräche 1985. Ed. Fritz Peter Knapp. 78–106. Heidelberg.

Stock, Brian. 1983. *The Implications of Literacy: Written Language and Models of Interpretation in the Eleventh and Twelfth Centuries.* Princeton, N.J.

Störmer, Wilhelm. 1973. *Früher Adel: Studien zur politischen Führungsschicht im fränkisch-deutschen Reich vom 8.–11. Jahrhundert.* 2 vols. Monographien zur Geschichte des Mittelalters 6, 1; 6, 2. Stuttgart.

———.1974. "Die Herkunft Bischof Pilgrims von Passau (971–991) und die Nibelungen-Überlieferung." In *Ostbairische Grenzmarken: Passauer Jb. f. Geschichte, Kunst u. Volkskunde.* Ed. August Leidl. 62–67. Passau.

———. 1987. "Nibelungentradition als Hausüberlieferung in frühmittelalterlichen Adelsfamilien?: Beobachtungen zu Nibelungennamen im 8./9. Jahrhundert vornehmlich in Bayern." In *Nibelungenlied und Klage: Sage und Geschichte, Struktur und Gattung.* Passauer Nibelungengespräche 1985. Ed. Fritz Peter Knapp. 1–20. Heidelberg.

Strohschneider, Peter, and Herfried Vögel. 1989. "Flußübergänge: Zur Konzeption des 'Straßburger Alexander.'" *ZfdA* 118: 85–108.

Strohschneider, Peter. 1995. "Die Zeichen der Mediävistik: Ein Diskussionsbeitrag zum Mittelalter-Entwurf in Peter Czerwinskis 'Gegenwärtigkeit.'" *IASL* 20, 2: 173–91.

———. 1996. "'Nu sehent, wie der singet!': Vom Hervortreten des Sängers im Minnesang." In Jan-Dirk Müller, ed., *"Aufführung" und "Schrift" in Mittelalter und früher Neuzeit.* DFG-Symposium 1994. 7–30. Stuttgart.

———. 1997. "Einfache Regeln, komplexe Strukturen: Ein strukturanalytisches Element zum 'Nibelungenlied.'" In *Mediävistische Komparatistik: Festschrift für Franz Josef Worstbrock zum 60. Geburtstag.* Ed. Wolfgang Harms and Jan-Dirk Müller. 43–74. Stuttgart.

Stutz, Elfriede. 1990. "Über die Einheit und Einzigartigkeit der Siegfried-Gestalt." In *Helden und Heldensage: Otto Gschwantler zum 60. Geburtstag.* Ed. Hermann Reichert and Günter Zimmermann. Philologica Germanica 11. 411–30. Vienna.

Szklenar, Hans. 1977. "Die literarische Gattung der 'Nibelungenklage' und das Ende alter maere." *Poetica* 9: 41–61.

Thelen, Lynn. 1984. "The Internal Source and Function of King Gunther's Bridal Quest." *Monatshefte* 76: 143–55.

———. 1988. "The Vassalage Deception, or Siegfried's Folly." *JEGP* 87: 471–91.

———. 1997. "Hagen's Shields: The 37th *Aventiure* Revisited." *JEGP* 96: 385–402.

Thomas, Brook. 1991. *The New Historicism and Other Old Fashioned Topics.* Princeton, N.J.

Titzmann, Michael. [1977] 1993. *Strukturale Textanalyse: Theorie und Praxis der Interpretation.* 3rd ed. Munich.

Uhlig, Claus. 1973. *Hofkritik im England des Mittelalters und der Renaissance: Studien zu einem Gemeinplatz der europäischen Moralistik.* Quellen u. Forschungen z. Sprach-u. Kulturgeschichte d. germanischen Völker NF 56. Berlin.

Verletzte Ehre: Ehrkonflikte in Gesellschaften des Mittelalters und in der Frühen Neuzeit. 1995. Ed. Klaus Schreiner and Gerd Schwerhoff. Norm und Struktur 5. Cologne.

Vogt, Friedrich. 1913. "Zur Geschichte der Nibelungenklage." In *Rektoratsprogramm der Universität Marburg der 52. Versammlung deutscher Philologen und Schulmänner als Festgabe gewidmet.* 139–67. Marburg.

Vollrath, Hanna. 1981. "Das Mittelalter in der Typik oraler Gesellschaften." *HZ* 233: 571–94.

Voorwinden, Norbert. 1981. "Nibelungenklage und Nibelungenlied." In *Hohenemser Studien zum Nibelungenlied: Unter Mitarbeit von Irmtraud Albrecht.* Ed. Achim Masser. 102–13. Dornbirn.

———. 1987. "Die Markgrafen im 'Nibelungenlied': Gestalten des 10. Jahrhunderts?" In *Nibelungenlied und Klage: Sage und Geschichte, Struktur und Gattung.* Passauer Nibelungengespräche 1985. Ed. Fritz Peter Knapp. 21–42. Heidelberg.

———. 1990. "Kampfschilderung und Kampfmotivation in mittelalterlicher Dichtung: Zur Verschmelzung zweier Traditionen in der deutschen Heldenepik." In *Helden und Heldensage: Otto Gschwantler zum 60. Geburtstag.* Ed. Hermann Reichert and Günter Zimmermann. Philologica Germanica 11.431–46. Vienna.

Vorderstemann, Jürgen. 1976. "Eine unbekannte Handschrift des Nibelungenliedes in der Hessischen Landes-und Hochschulbibliothek Darmstadt." *ZfdA* 105: 115–22.

Vox intexta: Orality and Textuality in the Middle Ages. 1991. Ed. A. N. Doane and Carol Braun Pasternack. Madison, Wisc.

Wachinger, Burghart. 1960. *Studien zum Nibelungenlied: Vorausdeutungen, Aufbau, Motivierung.* Tübingen.

———. 1981. "Die 'Klage' und das Nibelungenlied." In *Hohenemser Studien zum Nibelungenlied: Unter Mitarbeit von Irmtraud Albrecht.* Ed. Achim Masser. 90–101. Dornbirn.

Wailes, Stephen L. 1982. *Wärbel und Swemmel: Zur verräterischen Botschaft im Nibelungenlied.* Archiv f. d. Studium der neueren Sprachen und Literaturen, 219, no. 134. 261–76.

Wapnewski, Peter. 1976. "Rüdigers Schild: Zur 37. Aventiure des 'Nibelungenliedes.'" *Euphorion* 54 (1960): 380–410. Reprinted in *Nibelungelied und Kudrun.* Ed. Heinz Rupp. WdF 54. 134–78. Darmstadt.

———. 1979. "Des Kürenbergers Falkenlied." In *Was ist minne? Studien zur mittelhochdeutschen Lyrik*². Beck'sche Schwarze Reihe 195. 23–46. Munich.

Warning, Rainer. 1979. "Lyrisches Ich und Öffentlichkeit bei den Trobadors." *Deutsche Literatur im Mittelalter: Kontakte und Perspektiven, Hugo Kuhn zum Gedenken.* Ed. Cristoph Cormeau. Stuttgart. 120–59.

———. "1983. Der inszenierte Diskurs: Bemerkungen zur pragmatischen Relation der Fiktion." In *Funktionen des Fiktiven.* Ed. Dieter Henrich and Wolfgang Iser.183–206. Munich.

Weber, Gerd Wolfgang. 1990. "*Sem konungr skyldi:* Heldendichtung und Semiotik. Griechische und germanische heroische Ethik als kollektives Normensystem einer archaischen Kultur." In *Helden und Heldensage: Otto Gschwantler zum 60. Geburtstag.* Ed. Hermann Reichert and Günter Zimmermann. Philologica Germanica 11. 447–81. Vienna.

Weber, Gottfried. 1963. *Das Nibelungenlied: Problem und Idee.* Stuttgart.

Weddige, Hilkert. 1989. *Heldensage und Stammessage: Iring und der Untergang des Thüringerreiches in Historiographie und heroischer Dichtung.* Hermaea, n.s., 61. Tübingen.

Wehrli, Max. 1972. "Die 'Klage' und der Untergang der Nibelungen." In *Zeiten und Formen in Sprache und Dichtung: Festschrift für Fritz Tschirch zum 70. Geburtstag.* Ed. Karl-Heinz Schirmer and Bernhard Sowinski. 96–112. Cologne.

Wenskus, Reinhard. 1973 "Wie die Nibelungen-Überlieferung nach Bayern kam." *Zs. f. bayr. Landesgeschichte* 36, 2: 393–449.

Wenzel, Horst. 1974. *Frauendienst und Gottesdienst: Studien zur Minne-Ideologie.* Philologische Studien und Quellen 74. Berlin.

———. 1986. "*Ze hove* and *ze holze:* Zur Darstellung und Deutung des Unhöfischen in der höfischen Epik und im Nibelungenlied." In *Höfische Literatur, Hofgesellschaft, höfische Lebensformen um 1200: Kolloquium am Zentrum für Interdisziplinäre Forschung der Universität Bielefeld (3. bis 5. November 1983).* Ed. Gert Kaiser and Jan-Dirk Müller. Studia humaniora 6. 277–300. Düsseldorf.

———. 1988. "Öffentlichkeit und Heimlichkeit in Gottfrieds 'Tristan.'" *ZfdPh* 107: 335–61.

———. 1990. "Repräsentation und schöner Schein am Hof und in der höfischen Literatur." In *Höfische Repräsentation: Das Zeremoniell und die Zeichen.* Ed. Hedda Ragotzky and Horst Wenzel. 171–208. Tübingen.

———. 1992. "Szene und Gebärde: Zur visuellen Imagination im Nibelungenlied." *ZfdPh* 111: 321–43.

———. 1995. *Hören und Sehen, Schrift und Bild: Kultur und Gedächtnis im Mittelalter.* Munich.

Willson, Bernard. 1963. "*Ordo* and *Inordinatio* in the Nibelungenlied." *PBB* (Tübingen) 85: 83–101, 325–51.

———. 1960. "Blood and Wounds in the 'Nibelungenlied.'" *MLR* 55: 40–50.

Wisniewski, Roswitha. 1973. "Das Versagen des Königs: Zur Interpretation des Nibelungenliedes." *PBB* (Tübingen) 95 Sonderheft: 170–86.

Wissen für den Hof: Der spätmittelalterliche Verschiftungsprozeß am Beispiel Heidelberg im 15. Jahrhundert. 1994. Ed. Jan-Dirk Müller. Münstersche Mittelalter-Schriften 67. Munich.

Wolf, Alois. 1976. "Mittelalterliche Heldensagen zwischen Vergil, Prudentius und raffinierter Klosterliteratur: Beobachtungen zum 'Waltharius.'" *Sprachkunst* 7: 180–212.

———. 1980 "'Der Abend wiegte schon die Erde, und an den Bergen hing die Nacht.'" In *Bild und Gedanke: Festschrift für Gerhart Baumann zum 60. Geburtstag.* Ed. Günter Schnitzler. 187–205. Munich.

———. 1981. "Die Verschriftlichung der Nibelungensage und die französischdeutschen Literaturbeziehungen im Mittelalter." In *Hohenemser Studien zum Nibelungenlied: Unter Mitarbeit von Irmtraud Albrecht.* Ed. Achim Masser. 53–71. Dornbirn.

———. 1987. "Nibelungenlied, Chanson de geste, höfischer Roman: Zur Problematik der Verschriftlichung der deutschen Nibelungensagen." In *Nibelungenlied und Klage: Sage und Geschichte, Struktur und Gattung.* Passauer Nibelungengespräche 1985. Ed. Fritz Peter Knapp. 171–201. Heidelberg.

———. 1988. "Altisländische theoretische Äußerungen zur Verschriftlichung und die Verschriftlichung der Nibelungensagen im Norden." In *Zwischen Festtag und Alltag: Zehn Beiträge zum Thema 'Mündlichkeit und Schriftlichkeit.'* Ed. Wolgang Raible. Script-Oralia 6. 167–89. Tübingen.

———. 1991a. "Frühmittelalterliches Erzählen im Spannungsfeld von Vers, Abschnitt und Strophe: Versuch einer Bestandsaufnahme." In *Metrik und Medienwechsel, Metrics and Media.* Ed. Hildegard L. C. Tristram. Script-Oralia 35.107–28. Tübingen.

———. 1991b. "Medieval Heroic Traditions and Their Transitions from Orality to Literacy." In *Vox intexta: Orality and Textuality in the Middle Ages.* Ed. A. N. Doane and Carol Braun Pasternack. 57–88. Madison, Wisc.

———. 1995. *Heldensage und Epos: Zur Konstituierung einer mittelalterlichen volkssprachlichen Gattung im Spannungsfeld von Mündlichkeit und Schriftlichkeit.* Script-Oralia 68. Tübingen.

Wolf, Werner. 1948,1950. "Zu den Hinweisstrophen auf Wolframfragmente in der kleinen Heidelberger Handschrift des Jüngeren Titurel." *ZfdA* 82: 256–64.

Wynn, Marianne. 1965. "Hagen's Defiance of Kriemhilt." In *Mediaeval German Studies Presented to Frederick Norman.* 104–14. London.

Wyss, Ulrich. 1990. "Zum letzten Mal: Die teutsche Ilias." In *Pöchlarner Heldenliedgespräch: Das Nibelungenlied und der mittlere Donauraum.* Ed. Klaus Zatloukal. Philologica Germanica 12. 157–79. Vienna.

Zimmermann, Günter. 1990. "Der Krieg, die Schuld und die 'Klage.'" In *Helden und Heldensage: Otto Gschwantler zum 60. Geburtstag.* Ed. Hermann Reichert and Günter Zimmermann. Philologica Germanica 11. 513–36. Vienna.

Zumthor, Paul. 1983. *Introduction à la poésie orale.* Paris.

———. 1987. *La lettre et la voix: De la "littérature" médiévale.* Paris.

Index